HIGH-RISE INVASION

9

STORY / Tsuina Miura
ART / Takahiro Oba

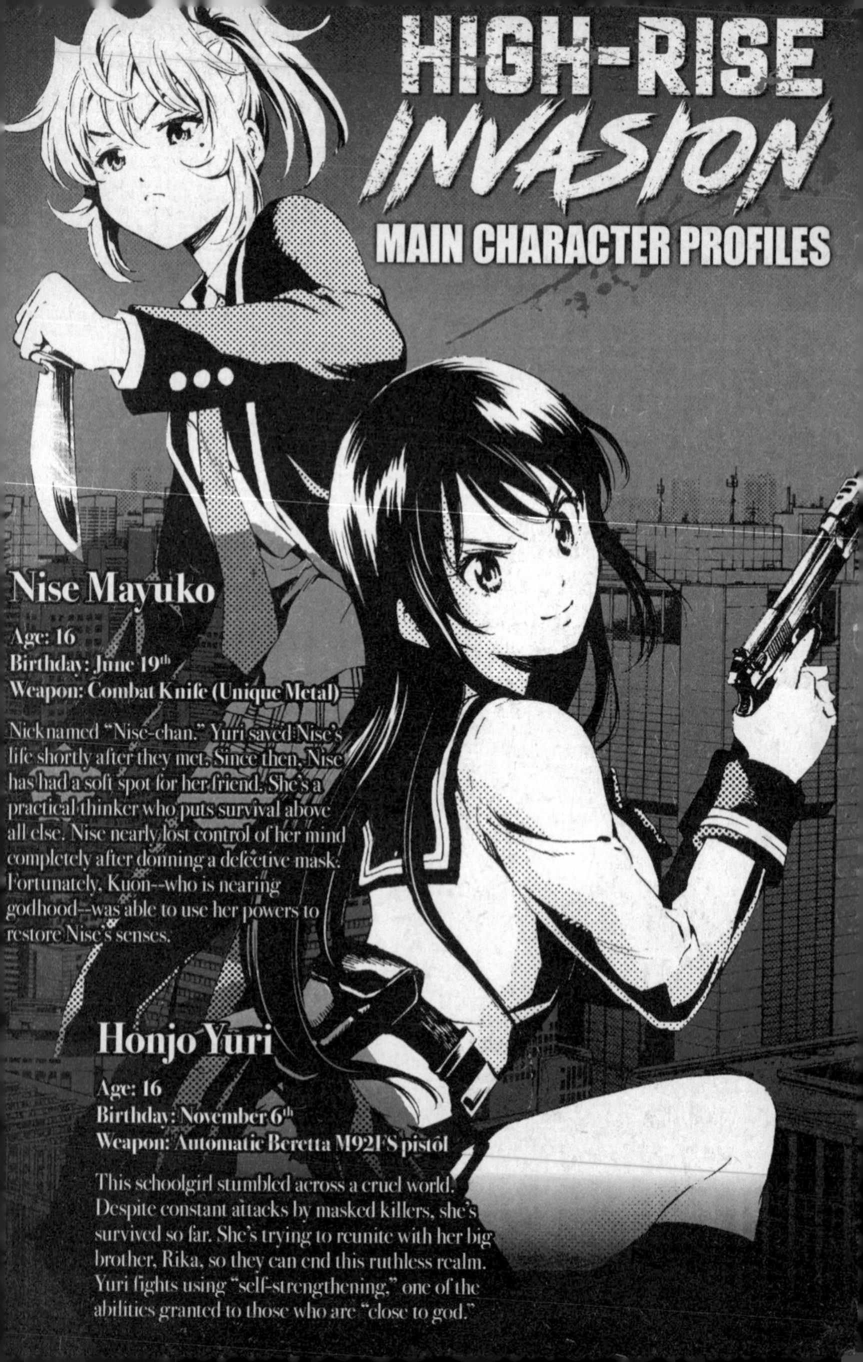

HIGH-RISE INVASION

MAIN CHARACTER PROFILES

Nise Mayuko

Age: 16
Birthday: June 19th
Weapon: Combat Knife (Unique Metal)

Nicknamed "Nise-chan." Yuri saved Nise's life shortly after they met. Since then, Nise has had a soft spot for her friend. She's a practical thinker who puts survival above all else. Nise nearly lost control of her mind completely after donning a defective mask. Fortunately, Kuon--who is nearing godhood--was able to use her powers to restore Nise's senses.

Honjo Yuri

Age: 16
Birthday: November 6th
Weapon: Automatic Beretta M92FS pistol

This schoolgirl stumbled across a cruel world. Despite constant attacks by masked killers, she's survived so far. She's trying to reunite with her big brother, Rika, so they can end this ruthless realm. Yuri fights using "self-strengthening," one of the abilities granted to those who are "close to god."

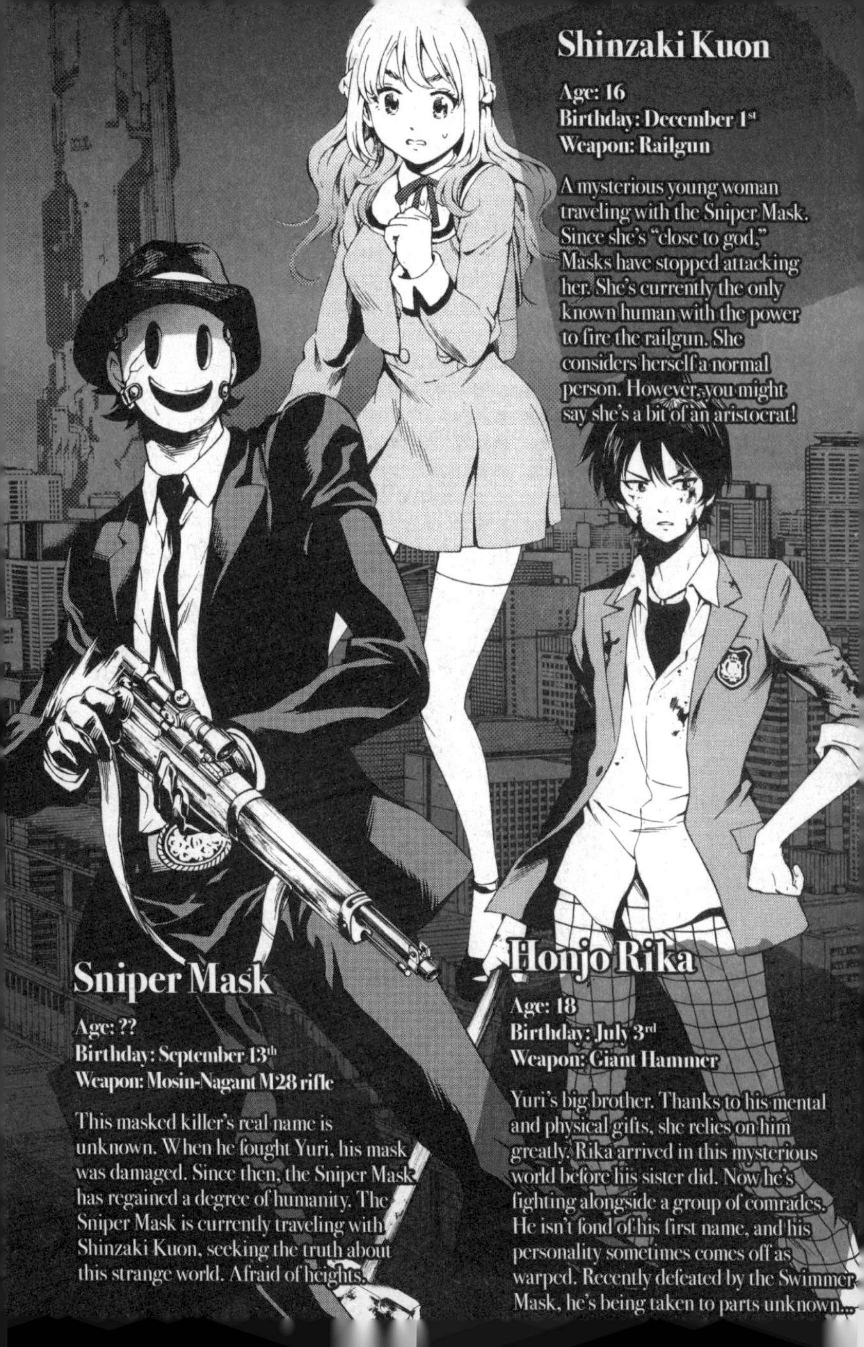
Shinzaki Kuon
Age: 16
Birthday: December 1st
Weapon: Railgun
A mysterious young woman traveling with the Sniper Mask. Since she's "close to god," Masks have stopped attacking her. She's currently the only known human with the power to fire the railgun. She considers herself a normal person. However, you might say she's a bit of an aristocrat!
Sniper Mask
Age: ??
Birthday: September 13th
Weapon: Mosin-Nagant M28 rifle
This masked killer's real name is unknown. When he fought Yuri, his mask was damaged. Since then, the Sniper Mask has regained a degree of humanity. The Sniper Mask is currently traveling with Shinzaki Kuon, seeking the truth about this strange world. Afraid of heights.
Honjo Rika
Age: 18
Birthday: July 3rd
Weapon: Giant Hammer
Yuri's big brother. Thanks to his mental and physical gifts, she relies on him greatly. Rika arrived in this mysterious world before his sister did. Now he's fighting alongside a group of comrades. He isn't fond of his first name, and his personality sometimes comes off as warped. Recently defeated by the Swimmer Mask, he's being taken to parts unknown...

HIGH-RISE INVASION

9

CONTENTS

CHAPTER 106: This Loser's Crap

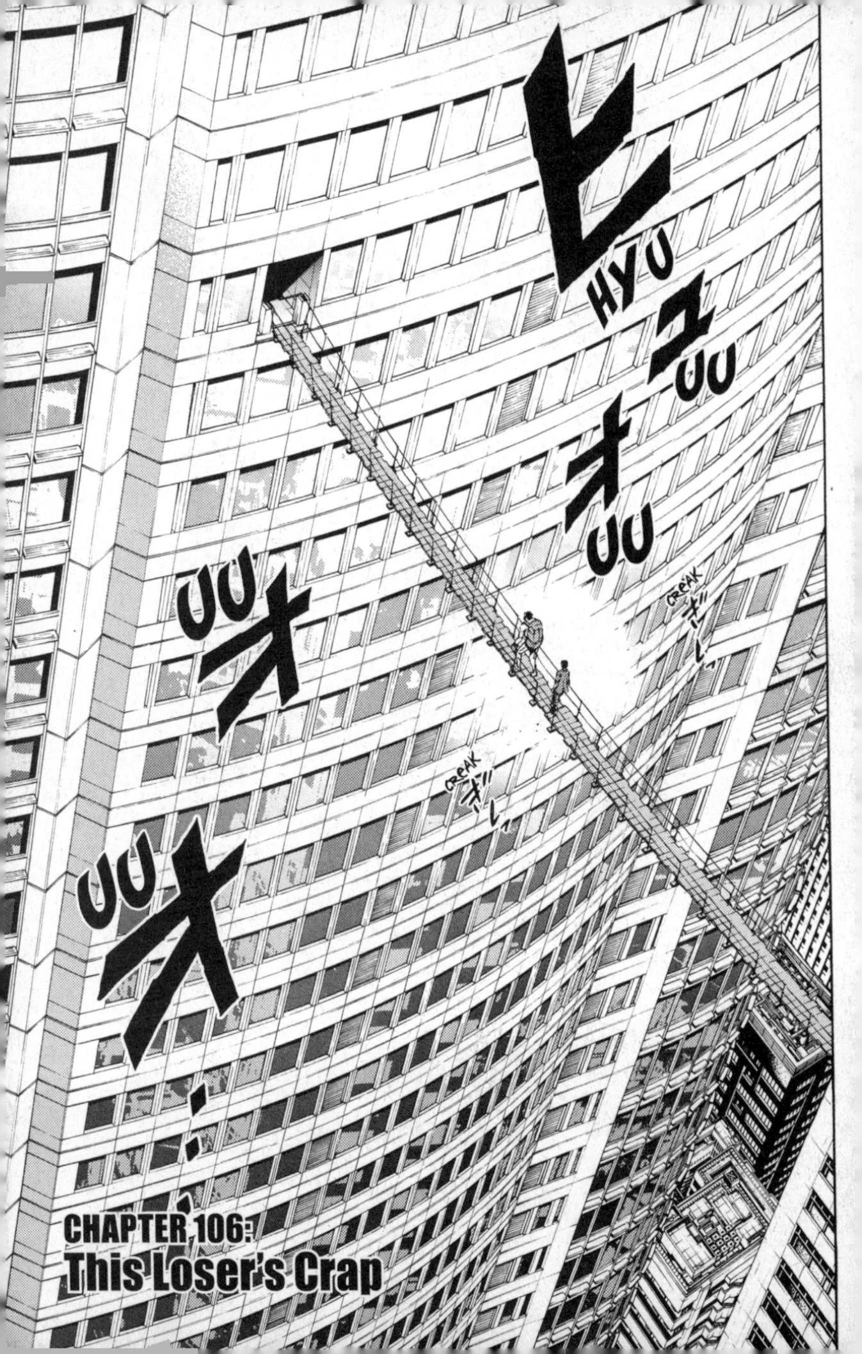
ヒ HYU
ユ UU
オ UU
オ UU
オ UU
CREAK
ギーし
CREAK
ギィし

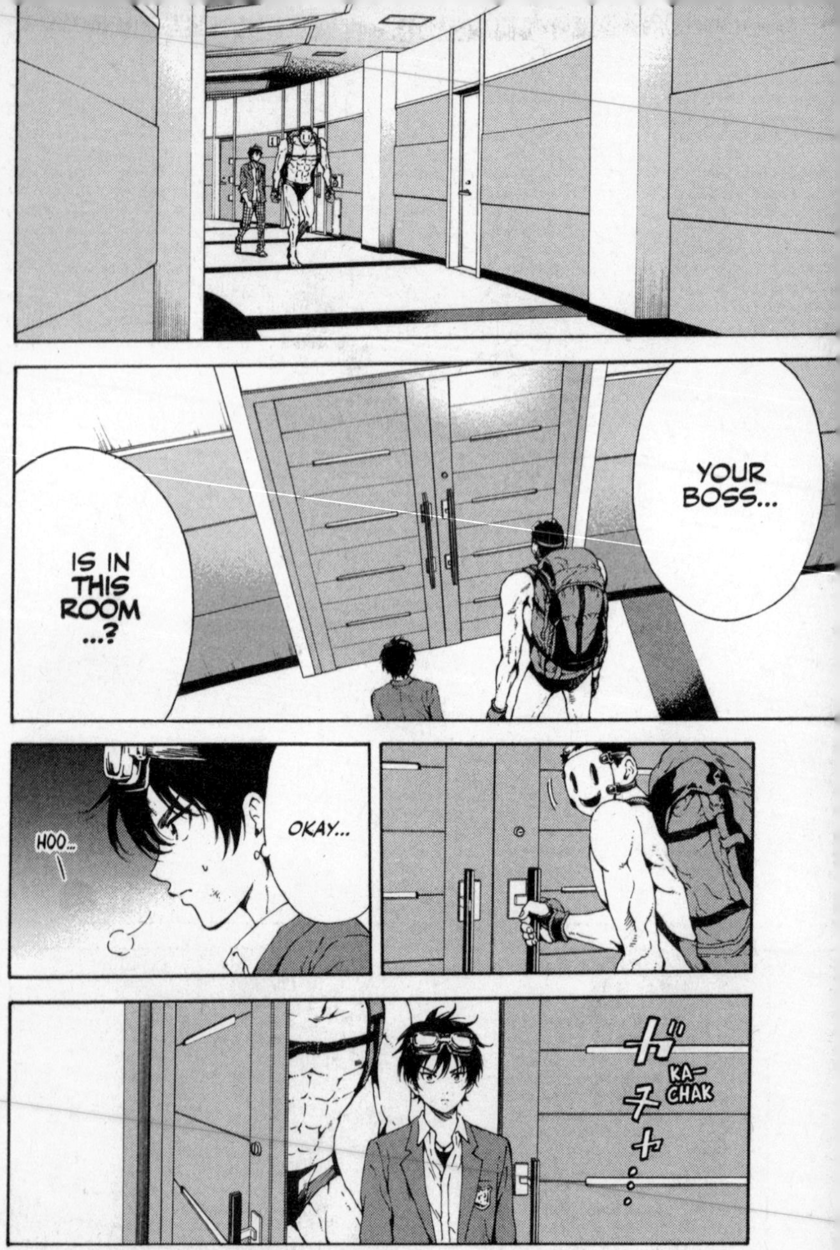
YOUR BOSS...
IS IN THIS ROOM ...?
OKAY...
HOO...
ガチャ…
KA-CHAK

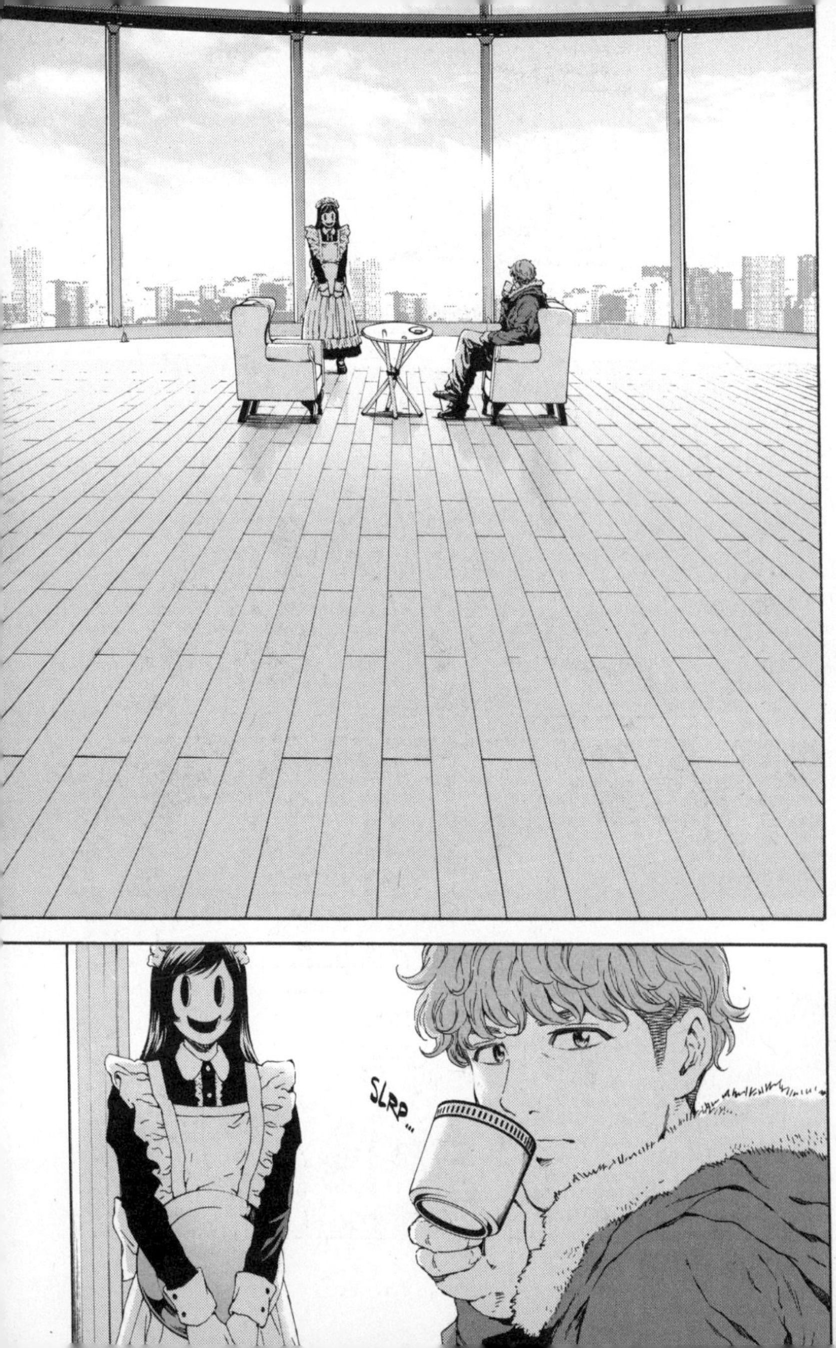
SLRP...

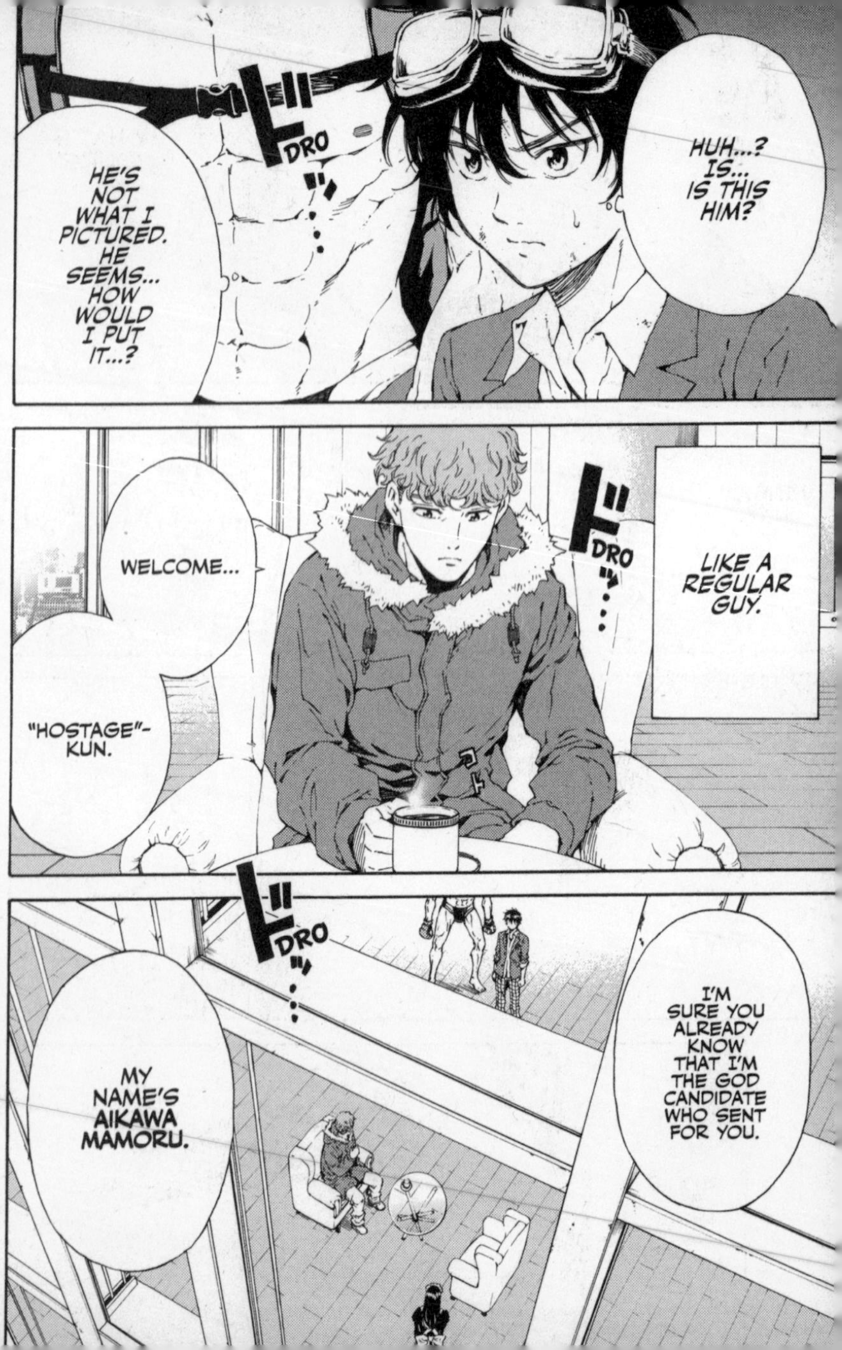
HUH...? IS... IS THIS HIM?
DRO...
HE'S NOT WHAT I PICTURED. HE SEEMS... HOW WOULD I PUT IT...?
LIKE A REGULAR GUY.
DRO...
WELCOME...
"HOSTAGE"-KUN.
I'M SURE YOU ALREADY KNOW THAT I'M THE GOD CANDIDATE WHO SENT FOR YOU.
DRO...
MY NAME'S AIKAWA MAMORU.

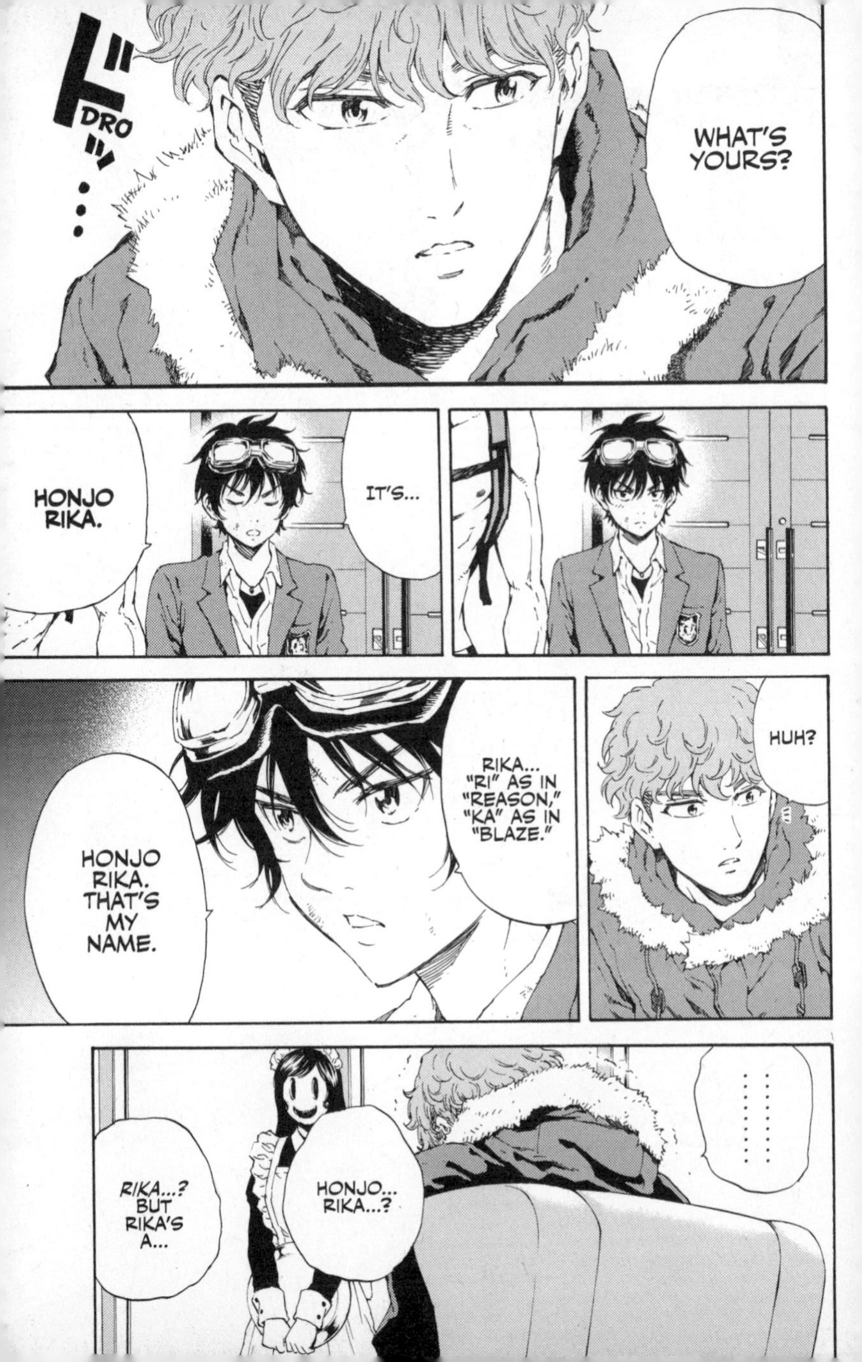
WHAT'S YOURS?
ド
DRO
...
IT'S...
HONJO RIKA.
HUH?
RIKA... "RI" AS IN "REASON," "KA" AS IN "BLAZE."
HONJO RIKA. THAT'S MY NAME.
......
HONJO... RIKA...?
RIKA...? BUT RIKA'S A...

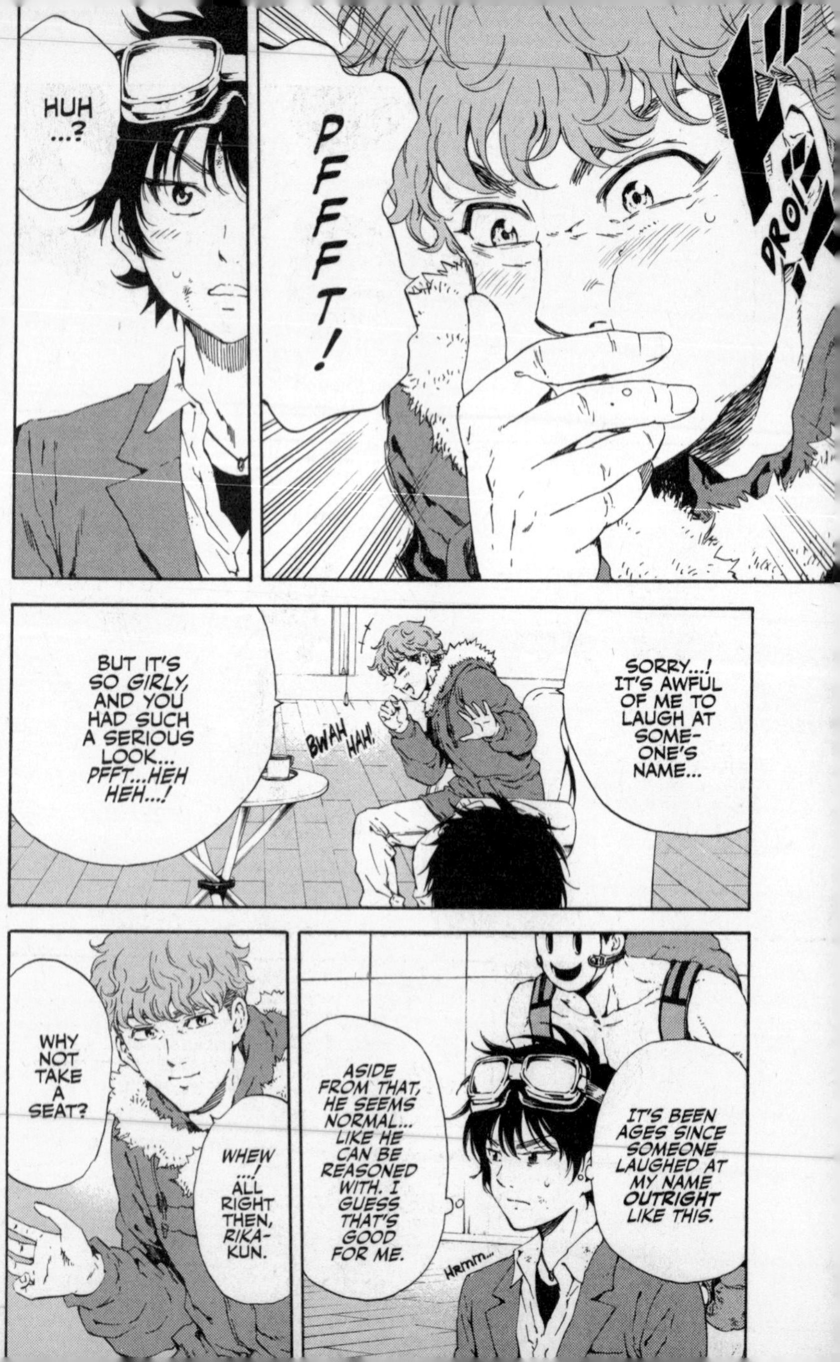
PFFFT!
HUH ...?
SORRY...! IT'S AWFUL OF ME TO LAUGH AT SOME-ONE'S NAME...
BWAH HAH!
BUT IT'S SO GIRLY, AND YOU HAD SUCH A SERIOUS LOOK... PFFT...HEH HEH...!
IT'S BEEN AGES SINCE SOMEONE LAUGHED AT MY NAME OUTRIGHT LIKE THIS.
ASIDE FROM THAT, HE SEEMS NORMAL... LIKE HE CAN BE REASONED WITH. I GUESS THAT'S GOOD FOR ME.
Hrmm...
WHY NOT TAKE A SEAT?
WHEW...! ALL RIGHT THEN, RIKA-KUN.

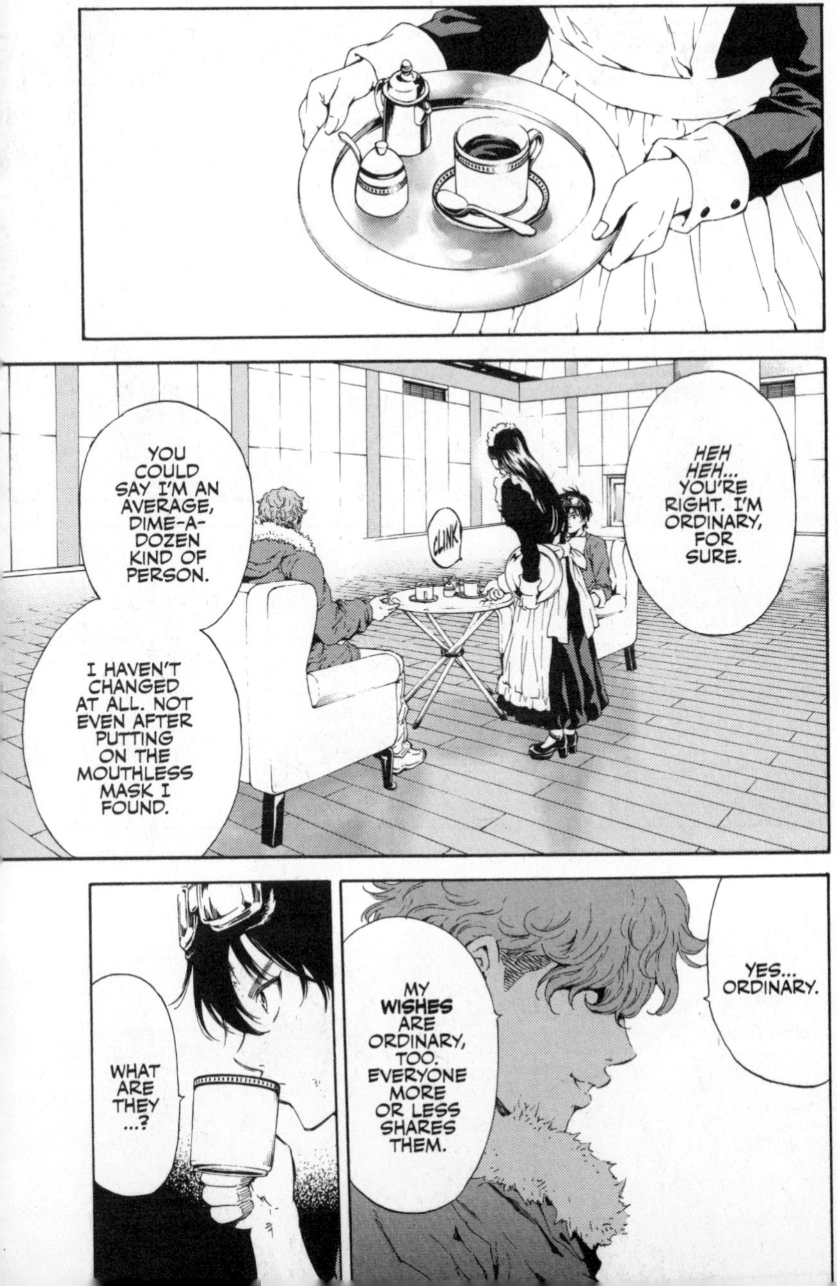
HEH HEH... YOU'RE RIGHT. I'M ORDINARY, FOR SURE.
CLINK!
YOU COULD SAY I'M AN AVERAGE, DIME-A-DOZEN KIND OF PERSON.
I HAVEN'T CHANGED AT ALL. NOT EVEN AFTER PUTTING ON THE MOUTHLESS MASK I FOUND.
YES... ORDINARY.
MY **WISHES** ARE ORDINARY, TOO. EVERYONE MORE OR LESS SHARES THEM.
WHAT ARE THEY ...?

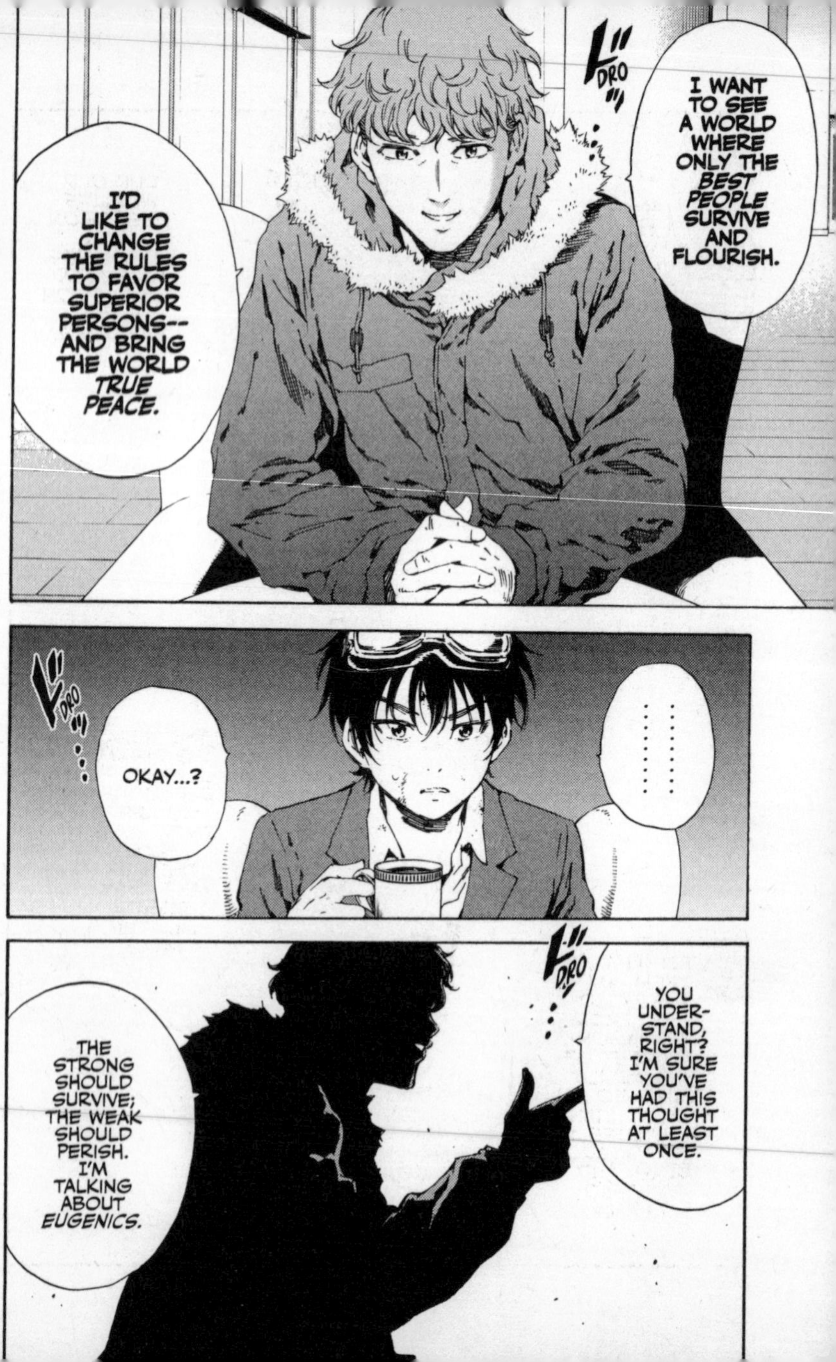
DRO
I WANT TO SEE A WORLD WHERE ONLY THE *BEST PEOPLE* SURVIVE AND FLOURISH.
I'D LIKE TO CHANGE THE RULES TO FAVOR SUPERIOR PERSONS-- AND BRING THE WORLD *TRUE PEACE.*
......
DRO
OKAY...?
DRO
YOU UNDER-STAND, RIGHT? I'M SURE YOU'VE HAD THIS THOUGHT AT LEAST ONCE.
THE STRONG SHOULD SURVIVE; THE WEAK SHOULD PERISH. I'M TALKING ABOUT *EUGENICS.*

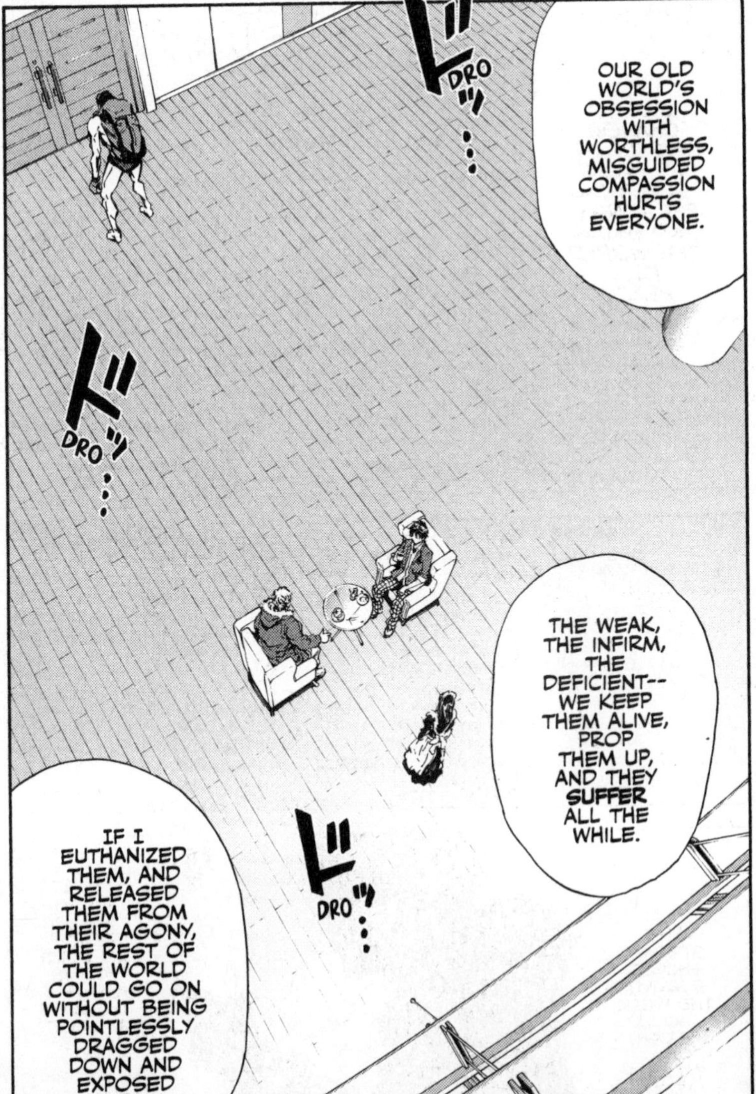
OUR OLD WORLD'S OBSESSION WITH WORTHLESS, MISGUIDED COMPASSION HURTS EVERYONE.
DRO...
THE WEAK, THE INFIRM, THE DEFICIENT-- WE KEEP THEM ALIVE, PROP THEM UP, AND THEY **SUFFER** ALL THE WHILE.
DRO...
DRO...
IF I EUTHANIZED THEM, AND RELEASED THEM FROM THEIR AGONY, THE REST OF THE WORLD COULD GO ON WITHOUT BEING POINTLESSLY DRAGGED DOWN AND EXPOSED TO PAIN.

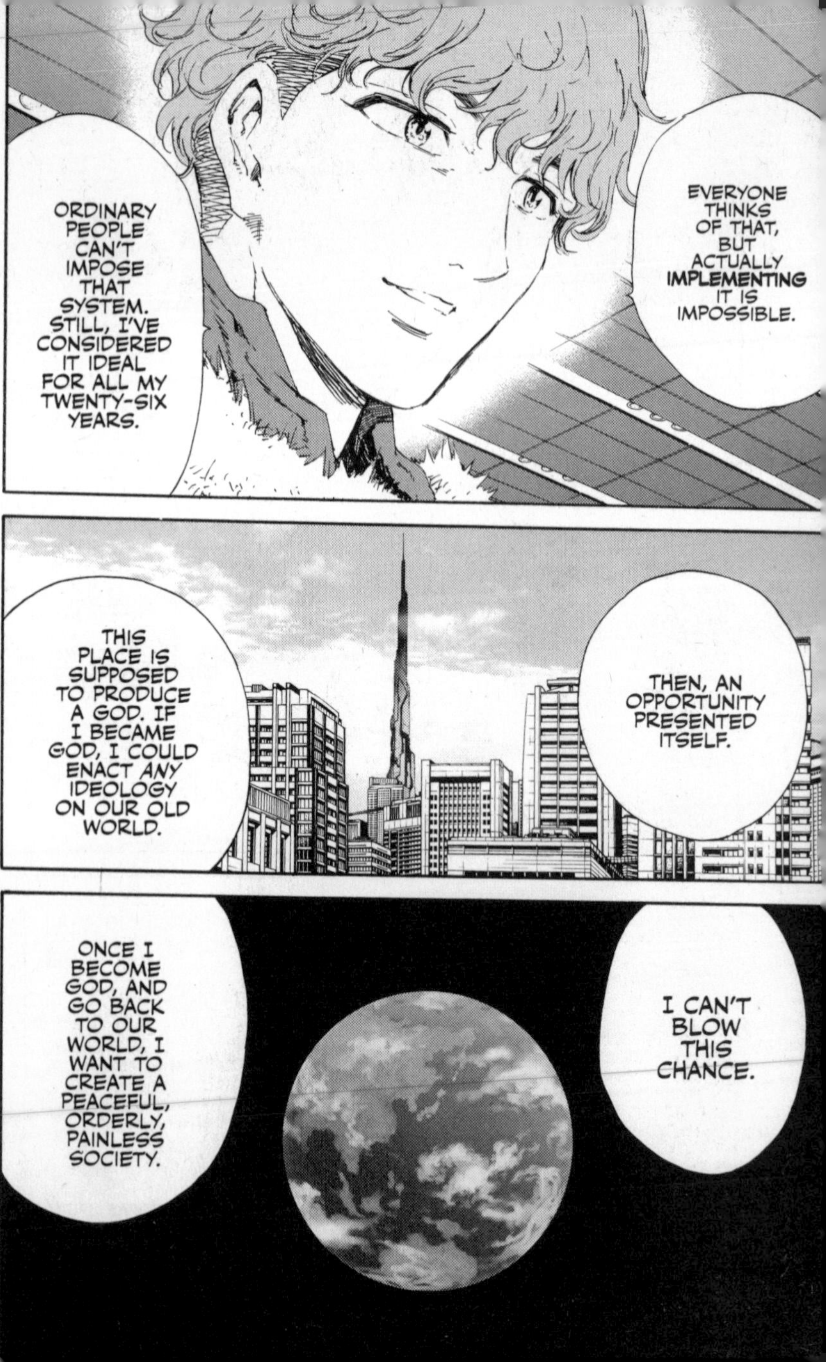
EVERYONE THINKS OF THAT, BUT ACTUALLY **IMPLEMENTING** IT IS IMPOSSIBLE.
ORDINARY PEOPLE CAN'T IMPOSE THAT SYSTEM. STILL, I'VE CONSIDERED IT IDEAL FOR ALL MY TWENTY-SIX YEARS.
THEN, AN OPPORTUNITY PRESENTED ITSELF.
THIS PLACE IS SUPPOSED TO PRODUCE A GOD. IF I BECAME GOD, I COULD ENACT *ANY* IDEOLOGY ON OUR OLD WORLD.
I CAN'T BLOW THIS CHANCE.
ONCE I BECOME GOD, AND GO BACK TO OUR WORLD, I WANT TO CREATE A PEACEFUL, ORDERLY, PAINLESS SOCIETY.

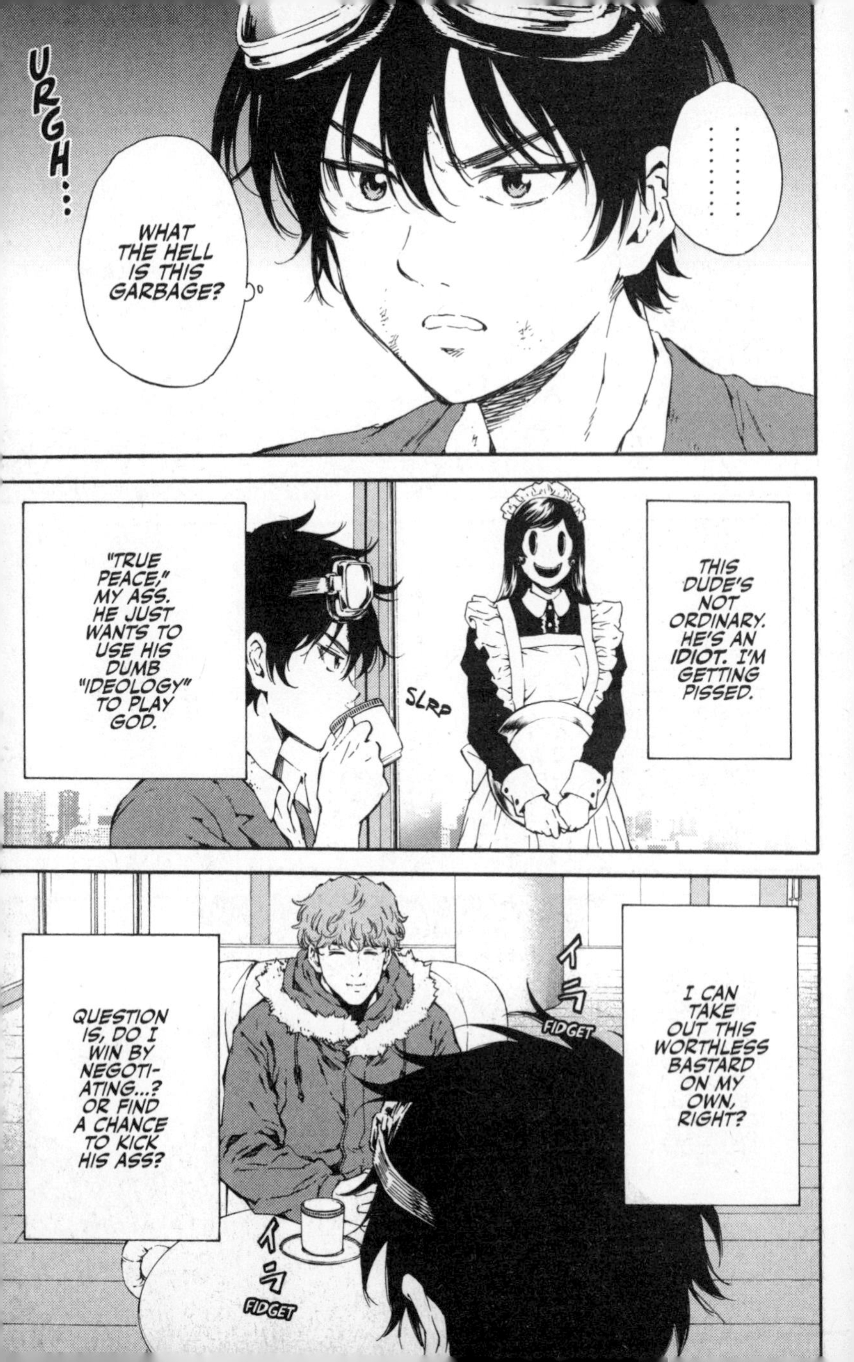
……
URGH…
WHAT THE HELL IS THIS GARBAGE?
THIS DUDE'S NOT ORDINARY. HE'S AN IDIOT. I'M GETTING PISSED.
SLRP
"TRUE PEACE," MY ASS. HE JUST WANTS TO USE HIS DUMB "IDEOLOGY" TO PLAY GOD.
I CAN TAKE OUT THIS WORTHLESS BASTARD ON MY OWN, RIGHT?
イラ
FIDGET
QUESTION IS, DO I WIN BY NEGOTIATING...? OR FIND A CHANCE TO KICK HIS ASS?
イラ
FIDGET

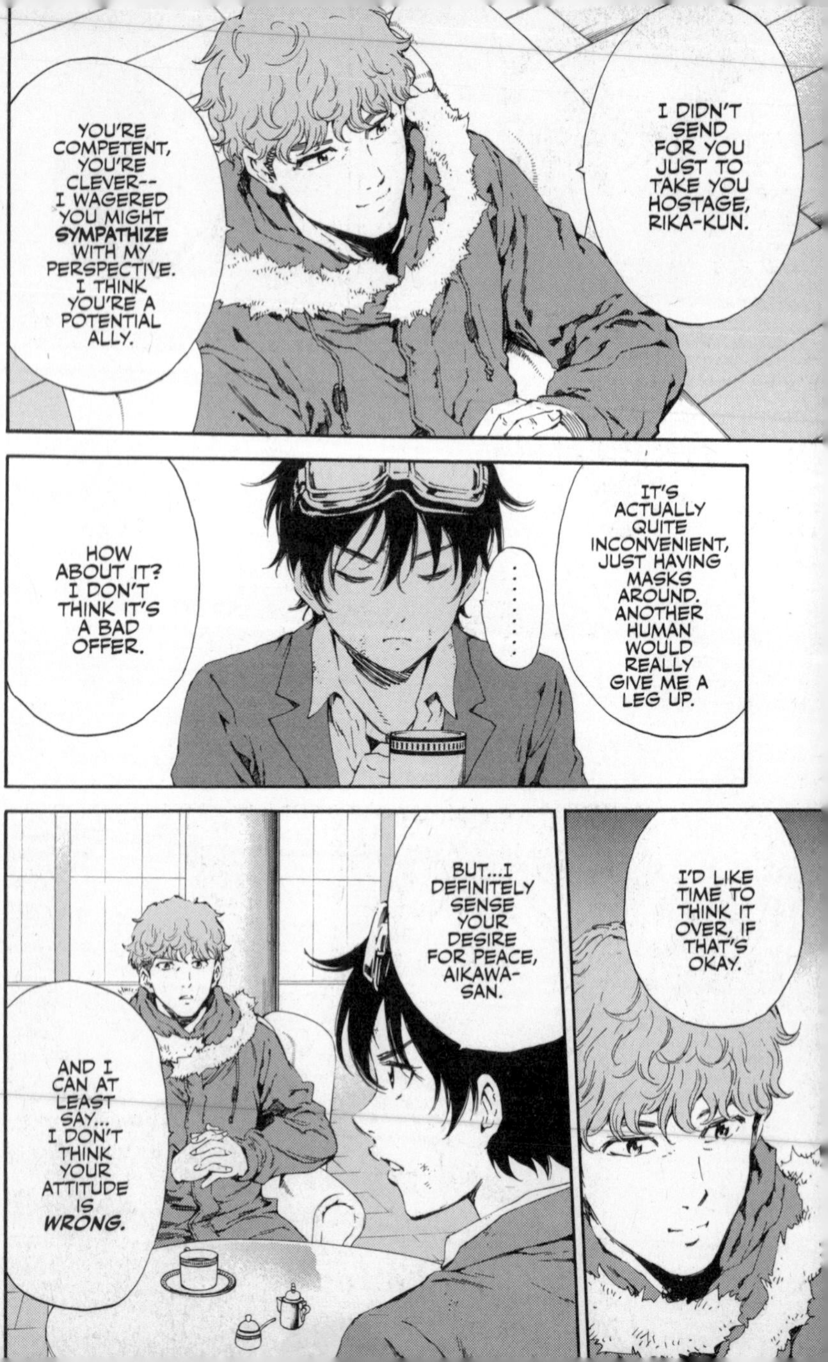
I DIDN'T SEND FOR YOU JUST TO TAKE YOU HOSTAGE, RIKA-KUN.
YOU'RE COMPETENT, YOU'RE CLEVER-- I WAGERED YOU MIGHT **SYMPATHIZE** WITH MY PERSPECTIVE. I THINK YOU'RE A POTENTIAL ALLY.
IT'S ACTUALLY QUITE INCONVENIENT, JUST HAVING MASKS AROUND. ANOTHER HUMAN WOULD REALLY GIVE ME A LEG UP.
......
HOW ABOUT IT? I DON'T THINK IT'S A BAD OFFER.
I'D LIKE TIME TO THINK IT OVER, IF THAT'S OKAY.
BUT...I DEFINITELY SENSE YOUR DESIRE FOR PEACE, AIKAWA-SAN.
AND I CAN AT LEAST SAY... I DON'T THINK YOUR ATTITUDE IS ***WRONG.***

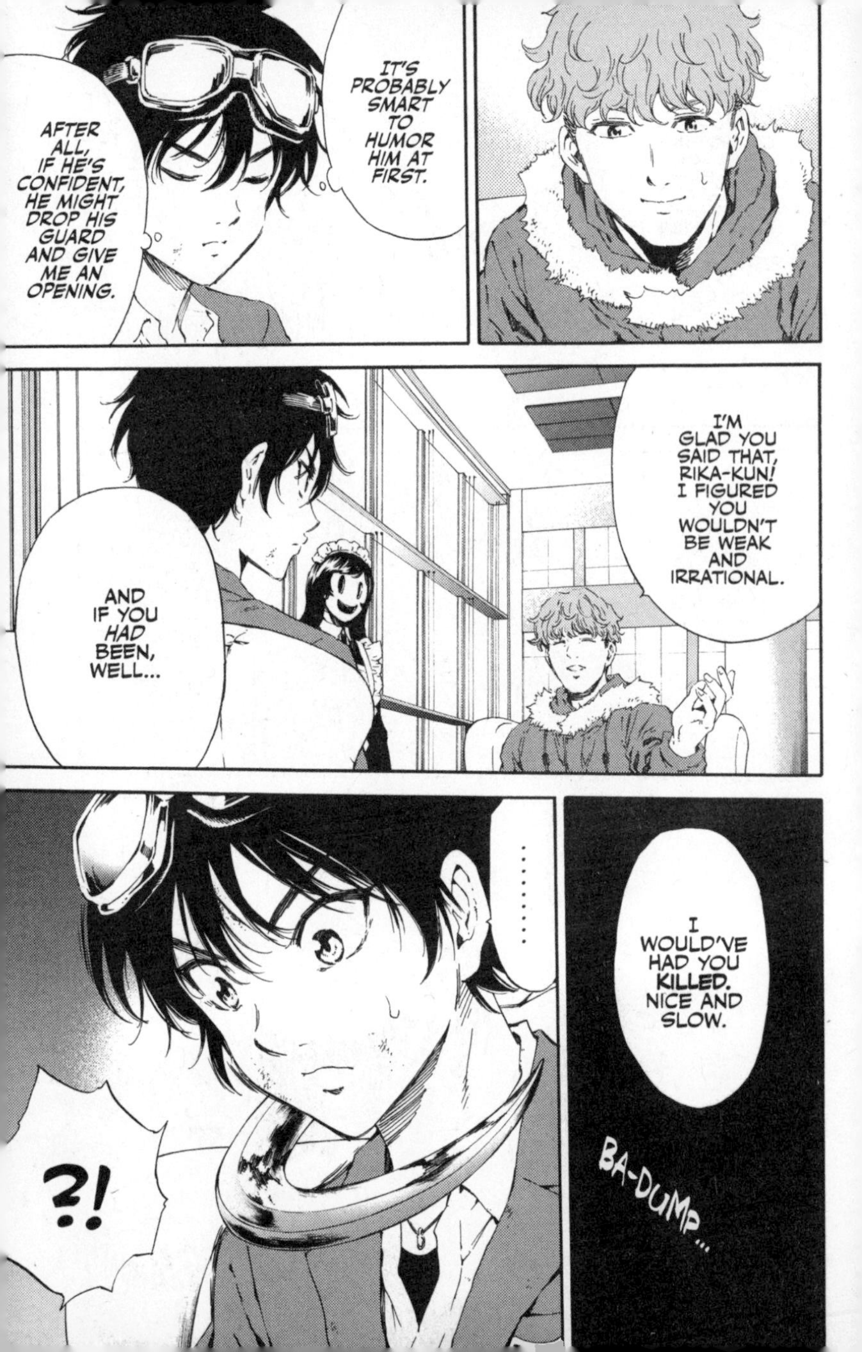
IT'S PROBABLY SMART TO HUMOR HIM AT FIRST.
AFTER ALL, IF HE'S CONFIDENT, HE MIGHT DROP HIS GUARD AND GIVE ME AN OPENING.
I'M GLAD YOU SAID THAT, RIKA-KUN! I FIGURED YOU WOULDN'T BE WEAK AND IRRATIONAL.
AND IF YOU HAD BEEN, WELL...
I WOULD'VE HAD YOU KILLED. NICE AND SLOW.
BA-DUMP...
......
?!

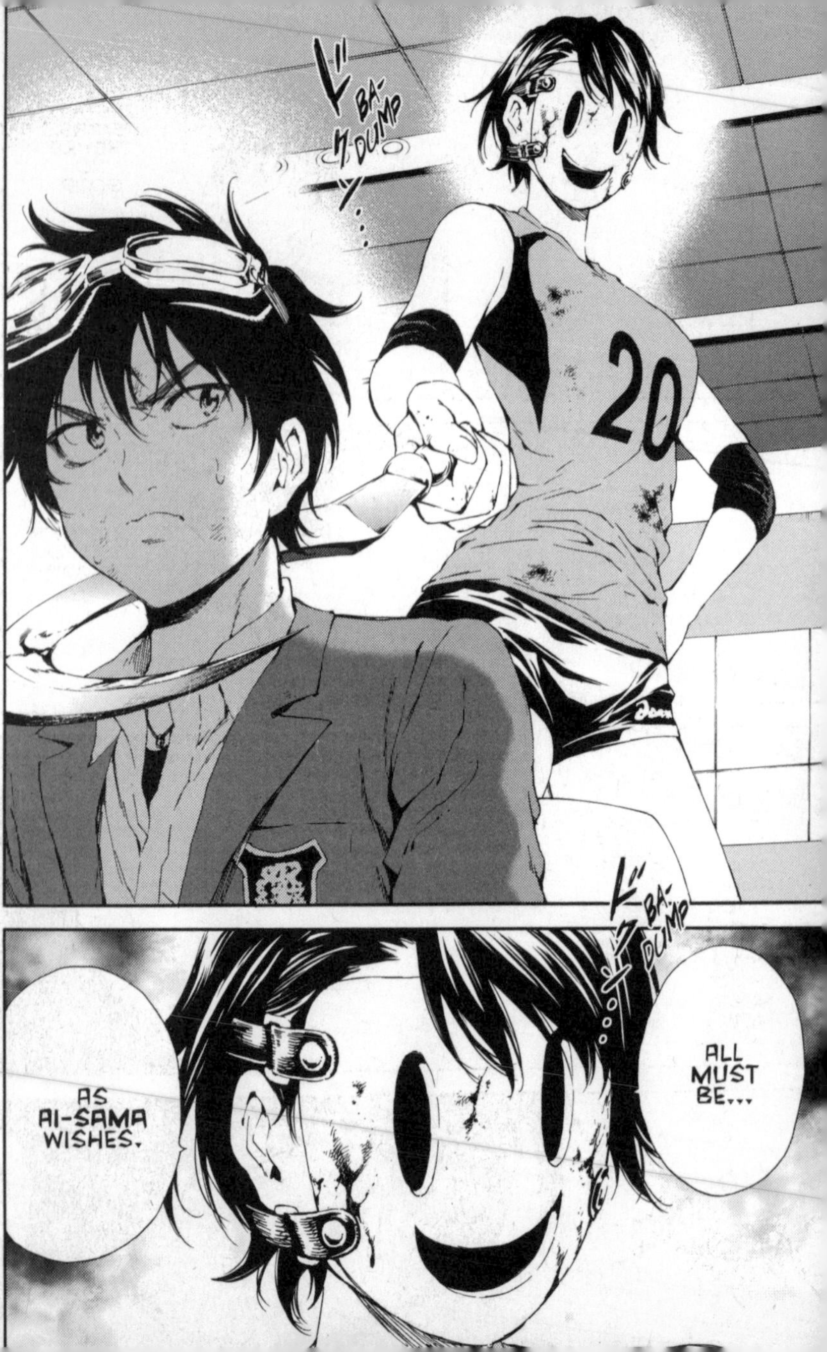
BA-DUMP
BA-DUMP
ALL MUST BE...
AS AI-SAMA WISHES.

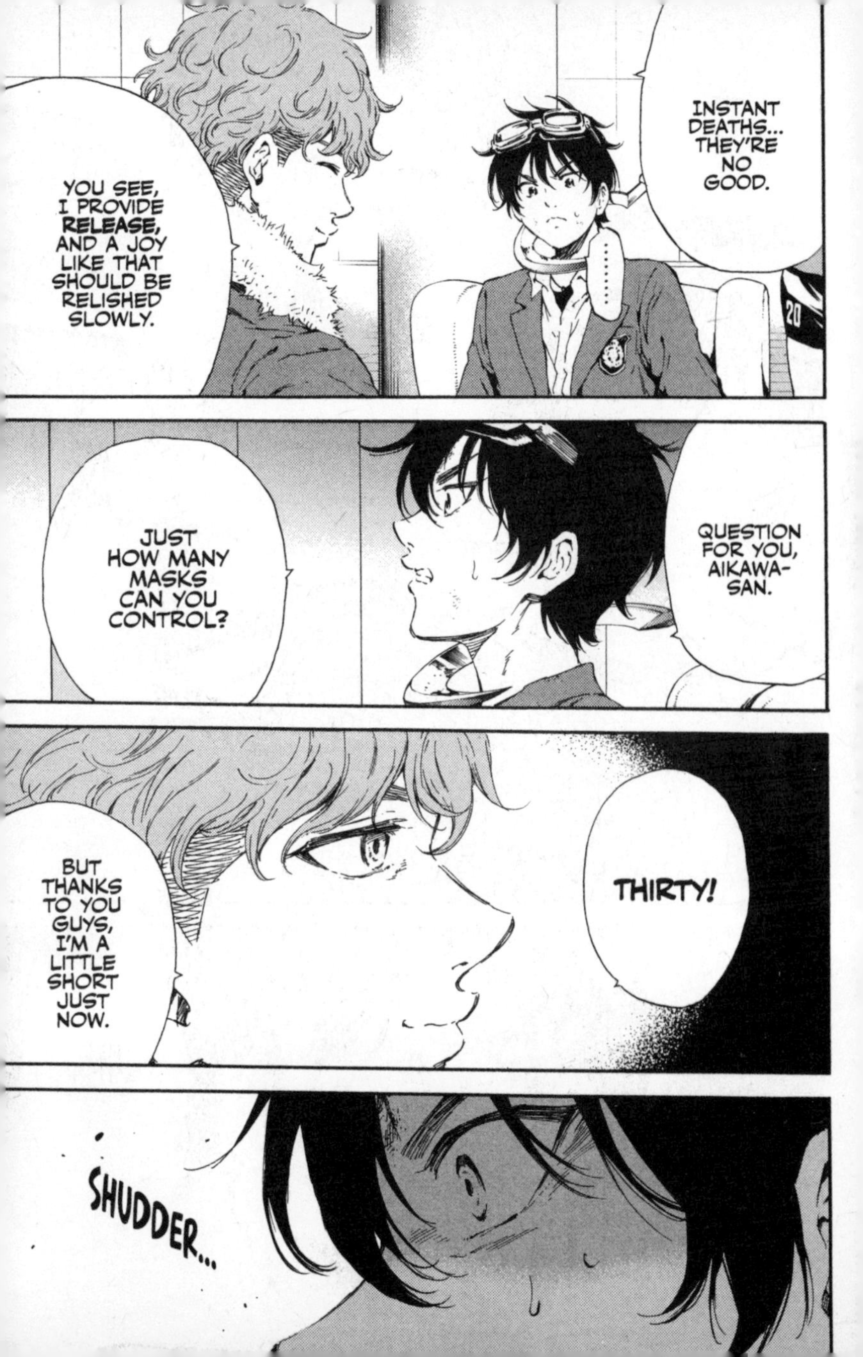
INSTANT DEATHS... THEY'RE NO GOOD.
YOU SEE, I PROVIDE RELEASE, AND A JOY LIKE THAT SHOULD BE RELISHED SLOWLY.
QUESTION FOR YOU, AIKAWA-SAN.
JUST HOW MANY MASKS CAN YOU CONTROL?
THIRTY!
BUT THANKS TO YOU GUYS, I'M A LITTLE SHORT JUST NOW.
SHUDDER...

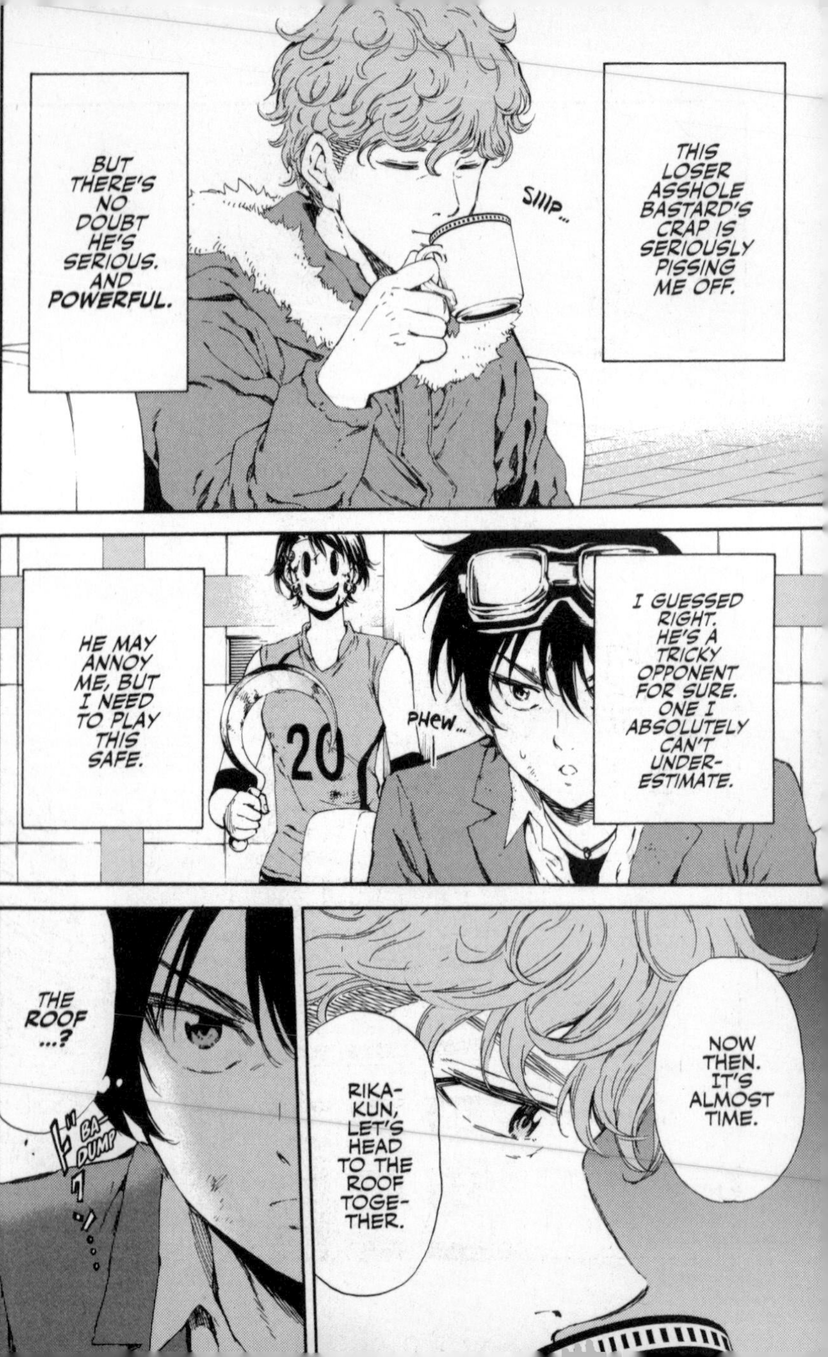
THIS LOSER ASSHOLE BASTARD'S CRAP IS SERIOUSLY PISSING ME OFF.
SIIIP...
BUT THERE'S NO DOUBT HE'S SERIOUS. AND POWERFUL.
I GUESSED RIGHT. HE'S A TRICKY OPPONENT FOR SURE. ONE I ABSOLUTELY CAN'T UNDER-ESTIMATE.
PHEW...
HE MAY ANNOY ME, BUT I NEED TO PLAY THIS SAFE.
NOW THEN. IT'S ALMOST TIME.
RIKA-KUN, LET'S HEAD TO THE ROOF TOGE-THER.
THE ROOF ...?
BA-DUMP

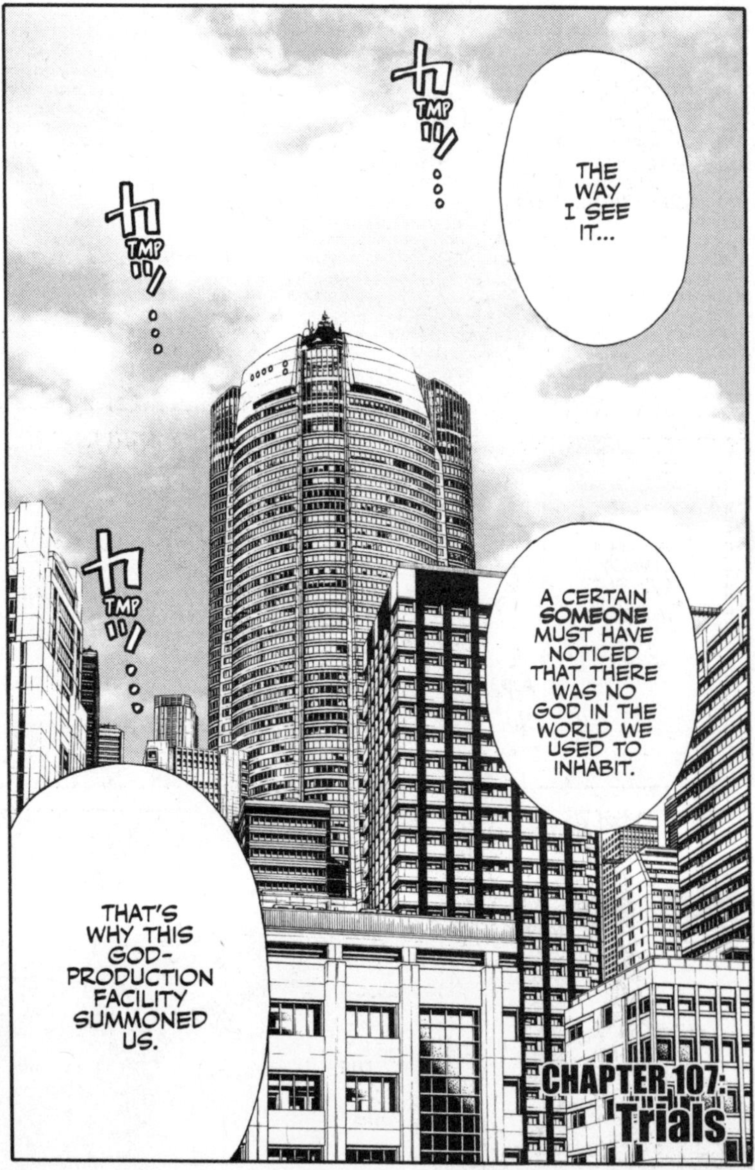
THE WAY I SEE IT...
TMP
TMP
A CERTAIN SOMEONE MUST HAVE NOTICED THAT THERE WAS NO GOD IN THE WORLD WE USED TO INHABIT.
TMP
THAT'S WHY THIS GOD-PRODUCTION FACILITY SUMMONED US.
CHAPTER 107:
Trials

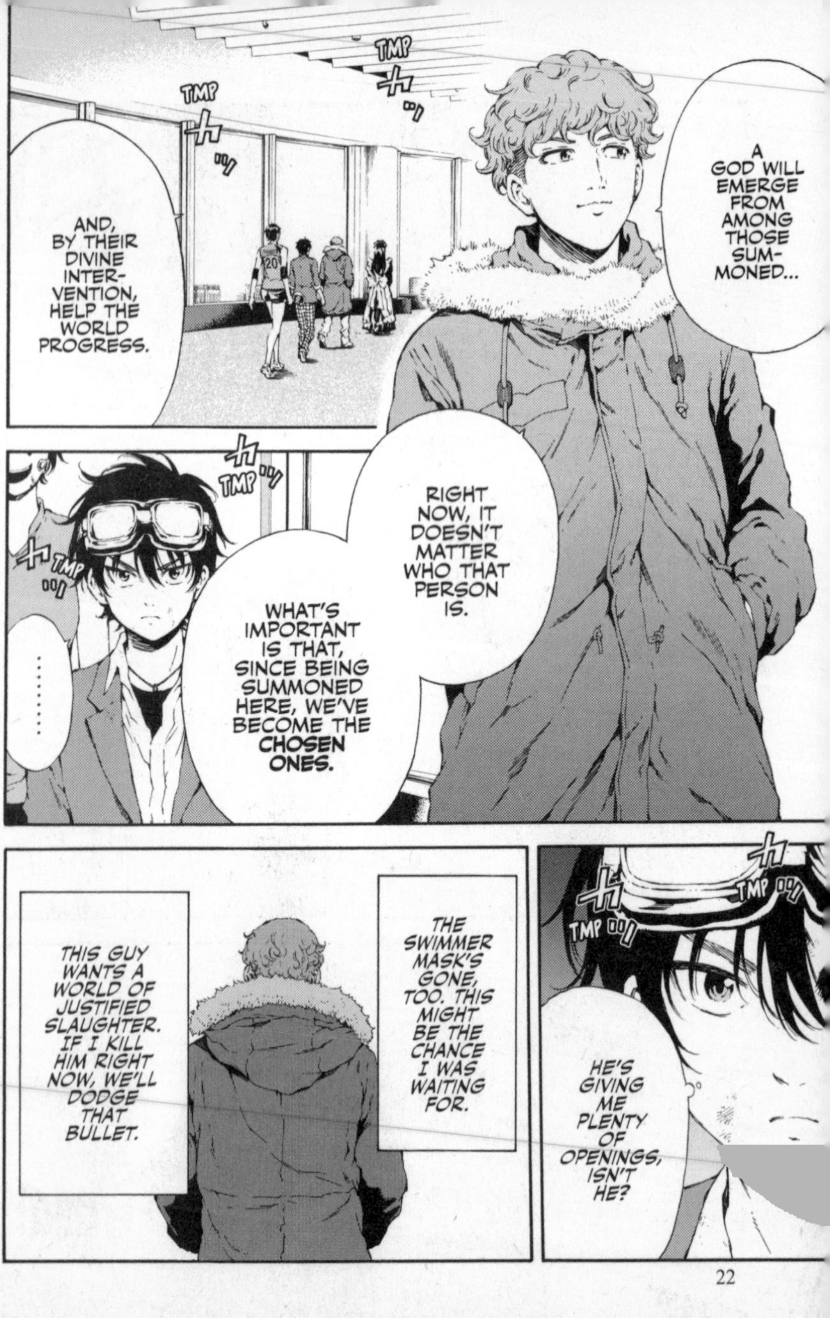
A GOD WILL EMERGE FROM AMONG THOSE SUM-MONED...
TMP
TMP
AND, BY THEIR DIVINE INTER-VENTION, HELP THE WORLD PROGRESS.
RIGHT NOW, IT DOESN'T MATTER WHO THAT PERSON IS.
TMP
WHAT'S IMPORTANT IS THAT, SINCE BEING SUMMONED HERE, WE'VE BECOME THE **CHOSEN ONES.**
TMP
......
TMP
TMP
HE'S GIVING ME PLENTY OF OPENINGS, ISN'T HE?
THE SWIMMER MASK'S GONE, TOO. THIS MIGHT BE THE CHANCE I WAS WAITING FOR.
THIS GUY WANTS A WORLD OF JUSTIFIED SLAUGHTER. IF I KILL HIM RIGHT NOW, WE'LL DODGE THAT BULLET.

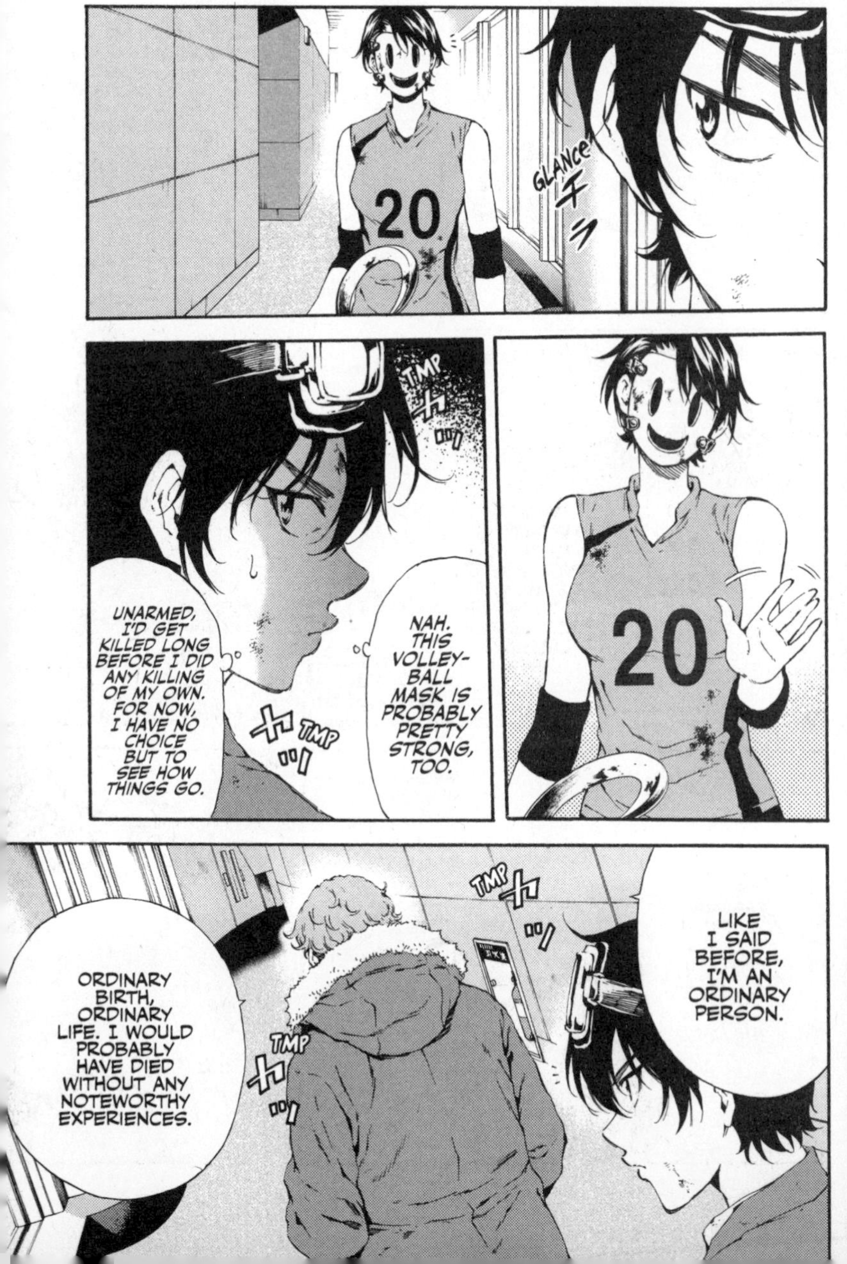
GLANCE
チラ
TMP
NAH. THIS VOLLEY-BALL MASK IS PROBABLY PRETTY STRONG, TOO.
UNARMED, I'D GET KILLED LONG BEFORE I DID ANY KILLING OF MY OWN. FOR NOW, I HAVE NO CHOICE BUT TO SEE HOW THINGS GO.
TMP
TMP
LIKE I SAID BEFORE, I'M AN ORDINARY PERSON.
ORDINARY BIRTH, ORDINARY LIFE. I WOULD PROBABLY HAVE DIED WITHOUT ANY NOTEWORTHY EXPERIENCES.
TMP

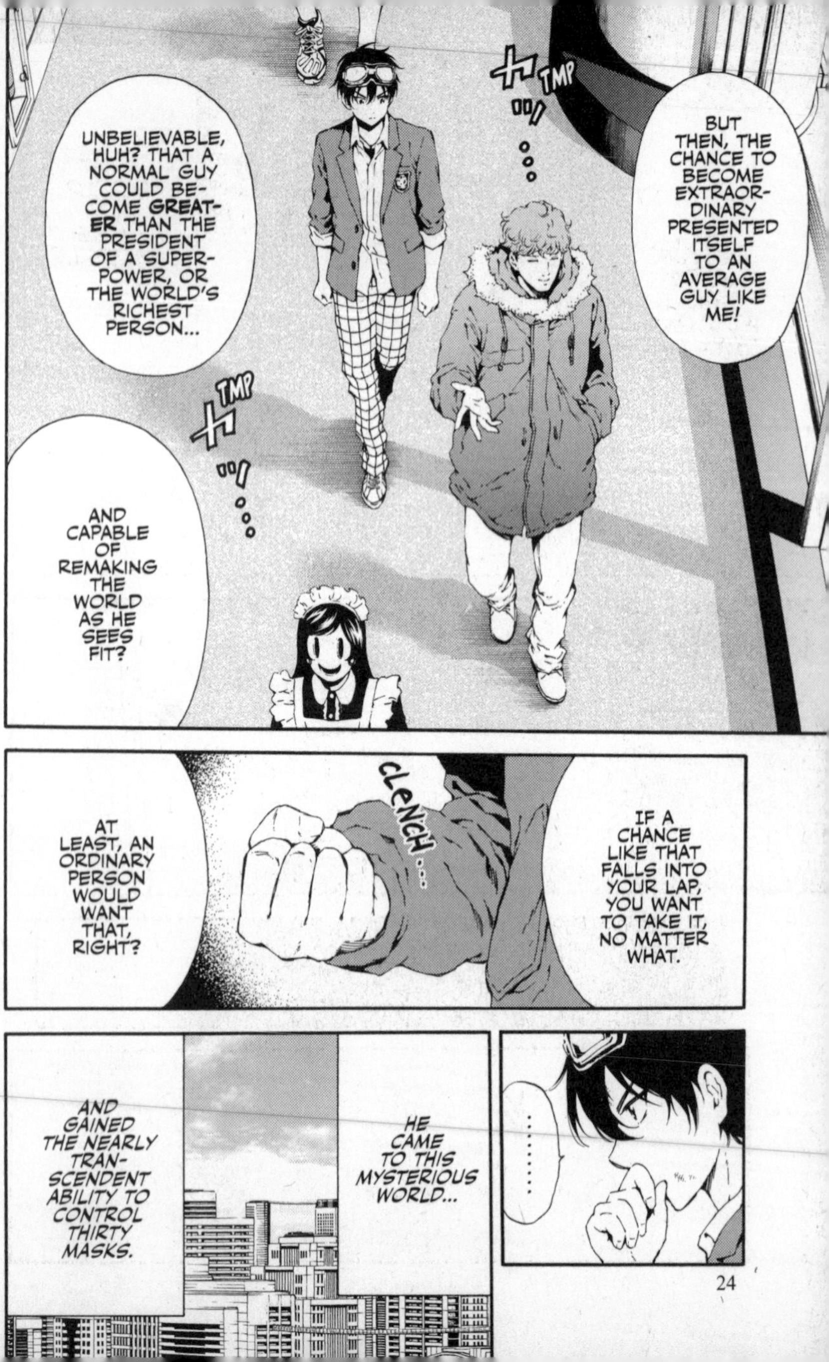
BUT THEN, THE CHANCE TO BECOME EXTRAORDINARY PRESENTED ITSELF TO AN AVERAGE GUY LIKE ME!
TMP
UNBELIEVABLE, HUH? THAT A NORMAL GUY COULD BECOME **GREATER** THAN THE PRESIDENT OF A SUPERPOWER, OR THE WORLD'S RICHEST PERSON...
TMP
AND CAPABLE OF REMAKING THE WORLD AS HE SEES FIT?
IF A CHANCE LIKE THAT FALLS INTO YOUR LAP, YOU WANT TO TAKE IT, NO MATTER WHAT.
CLENCH...
AT LEAST, AN ORDINARY PERSON WOULD WANT THAT, RIGHT?
......
HE CAME TO THIS MYSTERIOUS WORLD...
AND GAINED THE NEARLY TRANSCENDENT ABILITY TO CONTROL THIRTY MASKS.

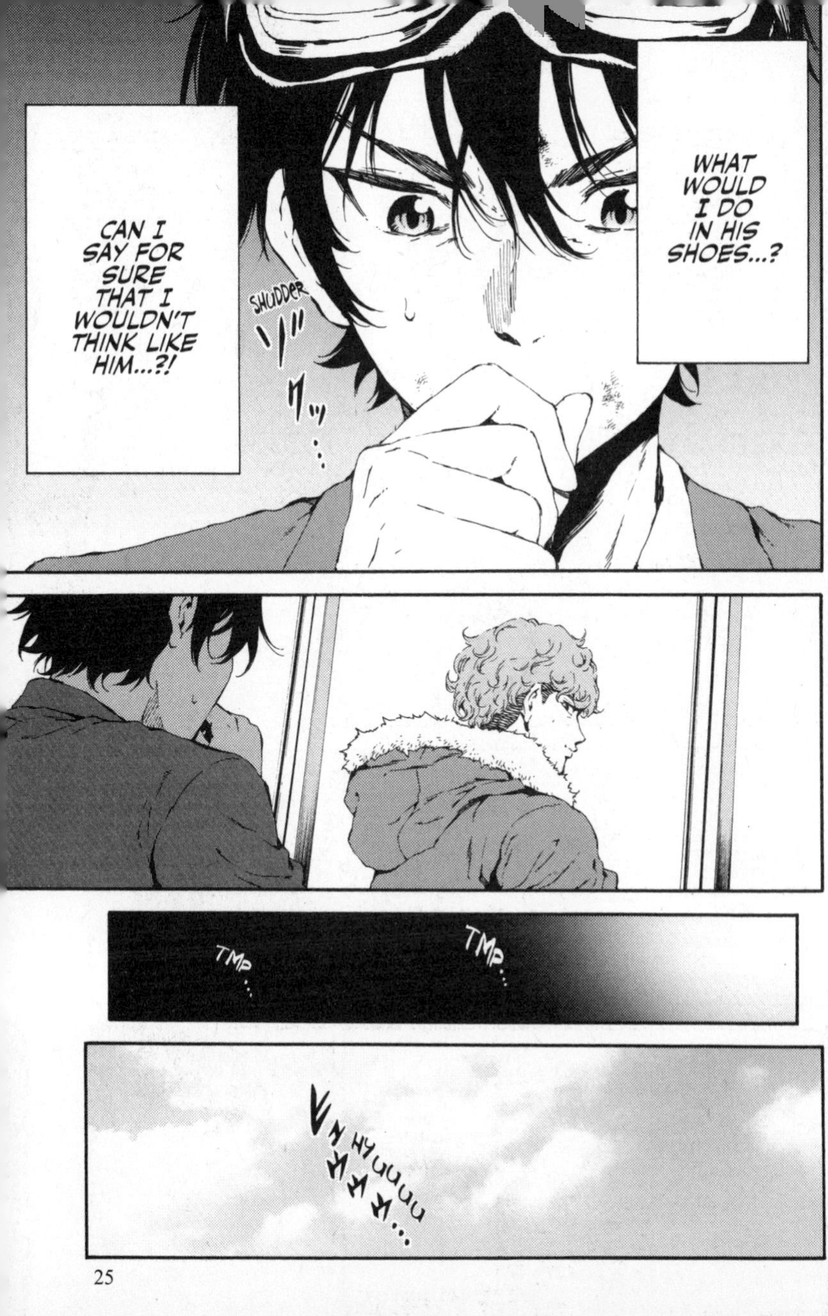
WHAT WOULD I DO IN HIS SHOES...?
SHUDDER
CAN I SAY FOR SURE THAT I WOULDN'T THINK LIKE HIM...?!
TMP...
TMP...
HYUUUU

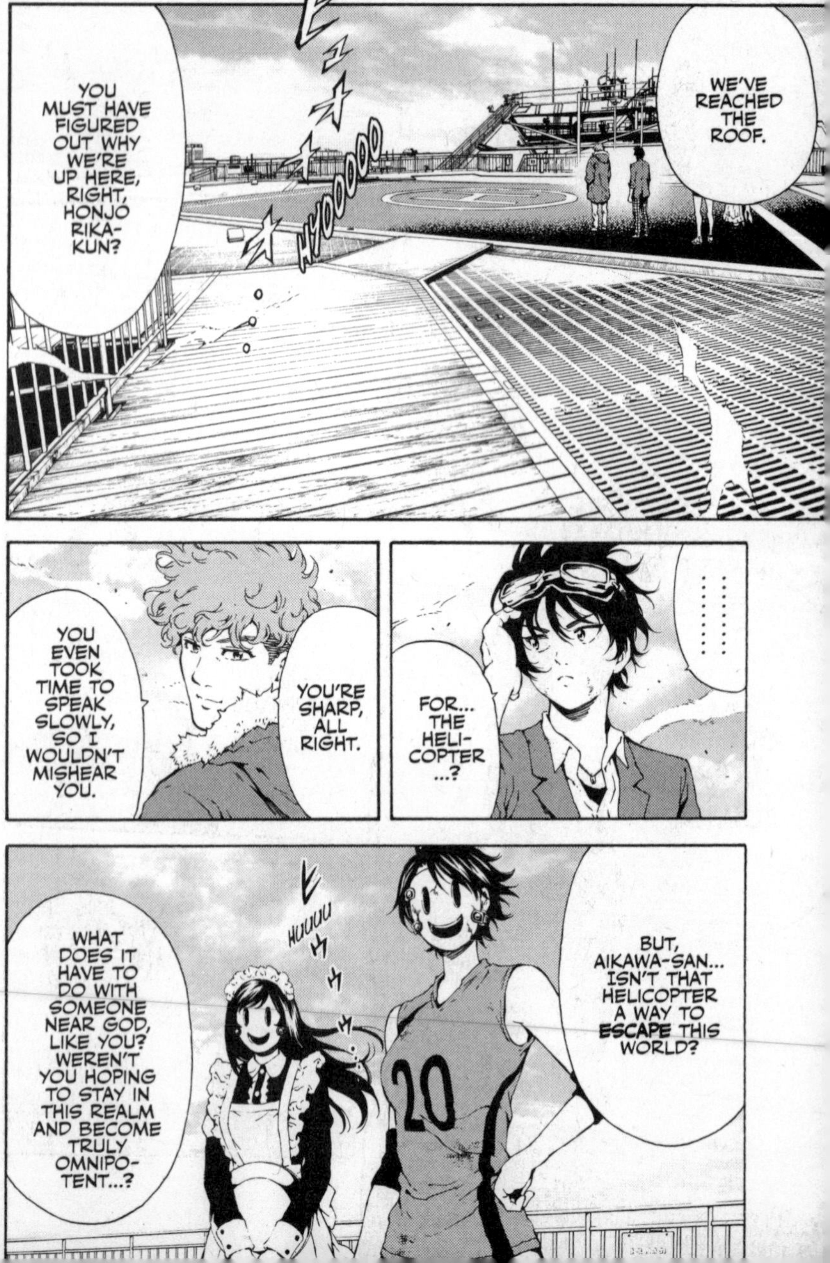
WE'VE REACHED THE ROOF.
HYOOOOO
YOU MUST HAVE FIGURED OUT WHY WE'RE UP HERE, RIGHT, HONJO RIKA-KUN?
......
FOR... THE HELI-COPTER ...?
YOU'RE SHARP, ALL RIGHT.
YOU EVEN TOOK TIME TO SPEAK SLOWLY, SO I WOULDN'T MISHEAR YOU.
BUT, AIKAWA-SAN... ISN'T THAT HELICOPTER A WAY TO ESCAPE THIS WORLD?
HUUUU
WHAT DOES IT HAVE TO DO WITH SOMEONE NEAR GOD, LIKE YOU? WEREN'T YOU HOPING TO STAY IN THIS REALM AND BECOME TRULY OMNIPO-TENT...?

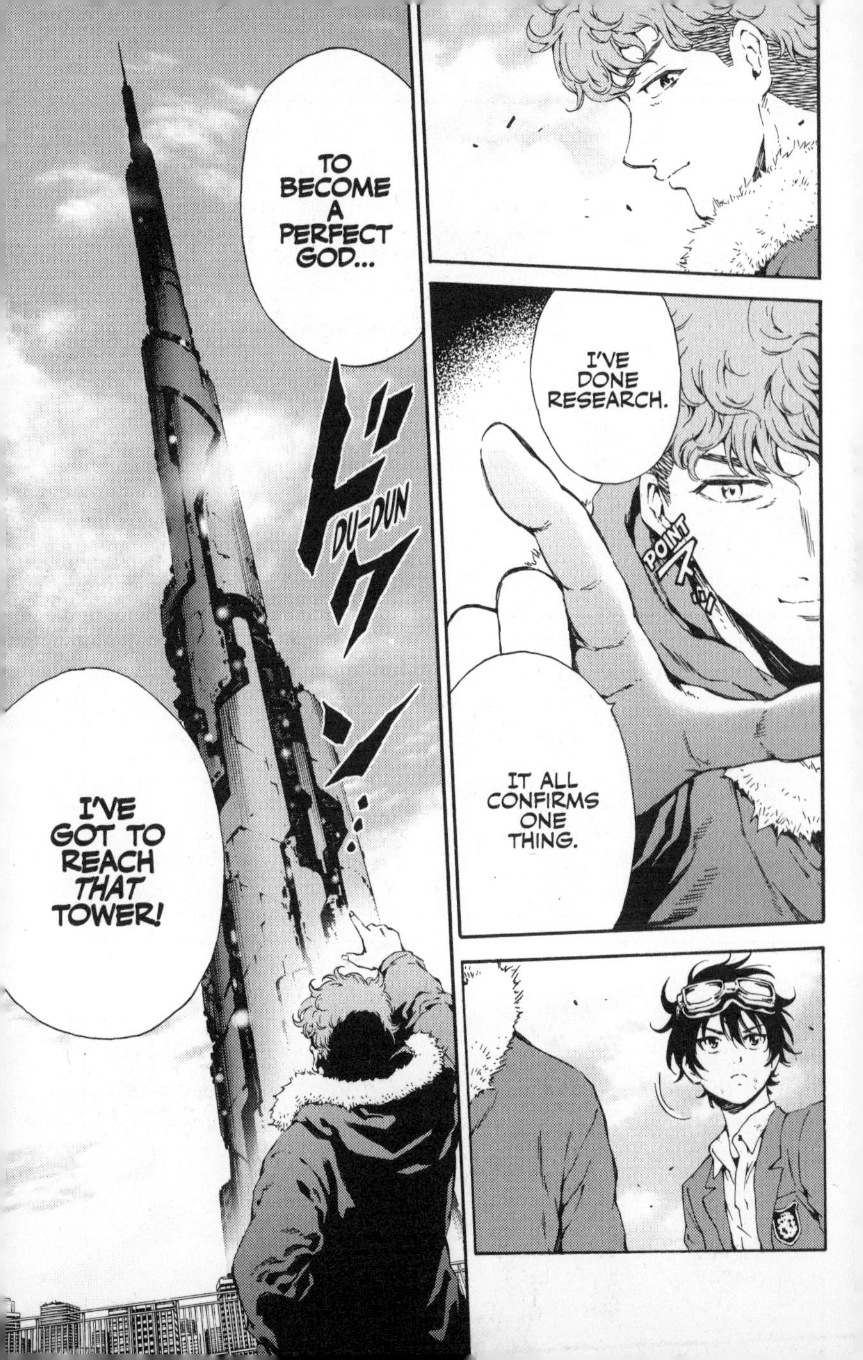
I'VE DONE RESEARCH.
POINT
IT ALL CONFIRMS ONE THING.
TO BECOME A PERFECT GOD...
DU-DUN
I'VE GOT TO REACH *THAT* TOWER!

THE TALLEST TOWER... I FIGURED IT WASN'T JUST THE RAILGUN'S BATTERY. BUT...

I... I SEE...

HOWEVER, NO BRIDGE LEADS TO THAT PLACE.

AND A HIGH WALL BLOCKS THE GROUND FLOORS COMPLETELY.

SO... HOW DO YOU GET IN?

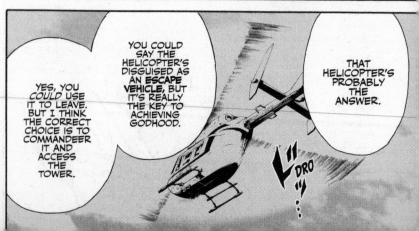

THAT HELICOPTER'S PROBABLY THE ANSWER.

YOU COULD SAY THE HELICOPTER'S DISGUISED AS AN **ESCAPE VEHICLE**, BUT IT'S REALLY THE KEY TO ACHIEVING GODHOOD.

YES, YOU *COULD* USE IT TO LEAVE. BUT I THINK THE CORRECT CHOICE IS TO COMMANDEER IT AND ACCESS THE TOWER.

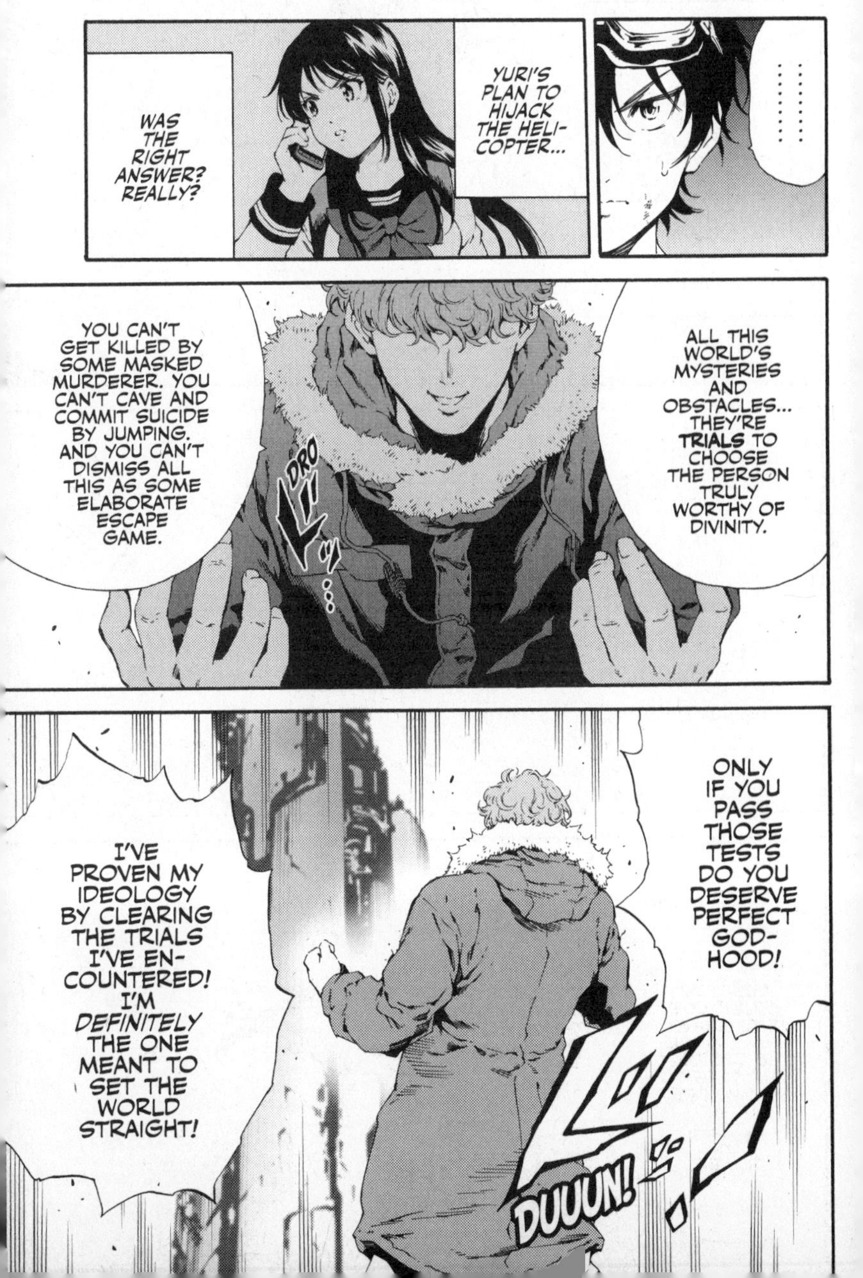
......
YURI'S PLAN TO HIJACK THE HELI-COPTER...
WAS THE RIGHT ANSWER? REALLY?
ALL THIS WORLD'S MYSTERIES AND OBSTACLES... THEY'RE **TRIALS** TO CHOOSE THE PERSON TRULY WORTHY OF DIVINITY.
YOU CAN'T GET KILLED BY SOME MASKED MURDERER. YOU CAN'T CAVE AND COMMIT SUICIDE BY JUMPING. AND YOU CAN'T DISMISS ALL THIS AS SOME ELABORATE ESCAPE GAME.
DRO
ONLY IF YOU PASS THOSE TESTS DO YOU DESERVE PERFECT GOD-HOOD!
I'VE PROVEN MY IDEOLOGY BY CLEARING THE TRIALS I'VE EN-COUNTERED! I'M *DEFINITELY* THE ONE MEANT TO SET THE WORLD STRAIGHT!
DUUUN!

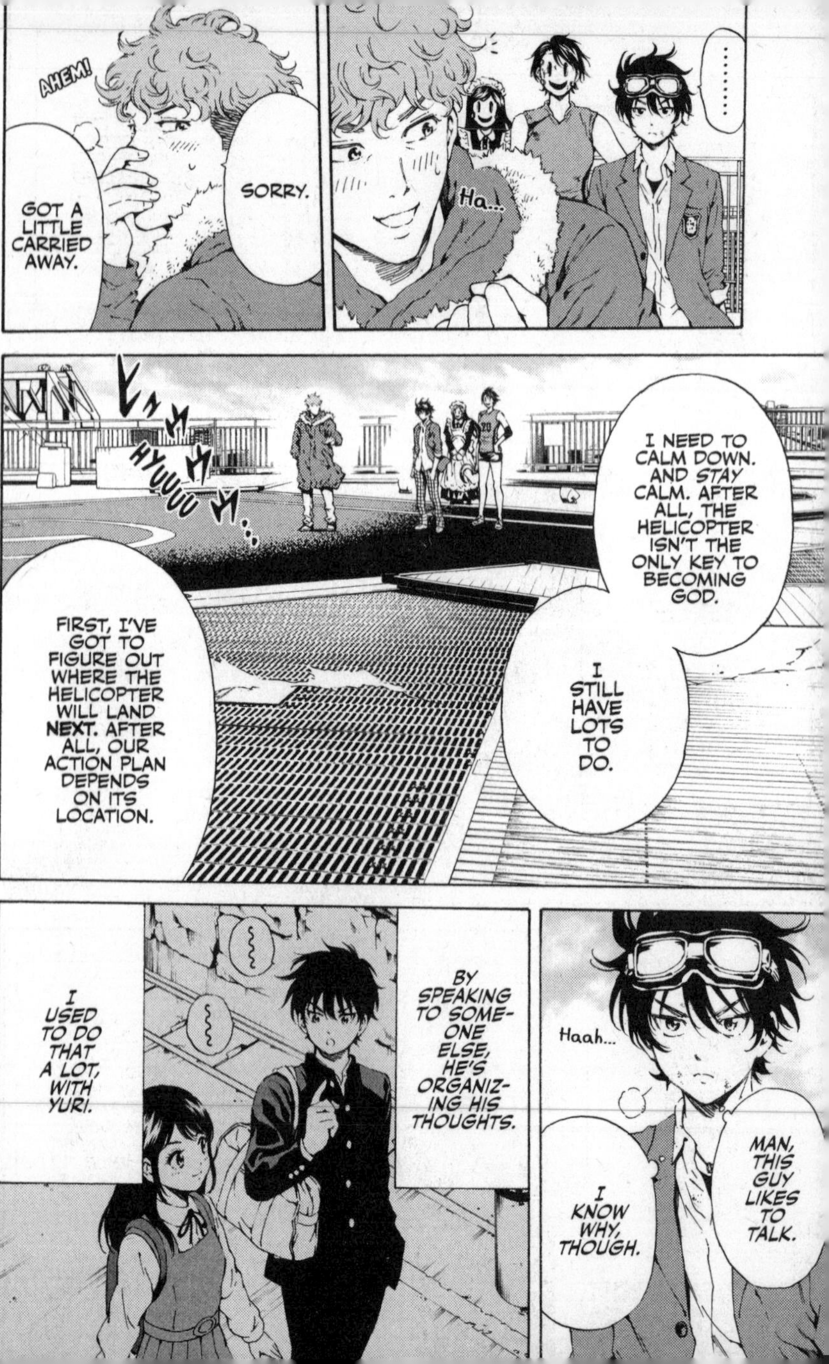
......
Ha...
AHEM!
SORRY.
GOT A LITTLE CARRIED AWAY.
I NEED TO CALM DOWN. AND STAY CALM. AFTER ALL, THE HELICOPTER ISN'T THE ONLY KEY TO BECOMING GOD.
I STILL HAVE LOTS TO DO.
HYUUUU...
FIRST, I'VE GOT TO FIGURE OUT WHERE THE HELICOPTER WILL LAND NEXT. AFTER ALL, OUR ACTION PLAN DEPENDS ON ITS LOCATION.
Haah...
MAN, THIS GUY LIKES TO TALK.
I KNOW WHY, THOUGH.
BY SPEAKING TO SOMEONE ELSE, HE'S ORGANIZING HIS THOUGHTS.
I USED TO DO THAT A LOT, WITH YURI.

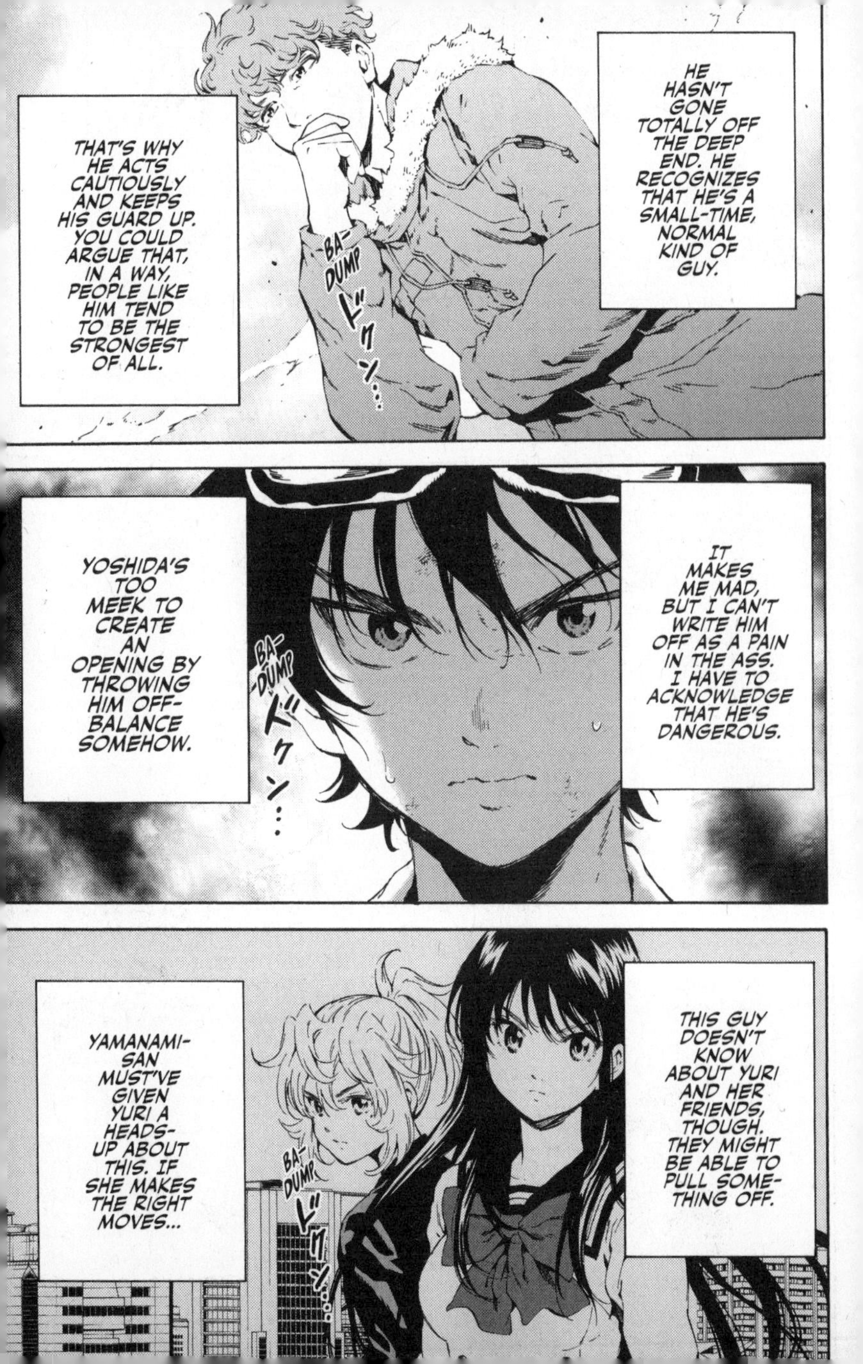
HE HASN'T GONE TOTALLY OFF THE DEEP END. HE RECOGNIZES THAT HE'S A SMALL-TIME, NORMAL KIND OF GUY.
BA-DUMP
ドクン…
THAT'S WHY HE ACTS CAUTIOUSLY AND KEEPS HIS GUARD UP. YOU COULD ARGUE THAT, IN A WAY, PEOPLE LIKE HIM TEND TO BE THE STRONGEST OF ALL.
IT MAKES ME MAD, BUT I CAN'T WRITE HIM OFF AS A PAIN IN THE ASS. I HAVE TO ACKNOWLEDGE THAT HE'S DANGEROUS.
BA-DUMP
ドクン…
YOSHIDA'S TOO MEEK TO CREATE AN OPENING BY THROWING HIM OFF-BALANCE SOMEHOW.
THIS GUY DOESN'T KNOW ABOUT YURI AND HER FRIENDS, THOUGH. THEY MIGHT BE ABLE TO PULL SOME-THING OFF.
BA-DUMP
ドクン…
YAMANAMI-SAN MUST'VE GIVEN YURI A HEADS-UP ABOUT THIS. IF SHE MAKES THE RIGHT MOVES...

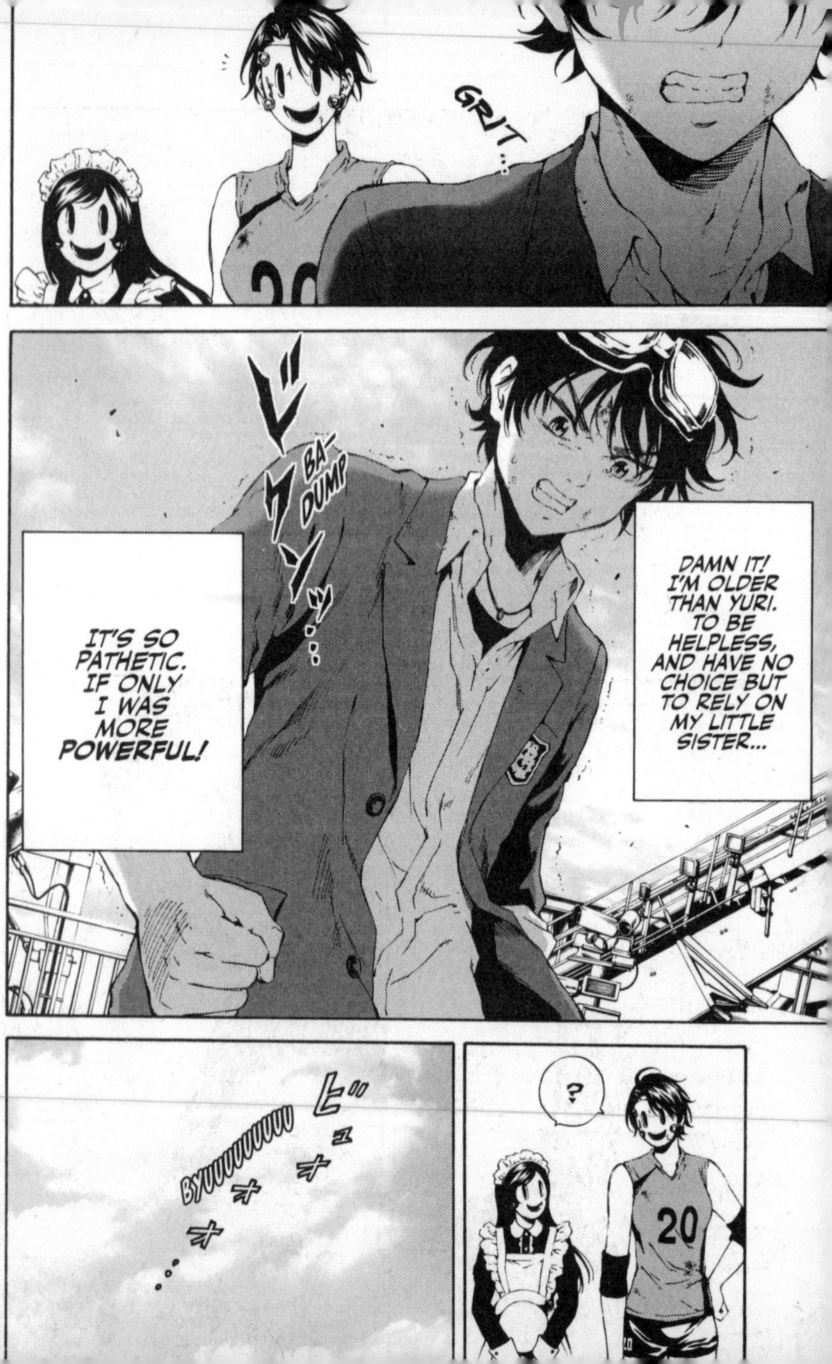
GRIT...
DAMN IT! I'M OLDER THAN YURI. TO BE HELPLESS, AND HAVE NO CHOICE BUT TO RELY ON MY LITTLE SISTER...
BA-DUMP
IT'S SO PATHETIC. IF ONLY I WAS MORE POWERFUL!
?
BYUUUUUUUUU

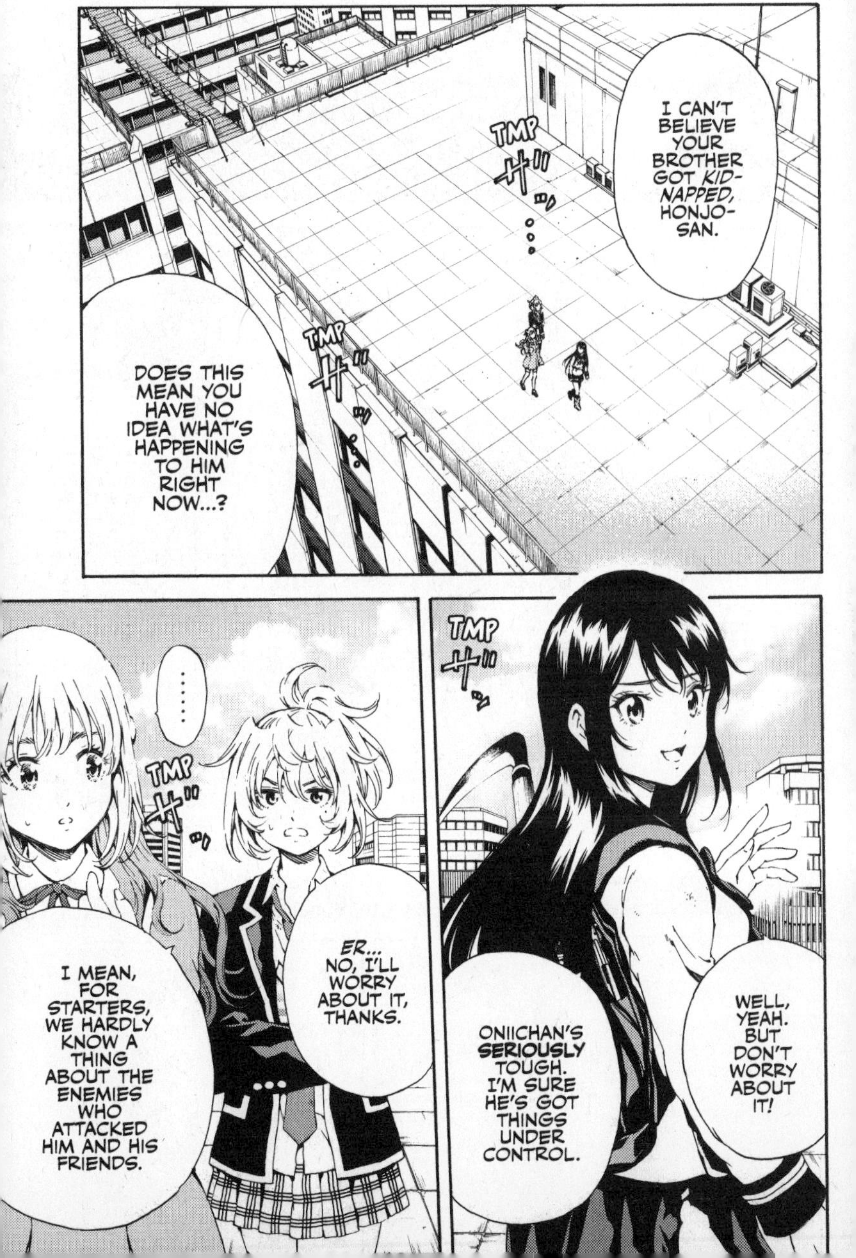
I CAN'T BELIEVE YOUR BROTHER GOT KID-NAPPED, HONJO-SAN.
TMP
TMP
DOES THIS MEAN YOU HAVE NO IDEA WHAT'S HAPPENING TO HIM RIGHT NOW...?
TMP
WELL, YEAH. BUT DON'T WORRY ABOUT IT!
ONIICHAN'S SERIOUSLY TOUGH. I'M SURE HE'S GOT THINGS UNDER CONTROL.
......
TMP
ER... NO, I'LL WORRY ABOUT IT, THANKS.
I MEAN, FOR STARTERS, WE HARDLY KNOW A THING ABOUT THE ENEMIES WHO ATTACKED HIM AND HIS FRIENDS.

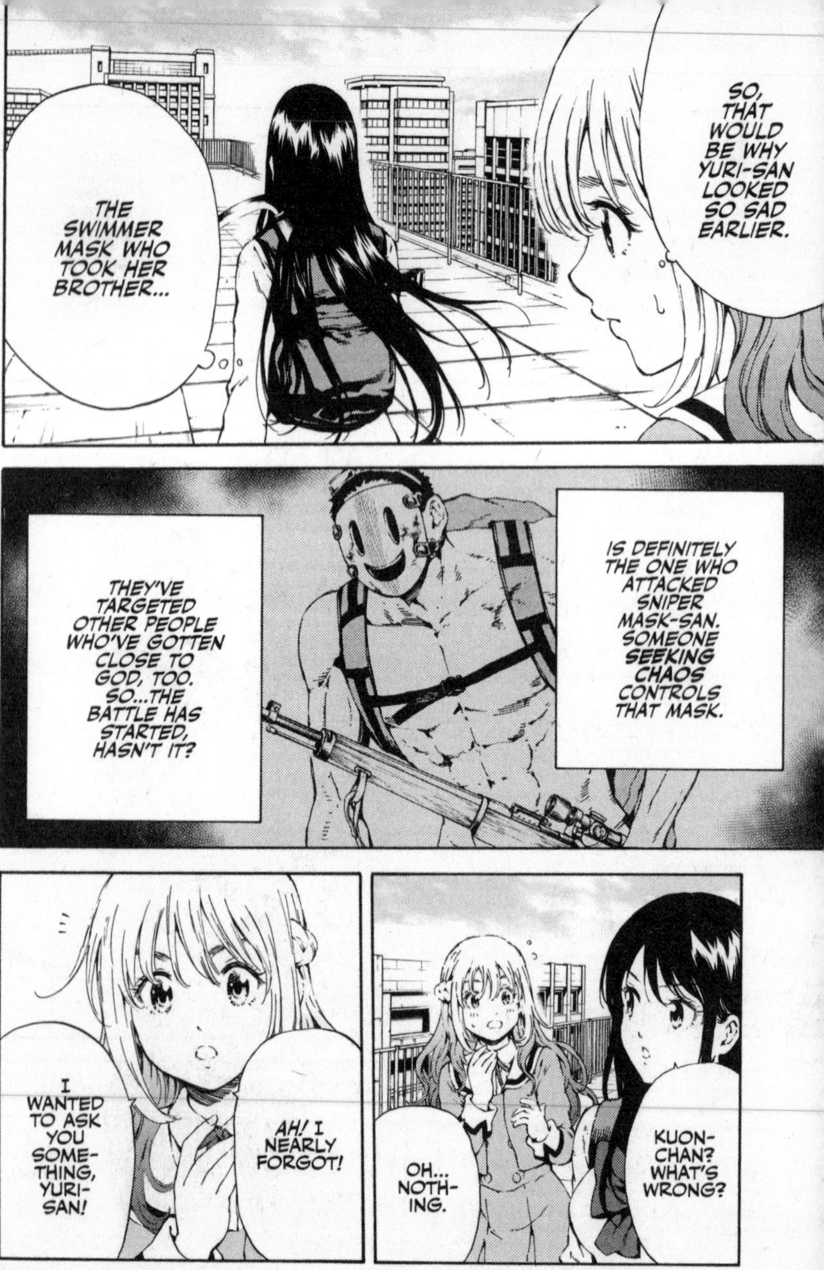
SO, THAT WOULD BE WHY YURI-SAN LOOKED SO SAD EARLIER.
THE SWIMMER MASK WHO TOOK HER BROTHER...
IS DEFINITELY THE ONE WHO ATTACKED SNIPER MASK-SAN. SOMEONE SEEKING CHAOS CONTROLS THAT MASK.
THEY'VE TARGETED OTHER PEOPLE WHO'VE GOTTEN CLOSE TO GOD, TOO. SO...THE BATTLE HAS STARTED, HASN'T IT?
KUON-CHAN? WHAT'S WRONG?
OH... NOTHING.
AH! I NEARLY FORGOT!
I WANTED TO ASK YOU SOMETHING, YURI-SAN!

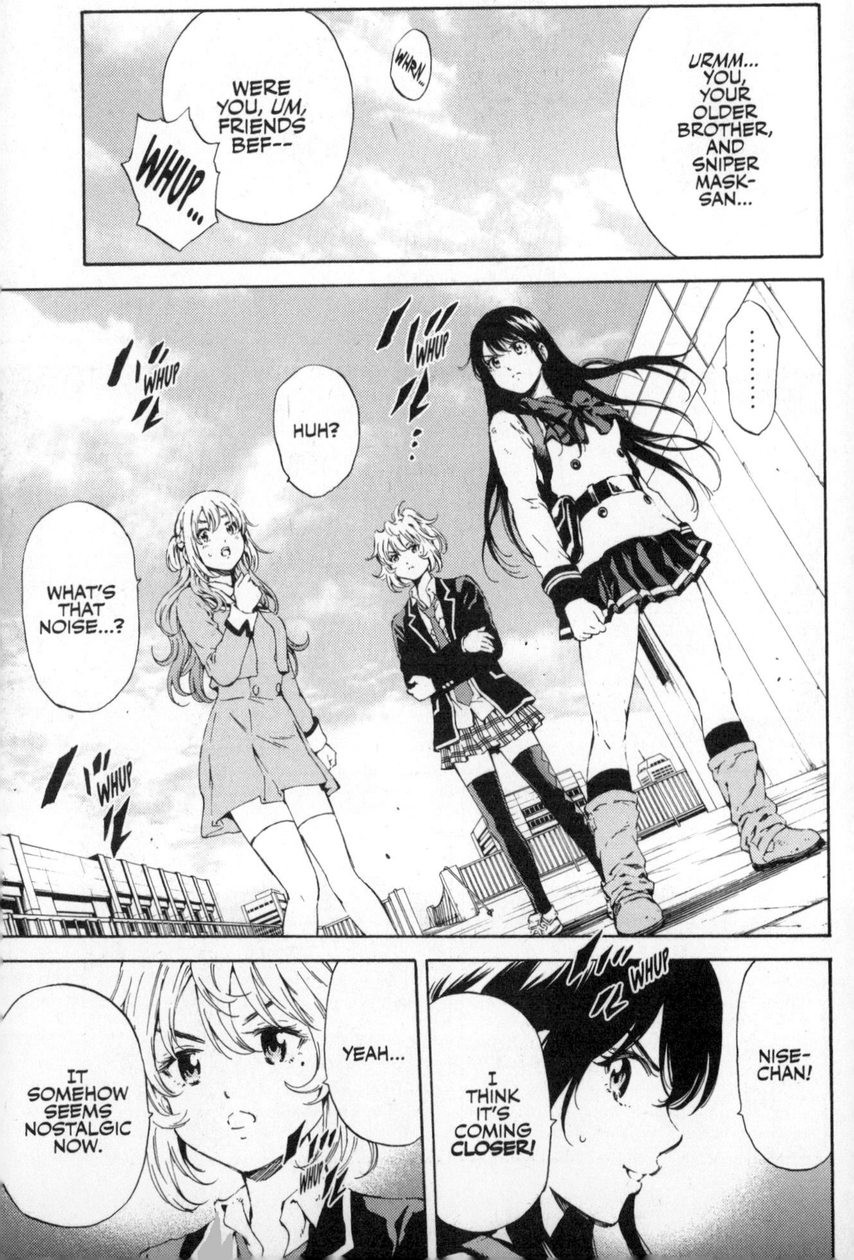
URMM... YOU, YOUR OLDER BROTHER, AND SNIPER MASK-SAN...
WHRN...
WERE YOU, UM, FRIENDS BEF--
WHUP...
......
WHUP
HUH?
WHUP
WHAT'S THAT NOISE...?
WHUP
WHUP
NISE-CHAN!
I THINK IT'S COMING CLOSER!
YEAH...
IT SOMEHOW SEEMS NOSTALGIC NOW.
WHUP

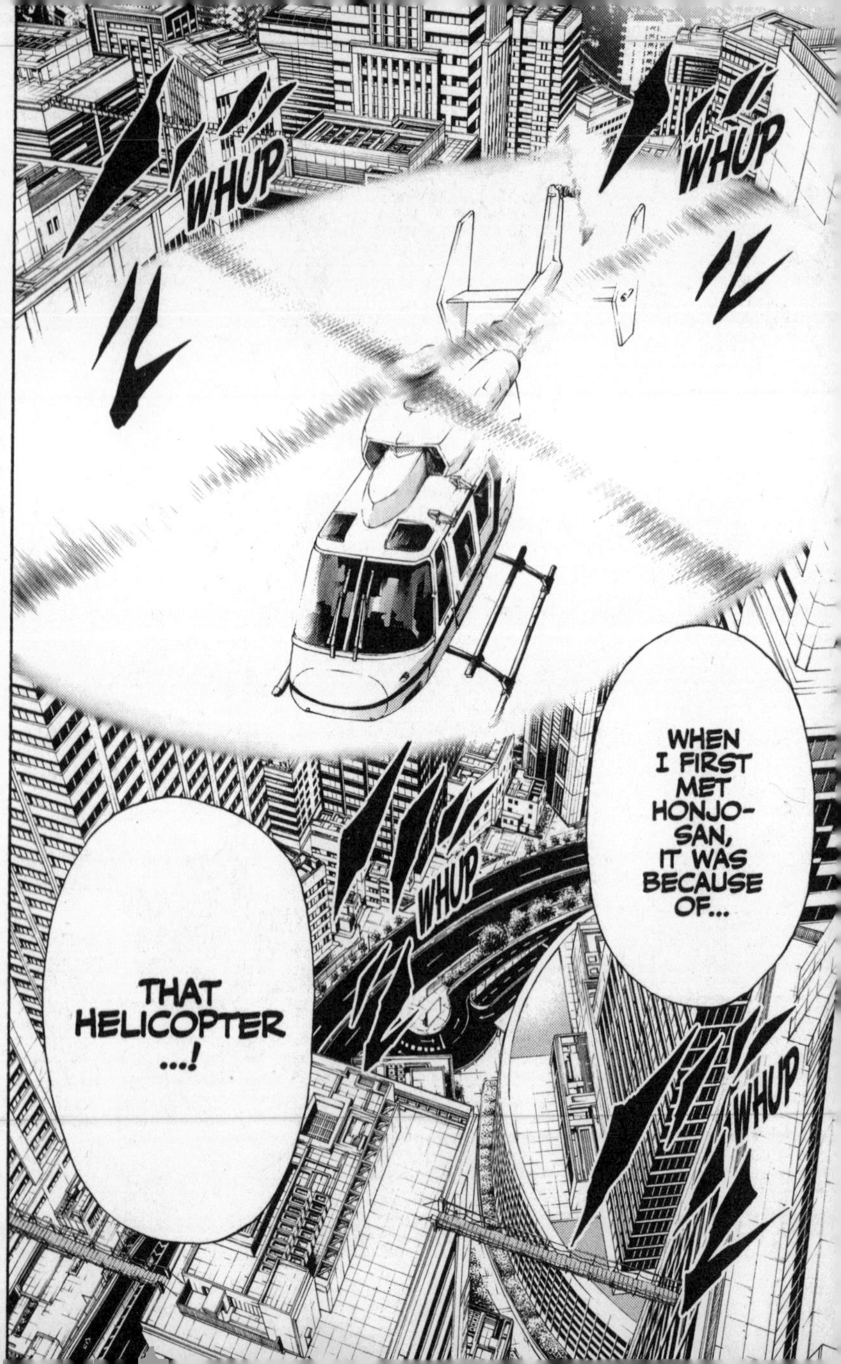
WHUP
WHUP
WHEN I FIRST MET HONJO-SAN, IT WAS BECAUSE OF...
WHUP
WHUP
THAT HELICOPTER ...!

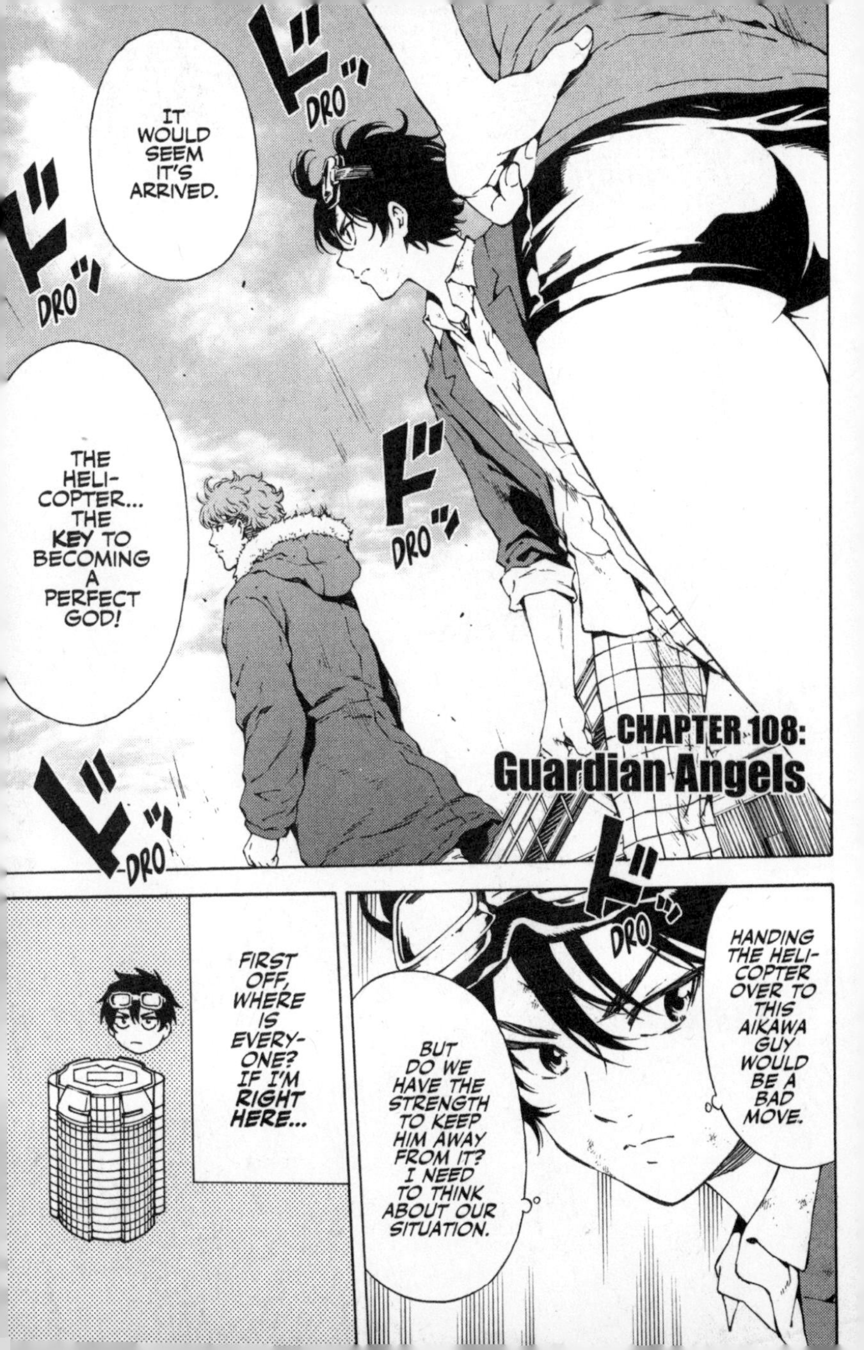
DRO
IT WOULD SEEM IT'S ARRIVED.
DRO
DRO
THE HELI-COPTER... THE KEY TO BECOMING A PERFECT GOD!
CHAPTER 108: Guardian Angels
DRO
DRO
HANDING THE HELI-COPTER OVER TO THIS AIKAWA GUY WOULD BE A BAD MOVE.
BUT DO WE HAVE THE STRENGTH TO KEEP HIM AWAY FROM IT? I NEED TO THINK ABOUT OUR SITUATION.
FIRST OFF, WHERE IS EVERY-ONE? IF I'M RIGHT HERE...

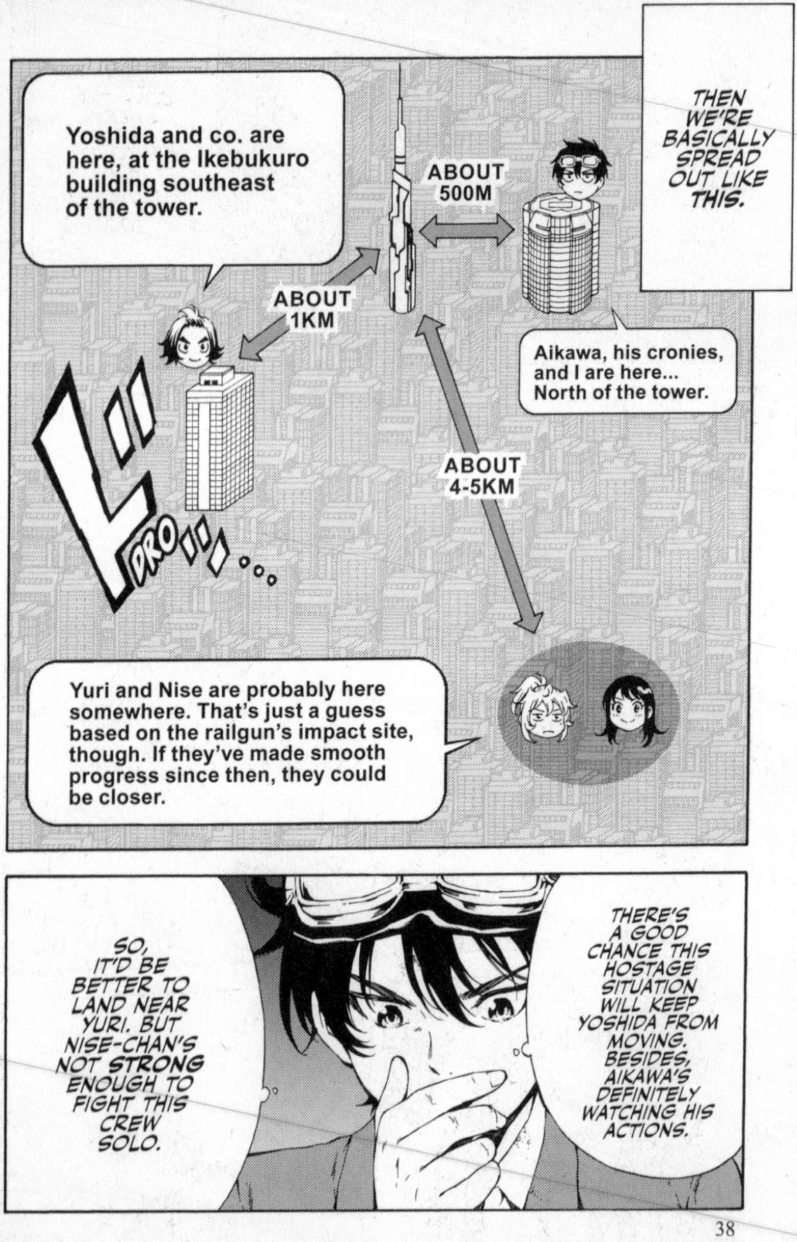
THEN WE'RE BASICALLY SPREAD OUT LIKE THIS.
ABOUT 500M
Aikawa, his cronies, and I are here... North of the tower.
Yoshida and co. are here, at the Ikebukuro building southeast of the tower.
ABOUT 1KM
ABOUT 4-5KM
DRO...
Yuri and Nise are probably here somewhere. That's just a guess based on the railgun's impact site, though. If they've made smooth progress since then, they could be closer.
THERE'S A GOOD CHANCE THIS HOSTAGE SITUATION WILL KEEP YOSHIDA FROM MOVING. BESIDES, AIKAWA'S DEFINITELY WATCHING HIS ACTIONS.
SO, IT'D BE BETTER TO LAND NEAR YURI. BUT NISE-CHAN'S NOT STRONG ENOUGH TO FIGHT THIS CREW SOLO.

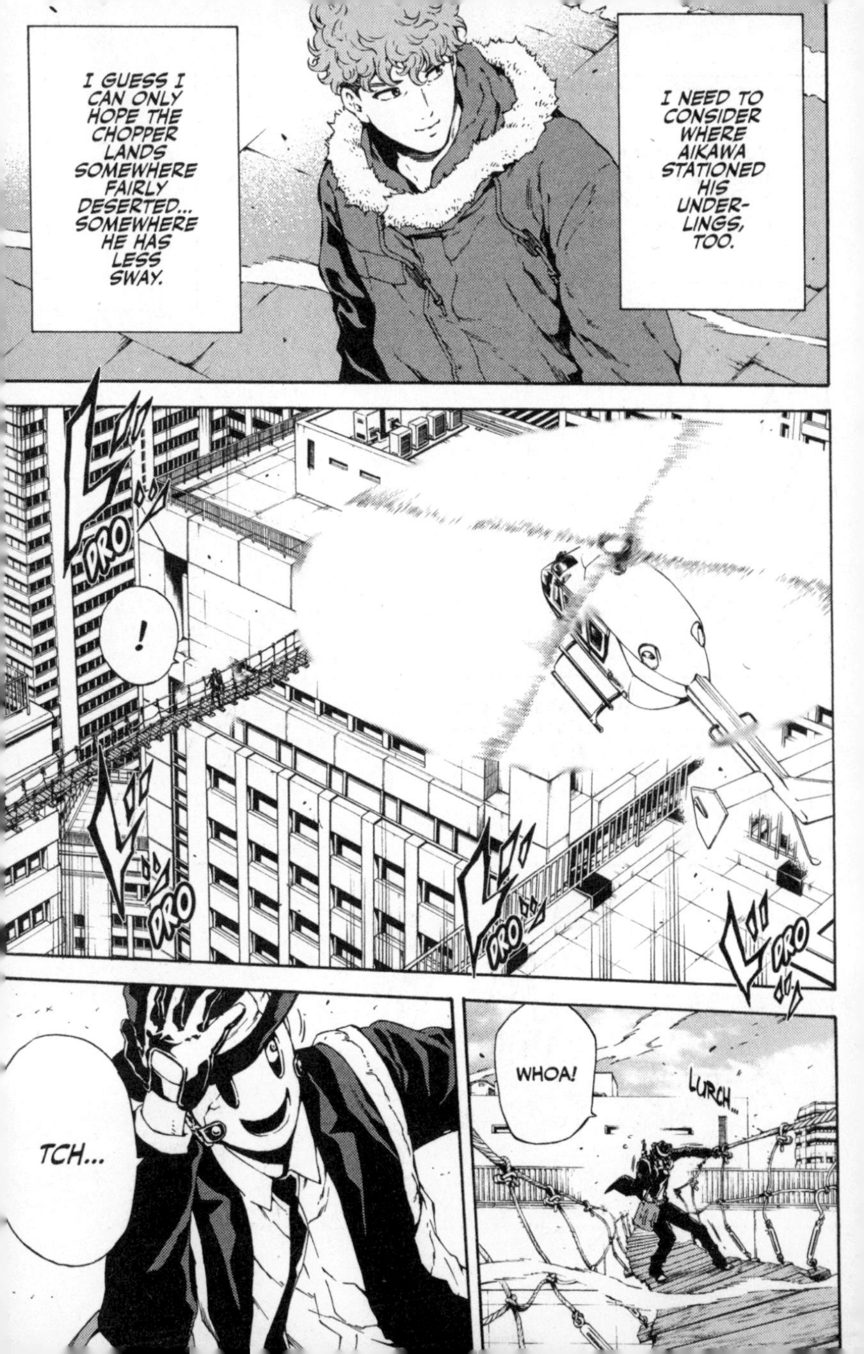
I NEED TO CONSIDER WHERE AIKAWA STATIONED HIS UNDER-LINGS, TOO.
I GUESS I CAN ONLY HOPE THE CHOPPER LANDS SOMEWHERE FAIRLY DESERTED... SOMEWHERE HE HAS LESS SWAY.
DRO
DRO
!
DRO
DRO
WHOA!
LURCH...
TCH...

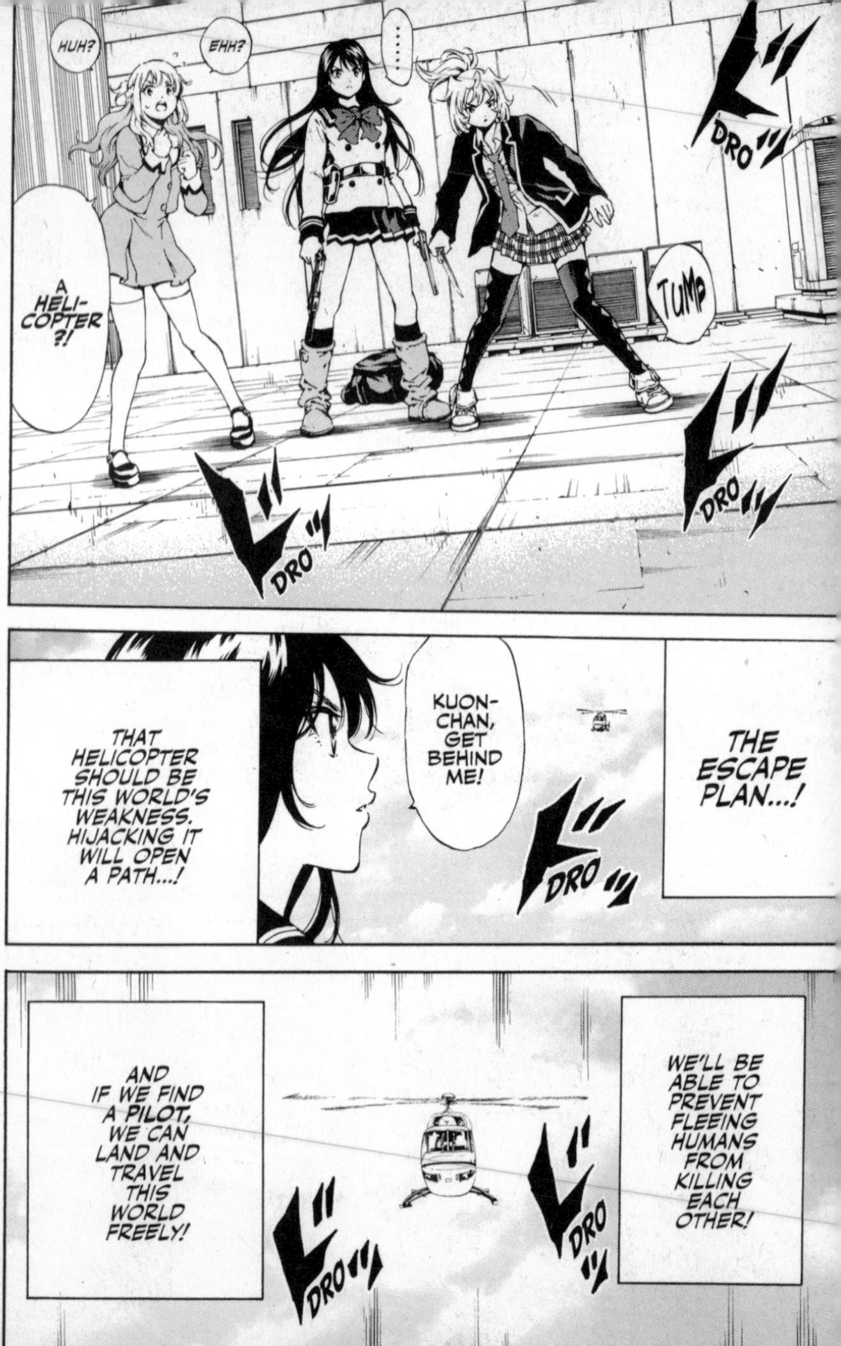
DRO
......
EHH?
HUH?
TUMP
A HELI-COPTER?!
DRO
DRO
THE ESCAPE PLAN...!
KUON-CHAN, GET BEHIND ME!
DRO
THAT HELICOPTER SHOULD BE THIS WORLD'S WEAKNESS. HIJACKING IT WILL OPEN A PATH...!
WE'LL BE ABLE TO PREVENT FLEEING HUMANS FROM KILLING EACH OTHER!
DRO
DRO
AND IF WE FIND A PILOT, WE CAN LAND AND TRAVEL THIS WORLD FREELY!

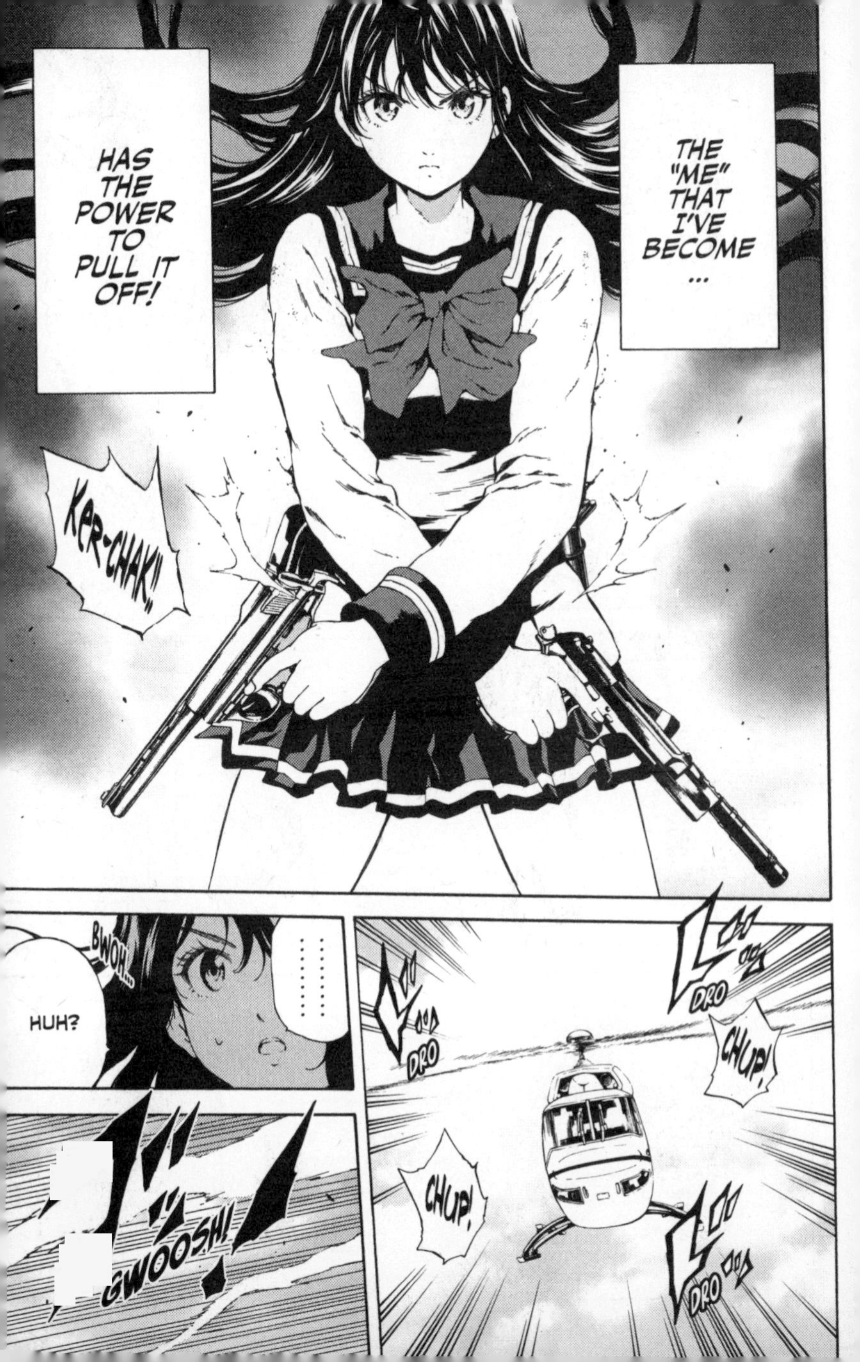
THE "ME" THAT I'VE BECOME ...
HAS THE POWER TO PULL IT OFF!
KER-CHAK!!
DRO
CHUP!
DRO
CHUP!
DRO
BWOH...
......
HUH?
GWOOSH!

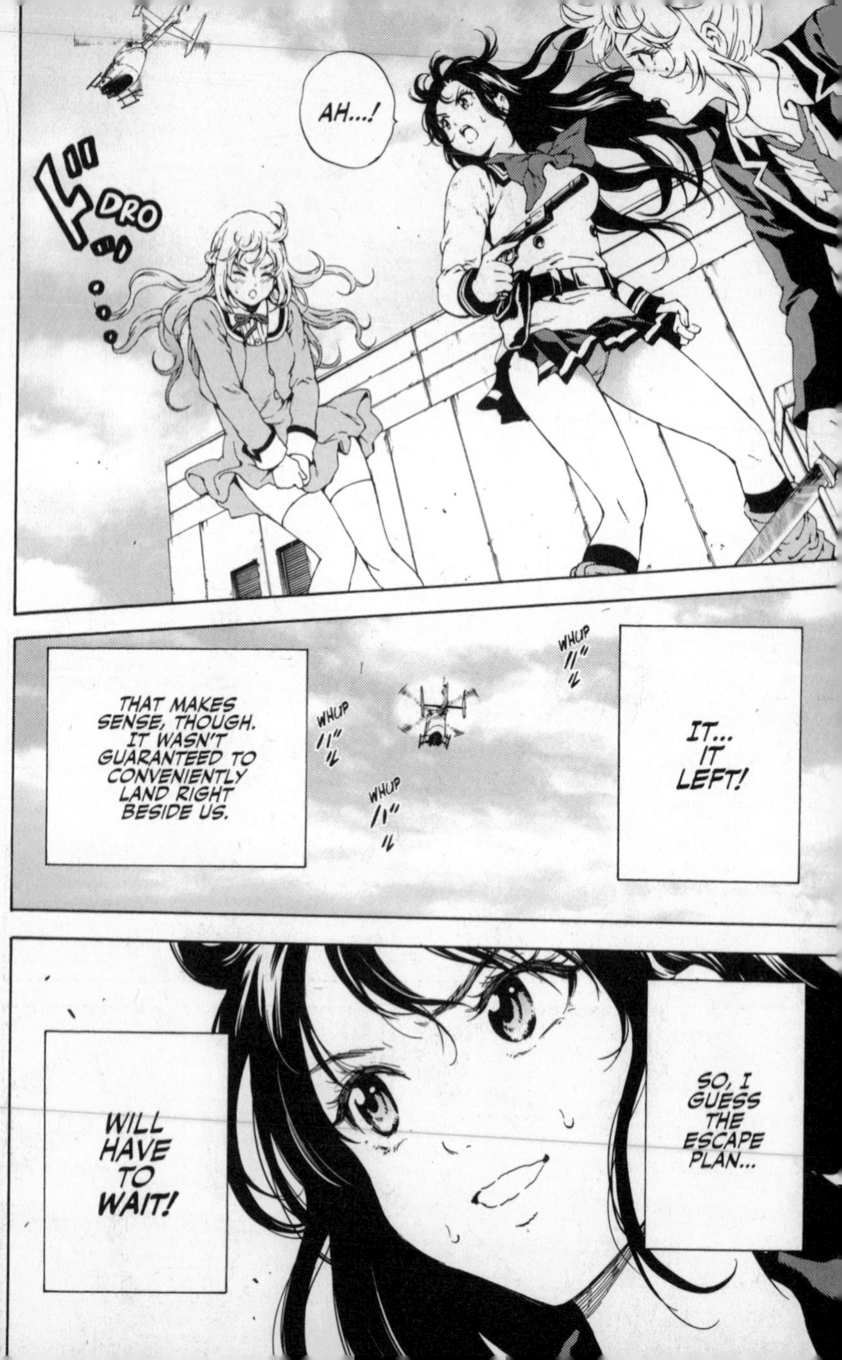
AH...!
DRO
IT... IT LEFT!
WHUP
WHUP
WHUP
THAT MAKES SENSE, THOUGH. IT WASN'T GUARANTEED TO CONVENIENTLY LAND RIGHT BESIDE US.
SO, I GUESS THE ESCAPE PLAN...
WILL HAVE TO WAIT!

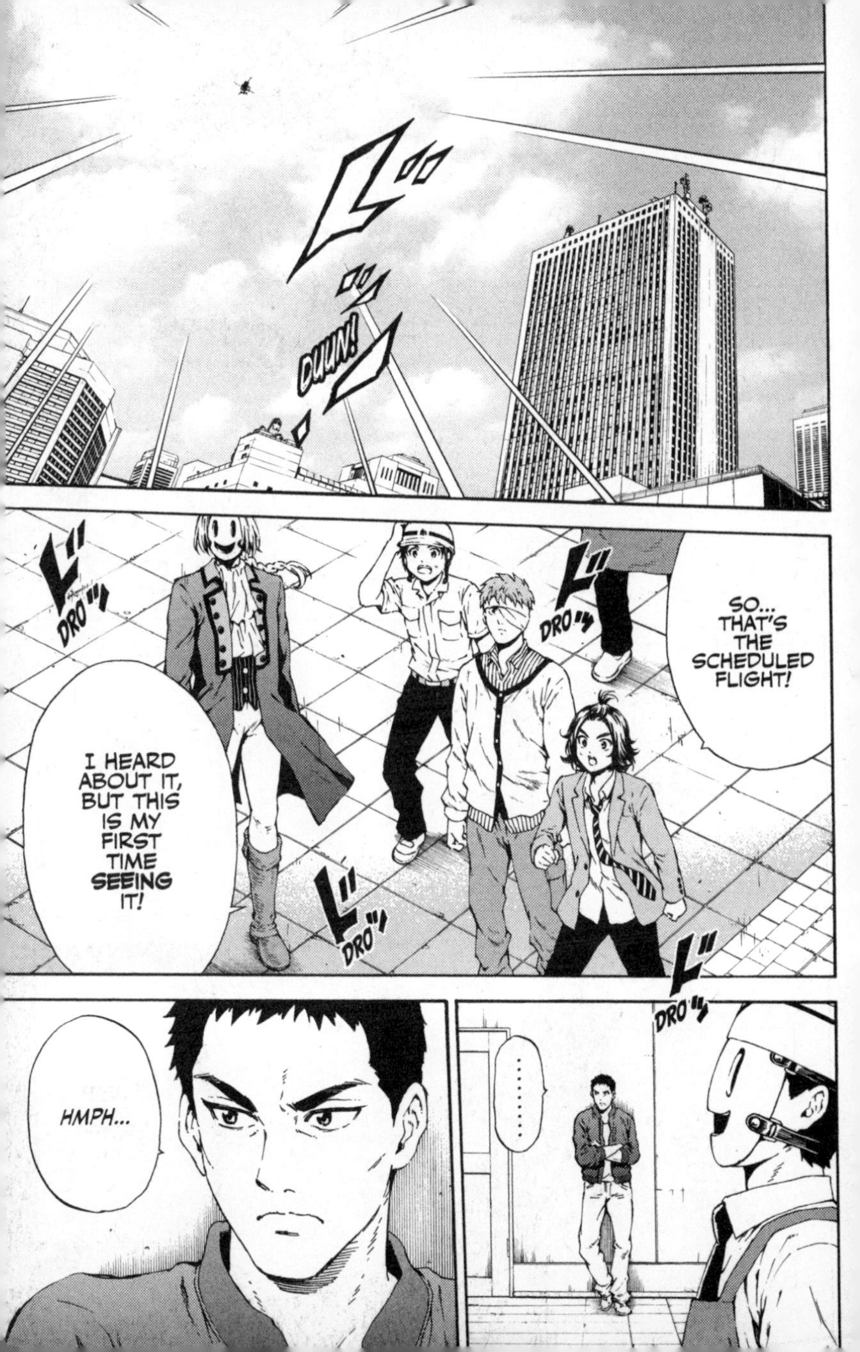
DUUN!
DRO
SO... THAT'S THE SCHEDULED FLIGHT!
DRO
I HEARD ABOUT IT, BUT THIS IS MY FIRST TIME SEEING IT!
DRO
DRO
......
HMPH...

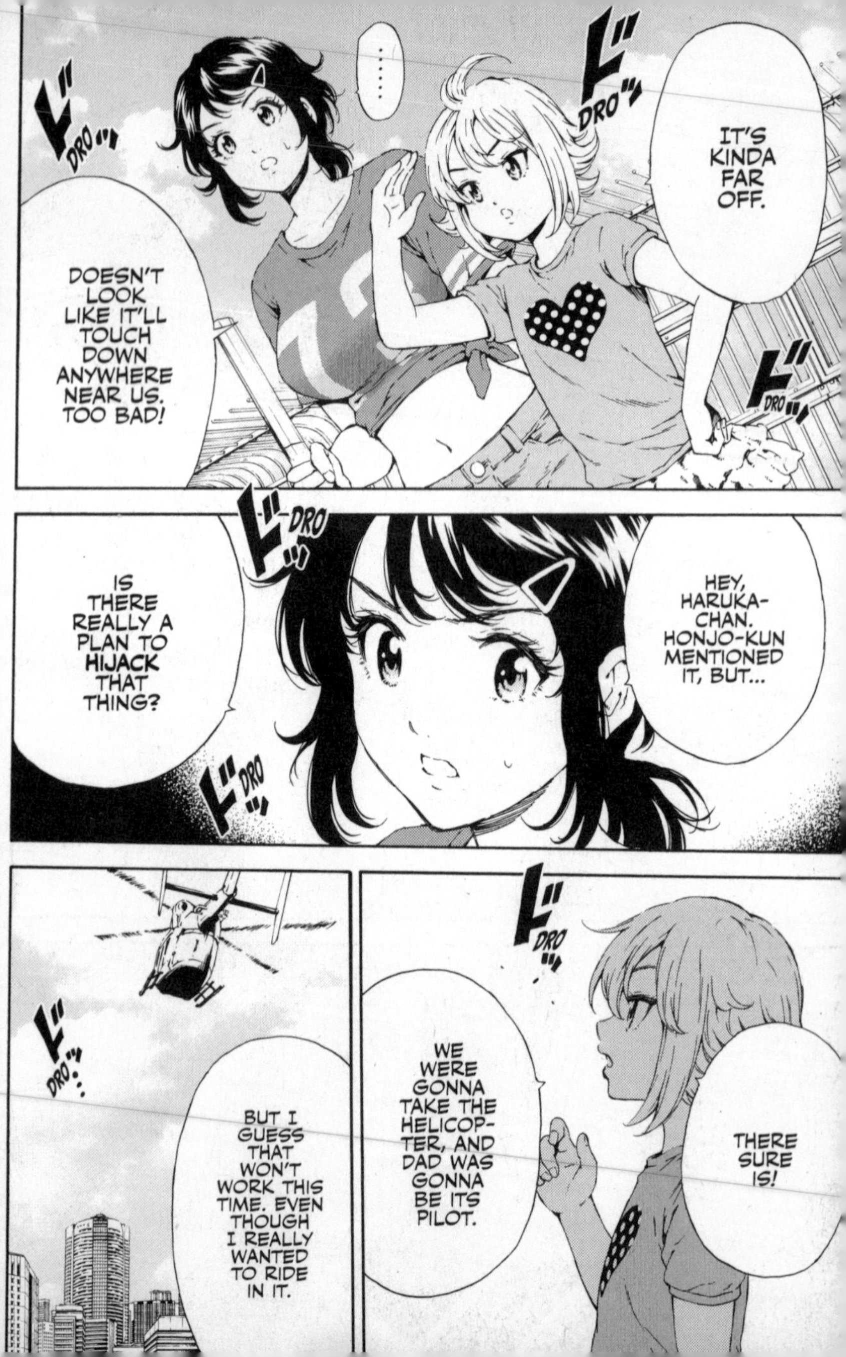
DRO
IT'S KINDA FAR OFF.
……
DRO
DOESN'T LOOK LIKE IT'LL TOUCH DOWN ANYWHERE NEAR US. TOO BAD!
DRO
HEY, HARUKA-CHAN. HONJO-KUN MENTIONED IT, BUT...
DRO
IS THERE REALLY A PLAN TO **HIJACK** THAT THING?
DRO
DRO
THERE SURE IS!
WE WERE GONNA TAKE THE HELICOPTER, AND DAD WAS GONNA BE ITS PILOT.
DRO
BUT I GUESS THAT WON'T WORK THIS TIME. EVEN THOUGH I REALLY WANTED TO RIDE IN IT.

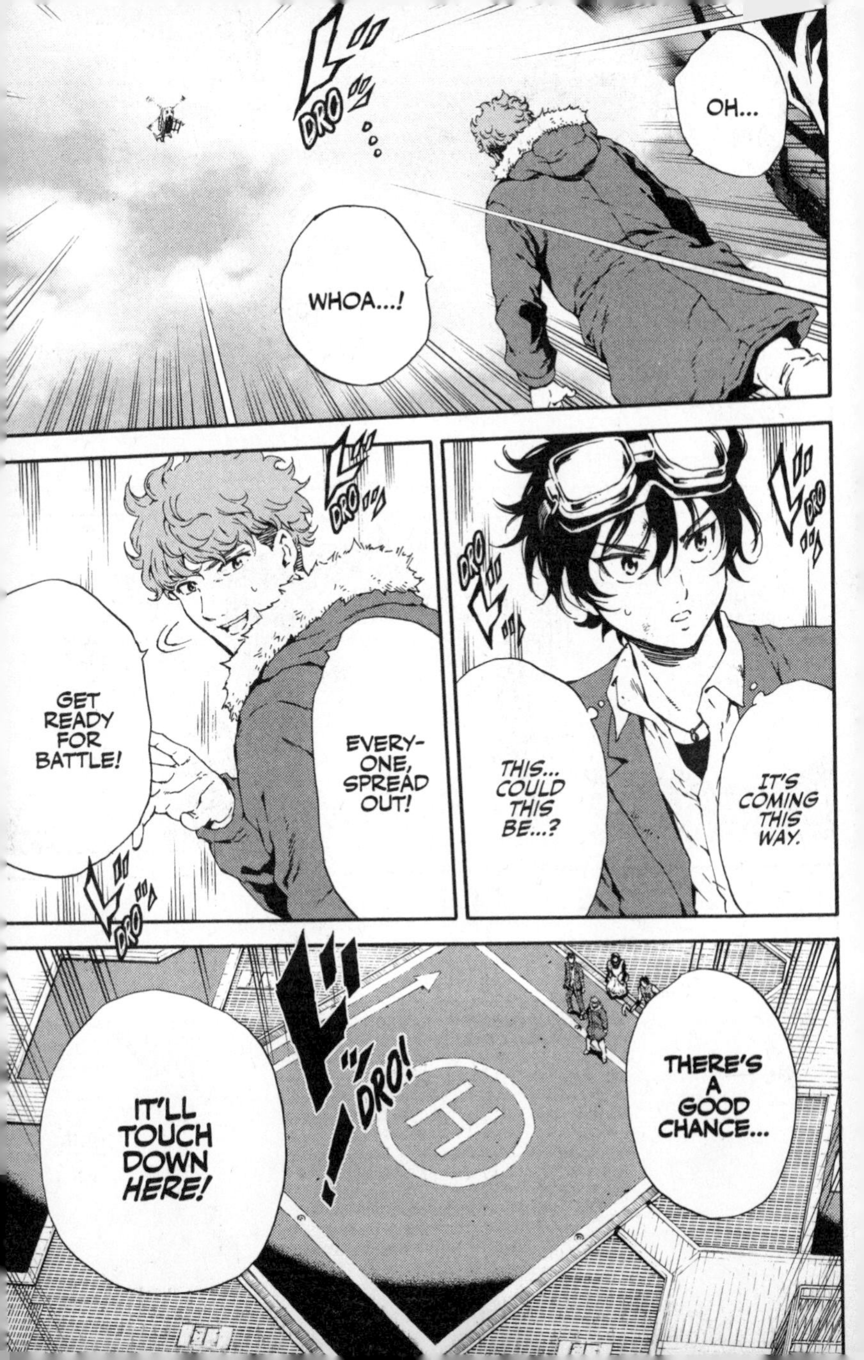
OH...
DRO
WHOA...!
DRO
DRO
IT'S COMING THIS WAY.
THIS... COULD THIS BE...?
DRO
EVERY-ONE, SPREAD OUT!
GET READY FOR BATTLE!
DRO
THERE'S A GOOD CHANCE...
DRO!
IT'LL TOUCH DOWN HERE!

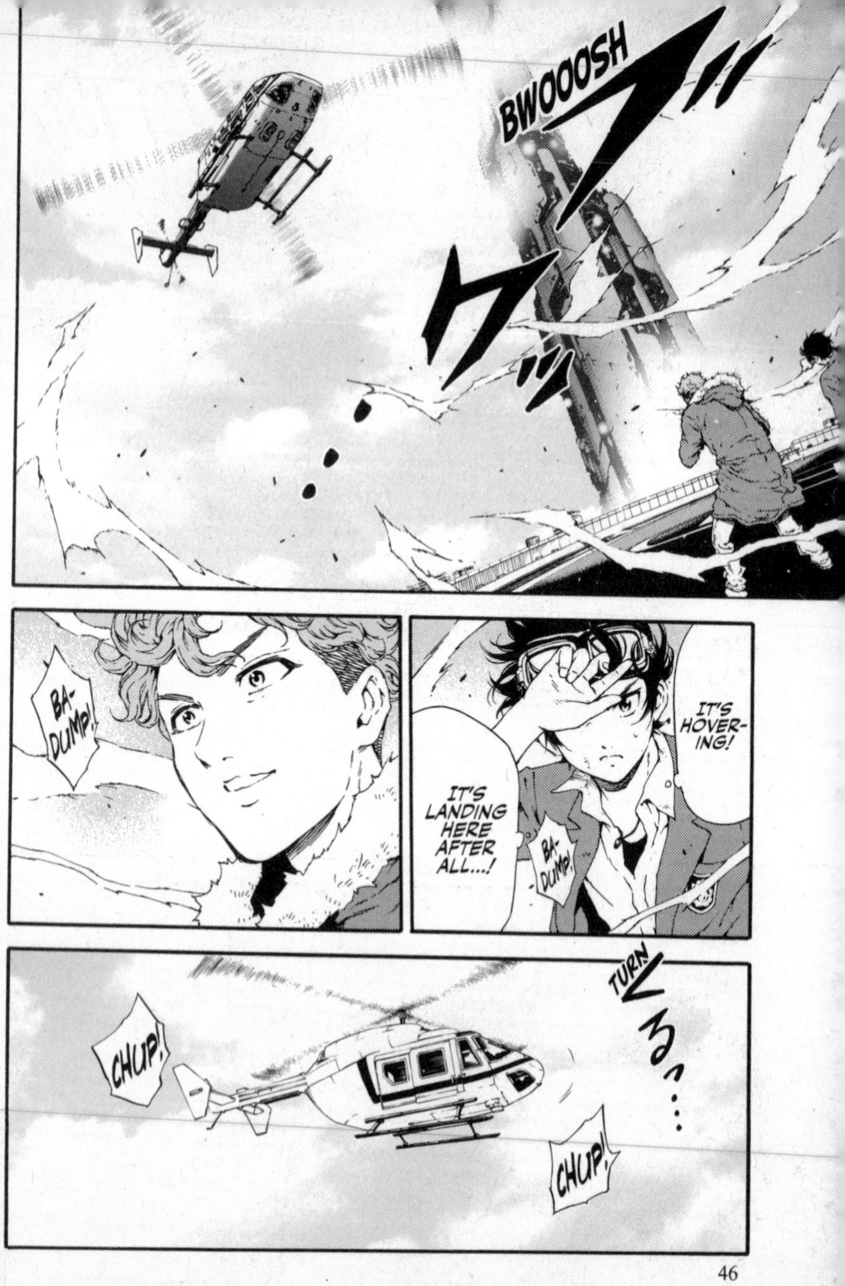
BWOOOSH
IT'S HOVER-ING!
IT'S LANDING HERE AFTER ALL...!
BA-DUMP!
BA-DUMP!
TURN
CHUP!
CHUP!

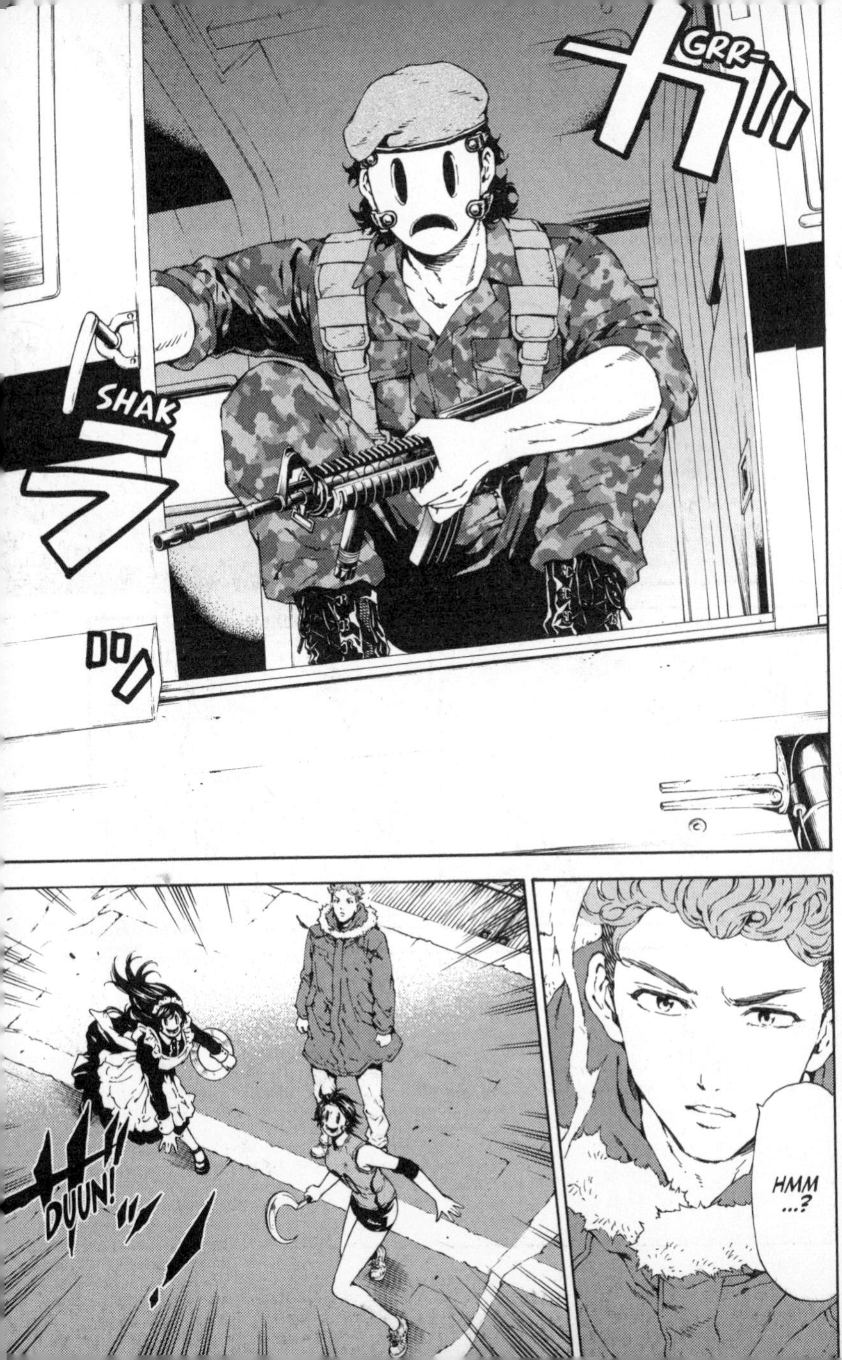
GRR-
SHAK
HMM ...?
DUUN!!

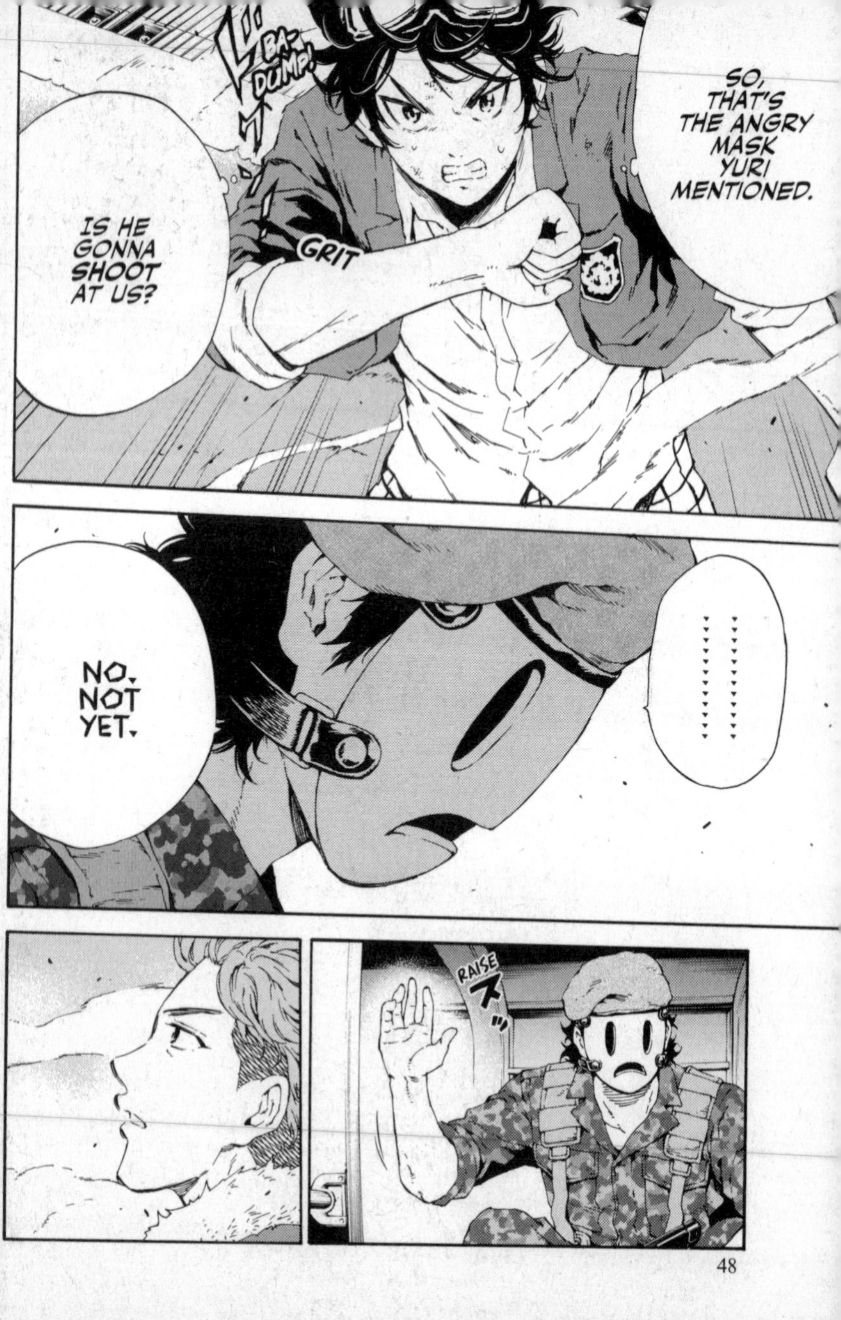

SO, THAT'S THE ANGRY MASK YURI MENTIONED.
BA-DUMP!
GRIT
IS HE GONNA SHOOT AT US?
......
NO. NOT YET.
RAISE

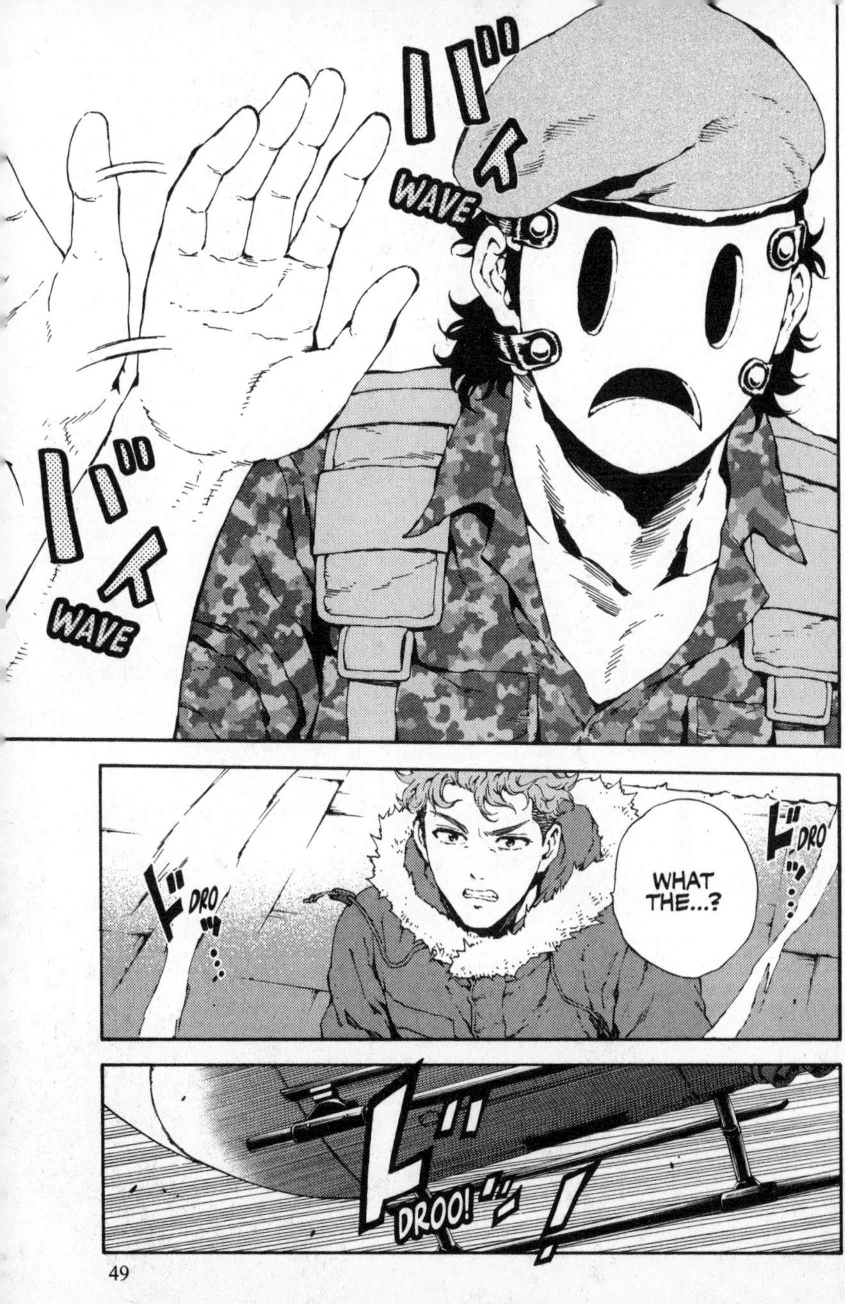
WAVE
WAVE
DRO
WHAT THE...?
DRO
DROO!

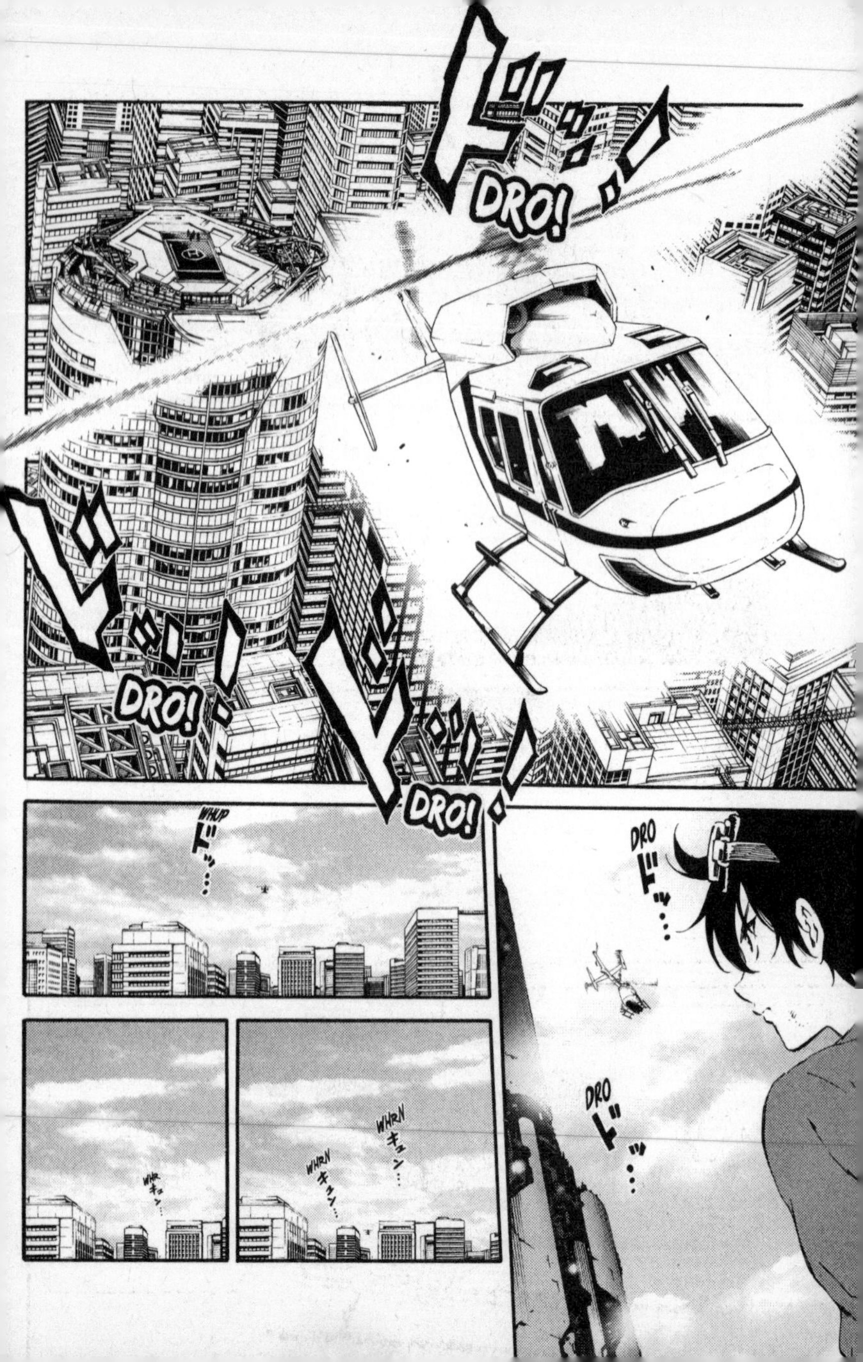

DRO!
DRO!
DRO!
DRO
ドッ…
DRO
ドッ…
WHUP
ドッ…
WHRN
キュン…
WHRN
キュン…
WHR
キュン…

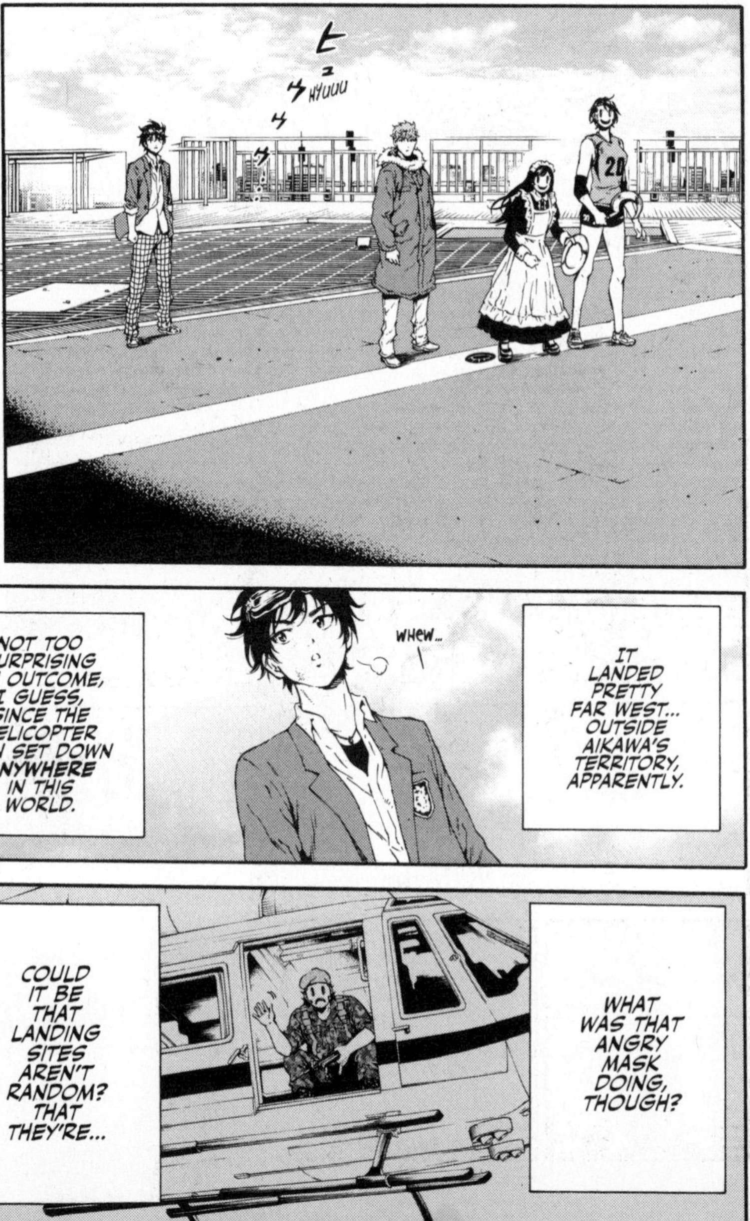
ヒュゥゥゥ
HYUUU
IT LANDED PRETTY FAR WEST... OUTSIDE AIKAWA'S TERRITORY, APPARENTLY.
WHEW...
NOT TOO SURPRISING AN OUTCOME, I GUESS, SINCE THE HELICOPTER CAN SET DOWN ANYWHERE IN THIS WORLD.
WHAT WAS THAT ANGRY MASK DOING, THOUGH?
COULD IT BE THAT LANDING SITES AREN'T RANDOM? THAT THEY'RE...

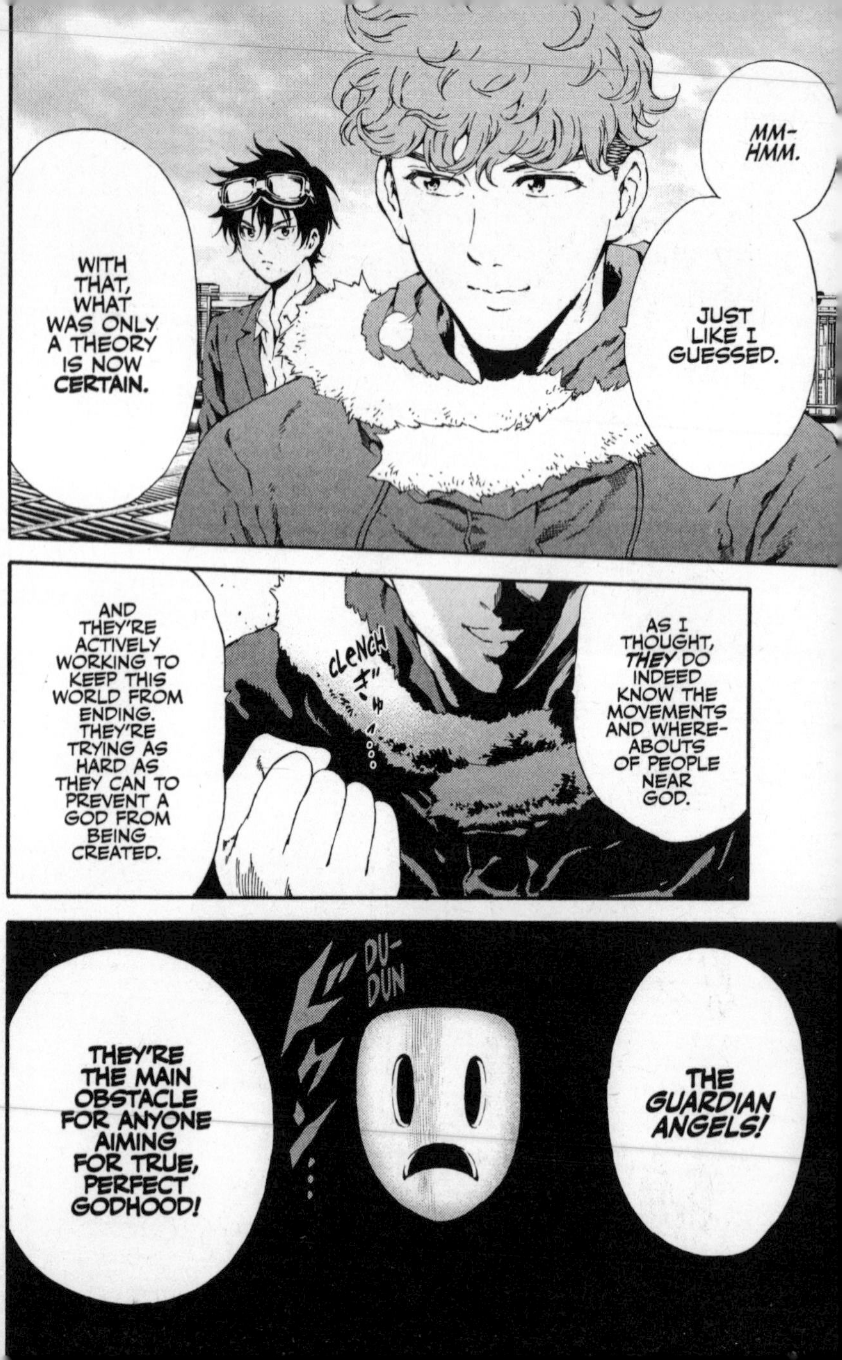
MM-HMM.
JUST LIKE I GUESSED.
WITH THAT, WHAT WAS ONLY A THEORY IS NOW **CERTAIN.**
AS I THOUGHT, *THEY* DO INDEED KNOW THE MOVEMENTS AND WHEREABOUTS OF PEOPLE NEAR GOD.
CLENCH
AND THEY'RE ACTIVELY WORKING TO KEEP THIS WORLD FROM ENDING. THEY'RE TRYING AS HARD AS THEY CAN TO PREVENT A GOD FROM BEING CREATED.
THE *GUARDIAN ANGELS!*
DU-DUN
THEY'RE THE MAIN OBSTACLE FOR ANYONE AIMING FOR TRUE, PERFECT GODHOOD!

Hostage Rika

Being flanked by this pair feels like...

HIGH-RISE INVASION

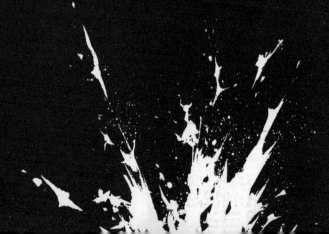

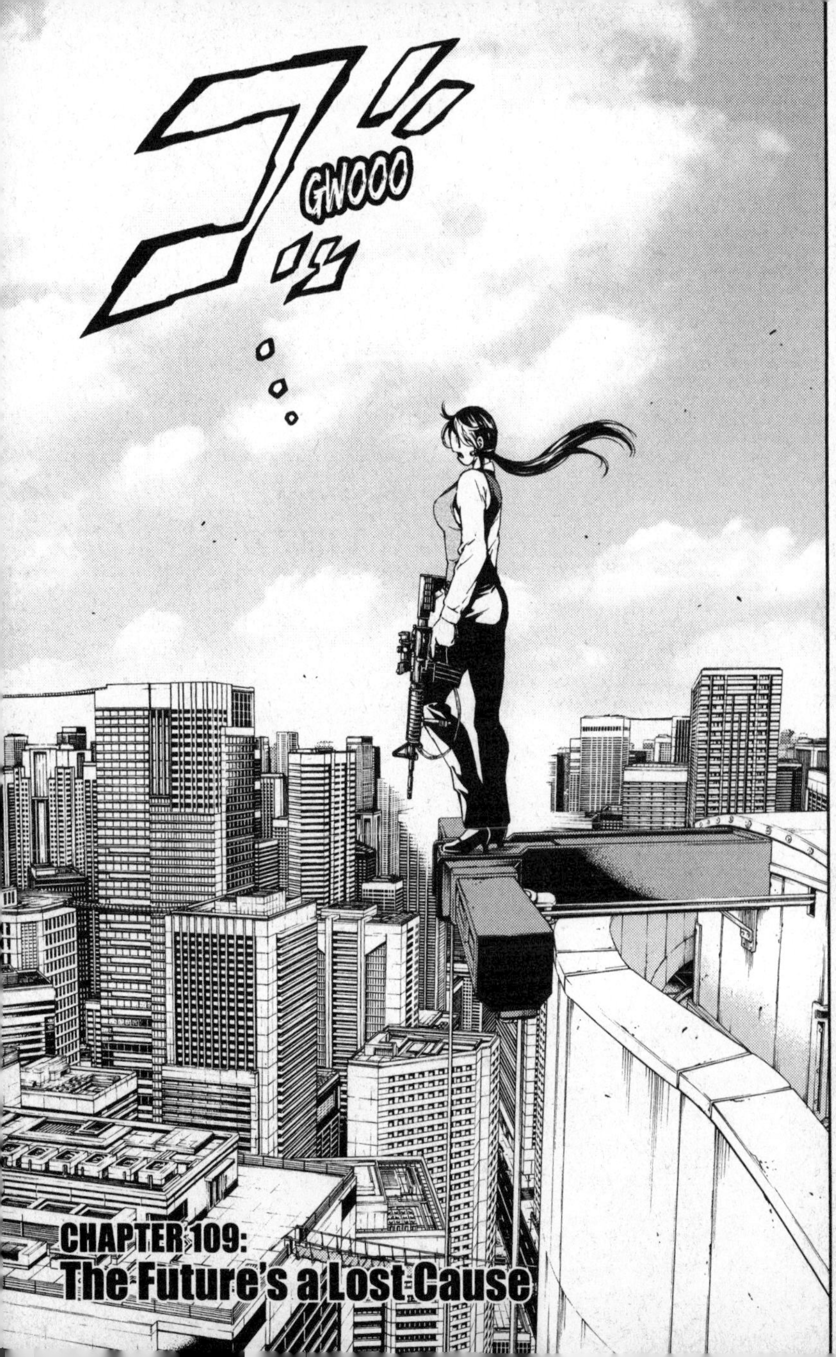
GWOOO
CHAPTER 109:
The Future's a Lost Cause

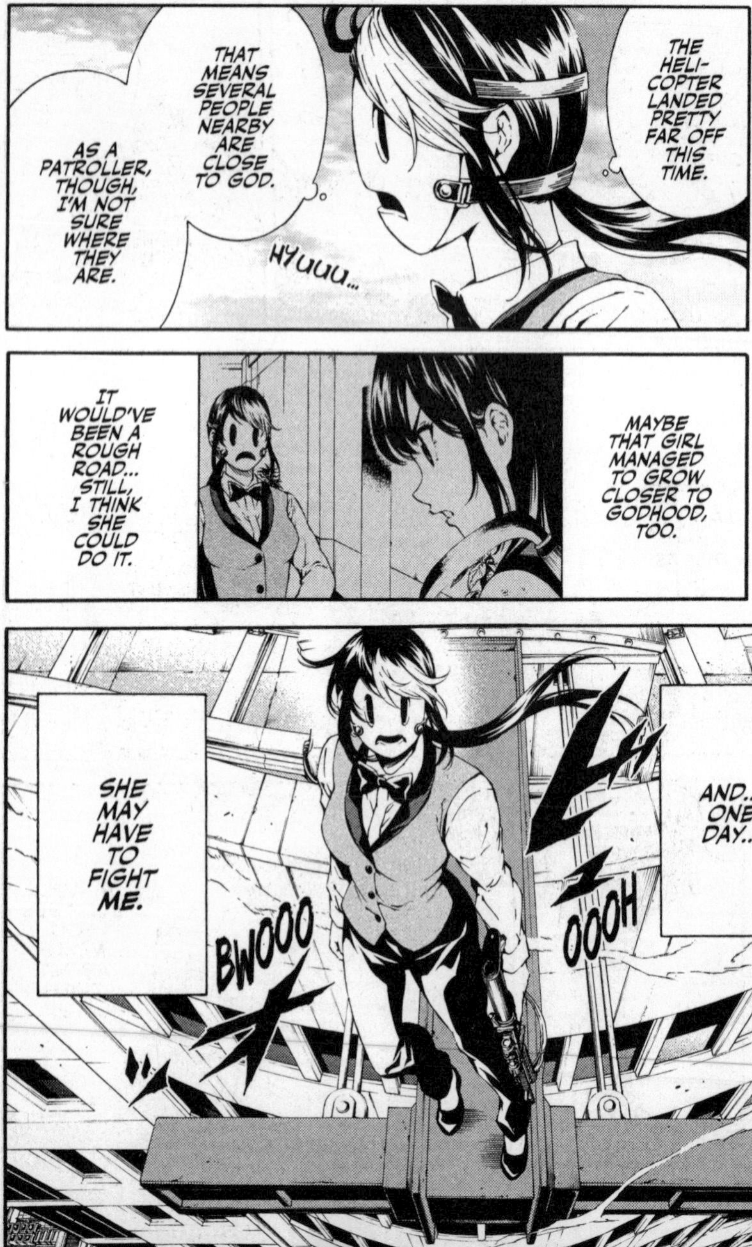
THE HELI-COPTER LANDED PRETTY FAR OFF THIS TIME.
THAT MEANS SEVERAL PEOPLE NEARBY ARE CLOSE TO GOD.
AS A PATROLLER, THOUGH, I'M NOT SURE WHERE THEY ARE.
HYUUU...
MAYBE THAT GIRL MANAGED TO GROW CLOSER TO GODHOOD, TOO.
IT WOULD'VE BEEN A ROUGH ROAD... STILL, I THINK SHE COULD DO IT.
AND... ONE DAY...
SHE MAY HAVE TO FIGHT ME.
OOOH
BWOOO

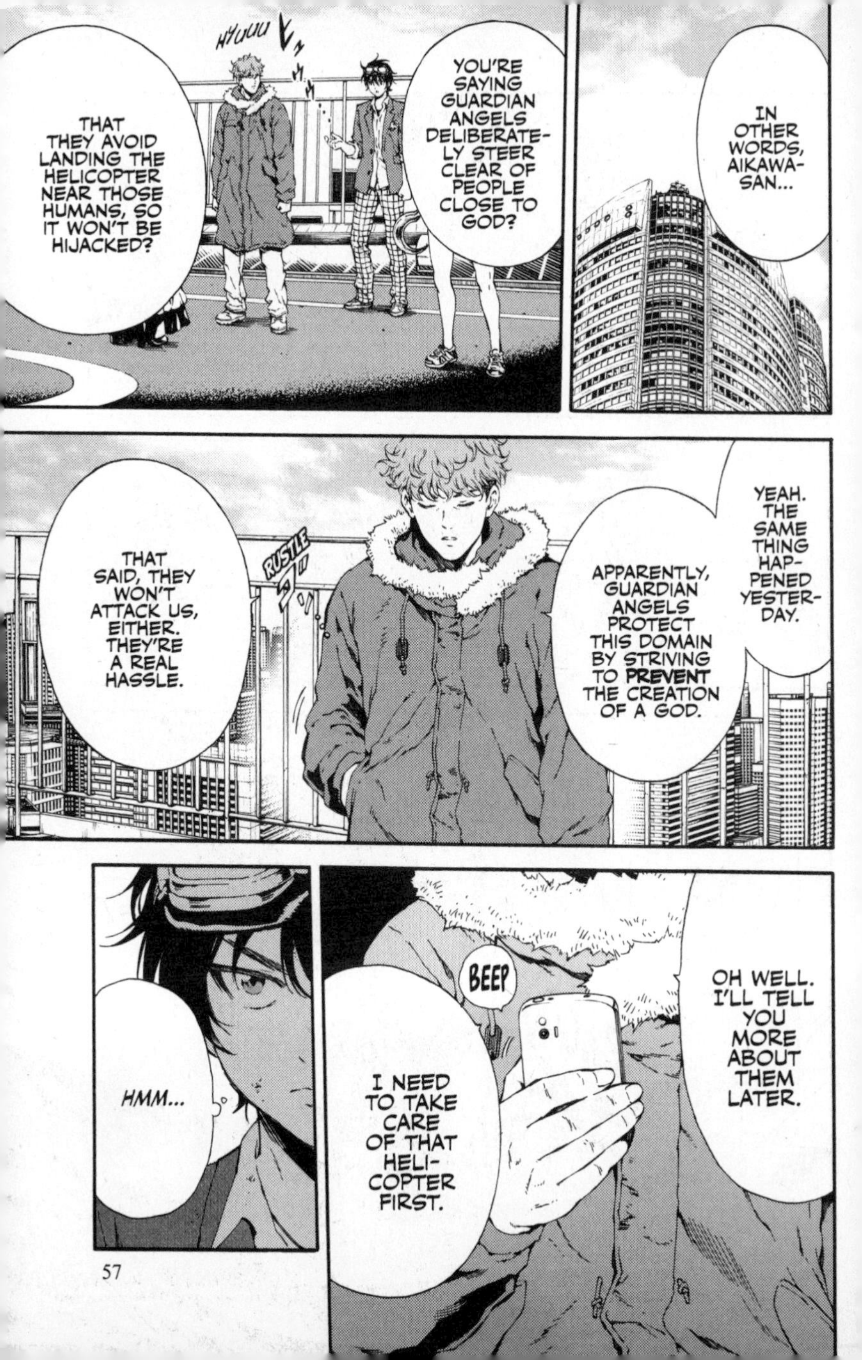
IN OTHER WORDS, AIKAWA-SAN...
HYUUU
YOU'RE SAYING GUARDIAN ANGELS DELIBERATE-LY STEER CLEAR OF PEOPLE CLOSE TO GOD?
THAT THEY AVOID LANDING THE HELICOPTER NEAR THOSE HUMANS, SO IT WON'T BE HIJACKED?
YEAH. THE SAME THING HAP-PENED YESTER-DAY.
APPARENTLY, GUARDIAN ANGELS PROTECT THIS DOMAIN BY STRIVING TO **PREVENT** THE CREATION OF A GOD.
RUSTLE
THAT SAID, THEY WON'T ATTACK US, EITHER. THEY'RE A REAL HASSLE.
OH WELL. I'LL TELL YOU MORE ABOUT THEM LATER.
BEEP
I NEED TO TAKE CARE OF THAT HELI-COPTER FIRST.
HMM...

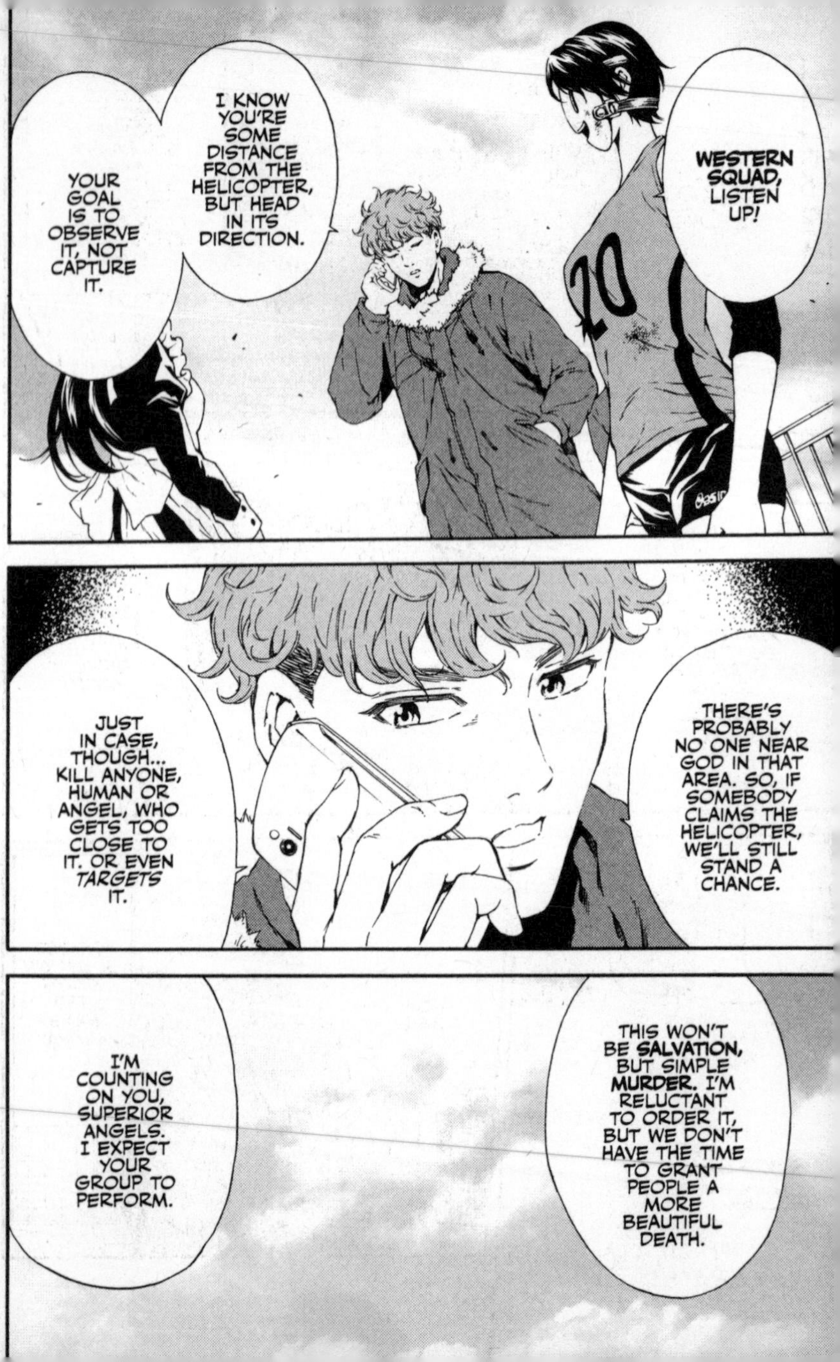
WESTERN SQUAD, LISTEN UP!
I KNOW YOU'RE SOME DISTANCE FROM THE HELICOPTER, BUT HEAD IN ITS DIRECTION.
YOUR GOAL IS TO OBSERVE IT, NOT CAPTURE IT.
THERE'S PROBABLY NO ONE NEAR GOD IN THAT AREA. SO, IF SOMEBODY CLAIMS THE HELICOPTER, WE'LL STILL STAND A CHANCE.
JUST IN CASE, THOUGH... KILL ANYONE, HUMAN OR ANGEL, WHO GETS TOO CLOSE TO IT. OR EVEN *TARGETS* IT.
THIS WON'T BE **SALVATION,** BUT SIMPLE **MURDER.** I'M RELUCTANT TO ORDER IT, BUT WE DON'T HAVE THE TIME TO GRANT PEOPLE A MORE BEAUTIFUL DEATH.
I'M COUNTING ON YOU, SUPERIOR ANGELS. I EXPECT YOUR GROUP TO PERFORM.

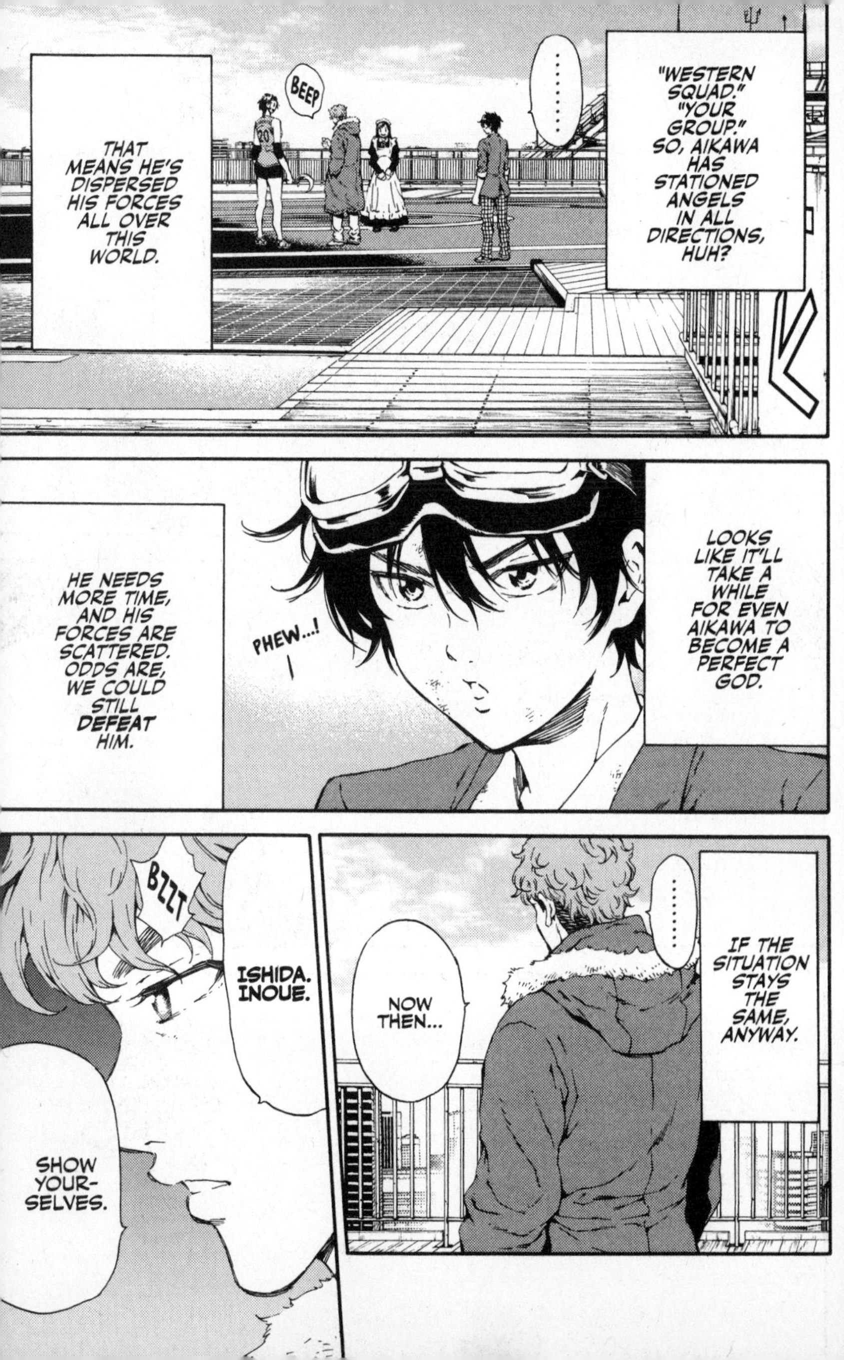
"WESTERN SQUAD." "YOUR GROUP." SO, AIKAWA HAS STATIONED ANGELS IN ALL DIRECTIONS, HUH?
......
BEEP
THAT MEANS HE'S DISPERSED HIS FORCES ALL OVER THIS WORLD.
LOOKS LIKE IT'LL TAKE A WHILE FOR EVEN AIKAWA TO BECOME A PERFECT GOD.
PHEW...!
HE NEEDS MORE TIME, AND HIS FORCES ARE SCATTERED. ODDS ARE, WE COULD STILL DEFEAT HIM.
IF THE SITUATION STAYS THE SAME, ANYWAY.
......
NOW THEN...
BZZT
ISHIDA. INOUE.
SHOW YOUR-SELVES.

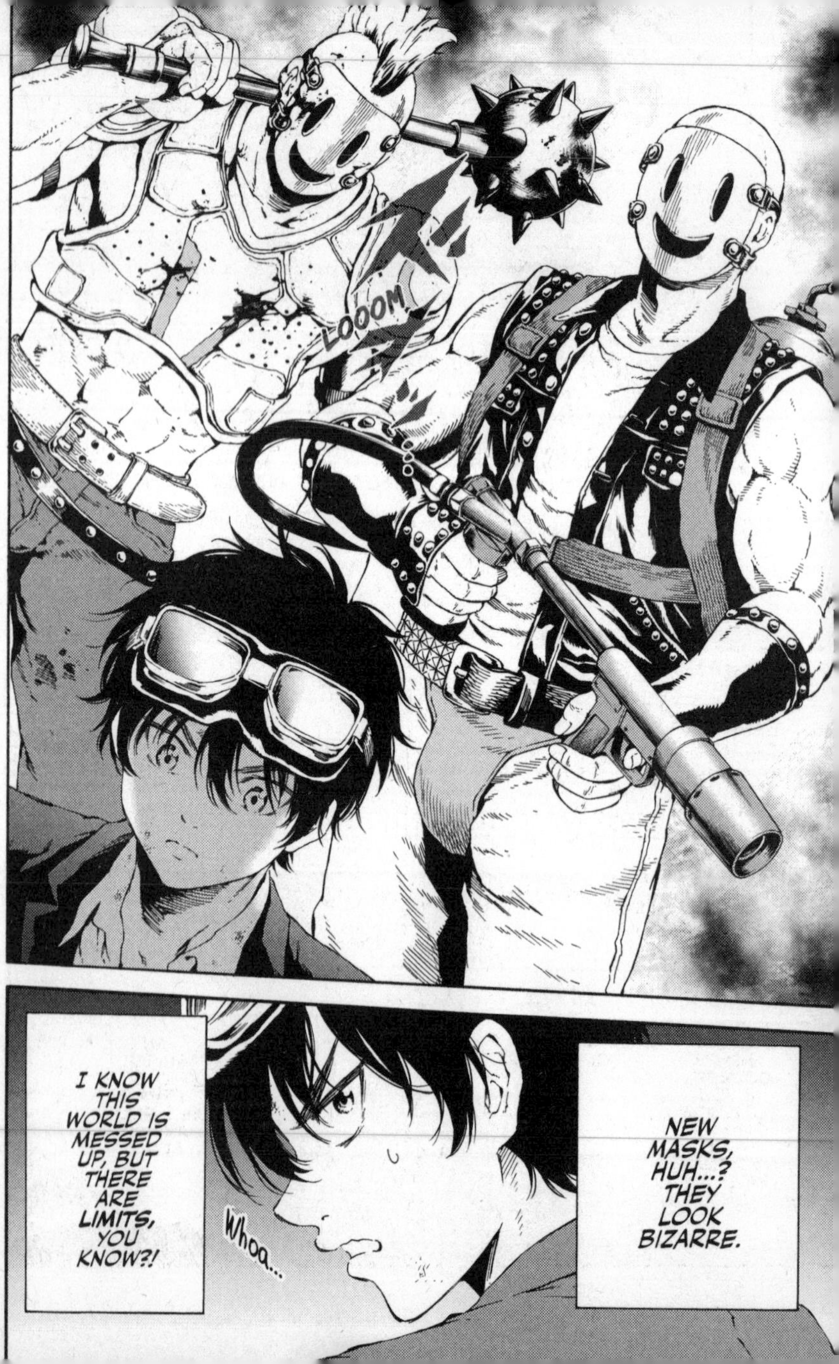
LOOOM
NEW MASKS, HUH...? THEY LOOK BIZARRE.
Whoa...
I KNOW THIS WORLD IS MESSED UP, BUT THERE ARE LIMITS, YOU KNOW?!

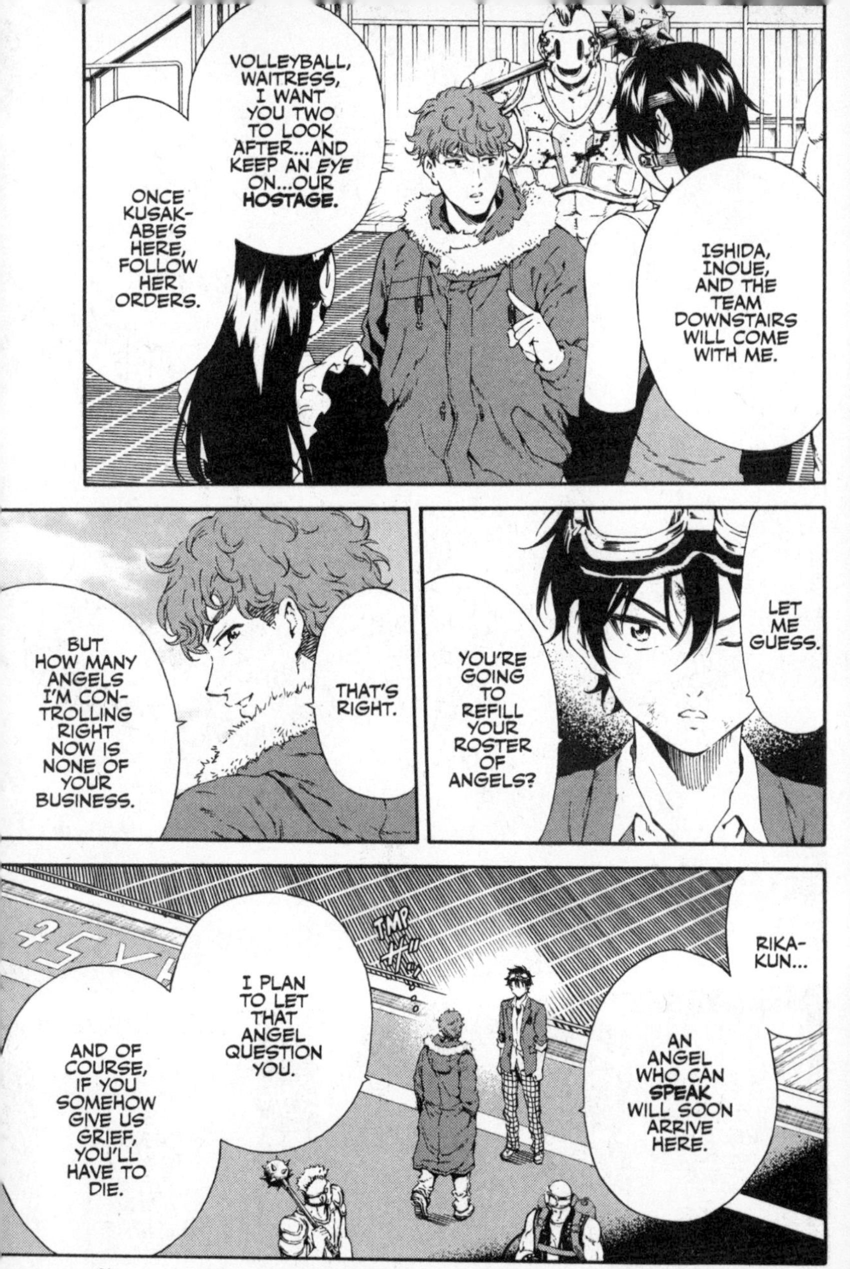
ISHIDA, INOUE, AND THE TEAM DOWNSTAIRS WILL COME WITH ME.
VOLLEYBALL, WAITRESS, I WANT YOU TWO TO LOOK AFTER...AND KEEP AN *EYE* ON...OUR **HOSTAGE.**
ONCE KUSAK-ABE'S HERE, FOLLOW HER ORDERS.
LET ME GUESS.
YOU'RE GOING TO REFILL YOUR ROSTER OF ANGELS?
THAT'S RIGHT.
BUT HOW MANY ANGELS I'M CON-TROLLING RIGHT NOW IS NONE OF YOUR BUSINESS.
RIKA-KUN...
AN ANGEL WHO CAN **SPEAK** WILL SOON ARRIVE HERE.
TMP
I PLAN TO LET THAT ANGEL QUESTION YOU.
AND OF COURSE, IF YOU SOMEHOW GIVE US GRIEF, YOU'LL HAVE TO DIE.

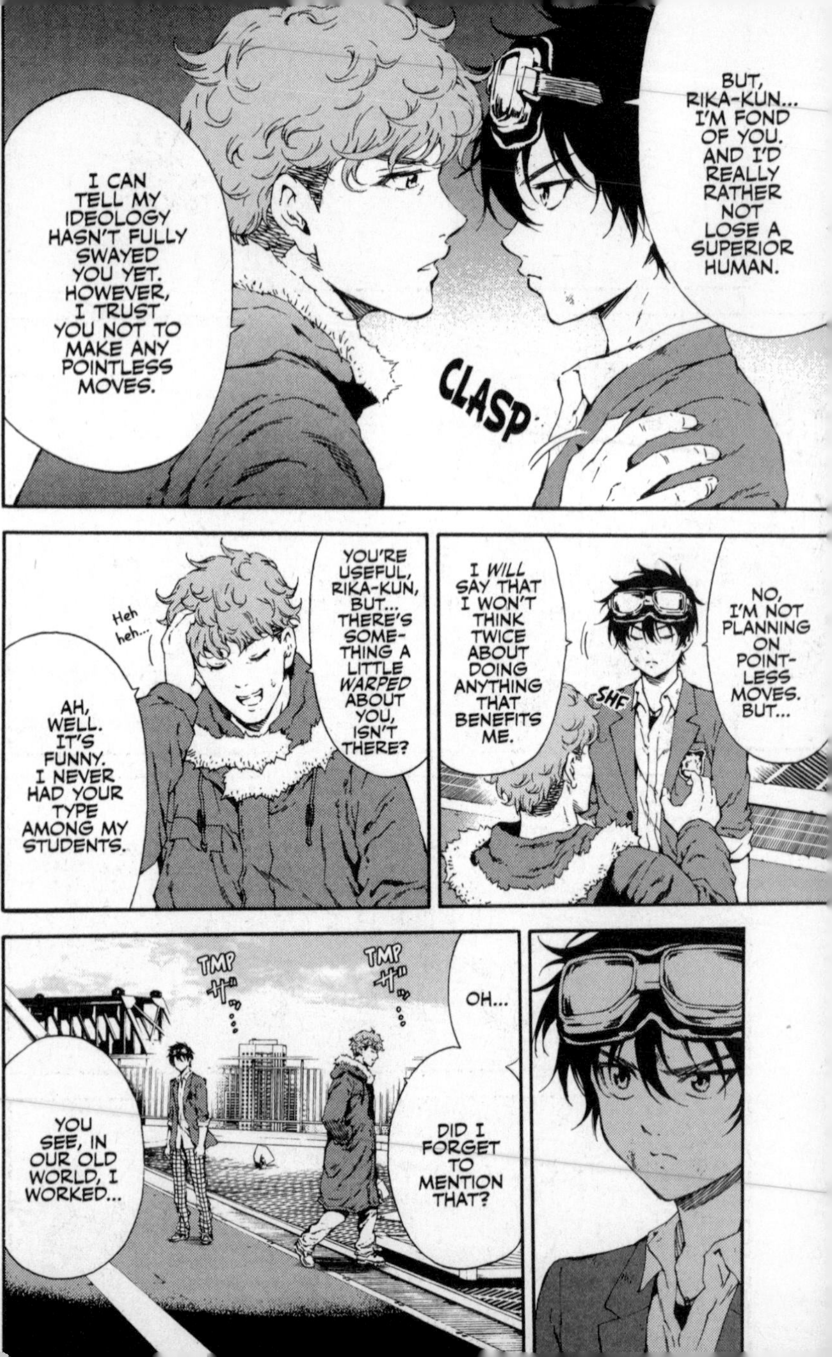
BUT, RIKA-KUN... I'M FOND OF YOU. AND I'D REALLY RATHER NOT LOSE A SUPERIOR HUMAN.
I CAN TELL MY IDEOLOGY HASN'T FULLY SWAYED YOU YET. HOWEVER, I TRUST YOU NOT TO MAKE ANY POINTLESS MOVES.
CLASP
NO, I'M NOT PLANNING ON POINT-LESS MOVES. BUT...
SHF
I *WILL* SAY THAT I WON'T THINK TWICE ABOUT DOING ANYTHING THAT BENEFITS ME.
YOU'RE USEFUL, RIKA-KUN, BUT... THERE'S SOME-THING A LITTLE *WARPED* ABOUT YOU, ISN'T THERE?
Heh heh...
AH, WELL. IT'S FUNNY. I NEVER HAD YOUR TYPE AMONG MY STUDENTS.
OH...
DID I FORGET TO MENTION THAT?
TMP
TMP
YOU SEE, IN OUR OLD WORLD, I WORKED...

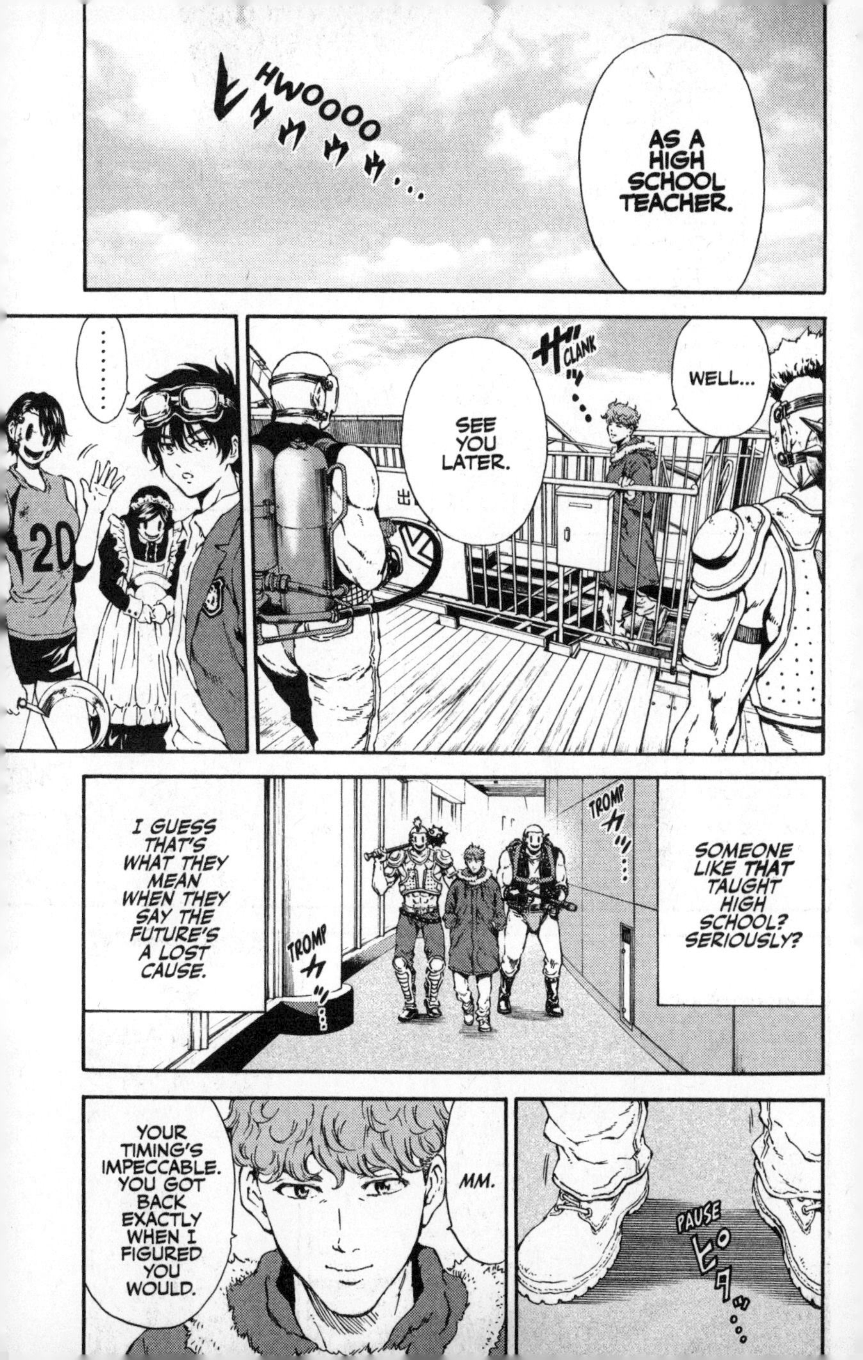
AS A HIGH SCHOOL TEACHER.
HWOOOO...
WELL...
CLANK
SEE YOU LATER.
......
TROMP
SOMEONE LIKE THAT TAUGHT HIGH SCHOOL? SERIOUSLY?
I GUESS THAT'S WHAT THEY MEAN WHEN THEY SAY THE FUTURE'S A LOST CAUSE.
TROMP
PAUSE
YOUR TIMING'S IMPECCABLE. YOU GOT BACK EXACTLY WHEN I FIGURED YOU WOULD.
MM.

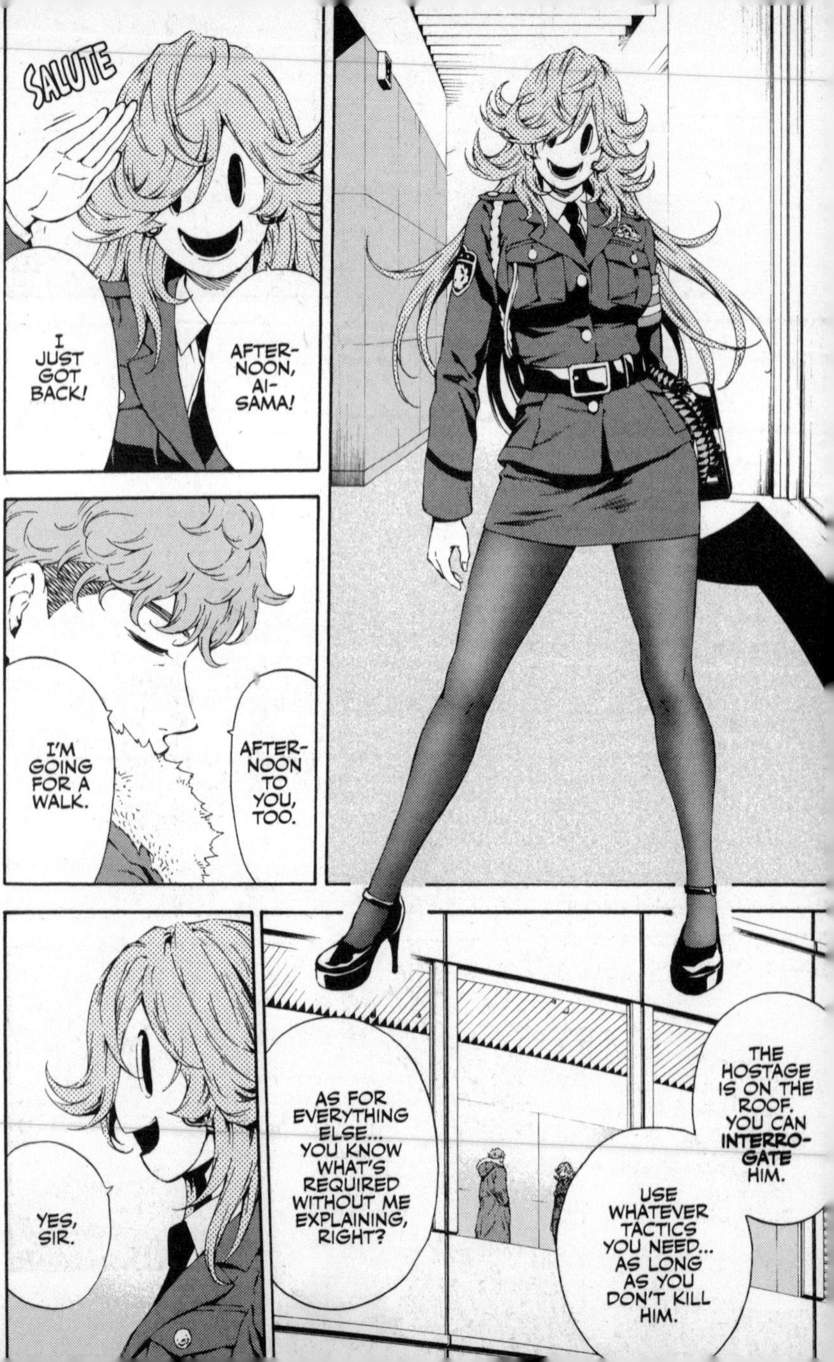
SALUTE
AFTERNOON, AI-SAMA!
I JUST GOT BACK!
AFTERNOON TO YOU, TOO.
I'M GOING FOR A WALK.
THE HOSTAGE IS ON THE ROOF. YOU CAN INTERROGATE HIM.
USE WHATEVER TACTICS YOU NEED... AS LONG AS YOU DON'T KILL HIM.
AS FOR EVERYTHING ELSE... YOU KNOW WHAT'S REQUIRED WITHOUT ME EXPLAINING, RIGHT?
YES, SIR.

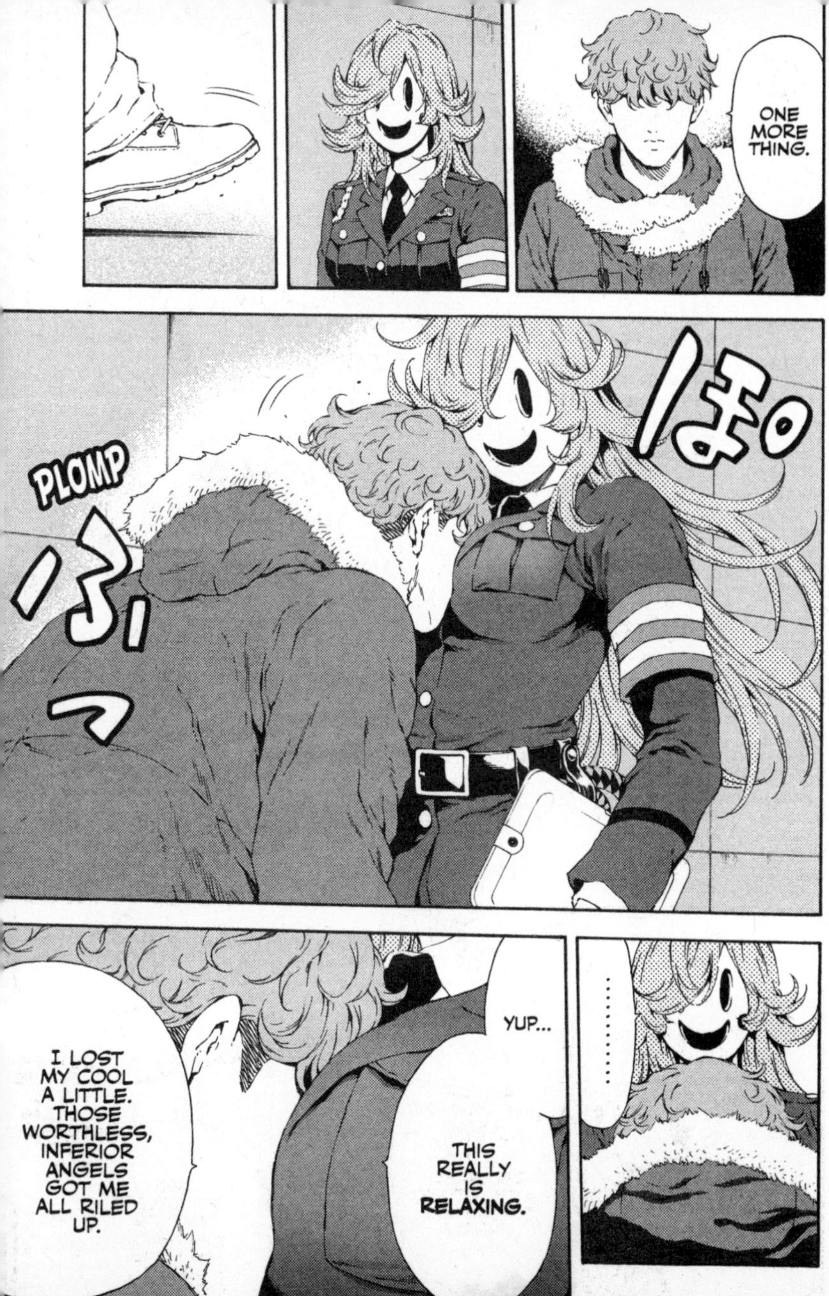

ONE MORE THING.
ぽ
ふっ
PLOMP
……
YUP...
THIS REALLY IS RELAXING.
I LOST MY COOL A LITTLE. THOSE WORTHLESS, INFERIOR ANGELS GOT ME ALL RILED UP.

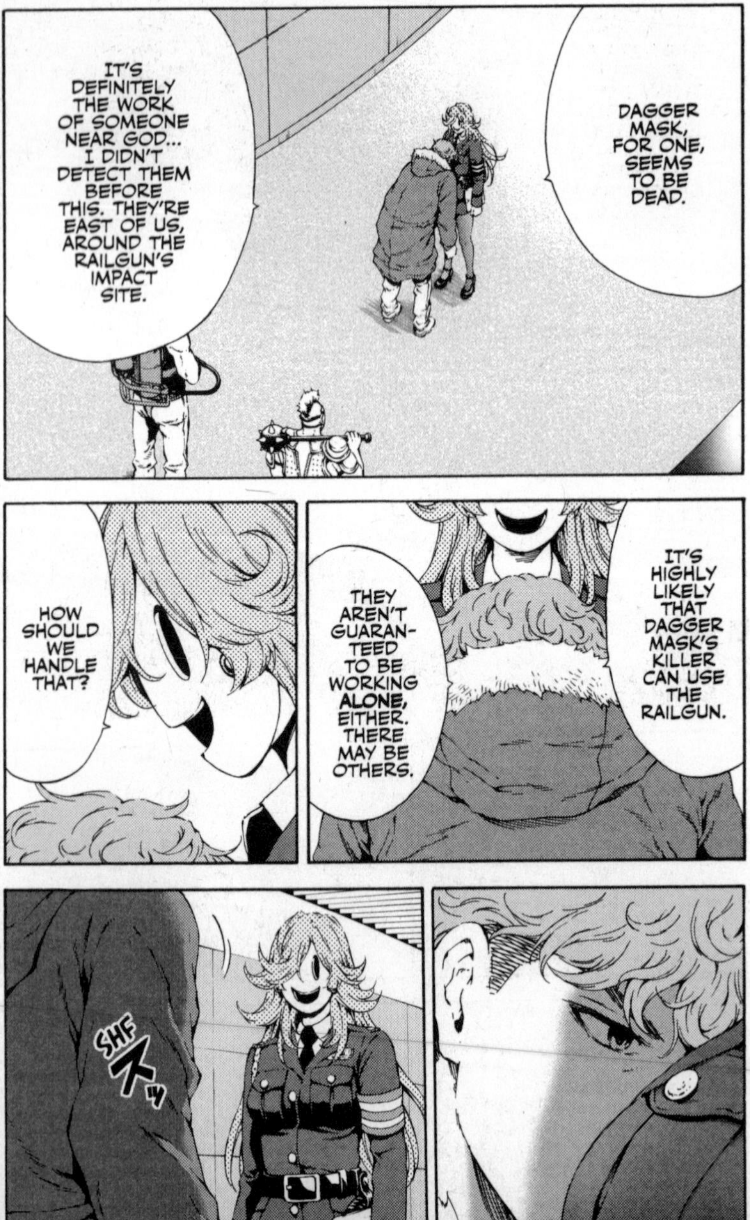
DAGGER MASK, FOR ONE, SEEMS TO BE DEAD.
IT'S DEFINITELY THE WORK OF SOMEONE NEAR GOD... I DIDN'T DETECT THEM BEFORE THIS. THEY'RE EAST OF US, AROUND THE RAILGUN'S IMPACT SITE.
IT'S HIGHLY LIKELY THAT DAGGER MASK'S KILLER CAN USE THE RAILGUN.
THEY AREN'T GUARANTEED TO BE WORKING ALONE, EITHER. THERE MAY BE OTHERS.
HOW SHOULD WE HANDLE THAT?
SHF

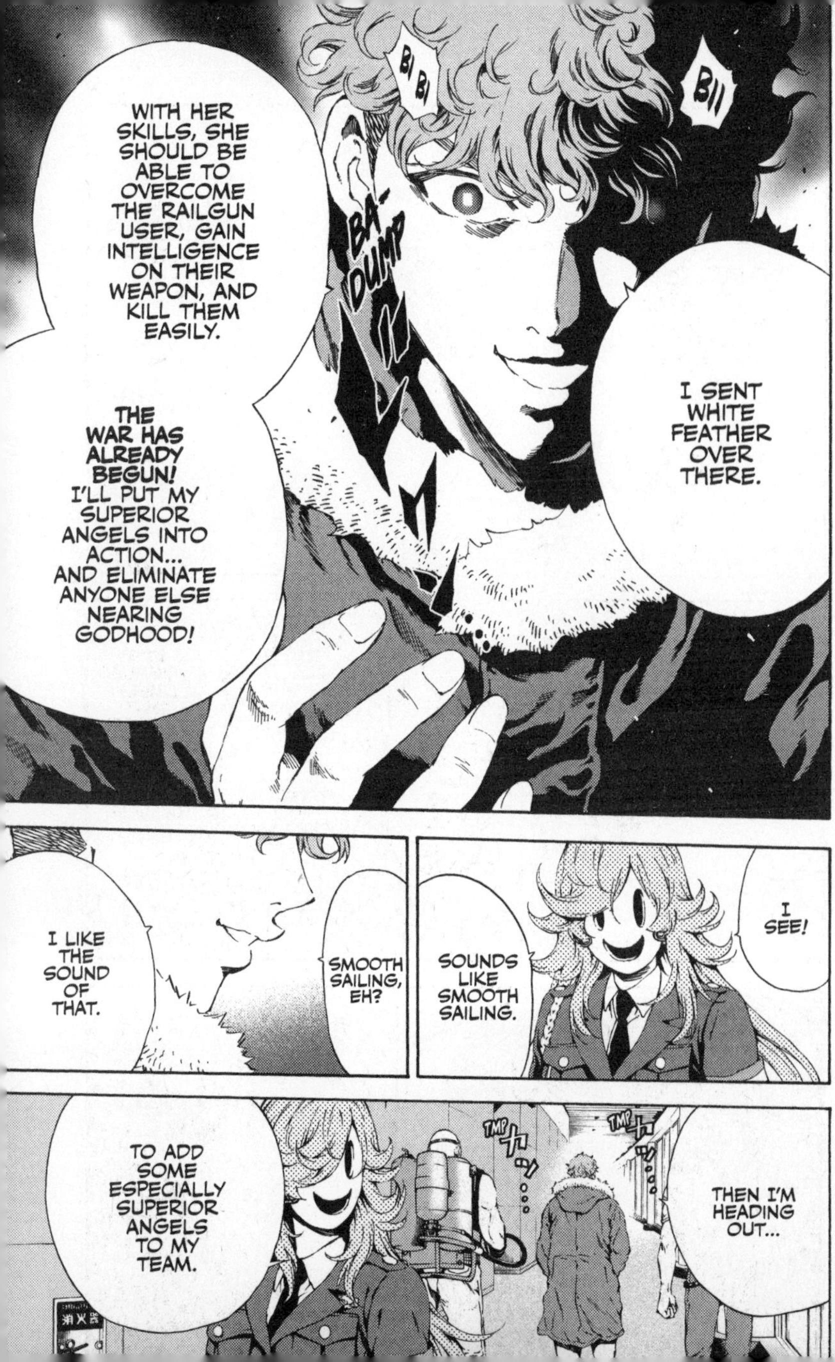
BII
BI BI
I SENT WHITE FEATHER OVER THERE.
WITH HER SKILLS, SHE SHOULD BE ABLE TO OVERCOME THE RAILGUN USER, GAIN INTELLIGENCE ON THEIR WEAPON, AND KILL THEM EASILY.
BA-DUMP
THE WAR HAS ALREADY BEGUN! I'LL PUT MY SUPERIOR ANGELS INTO ACTION... AND ELIMINATE ANYONE ELSE NEARING GODHOOD!
I SEE!
SOUNDS LIKE SMOOTH SAILING.
SMOOTH SAILING, EH?
I LIKE THE SOUND OF THAT.
THEN I'M HEADING OUT...
TMP
TMP
TO ADD SOME ESPECIALLY SUPERIOR ANGELS TO MY TEAM.
消火器

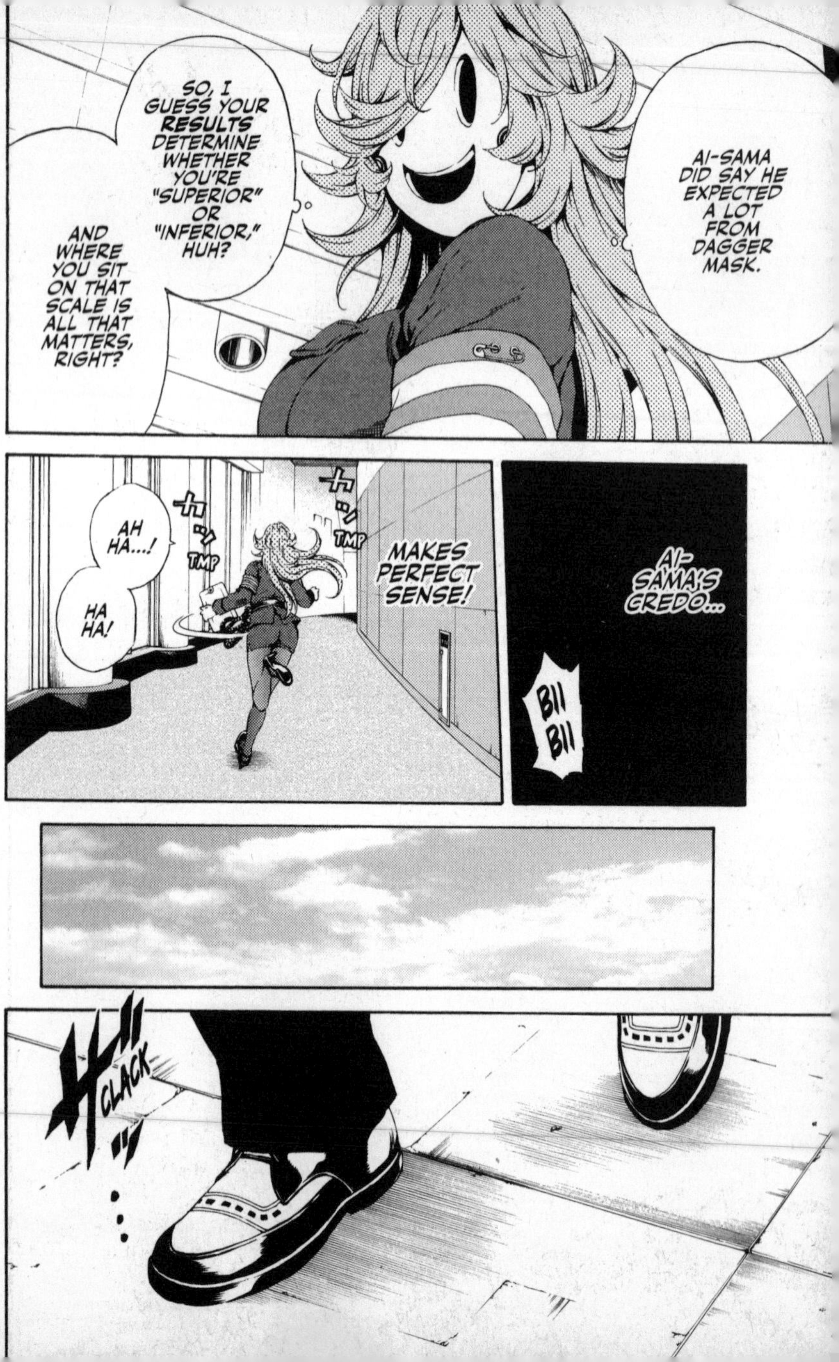
AI-SAMA DID SAY HE EXPECTED A LOT FROM DAGGER MASK.
SO, I GUESS YOUR RESULTS DETERMINE WHETHER YOU'RE "SUPERIOR" OR "INFERIOR," HUH?
AND WHERE YOU SIT ON THAT SCALE IS ALL THAT MATTERS, RIGHT?
AI-SAMA'S CREDO...
BII BII
TMP
MAKES PERFECT SENSE!
TMP
AH HA...!
HA HA!
CLACK

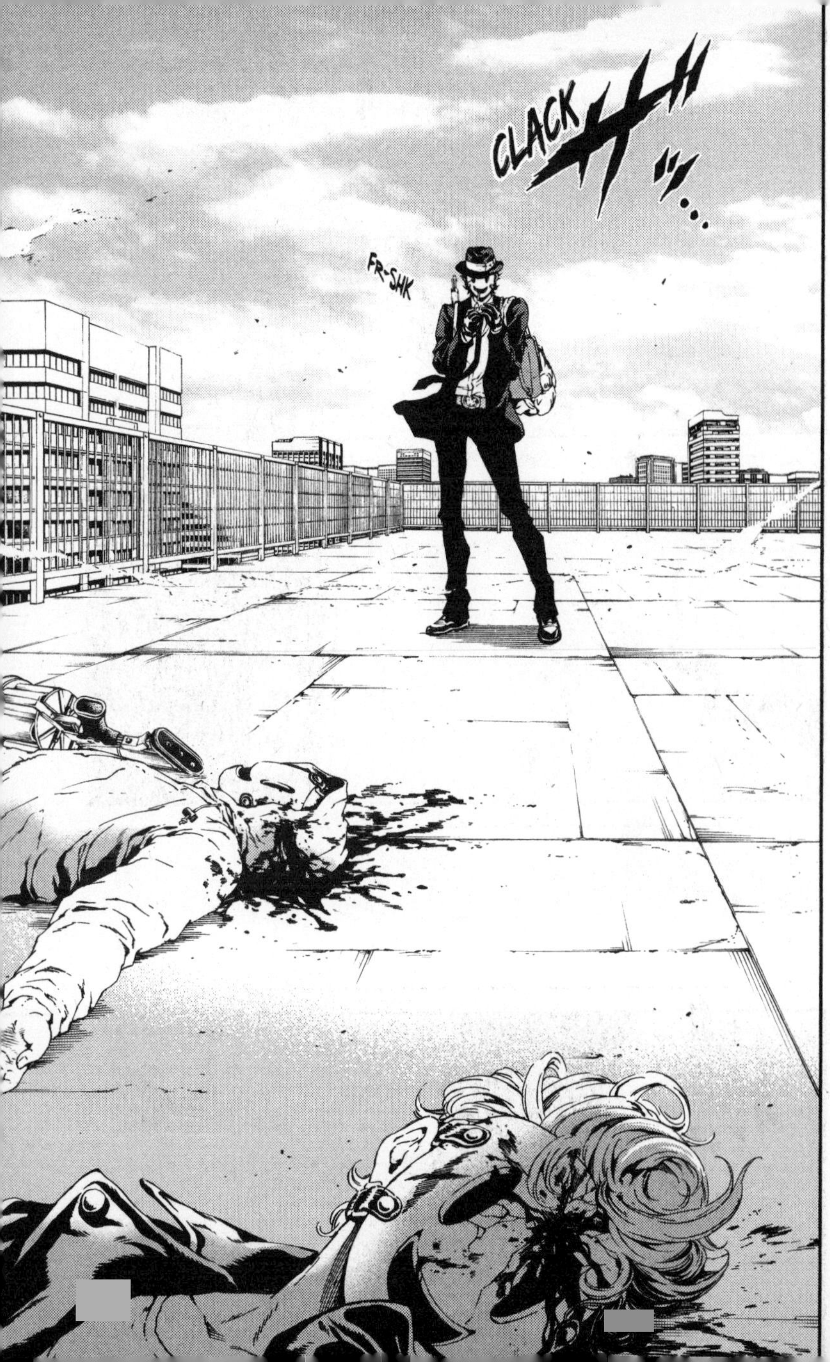
CLACK
FR-SHK

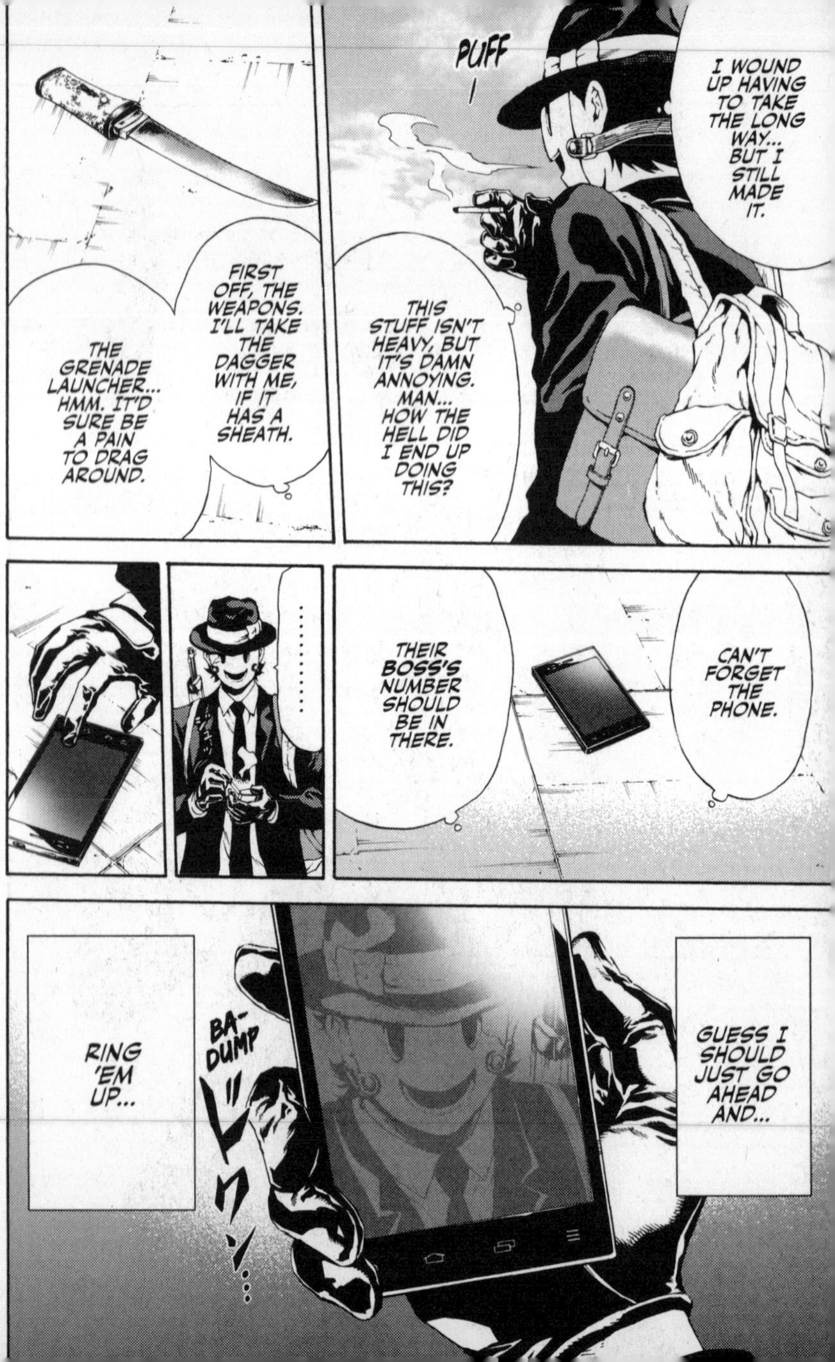
PUFF
I WOUND UP HAVING TO TAKE THE LONG WAY... BUT I STILL MADE IT.
THIS STUFF ISN'T HEAVY, BUT IT'S DAMN ANNOYING. MAN... HOW THE HELL DID I END UP DOING THIS?
FIRST OFF, THE WEAPONS. I'LL TAKE THE DAGGER WITH ME, IF IT HAS A SHEATH.
THE GRENADE LAUNCHER... HMM. IT'D SURE BE A PAIN TO DRAG AROUND.
CAN'T FORGET THE PHONE.
THEIR BOSS'S NUMBER SHOULD BE IN THERE.
......
GUESS I SHOULD JUST GO AHEAD AND...
BA-DUMP
RING 'EM UP...

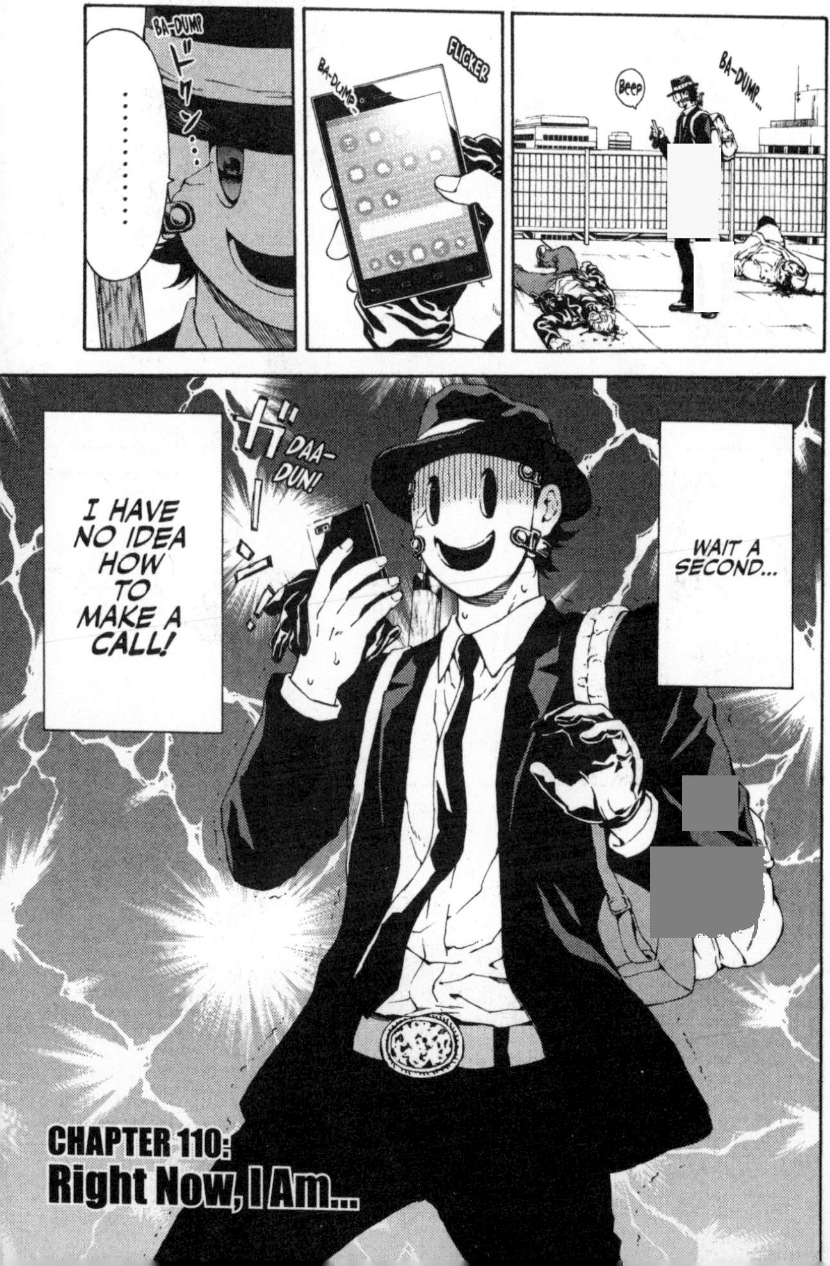

BA-DUMP...
Beep
FLICKER
BA-DUMP...
BA-DUMP
ドクン…
....
WAIT A SECOND...
DAA-DUN!
I HAVE NO IDEA HOW TO MAKE A CALL!
CHAPTER 110:
Right Now, I Am...

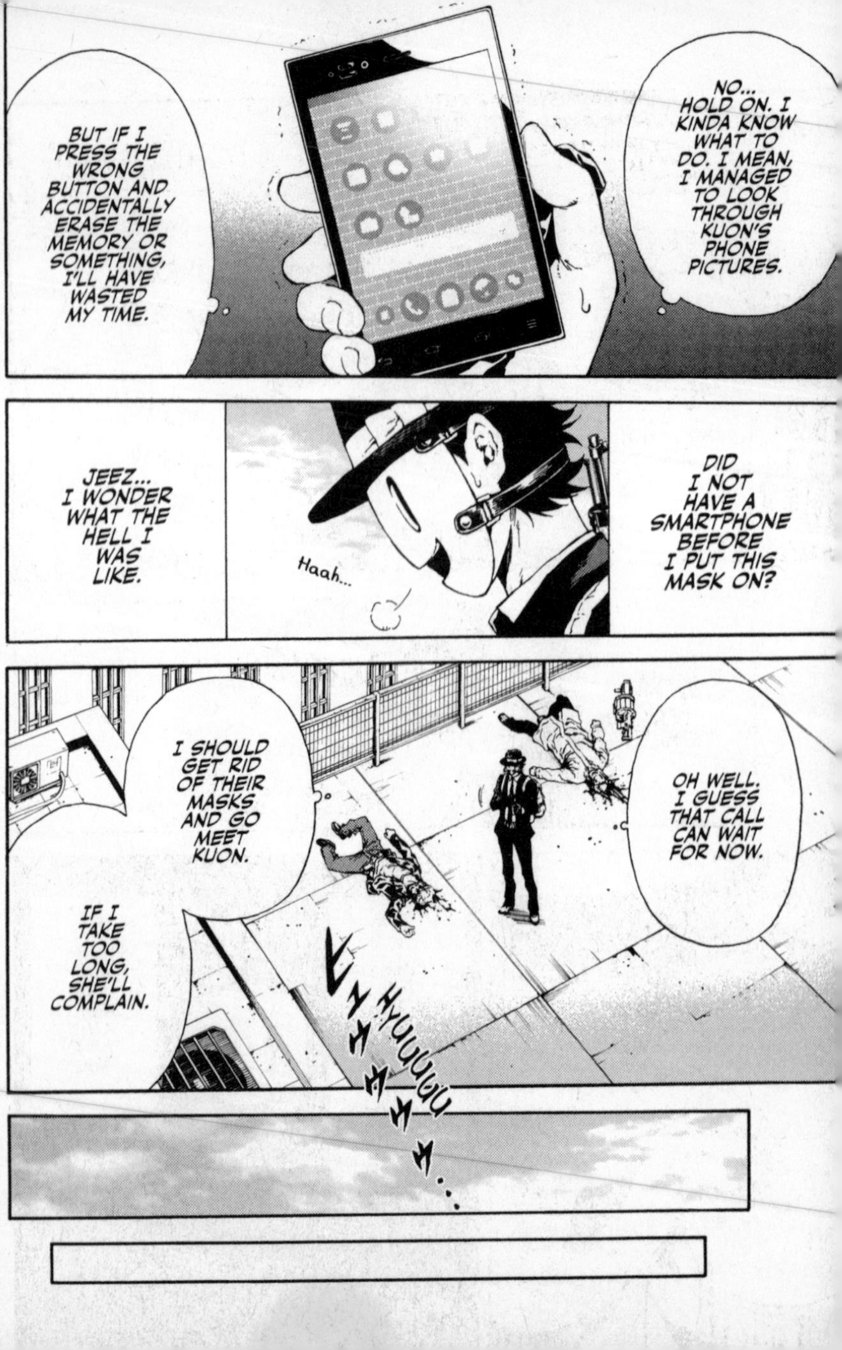
NO... HOLD ON. I KINDA KNOW WHAT TO DO. I MEAN, I MANAGED TO LOOK THROUGH KUON'S PHONE PICTURES.
BUT IF I PRESS THE WRONG BUTTON AND ACCIDENTALLY ERASE THE MEMORY OR SOMETHING, I'LL HAVE WASTED MY TIME.
DID I NOT HAVE A SMARTPHONE BEFORE I PUT THIS MASK ON?
Haah...
JEEZ... I WONDER WHAT THE HELL I WAS LIKE.
OH WELL. I GUESS THAT CALL CAN WAIT FOR NOW.
I SHOULD GET RID OF THEIR MASKS AND GO MEET KUON.
IF I TAKE TOO LONG, SHE'LL COMPLAIN.

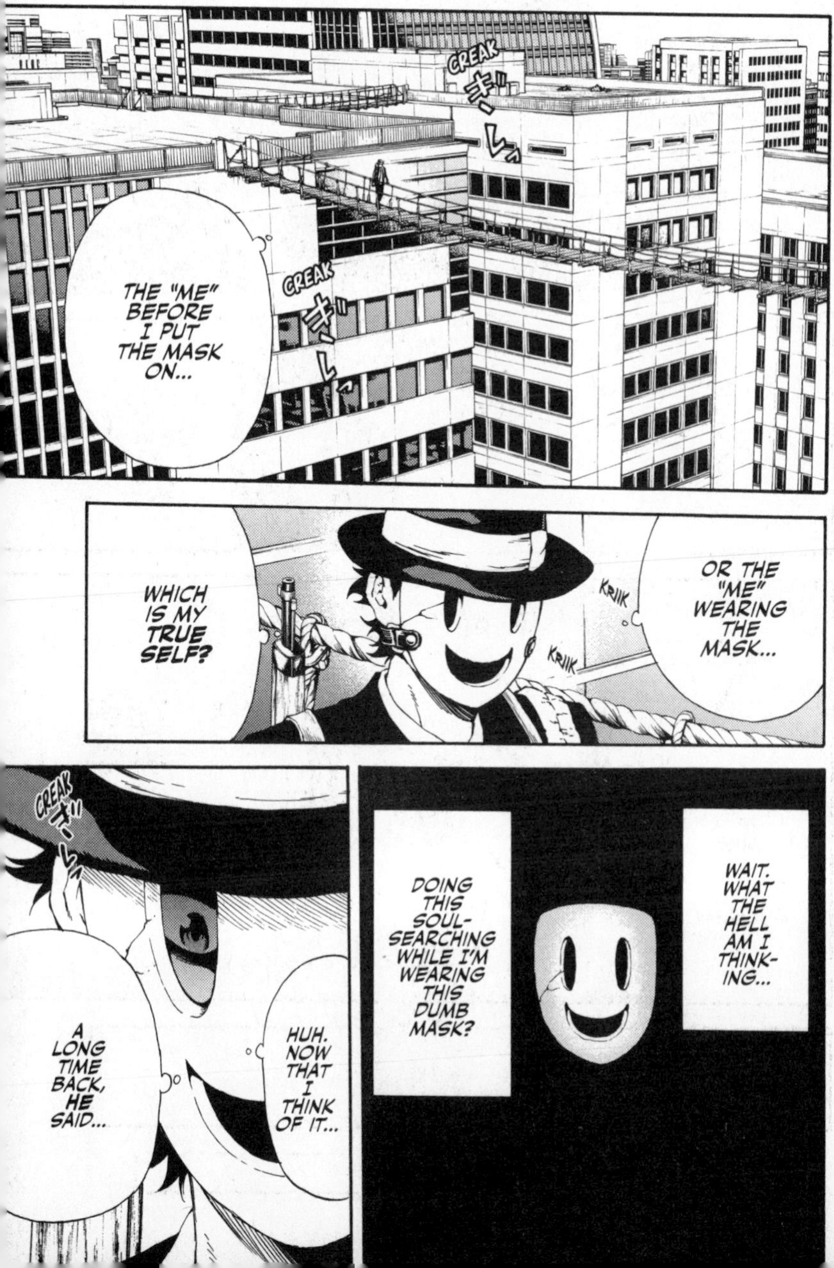
CREAK
CREAK
THE "ME" BEFORE I PUT THE MASK ON...
OR THE "ME" WEARING THE MASK...
KRIIK
KRIIK
WHICH IS MY TRUE SELF?
WAIT. WHAT THE HELL AM I THINKING...
DOING THIS SOUL-SEARCHING WHILE I'M WEARING THIS DUMB MASK?
CREAK
HUH. NOW THAT I THINK OF IT...
A LONG TIME BACK, HE SAID...

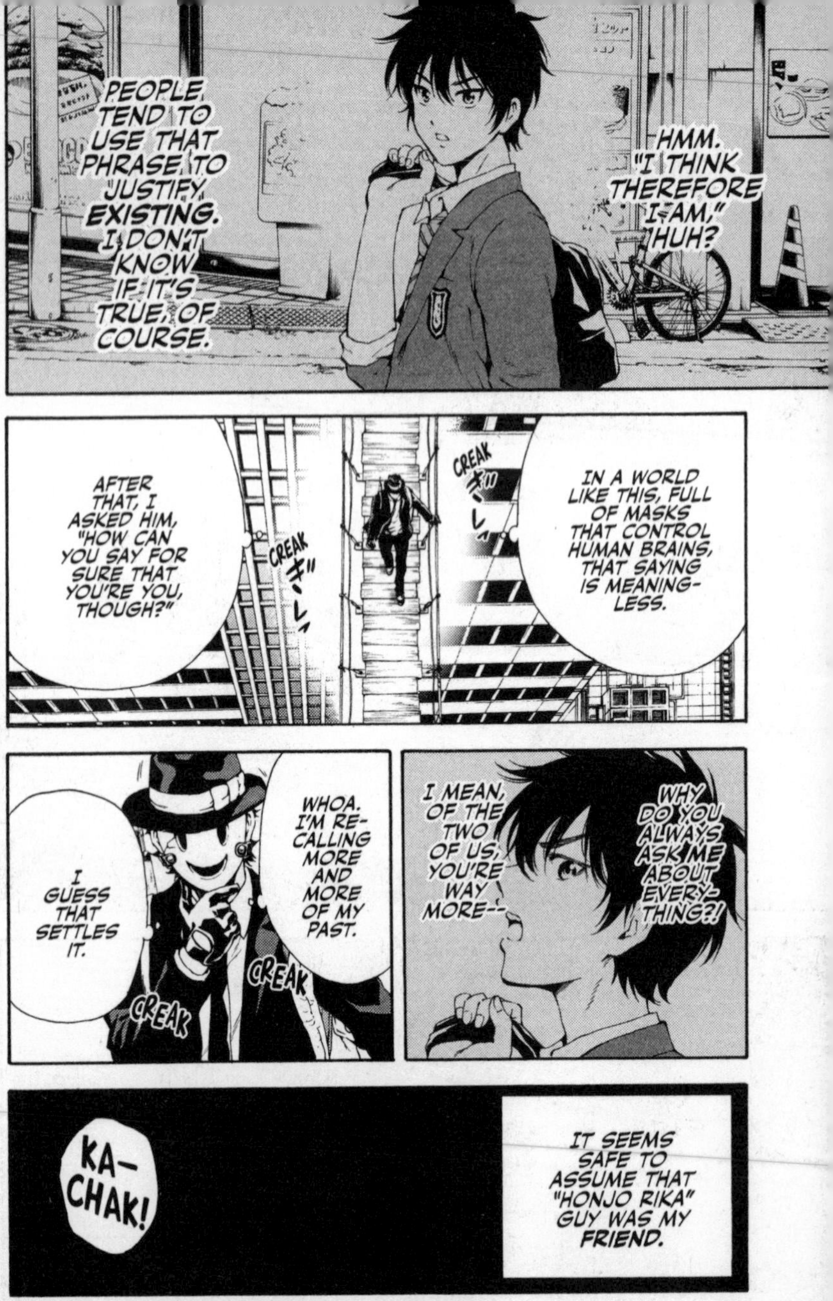
HMM. "I THINK THEREFORE I AM," HUH?
PEOPLE TEND TO USE THAT PHRASE TO JUSTIFY EXISTING. I DON'T KNOW IF IT'S TRUE, OF COURSE.
IN A WORLD LIKE THIS, FULL OF MASKS THAT CONTROL HUMAN BRAINS, THAT SAYING IS MEANING-LESS.
CREAK
CREAK
AFTER THAT, I ASKED HIM, "HOW CAN YOU SAY FOR SURE THAT YOU'RE YOU, THOUGH?"
WHY DO YOU ALWAYS ASK ME ABOUT EVERY-THING?!
I MEAN, OF THE TWO OF US, YOU'RE WAY MORE--
WHOA. I'M RE-CALLING MORE AND MORE OF MY PAST.
CREAK
CREAK
I GUESS THAT SETTLES IT.
IT SEEMS SAFE TO ASSUME THAT "HONJO RIKA" GUY WAS MY FRIEND.
KA-CHAK!

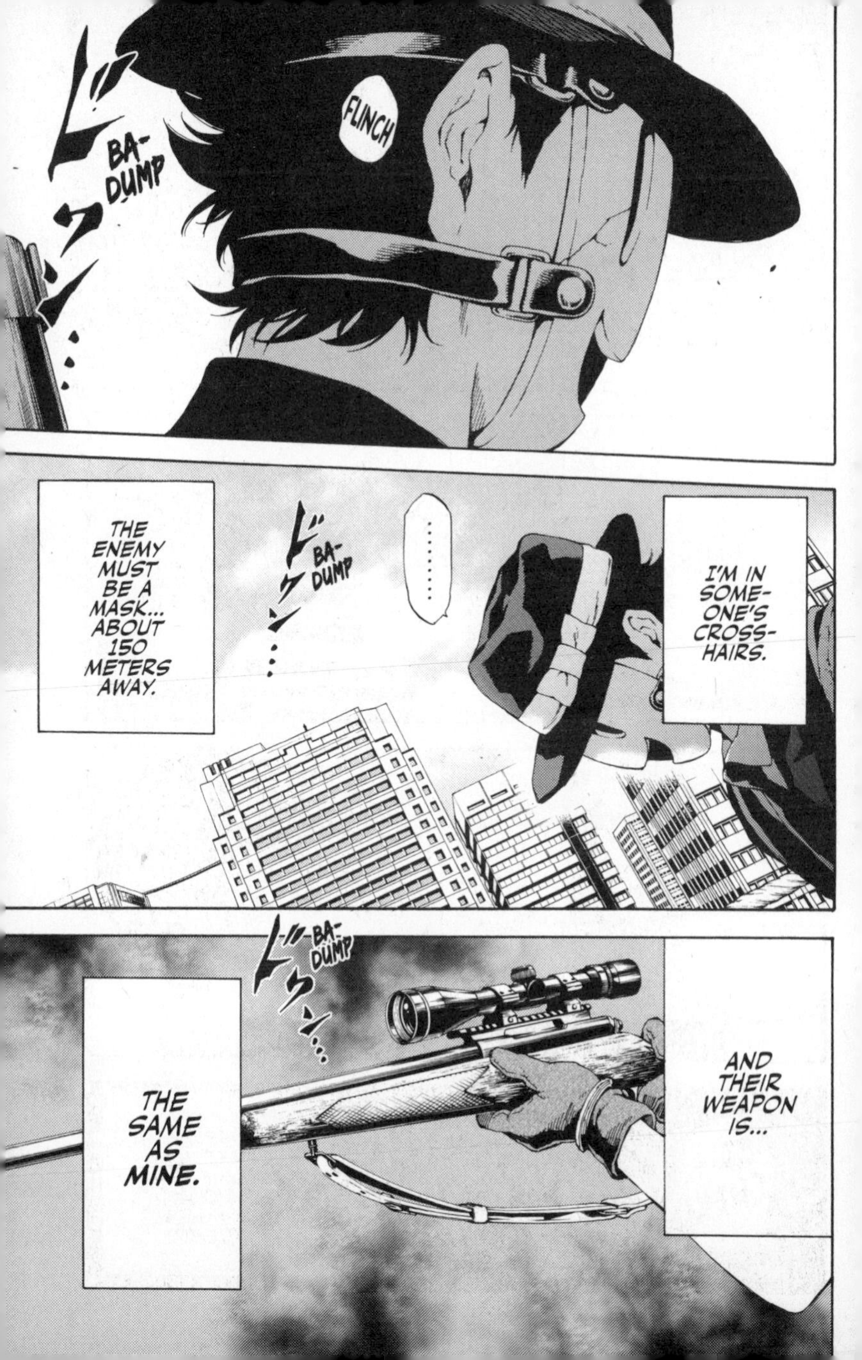
FLINCH
BA-DUMP
I'M IN SOMEONE'S CROSSHAIRS.
......
BA-DUMP
THE ENEMY MUST BE A MASK... ABOUT 150 METERS AWAY.
AND THEIR WEAPON IS...
BA-DUMP
THE SAME AS MINE.

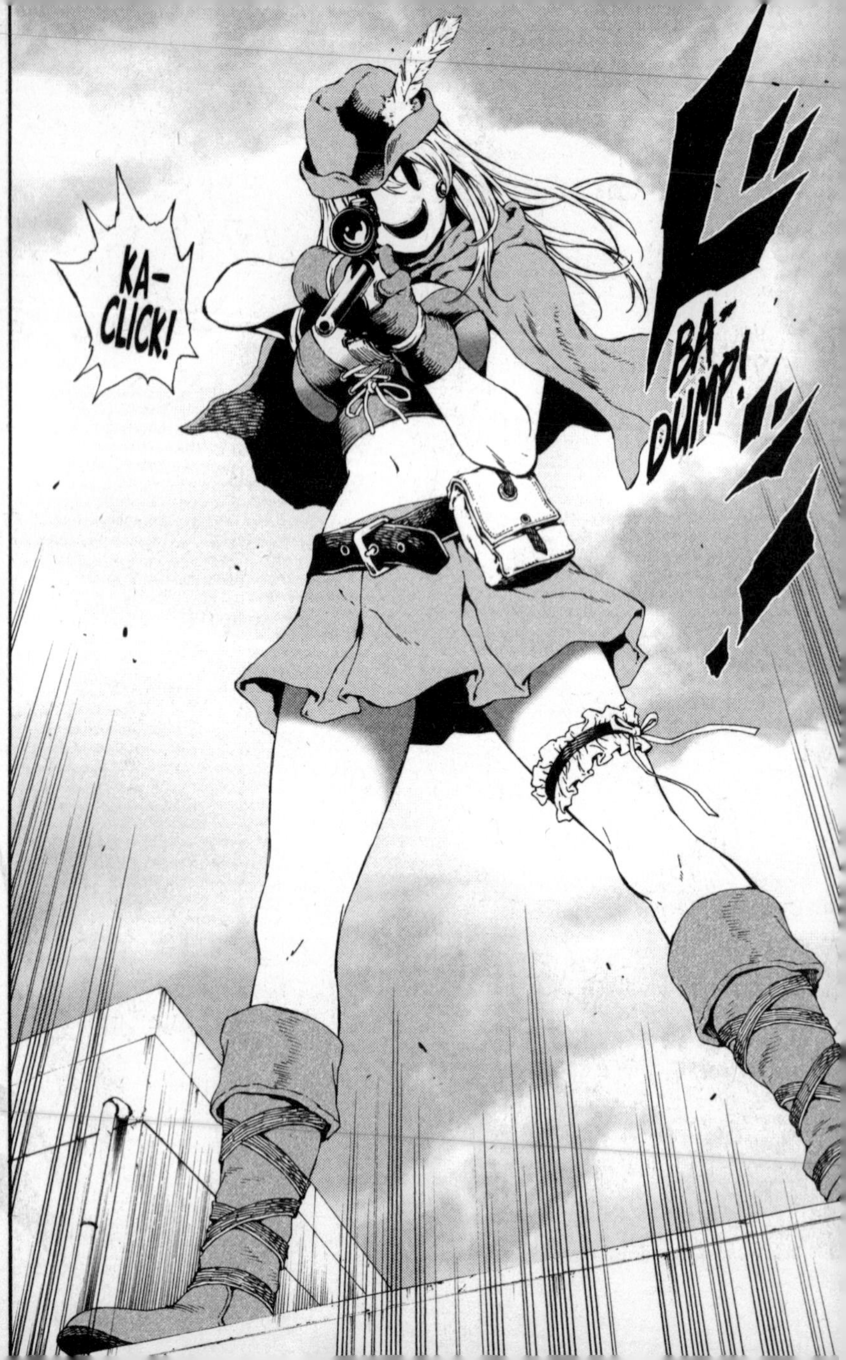
BA-DUMP!
KA-CLICK!

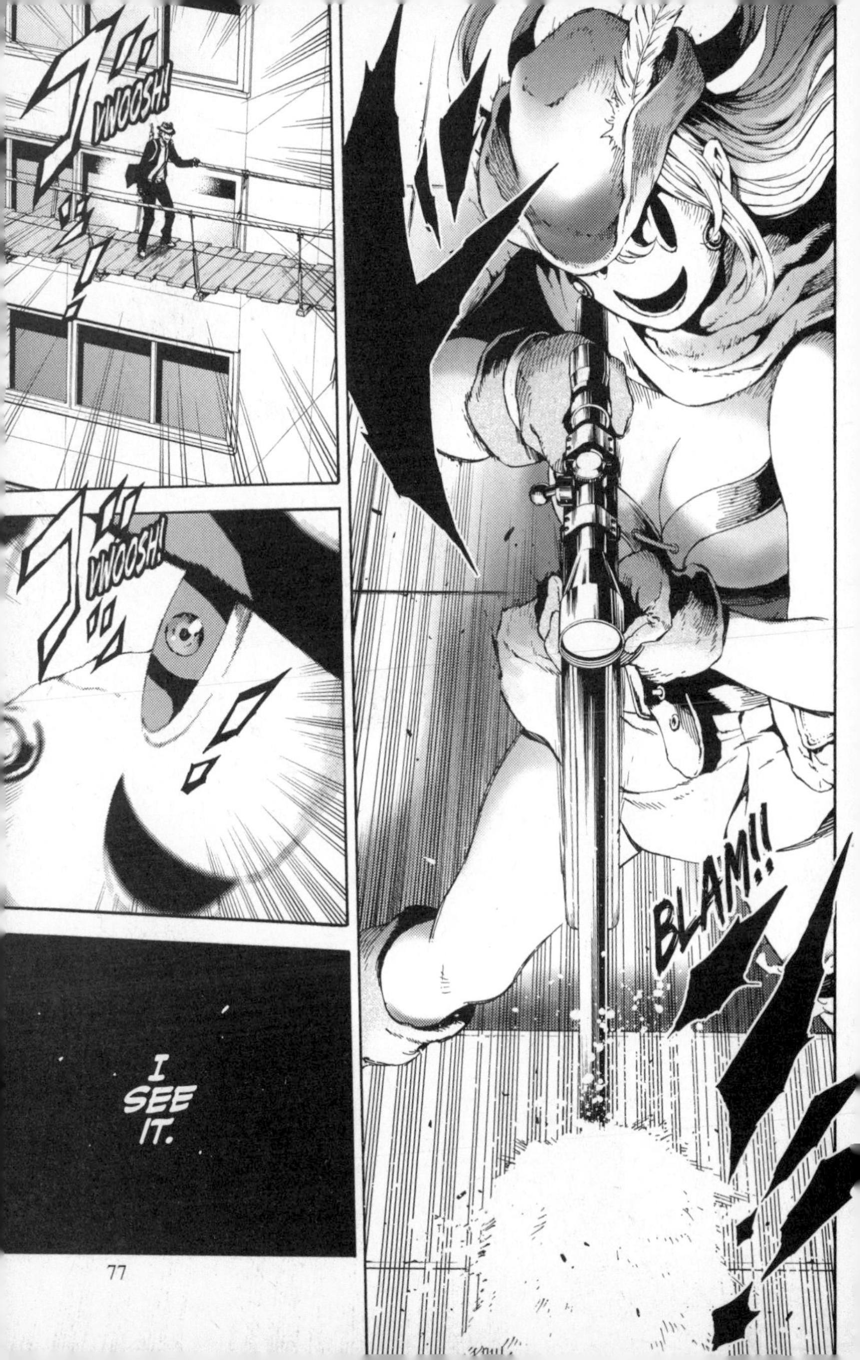
BLAM!!
VVOOSH!
VVOOSH!
I SEE IT.

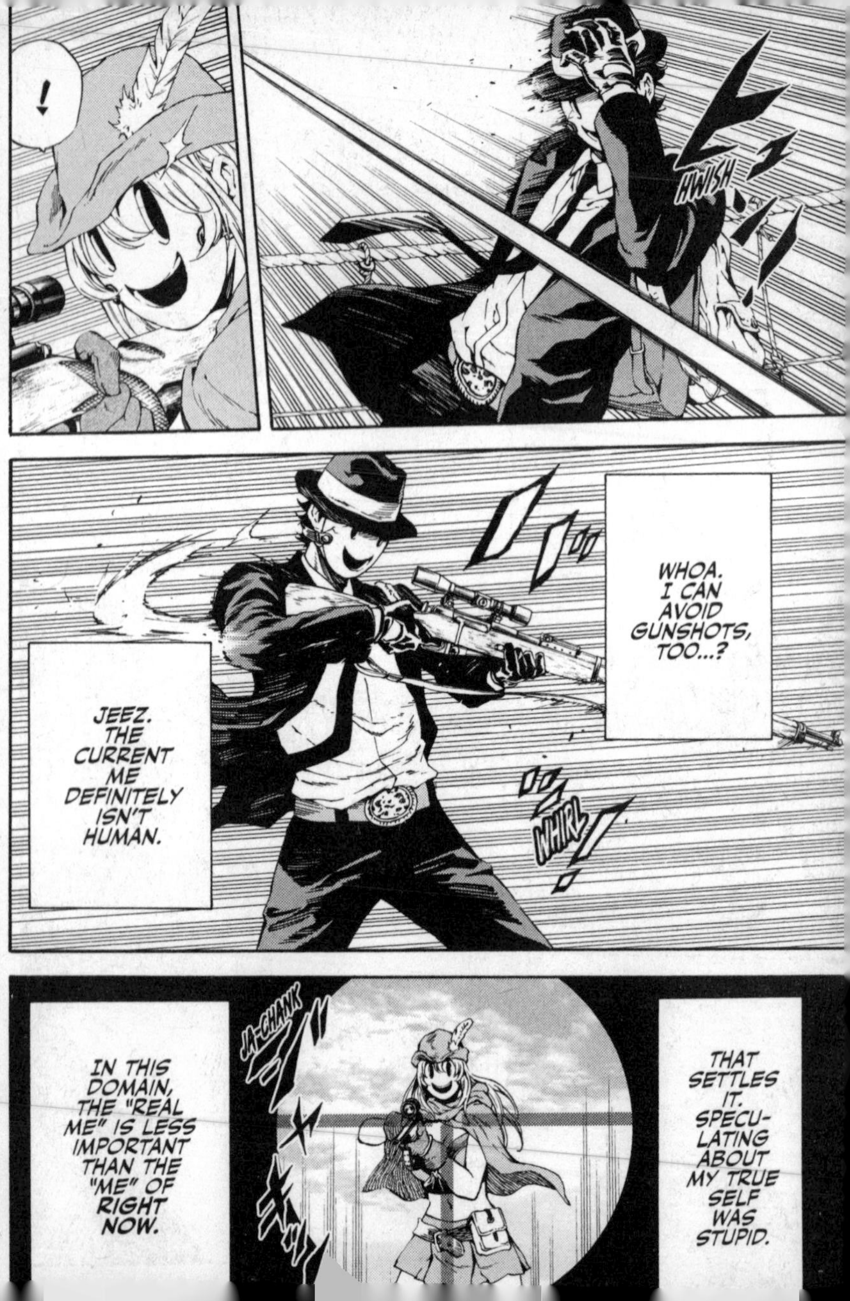
HWISH
!
WHOA. I CAN AVOID GUNSHOTS, TOO...?
WHIRL
JEEZ. THE CURRENT ME DEFINITELY ISN'T HUMAN.
THAT SETTLES IT. SPECU-LATING ABOUT MY TRUE SELF WAS STUPID.
JA-CHANK
IN THIS DOMAIN, THE "REAL ME" IS LESS IMPORTANT THAN THE "ME" OF RIGHT NOW.

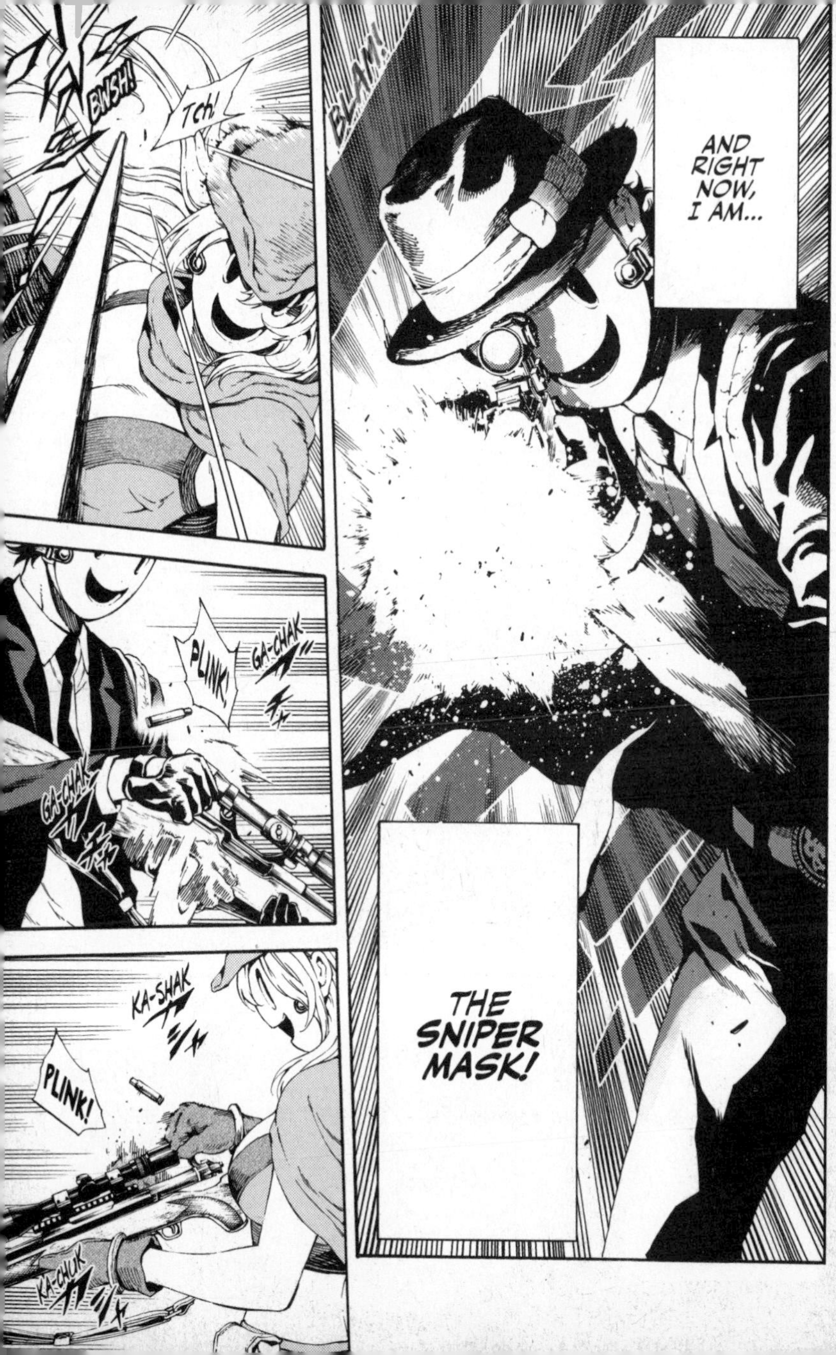
AND RIGHT NOW, I AM...
BLAM!
THE SNIPER MASK!
Tch!
BWSH!
GA-CHAK
PLINK!
GA-CHAK
KA-SHAK
PLINK!
KA-CHUK

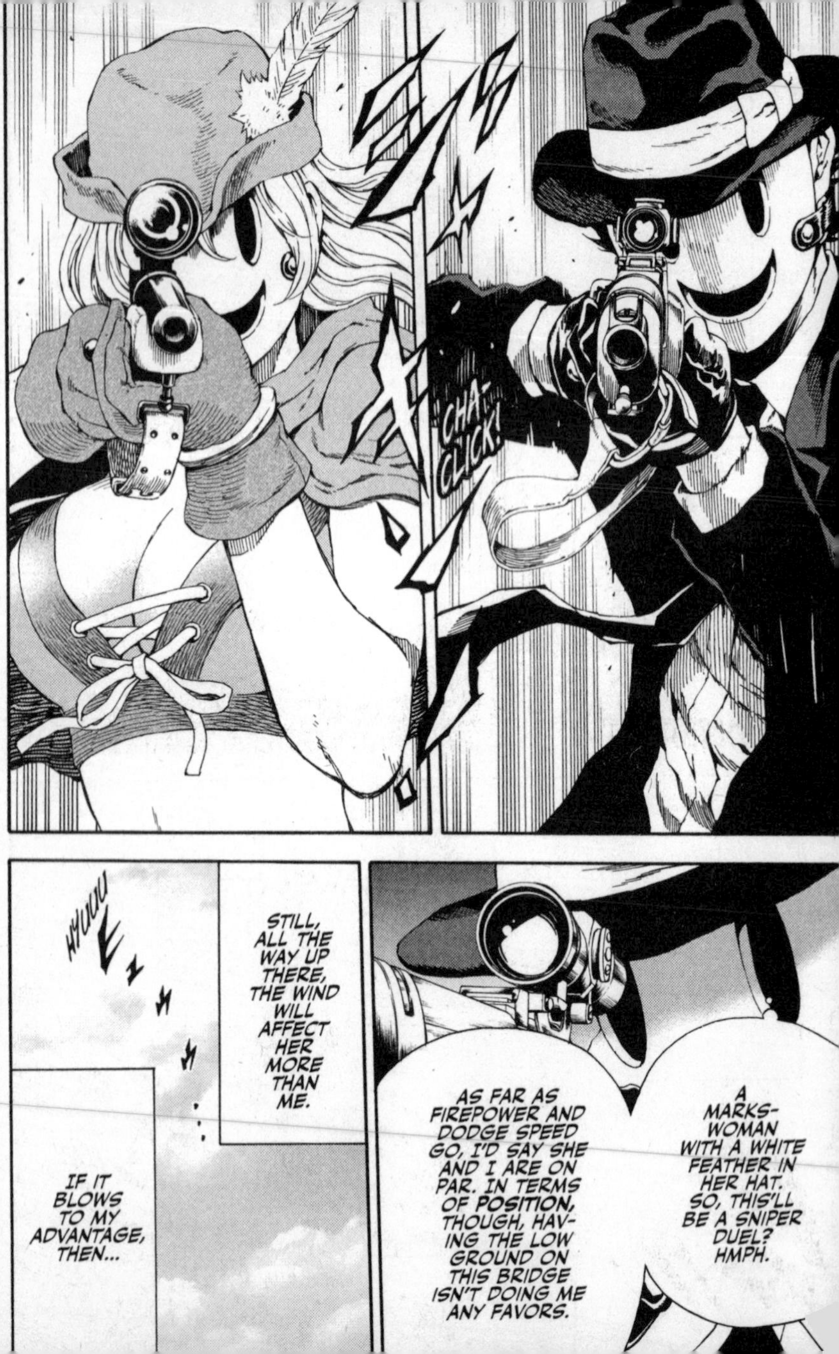
CHA-CLICK!
A MARKS-WOMAN WITH A WHITE FEATHER IN HER HAT. SO, THIS'LL BE A SNIPER DUEL? HMPH.
AS FAR AS FIREPOWER AND DODGE SPEED GO, I'D SAY SHE AND I ARE ON PAR. IN TERMS OF POSITION, THOUGH, HAV-ING THE LOW GROUND ON THIS BRIDGE ISN'T DOING ME ANY FAVORS.
STILL, ALL THE WAY UP THERE, THE WIND WILL AFFECT HER MORE THAN ME.
HYUUU
IF IT BLOWS TO MY ADVANTAGE, THEN...

....

<EVERYTHING IN THIS WORLD BELONGS TO *HIM*.>

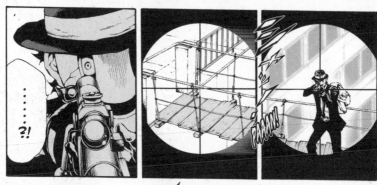

.....?!

PAAAN!

THIS ISN'T A SNIPER DUEL ANYMORE!

NOT GOOD ...!

BLAM!

KSHAK

BLAM!

BLAM!

KSHAK

BLAM!

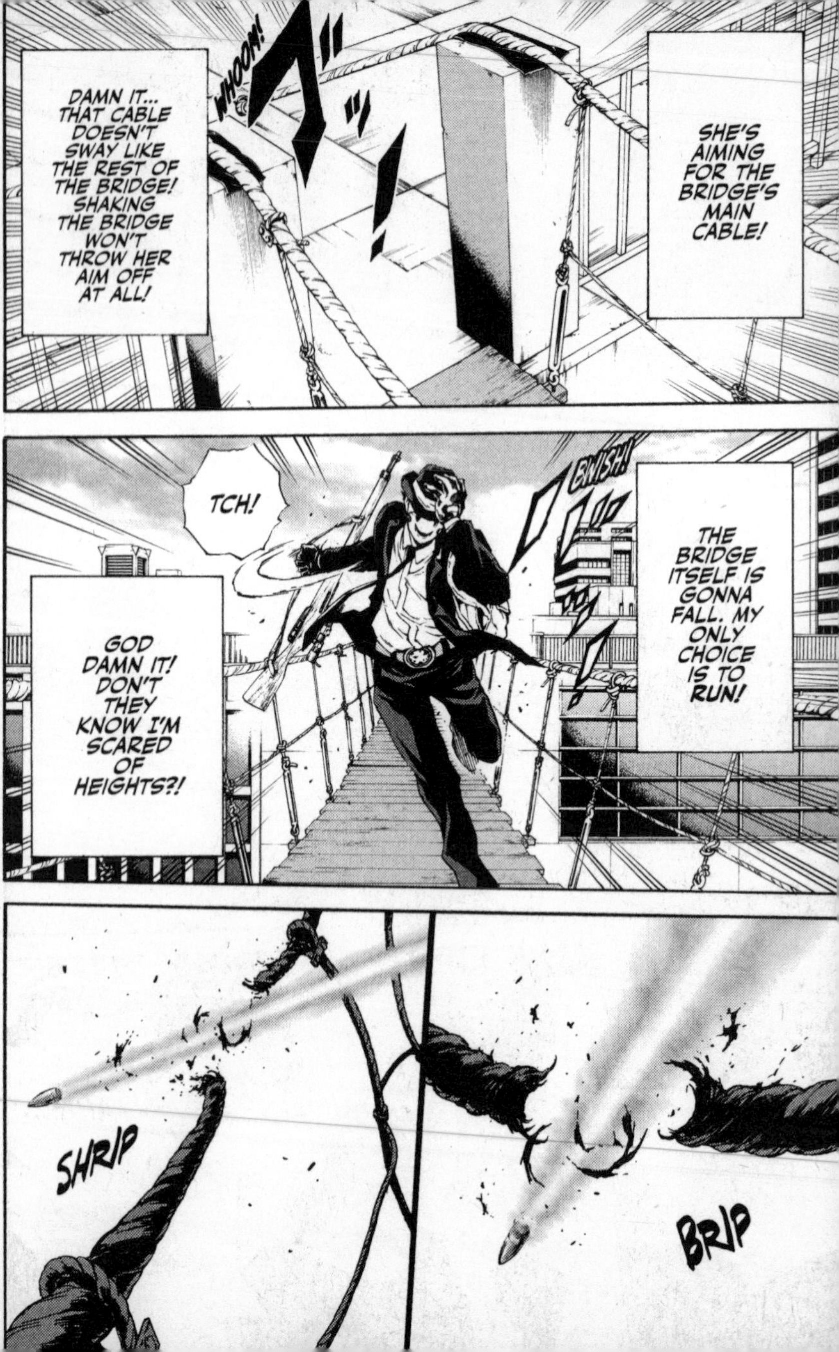
SHE'S AIMING FOR THE BRIDGE'S MAIN CABLE!
WHOOM!
DAMN IT... THAT CABLE DOESN'T SWAY LIKE THE REST OF THE BRIDGE! SHAKING THE BRIDGE WON'T THROW HER AIM OFF AT ALL!
THE BRIDGE ITSELF IS GONNA FALL. MY ONLY CHOICE IS TO RUN!
SWISH
TCH!
GOD DAMN IT! DON'T THEY KNOW I'M SCARED OF HEIGHTS?!
BRIP
SHRIP

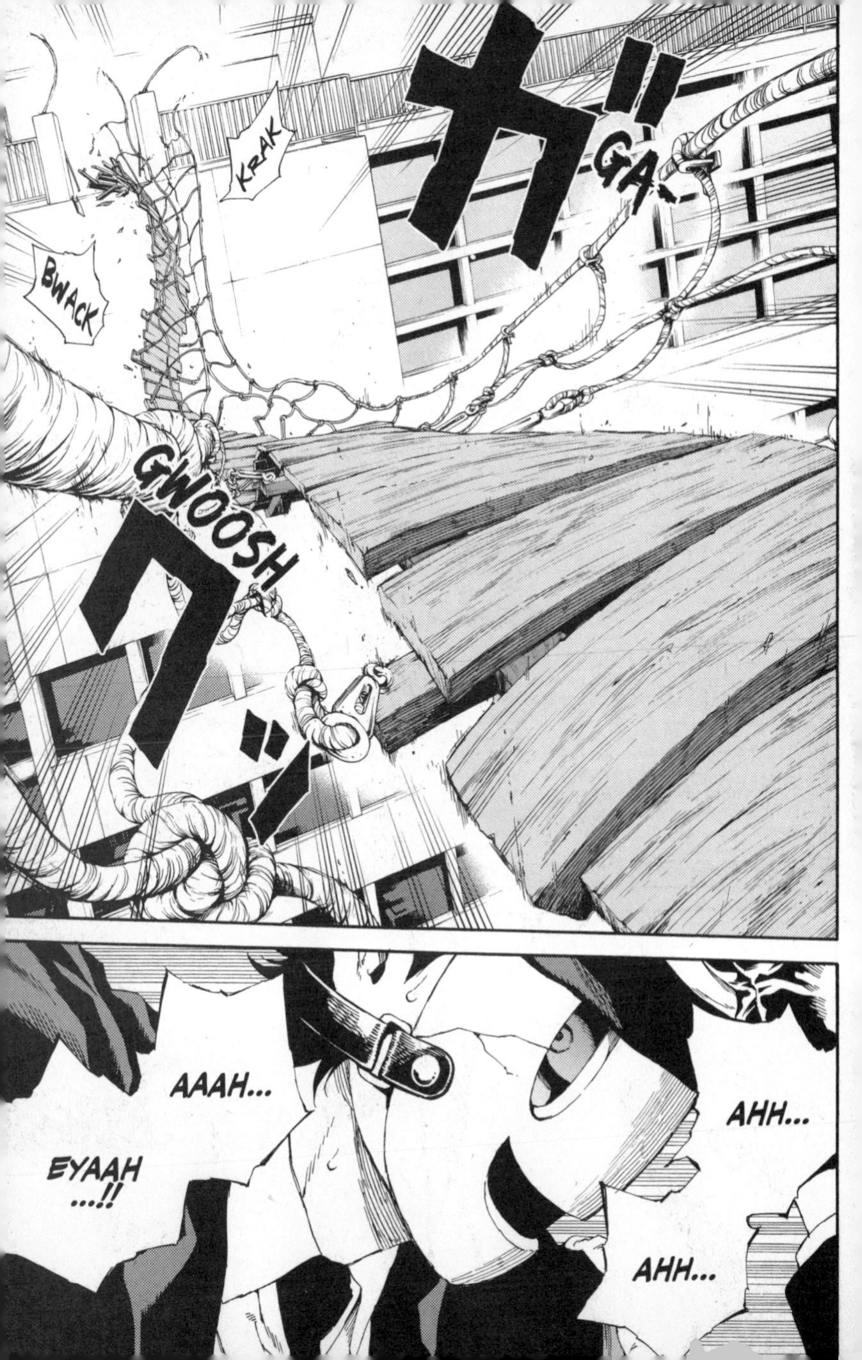
ガ
GA
KRAK
BWACK
GWOOSH
ブ
AHH...
AHH...
AAAH...
EYAAH ...!!

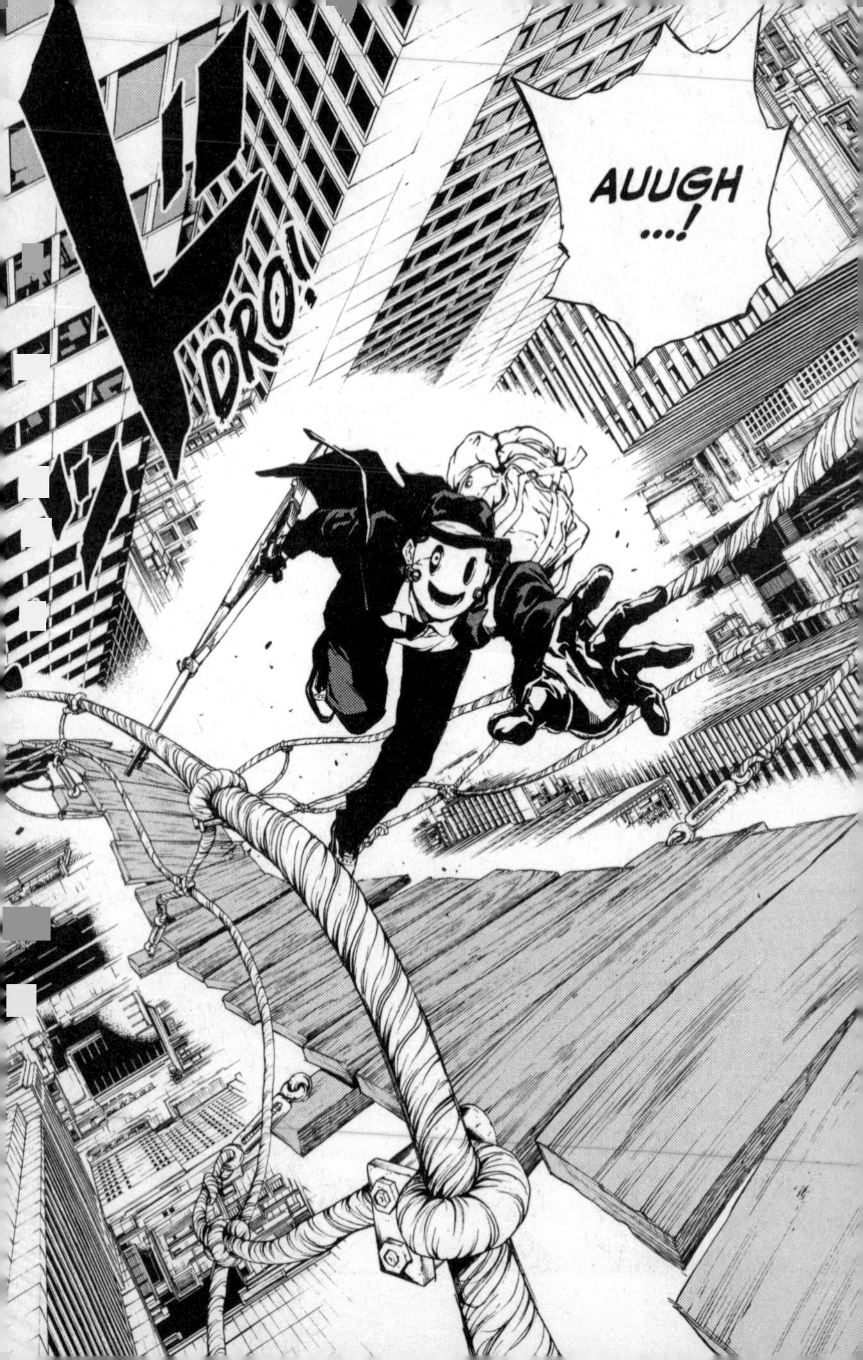
AUUGH ...!
DRO!!

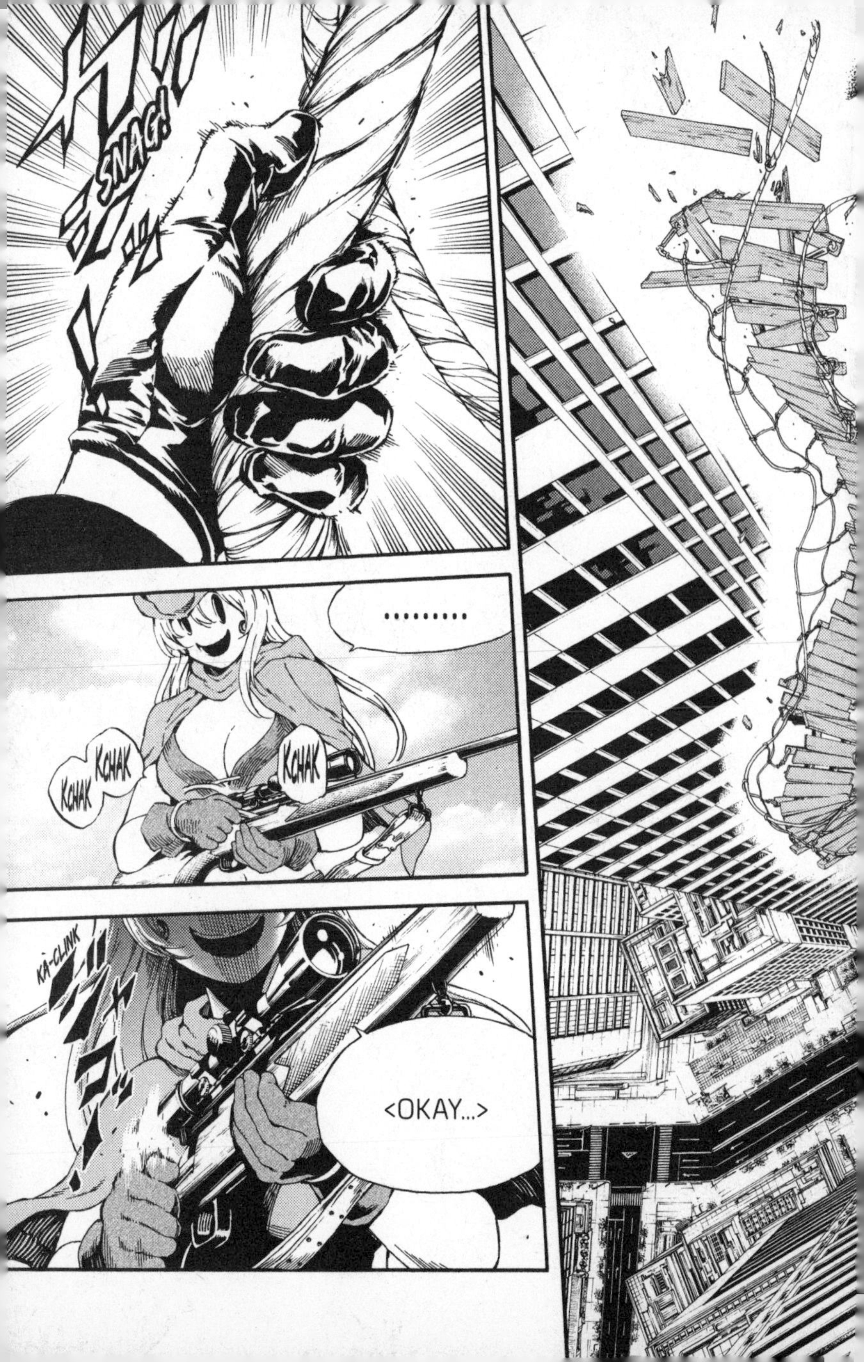
SNAG!
....
KCHAK
KCHAK
KCHAK
KA-CLINK
<OKAY...>

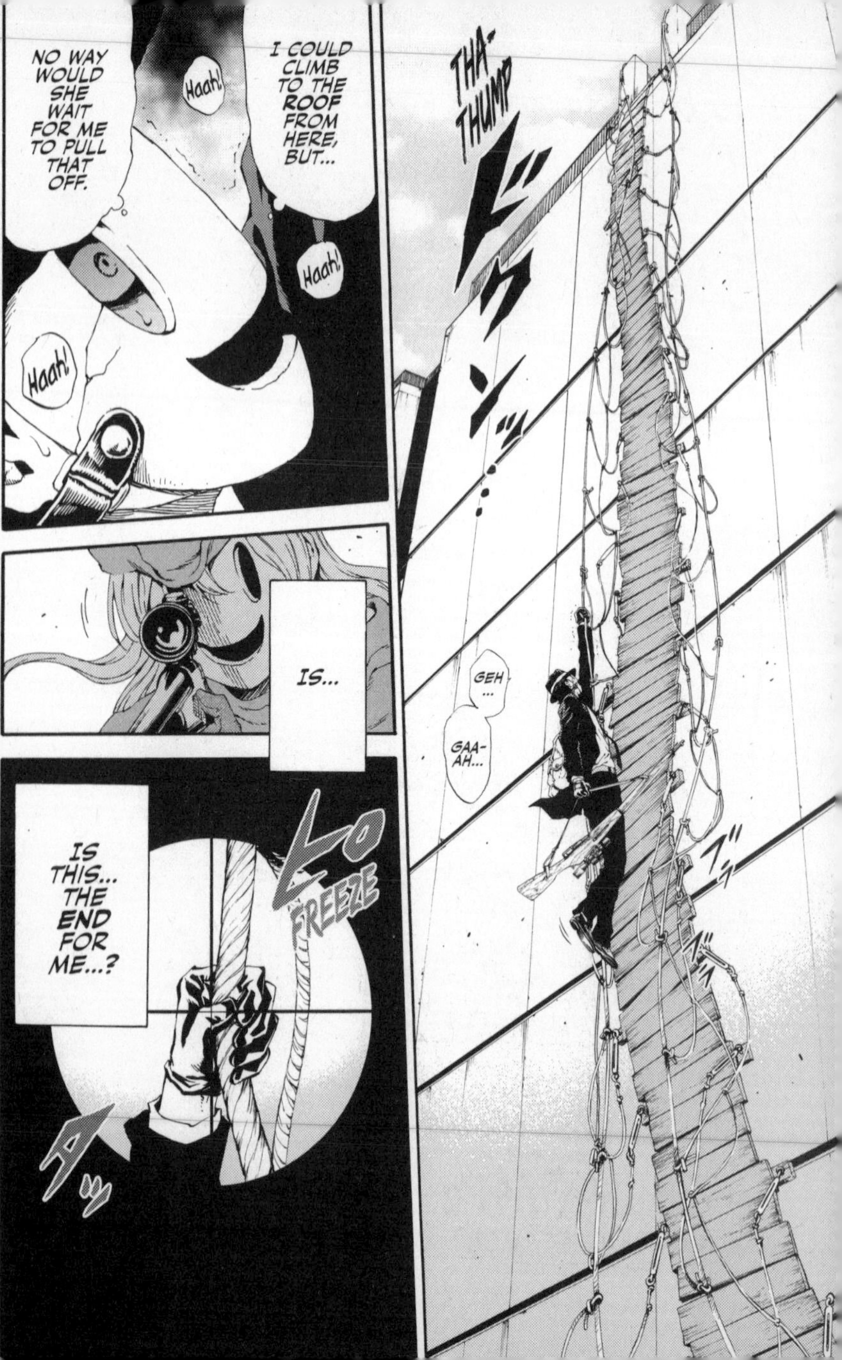
THA-THUMP
GEH...
GAAH...
I COULD CLIMB TO THE ROOF FROM HERE, BUT...
Haah!
NO WAY WOULD SHE WAIT FOR ME TO PULL THAT OFF.
Haah!
Haah!
IS...
FREEZE
IS THIS... THE END FOR ME...?

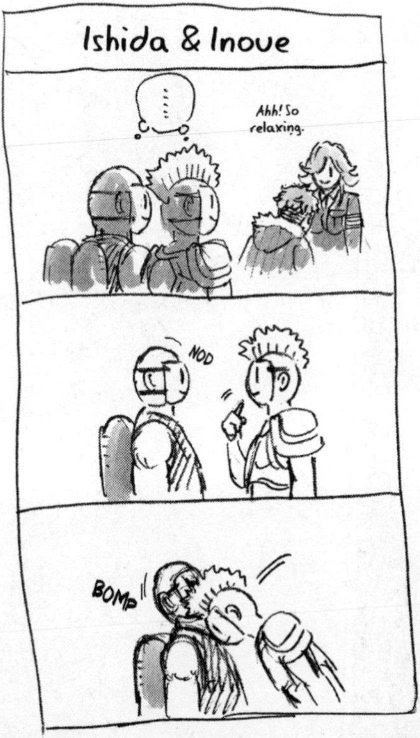
Ishida & Inoue
Ahh! So relaxing.
NOD
BOMP

HIGH-RISE
INVASION

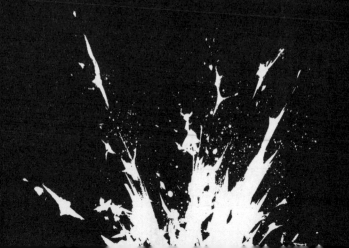

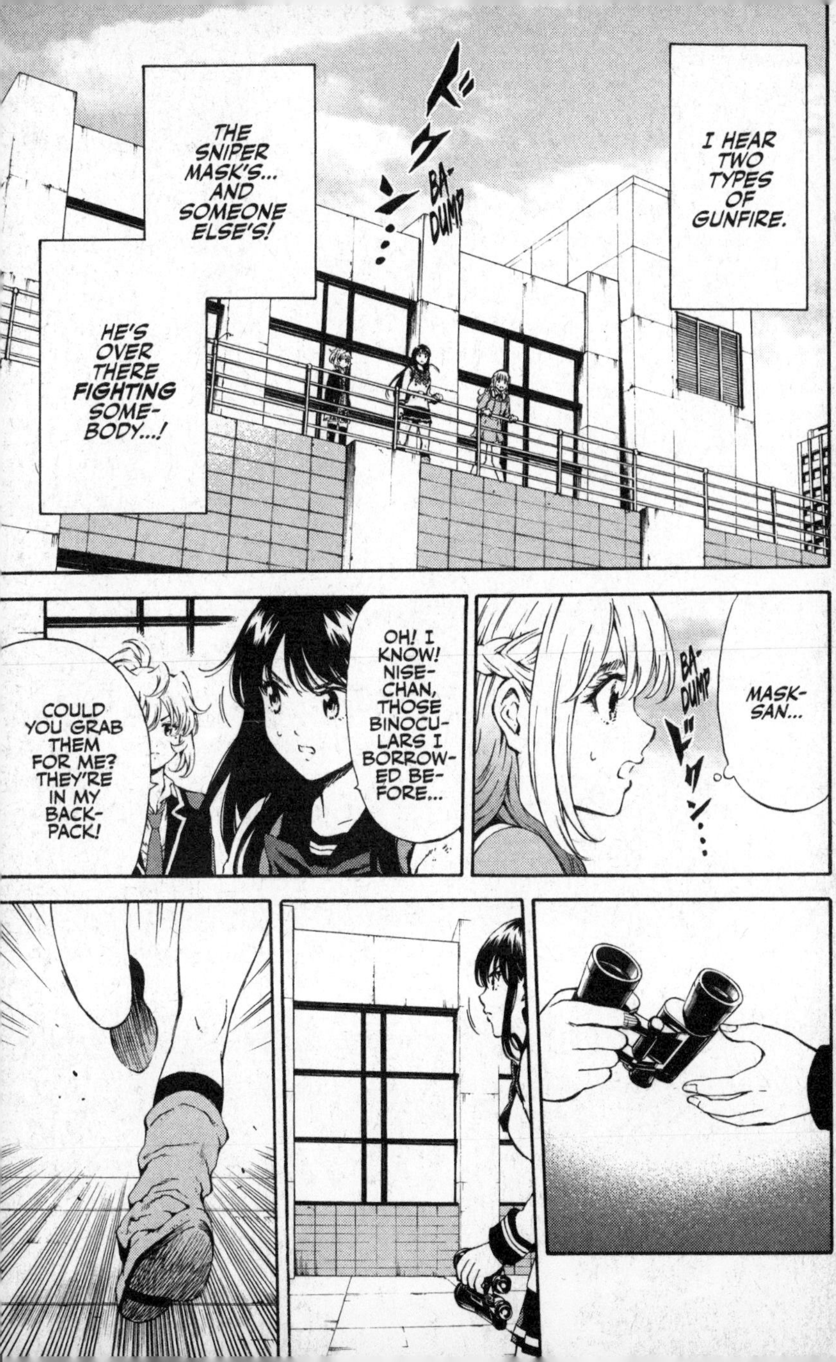
I HEAR TWO TYPES OF GUNFIRE.
BA-DUMP
THE SNIPER MASK'S... AND SOMEONE ELSE'S!
HE'S OVER THERE FIGHTING SOMEBODY...!
MASK-SAN...
BA-DUMP
OH! I KNOW! NISE-CHAN, THOSE BINOCULARS I BORROWED BEFORE...
COULD YOU GRAB THEM FOR ME? THEY'RE IN MY BACKPACK!

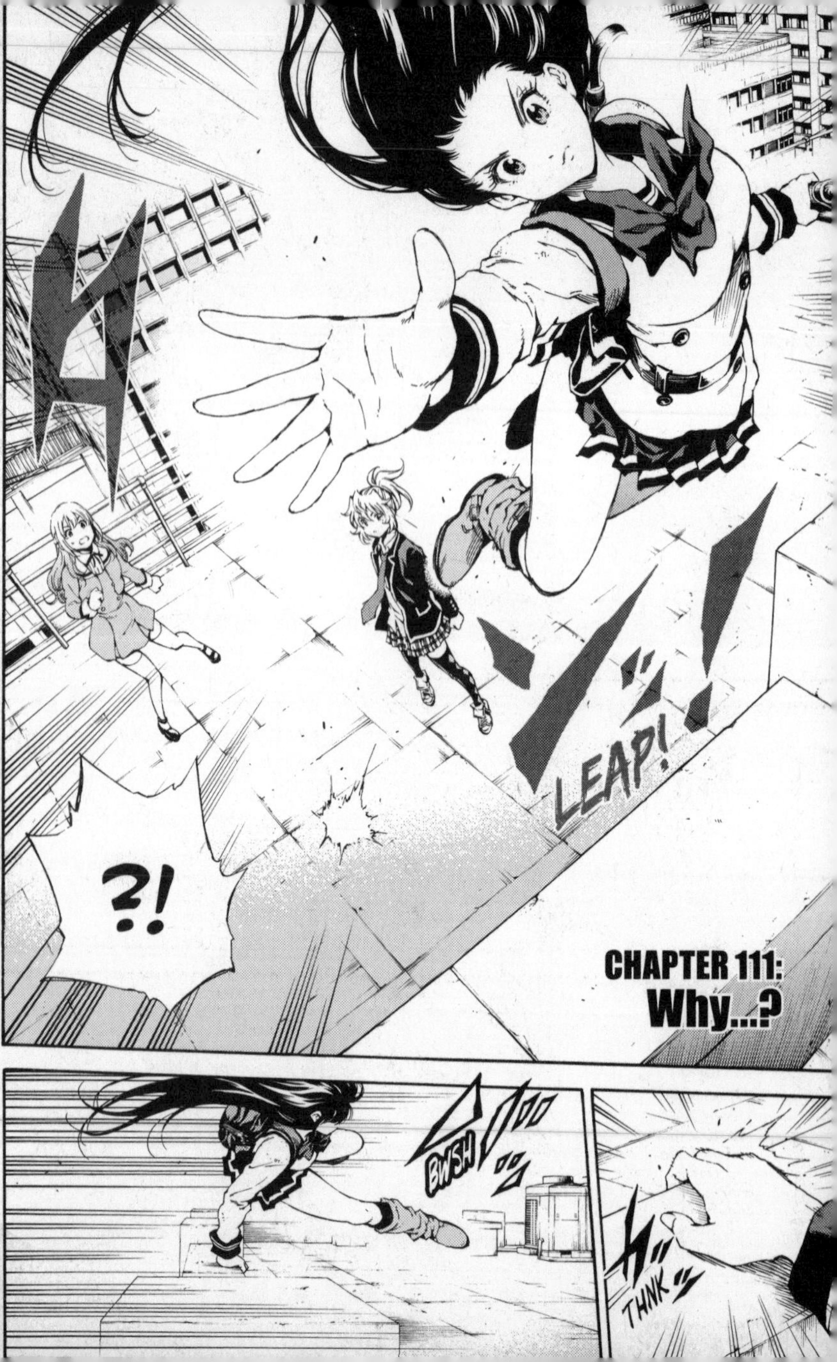
LEAP!
CHAPTER 111:
Why...?
?!
THINK
BWSH

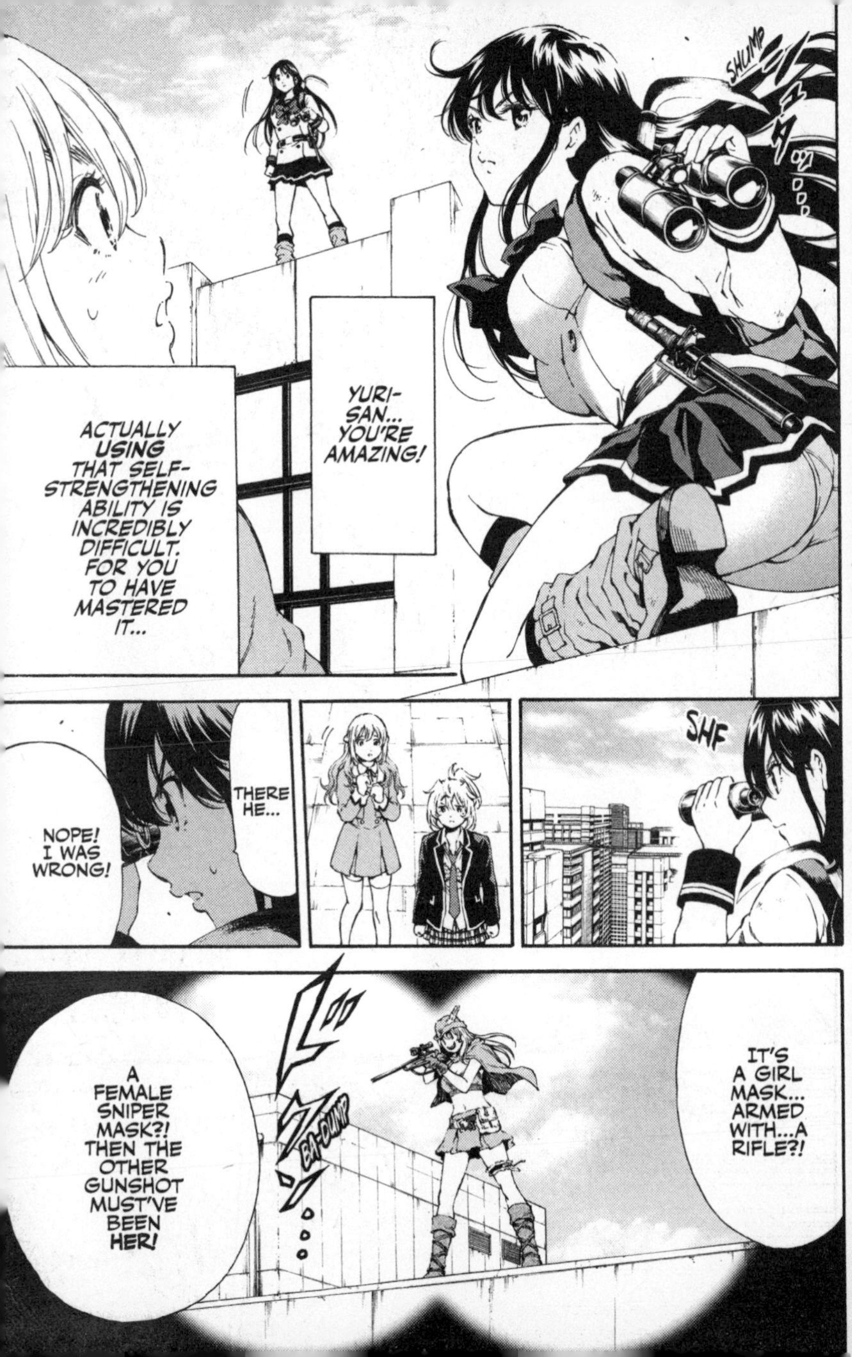
SHUMP
YURI-SAN... YOU'RE AMAZING!
ACTUALLY USING THAT SELF-STRENGTHENING ABILITY IS INCREDIBLY DIFFICULT. FOR YOU TO HAVE MASTERED IT...
SHF
THERE HE...
NOPE! I WAS WRONG!
IT'S A GIRL MASK... ARMED WITH...A RIFLE?!
BA-DUMP
A FEMALE SNIPER MASK?! THEN THE OTHER GUNSHOT MUST'VE BEEN HER!

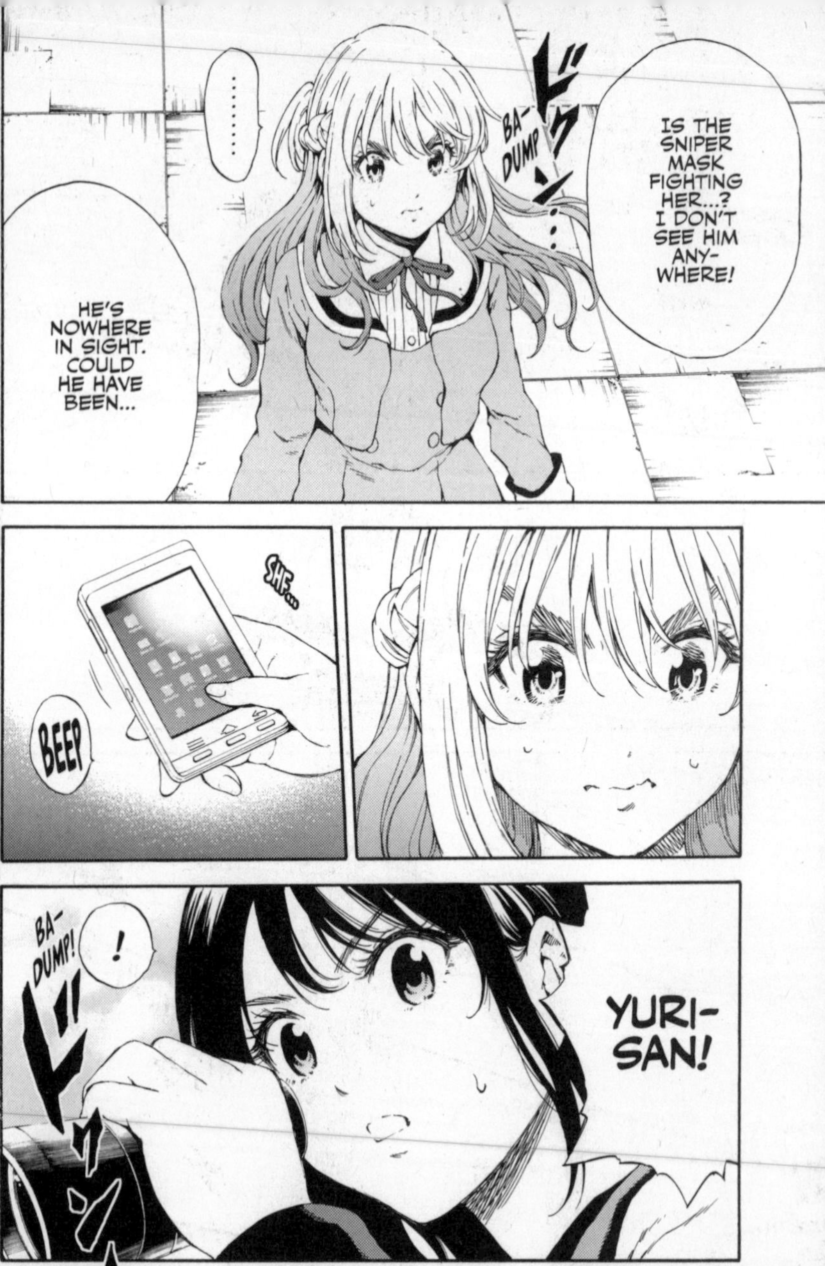
IS THE SNIPER MASK FIGHTING HER...? I DON'T SEE HIM ANYWHERE!
BA-DUMP
......
HE'S NOWHERE IN SIGHT. COULD HE HAVE BEEN...
SHF...
BEEP
YURI-SAN!
!
BA-DUMP!

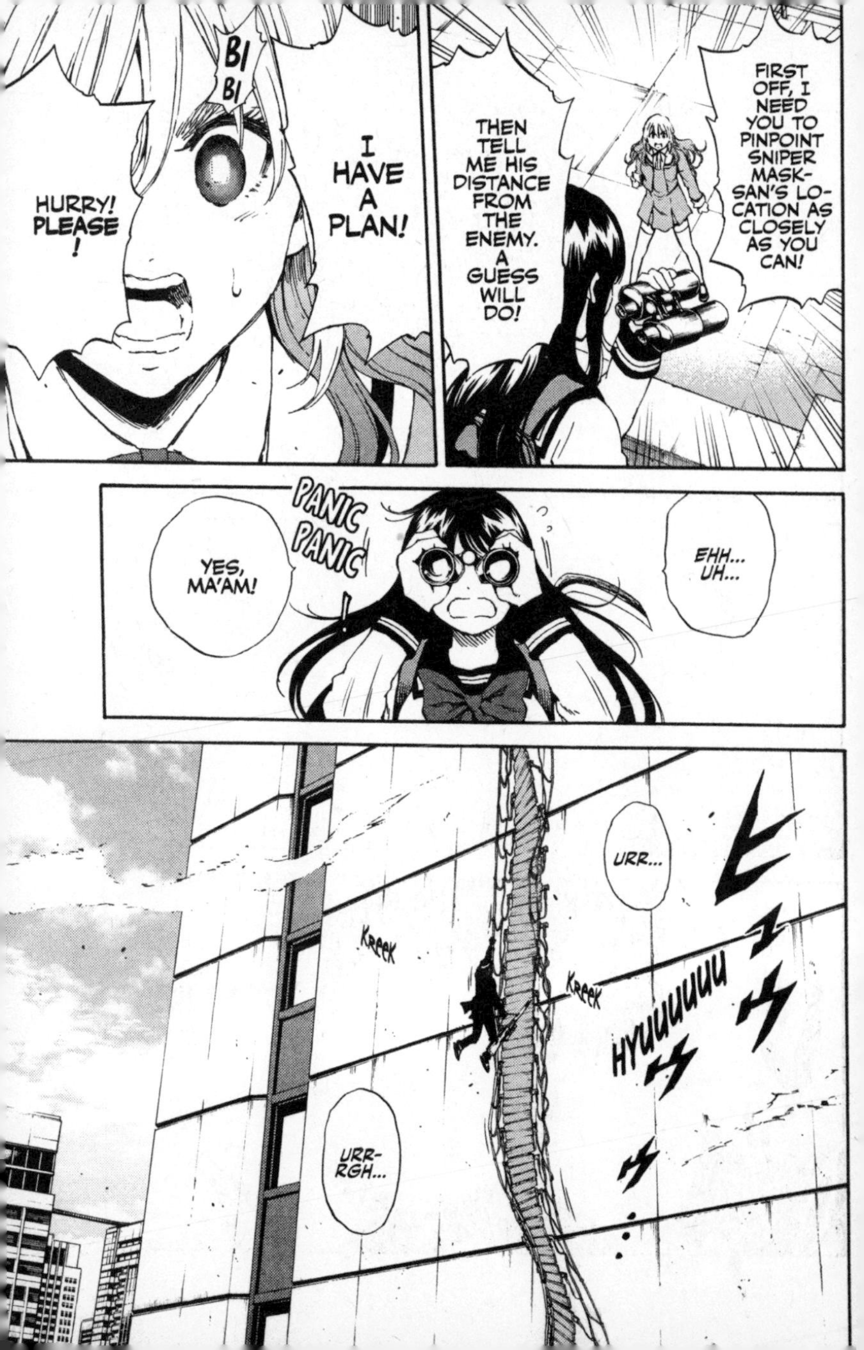
FIRST OFF, I NEED YOU TO PINPOINT SNIPER MASK-SAN'S LOCATION AS CLOSELY AS YOU CAN!
THEN TELL ME HIS DISTANCE FROM THE ENEMY. A GUESS WILL DO!
BI BI
I HAVE A PLAN!
HURRY! PLEASE!
EHH... UH...
PANIC PANIC
YES, MA'AM!
URR...
HYUUUUUU
Kreek
Kreek
URR-RGH...

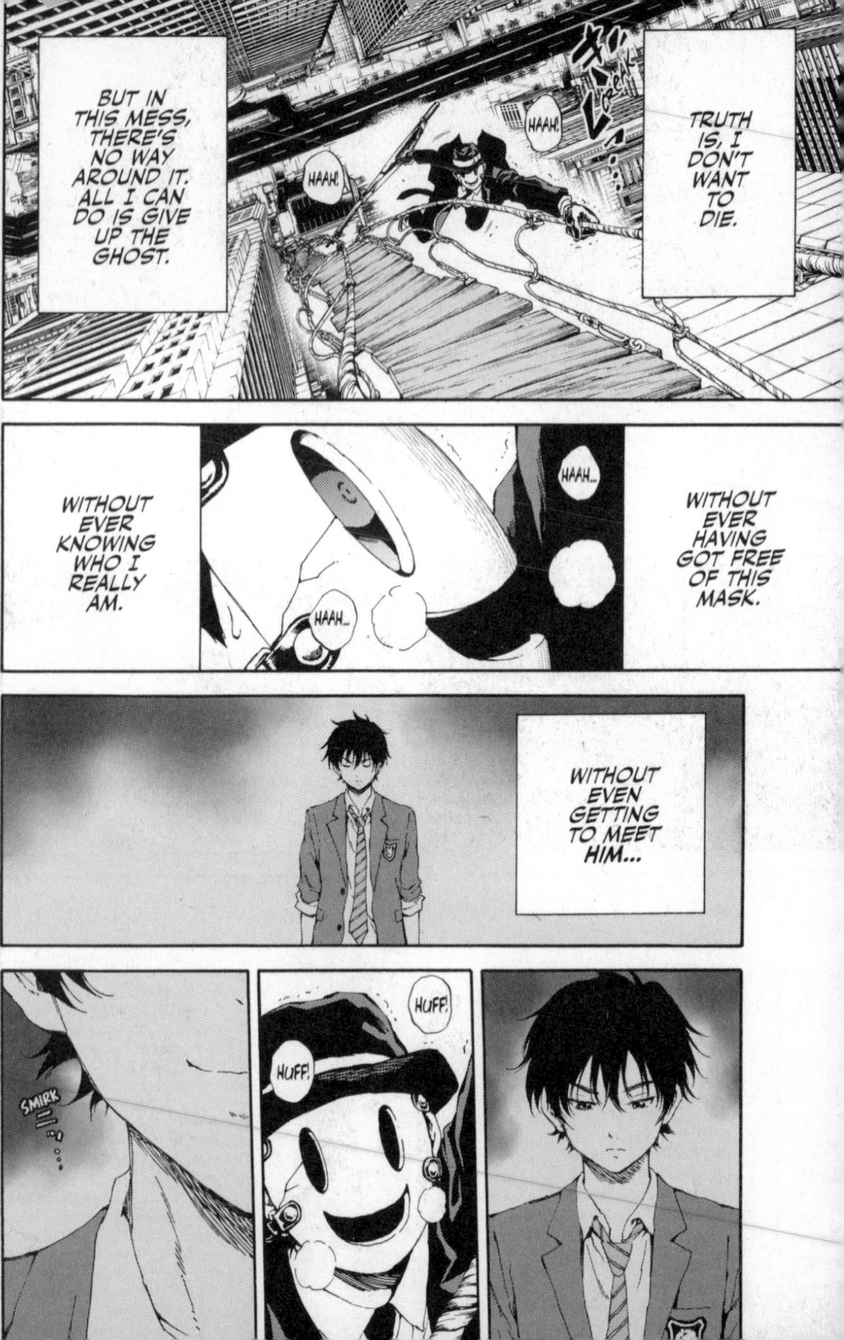
TRUTH IS, I DON'T WANT TO DIE.
creak
HAAH!
HAAH!
BUT IN THIS MESS, THERE'S NO WAY AROUND IT. ALL I CAN DO IS GIVE UP THE GHOST.
WITHOUT EVER HAVING GOT FREE OF THIS MASK.
HAAH...
HAAH...
WITHOUT EVER KNOWING WHO I REALLY AM.
WITHOUT EVEN GETTING TO MEET HIM...
HUFF!
HUFF!
SMIRK

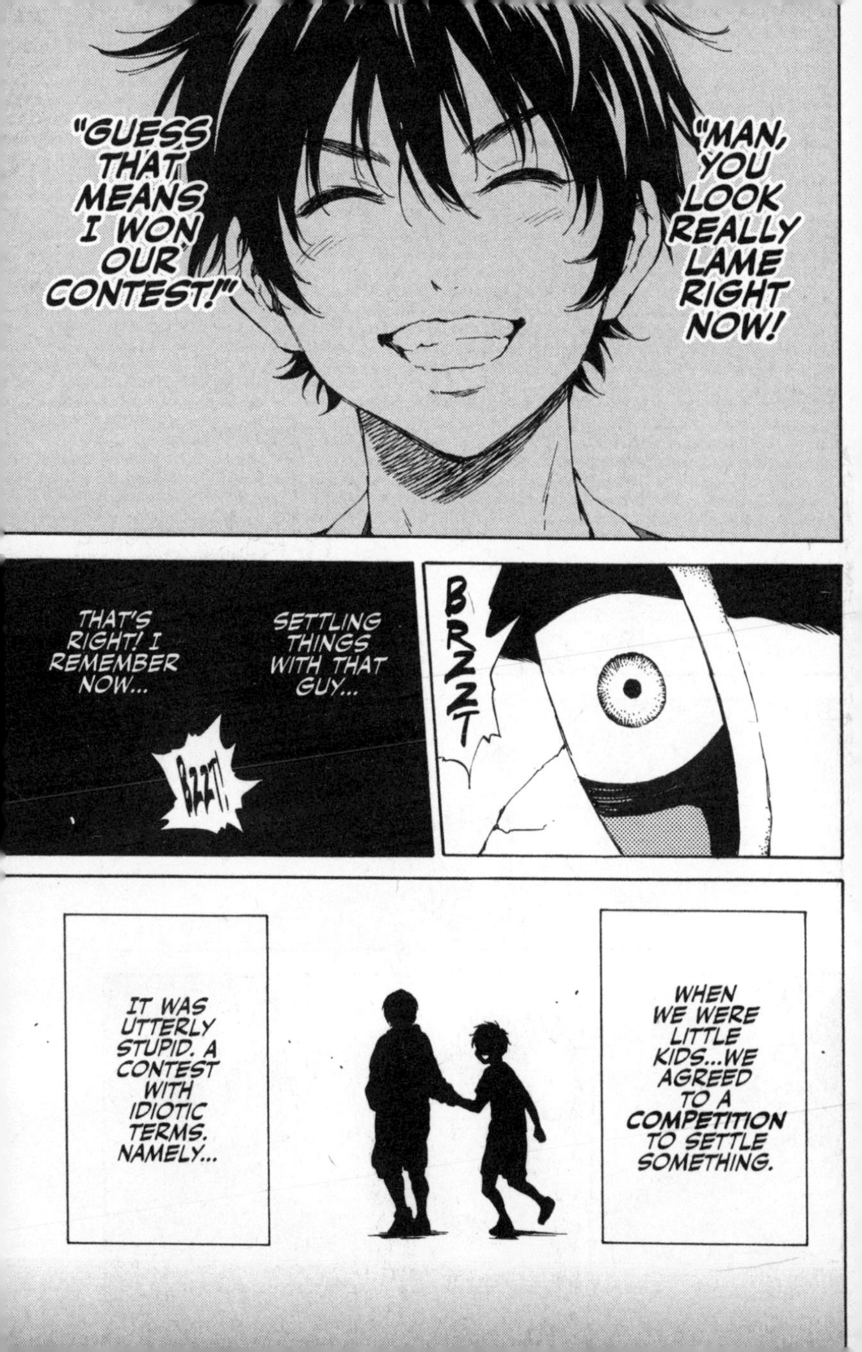
"MAN, YOU LOOK REALLY LAME RIGHT NOW!
"GUESS THAT MEANS I WON OUR CONTEST!"
BRZZT
SETTLING THINGS WITH THAT GUY...
THAT'S RIGHT! I REMEMBER NOW...
BZZT!
WHEN WE WERE LITTLE KIDS...WE AGREED TO A COMPETITION TO SETTLE SOMETHING.
IT WAS UTTERLY STUPID. A CONTEST WITH IDIOTIC TERMS. NAMELY...

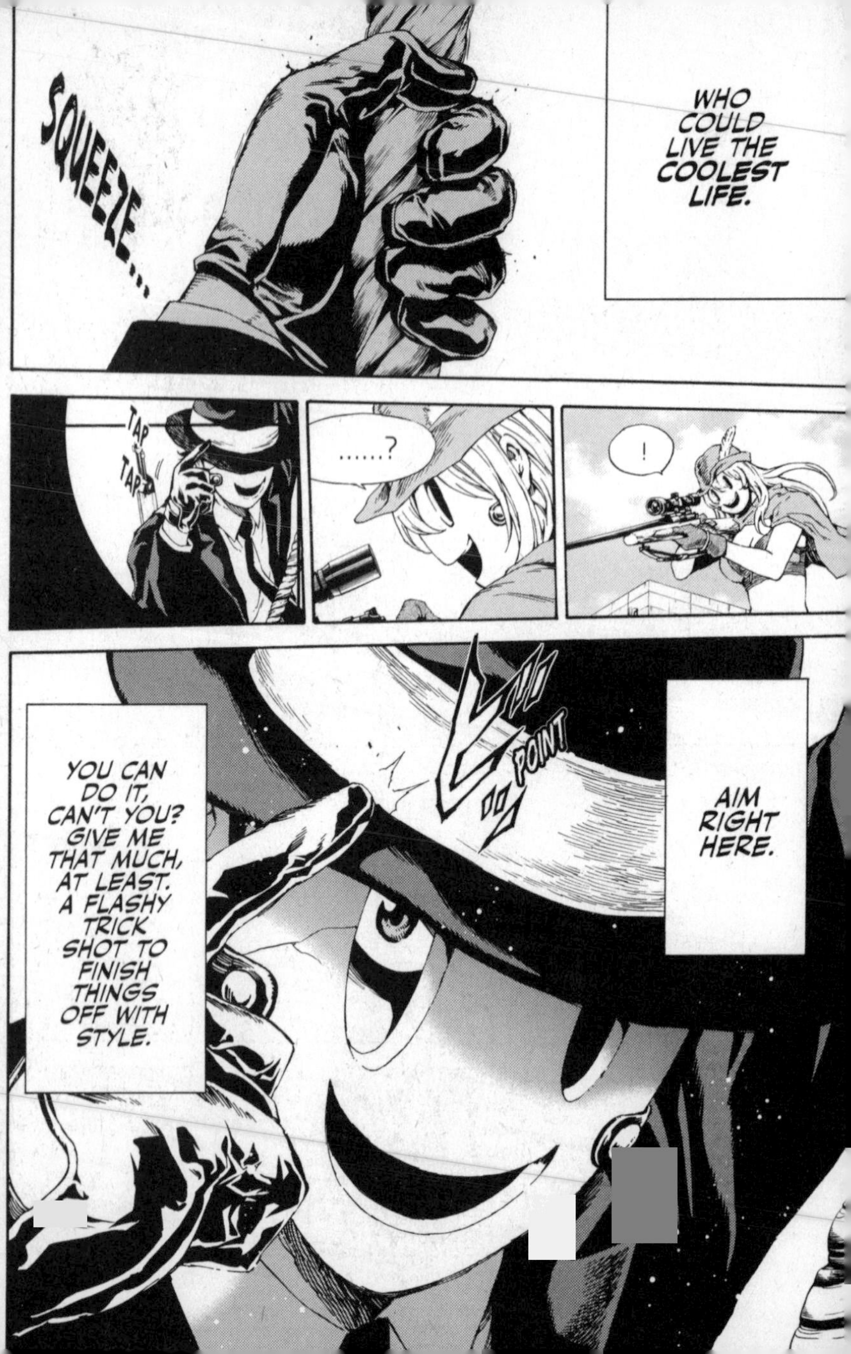
WHO COULD LIVE THE COOLEST LIFE.
SQUEEZE...
!
......?
TAP
TAP
AIM RIGHT HERE.
POINT
YOU CAN DO IT, CAN'T YOU? GIVE ME THAT MUCH, AT LEAST. A FLASHY TRICK SHOT TO FINISH THINGS OFF WITH STYLE.

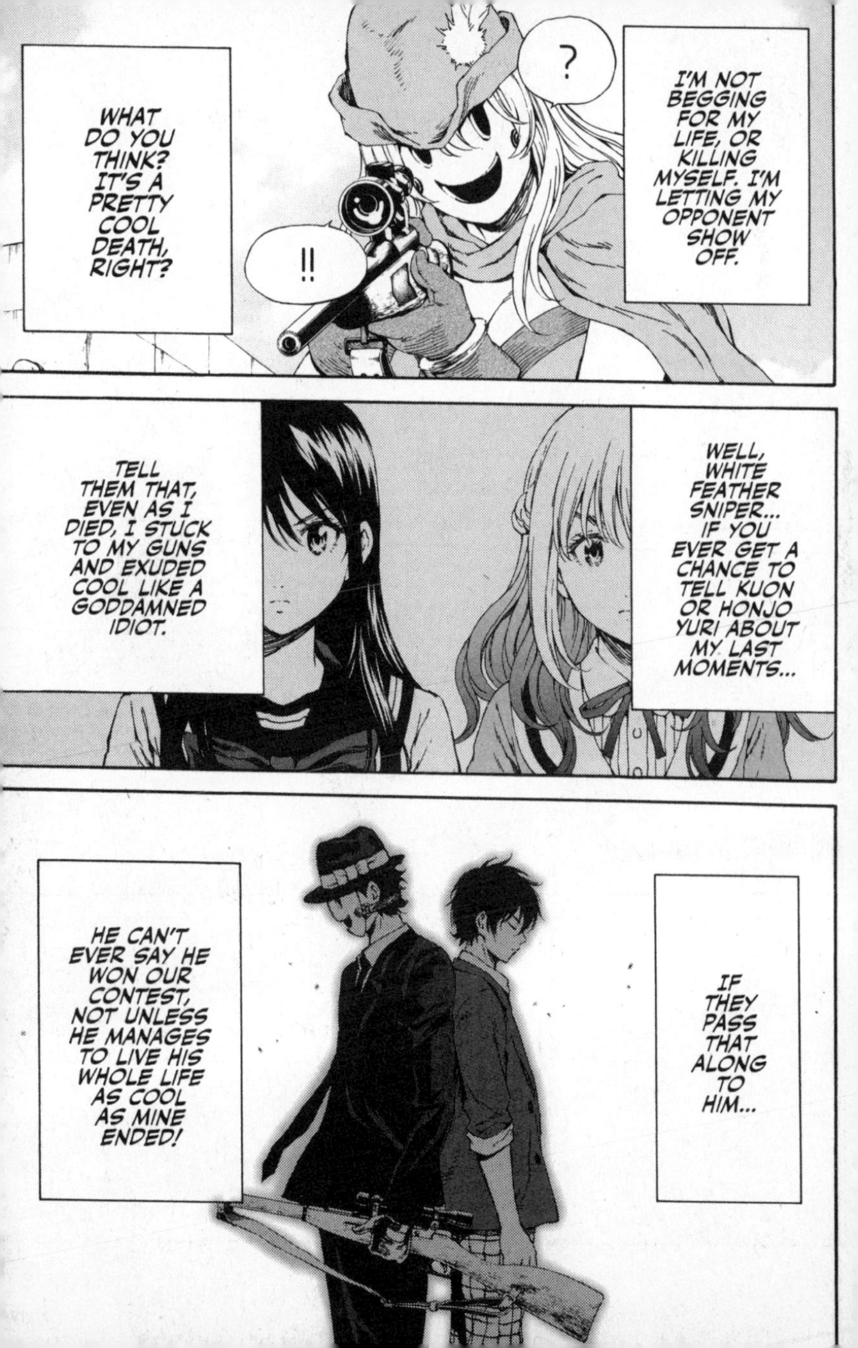
I'M NOT BEGGING FOR MY LIFE, OR KILLING MYSELF. I'M LETTING MY OPPONENT SHOW OFF.
?
!!
WHAT DO YOU THINK? IT'S A PRETTY COOL DEATH, RIGHT?
WELL, WHITE FEATHER SNIPER... IF YOU EVER GET A CHANCE TO TELL KUON OR HONJO YURI ABOUT MY LAST MOMENTS...
TELL THEM THAT, EVEN AS I DIED, I STUCK TO MY GUNS AND EXUDED COOL LIKE A GODDAMNED IDIOT.
IF THEY PASS THAT ALONG TO HIM...
HE CAN'T EVER SAY HE WON OUR CONTEST, NOT UNLESS HE MANAGES TO LIVE HIS WHOLE LIFE AS COOL AS MINE ENDED!

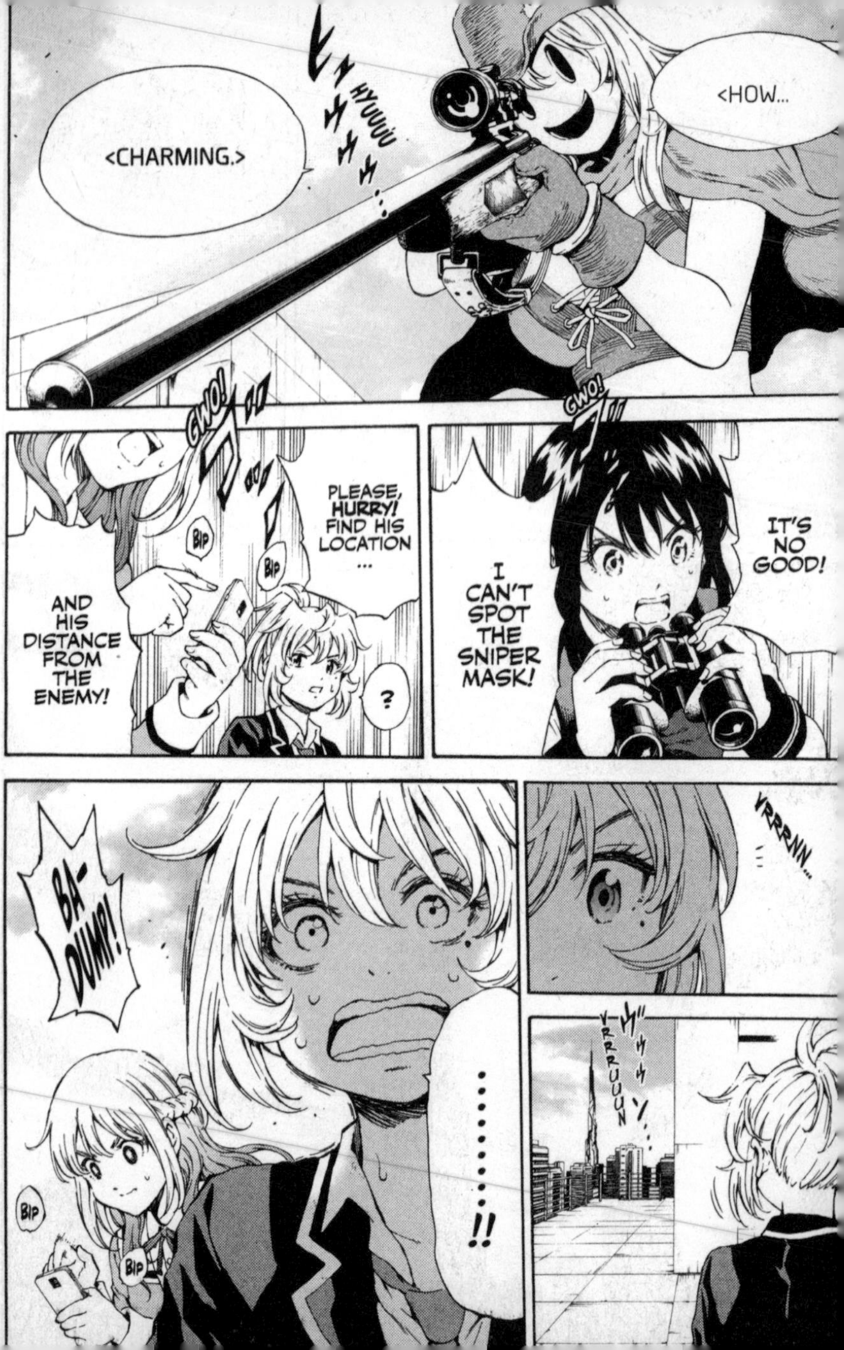

<HOW...
HYUUUU...
<CHARMING.>
GWO!
IT'S NO GOOD!
I CAN'T SPOT THE SNIPER MASK!
GWO!
PLEASE, HURRY! FIND HIS LOCATION...
BIP
BIP
AND HIS DISTANCE FROM THE ENEMY!
?
VRRRRNN...
VRRRUUUN...
BA-DUMP!
.........!!
BIP
BIP

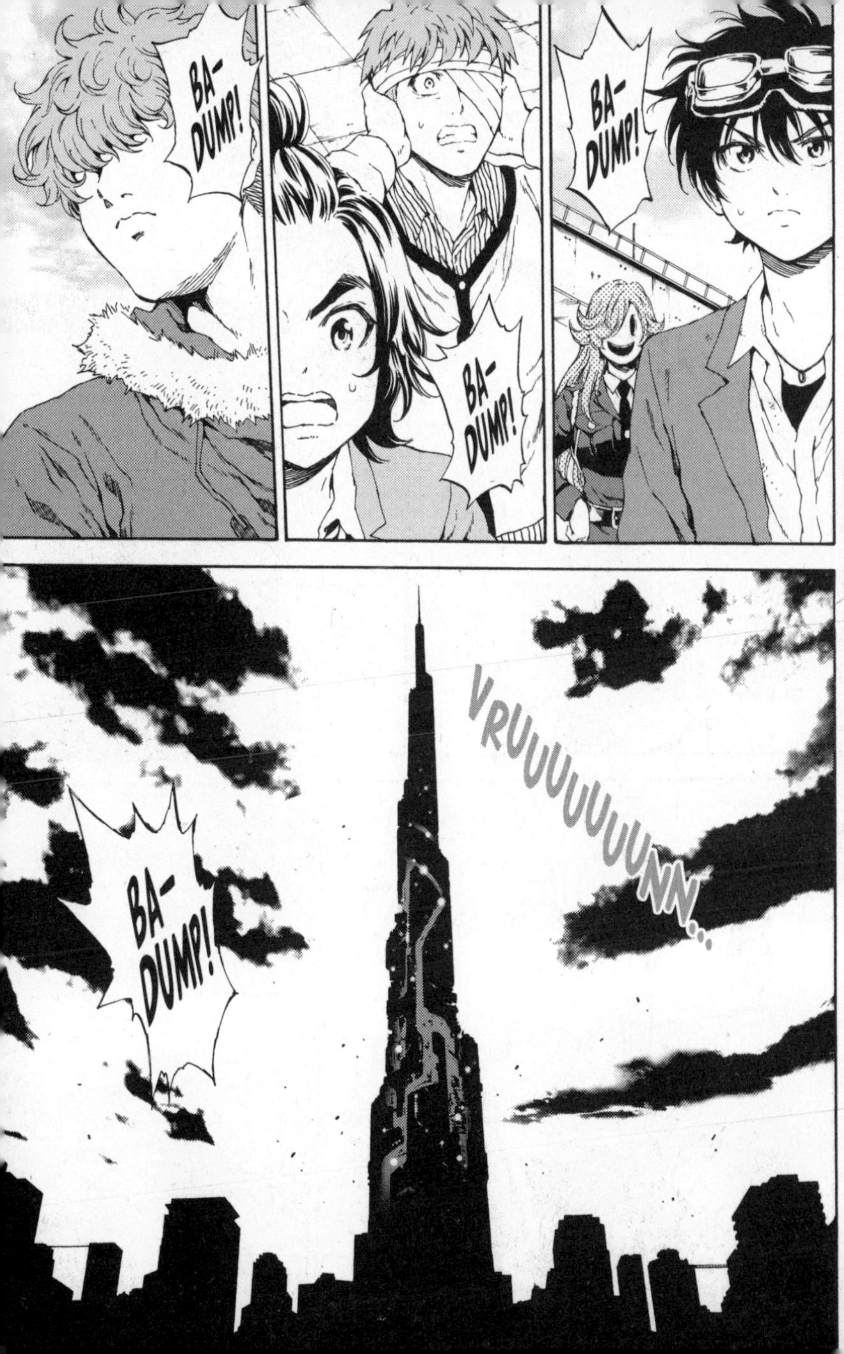
BA-DUMP!
BA-DUMP!
BA-DUMP!
VRUUUUUUUNN...
BA-DUMP!

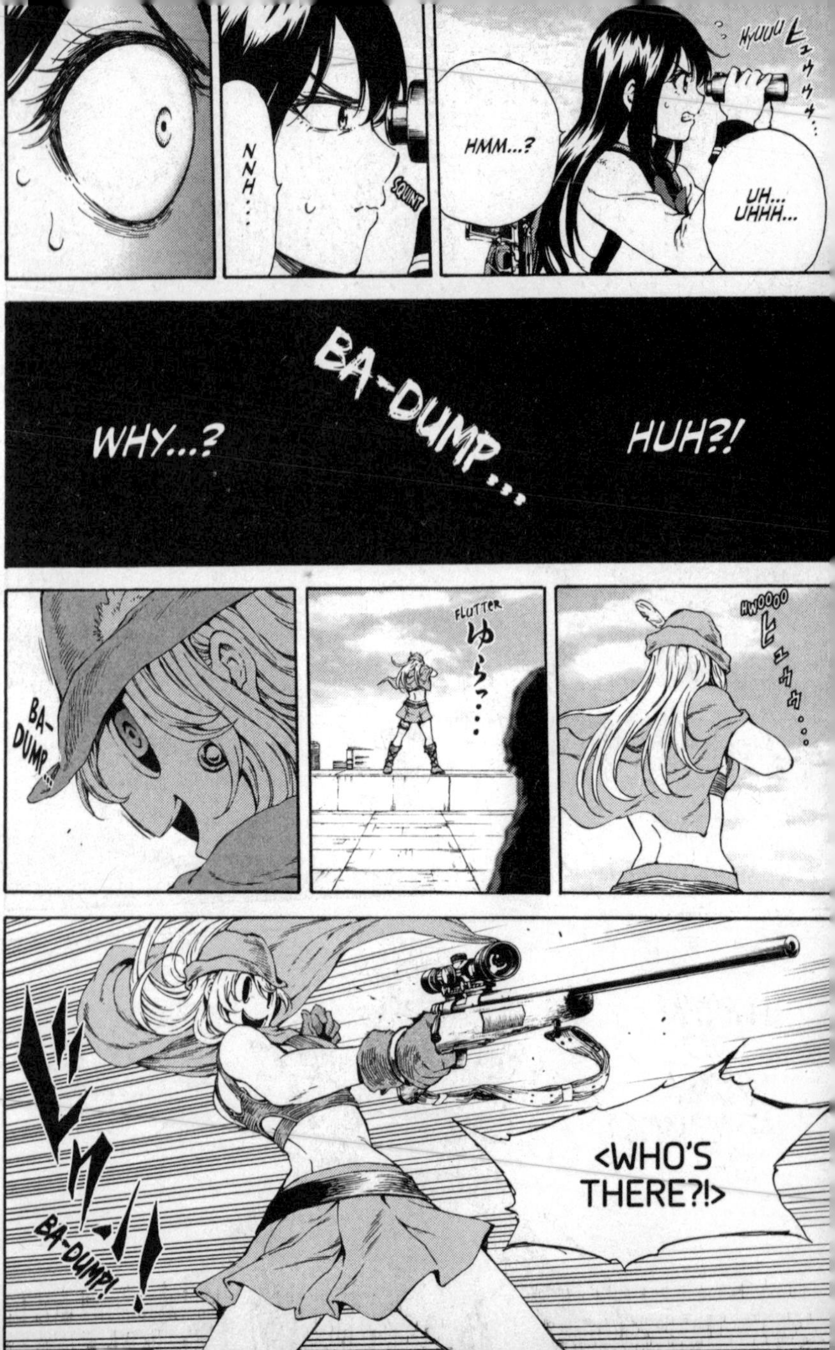
HYUUU ヒュウウウ…
UH... UHHH...
HMM...?
NNH...
SQUINT
HUH?!
BA-DUMP...
WHY...?
HWOOOO ヒュゥゥゥ...
FLUTTER ゆらっ...
BA-DUMP...
<WHO'S THERE?!>
BA-DUMP!

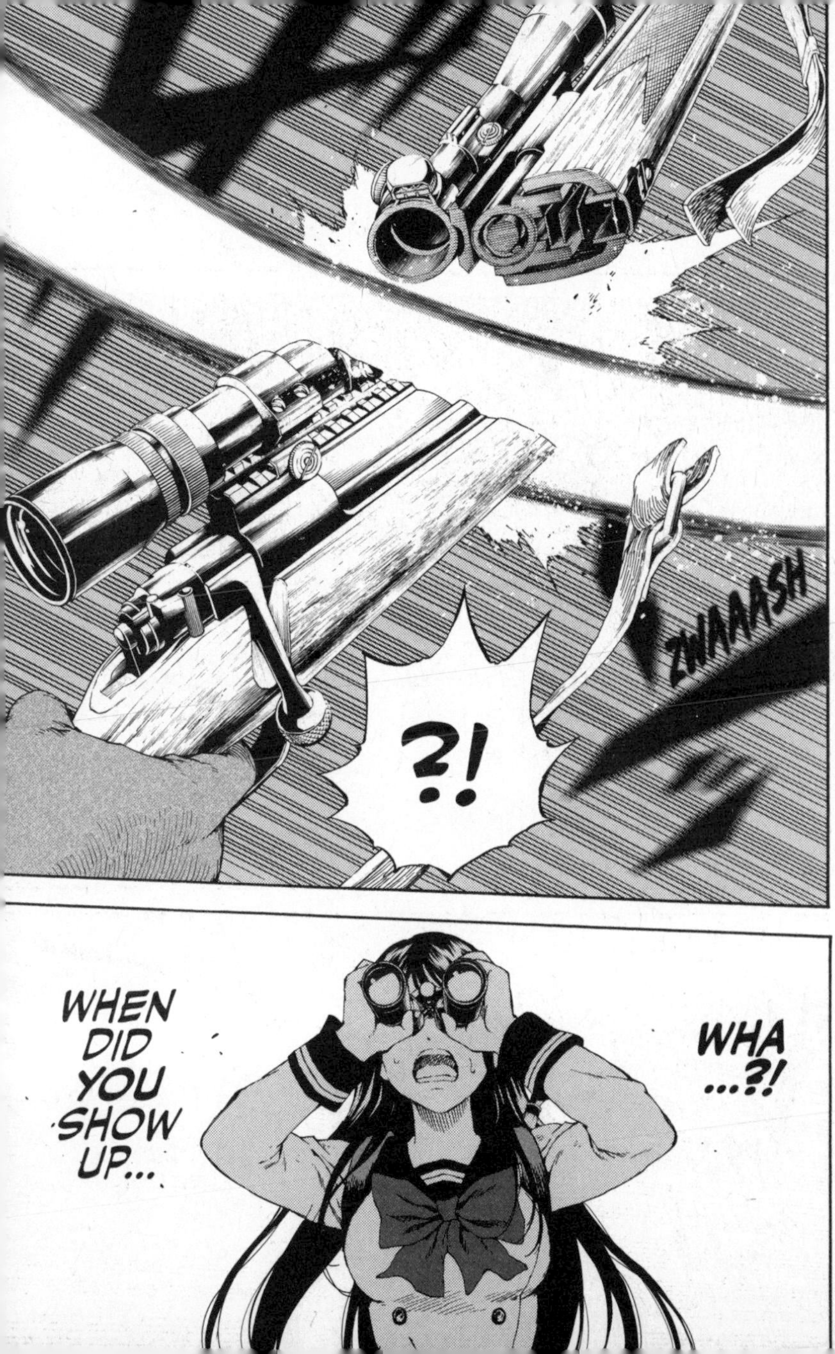
ZWAAASH
?!
WHA ...?!
WHEN DID YOU SHOW UP...

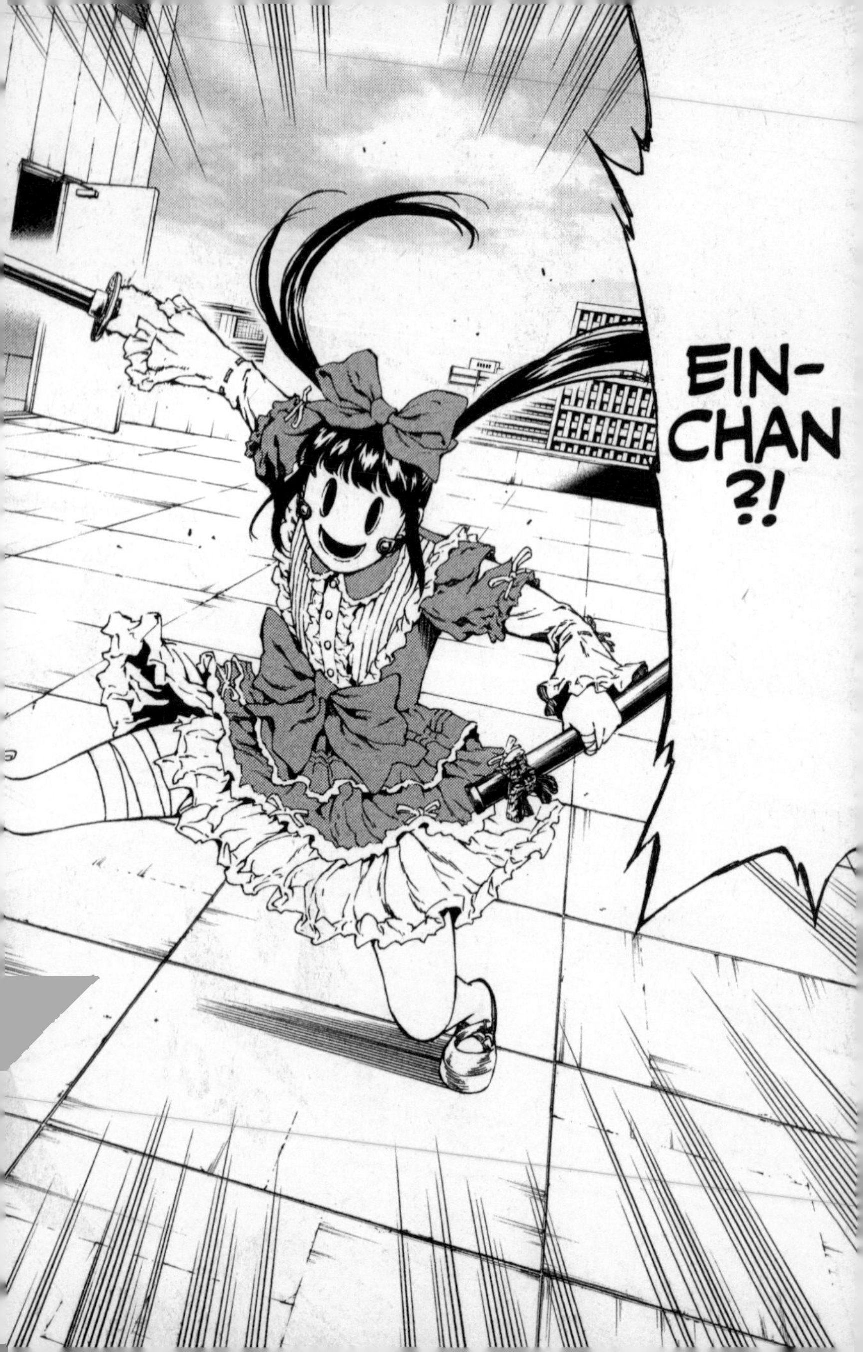
EIN-CHAN?!

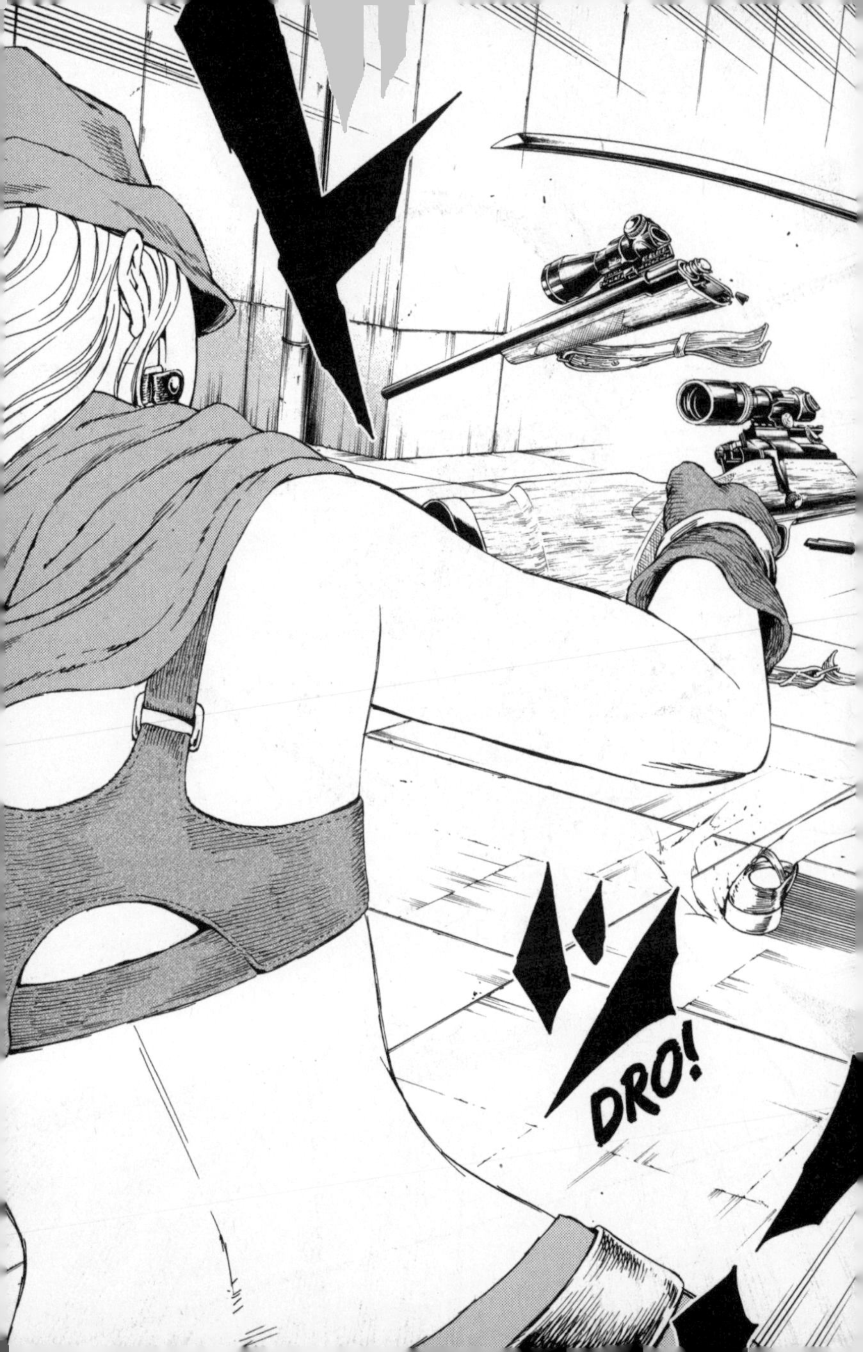
DRO!

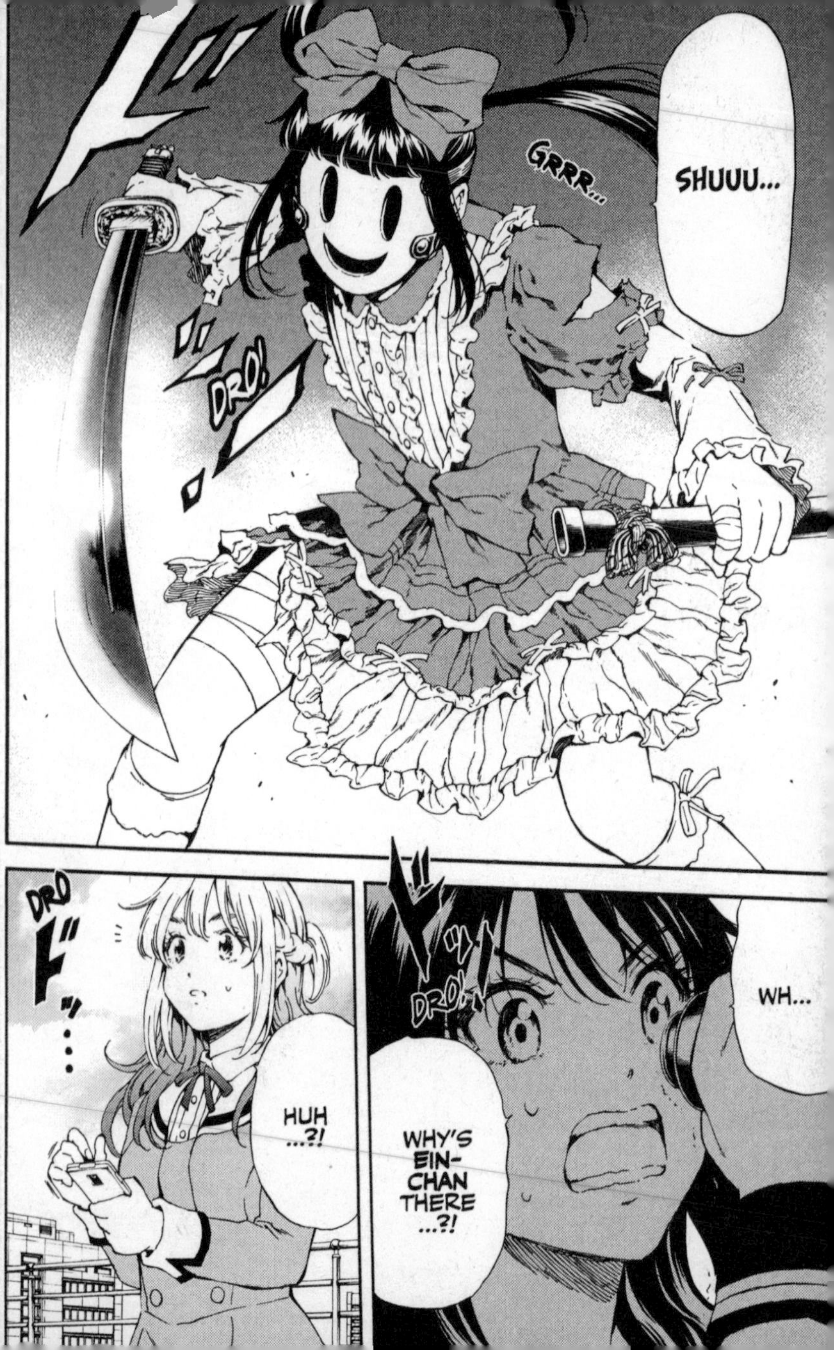
SHUUU...
GRRR...
DRO!
WH...
DRO!
WHY'S EIN-CHAN THERE ...?!
DRO
HUH ...?!

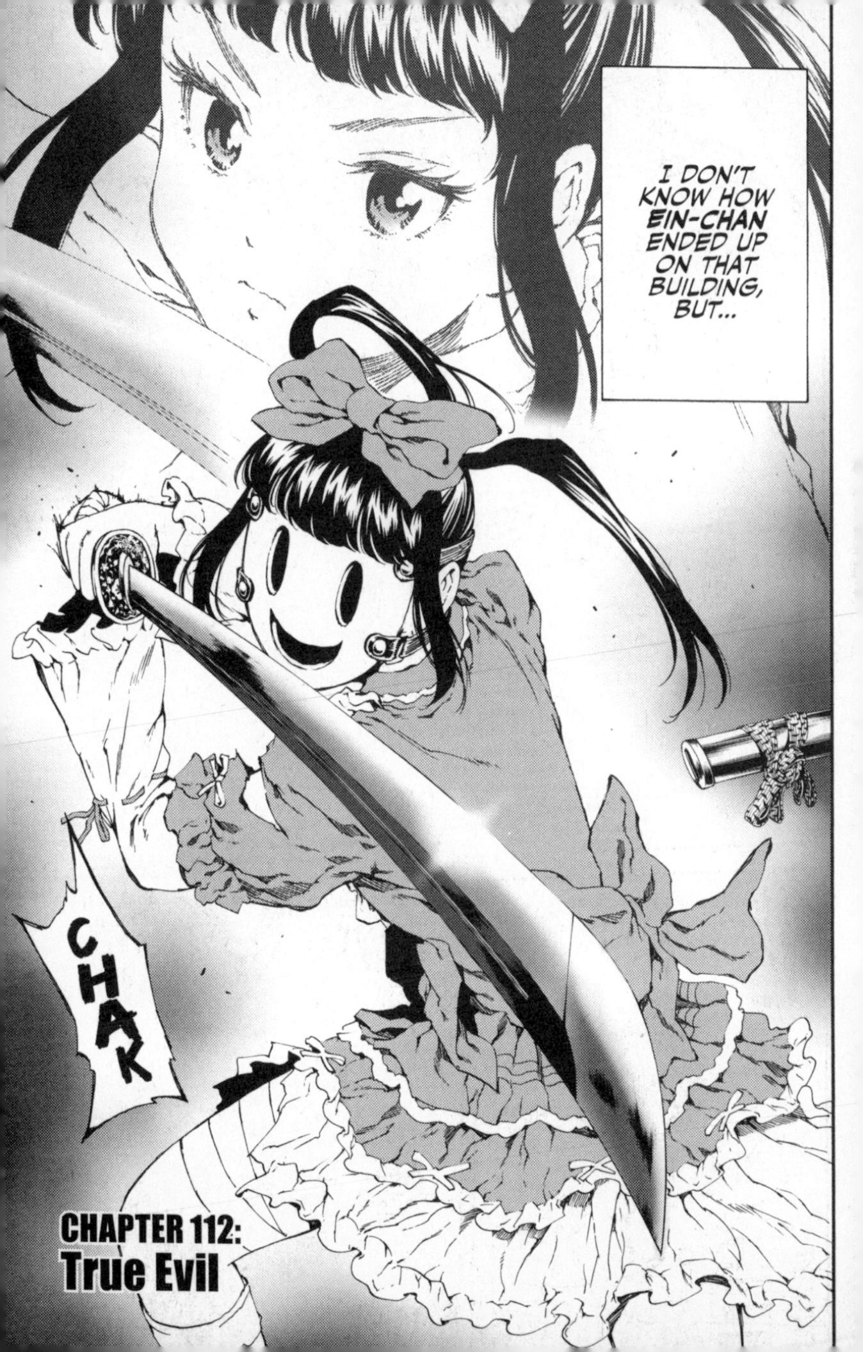
I DON'T KNOW HOW EIN-CHAN ENDED UP ON THAT BUILDING, BUT...
CHAK
CHAPTER 112:
True Evil

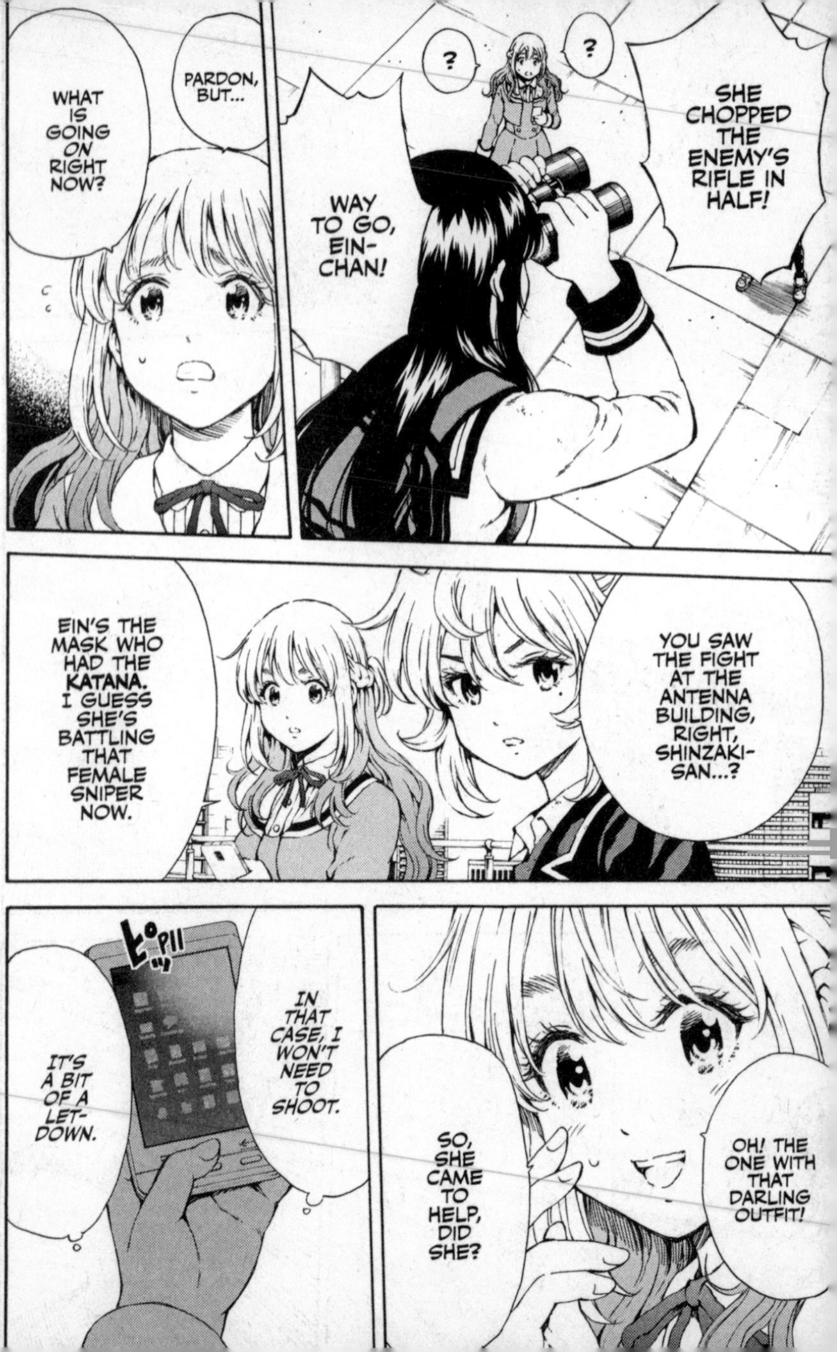
?
?
SHE CHOPPED THE ENEMY'S RIFLE IN HALF!
WAY TO GO, EIN-CHAN!
PARDON, BUT...
WHAT IS GOING ON RIGHT NOW?
YOU SAW THE FIGHT AT THE ANTENNA BUILDING, RIGHT, SHINZAKI-SAN...?
EIN'S THE MASK WHO HAD THE KATANA. I GUESS SHE'S BATTLING THAT FEMALE SNIPER NOW.
OH! THE ONE WITH THAT DARLING OUTFIT!
SO, SHE CAME TO HELP, DID SHE?
IN THAT CASE, I WON'T NEED TO SHOOT.
IT'S A BIT OF A LET-DOWN.

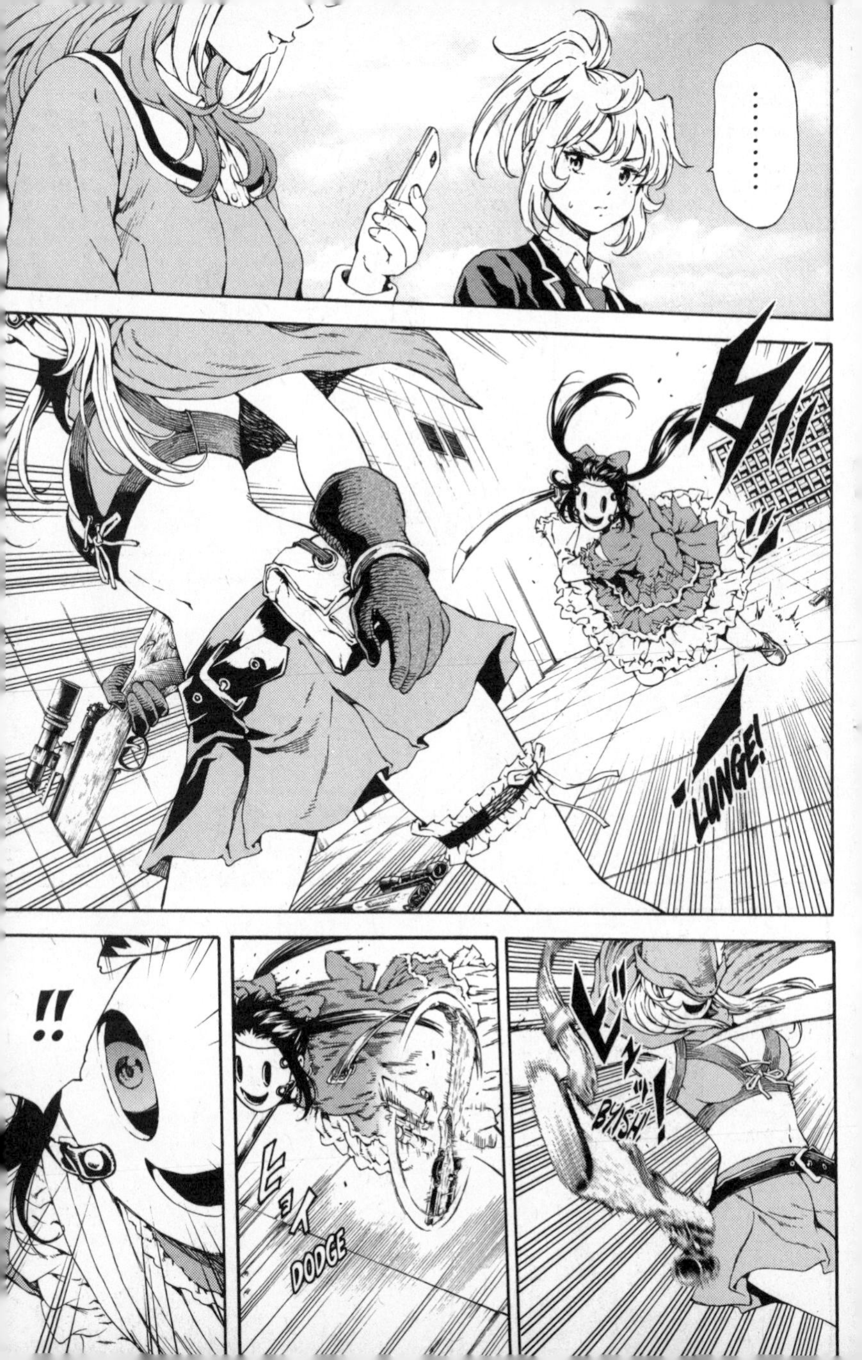
......
LUNGE!
BYISH!
ヒョイ
DODGE
!!

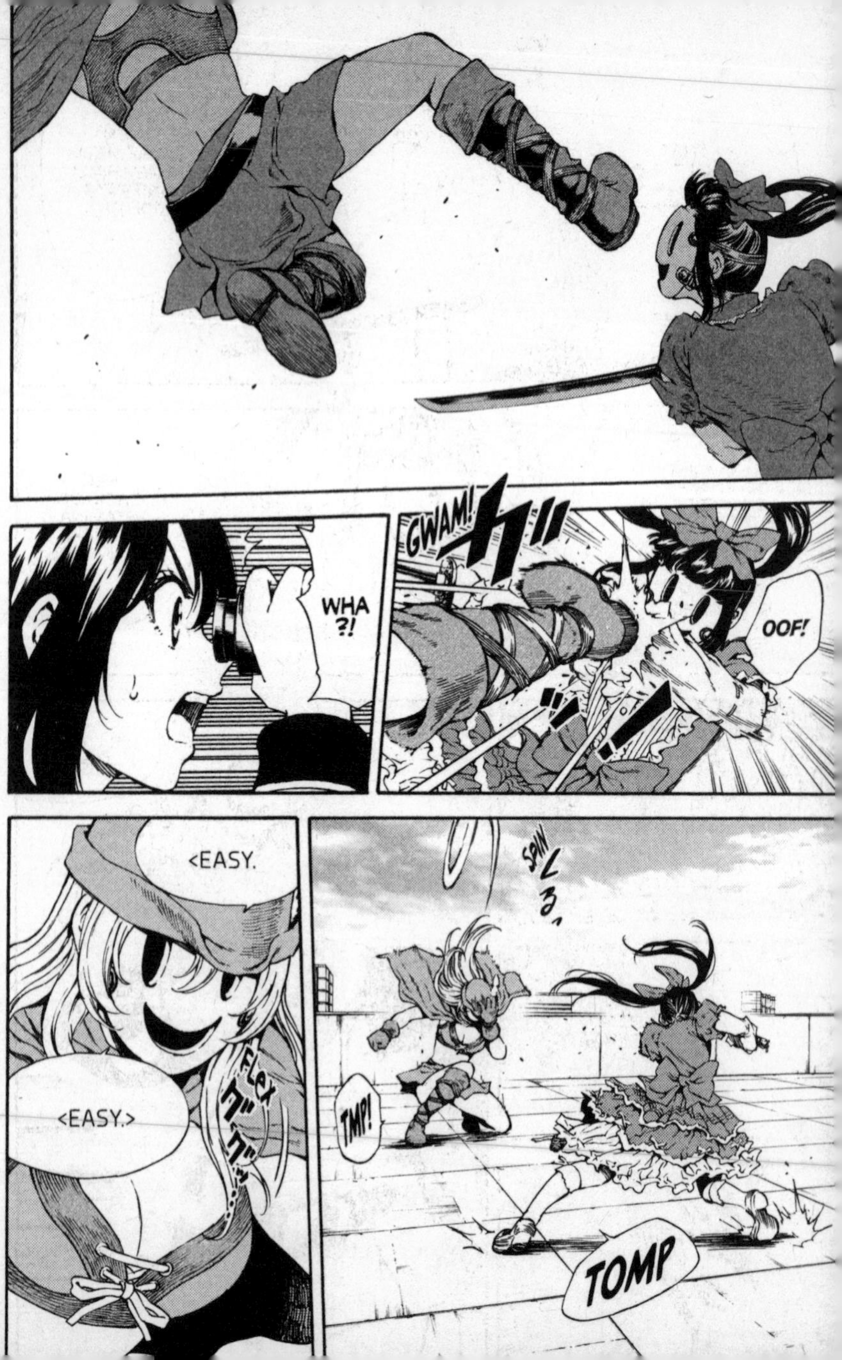
GWAM!
OOF!
WHA ?!
SPIN
TMP!
TOMP
<EASY.
<EASY.>
FLEX

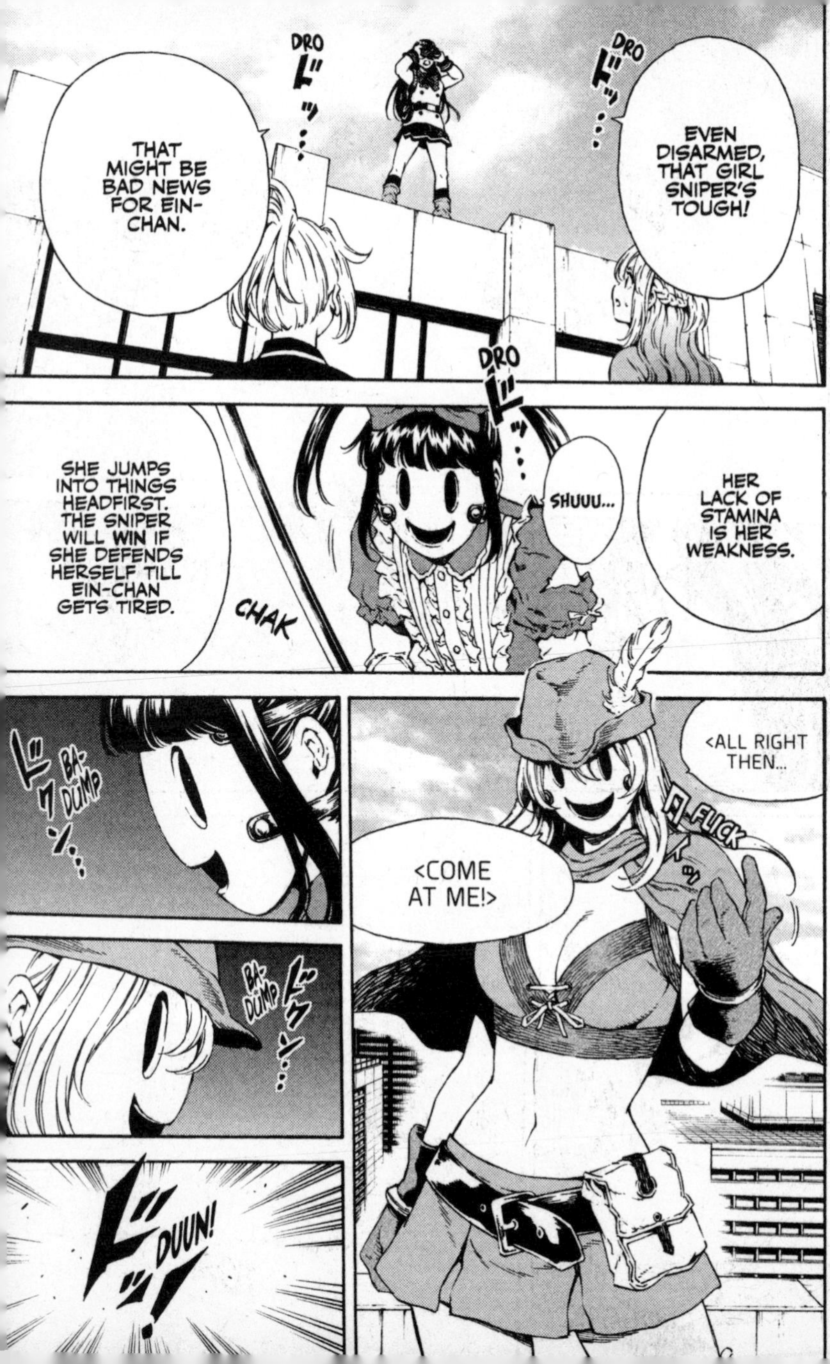
DRO
EVEN DISARMED, THAT GIRL SNIPER'S TOUGH!
DRO
THAT MIGHT BE BAD NEWS FOR EIN-CHAN.
HER LACK OF STAMINA IS HER WEAKNESS.
DRO
SHUUU...
CHAK
SHE JUMPS INTO THINGS HEADFIRST. THE SNIPER WILL WIN IF SHE DEFENDS HERSELF TILL EIN-CHAN GETS TIRED.
<ALL RIGHT THEN...
FLICK
<COME AT ME!>
BA-DUMP
BA-DUMP
DUUN!

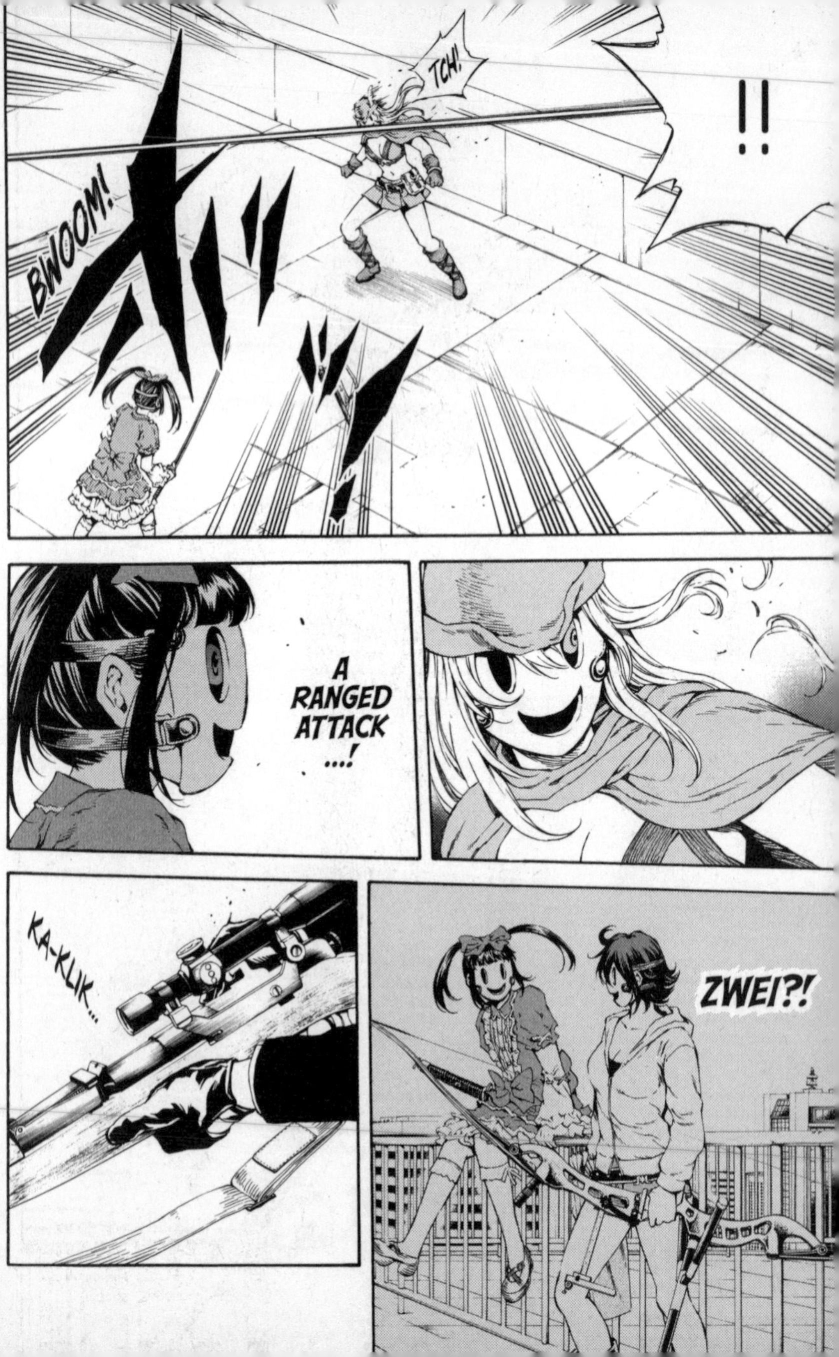
!!
TCH!
BWOOM!
A RANGED ATTACK ...!
ZWEI?!
KA-KLIK...

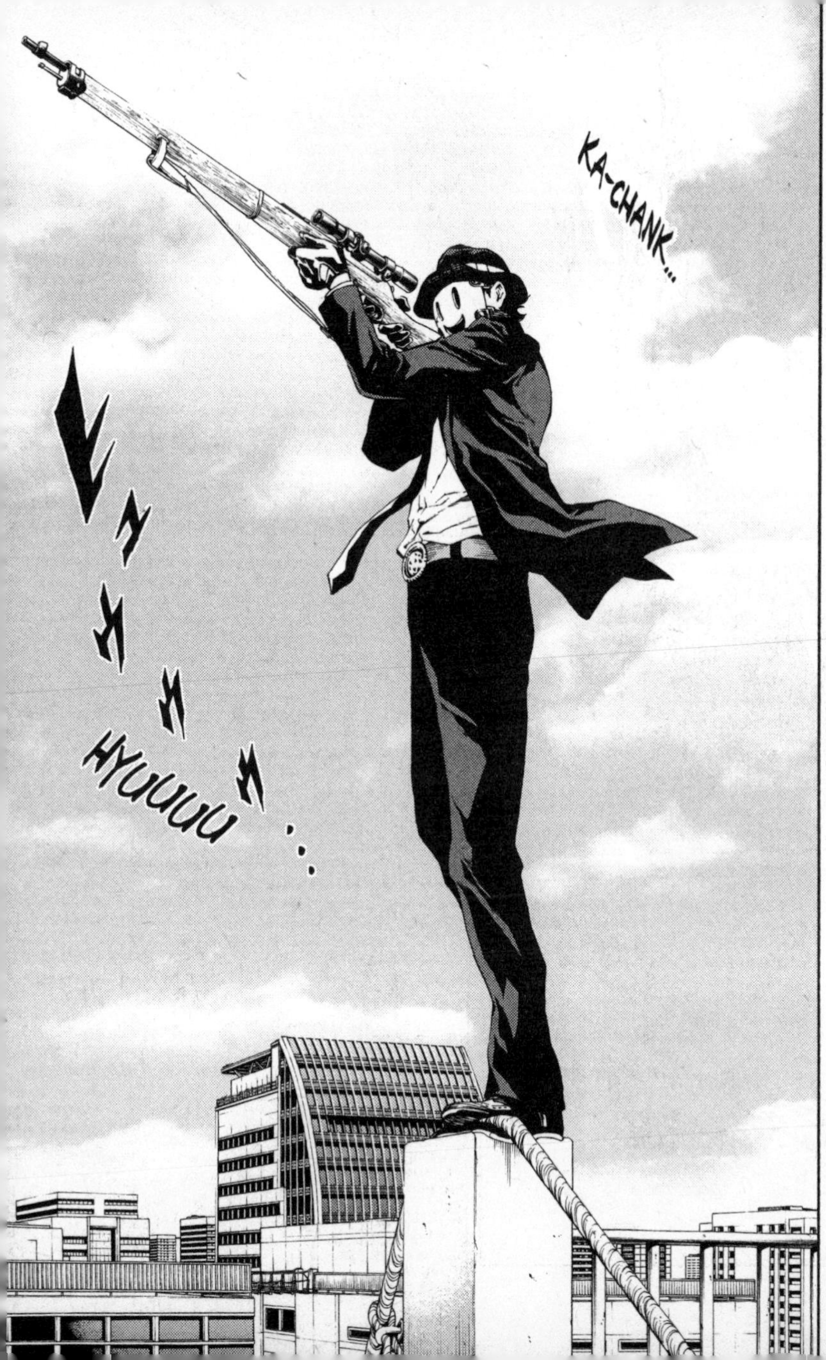

KA-CHANK...
HYUUUUU...

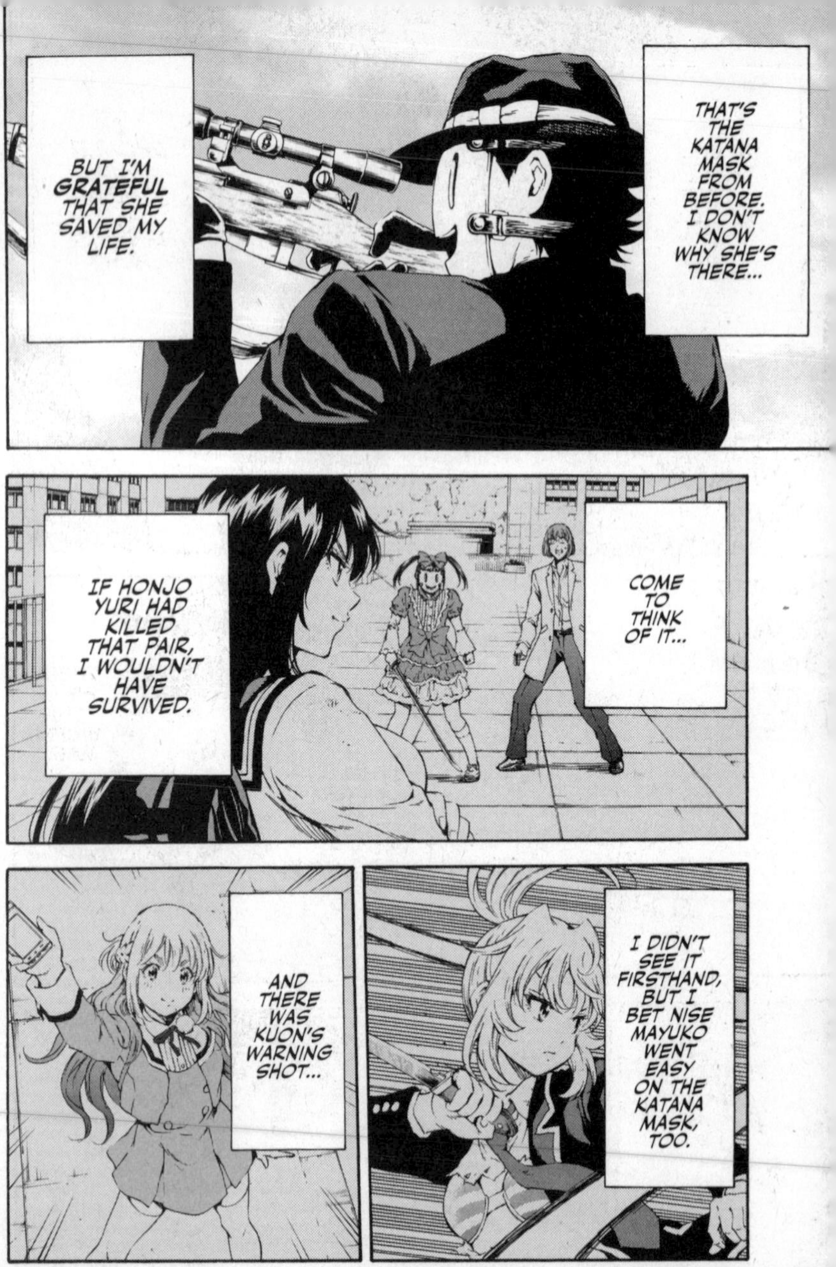
THAT'S THE KATANA MASK FROM BEFORE. I DON'T KNOW WHY SHE'S THERE...
BUT I'M GRATEFUL THAT SHE SAVED MY LIFE.
COME TO THINK OF IT...
IF HONJO YURI HAD KILLED THAT PAIR, I WOULDN'T HAVE SURVIVED.
I DIDN'T SEE IT FIRSTHAND, BUT I BET NISE MAYUKO WENT EASY ON THE KATANA MASK, TOO.
AND THERE WAS KUON'S WARNING SHOT...

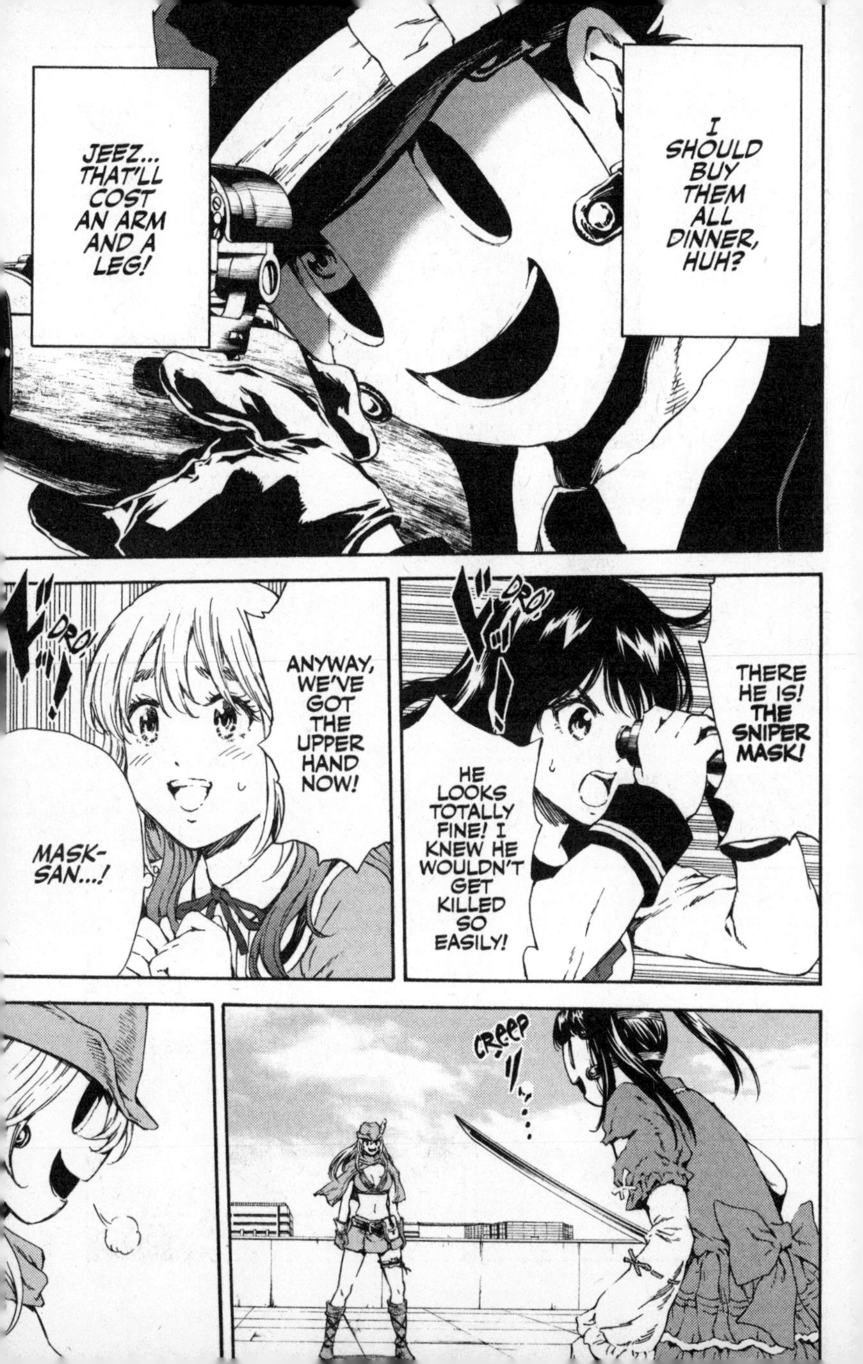
I SHOULD BUY THEM ALL DINNER, HUH?
JEEZ... THAT'LL COST AN ARM AND A LEG!
DRO!
THERE HE IS! THE SNIPER MASK!
HE LOOKS TOTALLY FINE! I KNEW HE WOULDN'T GET KILLED SO EASILY!
DRO!
ANYWAY, WE'VE GOT THE UPPER HAND NOW!
MASK-SAN...!
CREEP

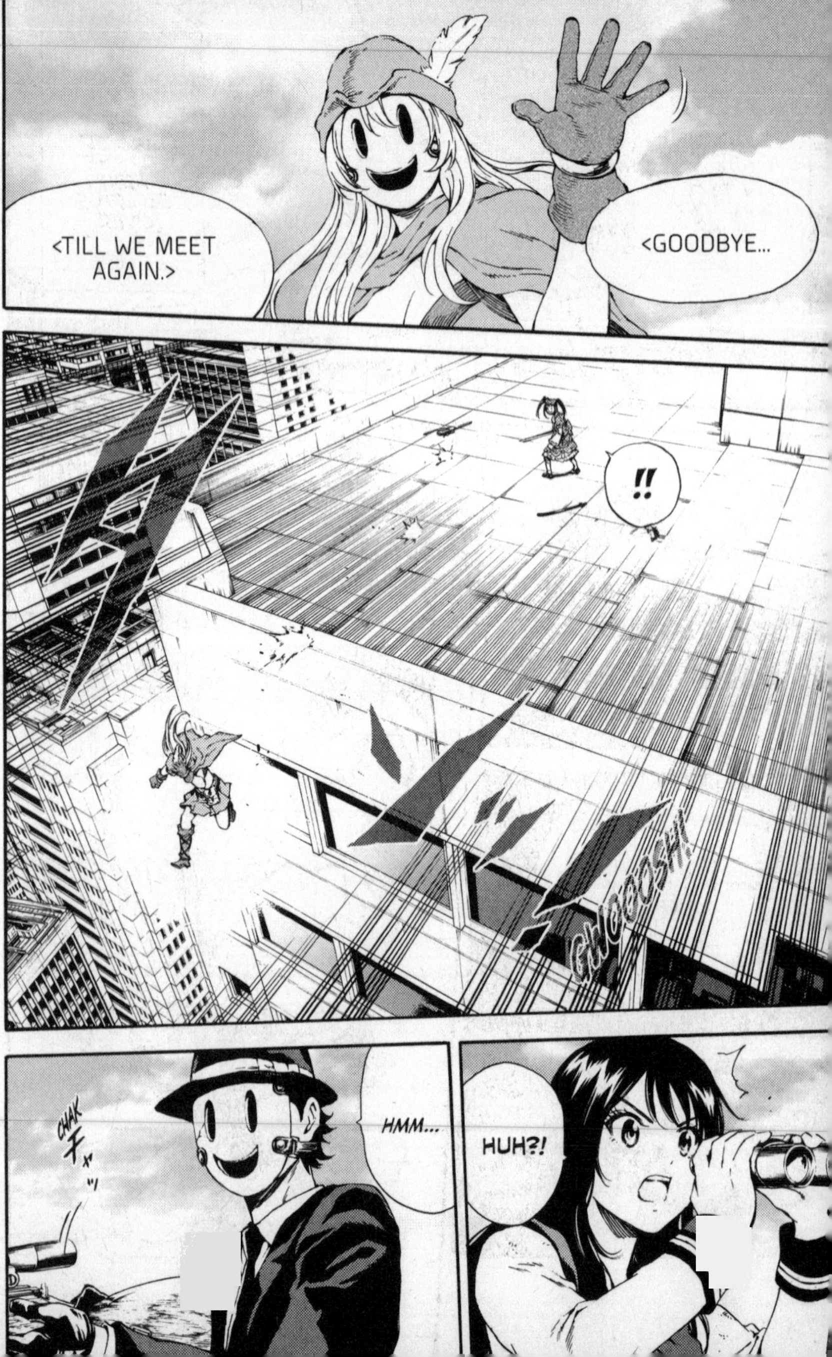
<GOODBYE...
<TILL WE MEET AGAIN.>
!!
GWOOOSH!
HUH?!
HMM...
CHAK
チャッ

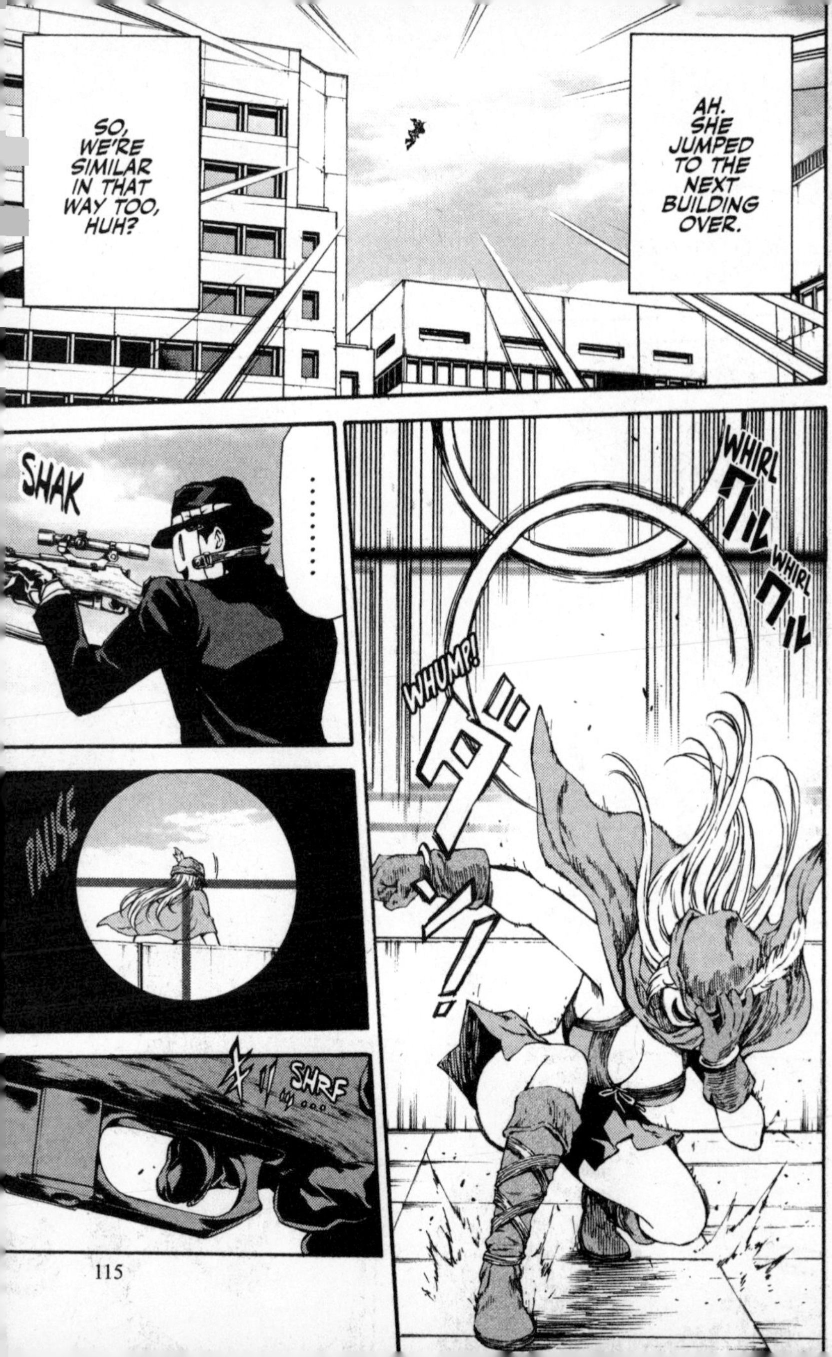
AH. SHE JUMPED TO THE NEXT BUILDING OVER.
SO, WE'RE SIMILAR IN THAT WAY TOO, HUH?
WHIRL
WHIRL
WHUMP!
SHAK
......
PAUSE
SHRF

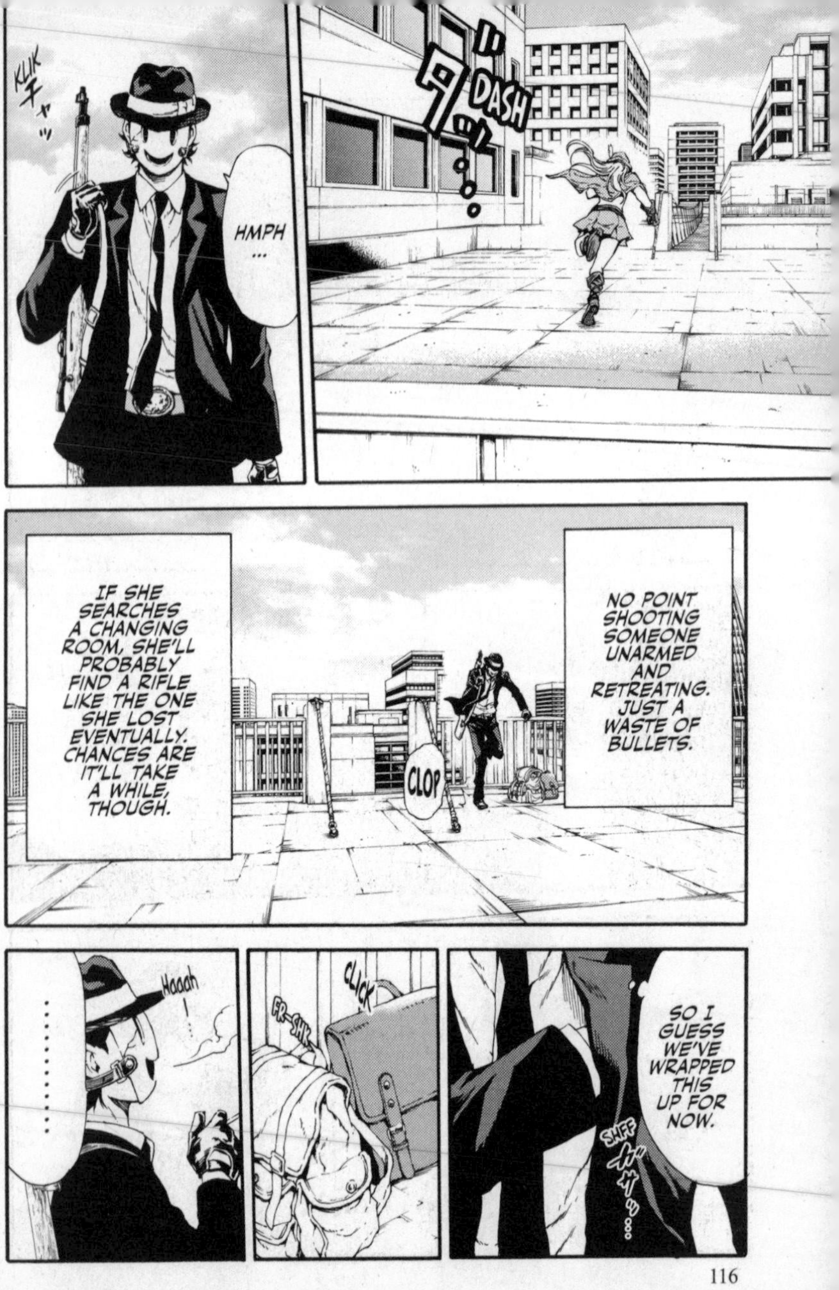
DASH
KLIK
HMPH ...
NO POINT SHOOTING SOMEONE UNARMED AND RETREATING. JUST A WASTE OF BULLETS.
IF SHE SEARCHES A CHANGING ROOM, SHE'LL PROBABLY FIND A RIFLE LIKE THE ONE SHE LOST EVENTUALLY. CHANCES ARE IT'LL TAKE A WHILE, THOUGH.
CLOP
SO I GUESS WE'VE WRAPPED THIS UP FOR NOW.
SHFF
CLICK
FR-SHK
Haaah!
......

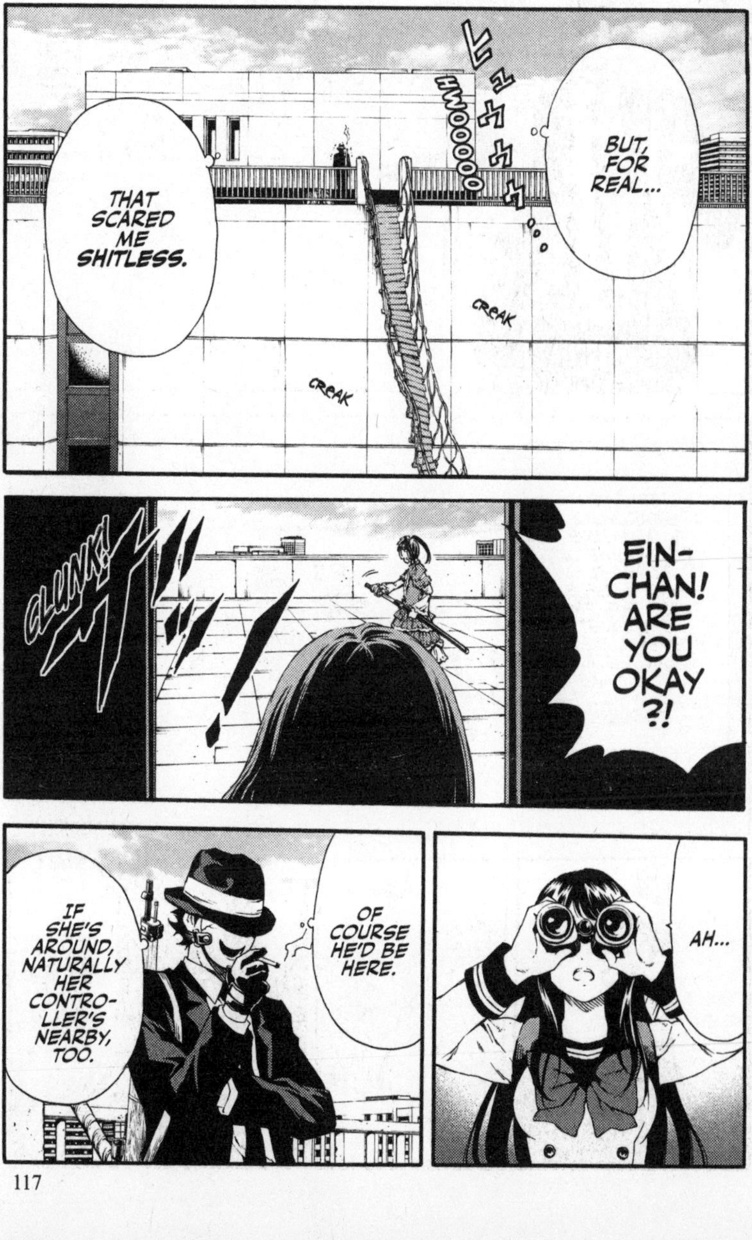
BUT, FOR REAL...
HWOOOOO
THAT SCARED ME SHITLESS.
CREAK
CREAK
EIN-CHAN! ARE YOU OKAY?!
CLUNK!!
AH...
OF COURSE HE'D BE HERE.
IF SHE'S AROUND, NATURALLY HER CONTROLLER'S NEARBY, TOO.

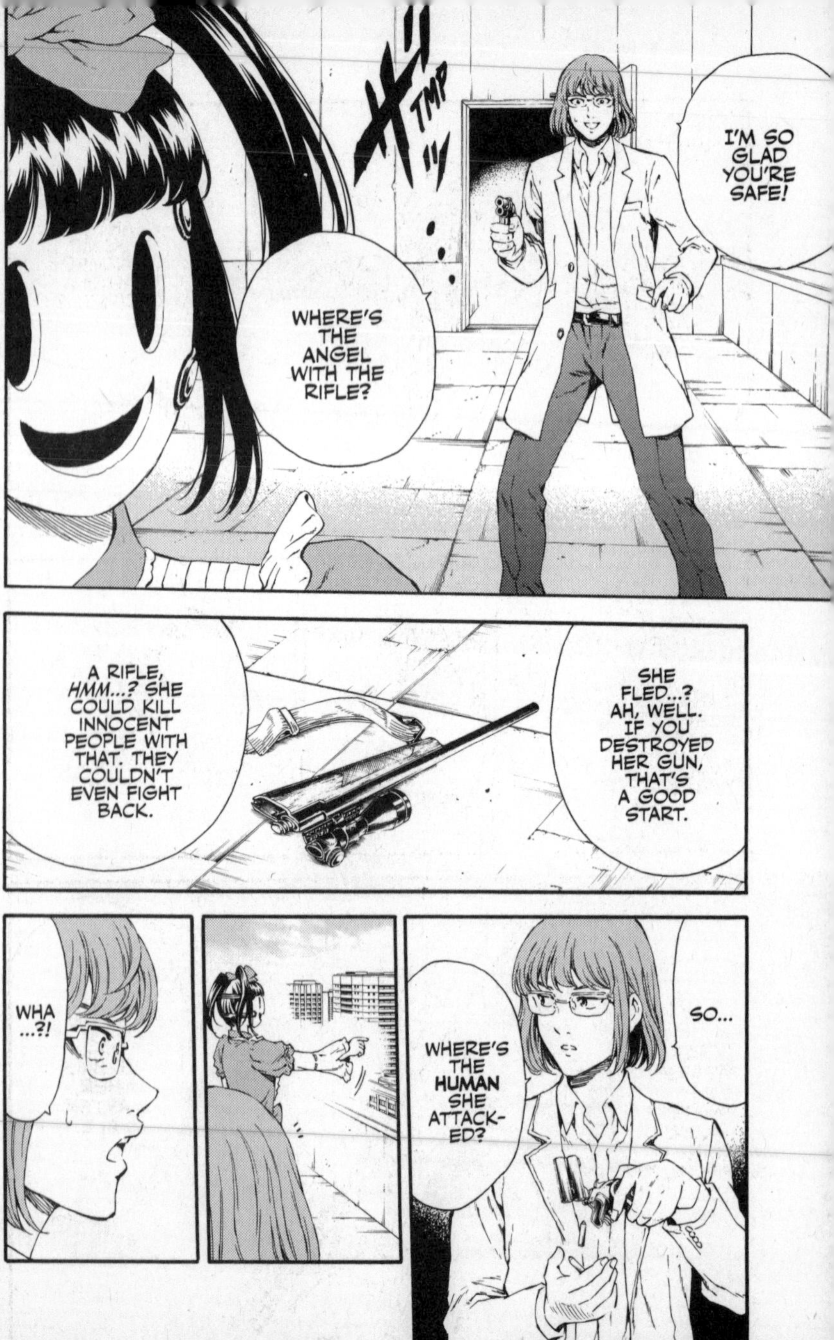
I'M SO GLAD YOU'RE SAFE!
TMP
WHERE'S THE ANGEL WITH THE RIFLE?
SHE FLED...? AH, WELL. IF YOU DESTROYED HER GUN, THAT'S A GOOD START.
A RIFLE, *HMM*...? SHE COULD KILL INNOCENT PEOPLE WITH THAT. THEY COULDN'T EVEN FIGHT BACK.
SO...
WHERE'S THE **HUMAN** SHE ATTACKED?
WHA ...?!

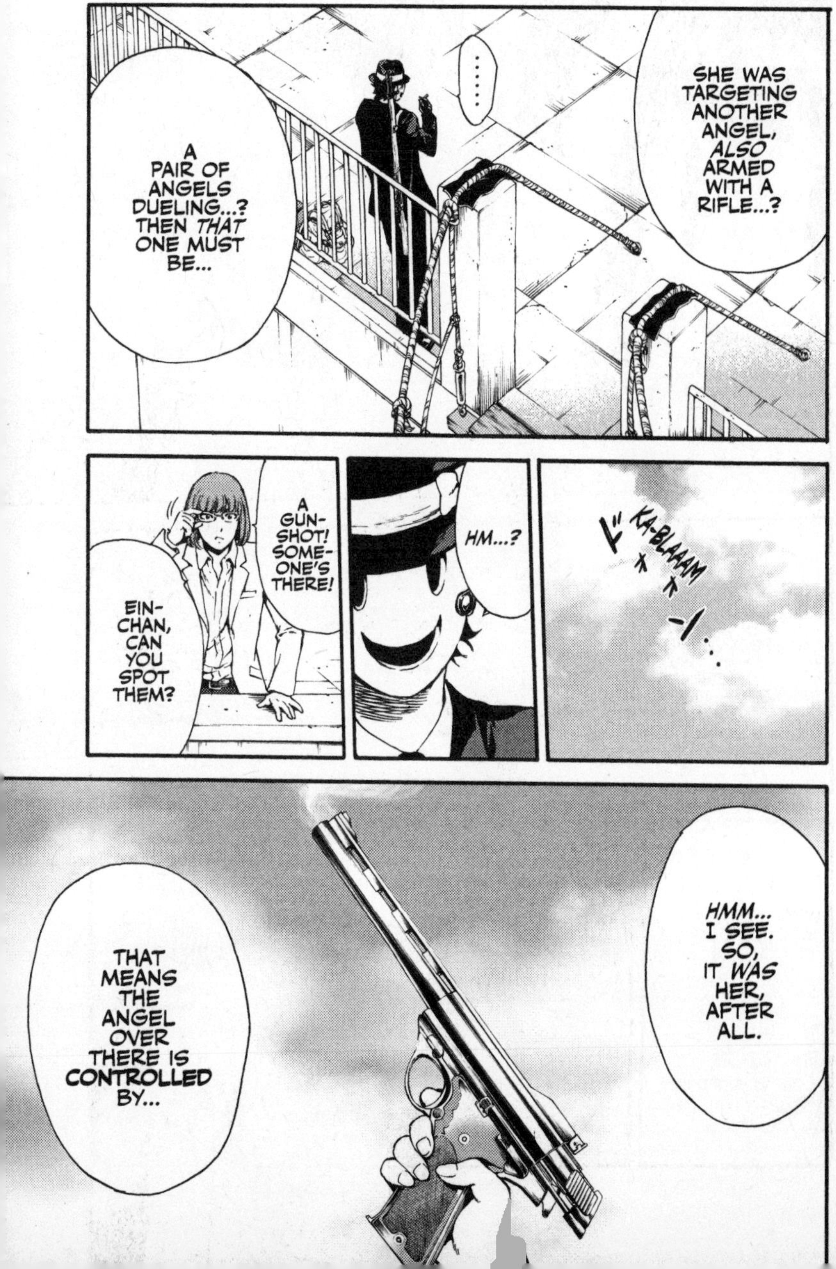
SHE WAS TARGETING ANOTHER ANGEL, *ALSO* ARMED WITH A RIFLE...?
......
A PAIR OF ANGELS DUELING...? THEN *THAT* ONE MUST BE...
KA-BLAAAM
HM...?
A GUN-SHOT! SOME-ONE'S THERE!
EIN-CHAN, CAN YOU SPOT THEM?
HMM... I SEE. SO, IT *WAS* HER, AFTER ALL.
THAT MEANS THE ANGEL OVER THERE IS **CONTROLLED** BY...

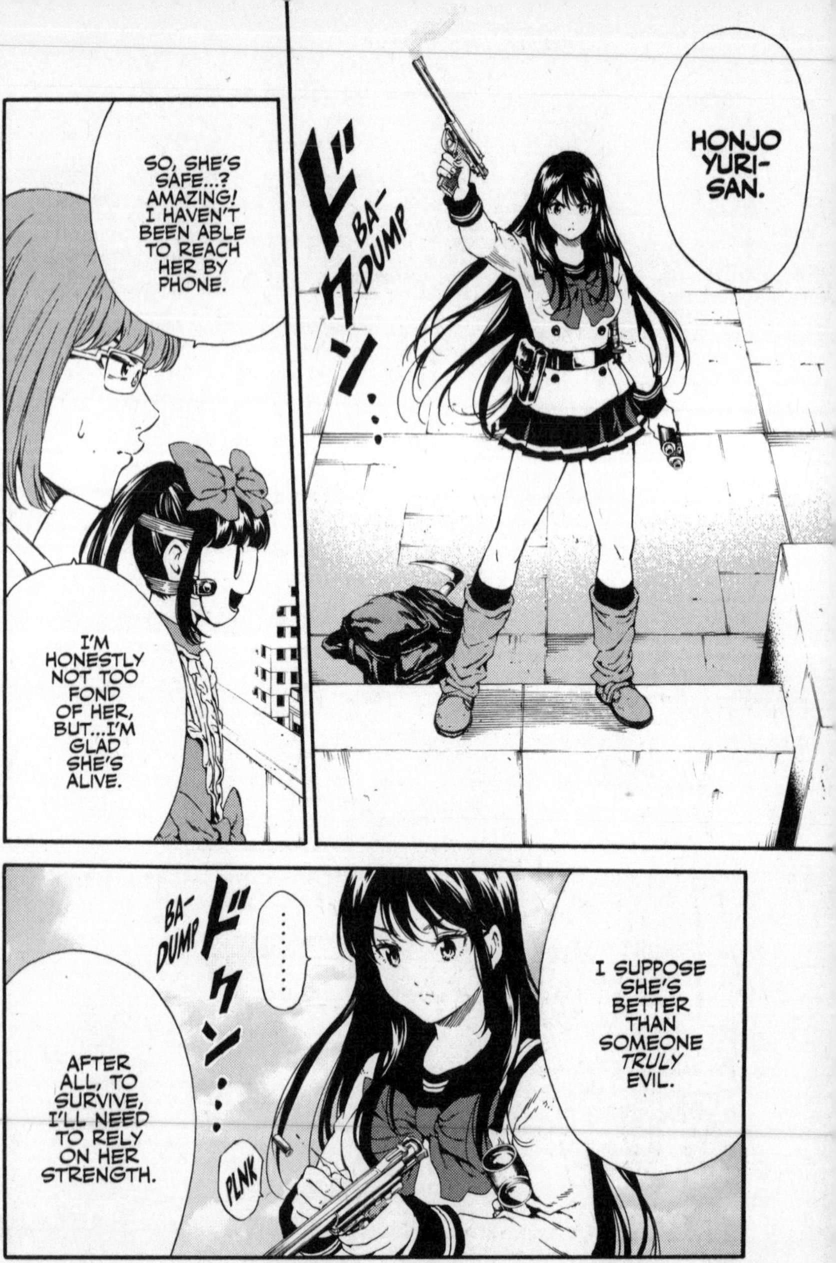
HONJO YURI-SAN.
ドクン…
BA-DUMP
SO, SHE'S SAFE...? AMAZING! I HAVEN'T BEEN ABLE TO REACH HER BY PHONE.
I'M HONESTLY NOT TOO FOND OF HER, BUT...I'M GLAD SHE'S ALIVE.
I SUPPOSE SHE'S BETTER THAN SOMEONE *TRULY* EVIL.
......
ドクン…
BA-DUMP
AFTER ALL, TO SURVIVE, I'LL NEED TO RELY ON HER STRENGTH.
PLNK

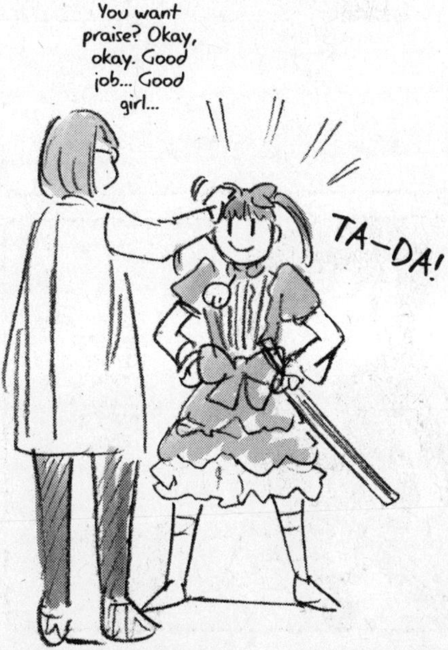
You want praise? Okay, okay. Good job... Good girl...
TA-DA!

HIGH-RISE INVASION

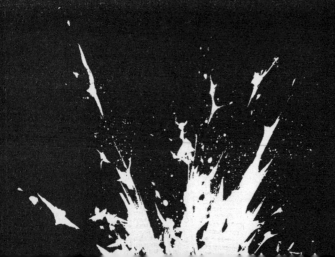

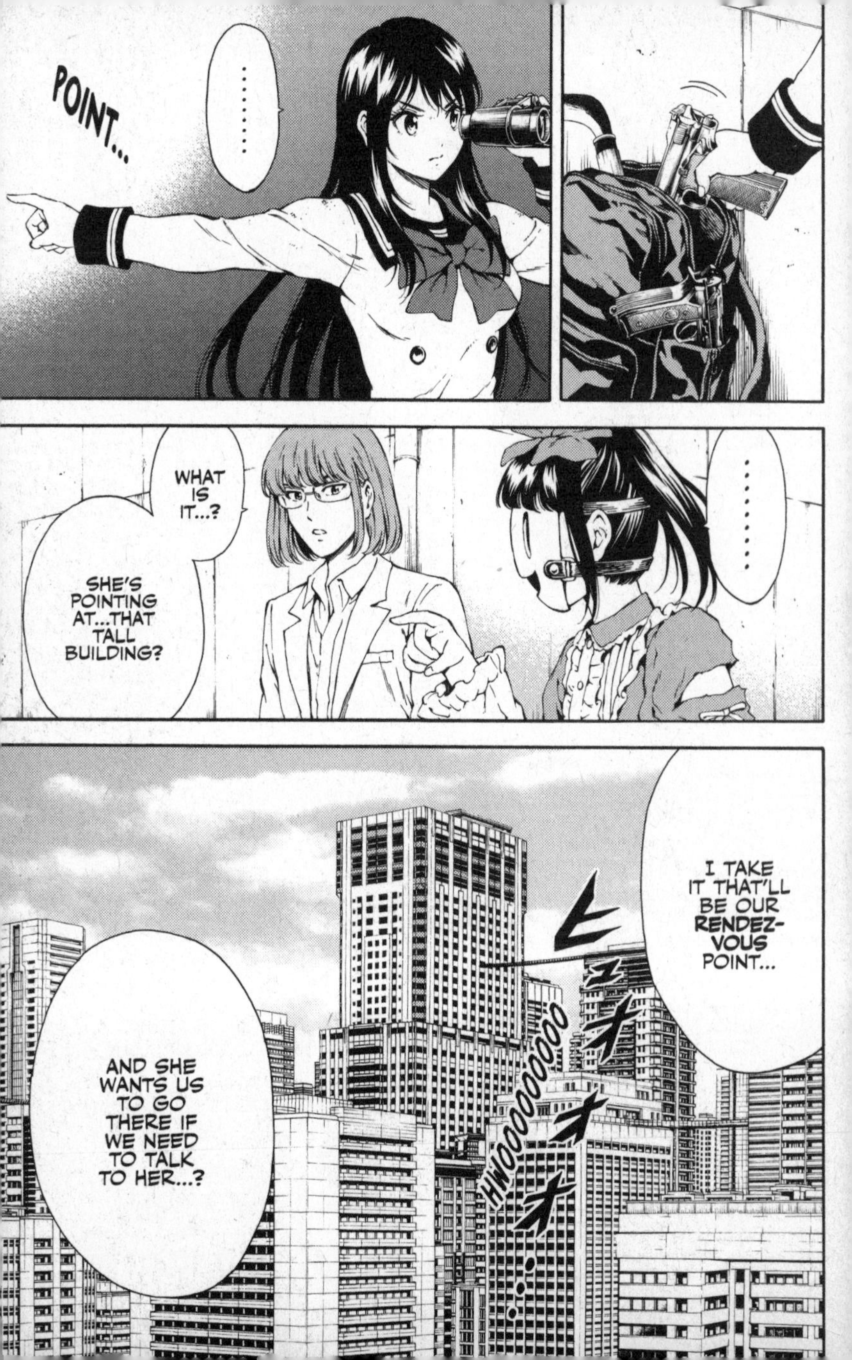
......
POINT...
......
WHAT IS IT...?
SHE'S POINTING AT...THAT TALL BUILDING?
I TAKE IT THAT'LL BE OUR RENDEZ-VOUS POINT...
HWOOOOOOOOOO...
AND SHE WANTS US TO GO THERE IF WE NEED TO TALK TO HER...?

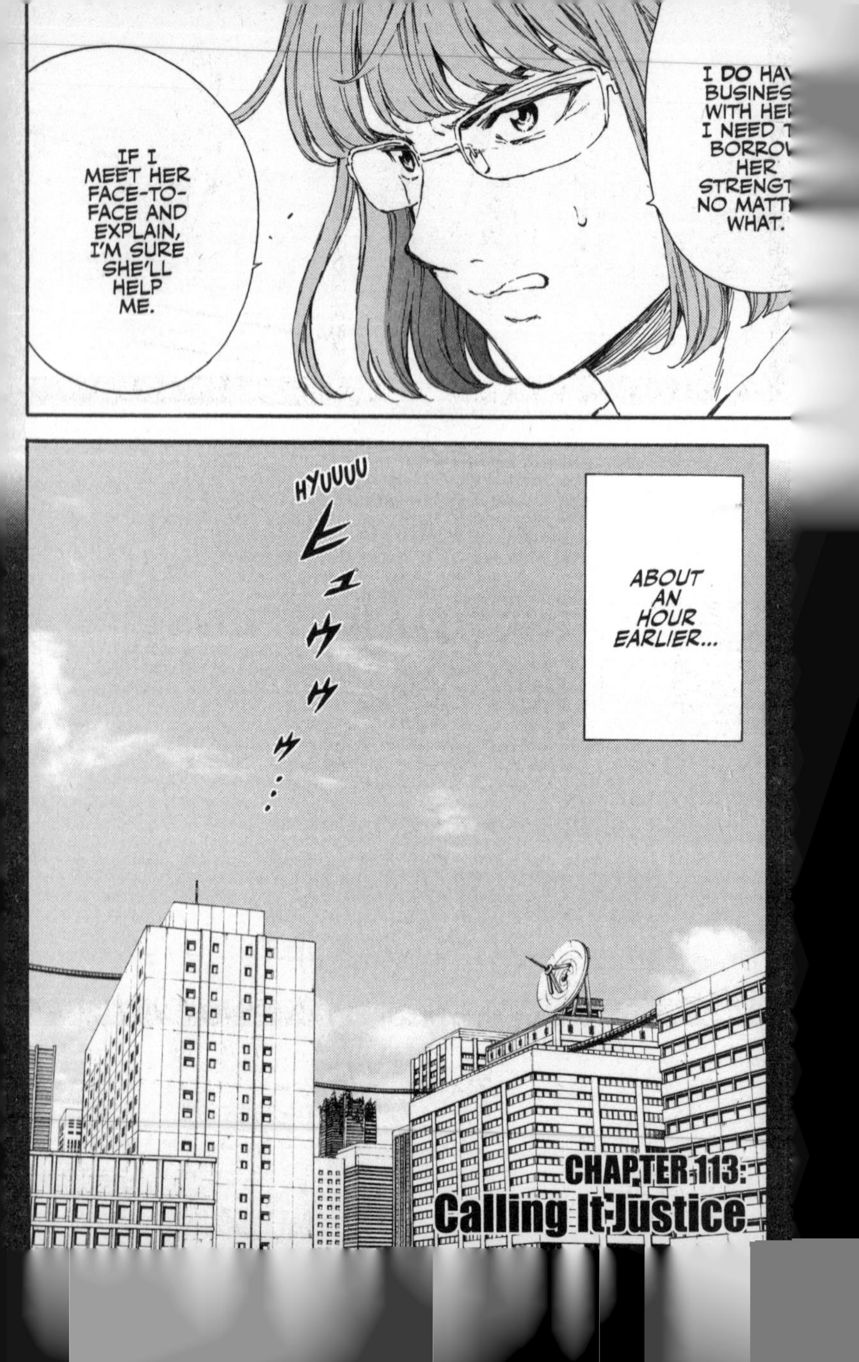
I DO HAV BUSINES WITH HE I NEED T BORROW HER STRENGT NO MATT WHAT.
IF I MEET HER FACE-TO-FACE AND EXPLAIN, I'M SURE SHE'LL HELP ME.
ABOUT AN HOUR EARLIER...
HYUUUU
CHAPTER 113:
Calling It Justice

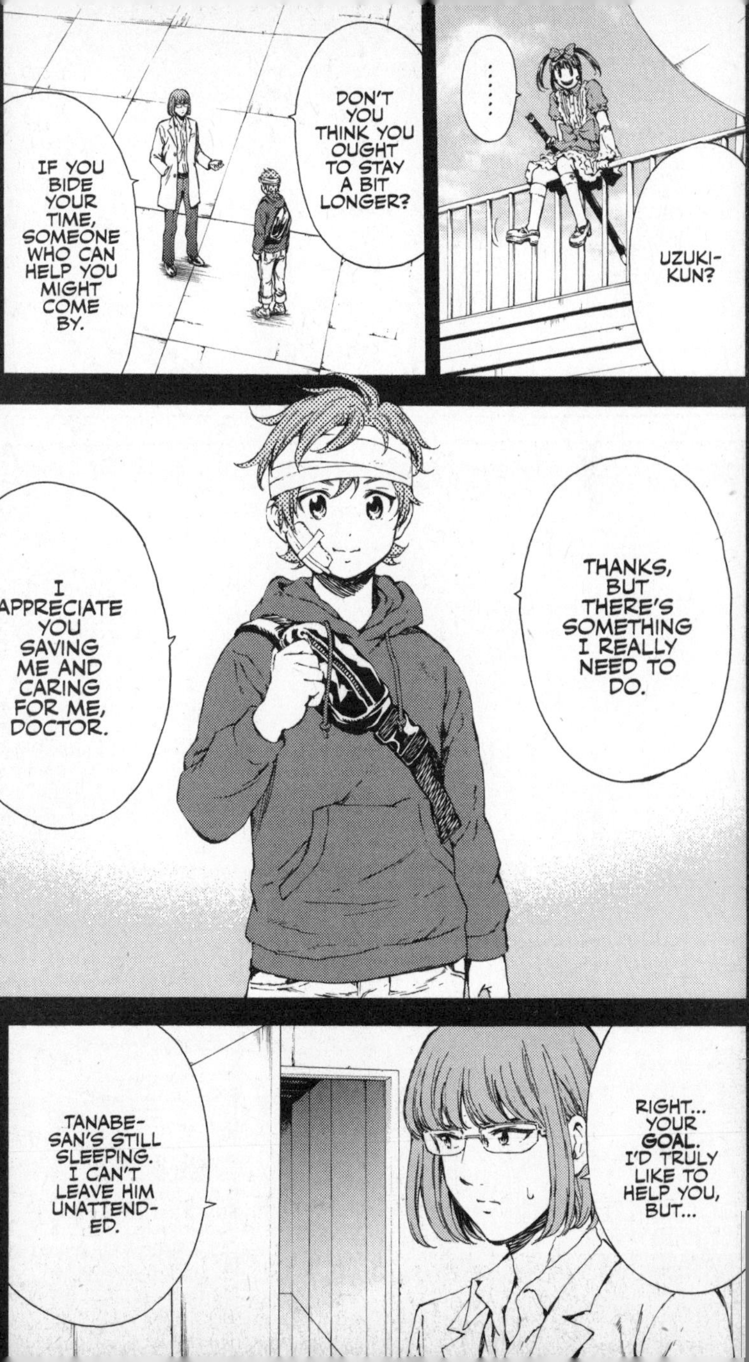
UZUKI-KUN?
......
DON'T YOU THINK YOU OUGHT TO STAY A BIT LONGER?
IF YOU BIDE YOUR TIME, SOMEONE WHO CAN HELP YOU MIGHT COME BY.
THANKS, BUT THERE'S SOMETHING I REALLY NEED TO DO.
I APPRECIATE YOU SAVING ME AND CARING FOR ME, DOCTOR.
RIGHT... YOUR GOAL. I'D TRULY LIKE TO HELP YOU, BUT...
TANABE-SAN'S STILL SLEEPING. I CAN'T LEAVE HIM UNATTEND-ED.

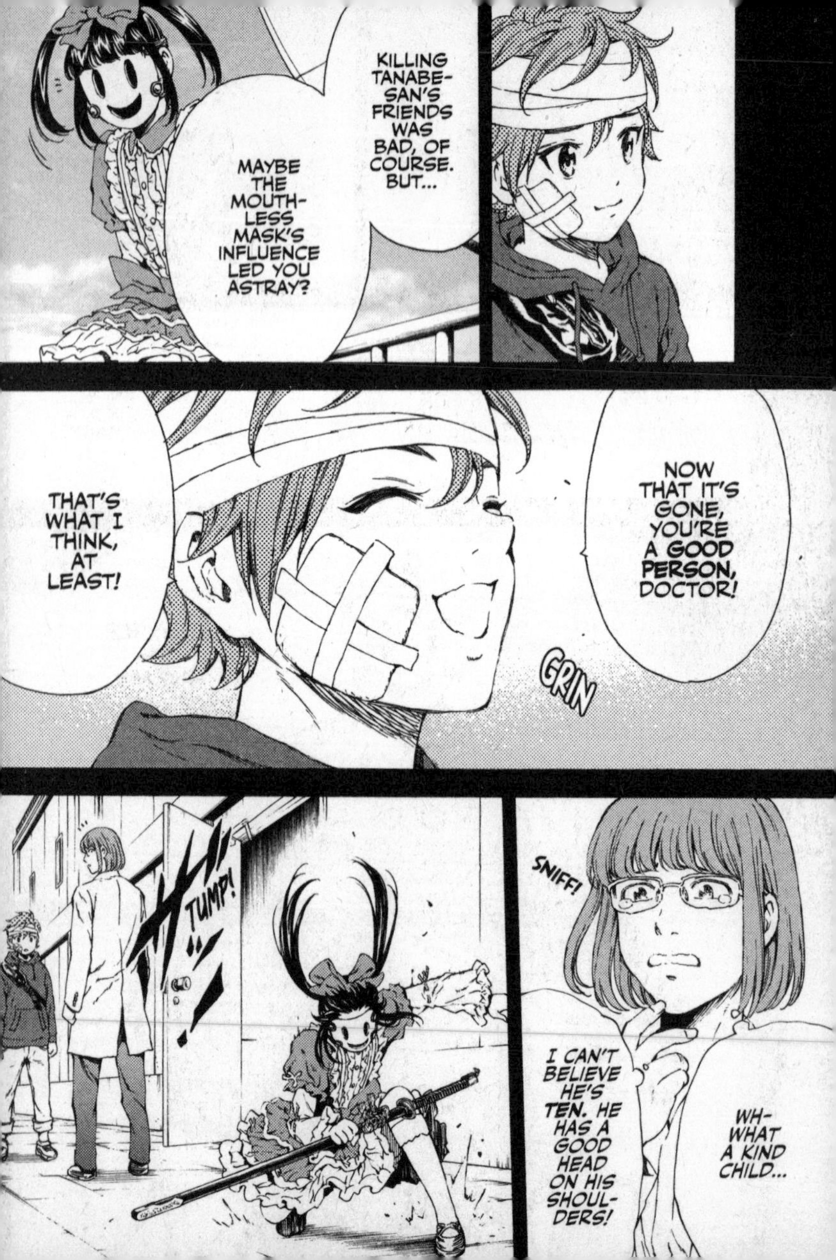
KILLING TANABE-SAN'S FRIENDS WAS BAD, OF COURSE. BUT...
MAYBE THE MOUTH-LESS MASK'S INFLUENCE LED YOU ASTRAY?
NOW THAT IT'S GONE, YOU'RE A GOOD PERSON, DOCTOR!
GRIN
THAT'S WHAT I THINK, AT LEAST!
SNIFF!
WH-WHAT A KIND CHILD...
I CAN'T BELIEVE HE'S TEN. HE HAS A GOOD HEAD ON HIS SHOUL-DERS!
TUMP!

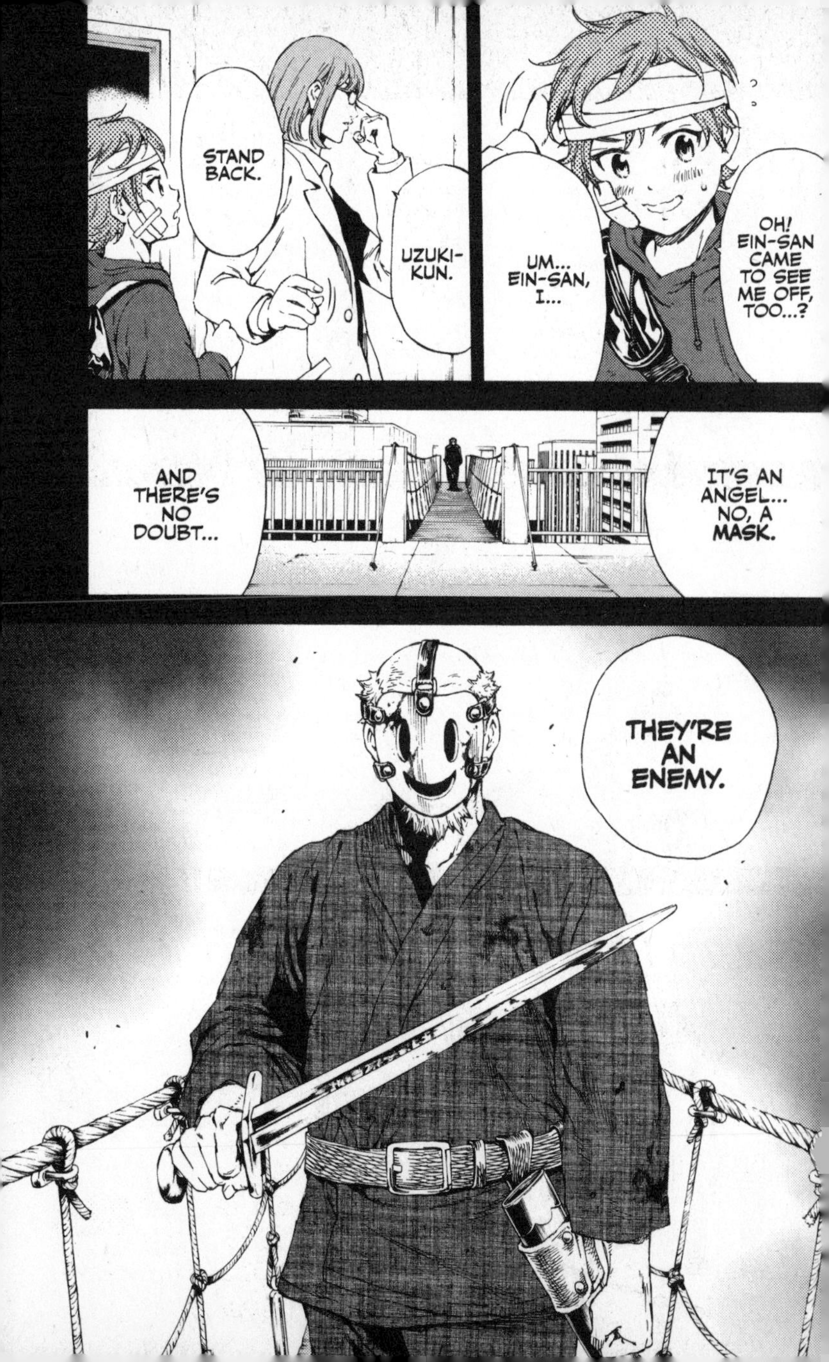
OH! EIN-SAN CAME TO SEE ME OFF, TOO...?
UM... EIN-SAN, I...
UZUKI-KUN.
STAND BACK.
IT'S AN ANGEL... NO, A MASK.
AND THERE'S NO DOUBT...
THEY'RE AN ENEMY.

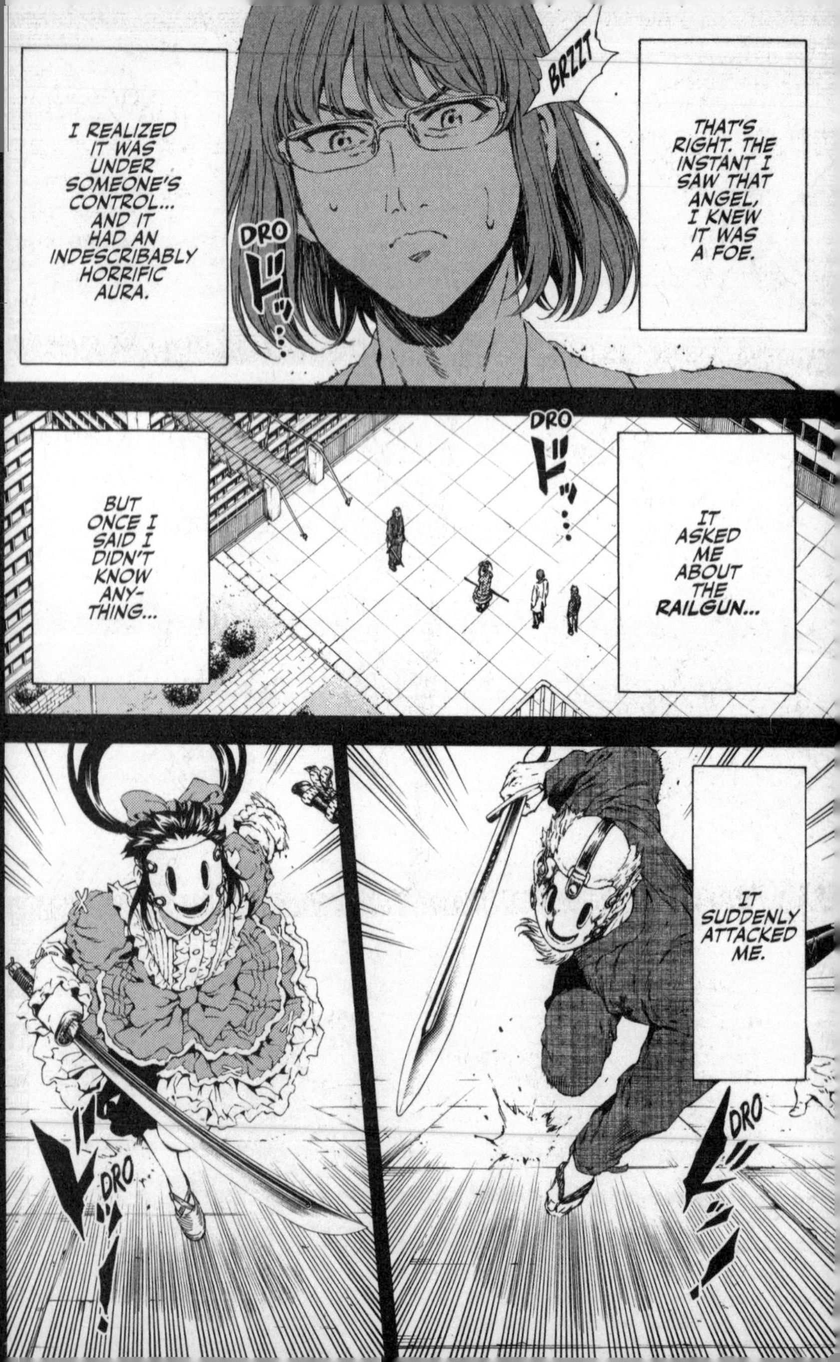
BRZZT
THAT'S RIGHT. THE INSTANT I SAW THAT ANGEL, I KNEW IT WAS A FOE.
I REALIZED IT WAS UNDER SOMEONE'S CONTROL... AND IT HAD AN INDESCRIBABLY HORRIFIC AURA.
DRO
ドッ…
IT ASKED ME ABOUT THE RAILGUN...
DRO
ドッ…
BUT ONCE I SAID I DIDN'T KNOW ANY-THING...
IT SUDDENLY ATTACKED ME.
DRO
DRO

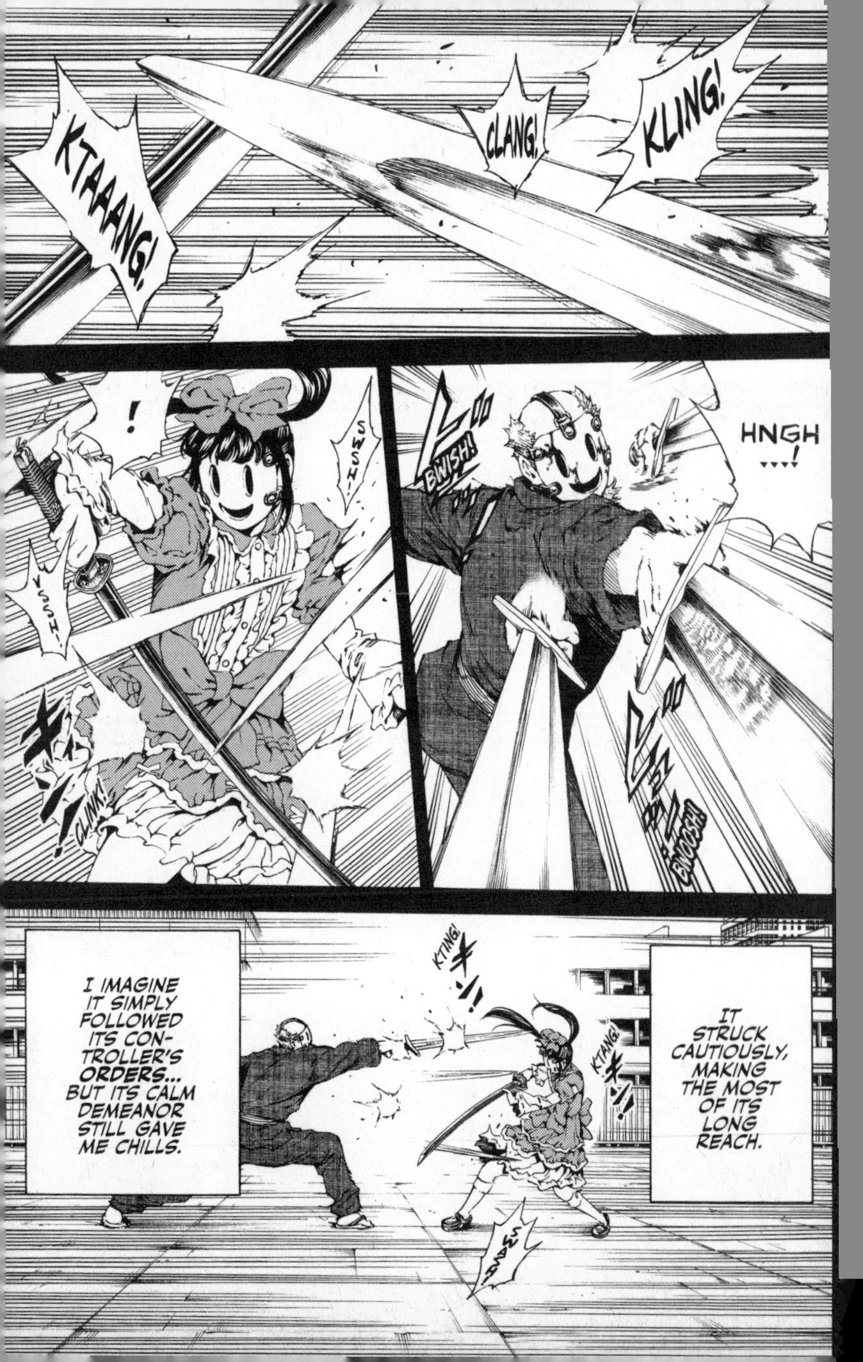
KLING!
CLANG!
KTAAANG!
HNGH ...!
BWISH!
BWOOSH!
SWSH!
!
VSSSH!
CLINK!
IT STRUCK CAUTIOUSLY, MAKING THE MOST OF ITS LONG REACH.
KTANG!
KTING!
SWAP!
I IMAGINE IT SIMPLY FOLLOWED ITS CON-TROLLER'S ORDERS... BUT ITS CALM DEMEANOR STILL GAVE ME CHILLS.

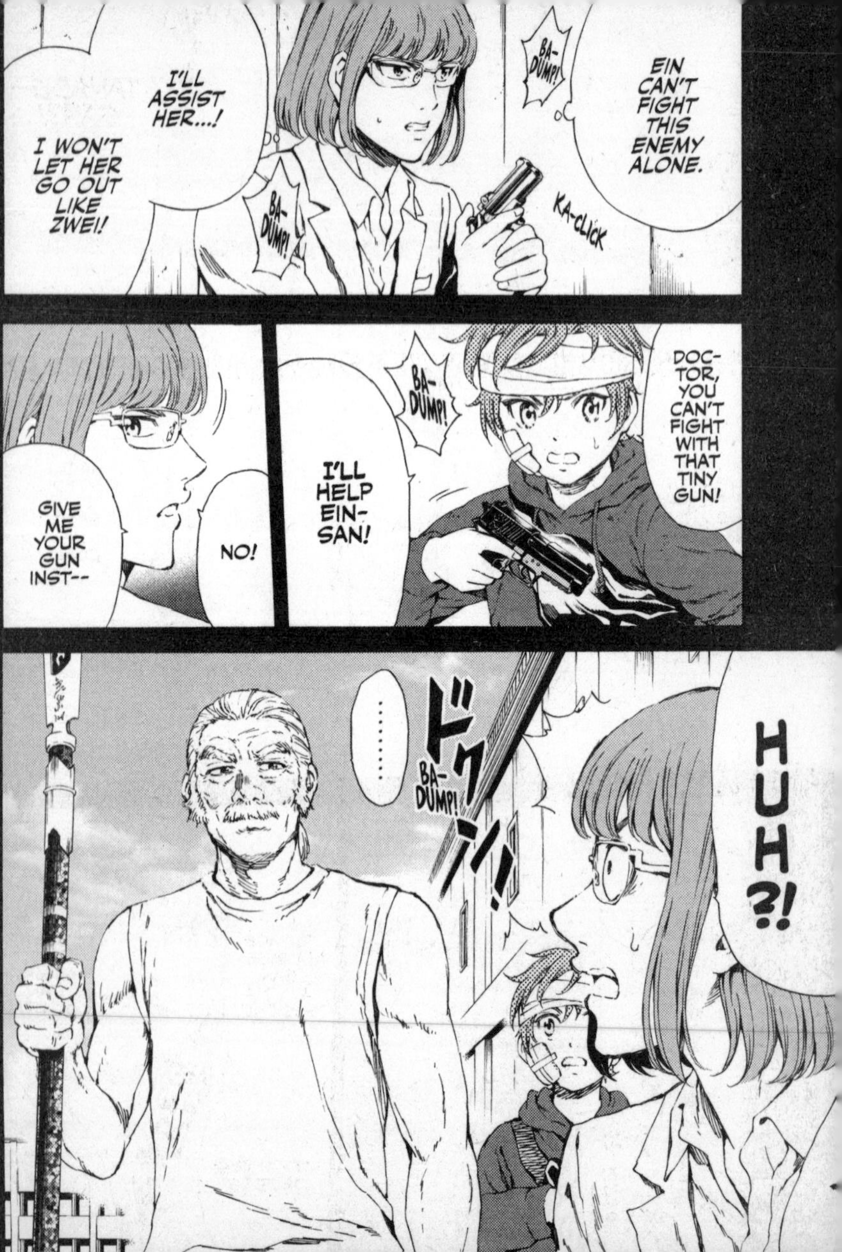
BA-DUMP!
EIN CAN'T FIGHT THIS ENEMY ALONE.
KA-CLICK
BA-DUMP!
I'LL ASSIST HER...!
I WON'T LET HER GO OUT LIKE ZWEI!
DOC-TOR, YOU CAN'T FIGHT WITH THAT TINY GUN!
BA-DUMP!
I'LL HELP EIN-SAN!
NO!
GIVE ME YOUR GUN INST--
HUH?!
BA-DUMP!
......

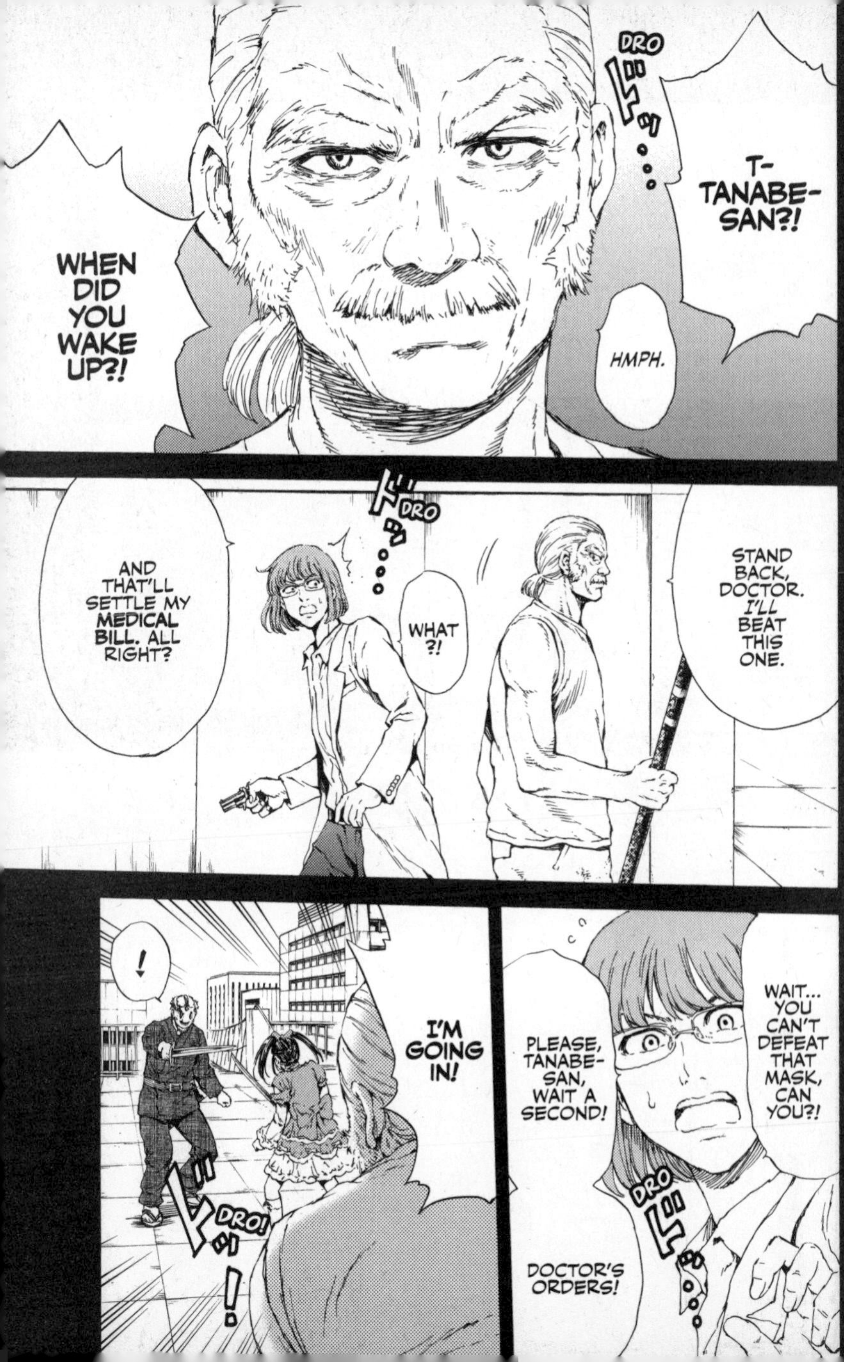
DRO
T-TANABE-SAN?!
HMPH.
WHEN DID YOU WAKE UP?!
STAND BACK, DOCTOR. *I'LL* BEAT THIS ONE.
DRO
WHAT?!
AND THAT'LL SETTLE MY MEDICAL BILL. ALL RIGHT?
WAIT... YOU CAN'T DEFEAT THAT MASK, CAN YOU?!
PLEASE, TANABE-SAN, WAIT A SECOND!
DRO
DOCTOR'S ORDERS!
I'M GOING IN!
!
DRO!
!

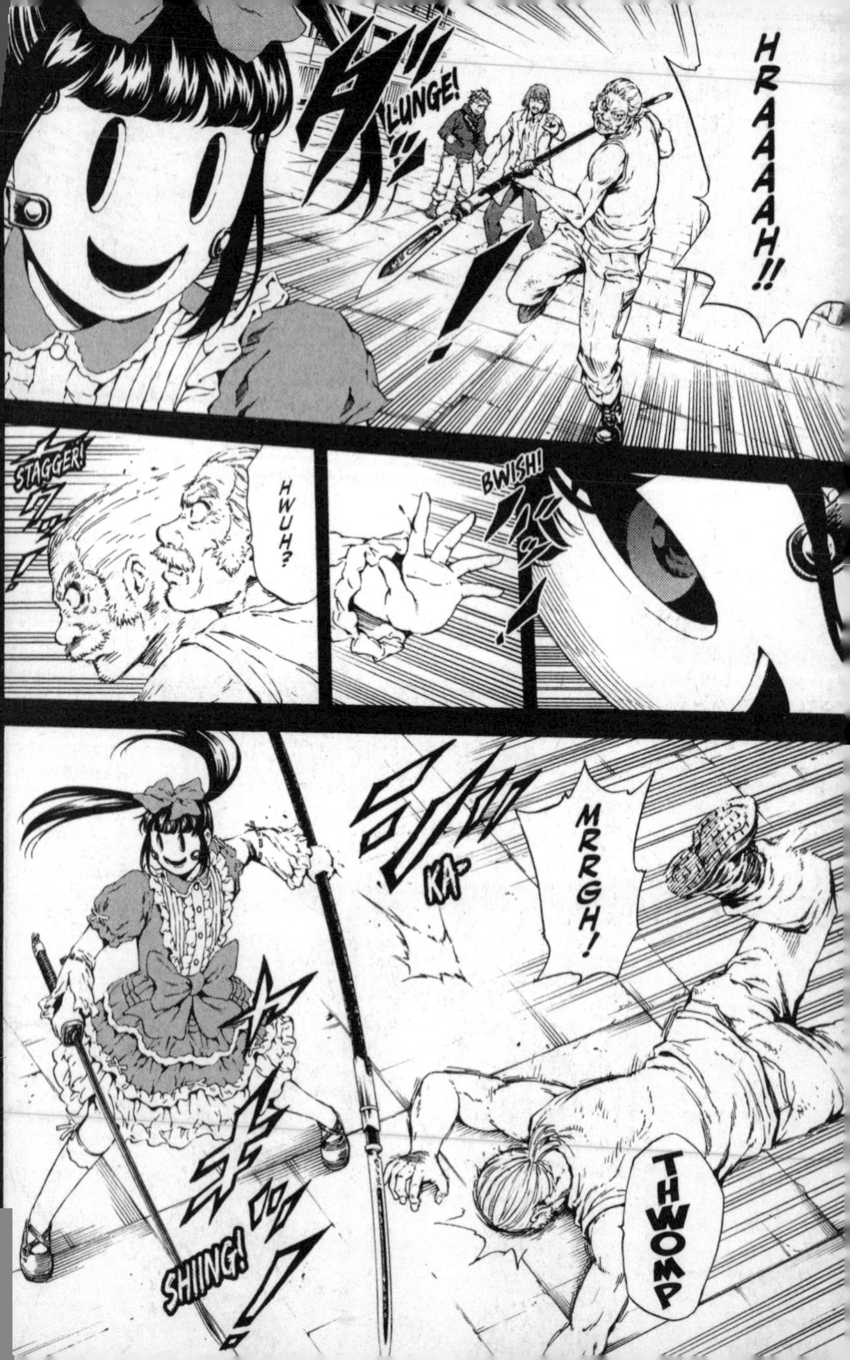
HRAAAAH!!
LUNGE!
BWISH!
HWUH?
STAGGER!
MRRGH!
KA-
THWOMP
SHIING!

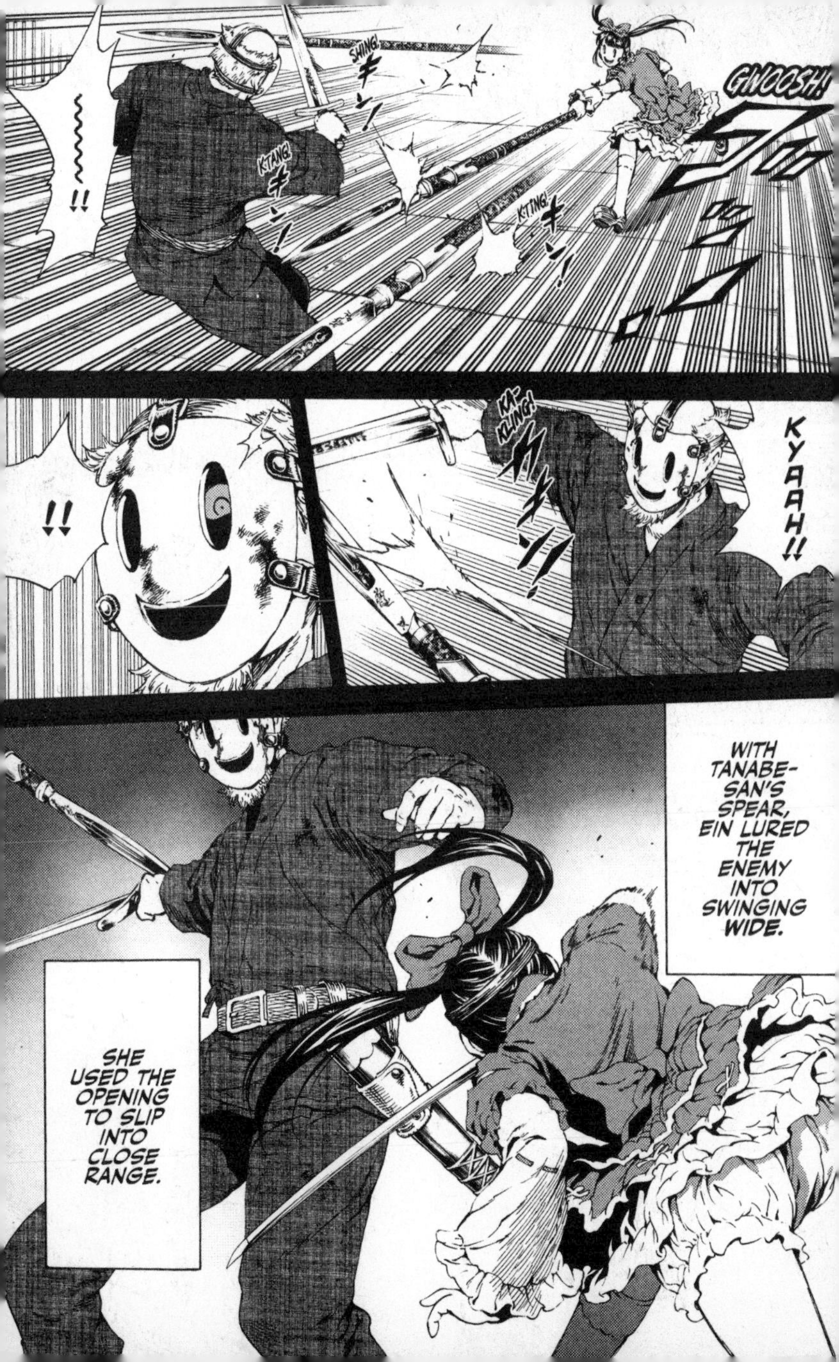
GWOOSH!
SHING!
KTING!
KTANG!
~~~~!!
KA-KLING!
KYAAH!!
!!
WITH TANABE-SAN'S SPEAR, EIN LURED THE ENEMY INTO SWINGING WIDE.
SHE USED THE OPENING TO SLIP INTO CLOSE RANGE.
~~~~

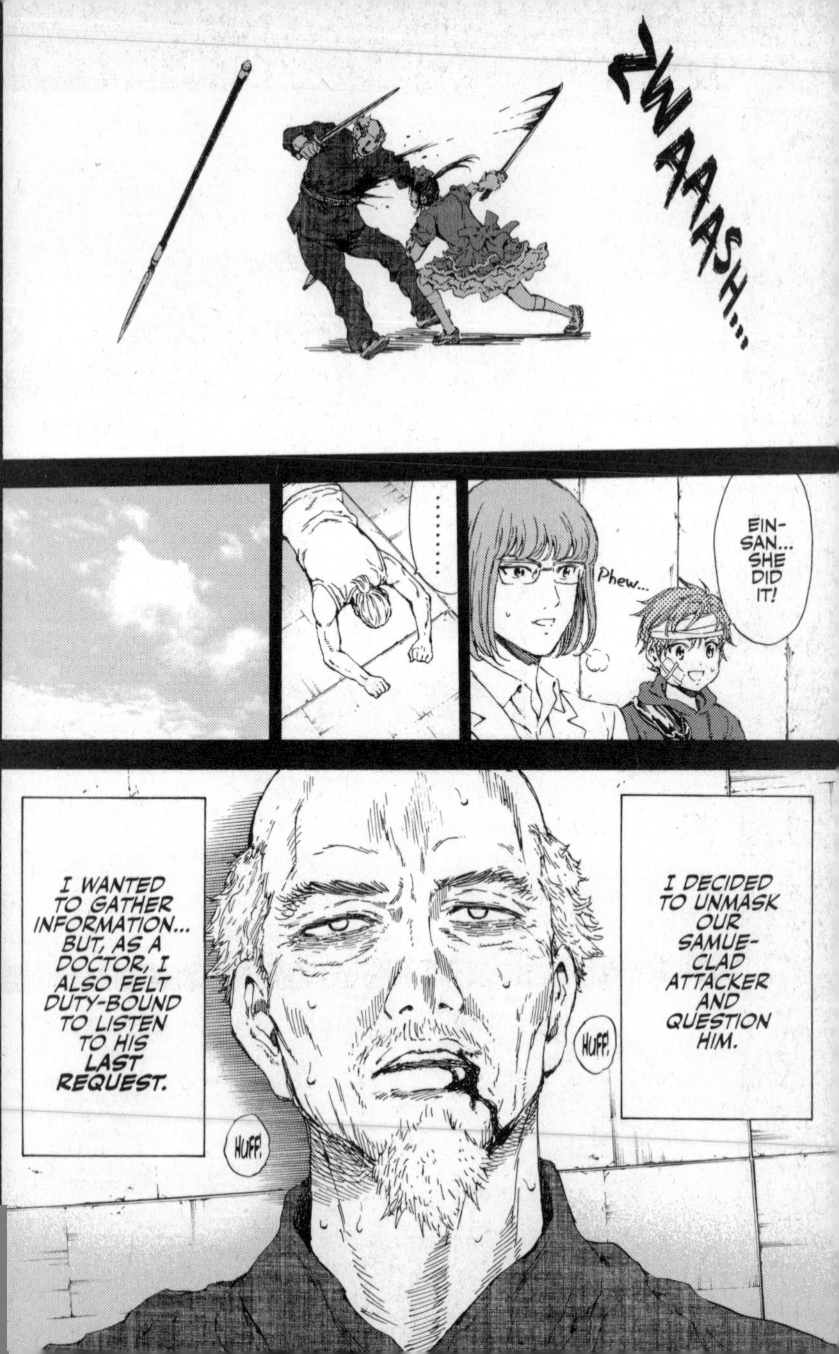
ZWAAASH...
EIN-SAN... SHE DID IT!
Phew...
......
I DECIDED TO UNMASK OUR SAMUE-CLAD ATTACKER AND QUESTION HIM.
HUFF!
I WANTED TO GATHER INFORMATION... BUT, AS A DOCTOR, I ALSO FELT DUTY-BOUND TO LISTEN TO HIS LAST REQUEST.
HUFF!

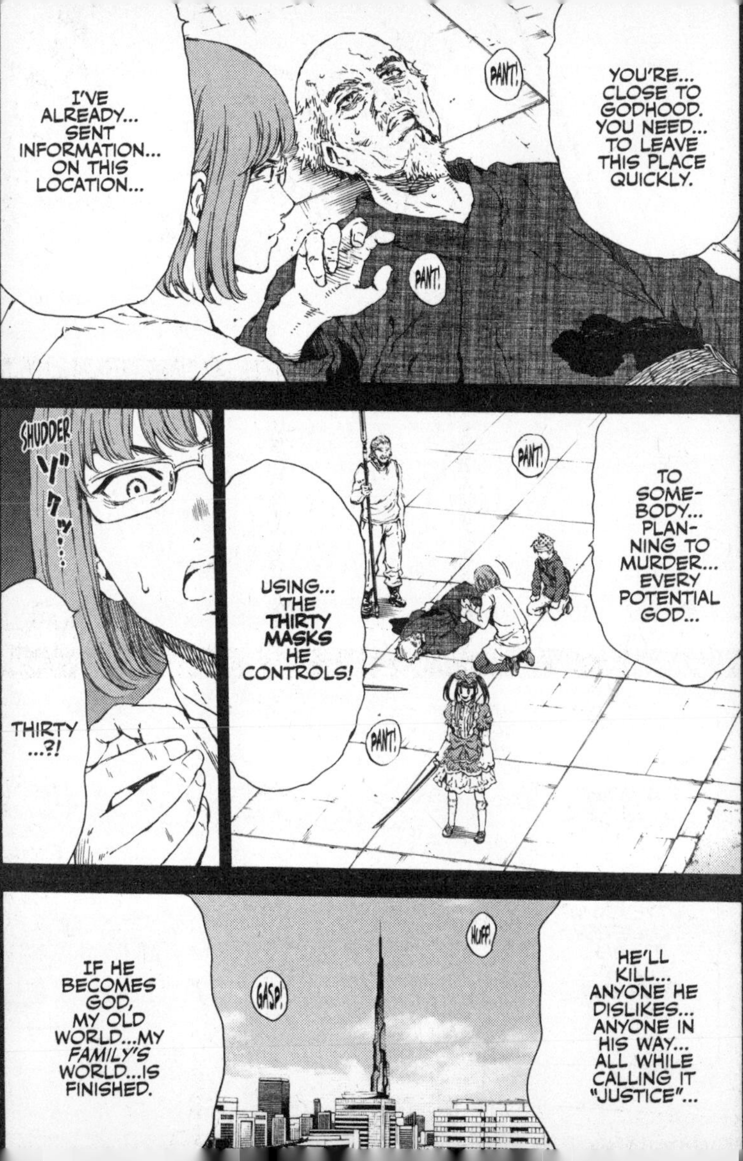
YOU'RE... CLOSE TO GODHOOD. YOU NEED... TO LEAVE THIS PLACE QUICKLY.
PANT!
I'VE ALREADY... SENT INFORMATION... ON THIS LOCATION...
PANT!
TO SOME-BODY... PLAN-NING TO MURDER... EVERY POTENTIAL GOD...
PANT!
USING... THE **THIRTY MASKS** HE CONTROLS!
PANT!
SHUDDER
ゾクッ…
THIRTY ...?!
HE'LL KILL... ANYONE HE DISLIKES... ANYONE IN HIS WAY... ALL WHILE CALLING IT "JUSTICE"...
HUFF!
GASP!
IF HE BECOMES GOD, MY OLD WORLD...MY *FAMILY'S* WORLD...IS FINISHED.

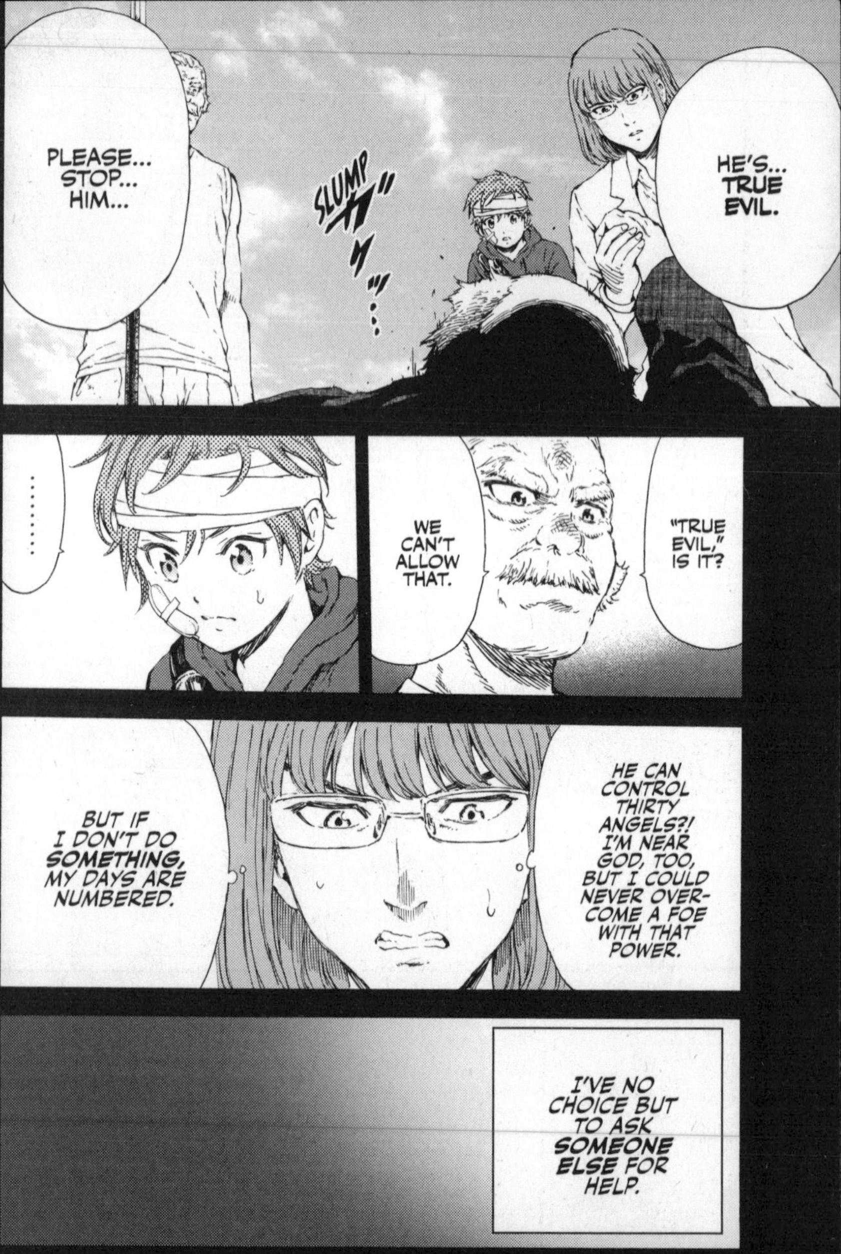
HE'S... TRUE EVIL.
SLUMP
PLEASE... STOP... HIM...
"TRUE EVIL," IS IT?
WE CAN'T ALLOW THAT.
......
HE CAN CONTROL THIRTY ANGELS?! I'M NEAR GOD, TOO, BUT I COULD NEVER OVER-COME A FOE WITH THAT POWER.
BUT IF I DON'T DO SOMETHING, MY DAYS ARE NUMBERED.
I'VE NO CHOICE BUT TO ASK SOMEONE ELSE FOR HELP.

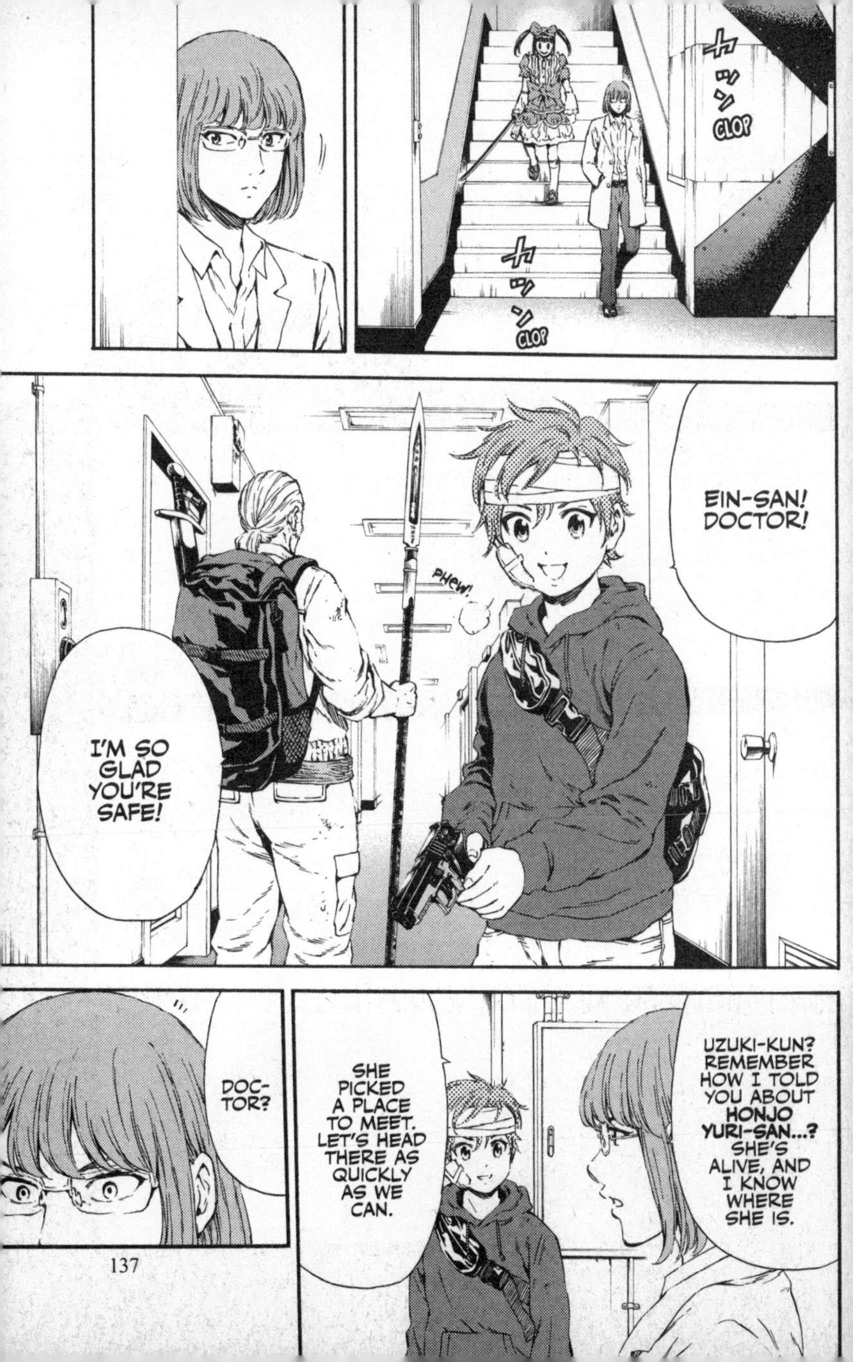
CLOP
CLOP
EIN-SAN! DOCTOR!
PHEW!
I'M SO GLAD YOU'RE SAFE!
UZUKI-KUN? REMEMBER HOW I TOLD YOU ABOUT **HONJO YURI-SAN...?** SHE'S ALIVE, AND I KNOW WHERE SHE IS.
SHE PICKED A PLACE TO MEET. LET'S HEAD THERE AS QUICKLY AS WE CAN.
DOC-TOR?

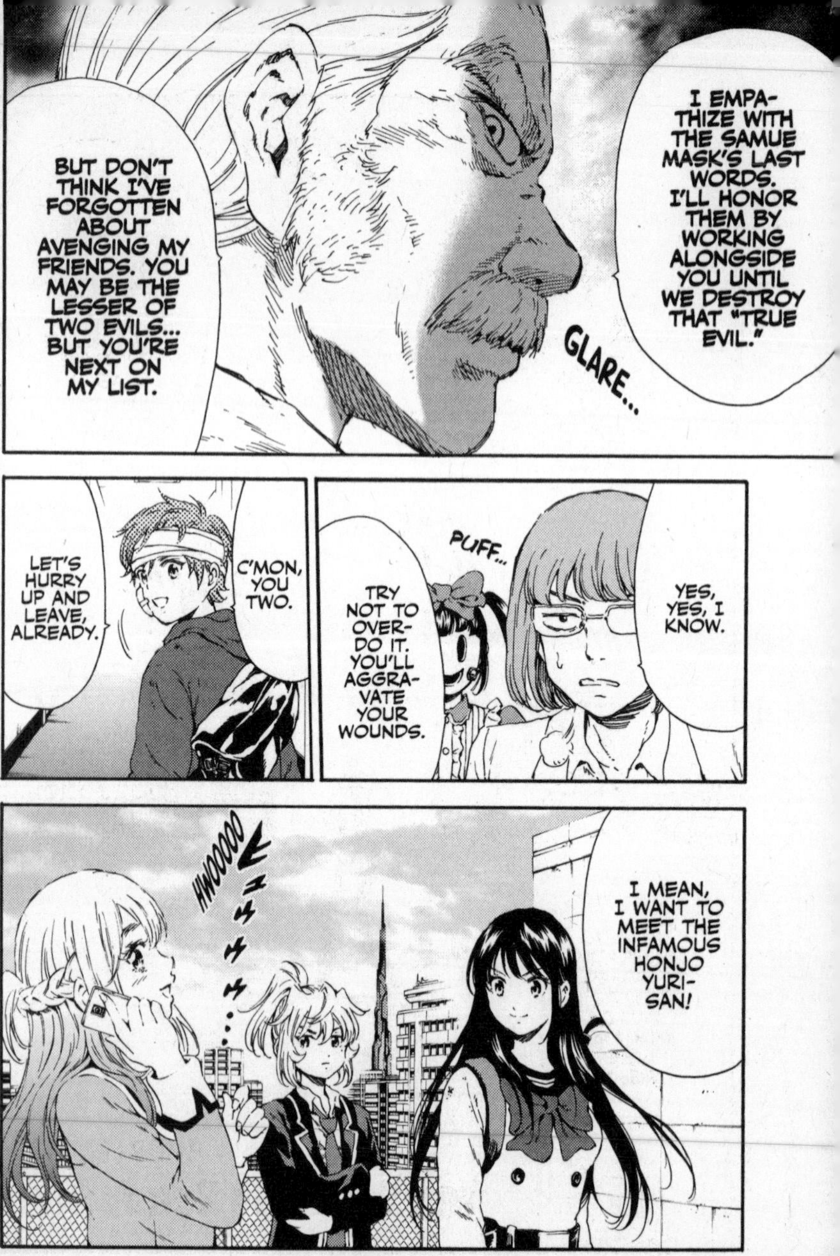
I EMPATHIZE WITH THE SAMUE MASK'S LAST WORDS. I'LL HONOR THEM BY WORKING ALONGSIDE YOU UNTIL WE DESTROY THAT "TRUE EVIL."
GLARE...
BUT DON'T THINK I'VE FORGOTTEN ABOUT AVENGING MY FRIENDS. YOU MAY BE THE LESSER OF TWO EVILS... BUT YOU'RE NEXT ON MY LIST.
YES, YES, I KNOW.
PUFF...
TRY NOT TO OVERDO IT. YOU'LL AGGRAVATE YOUR WOUNDS.
C'MON, YOU TWO.
LET'S HURRY UP AND LEAVE, ALREADY.
I MEAN, I WANT TO MEET THE INFAMOUS HONJO YURI-SAN!
HWOOOOO

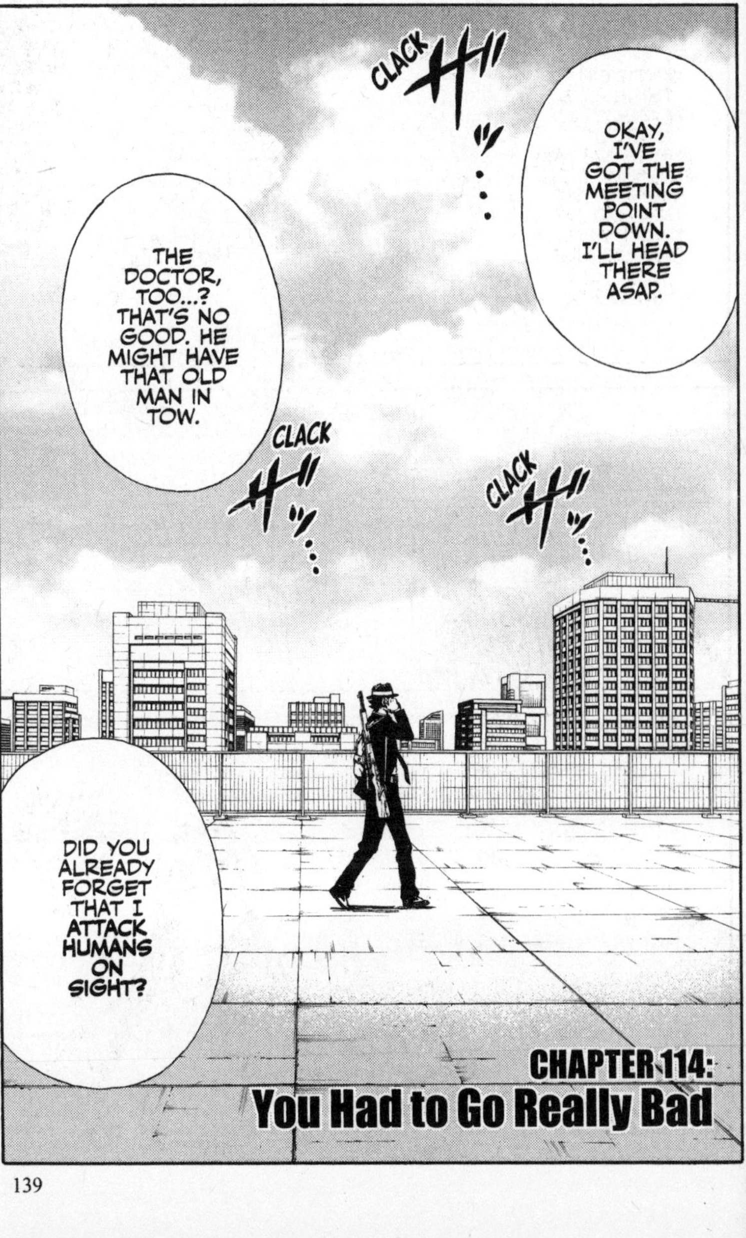
OKAY, I'VE GOT THE MEETING POINT DOWN. I'LL HEAD THERE ASAP.
CLACK
THE DOCTOR, TOO...? THAT'S NO GOOD. HE MIGHT HAVE THAT OLD MAN IN TOW.
CLACK
CLACK
DID YOU ALREADY FORGET THAT I ATTACK HUMANS ON SIGHT?

CHAPTER 114: You Had to Go Really Bad

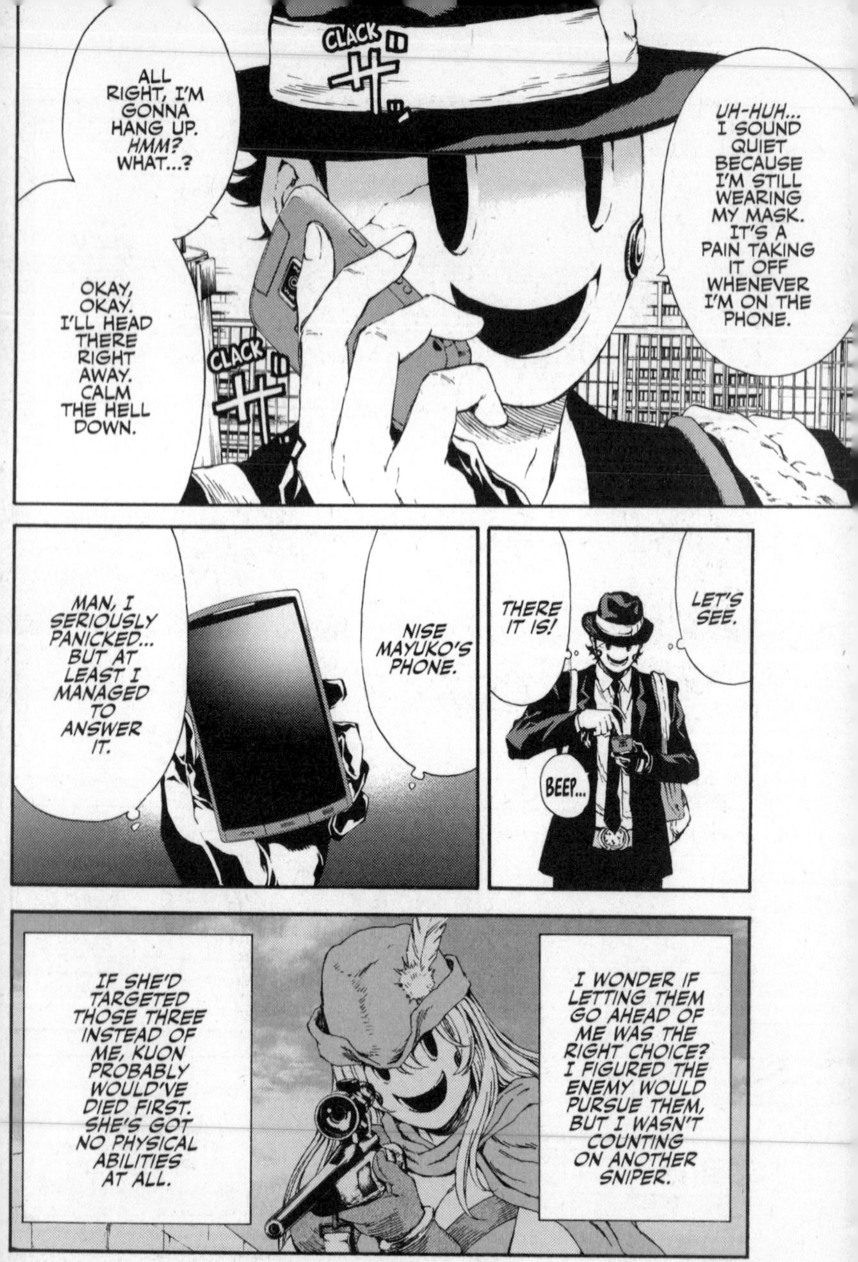
UH-HUH... I SOUND QUIET BECAUSE I'M STILL WEARING MY MASK. IT'S A PAIN TAKING IT OFF WHENEVER I'M ON THE PHONE.
ALL RIGHT, I'M GONNA HANG UP. HMM? WHAT...?
CLACK
OKAY, OKAY. I'LL HEAD THERE RIGHT AWAY. CALM THE HELL DOWN.
CLACK
LET'S SEE.
THERE IT IS!
BEEP...
NISE MAYUKO'S PHONE.
MAN, I SERIOUSLY PANICKED... BUT AT LEAST I MANAGED TO ANSWER IT.
I WONDER IF LETTING THEM GO AHEAD OF ME WAS THE RIGHT CHOICE? I FIGURED THE ENEMY WOULD PURSUE THEM, BUT I WASN'T COUNTING ON ANOTHER SNIPER.
IF SHE'D TARGETED THOSE THREE INSTEAD OF ME, KUON PROBABLY WOULD'VE DIED FIRST. SHE'S GOT NO PHYSICAL ABILITIES AT ALL.

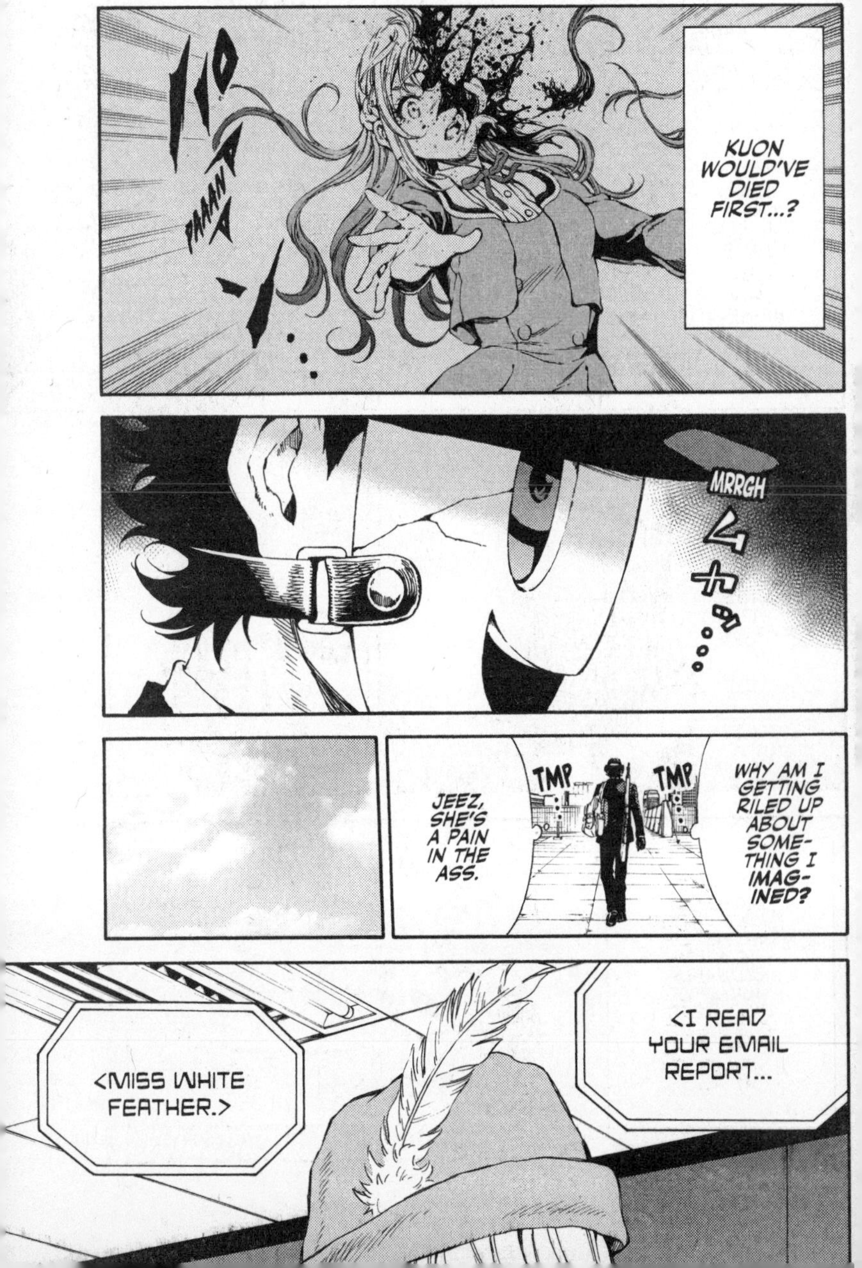
KUON WOULD'VE DIED FIRST...?
PAAAN
MRRGH
WHY AM I GETTING RILED UP ABOUT SOME-THING I IMAG-INED?
TMP
TMP
JEEZ, SHE'S A PAIN IN THE ASS.
<I READ YOUR EMAIL REPORT...
<MISS WHITE FEATHER.>

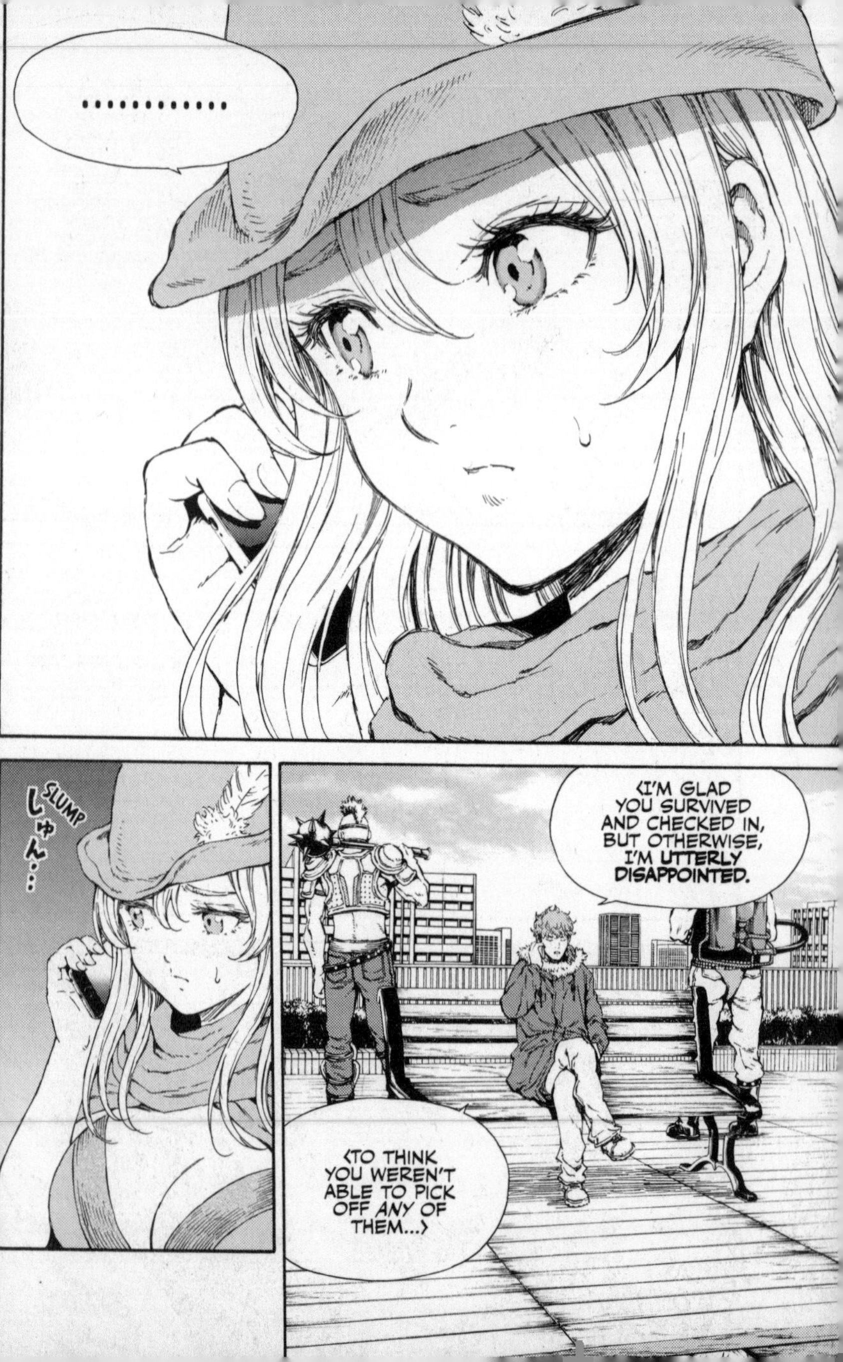
....
‹I'M GLAD YOU SURVIVED AND CHECKED IN, BUT OTHERWISE, I'M UTTERLY DISAPPOINTED.
‹TO THINK YOU WEREN'T ABLE TO PICK OFF ANY OF THEM...›
SLUMP
しゅん…

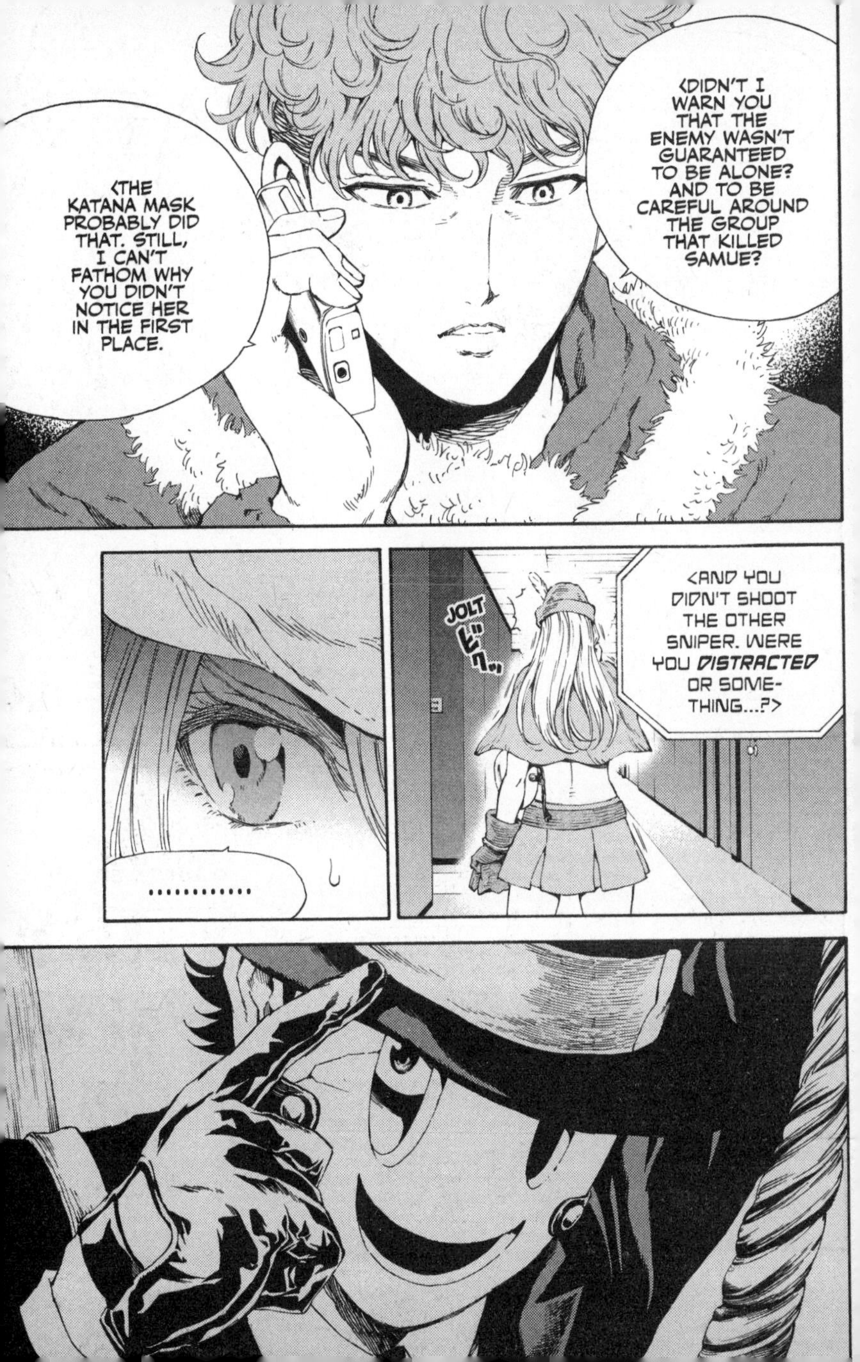
<DIDN'T I WARN YOU THAT THE ENEMY WASN'T GUARANTEED TO BE ALONE? AND TO BE CAREFUL AROUND THE GROUP THAT KILLED SAMUE?
<THE KATANA MASK PROBABLY DID THAT. STILL, I CAN'T FATHOM WHY YOU DIDN'T NOTICE HER IN THE FIRST PLACE.
<AND YOU DIDN'T SHOOT THE OTHER SNIPER. WERE YOU *DISTRACTED* OR SOME-THING...?>
JOLT
....

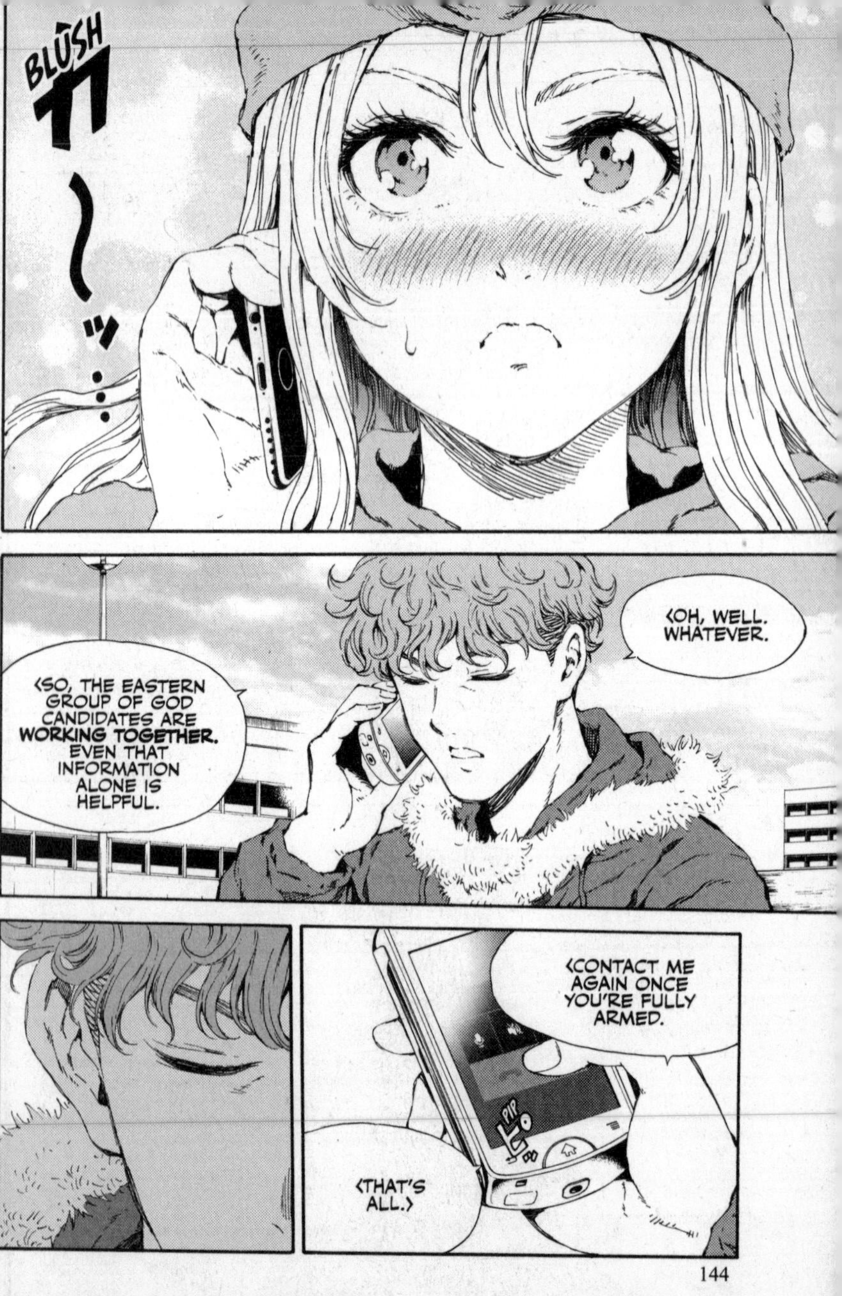
BLUSH
~ッ…
‹OH, WELL. WHATEVER.
‹SO, THE EASTERN GROUP OF GOD CANDIDATES ARE **WORKING TOGETHER.** EVEN THAT INFORMATION ALONE IS HELPFUL.
‹CONTACT ME AGAIN ONCE YOU'RE FULLY ARMED.
PIP
‹THAT'S ALL.›

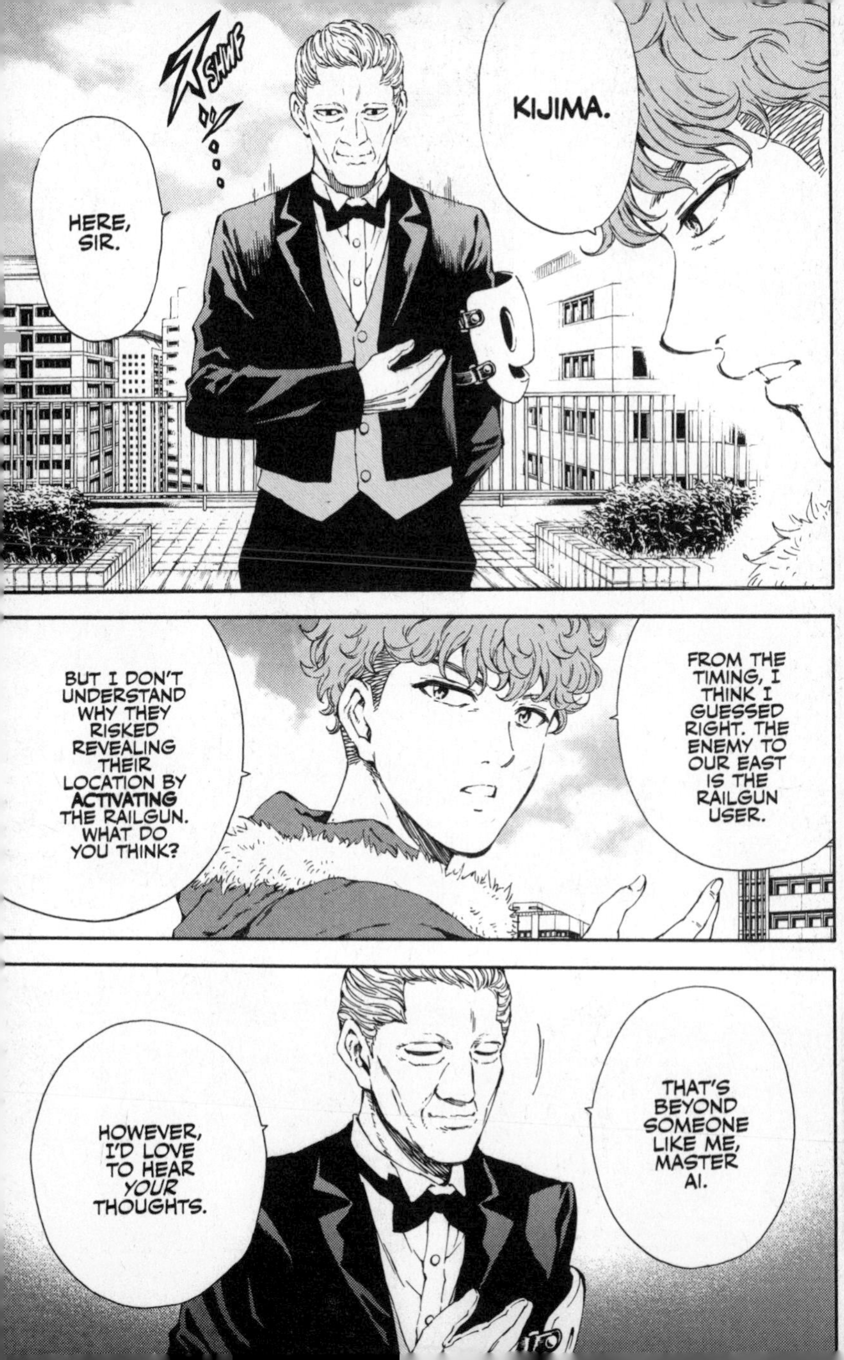
KIJIMA.
SHWF
HERE, SIR.
FROM THE TIMING, I THINK I GUESSED RIGHT. THE ENEMY TO OUR EAST IS THE RAILGUN USER.
BUT I DON'T UNDERSTAND WHY THEY RISKED REVEALING THEIR LOCATION BY ACTIVATING THE RAILGUN. WHAT DO YOU THINK?
THAT'S BEYOND SOMEONE LIKE ME, MASTER AI.
HOWEVER, I'D LOVE TO HEAR YOUR THOUGHTS.

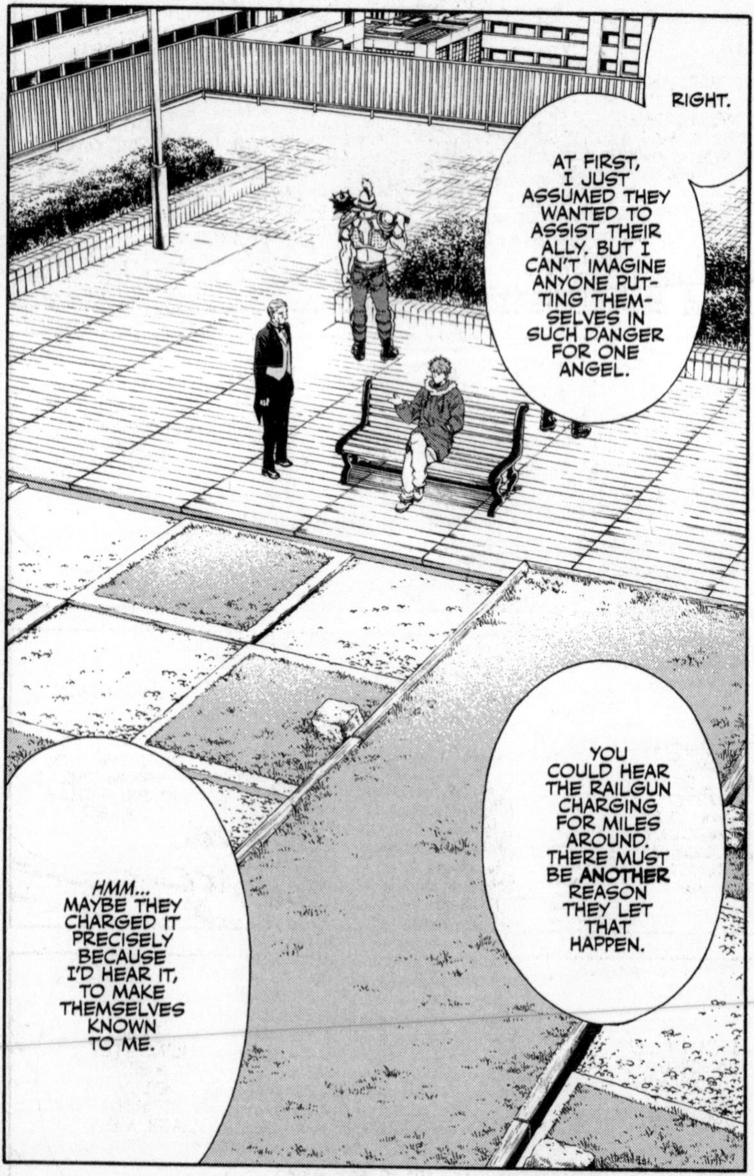
RIGHT.
AT FIRST, I JUST ASSUMED THEY WANTED TO ASSIST THEIR ALLY. BUT I CAN'T IMAGINE ANYONE PUTTING THEMSELVES IN SUCH DANGER FOR ONE ANGEL.
YOU COULD HEAR THE RAILGUN CHARGING FOR MILES AROUND. THERE MUST BE **ANOTHER** REASON THEY LET THAT HAPPEN.
HMM... MAYBE THEY CHARGED IT PRECISELY BECAUSE I'D HEAR IT, TO MAKE THEMSELVES KNOWN TO ME.

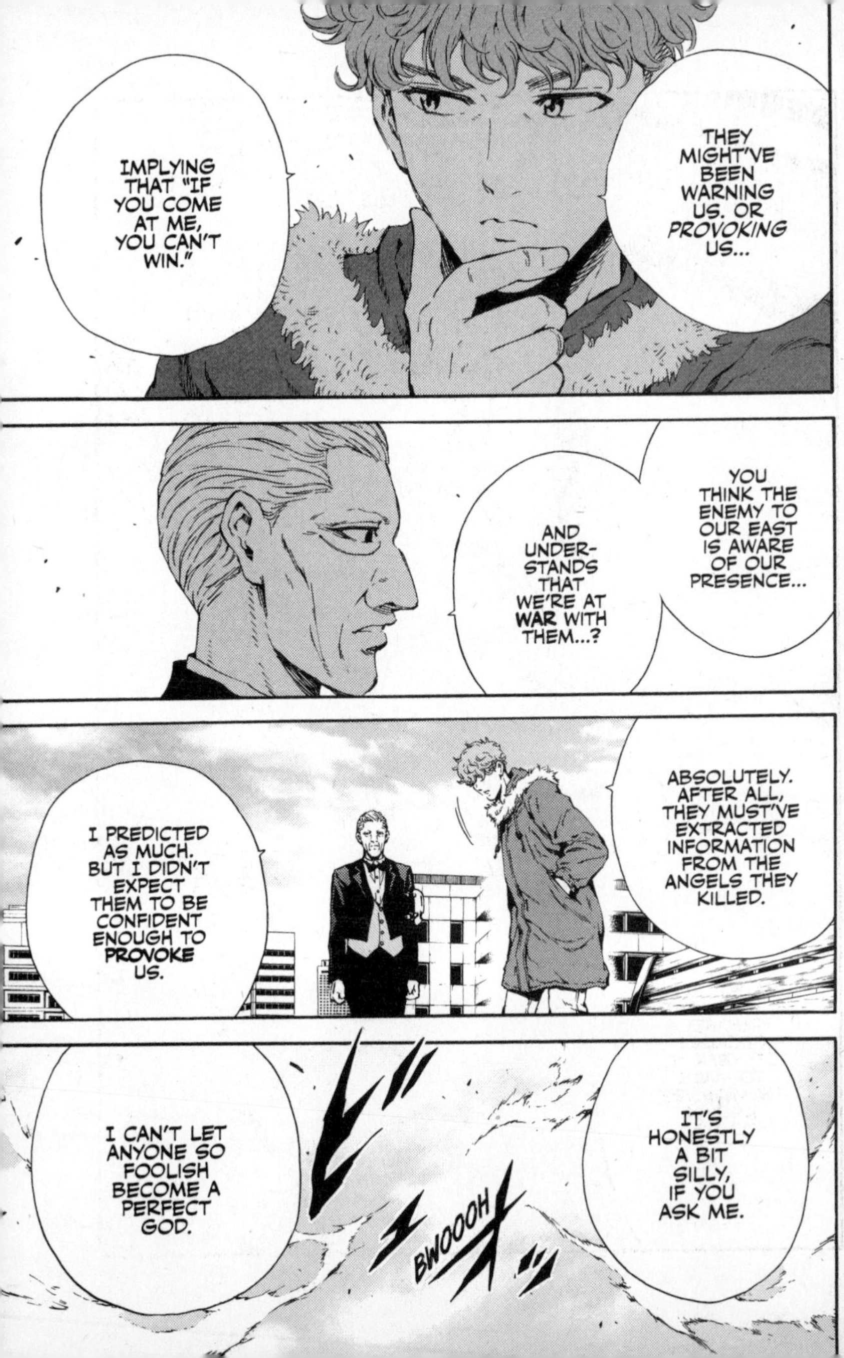
THEY MIGHT'VE BEEN WARNING US. OR *PROVOKING* US...
IMPLYING THAT "IF YOU COME AT ME, YOU CAN'T WIN."
YOU THINK THE ENEMY TO OUR EAST IS AWARE OF OUR PRESENCE...
AND UNDER-STANDS THAT WE'RE AT **WAR** WITH THEM...?
ABSOLUTELY. AFTER ALL, THEY MUST'VE EXTRACTED INFORMATION FROM THE ANGELS THEY KILLED.
I PREDICTED AS MUCH. BUT I DIDN'T EXPECT THEM TO BE CONFIDENT ENOUGH TO **PROVOKE** US.
IT'S HONESTLY A BIT SILLY, IF YOU ASK ME.
BWOOOH
I CAN'T LET ANYONE SO FOOLISH BECOME A PERFECT GOD.

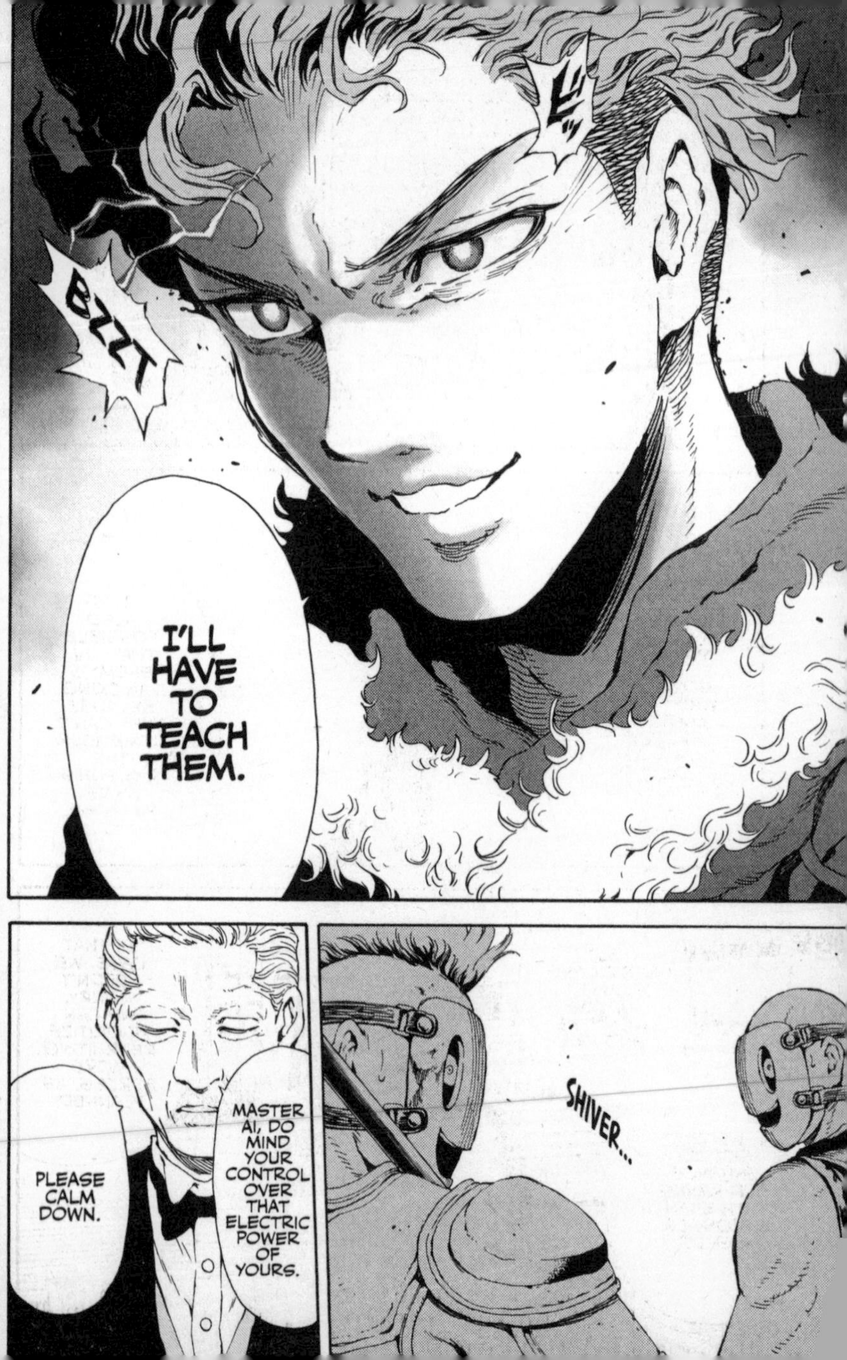
BZZT
I'LL HAVE TO TEACH THEM.
SHIVER...
MASTER AI, DO MIND YOUR CONTROL OVER THAT ELECTRIC POWER OF YOURS.
PLEASE CALM DOWN.

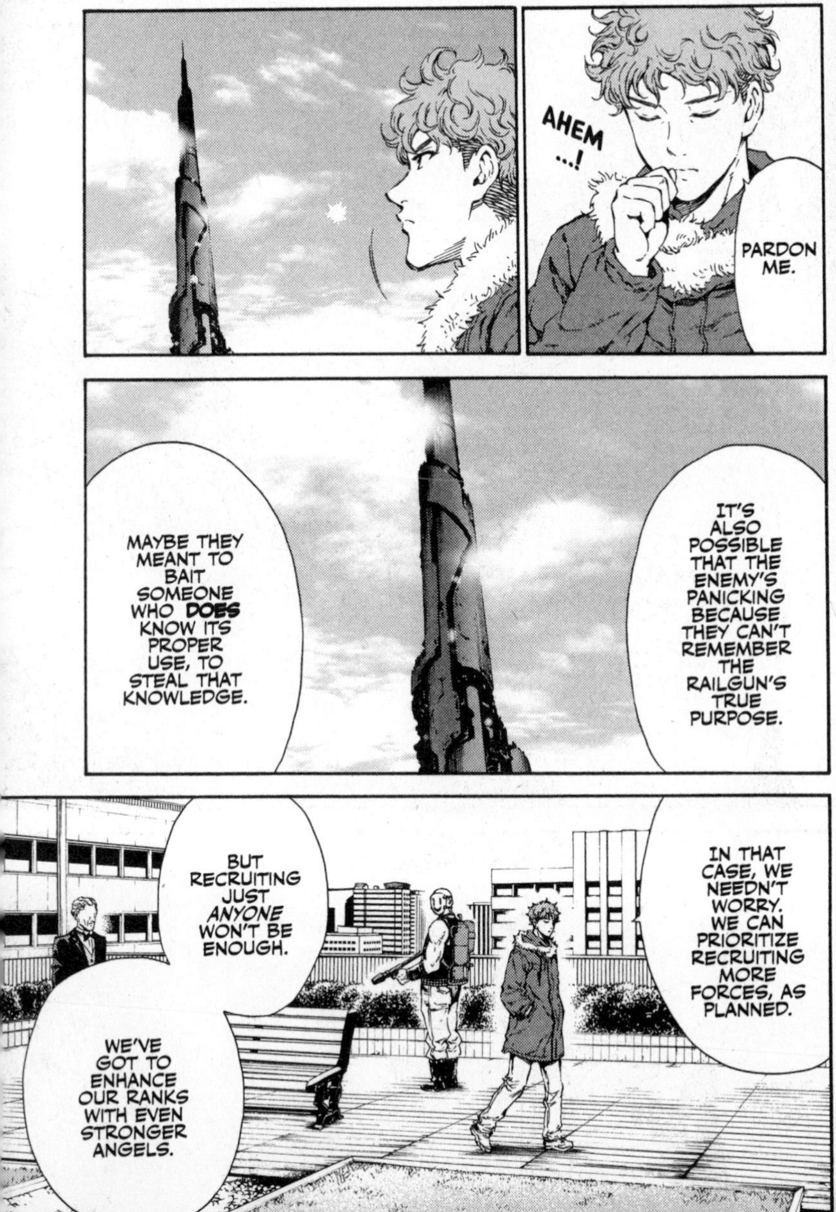
AHEM ...!
PARDON ME.
IT'S ALSO POSSIBLE THAT THE ENEMY'S PANICKING BECAUSE THEY CAN'T REMEMBER THE RAILGUN'S TRUE PURPOSE.
MAYBE THEY MEANT TO BAIT SOMEONE WHO **DOES** KNOW ITS PROPER USE, TO STEAL THAT KNOWLEDGE.
IN THAT CASE, WE NEEDN'T WORRY. WE CAN PRIORITIZE RECRUITING MORE FORCES, AS PLANNED.
BUT RECRUITING JUST *ANYONE* WON'T BE ENOUGH.
WE'VE GOT TO ENHANCE OUR RANKS WITH EVEN STRONGER ANGELS.

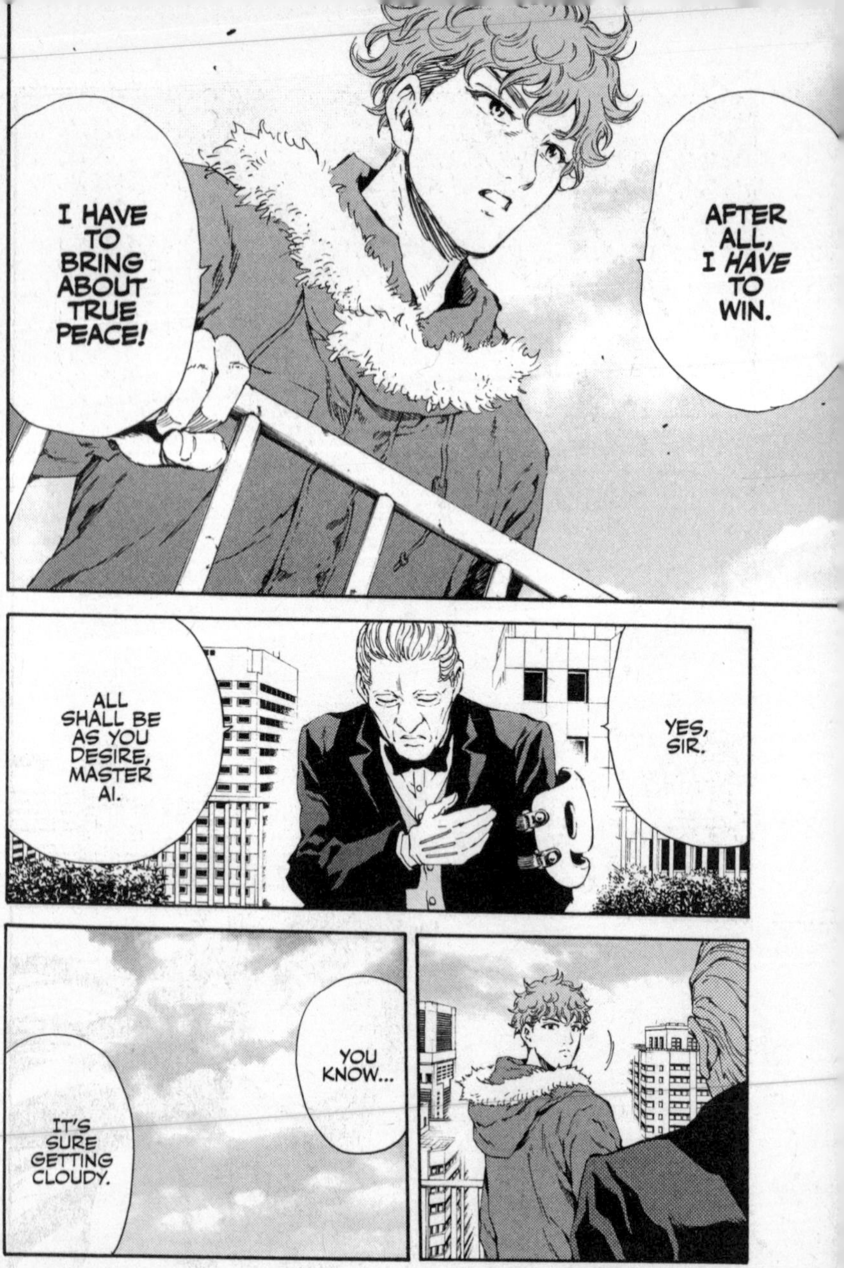
AFTER ALL, I *HAVE* TO WIN.
I HAVE TO BRING ABOUT TRUE PEACE!
YES, SIR.
ALL SHALL BE AS YOU DESIRE, MASTER AI.
YOU KNOW...
IT'S SURE GETTING CLOUDY.

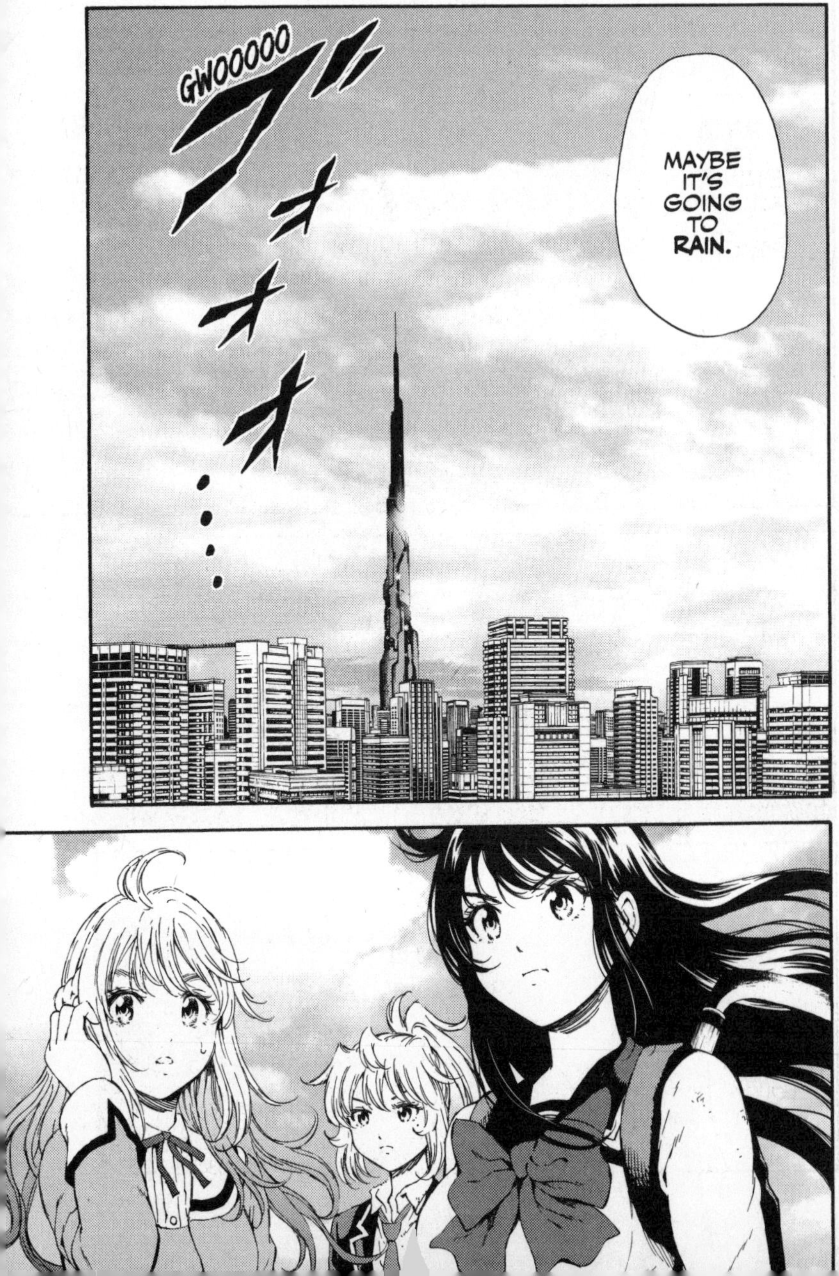
MAYBE IT'S GOING TO RAIN.
GWOOOOO
ブオオオ…

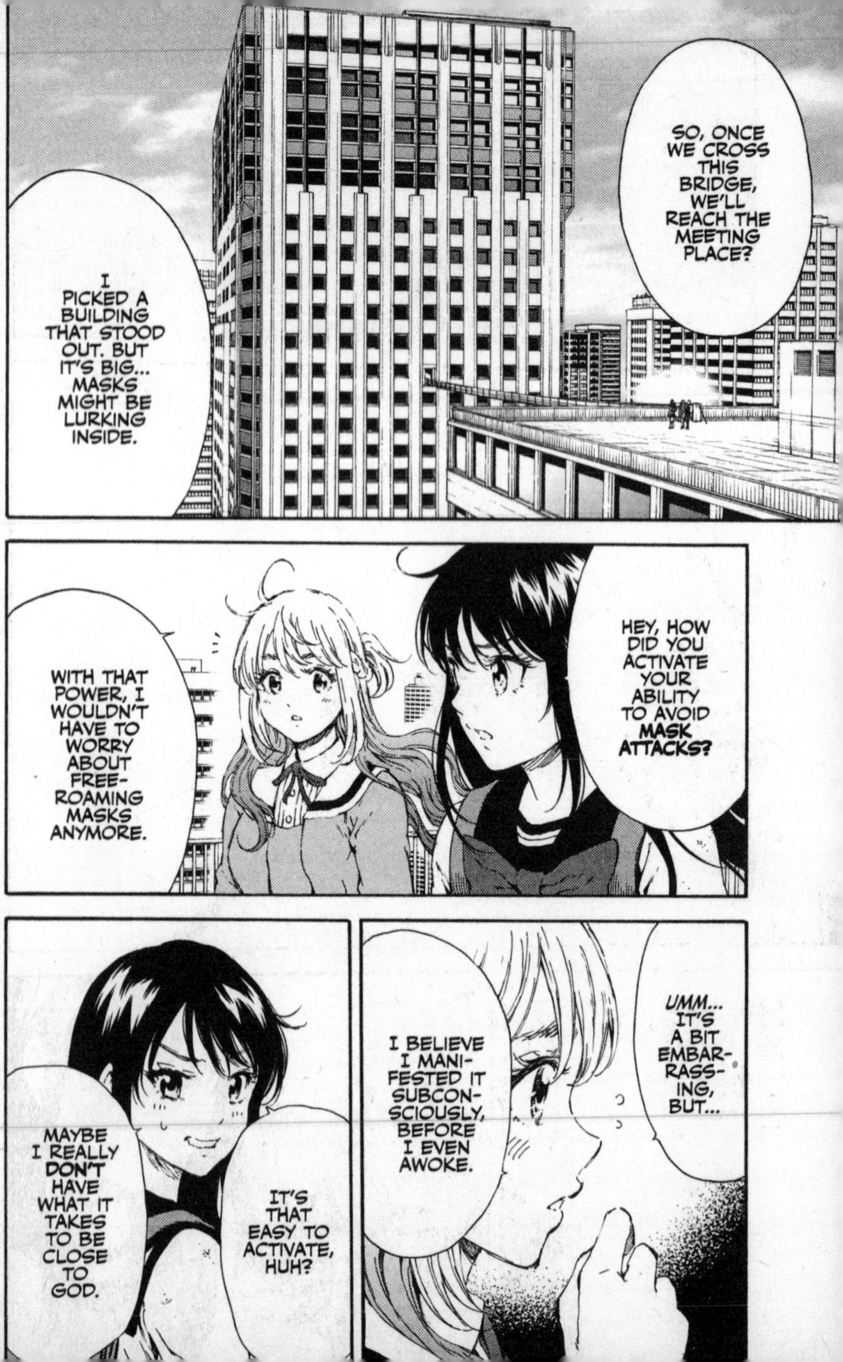
SO, ONCE WE CROSS THIS BRIDGE, WE'LL REACH THE MEETING PLACE?
I PICKED A BUILDING THAT STOOD OUT. BUT IT'S BIG... MASKS MIGHT BE LURKING INSIDE.
HEY, HOW DID YOU ACTIVATE YOUR ABILITY TO AVOID **MASK ATTACKS?**
WITH THAT POWER, I WOULDN'T HAVE TO WORRY ABOUT FREE-ROAMING MASKS ANYMORE.
UMM... IT'S A BIT EMBARRASSING, BUT...
I BELIEVE I MANIFESTED IT SUBCONSCIOUSLY, BEFORE I EVEN AWOKE.
IT'S THAT EASY TO ACTIVATE, HUH?
MAYBE I REALLY **DON'T** HAVE WHAT IT TAKES TO BE CLOSE TO GOD.

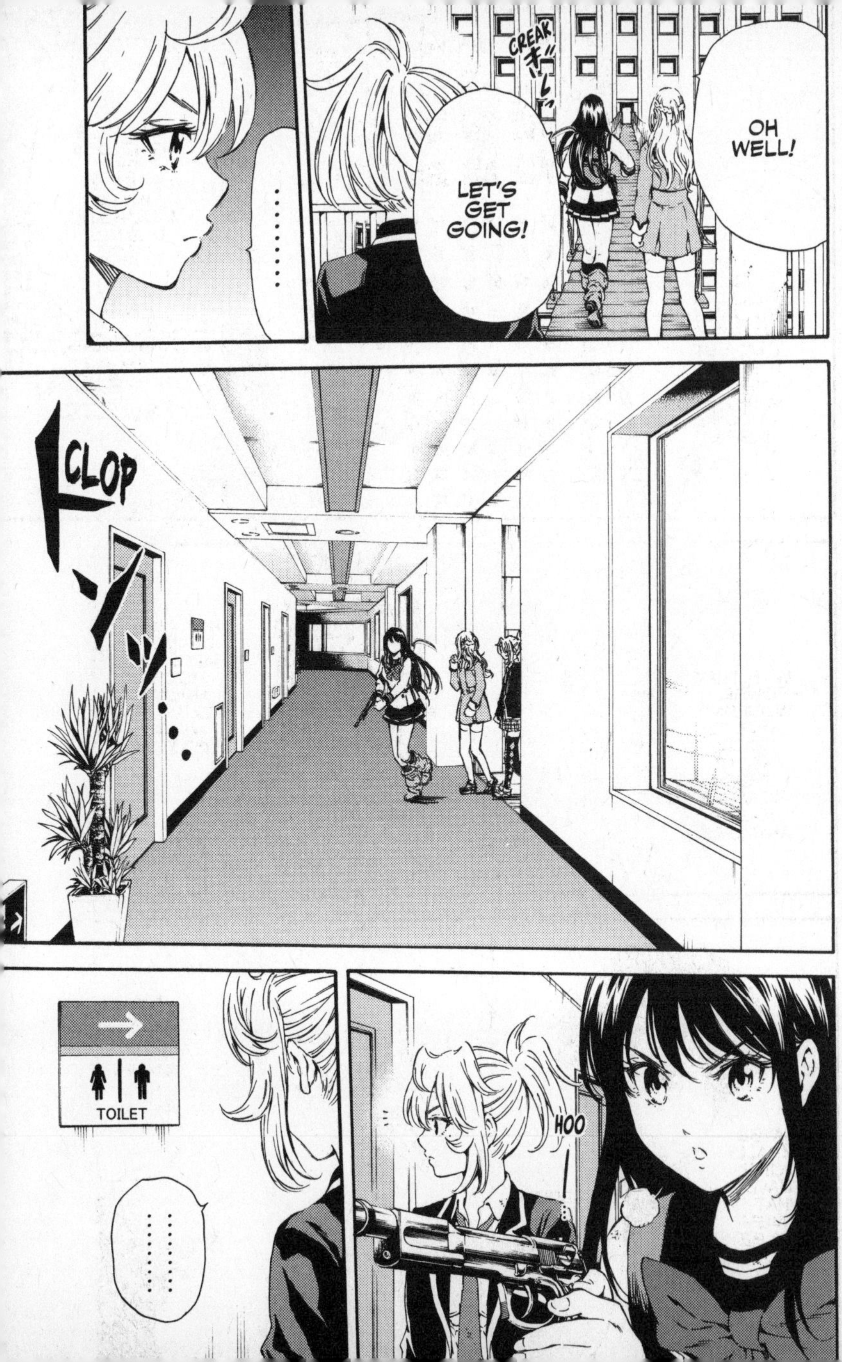
OH WELL!
CREAK
LET'S GET GOING!
......
CLOP
HOO
TOILET
......

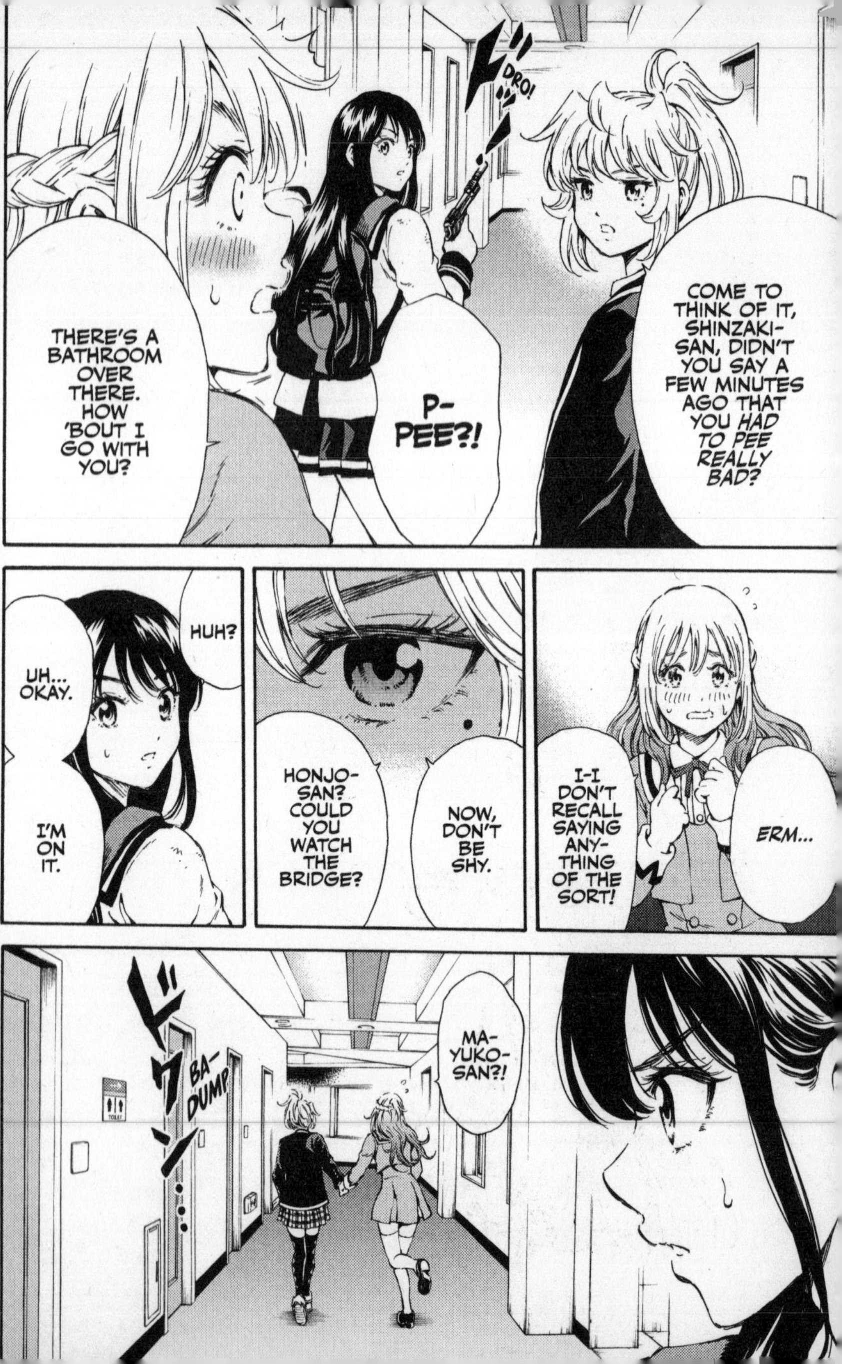
COME TO THINK OF IT, SHINZAKI-SAN, DIDN'T YOU SAY A FEW MINUTES AGO THAT YOU *HAD TO PEE REALLY BAD?*
DRO!
P-PEE?!
THERE'S A BATHROOM OVER THERE. HOW 'BOUT I GO WITH YOU?
ERM...
I-I DON'T RECALL SAYING ANY-THING OF THE SORT!
NOW, DON'T BE SHY.
HONJO-SAN? COULD YOU WATCH THE BRIDGE?
HUH?
UH... OKAY.
I'M ON IT.
MA-YUKO-SAN?!
BA-DUMP

HIGH-RISE INVASION

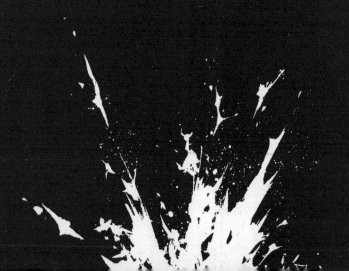

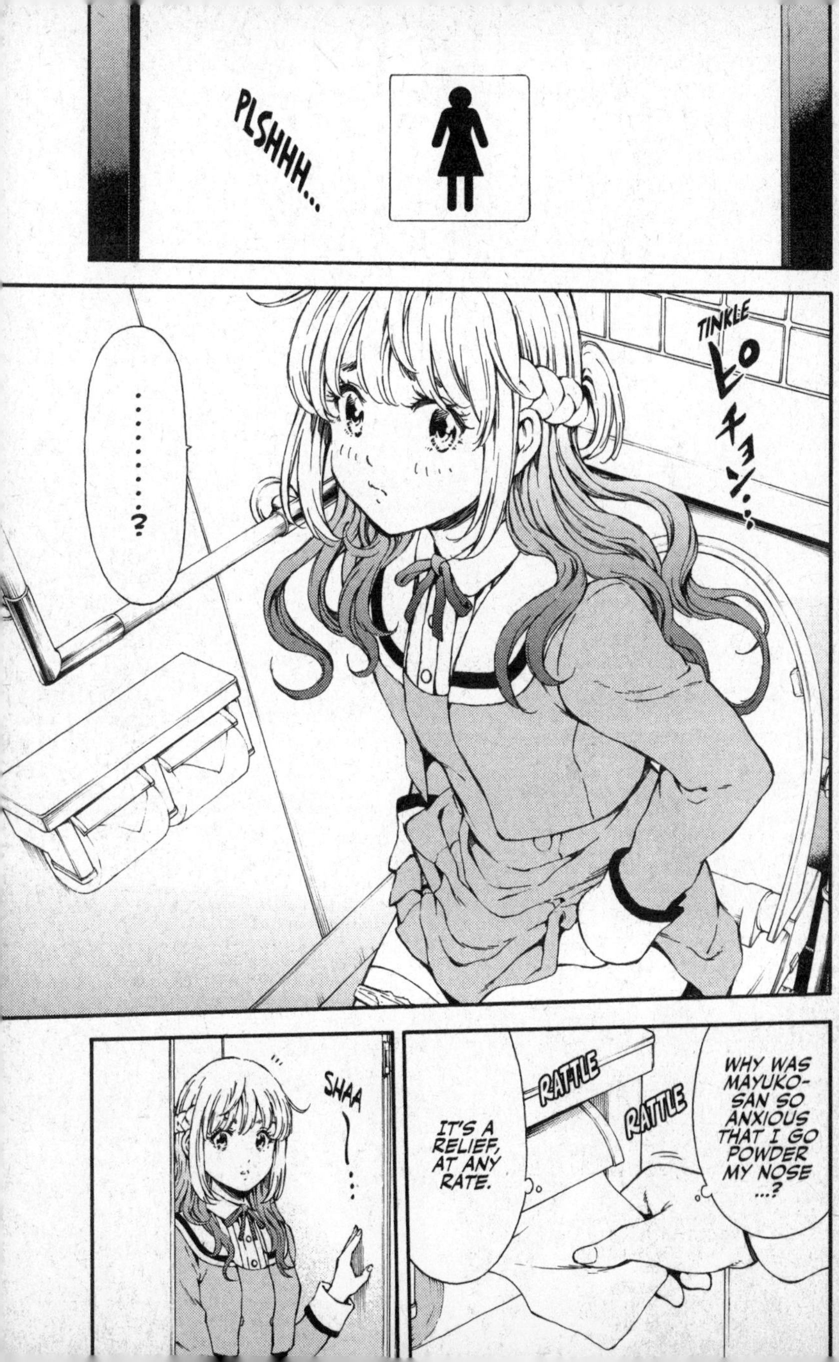
PLSHHH...
TINKLE
ピロチョン...
......?
WHY WAS MAYUKO-SAN SO ANXIOUS THAT I GO POWDER MY NOSE ...?
RATTLE
RATTLE
IT'S A RELIEF, AT ANY RATE.
SHAA ...

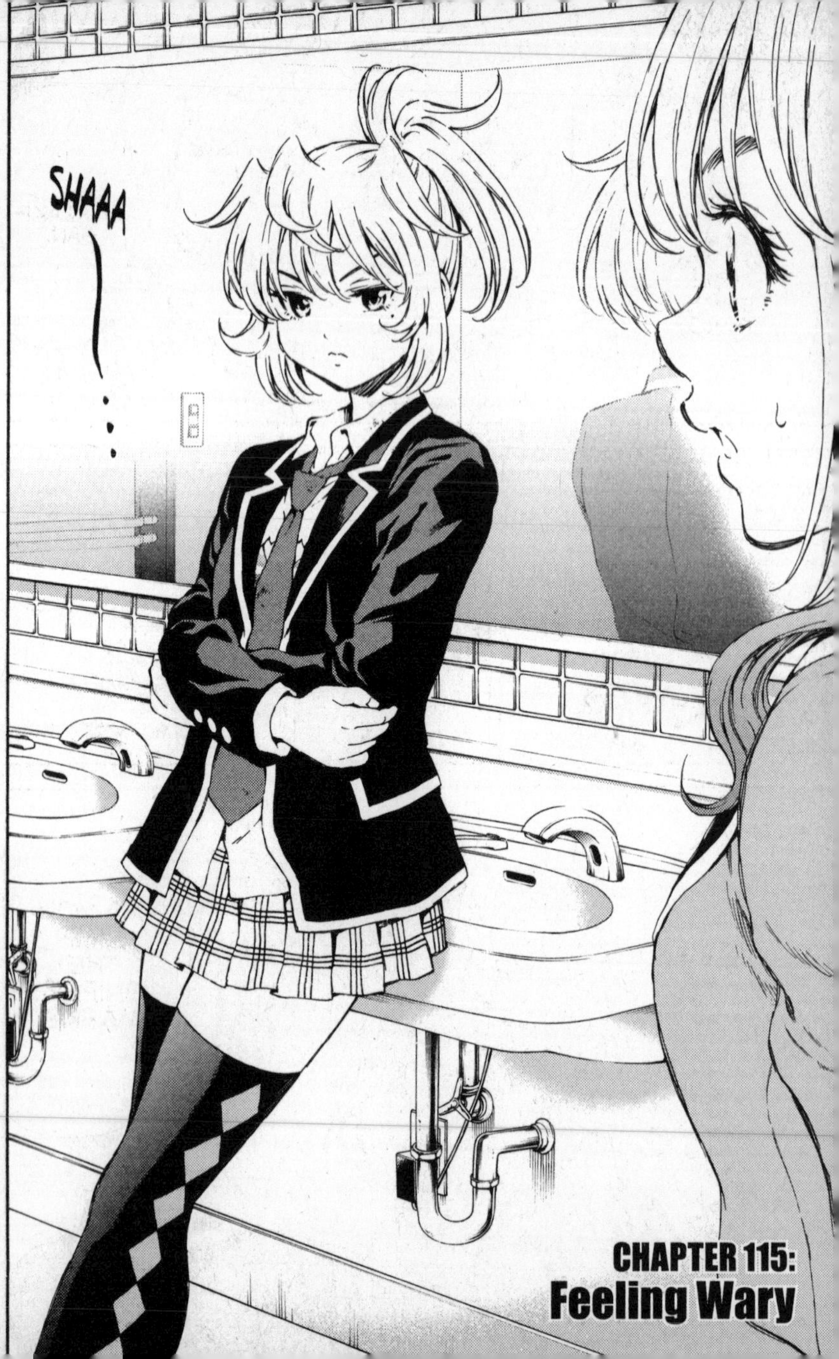
SHAAA

CHAPTER 115: Feeling Wary

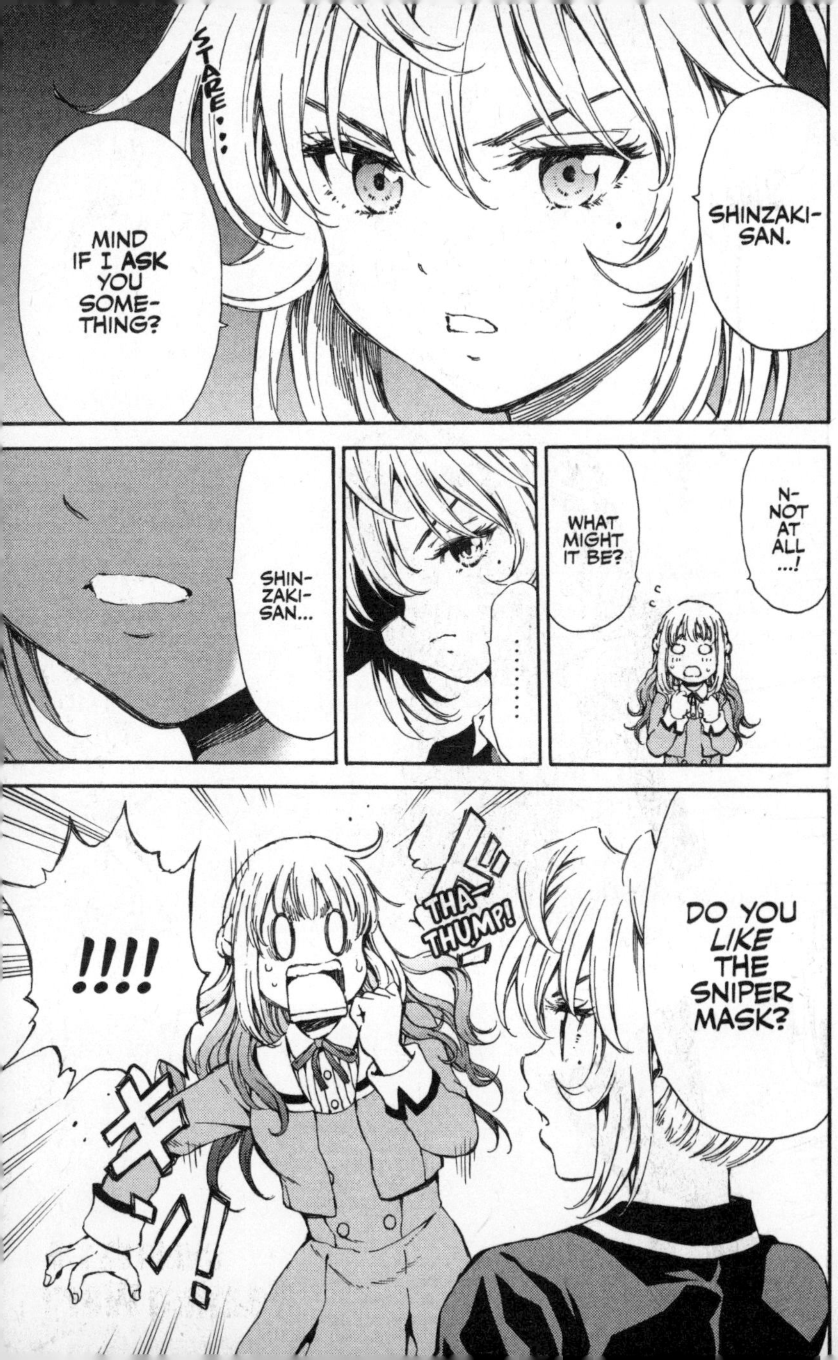
SHINZAKI-SAN.
STARE...
MIND IF I ASK YOU SOME-THING?
N-NOT AT ALL...!
WHAT MIGHT IT BE?
......
SHIN-ZAKI-SAN...
DO YOU *LIKE* THE SNIPER MASK?
THA-THUMP!
!!!!

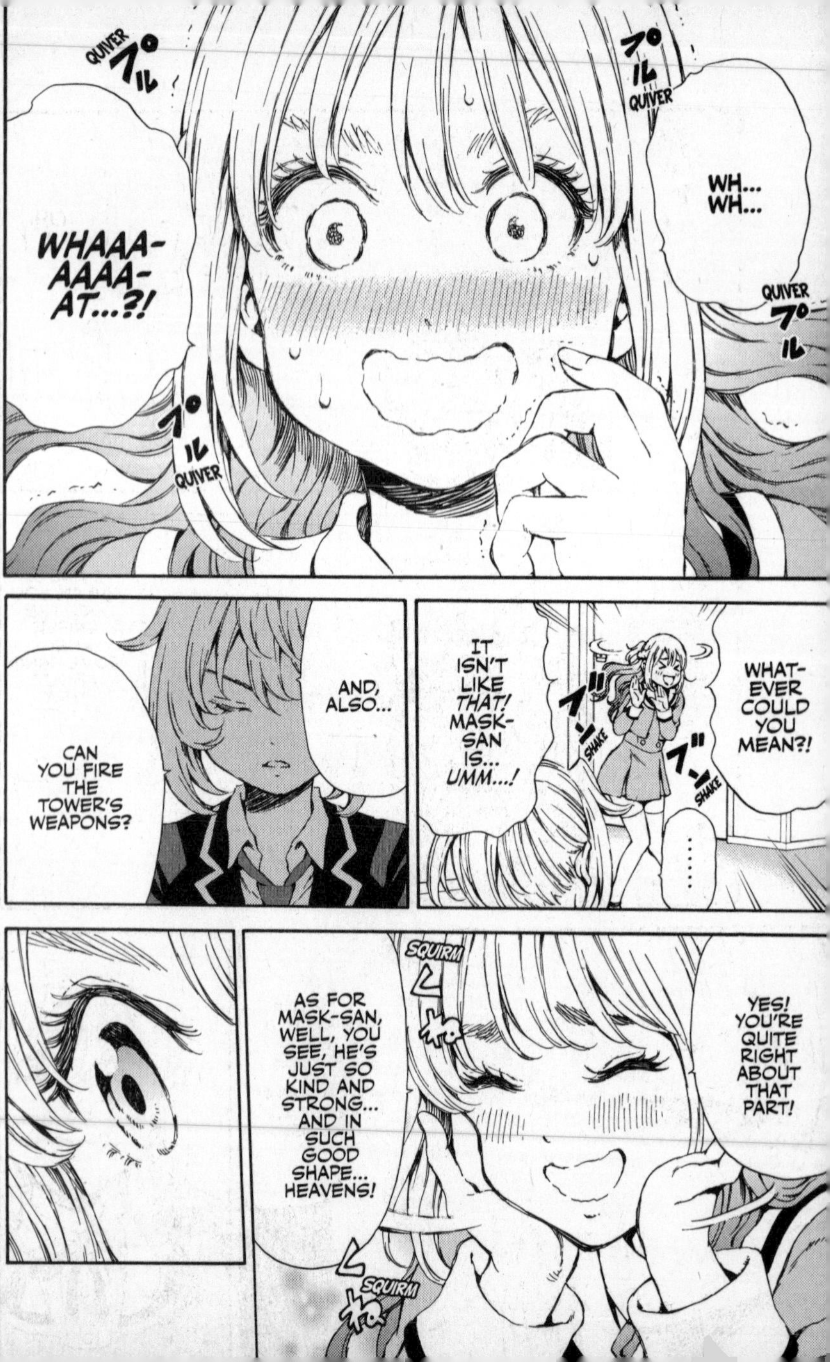
QUIVER
WH... WH...
QUIVER
QUIVER
WHAAAA-AAAA-AT...?!
QUIVER
WHAT-EVER COULD YOU MEAN?!
SHAKE
IT ISN'T LIKE *THAT!* MASK-SAN IS... *UMM...!*
SHAKE
......
AND, ALSO...
CAN YOU FIRE THE TOWER'S WEAPONS?
YES! YOU'RE QUITE RIGHT ABOUT THAT PART!
SQUIRM
AS FOR MASK-SAN, WELL, YOU SEE, HE'S JUST SO KIND AND STRONG... AND IN SUCH GOOD SHAPE... HEAVENS!
SQUIRM

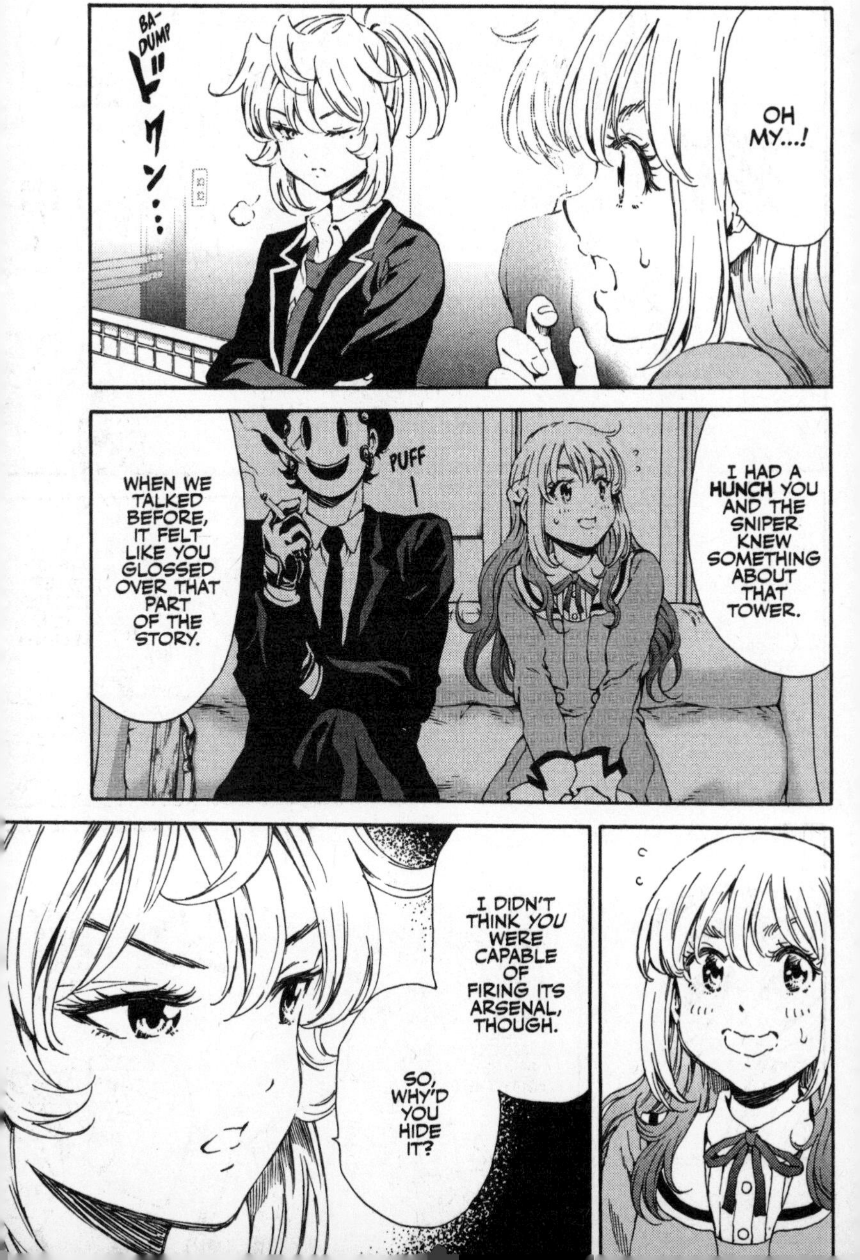
OH MY...!
BA-DUMP
ドクン…
I HAD A HUNCH YOU AND THE SNIPER KNEW SOMETHING ABOUT THAT TOWER.
PUFF
WHEN WE TALKED BEFORE, IT FELT LIKE YOU GLOSSED OVER THAT PART OF THE STORY.
I DIDN'T THINK YOU WERE CAPABLE OF FIRING ITS ARSENAL, THOUGH.
SO, WHY'D YOU HIDE IT?

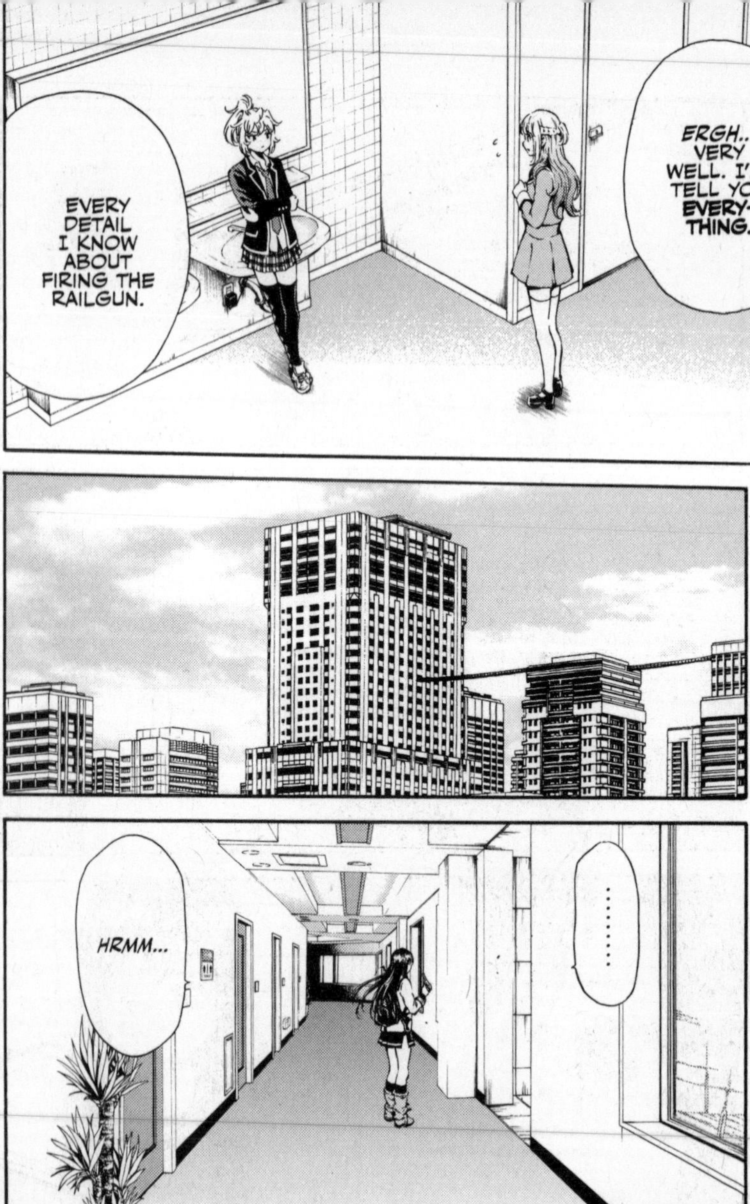
ERGH... VERY WELL. I'LL TELL YOU EVERYTHING.
EVERY DETAIL I KNOW ABOUT FIRING THE RAILGUN.
......
HRMM...

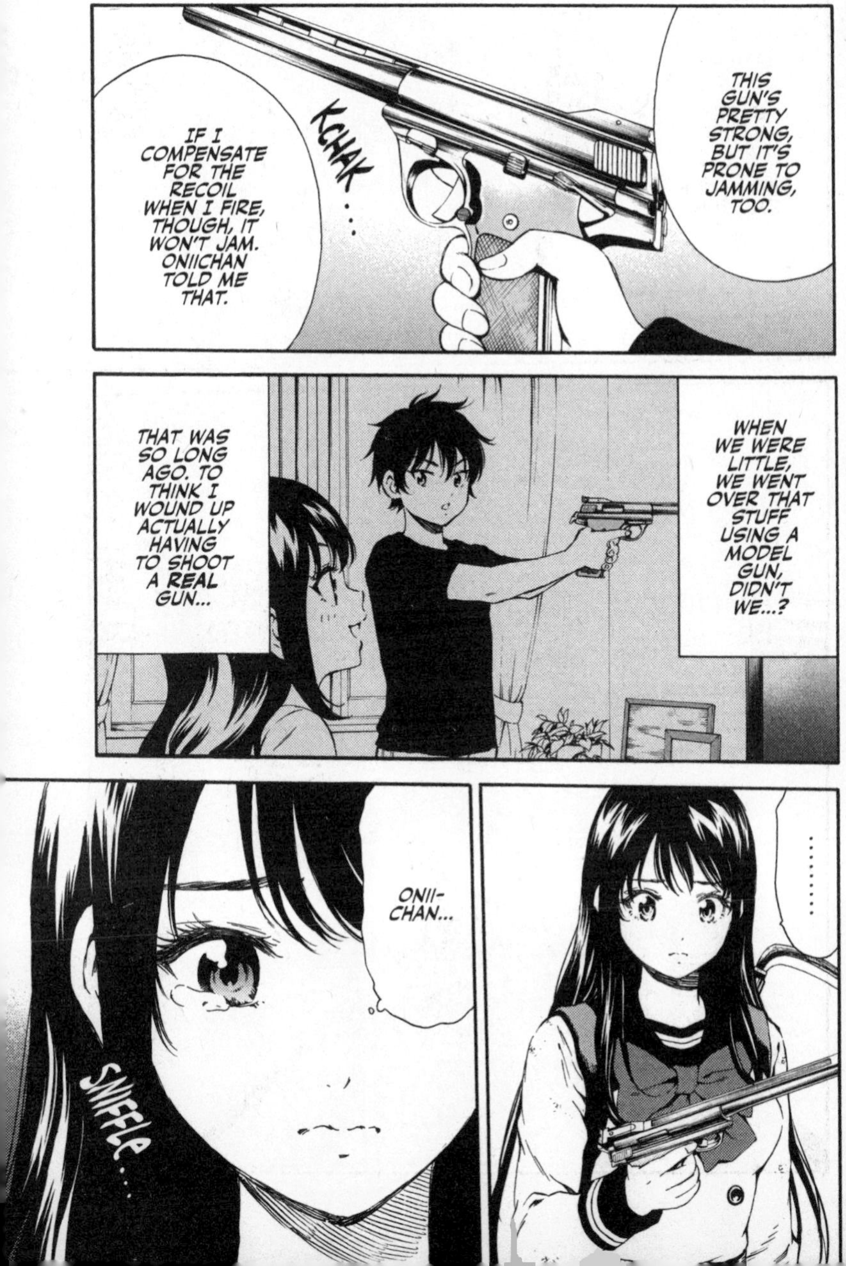
THIS GUN'S PRETTY STRONG, BUT IT'S PRONE TO JAMMING, TOO.
KCHAK...
IF I COMPENSATE FOR THE RECOIL WHEN I FIRE, THOUGH, IT WON'T JAM. ONIICHAN TOLD ME THAT.
WHEN WE WERE LITTLE, WE WENT OVER THAT STUFF USING A MODEL GUN, DIDN'T WE...?
THAT WAS SO LONG AGO. TO THINK I WOUND UP ACTUALLY HAVING TO SHOOT A **REAL** GUN...
....
ONII-CHAN...
SNIFFLE...

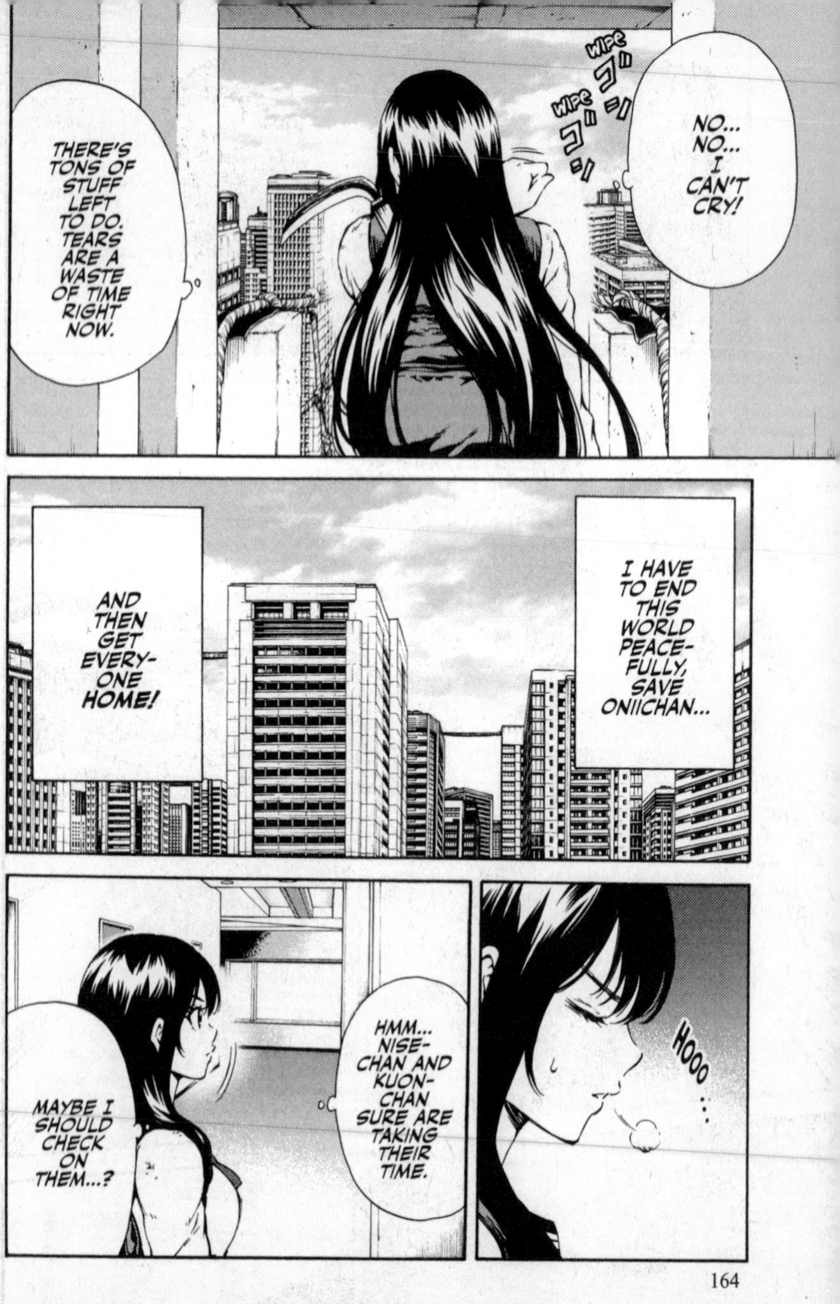
WIPE WIPE
NO... NO... I CAN'T CRY!
THERE'S TONS OF STUFF LEFT TO DO. TEARS ARE A WASTE OF TIME RIGHT NOW.
I HAVE TO END THIS WORLD PEACE-FULLY, SAVE ONIICHAN...
AND THEN GET EVERY-ONE HOME!
HOOO...
HMM... NISE-CHAN AND KUON-CHAN SURE ARE TAKING THEIR TIME.
MAYBE I SHOULD CHECK ON THEM...?

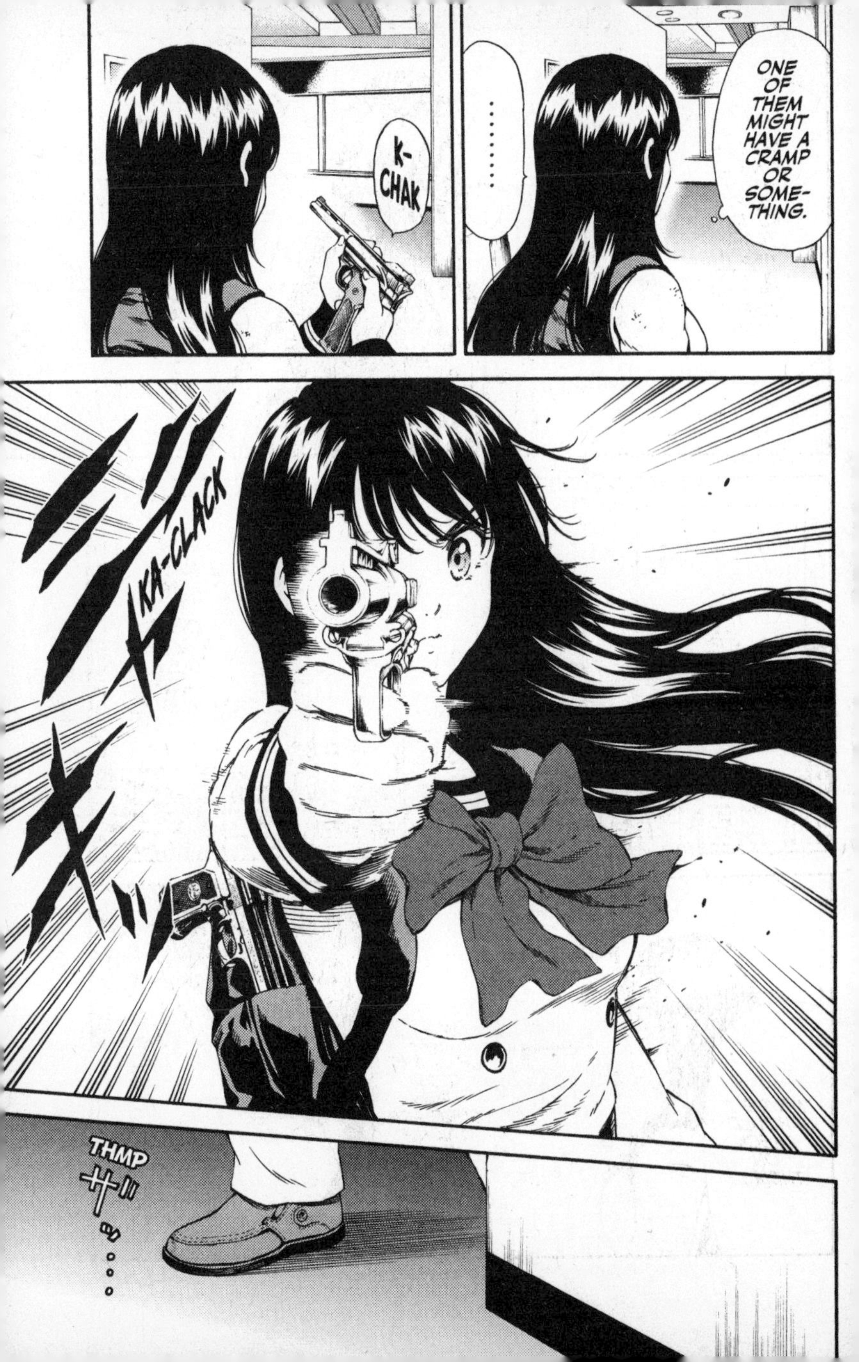
ONE OF THEM MIGHT HAVE A CRAMP OR SOME-THING.
......
K-CHAK
KA-CLACK
THMP

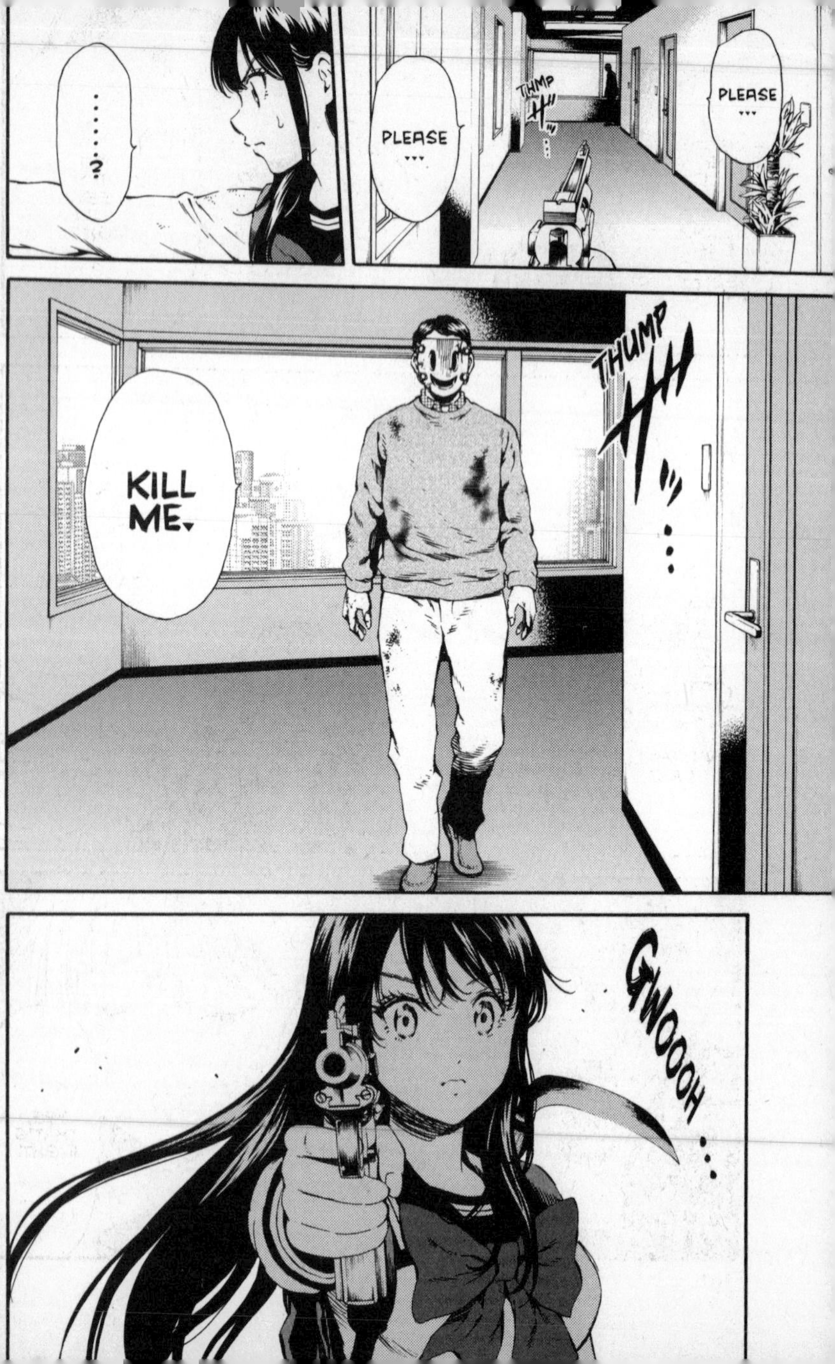
PLEASE ...
THUMP ...
PLEASE ...
......?
THUMP ...
KILL ME.
GWOOOH ...

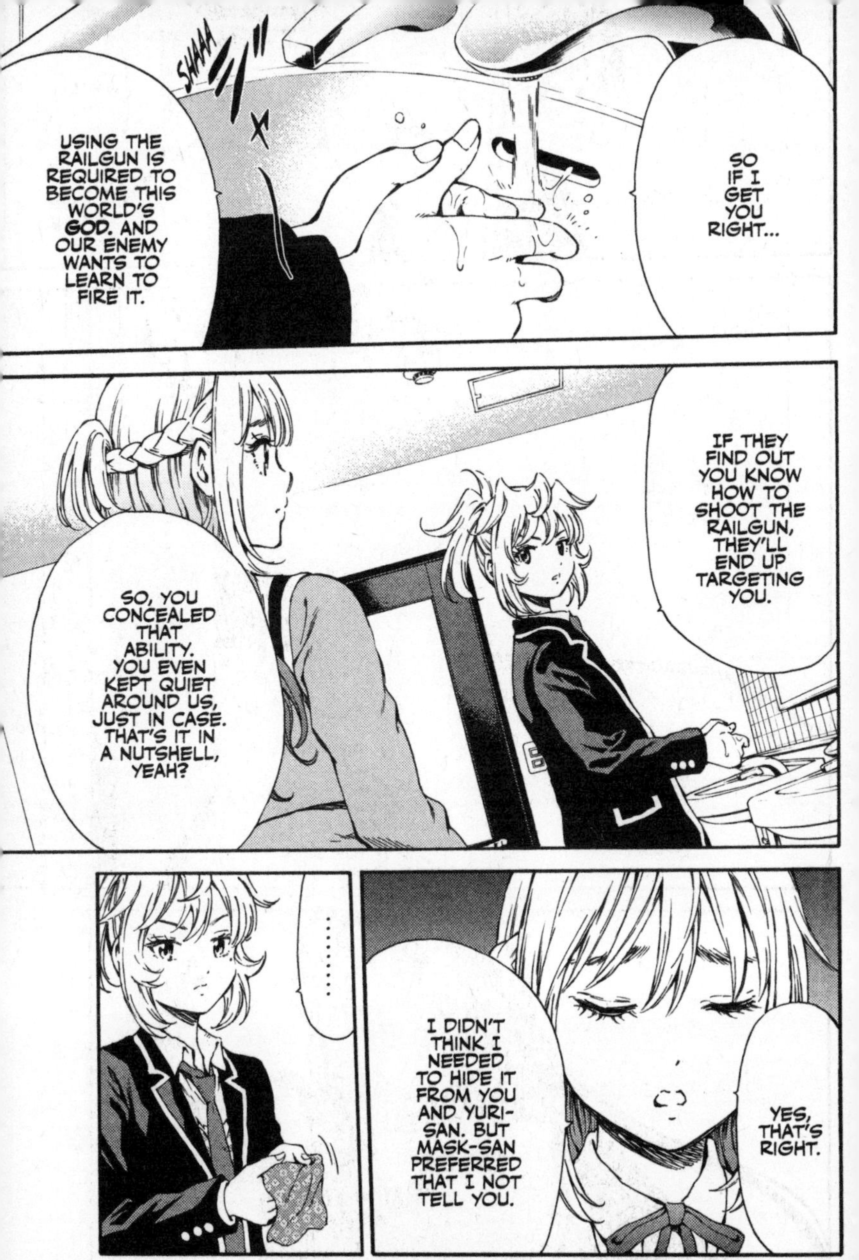
SO IF I GET YOU RIGHT...
SHAAA
USING THE RAILGUN IS REQUIRED TO BECOME THIS WORLD'S GOD. AND OUR ENEMY WANTS TO LEARN TO FIRE IT.
IF THEY FIND OUT YOU KNOW HOW TO SHOOT THE RAILGUN, THEY'LL END UP TARGETING YOU.
SO, YOU CONCEALED THAT ABILITY. YOU EVEN KEPT QUIET AROUND US, JUST IN CASE. THAT'S IT IN A NUTSHELL, YEAH?
YES, THAT'S RIGHT.
I DIDN'T THINK I NEEDED TO HIDE IT FROM YOU AND YURI-SAN. BUT MASK-SAN PREFERRED THAT I NOT TELL YOU.
......

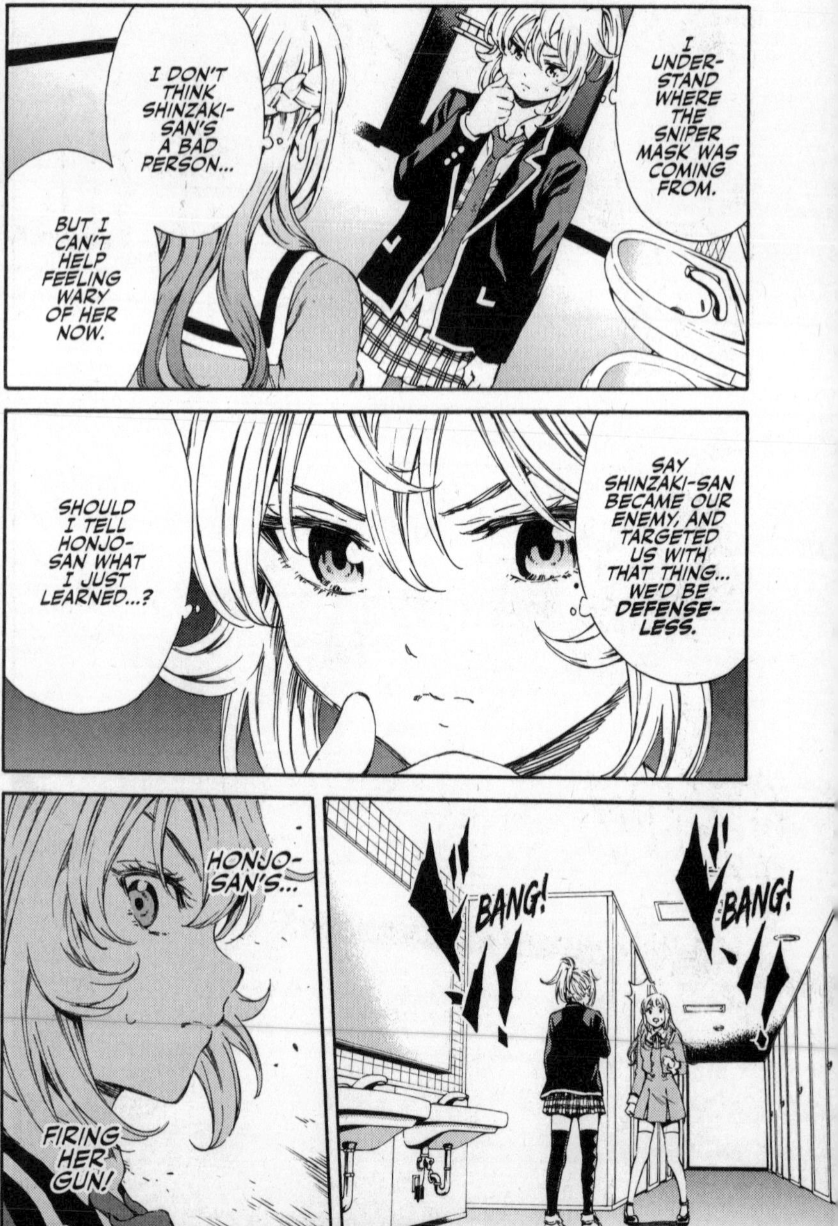
I UNDER-STAND WHERE THE SNIPER MASK WAS COMING FROM.
I DON'T THINK SHINZAKI-SAN'S A BAD PERSON...
BUT I CAN'T HELP FEELING WARY OF HER NOW.
SAY SHINZAKI-SAN BECAME OUR ENEMY, AND TARGETED US WITH THAT THING... WE'D BE **DEFENSE-LESS.**
SHOULD I TELL HONJO-SAN WHAT I JUST LEARNED...?
BANG!
BANG!
HONJO-SAN'S...
FIRING HER GUN!

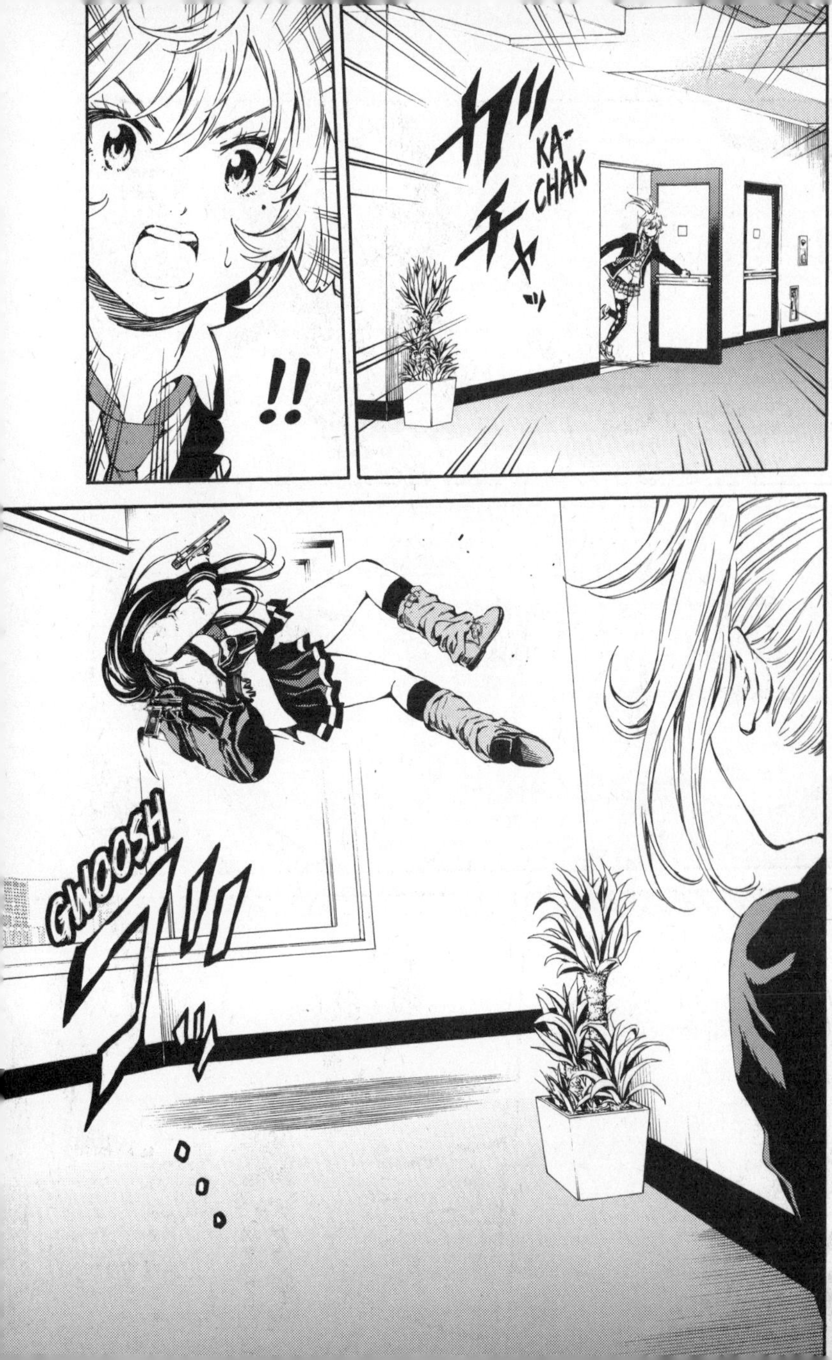
カチャッ
KA-CHAK
!!
GWOOSH

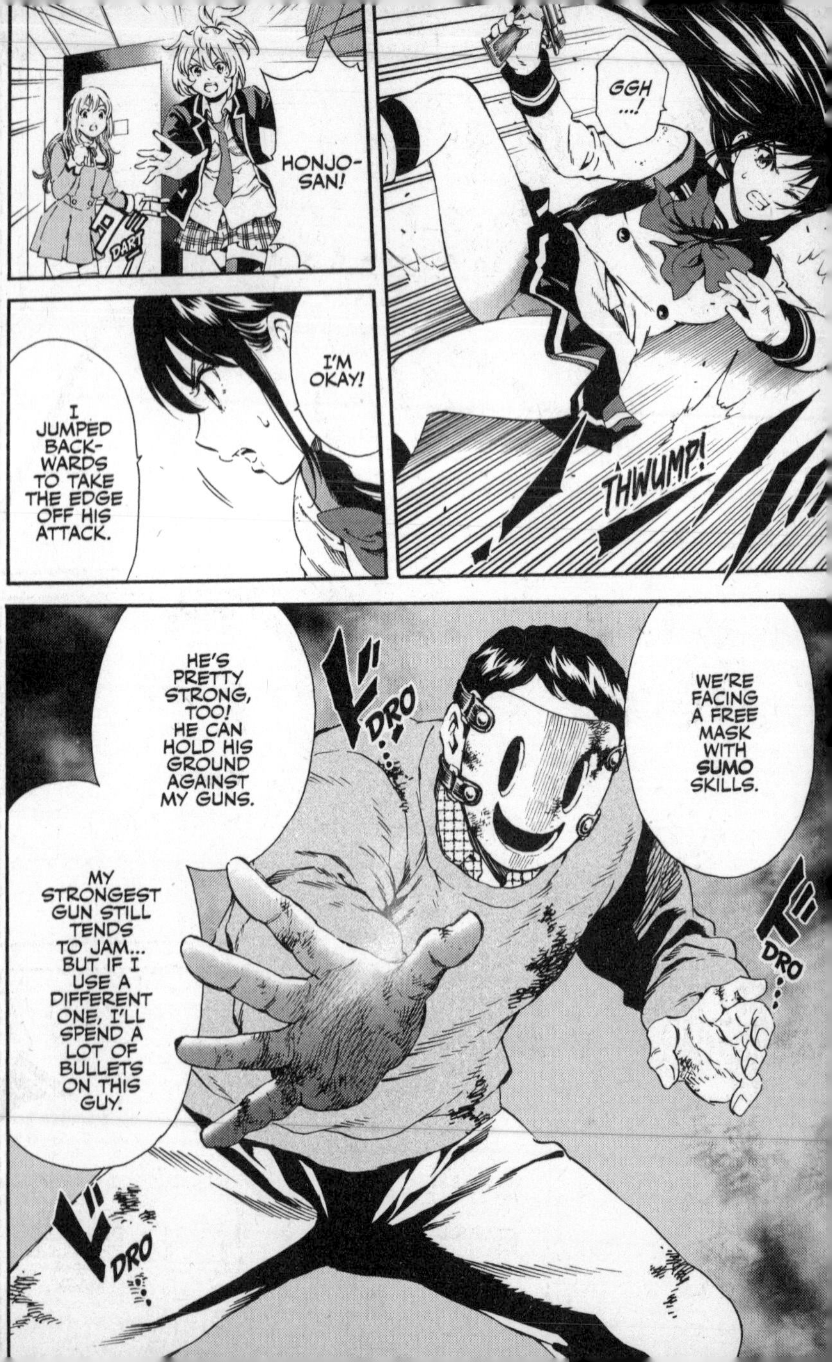
GGH ...!
THWUMP!
HONJO-SAN!
DART
I'M OKAY!
I JUMPED BACKWARDS TO TAKE THE EDGE OFF HIS ATTACK.
WE'RE FACING A FREE MASK WITH SUMO SKILLS.
DRO...
HE'S PRETTY STRONG, TOO! HE CAN HOLD HIS GROUND AGAINST MY GUNS.
DRO...
MY STRONGEST GUN STILL TENDS TO JAM... BUT IF I USE A DIFFERENT ONE, I'LL SPEND A LOT OF BULLETS ON THIS GUY.
DRO...

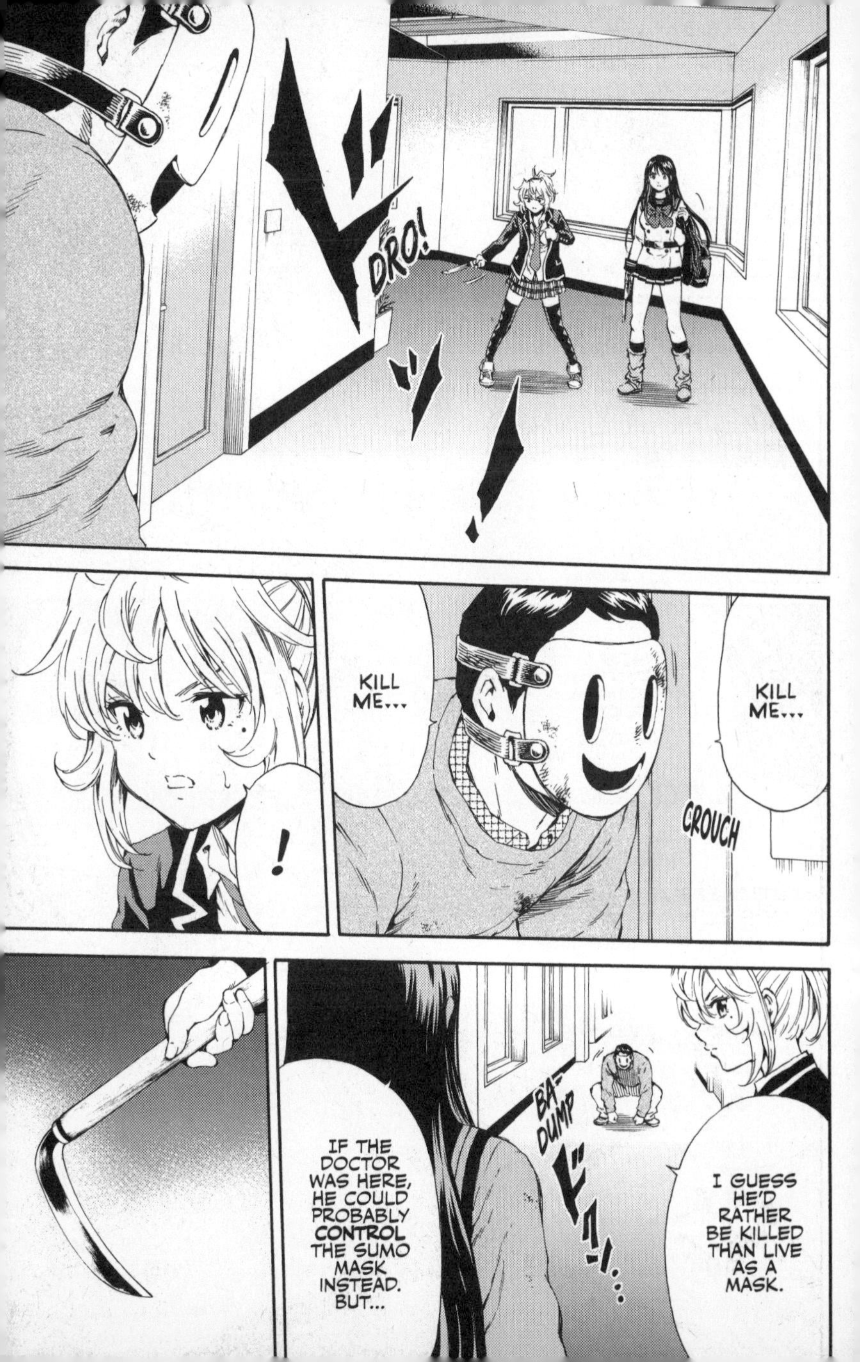
DRO!
KILL ME...
CROUCH
KILL ME...
!
I GUESS HE'D RATHER BE KILLED THAN LIVE AS A MASK.
BA-DUMP
IF THE DOCTOR WAS HERE, HE COULD PROBABLY **CONTROL** THE SUMO MASK INSTEAD. BUT...

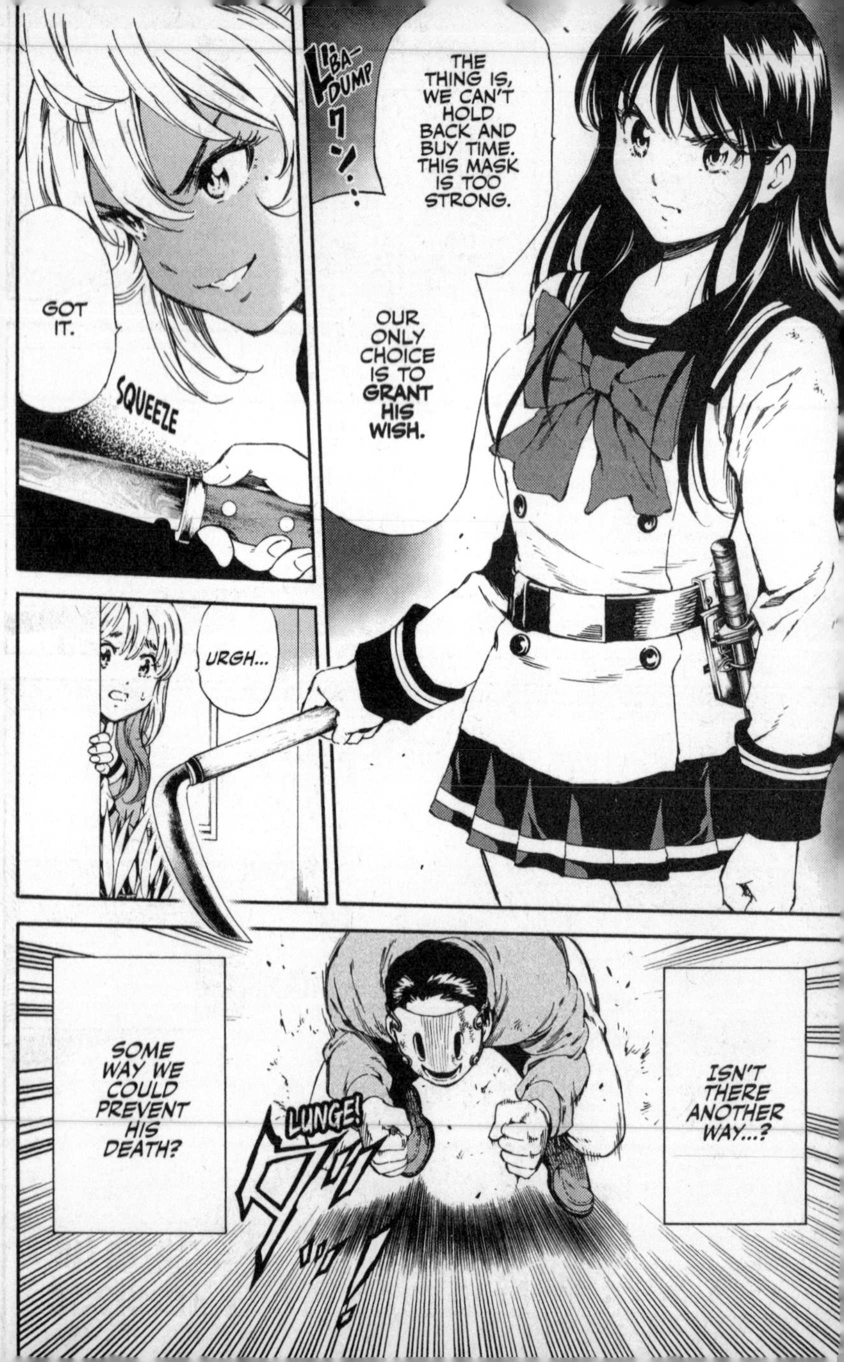
THE THING IS, WE CAN'T HOLD BACK AND BUY TIME. THIS MASK IS TOO STRONG.
OUR ONLY CHOICE IS TO GRANT HIS WISH.
BA-DUMP
GOT IT.
SQUEEZE
URGH...
ISN'T THERE ANOTHER WAY...?
SOME WAY WE COULD PREVENT HIS DEATH?
LUNGE!

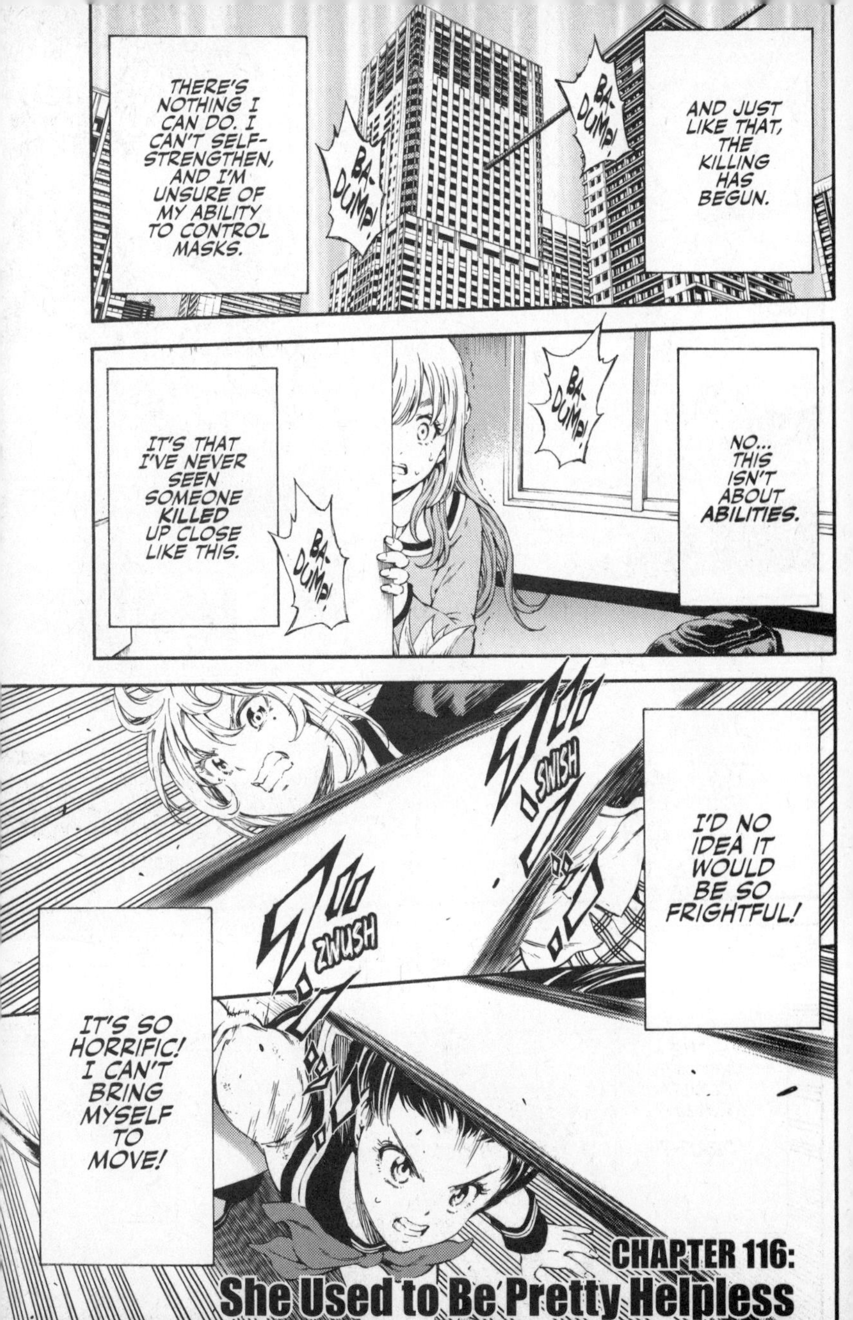
AND JUST LIKE THAT, THE KILLING HAS BEGUN.
BA-DUMP!
BA-DUMP!
THERE'S NOTHING I CAN DO. I CAN'T SELF-STRENGTHEN, AND I'M UNSURE OF MY ABILITY TO CONTROL MASKS.
NO... THIS ISN'T ABOUT ABILITIES.
BA-DUMP!
BA-DUMP!
IT'S THAT I'VE NEVER SEEN SOMEONE KILLED UP CLOSE LIKE THIS.
SWISH
I'D NO IDEA IT WOULD BE SO FRIGHTFUL!
ZWUSH
IT'S SO HORRIFIC! I CAN'T BRING MYSELF TO MOVE!
CHAPTER 116:
She Used to Be Pretty Helpless

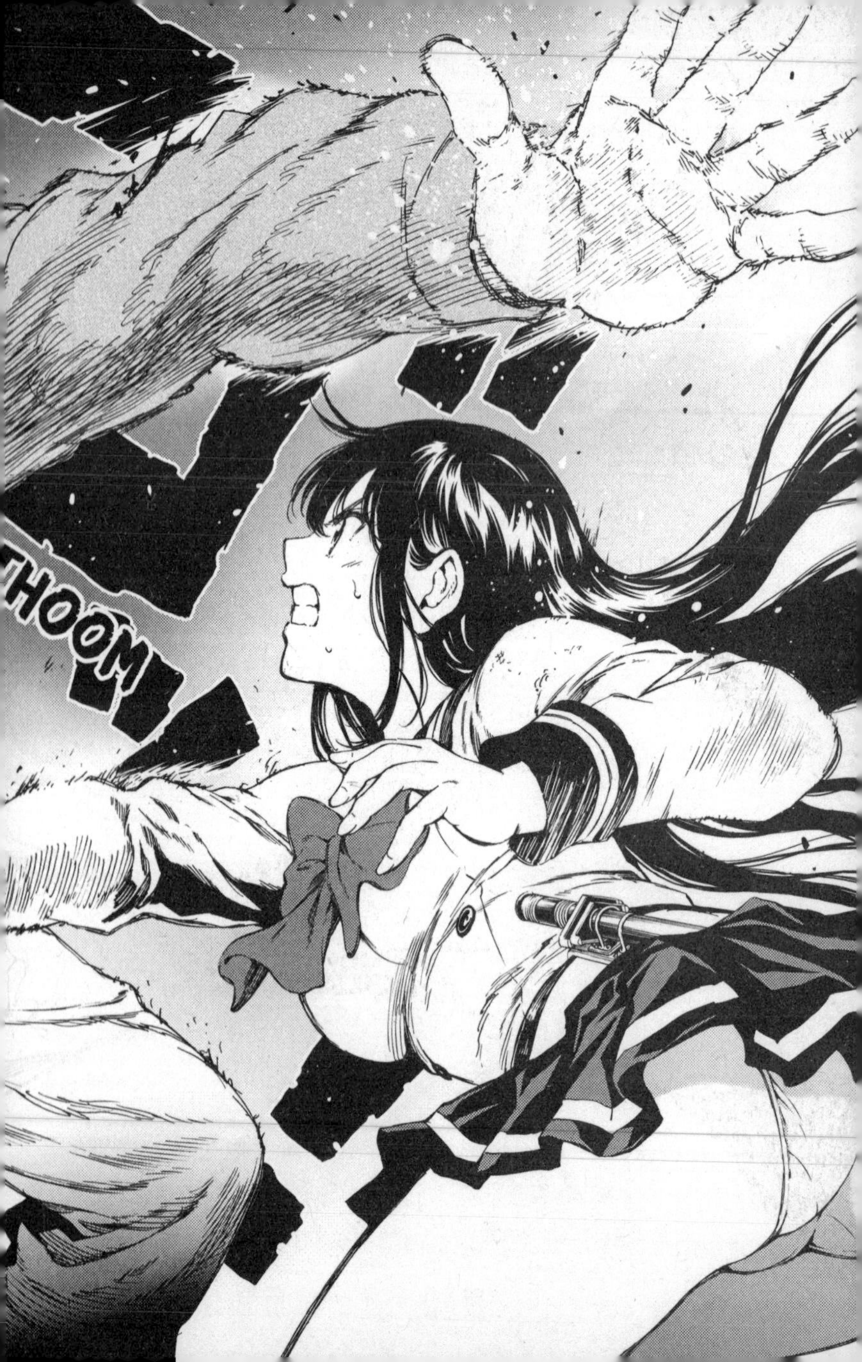
THOOM

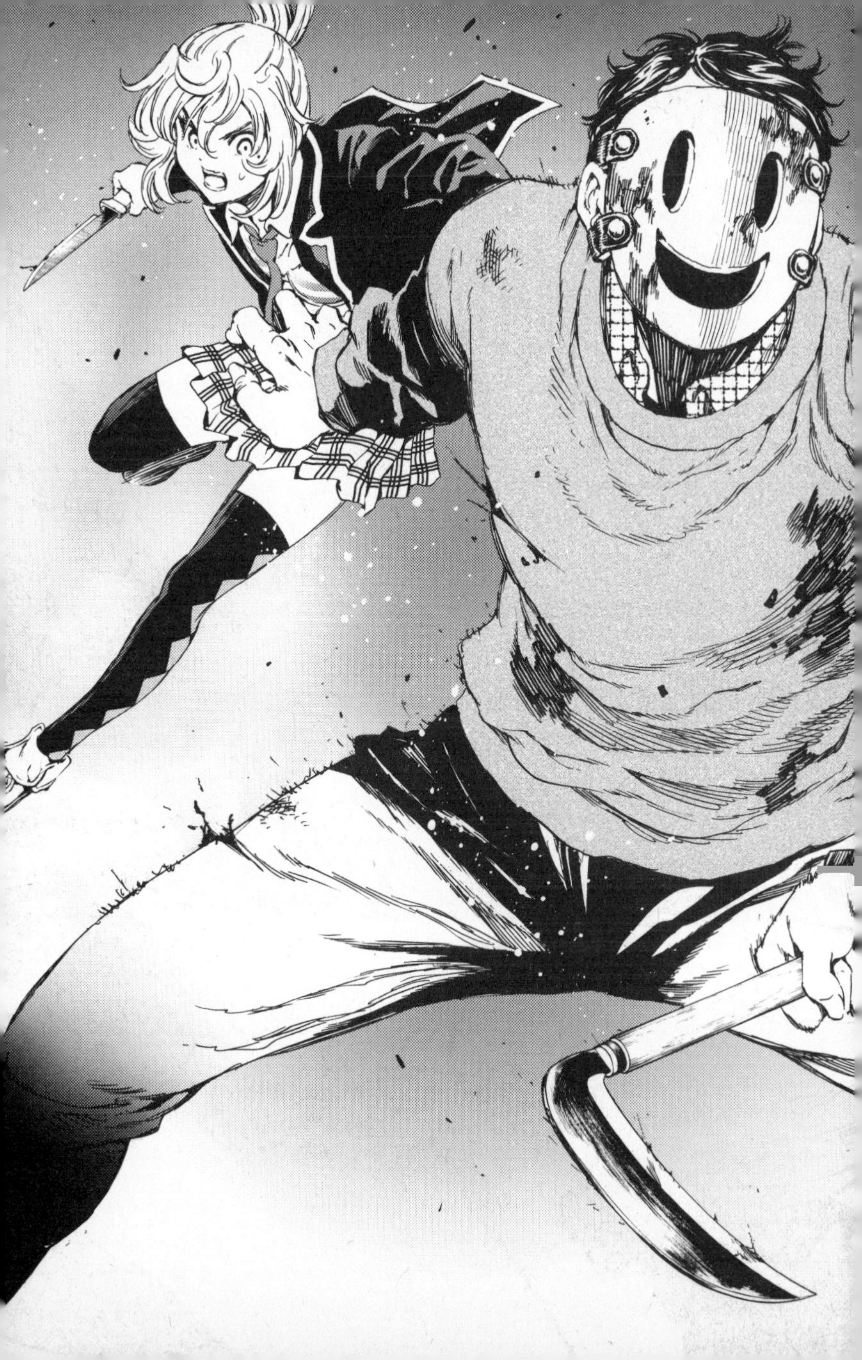

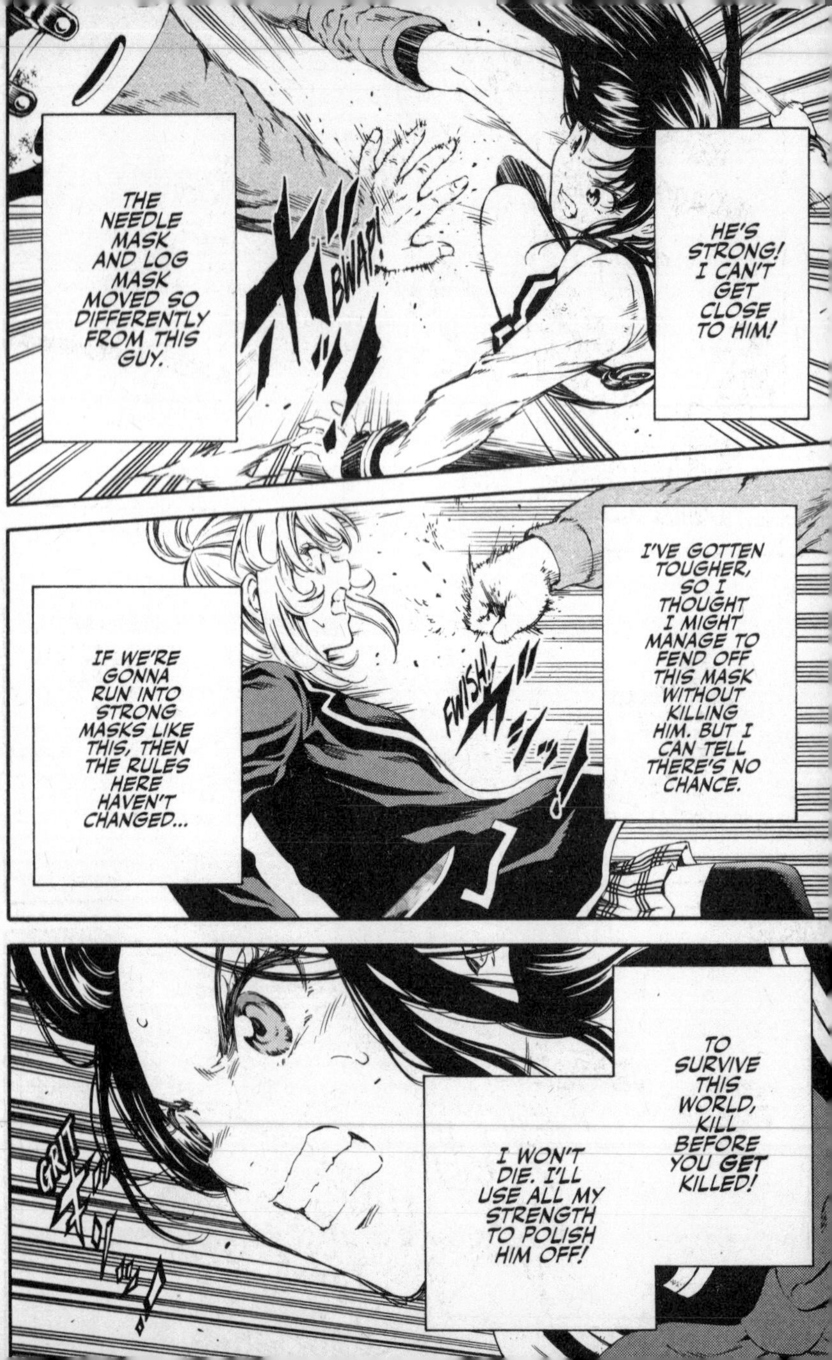
HE'S STRONG! I CAN'T GET CLOSE TO HIM!
BWAP!
THE NEEDLE MASK AND LOG MASK MOVED SO DIFFERENTLY FROM THIS GUY.
I'VE GOTTEN TOUGHER, SO I THOUGHT I MIGHT MANAGE TO FEND OFF THIS MASK WITHOUT KILLING HIM. BUT I CAN TELL THERE'S NO CHANCE.
FWISH
IF WE'RE GONNA RUN INTO STRONG MASKS LIKE THIS, THEN THE RULES HERE HAVEN'T CHANGED...
TO SURVIVE THIS WORLD, KILL BEFORE YOU GET KILLED!
I WON'T DIE. I'LL USE ALL MY STRENGTH TO POLISH HIM OFF!
GRIT

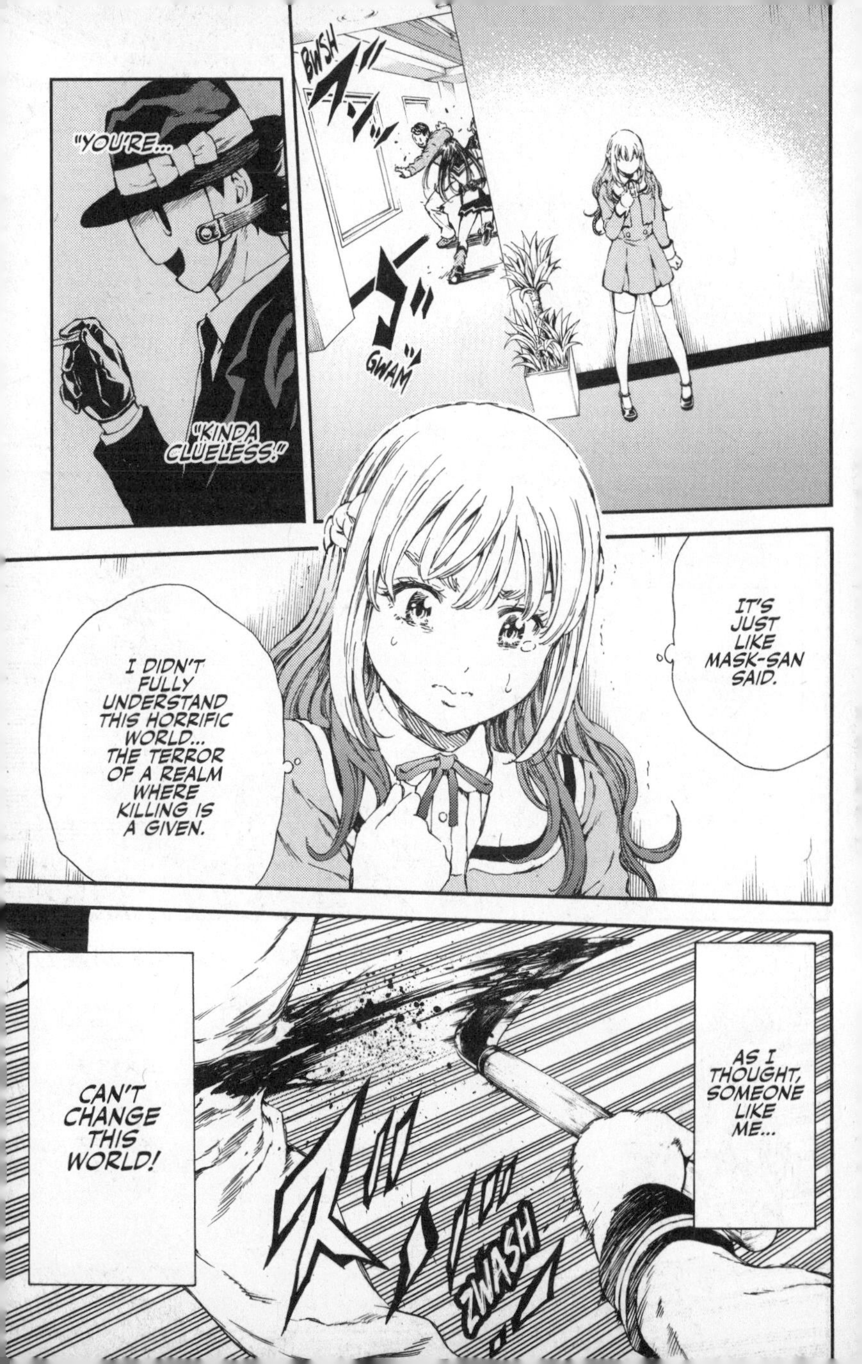
BWSH
GWAM
"YOU'RE...
"KINDA CLUELESS."
IT'S JUST LIKE MASK-SAN SAID.
I DIDN'T FULLY UNDERSTAND THIS HORRIFIC WORLD... THE TERROR OF A REALM WHERE KILLING IS A GIVEN.
AS I THOUGHT, SOMEONE LIKE ME...
CAN'T CHANGE THIS WORLD!
ZWASH

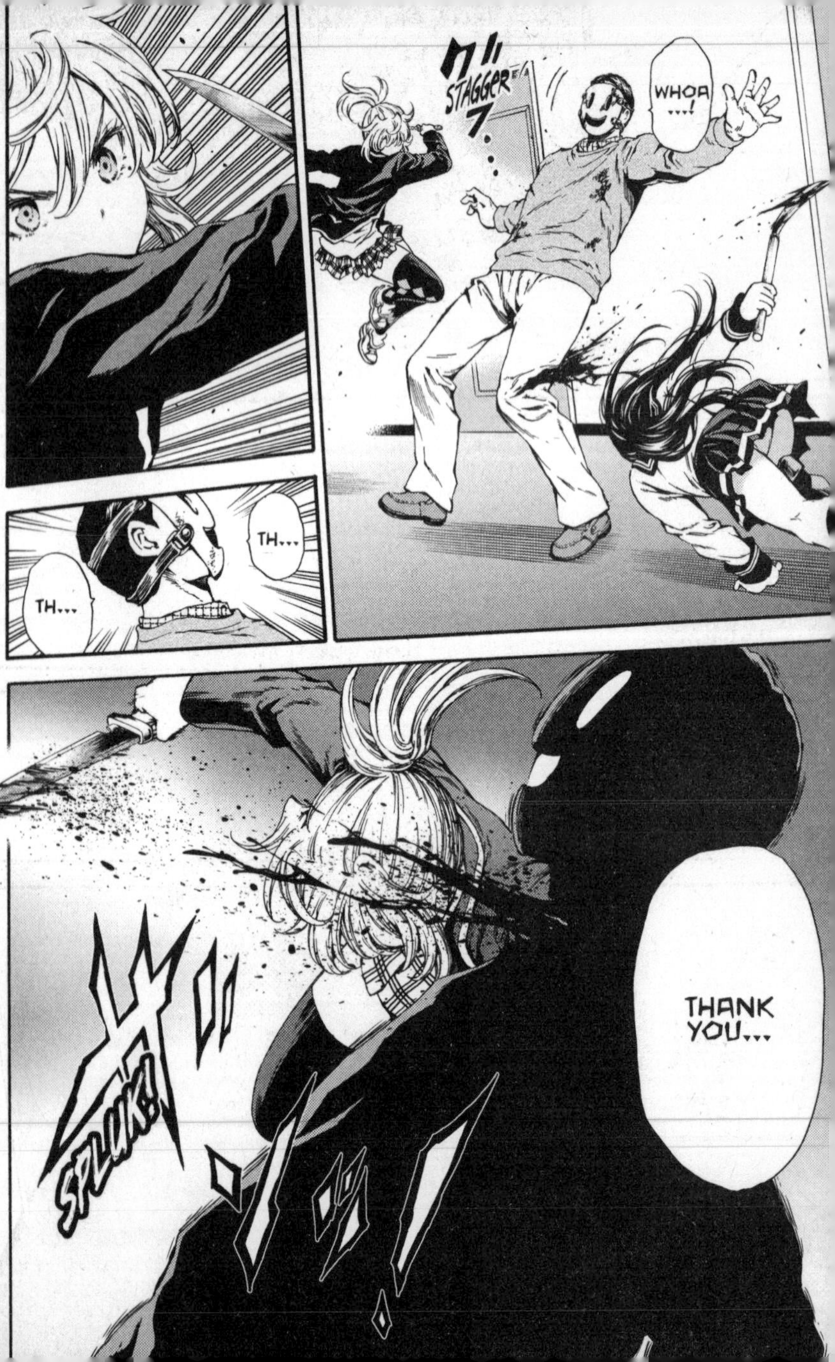
WHOA ...!
STAGGER
TH...
TH...
THANK YOU...
SPLUK!

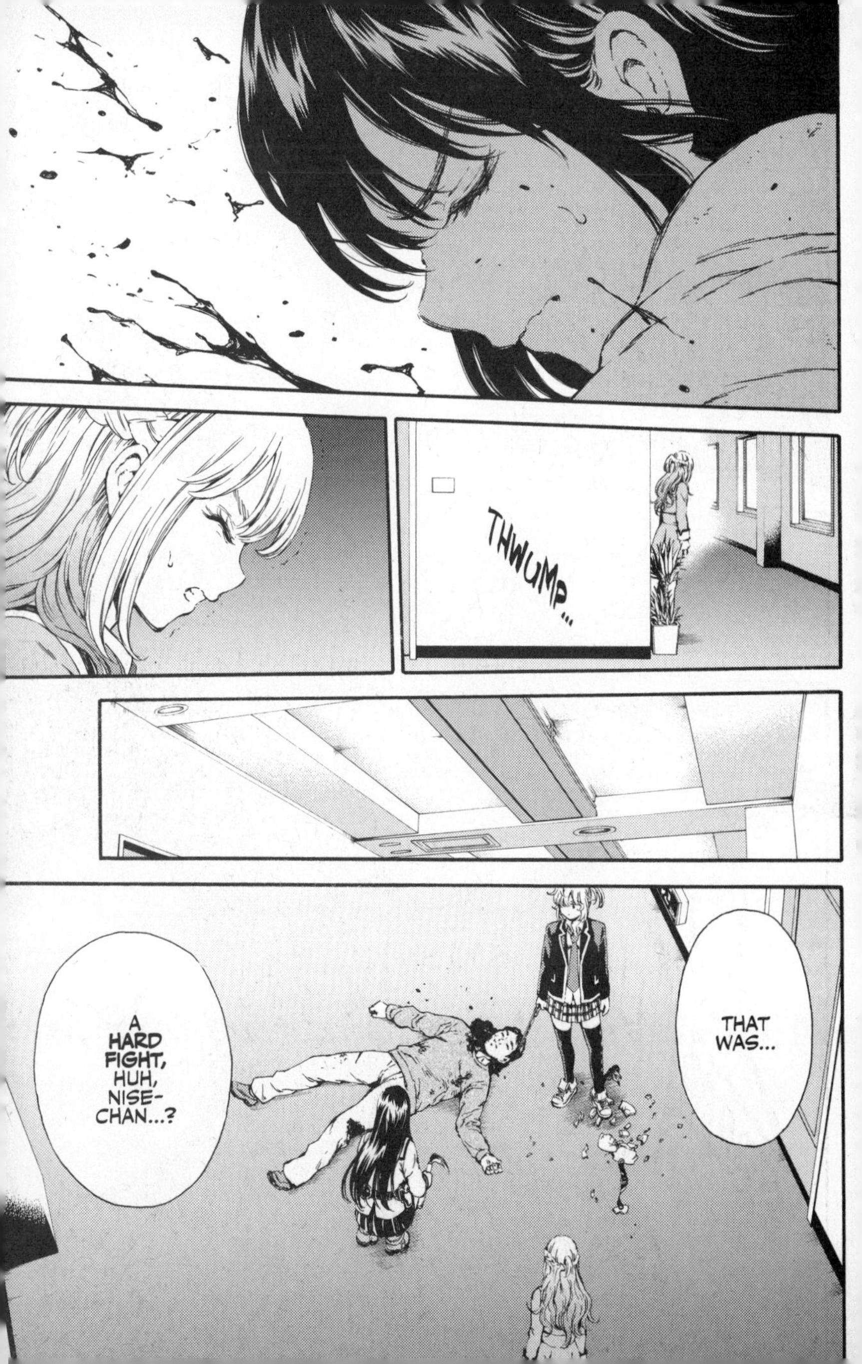
THWUMP...
THAT WAS...
A HARD FIGHT, HUH, NISE-CHAN...?

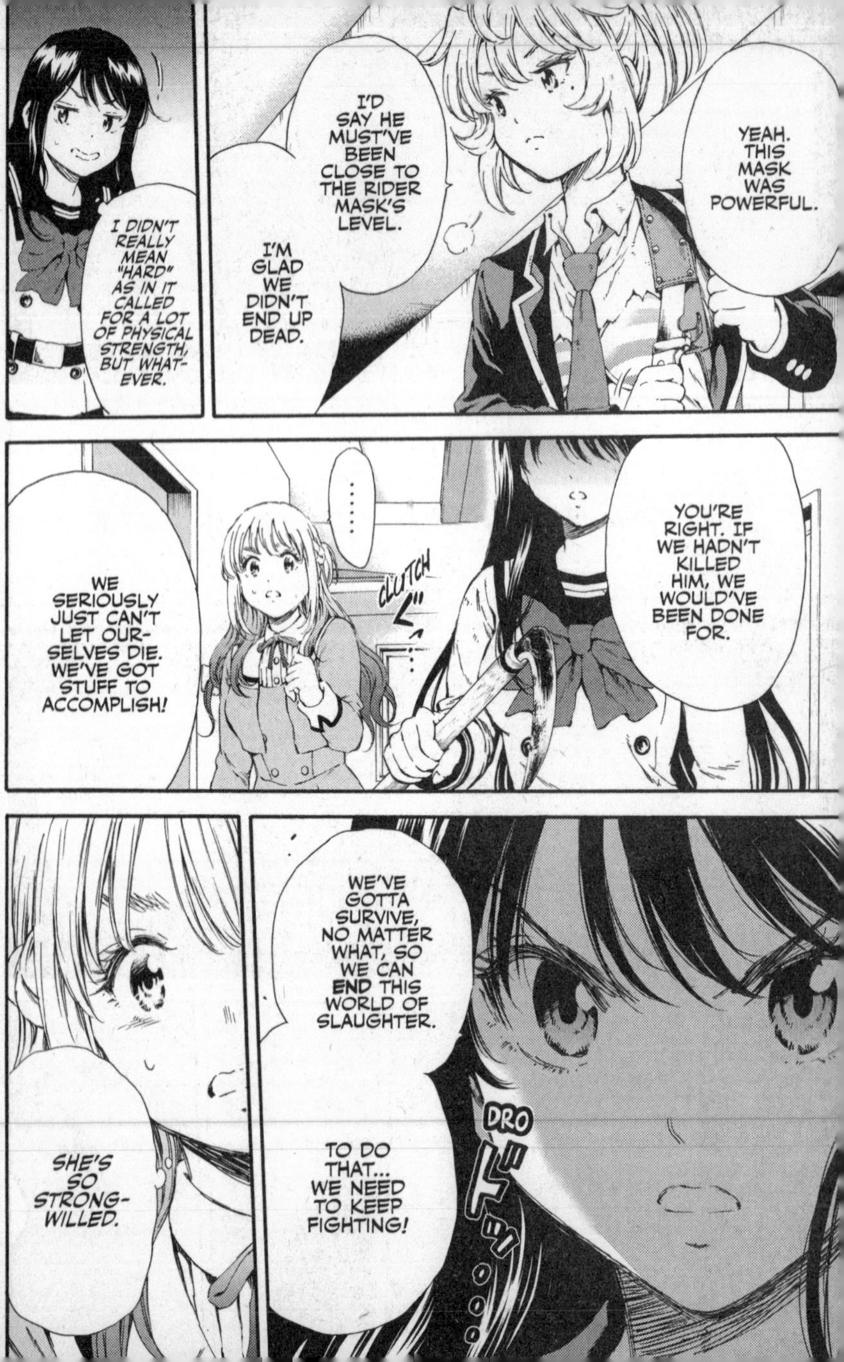
YEAH. THIS MASK WAS POWERFUL.
I'D SAY HE MUST'VE BEEN CLOSE TO THE RIDER MASK'S LEVEL.
I'M GLAD WE DIDN'T END UP DEAD.
I DIDN'T REALLY MEAN "HARD" AS IN IT CALLED FOR A LOT OF PHYSICAL STRENGTH, BUT WHATEVER.
YOU'RE RIGHT. IF WE HADN'T KILLED HIM, WE WOULD'VE BEEN DONE FOR.
CLUTCH
......
WE SERIOUSLY JUST CAN'T LET OURSELVES DIE. WE'VE GOT STUFF TO ACCOMPLISH!
WE'VE GOTTA SURVIVE, NO MATTER WHAT, SO WE CAN END THIS WORLD OF SLAUGHTER.
DRO
TO DO THAT... WE NEED TO KEEP FIGHTING!
SHE'S SO STRONG-WILLED.

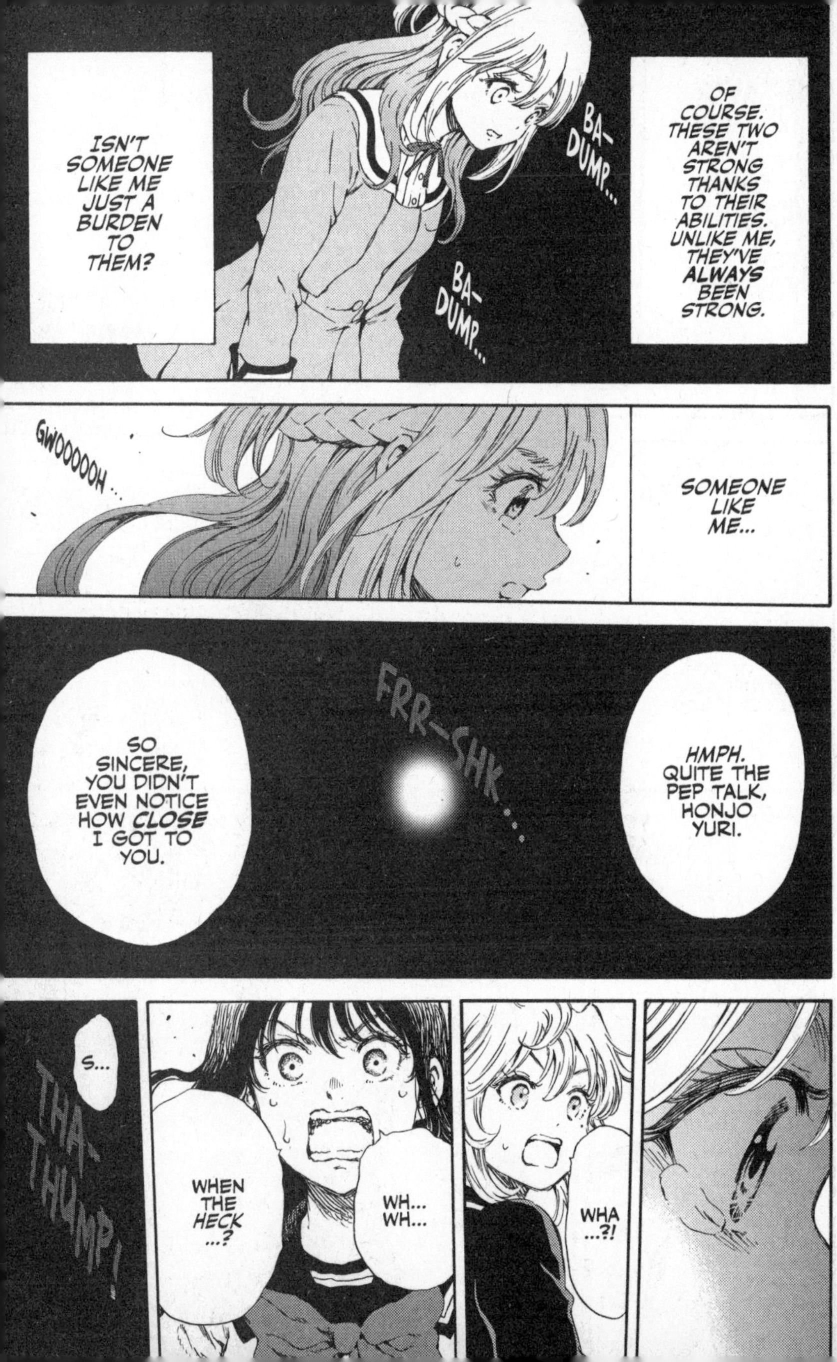
OF COURSE. THESE TWO AREN'T STRONG THANKS TO THEIR ABILITIES. UNLIKE ME, THEY'VE **ALWAYS** BEEN STRONG.
BA-DUMP...
BA-DUMP...
ISN'T SOMEONE LIKE ME JUST A BURDEN TO THEM?
SOMEONE LIKE ME...
GWOOOOOH...
HMPH. QUITE THE PEP TALK, HONJO YURI.
FRR-SHK...
SO SINCERE, YOU DIDN'T EVEN NOTICE HOW ***CLOSE*** I GOT TO YOU.
WHA...?!
WH... WH...
WHEN THE *HECK*...?
S...
THA-THUMP!

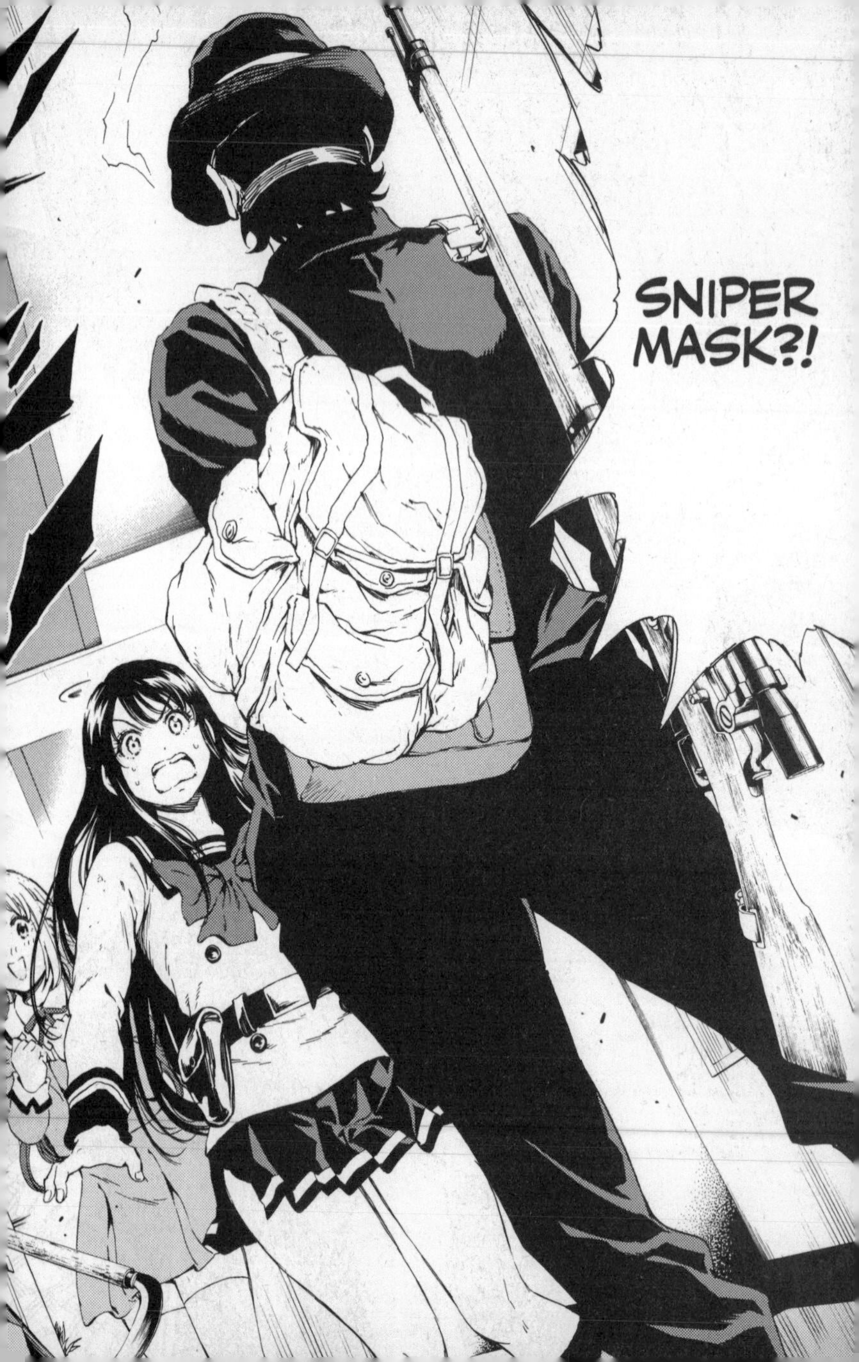
SNIPER MASK?!

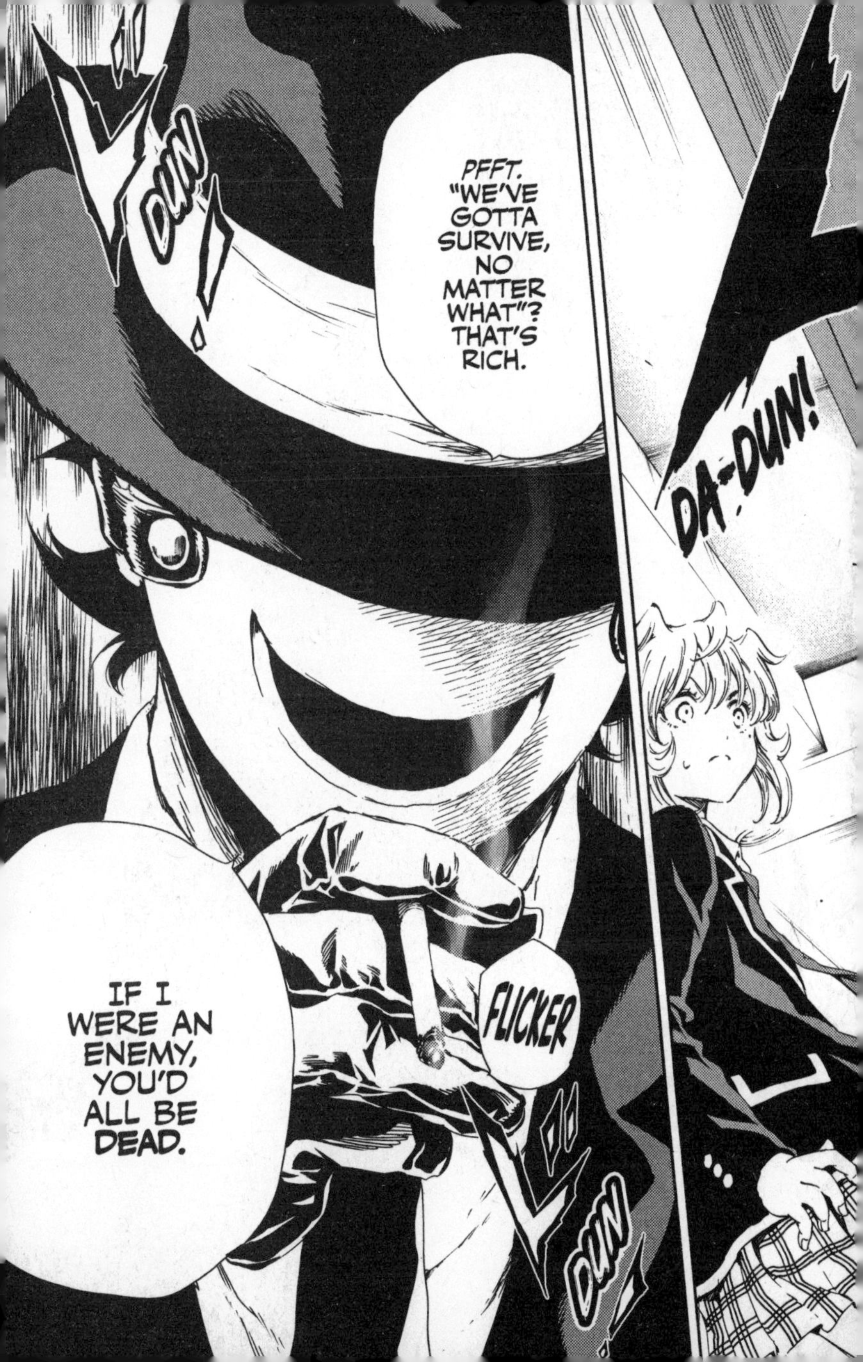
DA-DUN!
...
PFFT. "WE'VE GOTTA SURVIVE, NO MATTER WHAT"? THAT'S RICH.
DUN
FLICKER
IF I WERE AN ENEMY, YOU'D ALL BE DEAD.
DUN

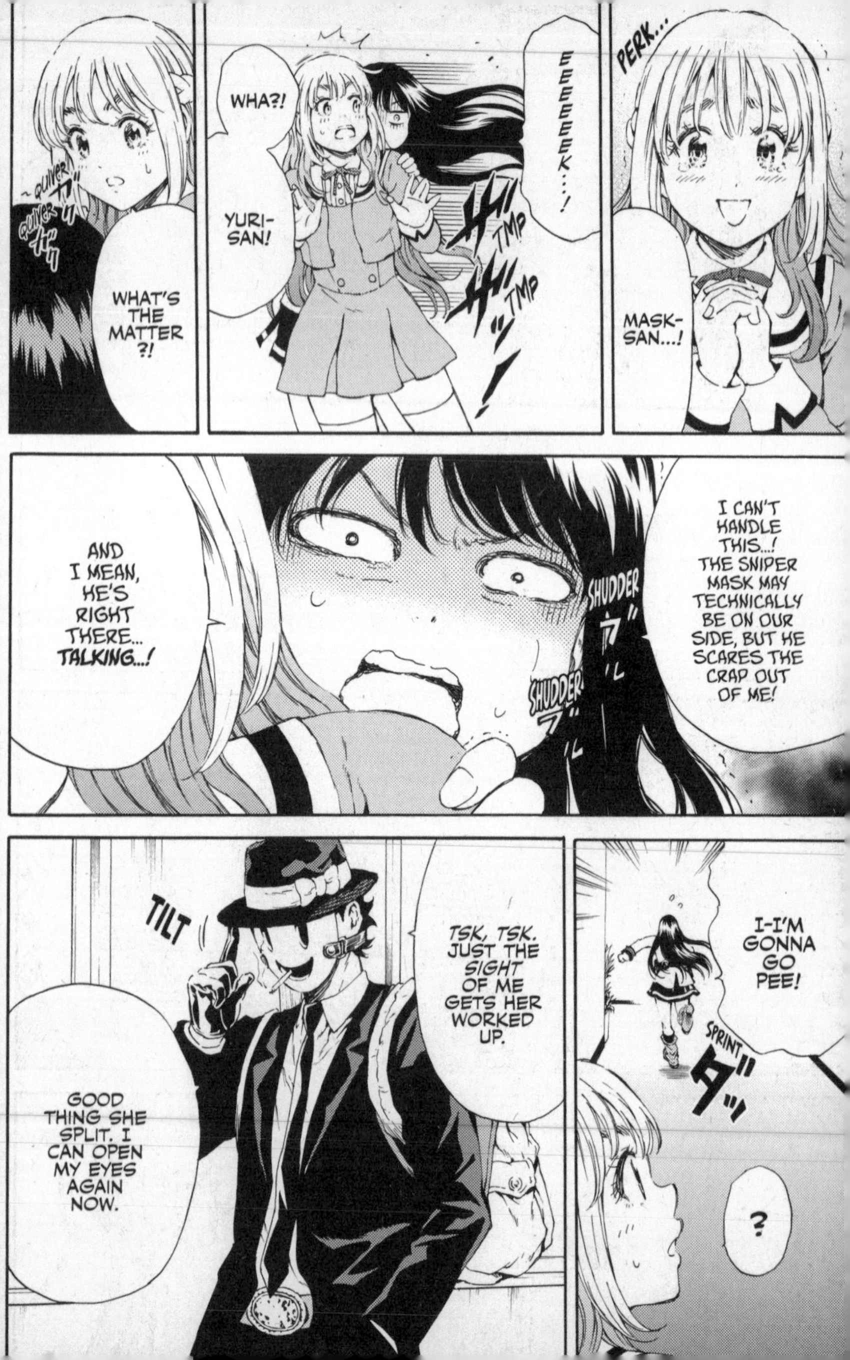
PERK...
MASK-SAN...!
EEEEEEK...!
TMP
TMP
WHA?!
YURI-SAN!
QUIVER
QUIVER
WHAT'S THE MATTER?!
I CAN'T HANDLE THIS...! THE SNIPER MASK MAY TECHNICALLY BE ON OUR SIDE, BUT HE SCARES THE CRAP OUT OF ME!
SHUDDER
SHUDDER
AND I MEAN, HE'S RIGHT THERE... TALKING...!
I-I'M GONNA GO PEE!
SPRINT
?
TSK, TSK. JUST THE SIGHT OF ME GETS HER WORKED UP.
TILT
GOOD THING SHE SPLIT. I CAN OPEN MY EYES AGAIN NOW.

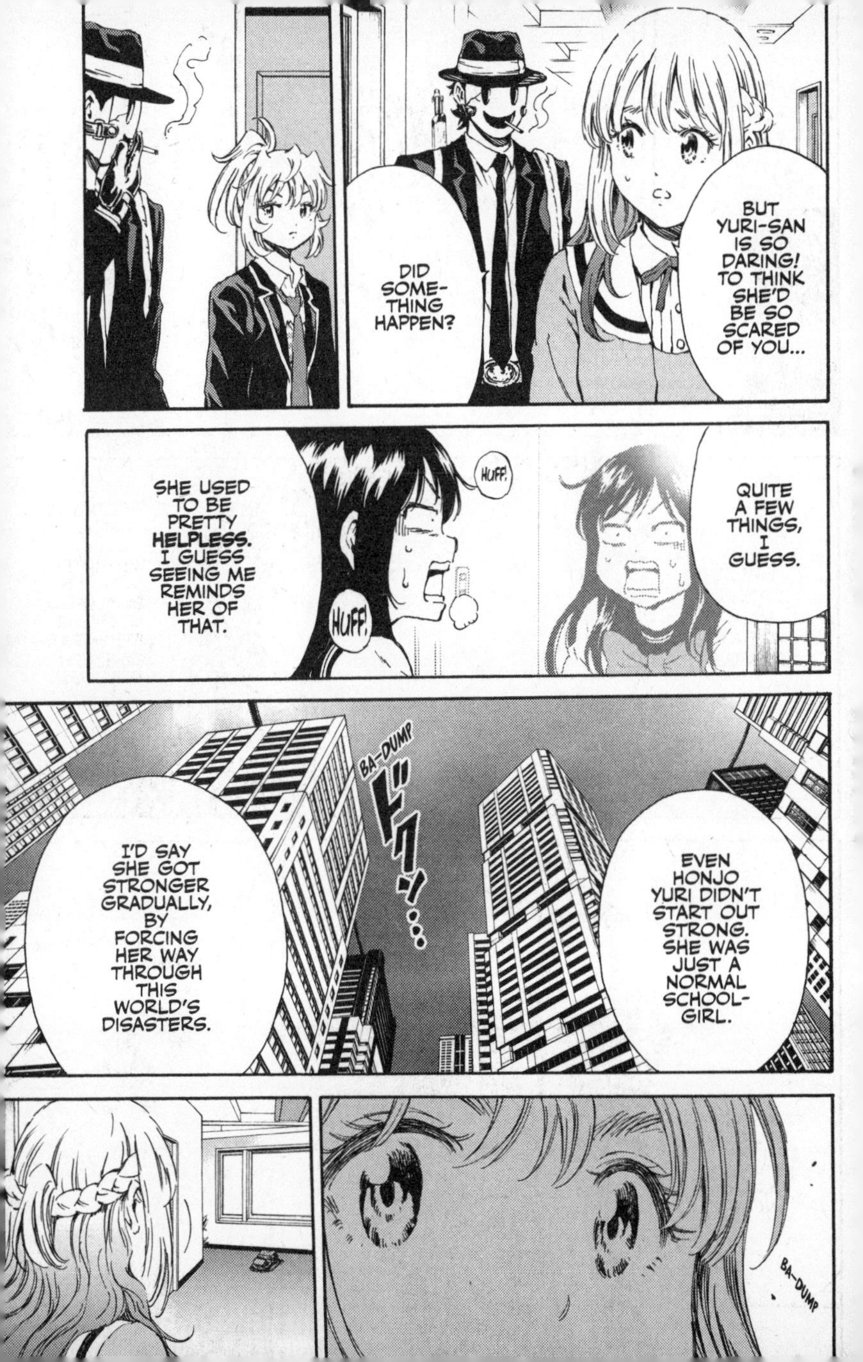
BUT YURI-SAN IS SO DARING! TO THINK SHE'D BE SO SCARED OF YOU...
DID SOMETHING HAPPEN?
QUITE A FEW THINGS, I GUESS.
HUFF!
SHE USED TO BE PRETTY **HELPLESS.** I GUESS SEEING ME REMINDS HER OF THAT.
HUFF!
EVEN HONJO YURI DIDN'T START OUT STRONG. SHE WAS JUST A NORMAL SCHOOLGIRL.
BA-DUMP
I'D SAY SHE GOT STRONGER GRADUALLY, BY FORCING HER WAY THROUGH THIS WORLD'S DISASTERS.
BA-DUMP

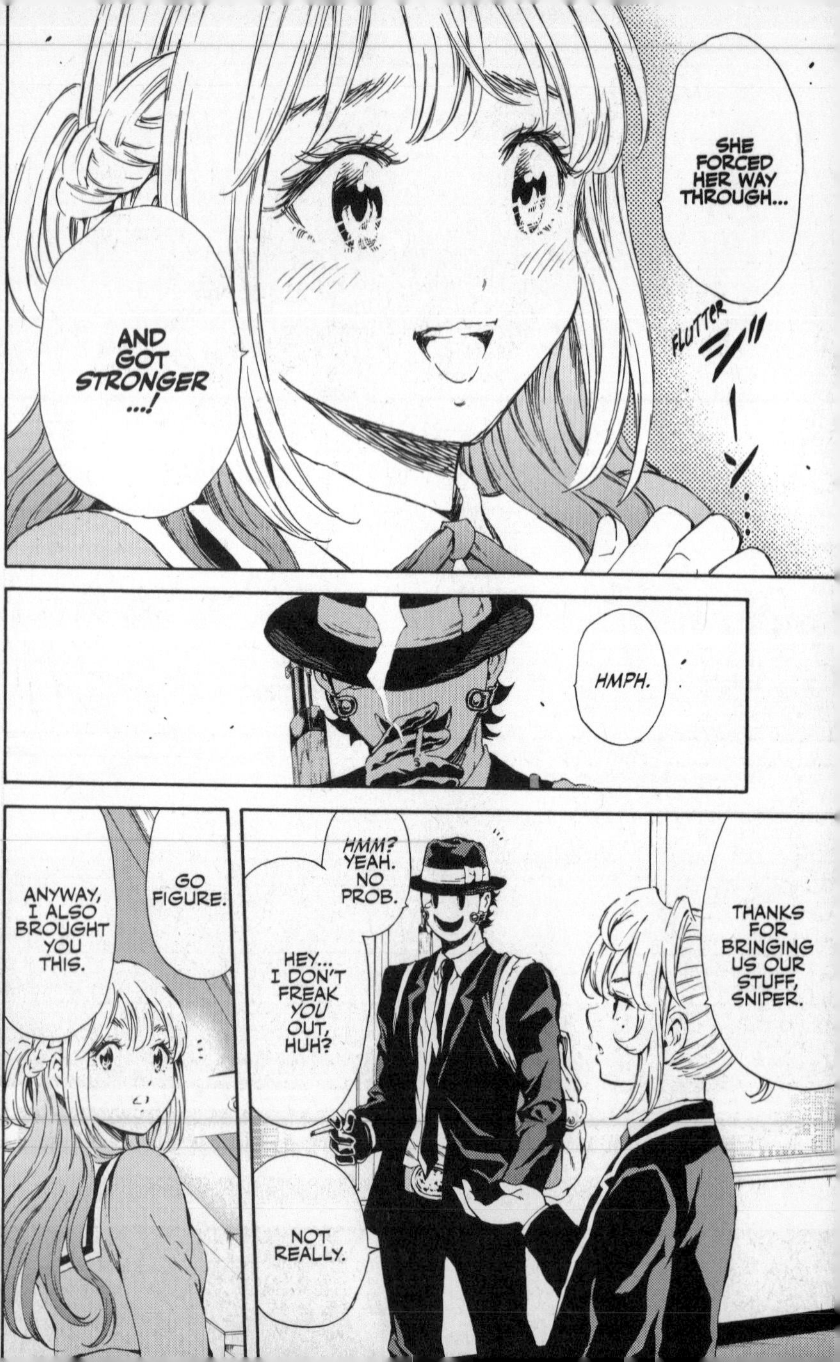
SHE FORCED HER WAY THROUGH...
AND GOT STRONGER ...!
FLUTTER
HMPH.
THANKS FOR BRINGING US OUR STUFF, SNIPER.
HMM? YEAH. NO PROB.
HEY... I DON'T FREAK *YOU* OUT, HUH?
NOT REALLY.
GO FIGURE.
ANYWAY, I ALSO BROUGHT YOU THIS.

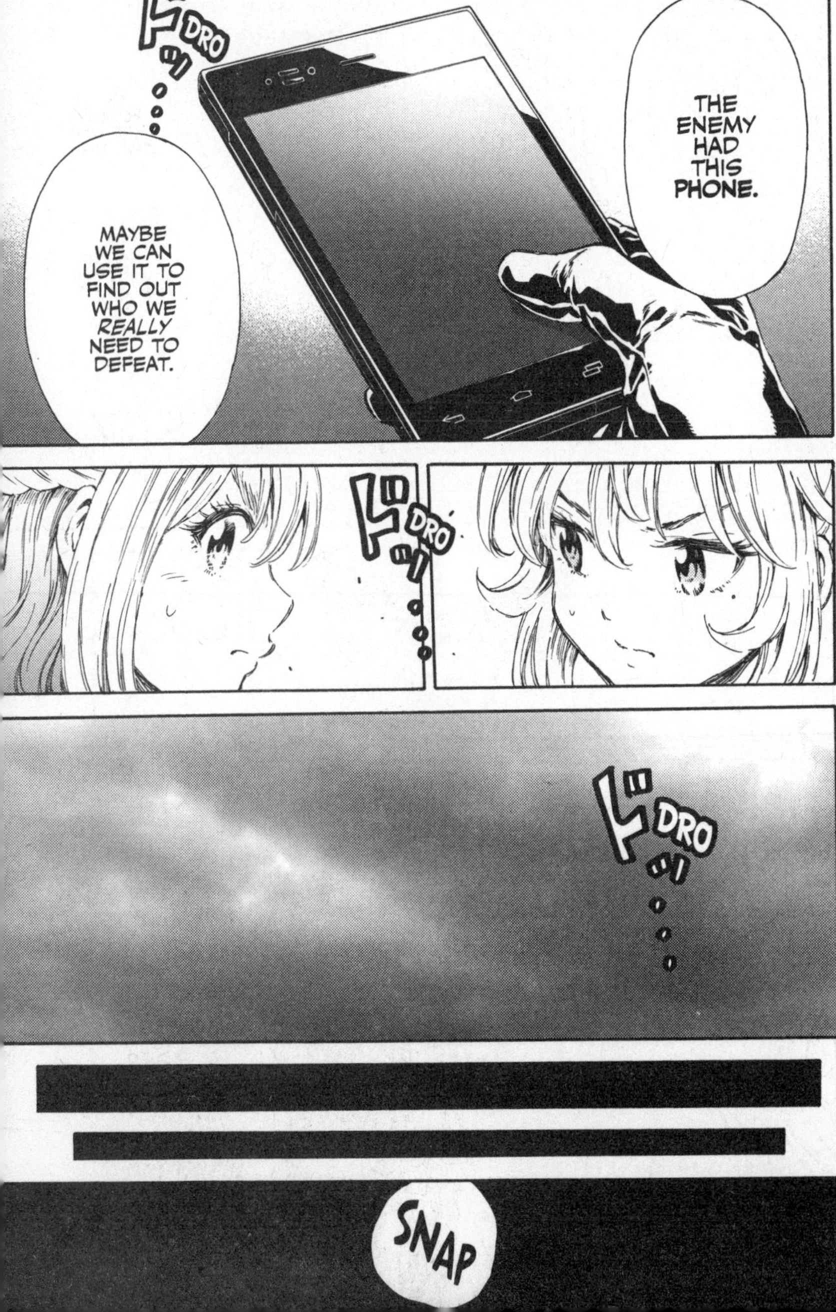
THE ENEMY HAD THIS PHONE.
DRO
MAYBE WE CAN USE IT TO FIND OUT WHO WE *REALLY* NEED TO DEFEAT.
DRO
DRO
SNAP

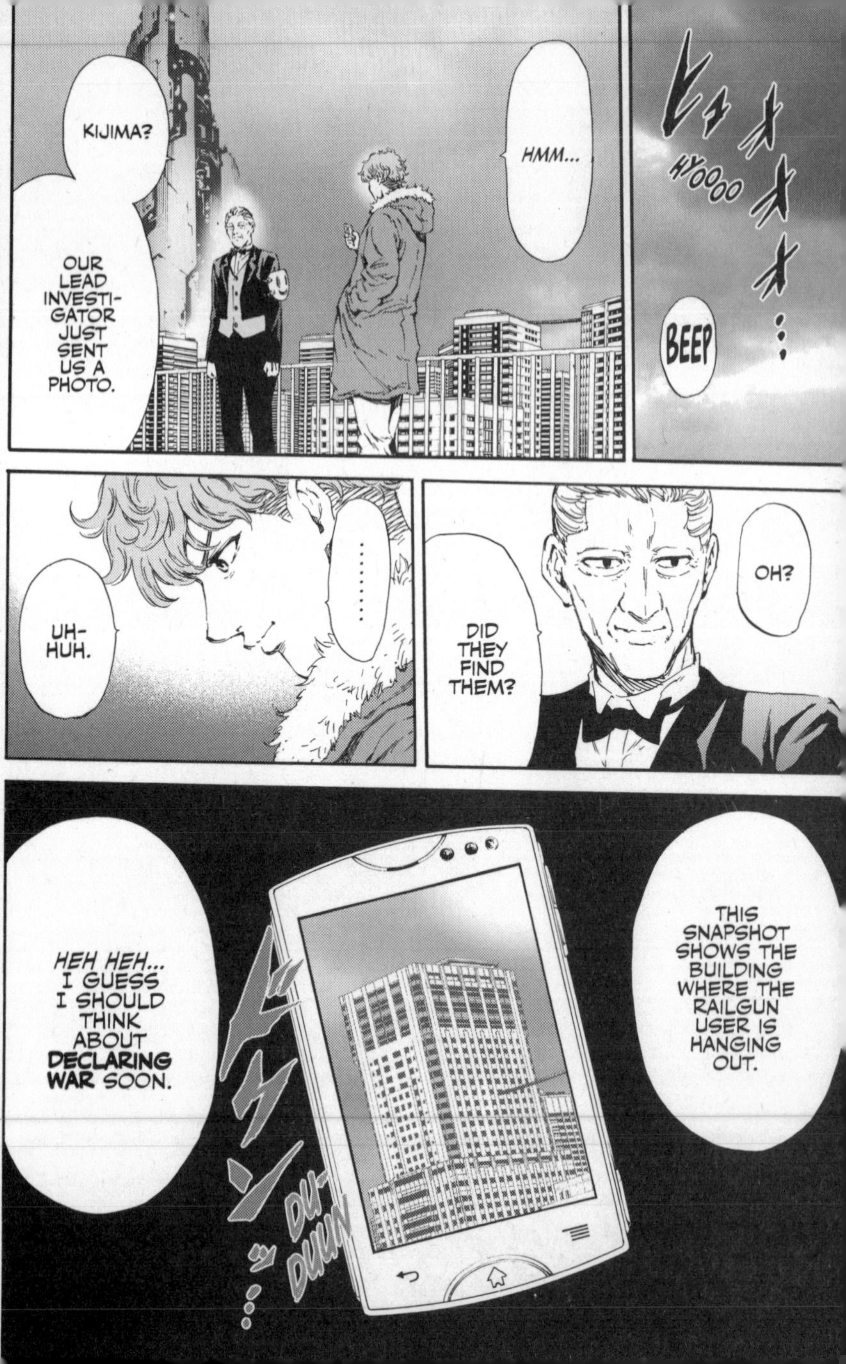
HYOOOO
BEEP
HMM...
KIJIMA?
OUR LEAD INVESTIGATOR JUST SENT US A PHOTO.
OH?
DID THEY FIND THEM?
......
UH-HUH.
THIS SNAPSHOT SHOWS THE BUILDING WHERE THE RAILGUN USER IS HANGING OUT.
HEH HEH... I GUESS I SHOULD THINK ABOUT **DECLARING WAR** SOON.
DU-DUUN

HIGH-RISE INVASION

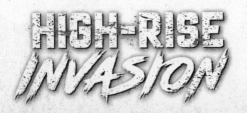

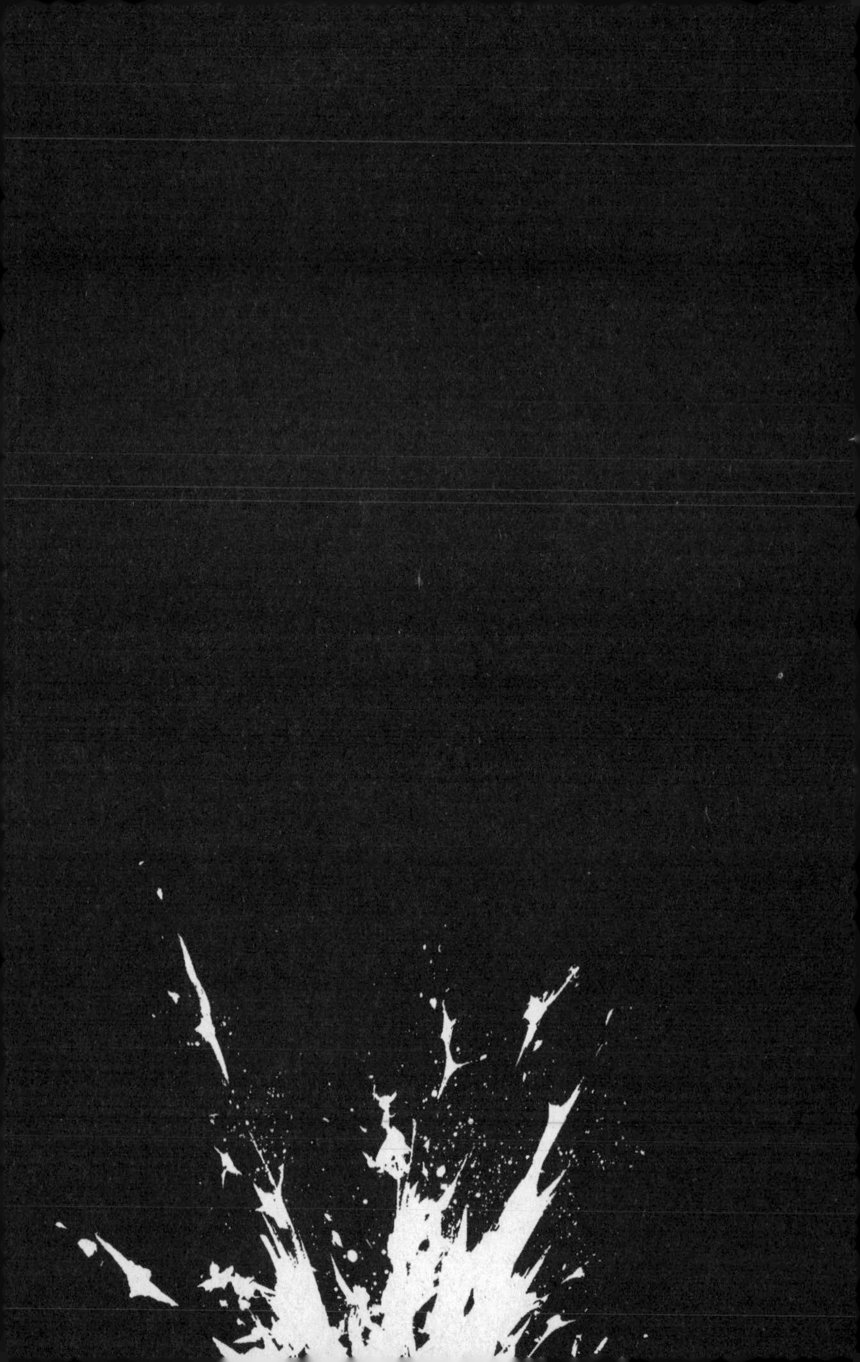

HIGH-RISE INVASION

10

STORY / Tsuina Miura
ART / Takahiro Oba

HIGH-RISE INVASION

INVASION

10

CONTENTS

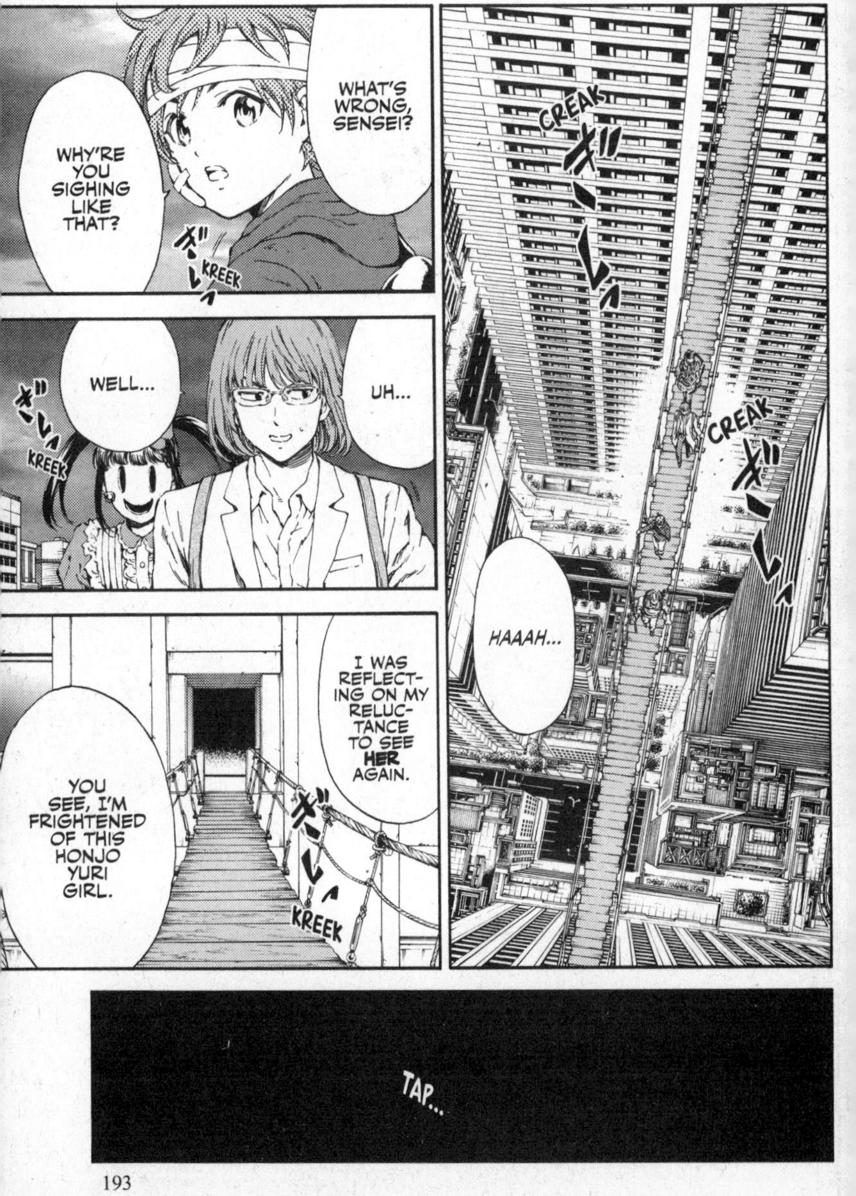
CREAK
CREAK
HAAAH...
WHAT'S WRONG, SENSEI?
WHY'RE YOU SIGHING LIKE THAT?
KREEK
UH...
WELL...
KREEK
I WAS REFLECTING ON MY RELUCTANCE TO SEE **HER** AGAIN.
YOU SEE, I'M FRIGHTENED OF THIS HONJO YURI GIRL.
KREEK
TAP...

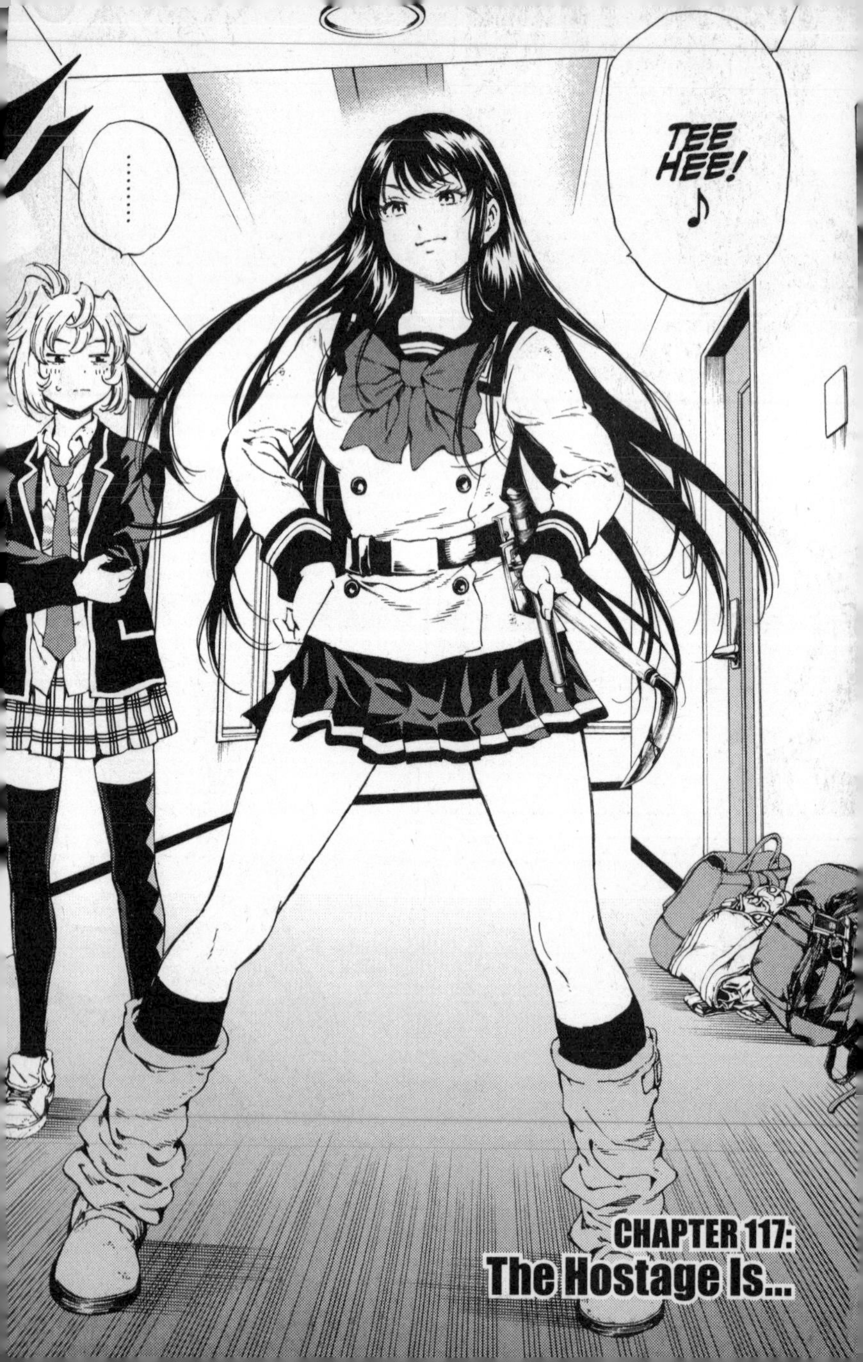
TEE HEE! ♪
......
CHAPTER 117:
The Hostage Is...

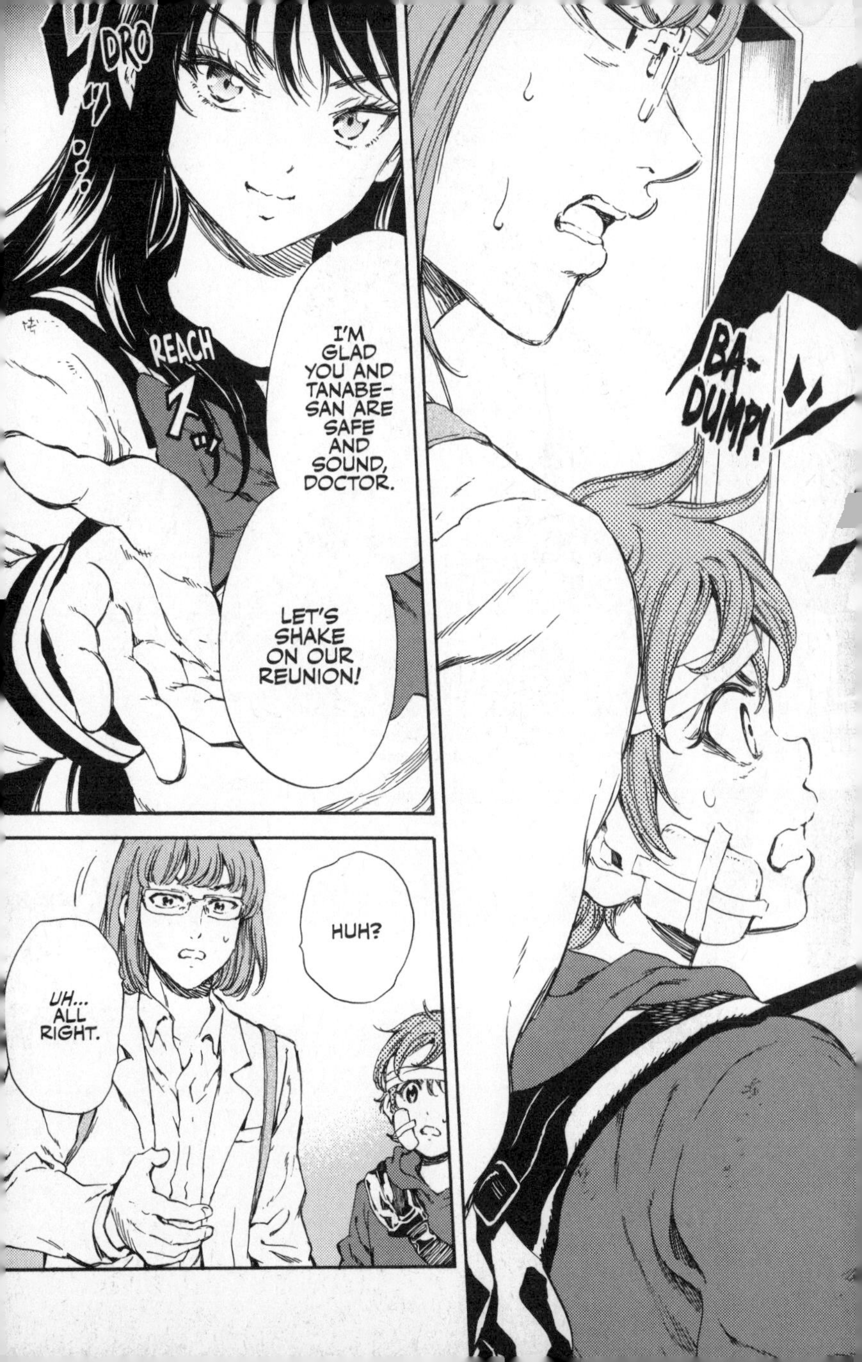

BA-DUMP!
DRO
REACH
I'M GLAD YOU AND TANABE-SAN ARE SAFE AND SOUND, DOCTOR.
LET'S SHAKE ON OUR REUNION!
HUH?
UH... ALL RIGHT.

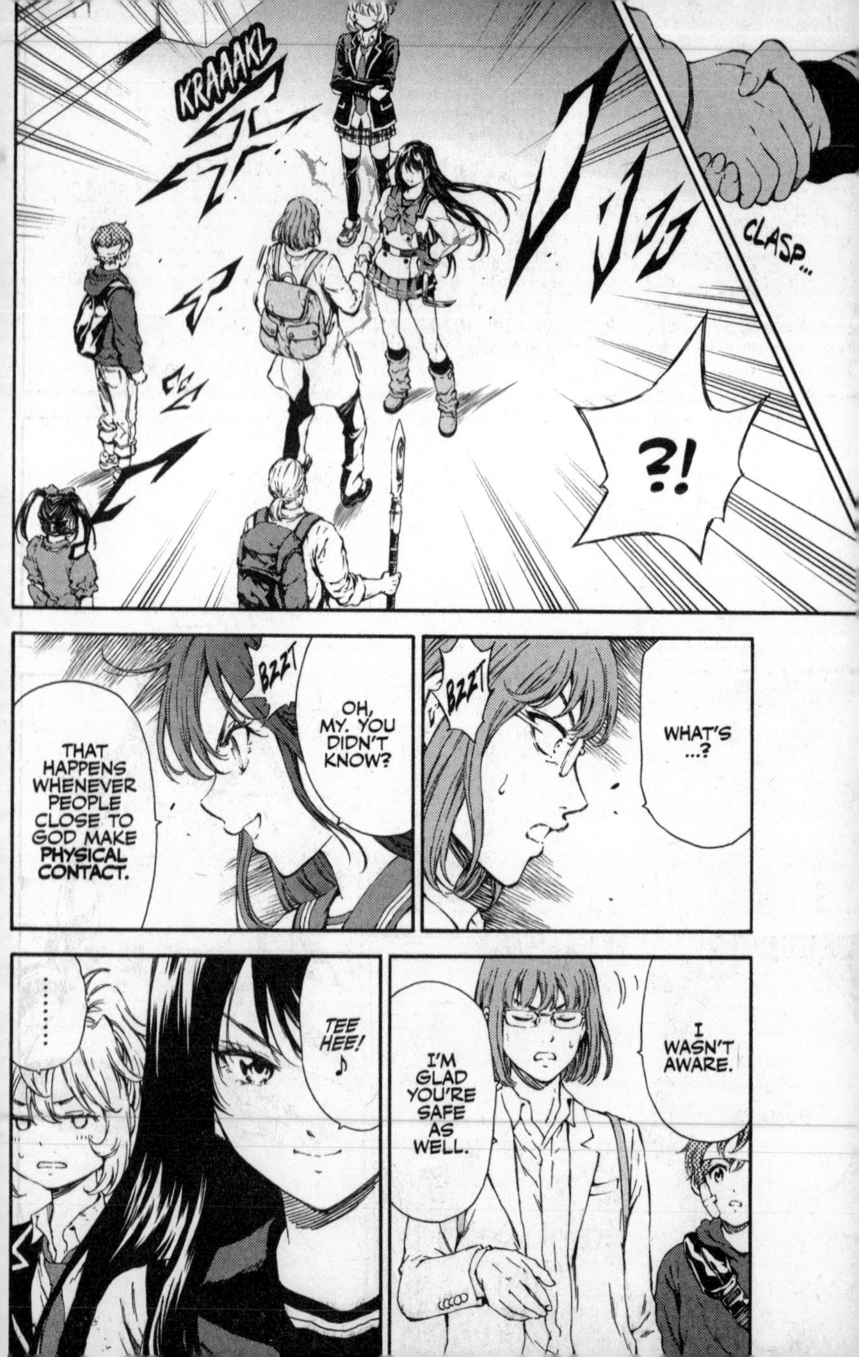
CLASP...
?!
KRAAAKL
BZZT
WHAT'S ...?
OH, MY. YOU DIDN'T KNOW?
BZZT
THAT HAPPENS WHENEVER PEOPLE CLOSE TO GOD MAKE PHYSICAL CONTACT.
I WASN'T AWARE.
I'M GLAD YOU'RE SAFE AS WELL.
TEE HEE! ♪
....

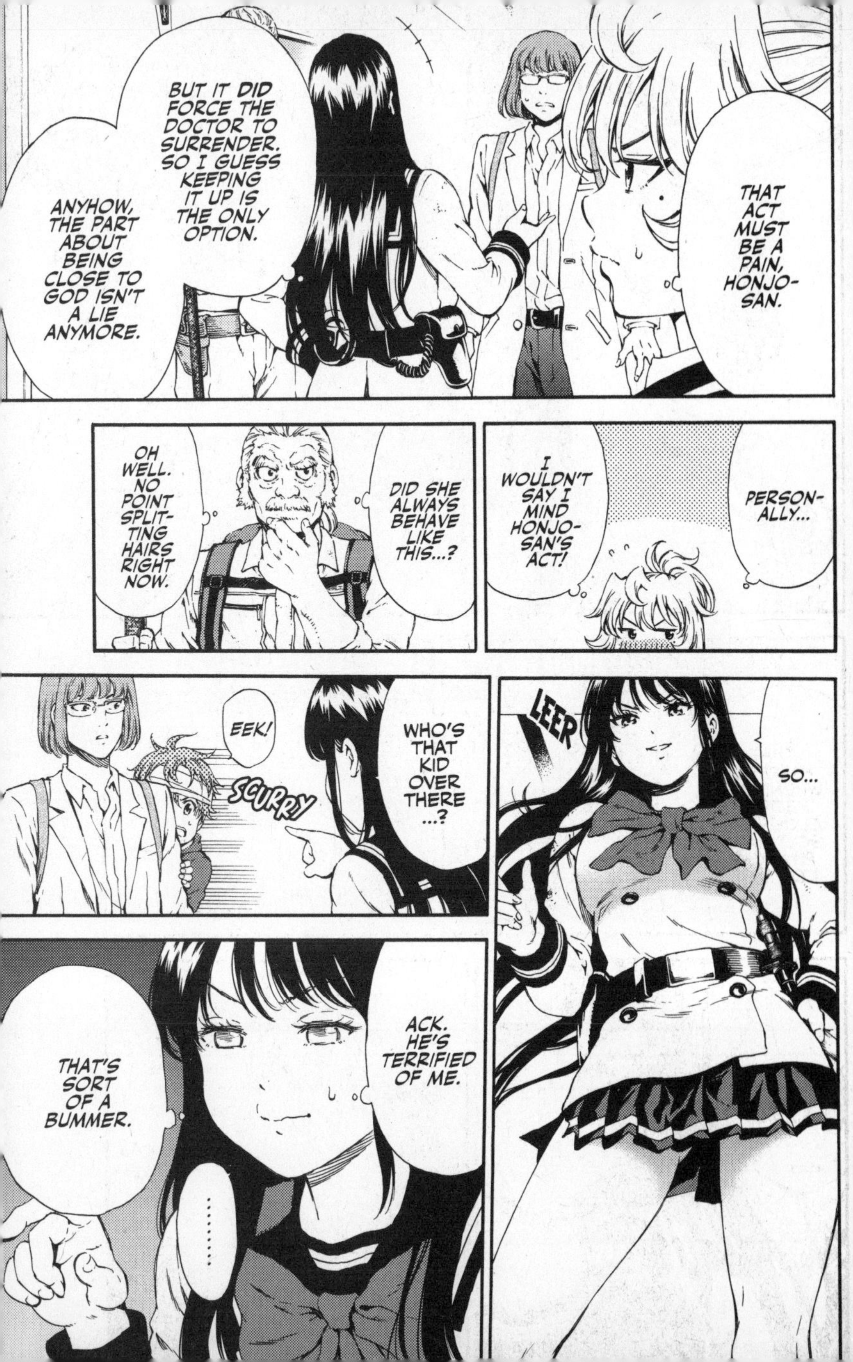
THAT ACT MUST BE A PAIN, HONJO-SAN.
BUT IT DID FORCE THE DOCTOR TO SURRENDER. SO I GUESS KEEPING IT UP IS THE ONLY OPTION.
ANYHOW, THE PART ABOUT BEING CLOSE TO GOD ISN'T A LIE ANYMORE.
PERSON-ALLY...
I WOULDN'T SAY I MIND HONJO-SAN'S ACT!
DID SHE ALWAYS BEHAVE LIKE THIS...?
OH WELL. NO POINT SPLIT-TING HAIRS RIGHT NOW.
SO...
LEER
WHO'S THAT KID OVER THERE ...?
EEK!
SCURRY
ACK. HE'S TERRIFIED OF ME.
THAT'S SORT OF A BUMMER.
......

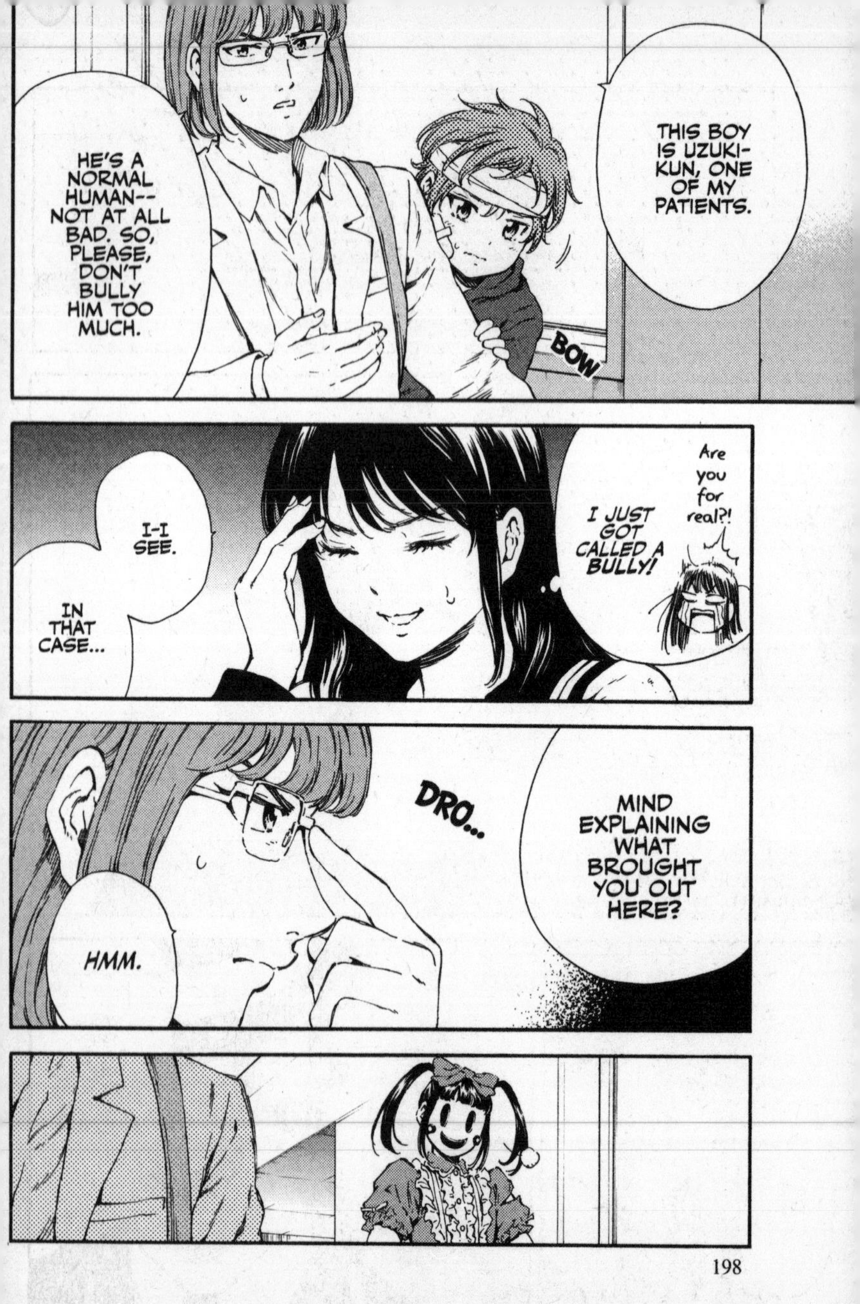
THIS BOY IS UZUKI-KUN, ONE OF MY PATIENTS.
HE'S A NORMAL HUMAN--NOT AT ALL BAD. SO, PLEASE, DON'T BULLY HIM TOO MUCH.
BOW
I JUST GOT CALLED A BULLY!
Are you for real?!
I-I SEE.
IN THAT CASE...
MIND EXPLAINING WHAT BROUGHT YOU OUT HERE?
DRO...
HMM.

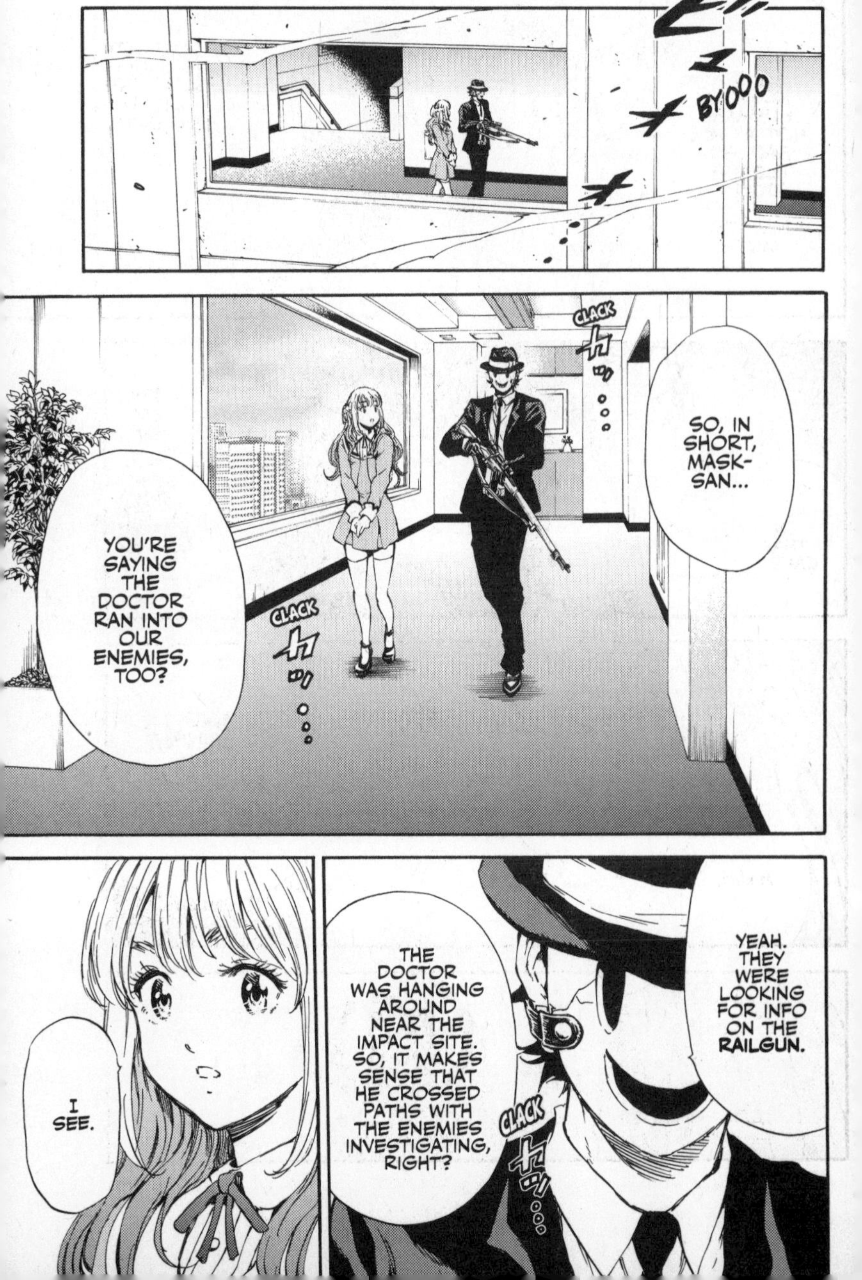
BYOOO
CLACK
SO, IN SHORT, MASK-SAN...
YOU'RE SAYING THE DOCTOR RAN INTO OUR ENEMIES, TOO?
CLACK
YEAH. THEY WERE LOOKING FOR INFO ON THE RAILGUN.
THE DOCTOR WAS HANGING AROUND NEAR THE IMPACT SITE. SO, IT MAKES SENSE THAT HE CROSSED PATHS WITH THE ENEMIES INVESTIGATING, RIGHT?
CLACK
I SEE.

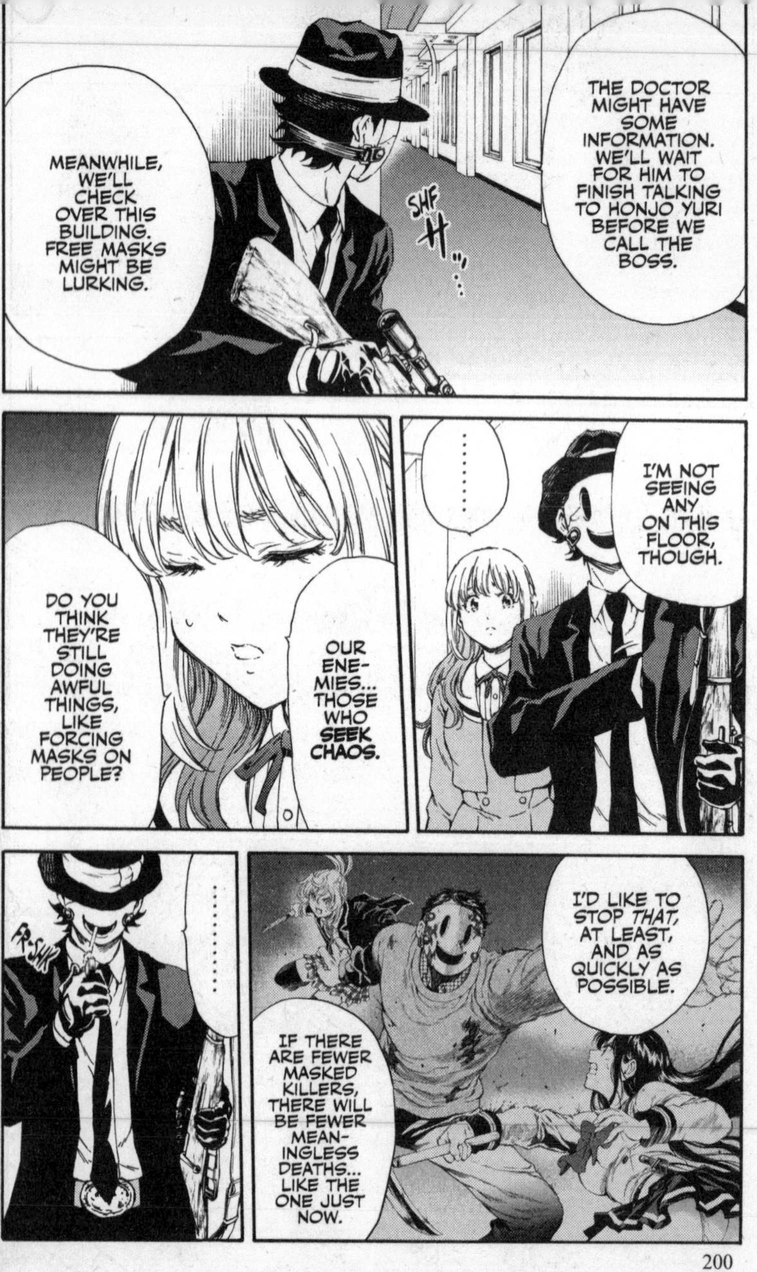
THE DOCTOR MIGHT HAVE SOME INFORMATION. WE'LL WAIT FOR HIM TO FINISH TALKING TO HONJO YURI BEFORE WE CALL THE BOSS.
SHFH...
MEANWHILE, WE'LL CHECK OVER THIS BUILDING. FREE MASKS MIGHT BE LURKING.
I'M NOT SEEING ANY ON THIS FLOOR, THOUGH.
......
OUR ENEMIES... THOSE WHO **SEEK CHAOS.**
DO YOU THINK THEY'RE STILL DOING AWFUL THINGS, LIKE FORCING MASKS ON PEOPLE?
I'D LIKE TO STOP *THAT,* AT LEAST, AND AS QUICKLY AS POSSIBLE.
IF THERE ARE FEWER MASKED KILLERS, THERE WILL BE FEWER MEANINGLESS DEATHS... LIKE THE ONE JUST NOW.
......
FR-SHK

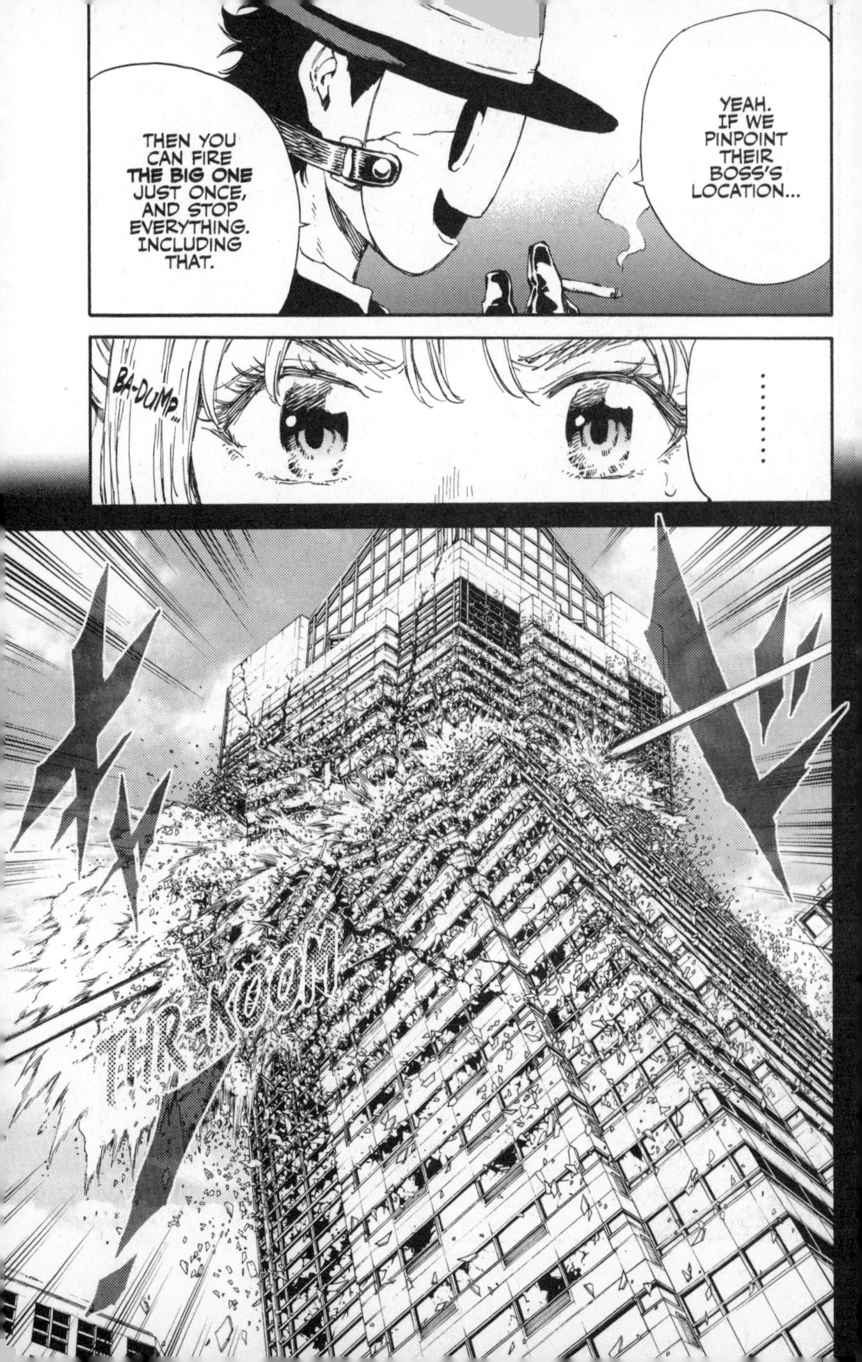
YEAH. IF WE PINPOINT THEIR BOSS'S LOCATION...
THEN YOU CAN FIRE THE BIG ONE JUST ONCE, AND STOP EVERYTHING. INCLUDING THAT.
....
BA-DUMP...
THR-KOOM

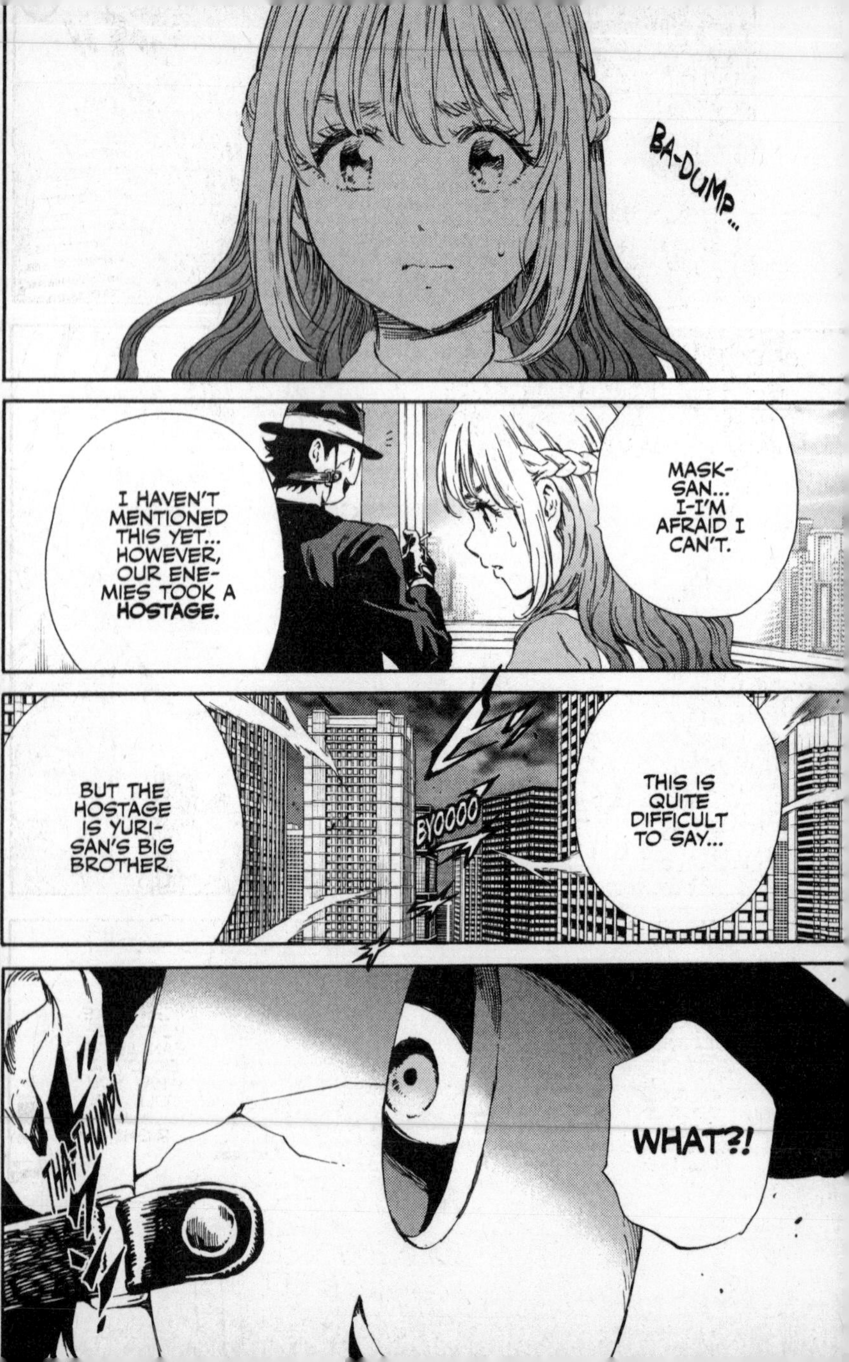
BA-DUMP...
MASK-SAN... I-I'M AFRAID I CAN'T.
I HAVEN'T MENTIONED THIS YET... HOWEVER, OUR ENE-MIES TOOK A HOSTAGE.
THIS IS QUITE DIFFICULT TO SAY...
BYOOOO
BUT THE HOSTAGE IS YURI-SAN'S BIG BROTHER.
WHAT?!
THA-THUMP!

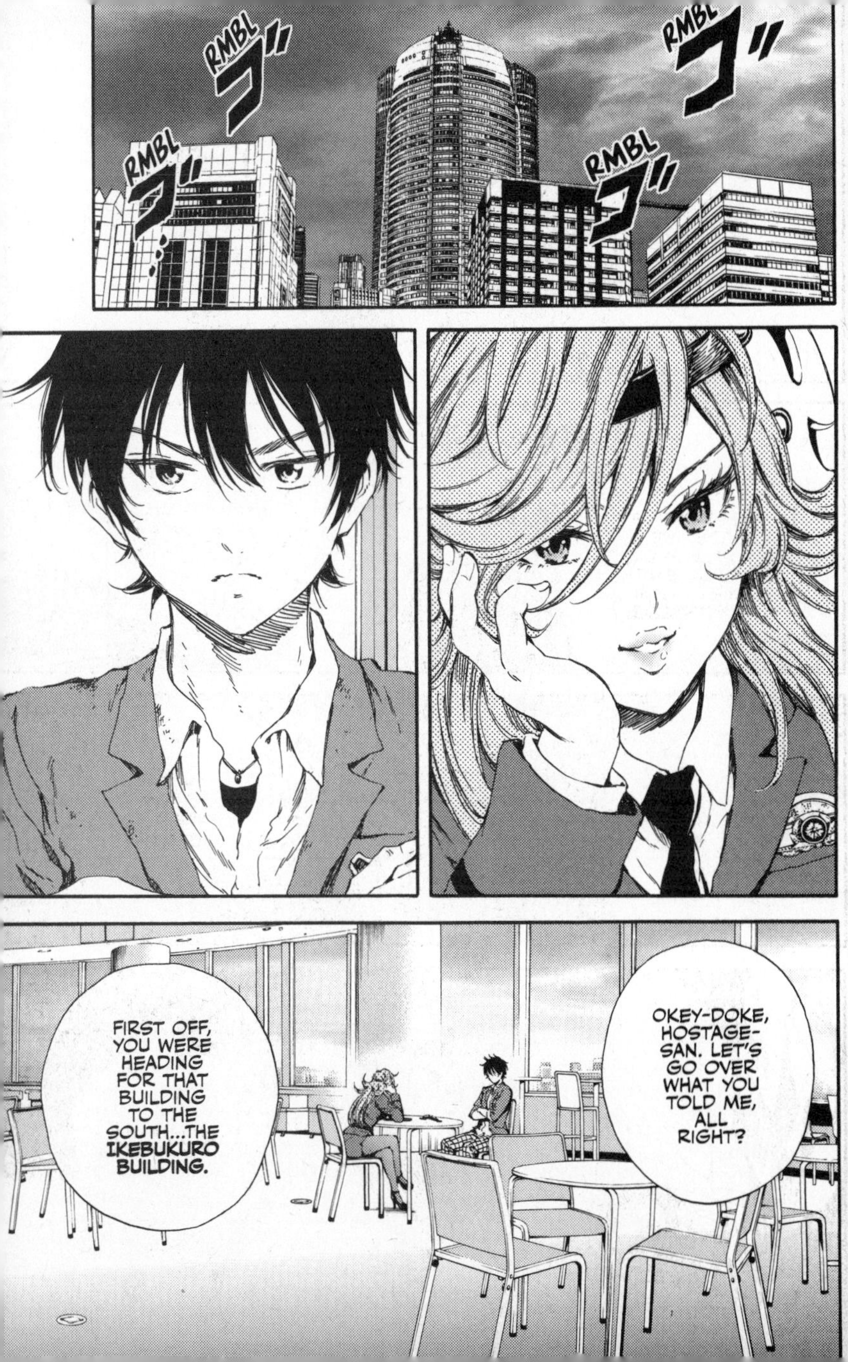
RMBL
ゴ
RMBL
ゴ
RMBL
ゴ
RMBL
ゴ
OKEY-DOKE, HOSTAGE-SAN. LET'S GO OVER WHAT YOU TOLD ME, ALL RIGHT?
FIRST OFF, YOU WERE HEADING FOR THAT BUILDING TO THE SOUTH...THE **IKEBUKURO** BUILDING.

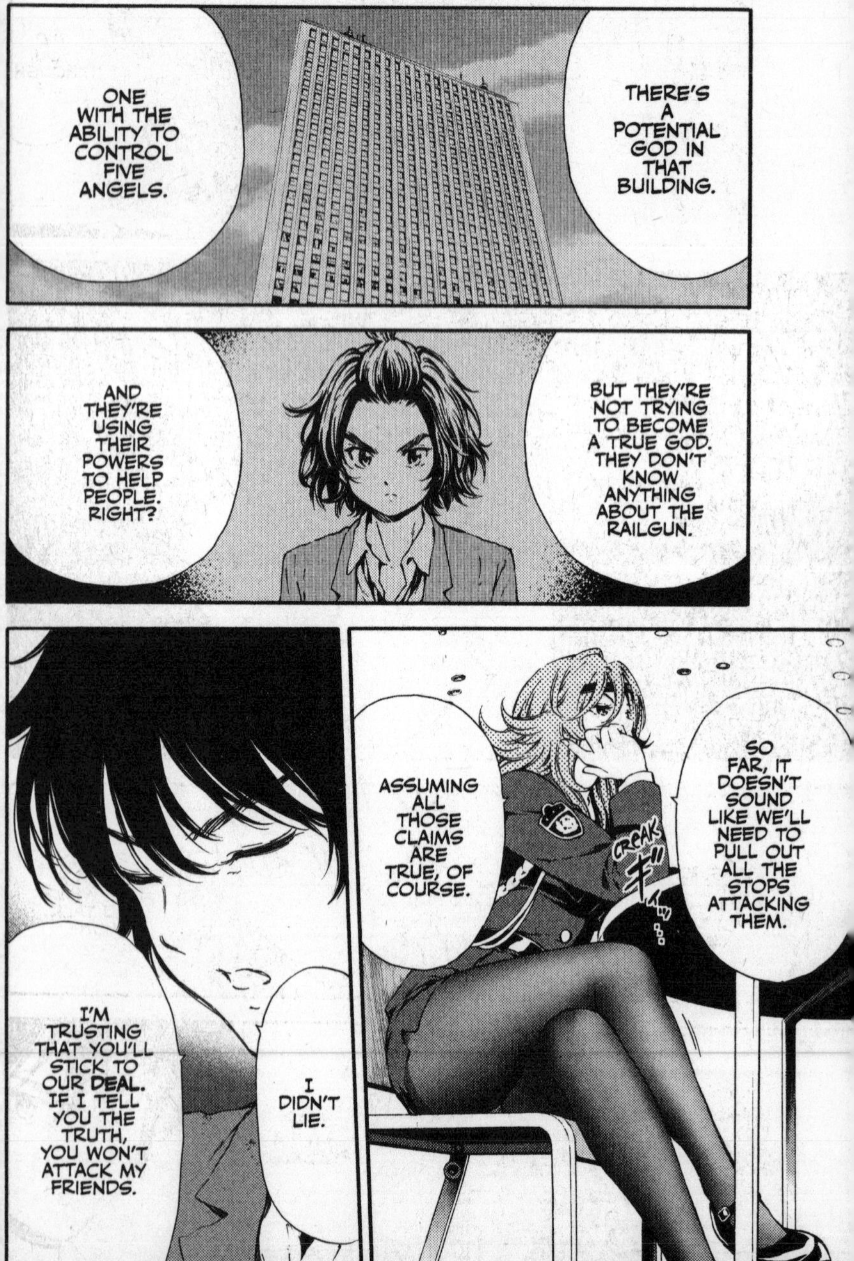
THERE'S A POTENTIAL GOD IN THAT BUILDING.
ONE WITH THE ABILITY TO CONTROL FIVE ANGELS.
BUT THEY'RE NOT TRYING TO BECOME A TRUE GOD. THEY DON'T KNOW ANYTHING ABOUT THE RAILGUN.
AND THEY'RE USING THEIR POWERS TO HELP PEOPLE. RIGHT?
SO FAR, IT DOESN'T SOUND LIKE WE'LL NEED TO PULL OUT ALL THE STOPS ATTACKING THEM.
CREAK
ASSUMING ALL THOSE CLAIMS ARE TRUE, OF COURSE.
I DIDN'T LIE.
I'M TRUSTING THAT YOU'LL STICK TO OUR DEAL. IF I TELL YOU THE TRUTH, YOU WON'T ATTACK MY FRIENDS.

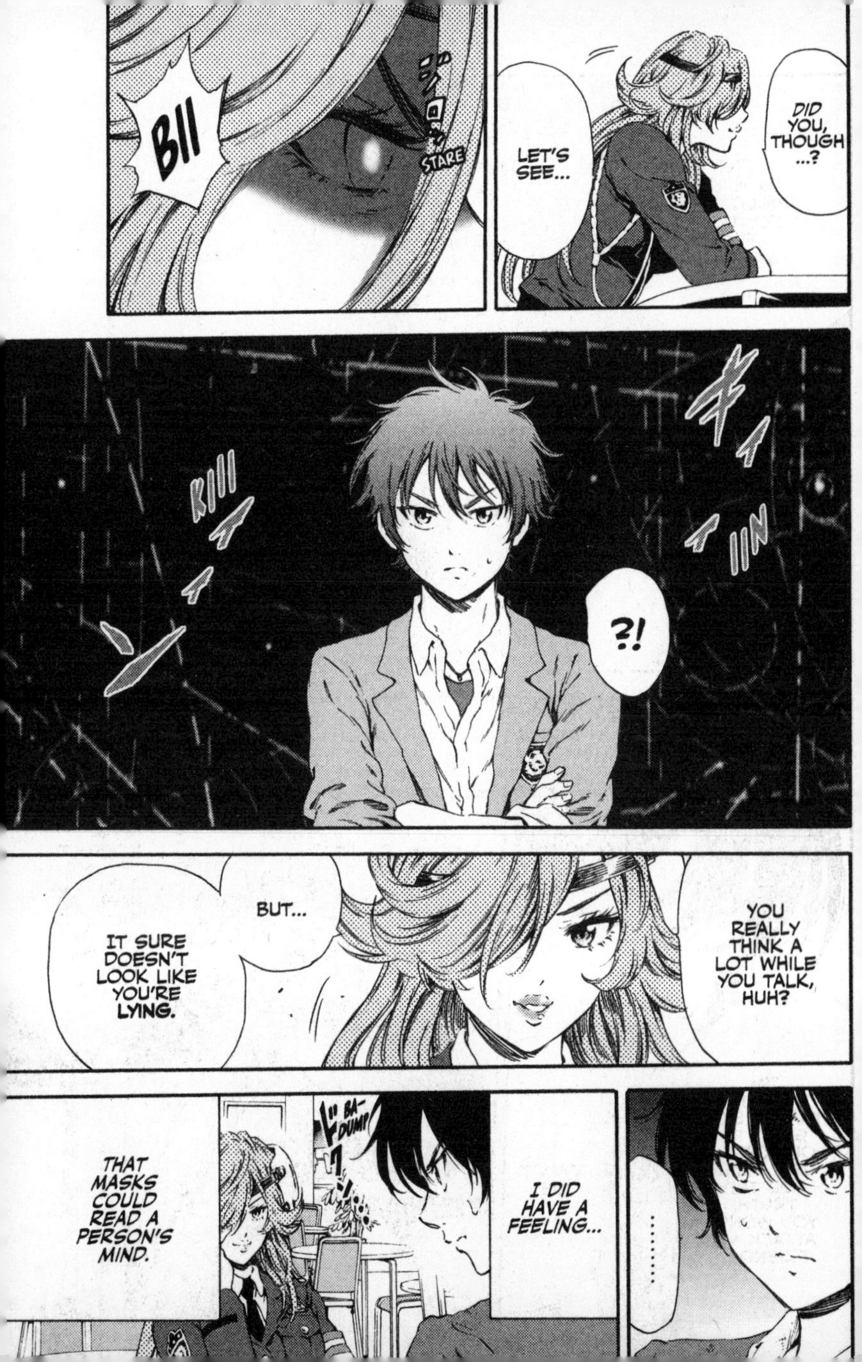
DID YOU, THOUGH ...?
LET'S SEE...
BII
STARE
IIN
?!
KIII
YOU REALLY THINK A LOT WHILE YOU TALK, HUH?
BUT...
IT SURE DOESN'T LOOK LIKE YOU'RE LYING.
......
I DID HAVE A FEELING...
BA-DUMP
THAT MASKS COULD READ A PERSON'S MIND.

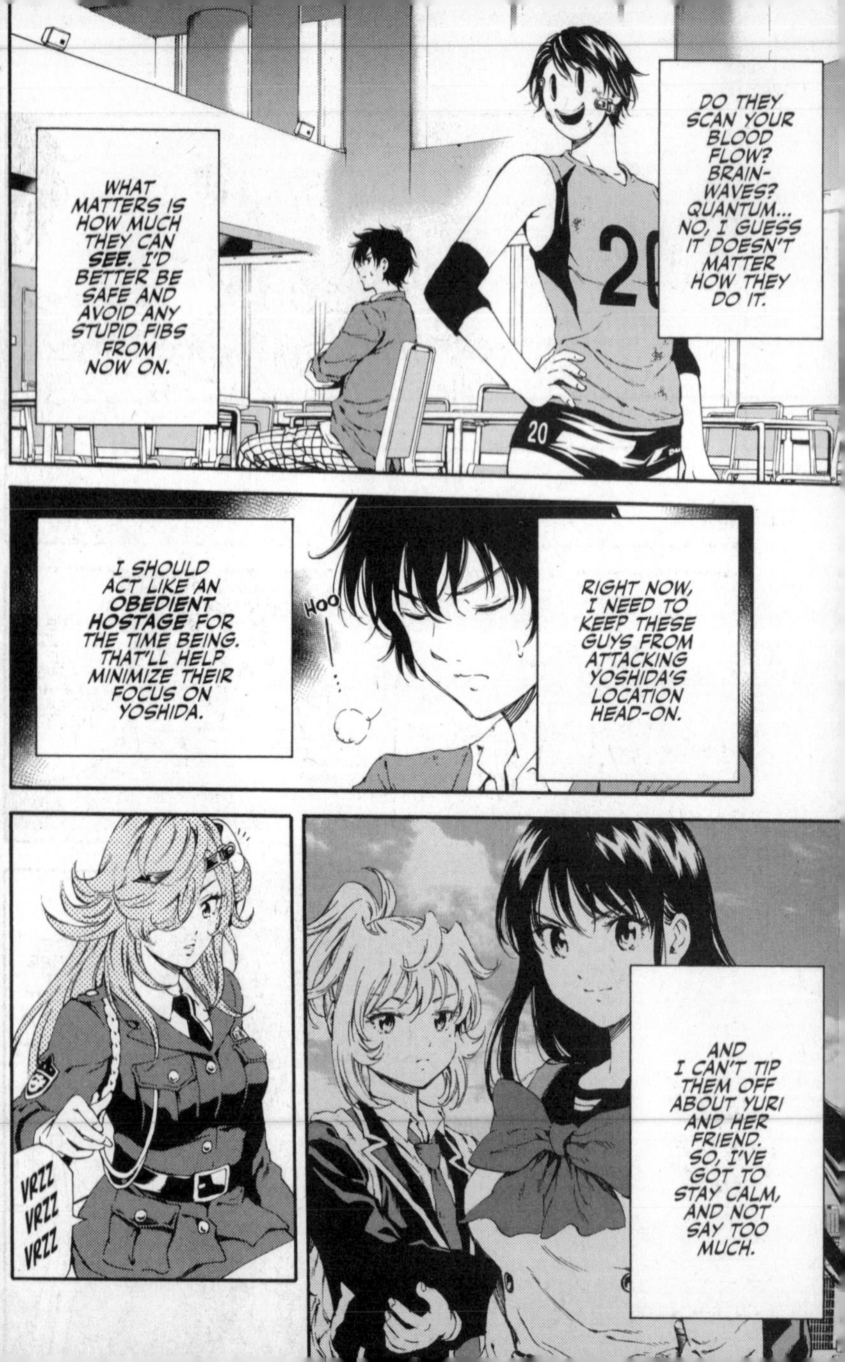
DO THEY SCAN YOUR BLOOD FLOW? BRAIN-WAVES? QUANTUM... NO, I GUESS IT DOESN'T MATTER HOW THEY DO IT.
WHAT MATTERS IS HOW MUCH THEY CAN **SEE**. I'D BETTER BE SAFE AND AVOID ANY STUPID FIBS FROM NOW ON.
RIGHT NOW, I NEED TO KEEP THESE GUYS FROM ATTACKING YOSHIDA'S LOCATION HEAD-ON.
HOO
I SHOULD ACT LIKE AN **OBEDIENT HOSTAGE** FOR THE TIME BEING. THAT'LL HELP MINIMIZE THEIR FOCUS ON YOSHIDA.
AND I CAN'T TIP THEM OFF ABOUT YURI AND HER FRIEND. SO, I'VE GOT TO STAY CALM, AND NOT SAY TOO MUCH.
VRZZ VRZZ VRZZ

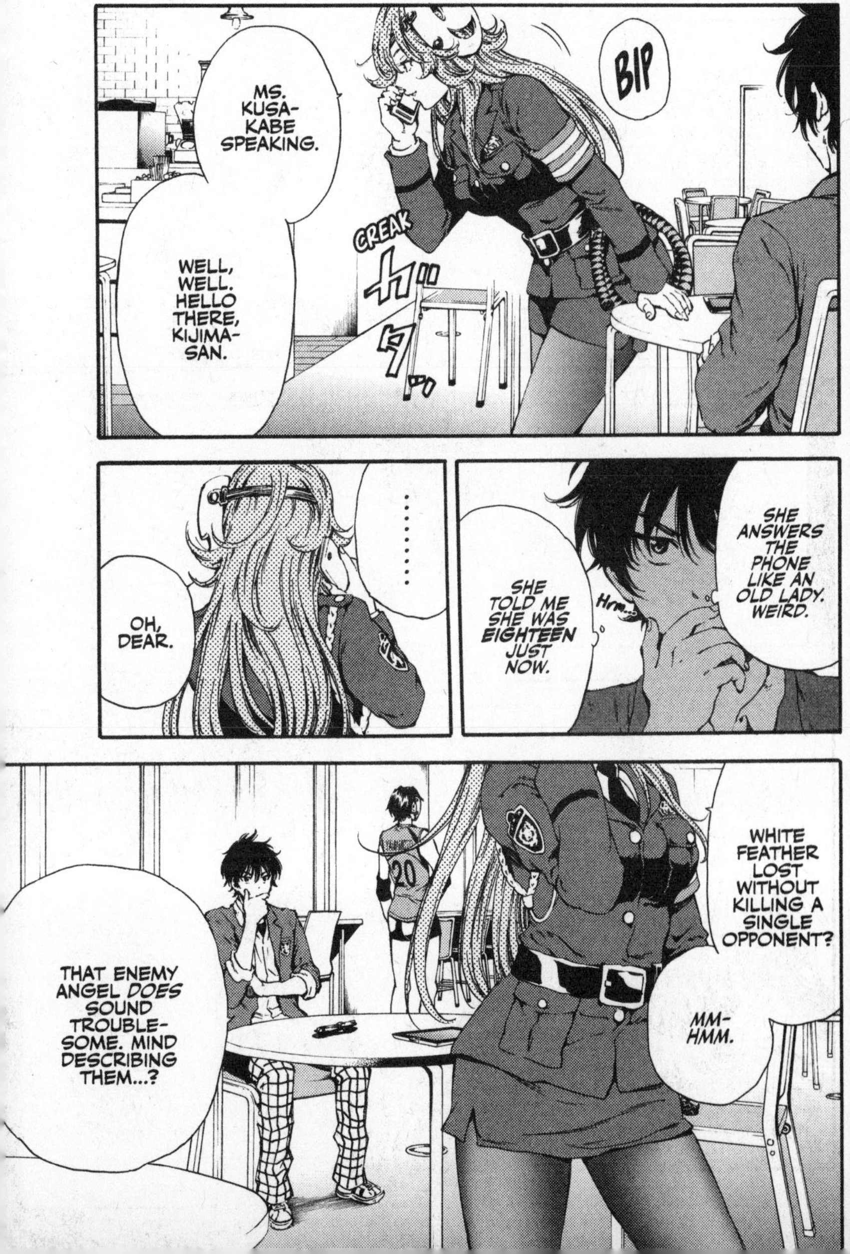
BIP
MS. KUSA-KABE SPEAKING.
CREAK
WELL, WELL. HELLO THERE, KIJIMA-SAN.
SHE ANSWERS THE PHONE LIKE AN OLD LADY. WEIRD.
Hrm...
SHE TOLD ME SHE WAS EIGHTEEN JUST NOW.
....
OH, DEAR.
WHITE FEATHER LOST WITHOUT KILLING A SINGLE OPPONENT?
MM-HMM.
THAT ENEMY ANGEL DOES SOUND TROUBLE-SOME. MIND DESCRIBING THEM...?

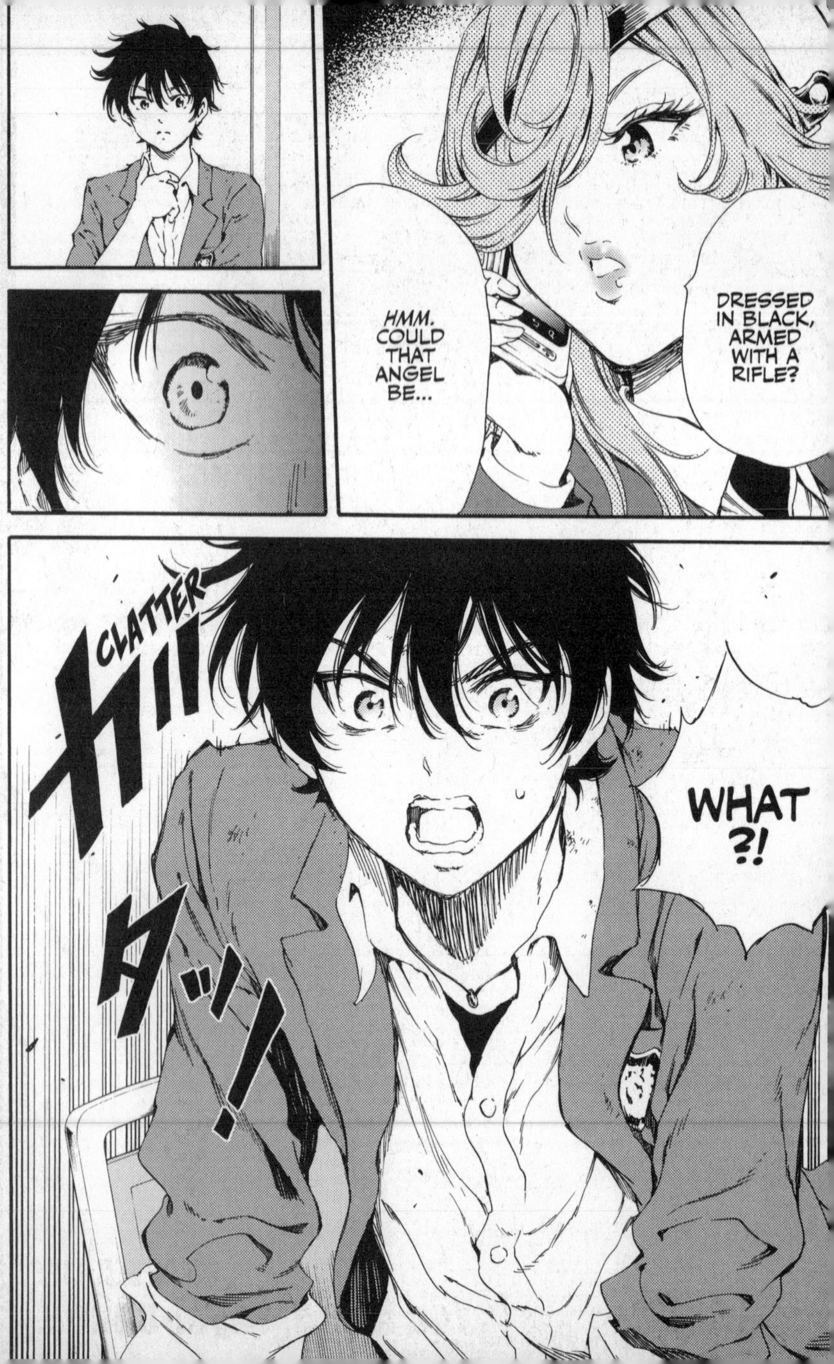
DRESSED IN BLACK, ARMED WITH A RIFLE?
HMM. COULD THAT ANGEL BE...
WHAT?!
CLATTER

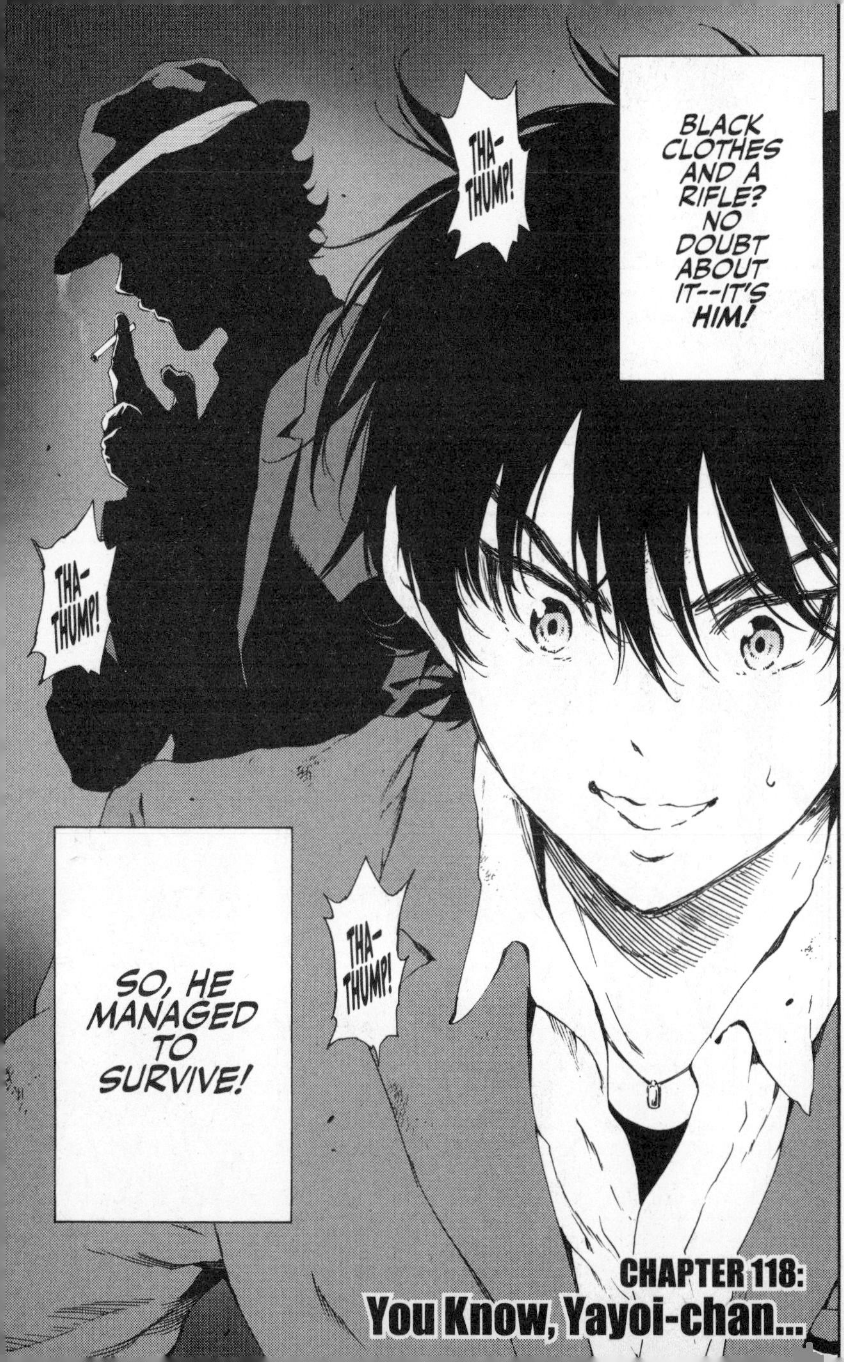
BLACK CLOTHES AND A RIFLE? NO DOUBT ABOUT IT--IT'S HIM!
THA-THUMP!
THA-THUMP!
THA-THUMP!
SO, HE MANAGED TO SURVIVE!
CHAPTER 118:
You Know, Yayoi-chan...

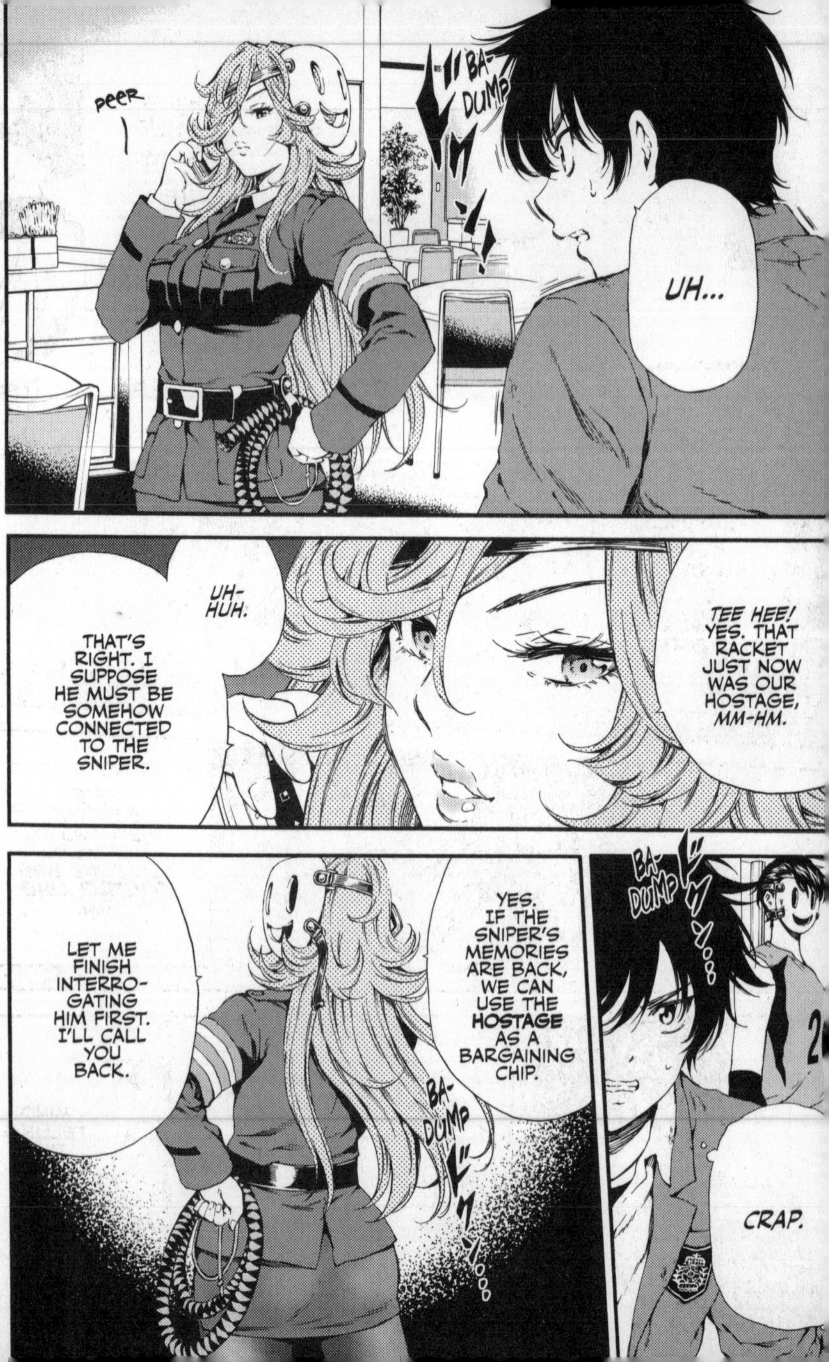
BA-DUMP
UH...
PEER
TEE HEE! YES. THAT RACKET JUST NOW WAS OUR HOSTAGE, MM-HM.
UH-HUH.
THAT'S RIGHT. I SUPPOSE HE MUST BE SOMEHOW CONNECTED TO THE SNIPER.
BA-DUMP
CRAP.
YES. IF THE SNIPER'S MEMORIES ARE BACK, WE CAN USE THE **HOSTAGE** AS A BARGAINING CHIP.
BA-DUMP
LET ME FINISH INTERRO-GATING HIM FIRST. I'LL CALL YOU BACK.

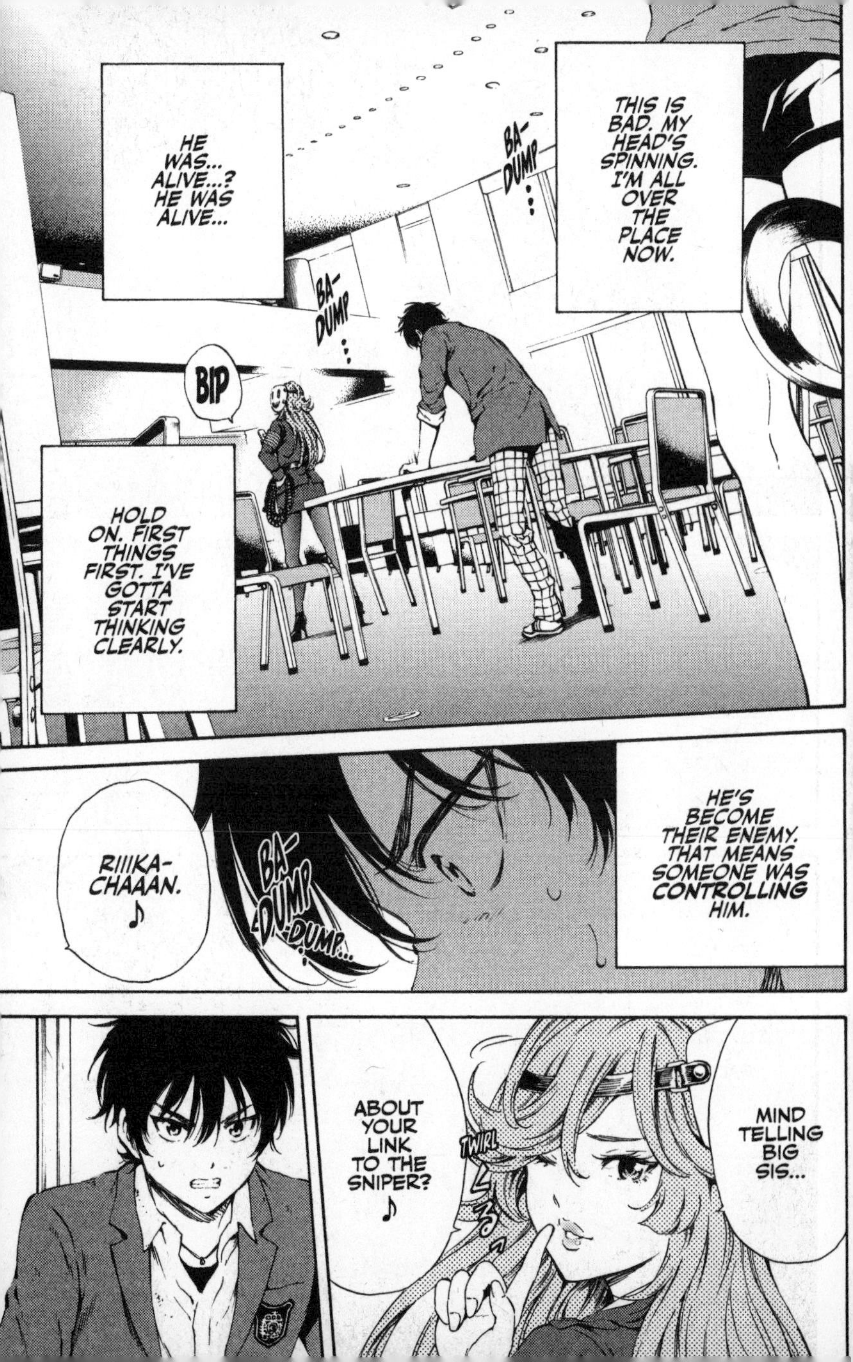
THIS IS BAD. MY HEAD'S SPINNING. I'M ALL OVER THE PLACE NOW.
BA-DUMP...
HE WAS... ALIVE...? HE WAS ALIVE...
BA-DUMP...
BIP
HOLD ON. FIRST THINGS FIRST. I'VE GOTTA START THINKING CLEARLY.
HE'S BECOME THEIR ENEMY. THAT MEANS SOMEONE WAS CONTROLLING HIM.
BA-DUMP-DUMP...
RIIIKA-CHAAAN. ♪
MIND TELLING BIG SIS...
TWIRL
ABOUT YOUR LINK TO THE SNIPER? ♪

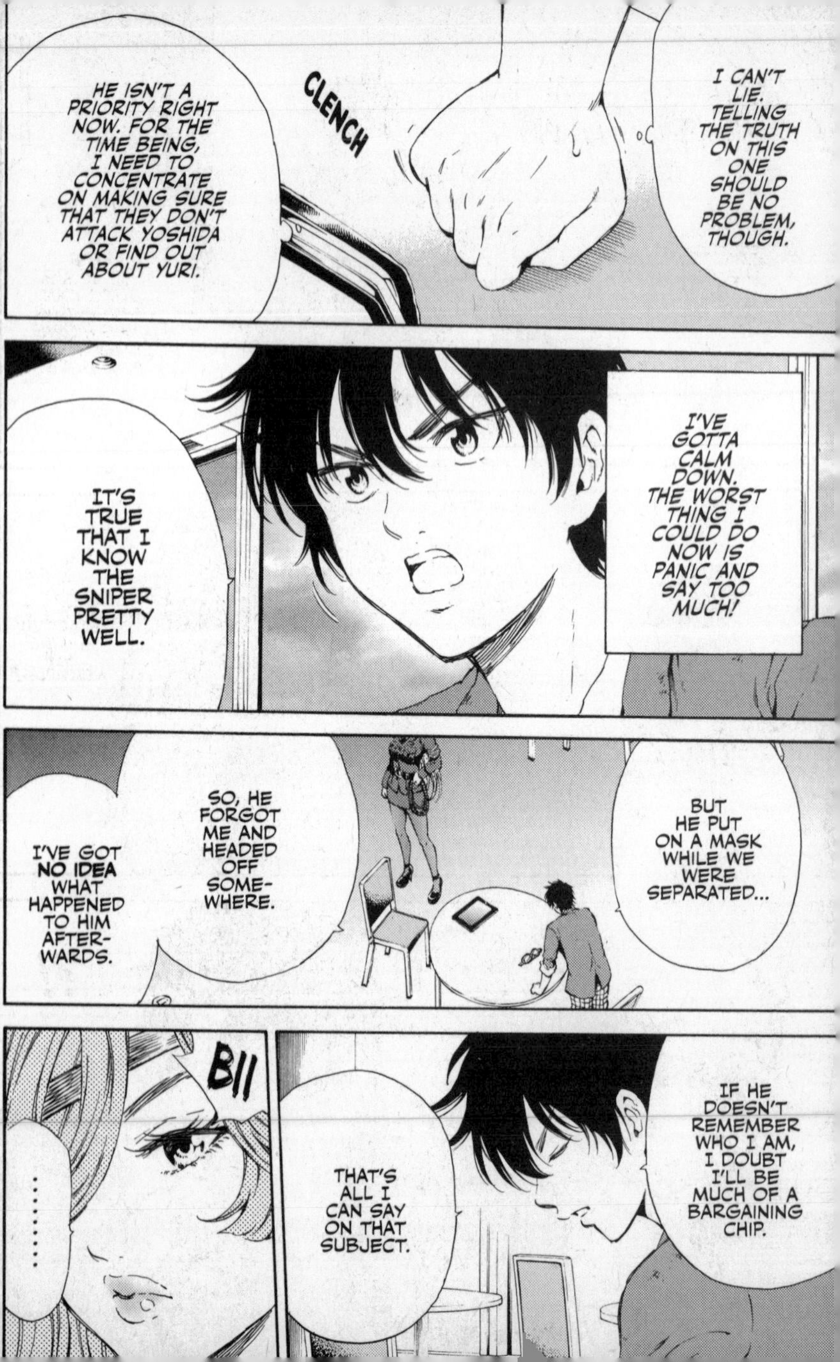
I CAN'T LIE. TELLING THE TRUTH ON THIS ONE SHOULD BE NO PROBLEM, THOUGH.
CLENCH
HE ISN'T A PRIORITY RIGHT NOW. FOR THE TIME BEING, I NEED TO CONCENTRATE ON MAKING SURE THAT THEY DON'T ATTACK YOSHIDA OR FIND OUT ABOUT YURI.
I'VE GOTTA CALM DOWN. THE WORST THING I COULD DO NOW IS PANIC AND SAY TOO MUCH!
IT'S TRUE THAT I KNOW THE SNIPER PRETTY WELL.
BUT HE PUT ON A MASK WHILE WE WERE SEPARATED...
SO, HE FORGOT ME AND HEADED OFF SOMEWHERE.
I'VE GOT **NO IDEA** WHAT HAPPENED TO HIM AFTERWARDS.
IF HE DOESN'T REMEMBER WHO I AM, I DOUBT I'LL BE MUCH OF A BARGAINING CHIP.
THAT'S ALL I CAN SAY ON THAT SUBJECT.
BII
......

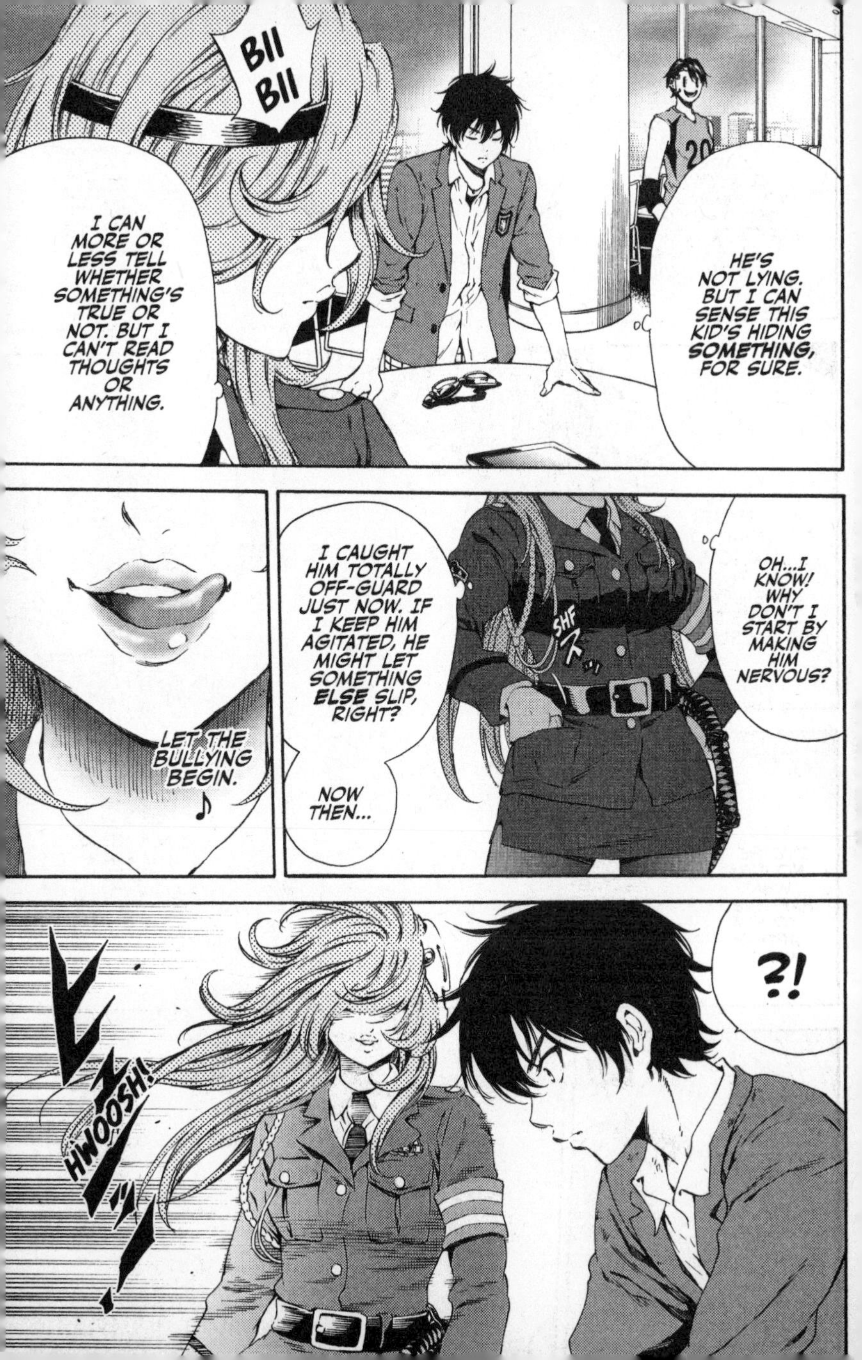
BII BII
HE'S NOT LYING. BUT I CAN SENSE THIS KID'S HIDING SOMETHING, FOR SURE.
I CAN MORE OR LESS TELL WHETHER SOMETHING'S TRUE OR NOT. BUT I CAN'T READ THOUGHTS OR ANYTHING.
OH...I KNOW! WHY DON'T I START BY MAKING HIM NERVOUS?
SHF
I CAUGHT HIM TOTALLY OFF-GUARD JUST NOW. IF I KEEP HIM AGITATED, HE MIGHT LET SOMETHING ELSE SLIP, RIGHT?
NOW THEN...
LET THE BULLYING BEGIN. ♪
?!
HWOOSH!

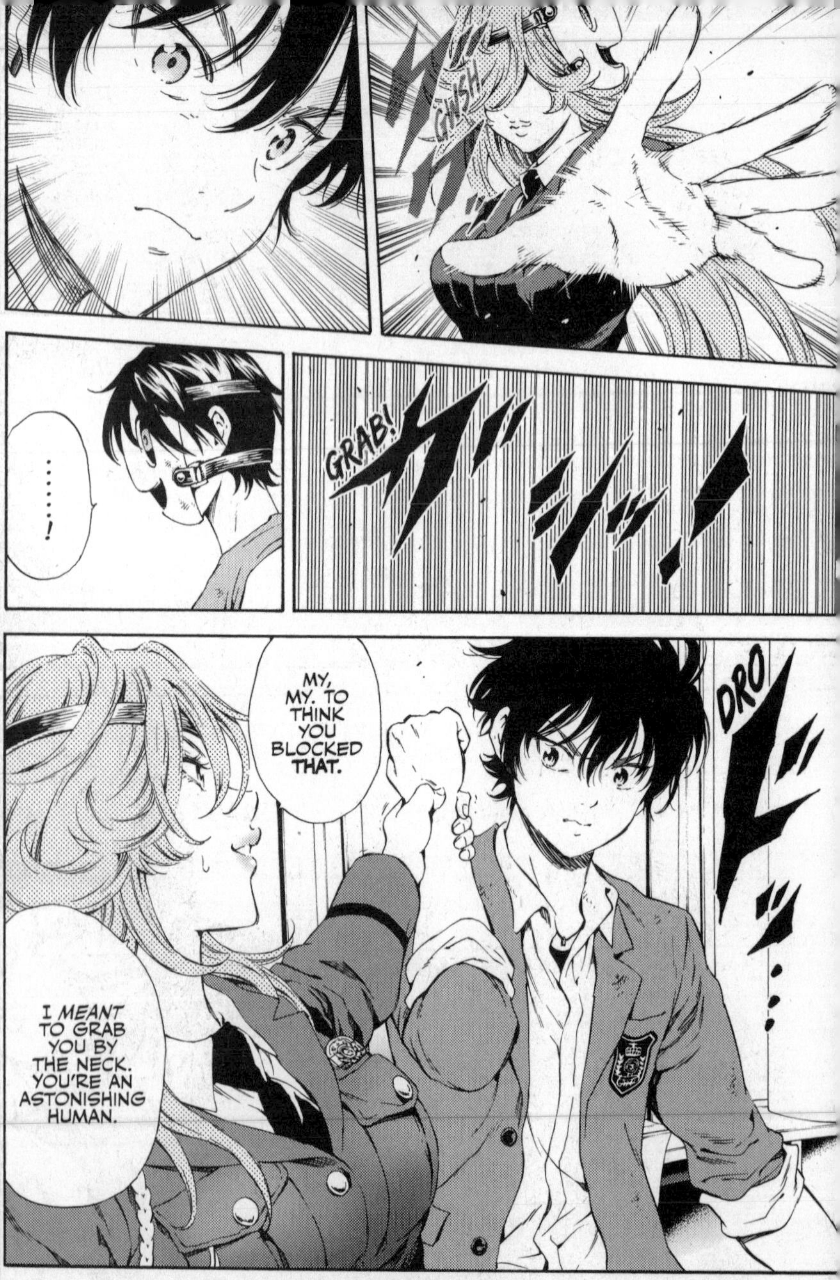
GWSH
GRAB!
......!
DRO
MY, MY. TO THINK YOU BLOCKED THAT.
I MEANT TO GRAB YOU BY THE NECK. YOU'RE AN ASTONISHING HUMAN.

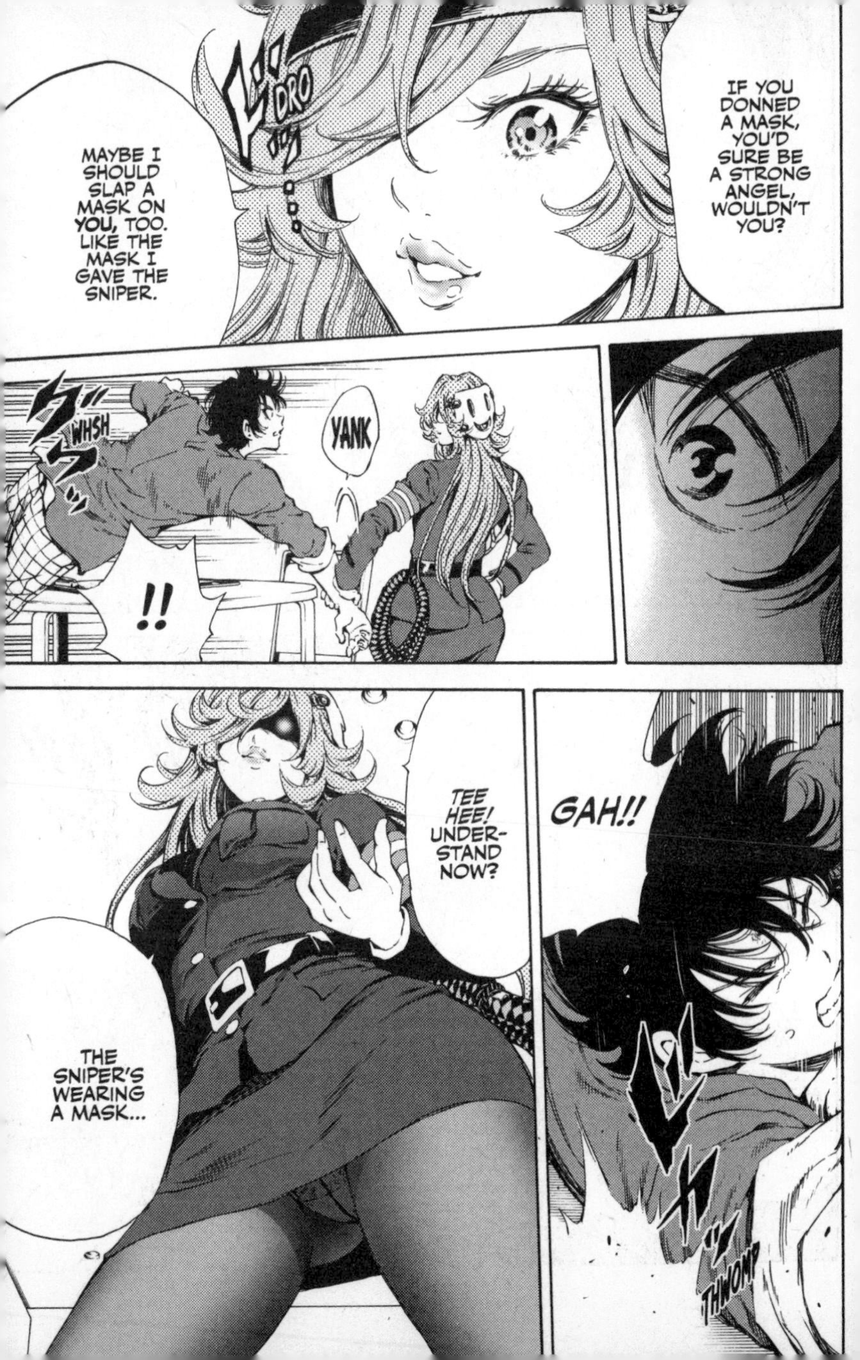
IF YOU DONNED A MASK, YOU'D SURE BE A STRONG ANGEL, WOULDN'T YOU?
DRO
MAYBE I SHOULD SLAP A MASK ON YOU, TOO. LIKE THE MASK I GAVE THE SNIPER.
YANK
WHSH
!!
GAH!!
THWOMP
TEE HEE! UNDER-STAND NOW?
THE SNIPER'S WEARING A MASK...

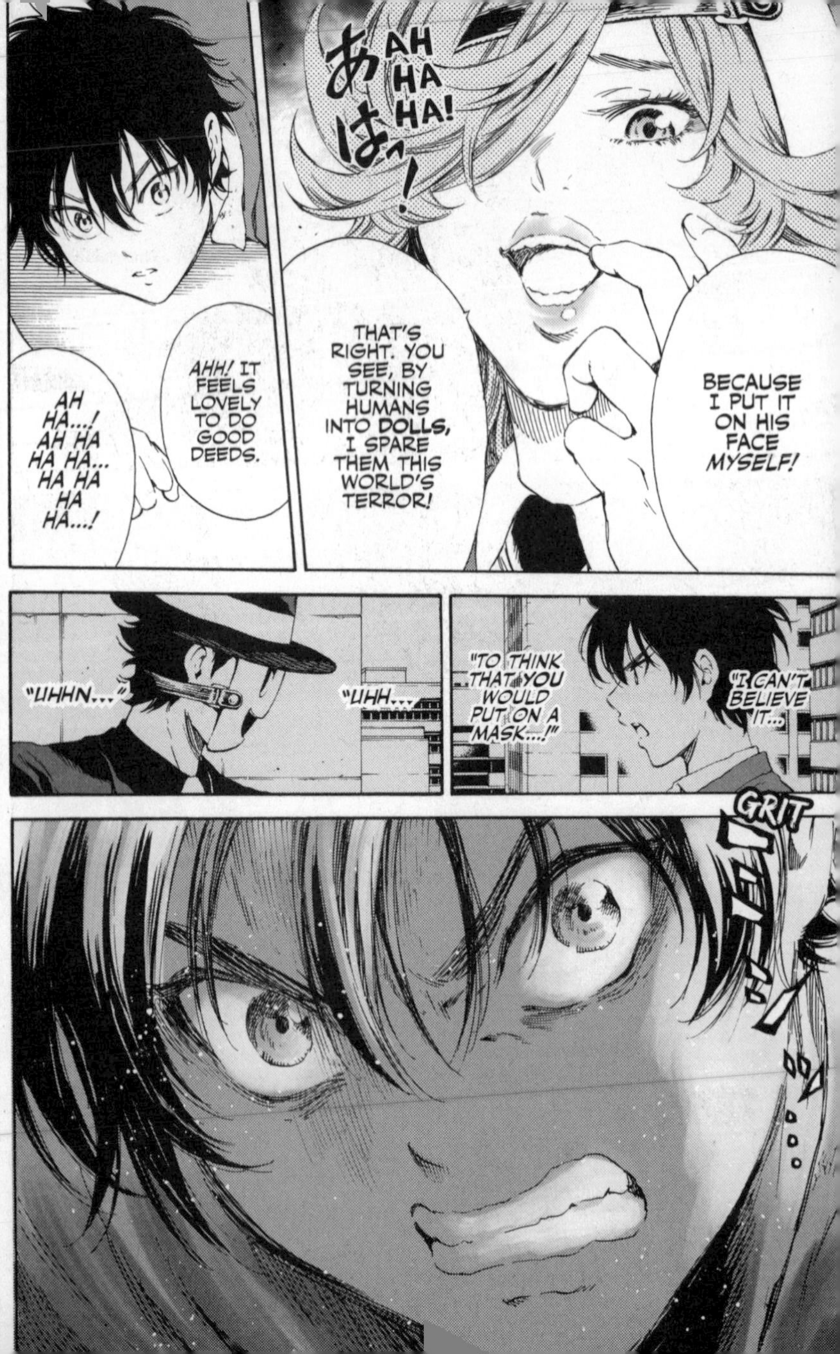
AH HA HA! あはっ!
BECAUSE I PUT IT ON HIS FACE MYSELF!
THAT'S RIGHT. YOU SEE, BY TURNING HUMANS INTO DOLLS, I SPARE THEM THIS WORLD'S TERROR!
AHH! IT FEELS LOVELY TO DO GOOD DEEDS.
AH HA...! AH HA HA HA... HA HA HA HA...!
"I CAN'T BELIEVE IT...
"TO THINK THAT YOU WOULD PUT ON A MASK...!"
"UHH...
"UHHN..."
GRIT

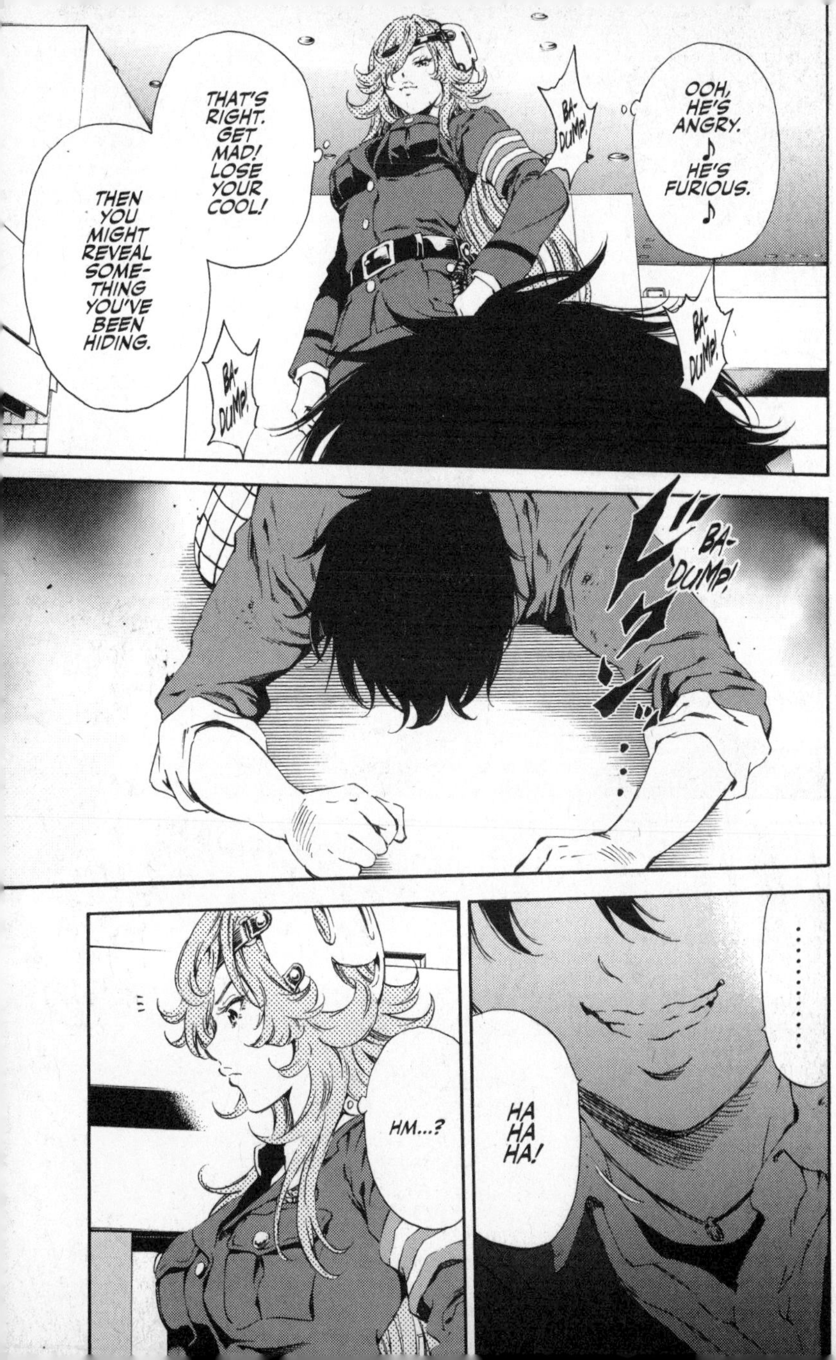
OOH, HE'S ANGRY. ♪ HE'S FURIOUS. ♪
BA-DUMP!
BA-DUMP!
THAT'S RIGHT. GET MAD! LOSE YOUR COOL!
THEN YOU MIGHT REVEAL SOME-THING YOU'VE BEEN HIDING.
BA-DUMP!
BA-DUMP!
......
HA HA HA!
HM...?

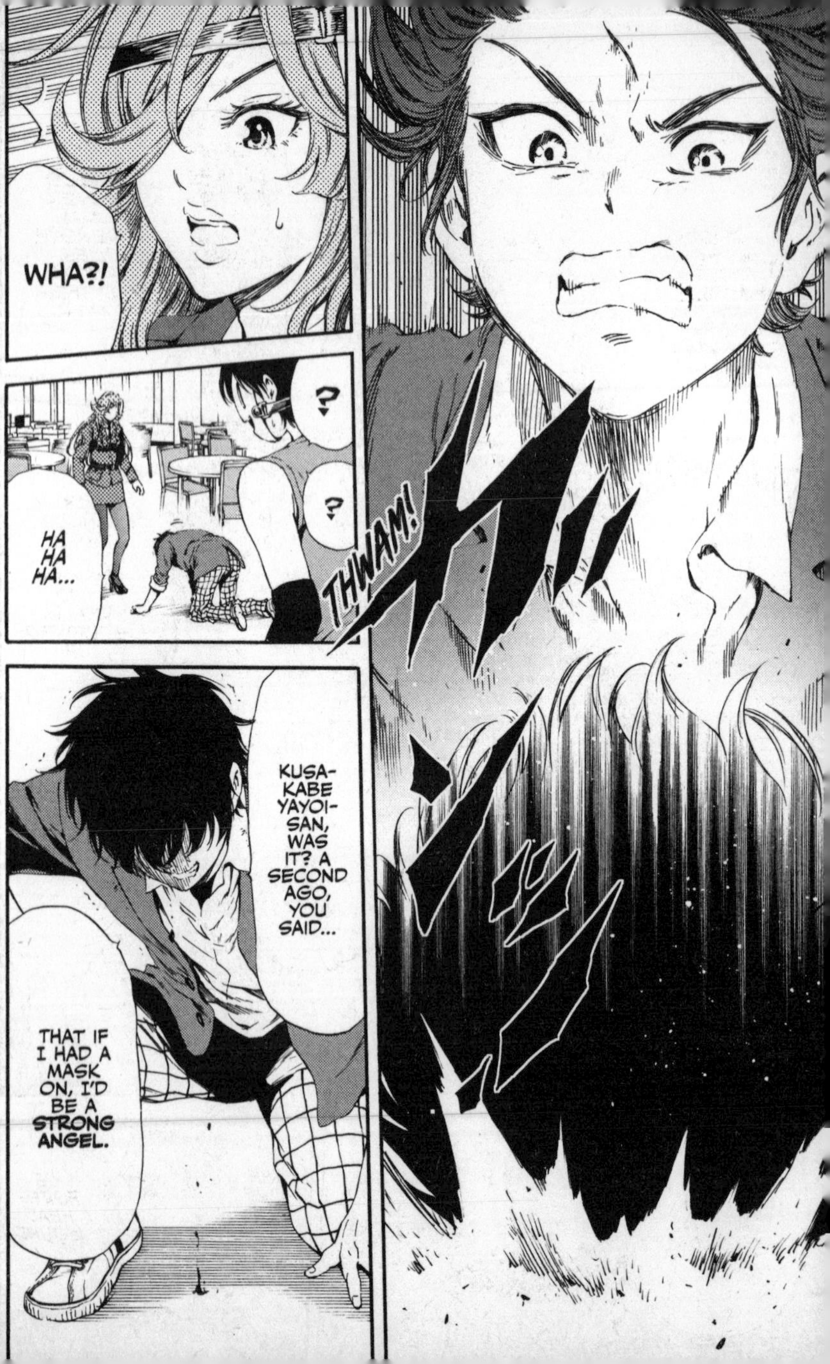
THWAM!
WHA?!
?
?
HA HA HA...
KUSAKABE YAYOI-SAN, WAS IT? A SECOND AGO, YOU SAID...
THAT IF I HAD A MASK ON, I'D BE A STRONG ANGEL.

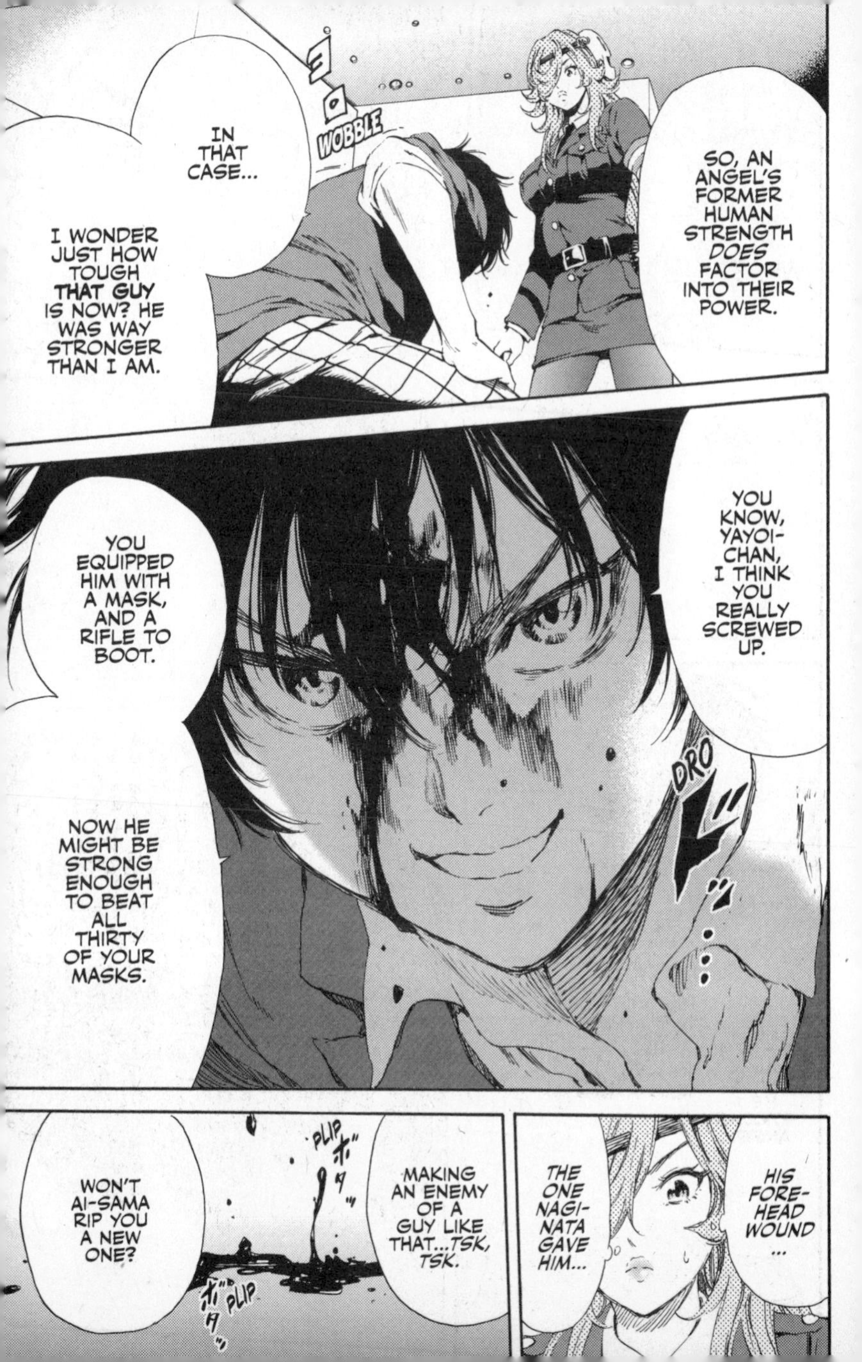
SO, AN ANGEL'S FORMER HUMAN STRENGTH *DOES* FACTOR INTO THEIR POWER.
WOBBLE
IN THAT CASE...
I WONDER JUST HOW TOUGH **THAT GUY** IS NOW? HE WAS WAY STRONGER THAN I AM.
YOU KNOW, YAYOI-CHAN, I THINK YOU REALLY SCREWED UP.
DRO
YOU EQUIPPED HIM WITH A MASK, AND A RIFLE TO BOOT.
NOW HE MIGHT BE STRONG ENOUGH TO BEAT ALL THIRTY OF YOUR MASKS.
HIS FORE-HEAD WOUND...
THE ONE NAGI-NATA GAVE HIM...
MAKING AN ENEMY OF A GUY LIKE THAT...*TSK, TSK.*
PLIP
PLIP
WON'T AI-SAMA RIP YOU A NEW ONE?

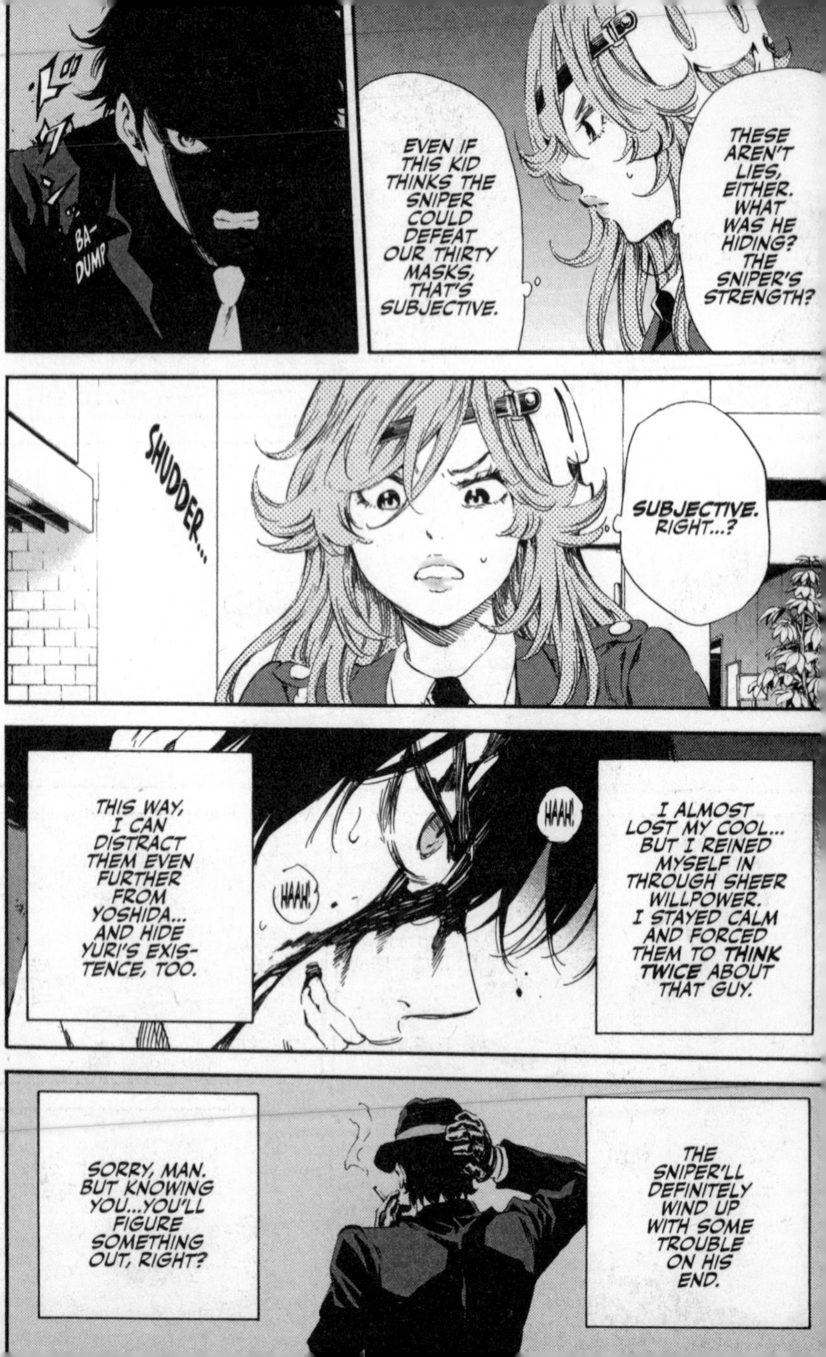
THESE AREN'T LIES, EITHER. WHAT WAS HE HIDING? THE SNIPER'S STRENGTH?
EVEN IF THIS KID THINKS THE SNIPER COULD DEFEAT OUR THIRTY MASKS, THAT'S SUBJECTIVE.
BA-DUMP
SUBJECTIVE. RIGHT...?
SHUDDER...
I ALMOST LOST MY COOL... BUT I REINED MYSELF IN THROUGH SHEER WILLPOWER. I STAYED CALM AND FORCED THEM TO THINK TWICE ABOUT THAT GUY.
HAAH
HAAH
THIS WAY, I CAN DISTRACT THEM EVEN FURTHER FROM YOSHIDA... AND HIDE YURI'S EXISTENCE, TOO.
THE SNIPER'LL DEFINITELY WIND UP WITH SOME TROUBLE ON HIS END.
SORRY, MAN. BUT KNOWING YOU...YOU'LL FIGURE SOMETHING OUT, RIGHT?

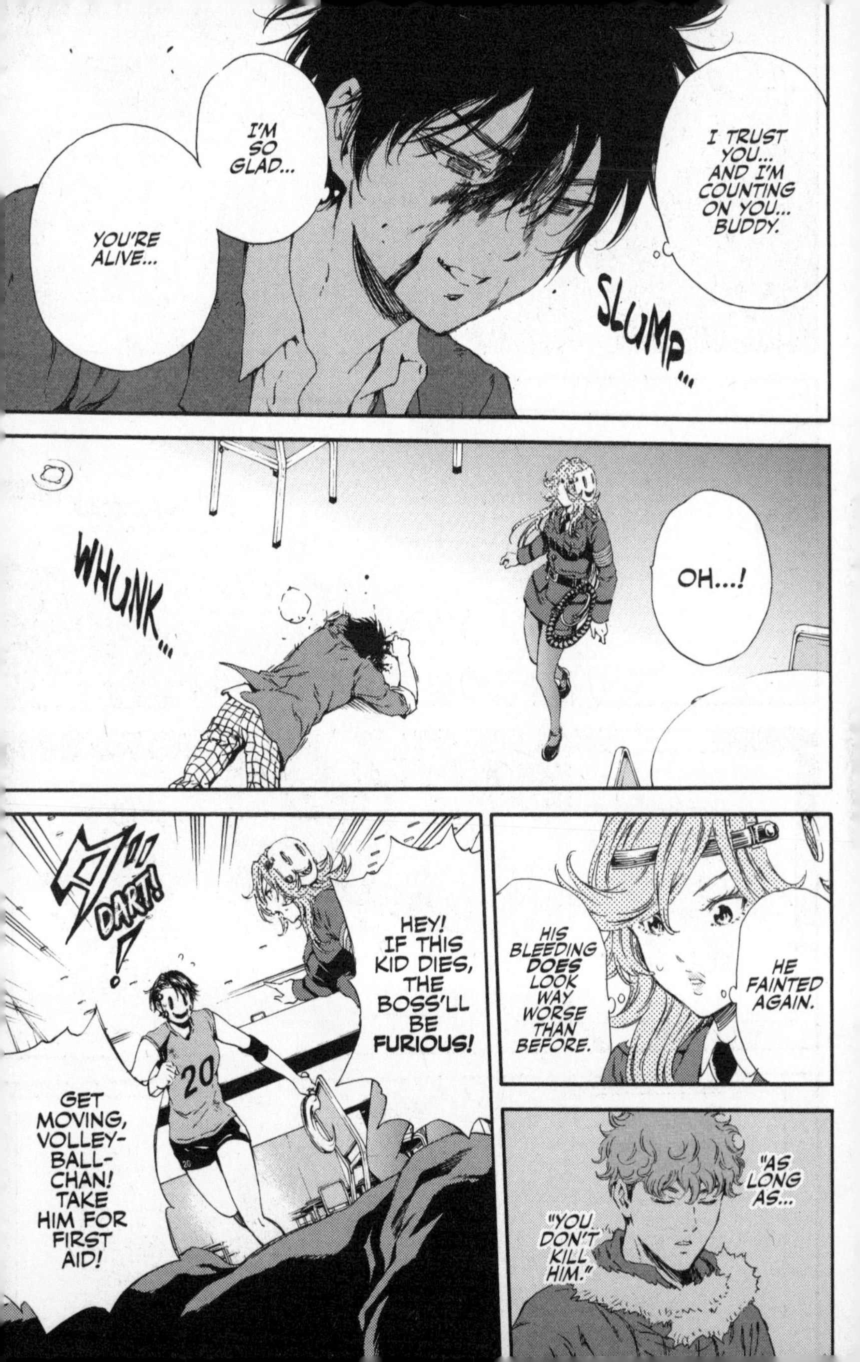
I TRUST YOU... AND I'M COUNTING ON YOU... BUDDY.
I'M SO GLAD...
YOU'RE ALIVE...
SLUMP...
OH...!
WHUNK...
HE FAINTED AGAIN.
HIS BLEEDING DOES LOOK WAY WORSE THAN BEFORE.
"AS LONG AS...
"YOU DON'T KILL HIM."
DART!
HEY! IF THIS KID DIES, THE BOSS'LL BE FURIOUS!
GET MOVING, VOLLEY-BALL-CHAN! TAKE HIM FOR FIRST AID!

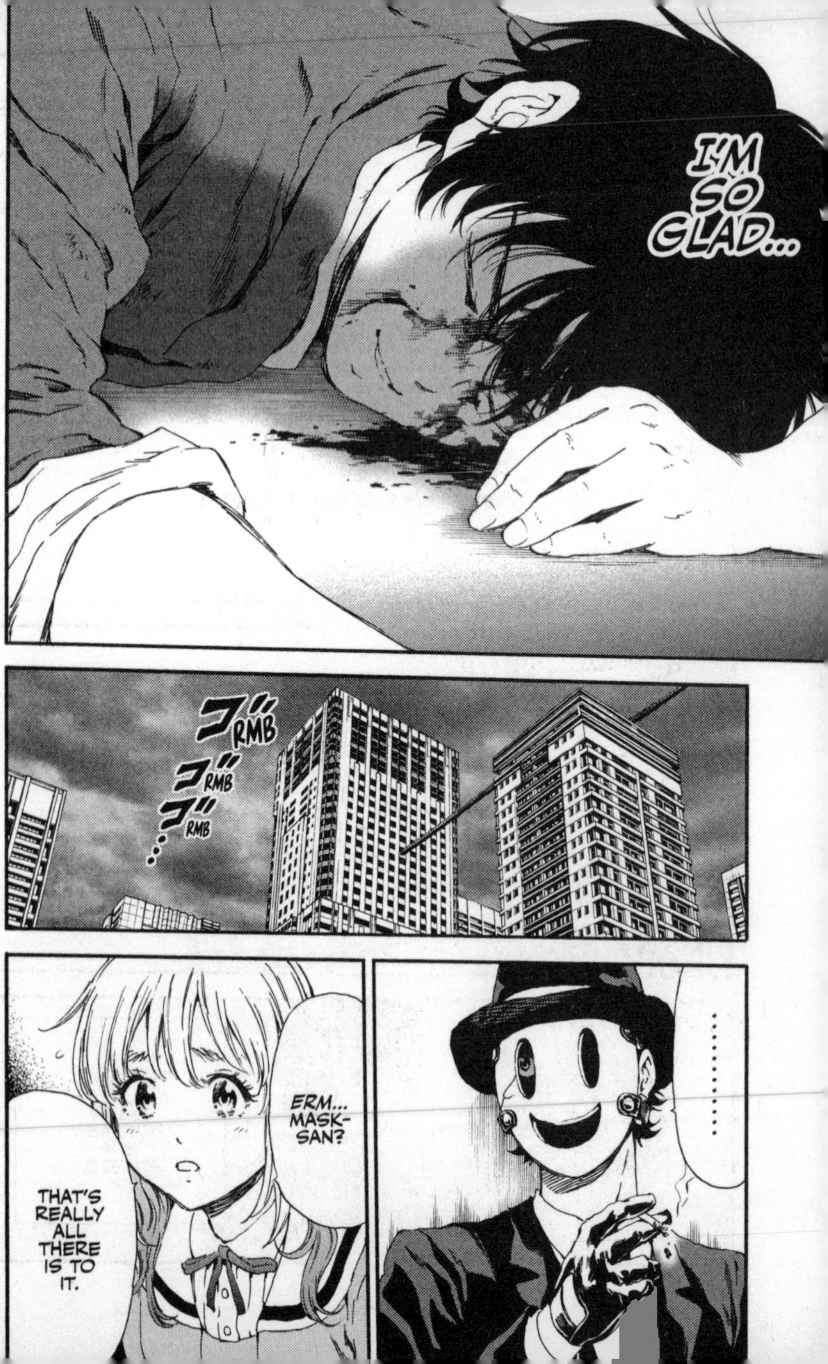
I'M SO GLAD...
ゴ RMB
ゴ RMB
ゴ RMB
...
....
ERM... MASK-SAN?
THAT'S REALLY ALL THERE IS TO IT.

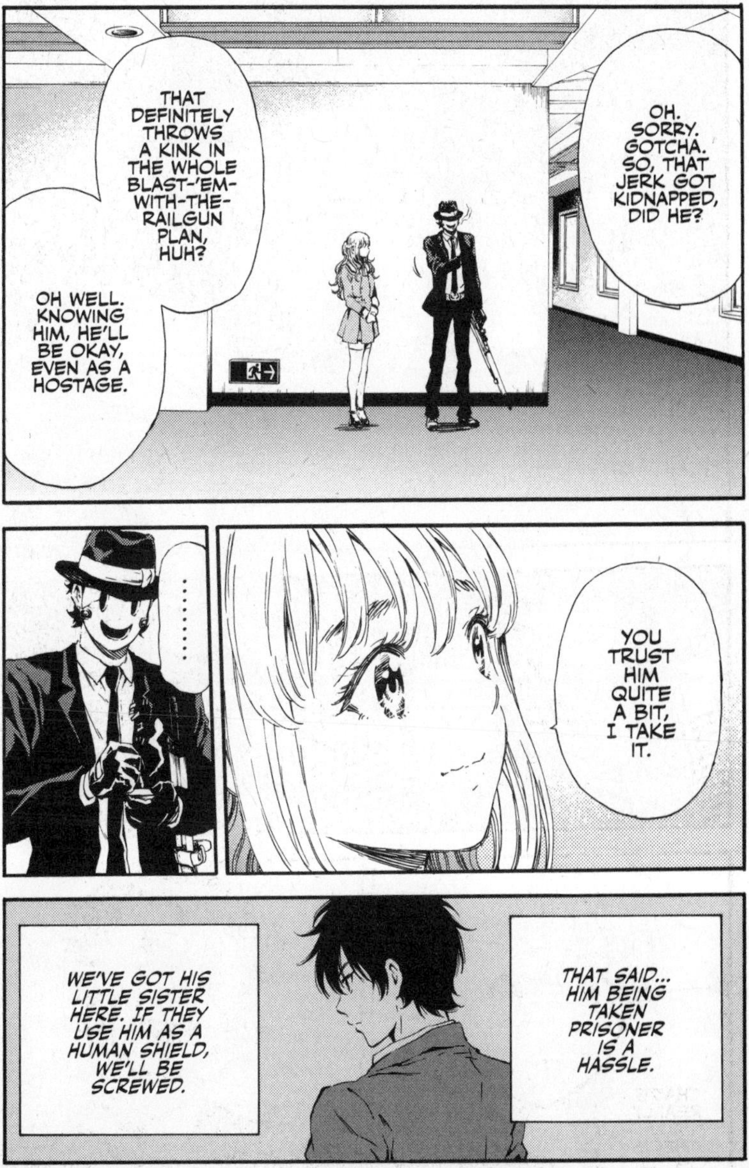
OH. SORRY. GOTCHA. SO, THAT JERK GOT KIDNAPPED, DID HE?
THAT DEFINITELY THROWS A KINK IN THE WHOLE BLAST-'EM-WITH-THE-RAILGUN PLAN, HUH?
OH WELL. KNOWING HIM, HE'LL BE OKAY, EVEN AS A HOSTAGE.
YOU TRUST HIM QUITE A BIT, I TAKE IT.
......
THAT SAID... HIM BEING TAKEN PRISONER IS A HASSLE.
WE'VE GOT HIS LITTLE SISTER HERE. IF THEY USE HIM AS A HUMAN SHIELD, WE'LL BE SCREWED.

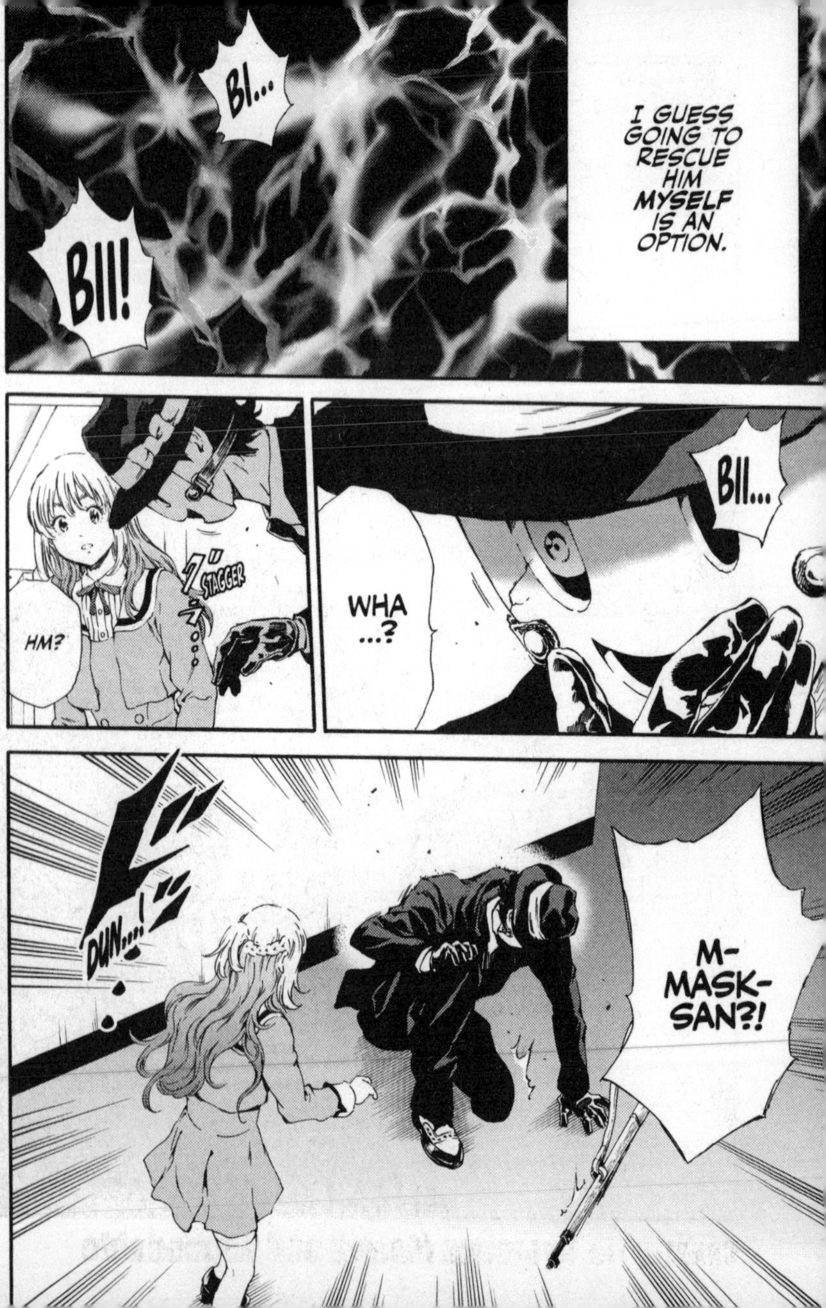
I GUESS GOING TO RESCUE HIM MYSELF IS AN OPTION.
BI...
BII!
BII...
WHA ...?
STAGGER
HM?
M-MASK-SAN?!
DUN...!

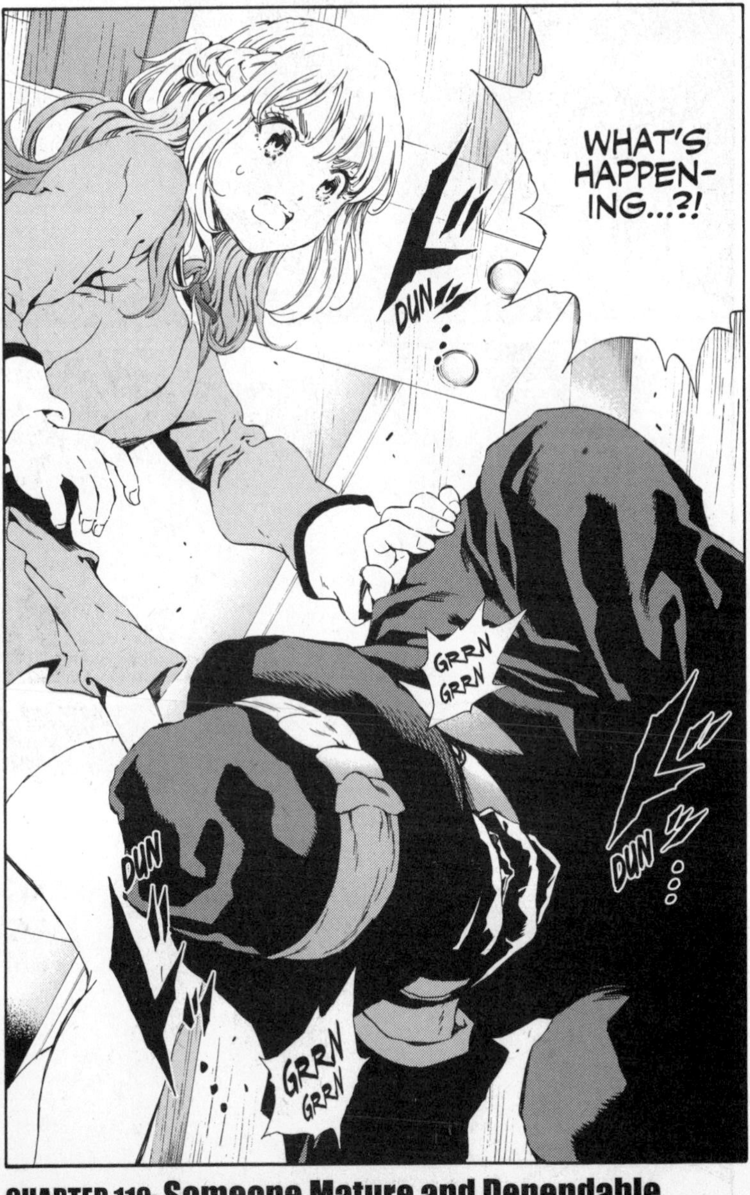
WHAT'S HAPPEN-ING...?!
DUN...
GRRN GRRN
DUN...
DUN...
GRRN GRRN

CHAPTER 119: Someone Mature and Dependable

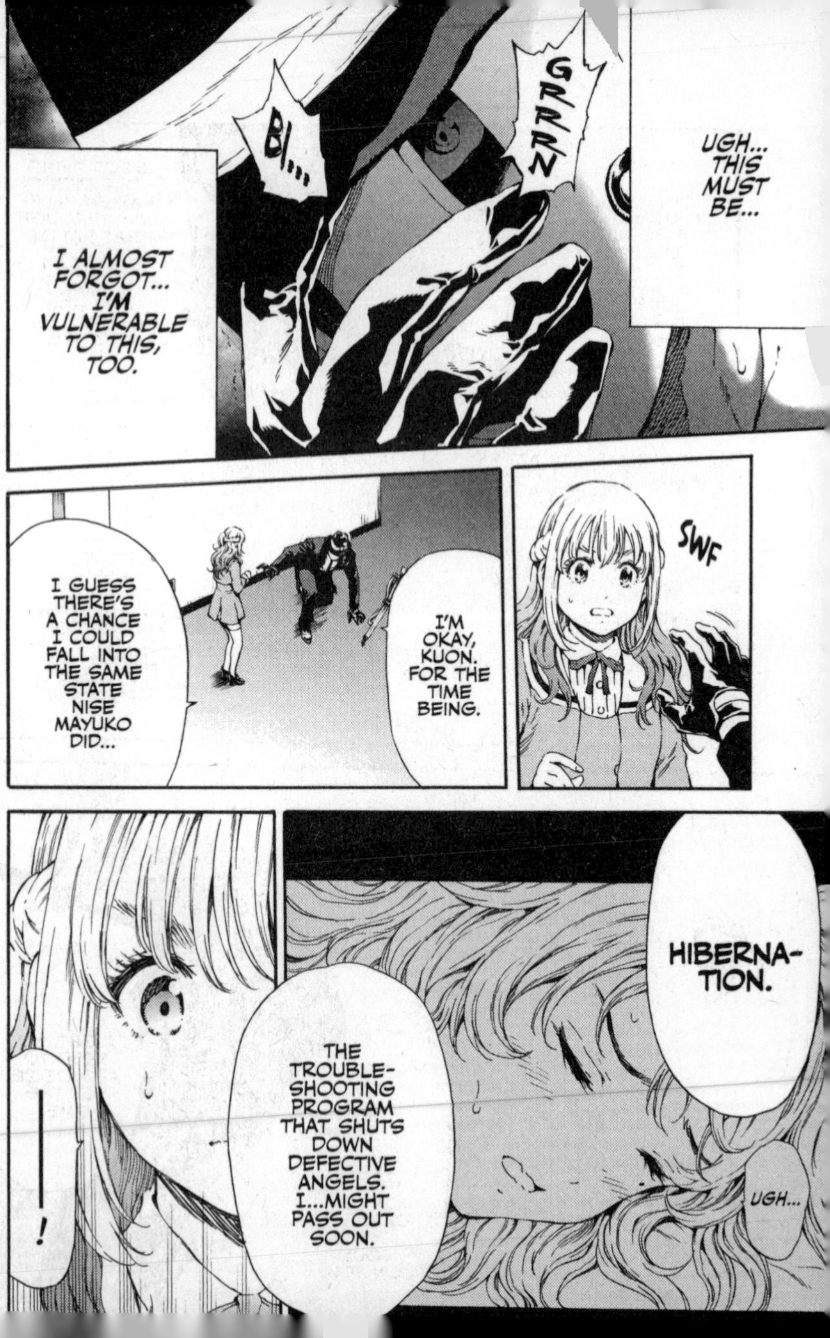
UGH... THIS MUST BE...
GRRRN
BI...
I ALMOST FORGOT... I'M VULNERABLE TO THIS, TOO.
SWF
I'M OKAY, KUON. FOR THE TIME BEING.
I GUESS THERE'S A CHANCE I COULD FALL INTO THE SAME STATE NISE MAYUKO DID...
HIBERNA-TION.
UGH...
THE TROUBLE-SHOOTING PROGRAM THAT SHUTS DOWN DEFECTIVE ANGELS. I...MIGHT PASS OUT SOON.
—!

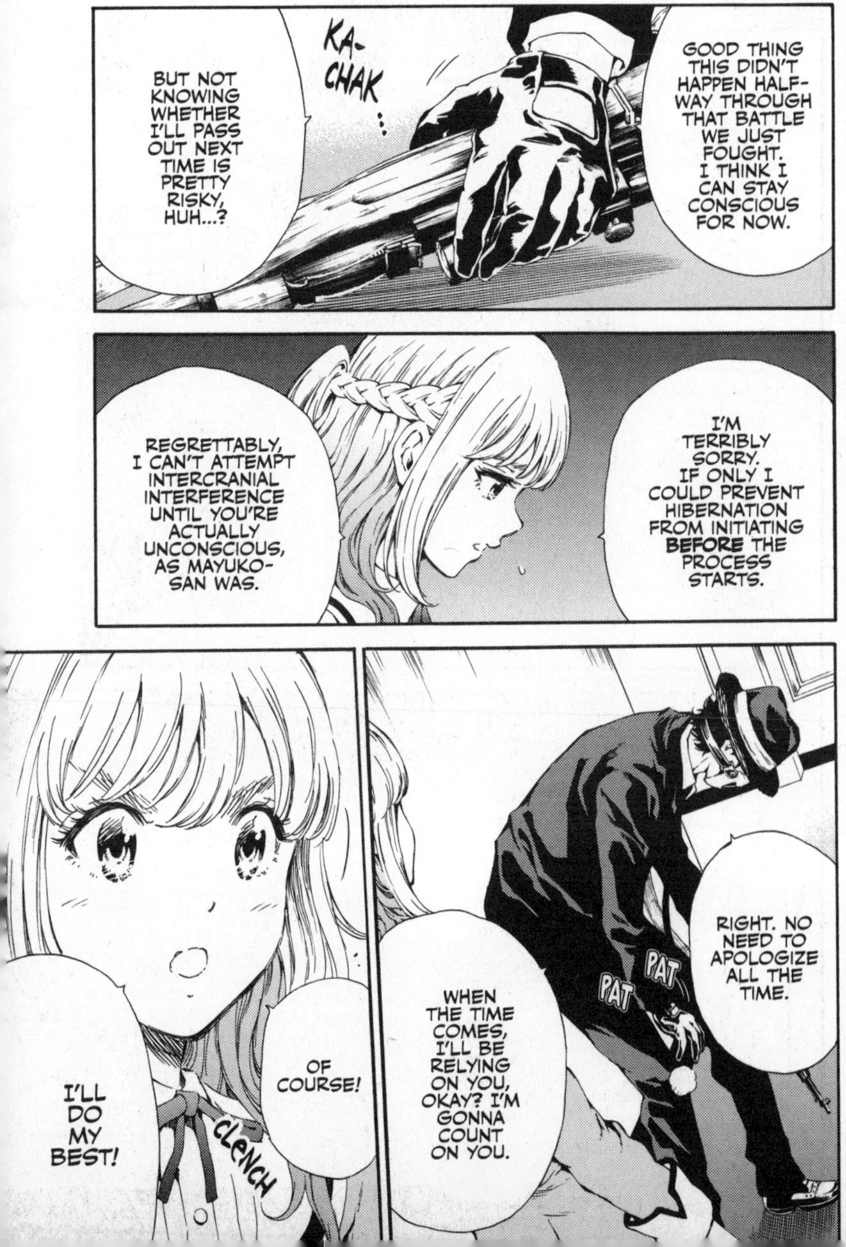
GOOD THING THIS DIDN'T HAPPEN HALF-WAY THROUGH THAT BATTLE WE JUST FOUGHT. I THINK I CAN STAY CONSCIOUS FOR NOW.
KA-CHAK
BUT NOT KNOWING WHETHER I'LL PASS OUT NEXT TIME IS PRETTY RISKY, HUH...?
I'M TERRIBLY SORRY. IF ONLY I COULD PREVENT HIBERNATION FROM INITIATING **BEFORE** THE PROCESS STARTS.
REGRETTABLY, I CAN'T ATTEMPT INTERCRANIAL INTERFERENCE UNTIL YOU'RE ACTUALLY UNCONSCIOUS, AS MAYUKO-SAN WAS.
RIGHT. NO NEED TO APOLOGIZE ALL THE TIME.
PAT
PAT
WHEN THE TIME COMES, I'LL BE RELYING ON YOU, OKAY? I'M GONNA COUNT ON YOU.
OF COURSE!
CLENCH
I'LL DO MY BEST!

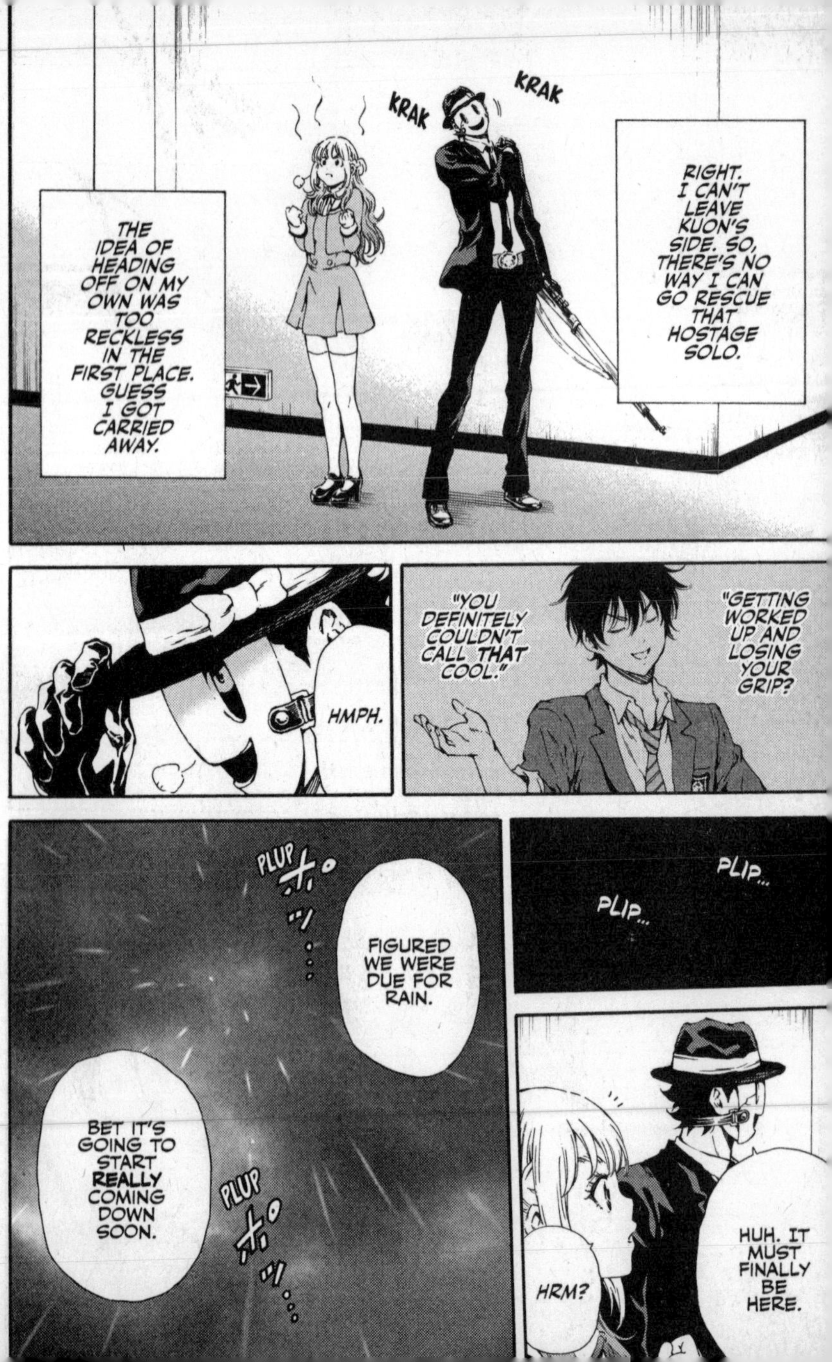
KRAK
KRAK
RIGHT. I CAN'T LEAVE KUON'S SIDE. SO, THERE'S NO WAY I CAN GO RESCUE THAT HOSTAGE SOLO.
THE IDEA OF HEADING OFF ON MY OWN WAS TOO RECKLESS IN THE FIRST PLACE. GUESS I GOT CARRIED AWAY.
"GETTING WORKED UP AND LOSING YOUR GRIP?
"YOU DEFINITELY COULDN'T CALL THAT COOL."
HMPH.
PLIP...
PLIP...
HUH. IT MUST FINALLY BE HERE.
HRM?
PLUP
FIGURED WE WERE DUE FOR RAIN.
BET IT'S GOING TO START **REALLY** COMING DOWN SOON.
PLUP

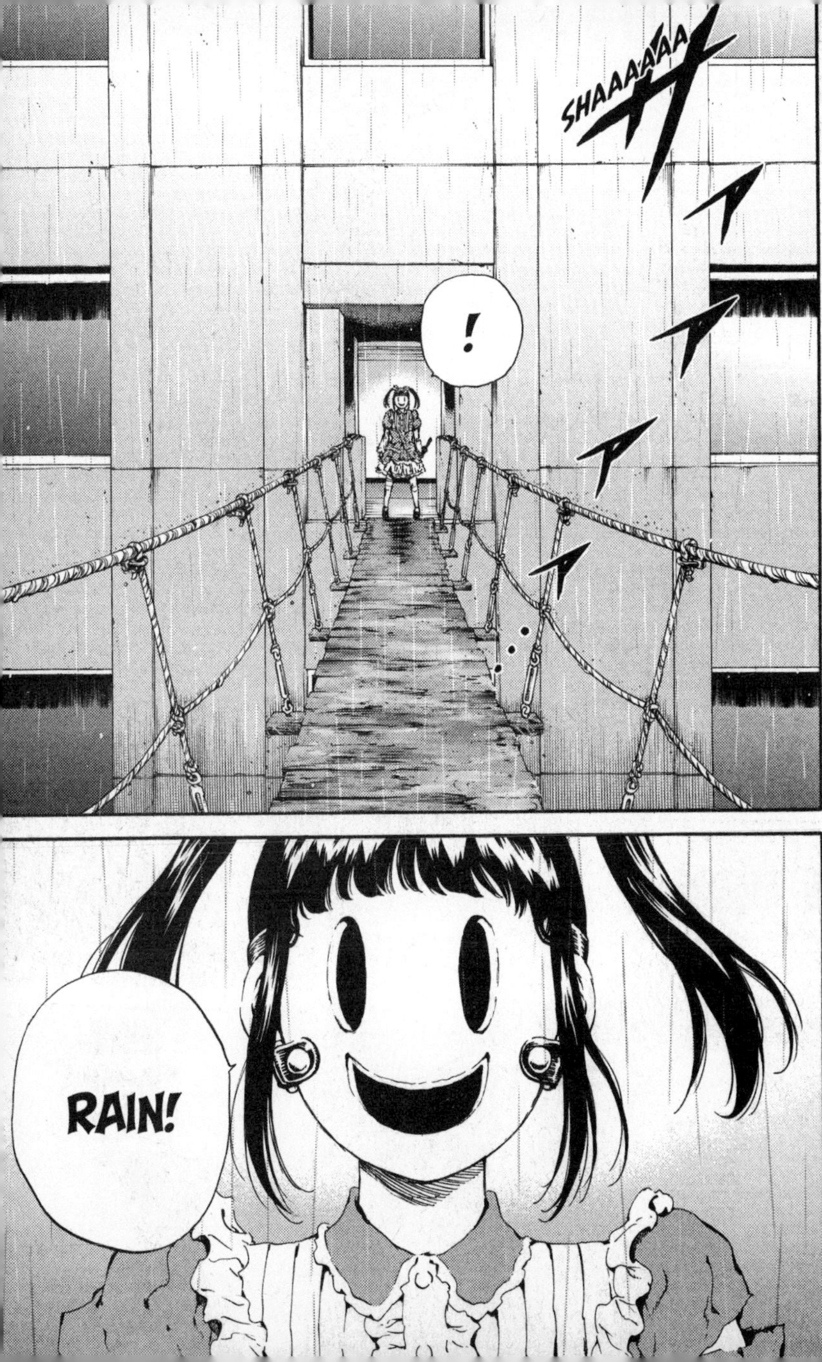
SHAAAAAA
!
RAIN!

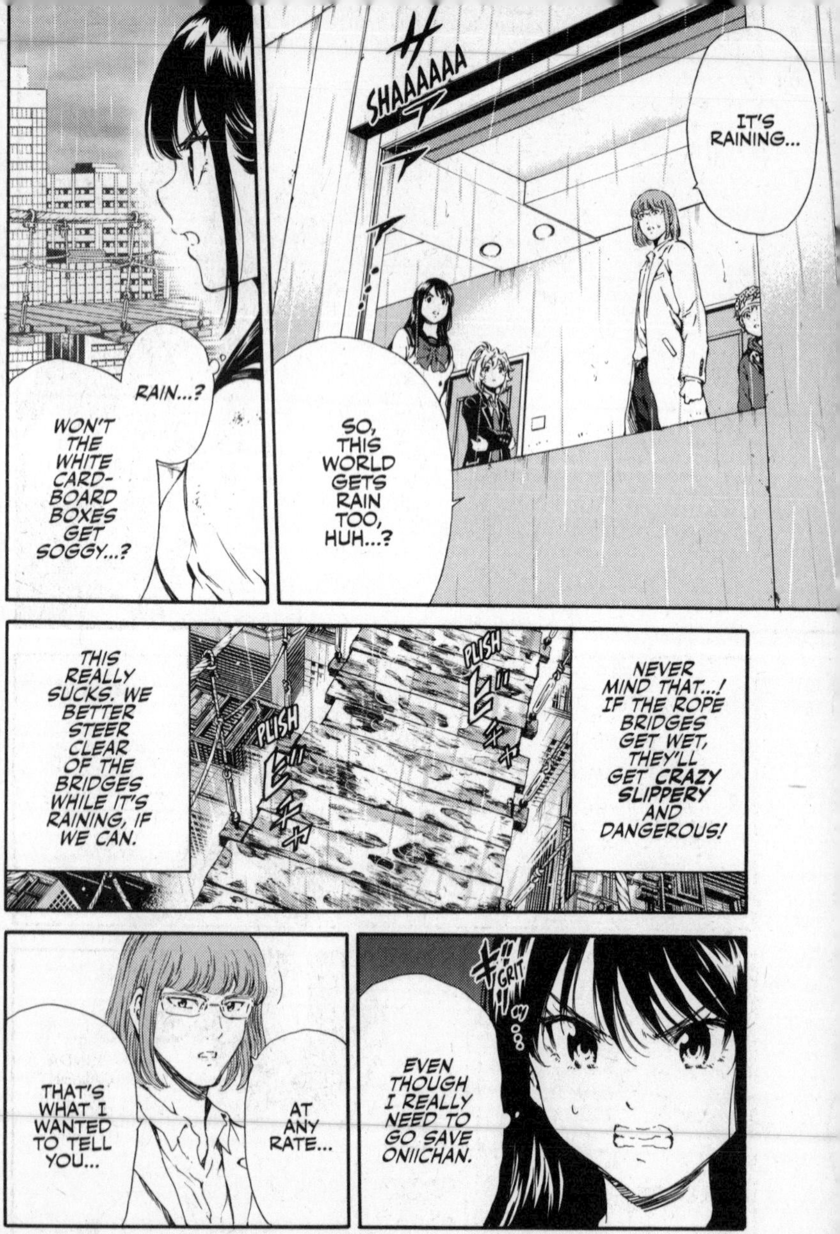
SHAAAAAA
IT'S RAINING...
SO, THIS WORLD GETS RAIN TOO, HUH...?
RAIN...?
WON'T THE WHITE CARD-BOARD BOXES GET SOGGY...?
NEVER MIND THAT...! IF THE ROPE BRIDGES GET WET, THEY'LL GET CRAZY SLIPPERY AND DANGEROUS!
PLISH
PLISH
THIS REALLY SUCKS. WE BETTER STEER CLEAR OF THE BRIDGES WHILE IT'S RAINING, IF WE CAN.
GRIT
EVEN THOUGH I REALLY NEED TO GO SAVE ONIICHAN.
AT ANY RATE...
THAT'S WHAT I WANTED TO TELL YOU...

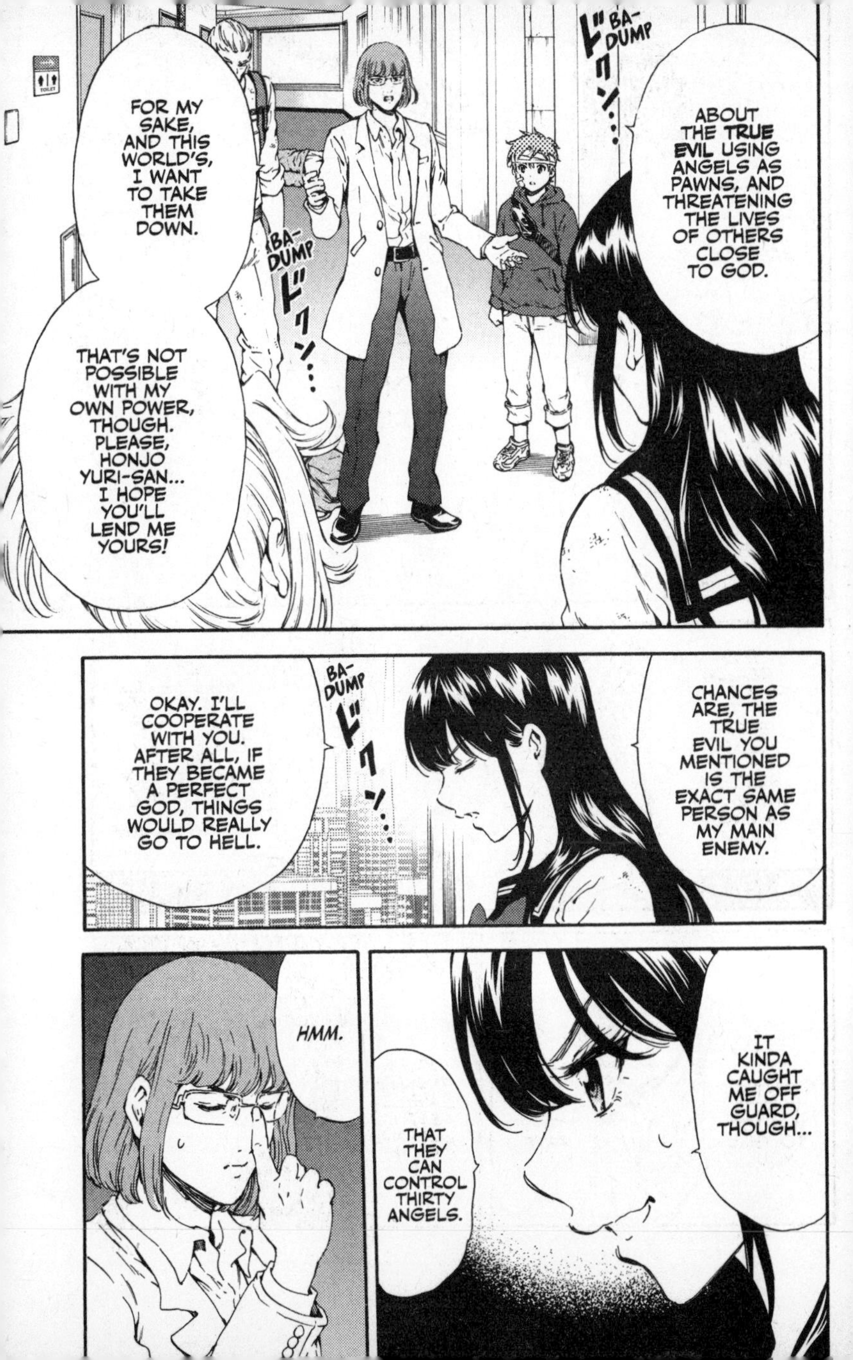
BA-DUMP
ABOUT THE TRUE EVIL USING ANGELS AS PAWNS, AND THREATENING THE LIVES OF OTHERS CLOSE TO GOD.
BA-DUMP
FOR MY SAKE, AND THIS WORLD'S, I WANT TO TAKE THEM DOWN.
THAT'S NOT POSSIBLE WITH MY OWN POWER, THOUGH. PLEASE, HONJO YURI-SAN... I HOPE YOU'LL LEND ME YOURS!
CHANCES ARE, THE TRUE EVIL YOU MENTIONED IS THE EXACT SAME PERSON AS MY MAIN ENEMY.
BA-DUMP
OKAY. I'LL COOPERATE WITH YOU. AFTER ALL, IF THEY BECAME A PERFECT GOD, THINGS WOULD REALLY GO TO HELL.
IT KINDA CAUGHT ME OFF GUARD, THOUGH...
THAT THEY CAN CONTROL THIRTY ANGELS.
HMM.

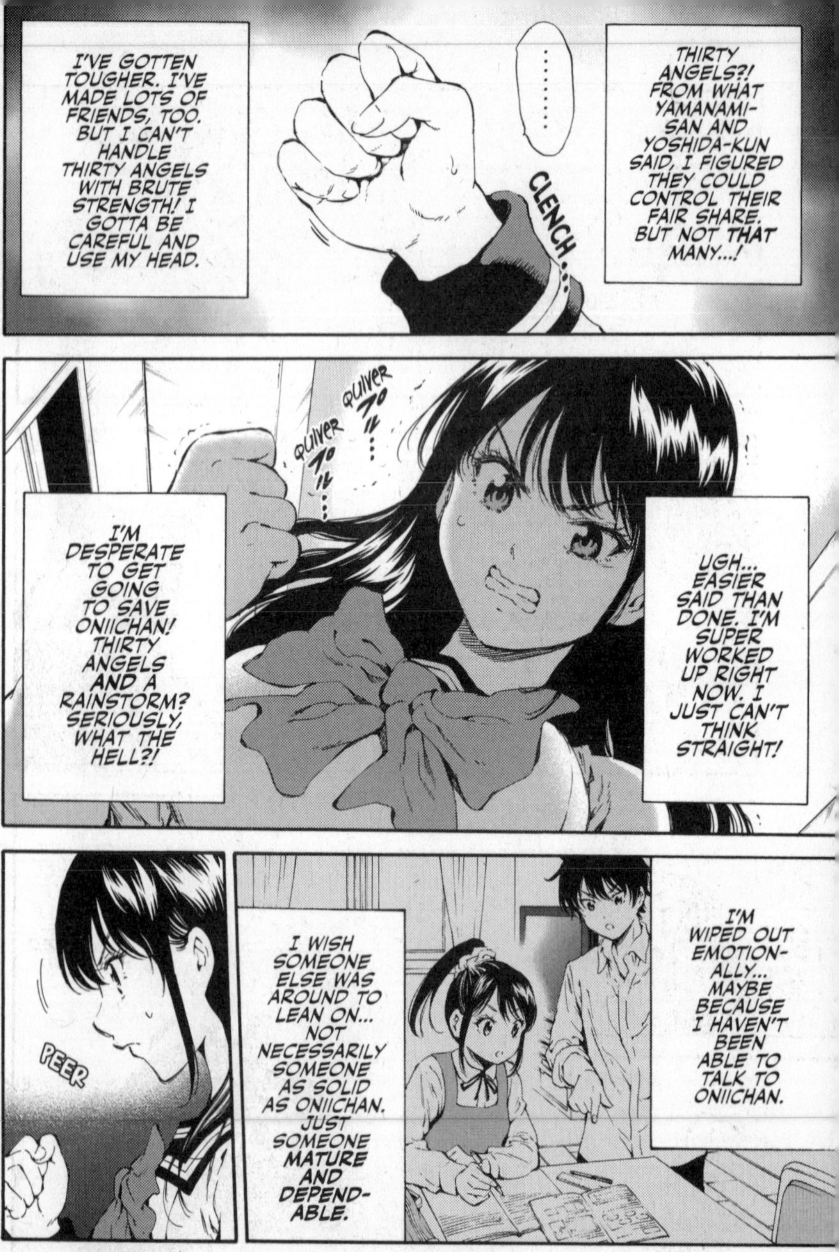
THIRTY ANGELS?! FROM WHAT YAMANAMI-SAN AND YOSHIDA-KUN SAID, I FIGURED THEY COULD CONTROL THEIR FAIR SHARE. BUT NOT THAT MANY...!
......
CLENCH...
I'VE GOTTEN TOUGHER. I'VE MADE LOTS OF FRIENDS, TOO. BUT I CAN'T HANDLE THIRTY ANGELS WITH BRUTE STRENGTH! I GOTTA BE CAREFUL AND USE MY HEAD.
UGH... EASIER SAID THAN DONE. I'M SUPER WORKED UP RIGHT NOW. I JUST CAN'T THINK STRAIGHT!
QUIVER
QUIVER
I'M DESPERATE TO GET GOING TO SAVE ONIICHAN! THIRTY ANGELS AND A RAINSTORM? SERIOUSLY, WHAT THE HELL?!
I'M WIPED OUT EMOTION-ALLY... MAYBE BECAUSE I HAVEN'T BEEN ABLE TO TALK TO ONIICHAN.
I WISH SOMEONE ELSE WAS AROUND TO LEAN ON... NOT NECESSARILY SOMEONE AS SOLID AS ONIICHAN. JUST SOMEONE MATURE AND DEPEND-ABLE.
PEER

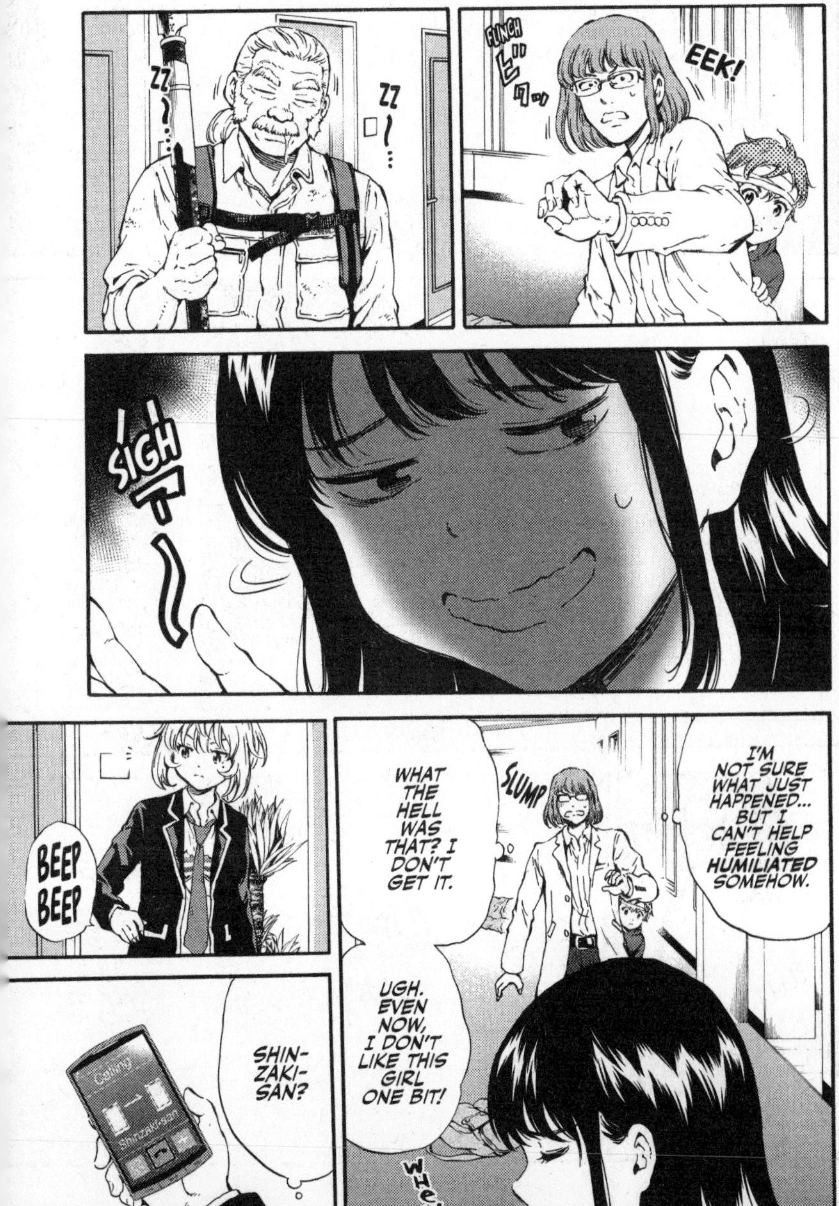
FLINCH
EEK!
ZZ...
ZZ...
SIGH
I'M NOT SURE WHAT JUST HAPPENED... BUT I CAN'T HELP FEELING **HUMILIATED** SOMEHOW.
SLUMP
WHAT THE HELL WAS THAT? I DON'T GET IT.
UGH. EVEN NOW, I DON'T LIKE THIS GIRL ONE BIT!
WHEW!
BEEP BEEP
SHIN-ZAKI-SAN?
Calling
Shinzaki-san

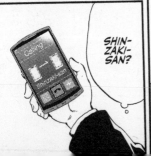

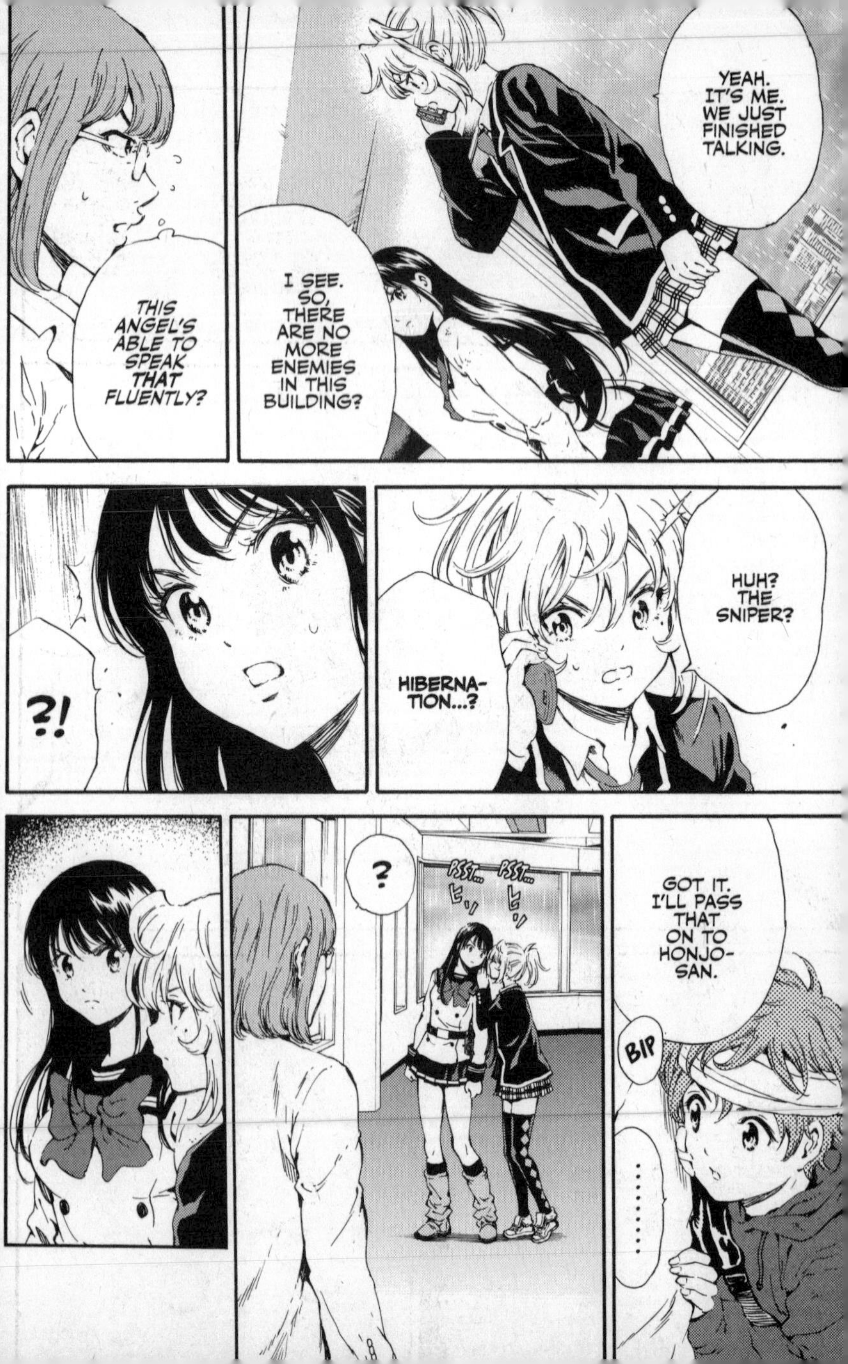
YEAH. IT'S ME. WE JUST FINISHED TALKING.
I SEE. SO, THERE ARE NO MORE ENEMIES IN THIS BUILDING?
THIS ANGEL'S ABLE TO SPEAK THAT FLUENTLY?
HUH? THE SNIPER?
HIBERNATION...?
?!
GOT IT. I'LL PASS THAT ON TO HONJO-SAN.
BIP
......
?
PSST... ヒソ
PSST... ヒソ

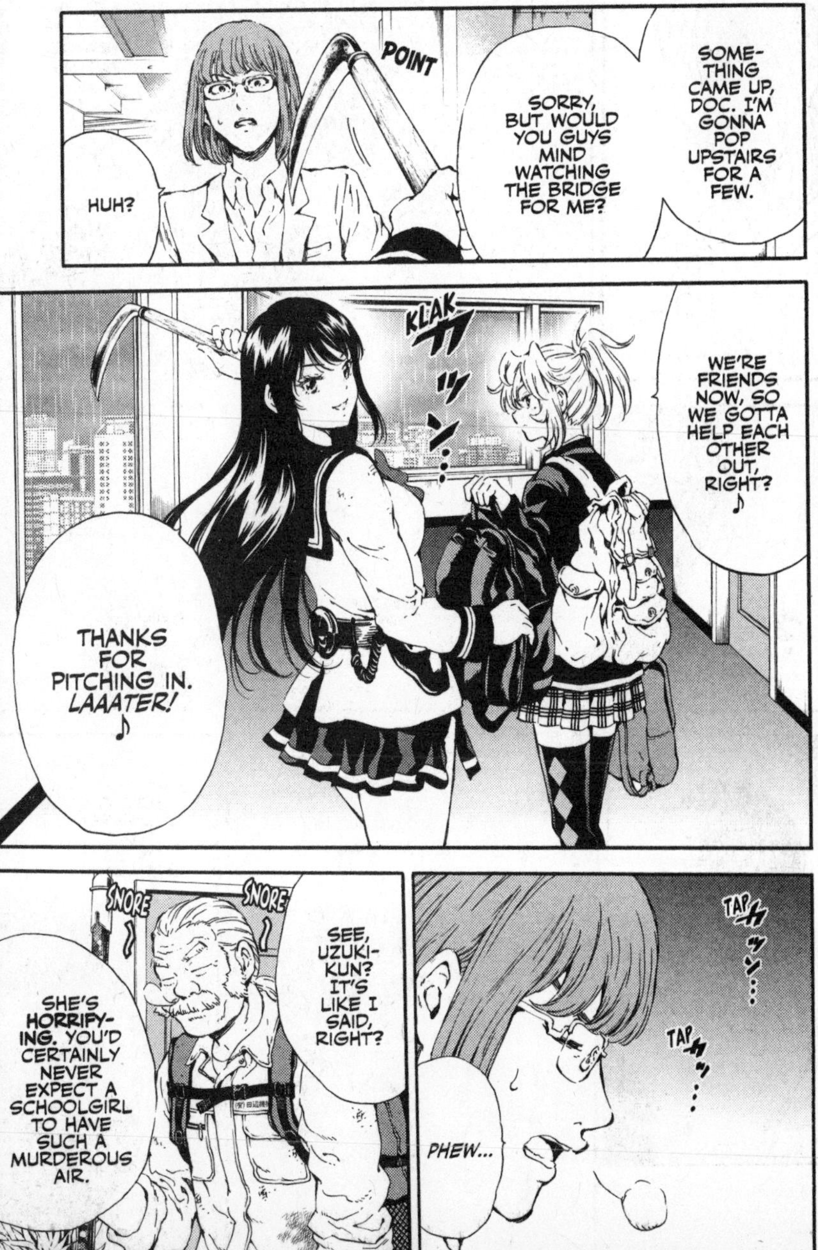
SOME-THING CAME UP, DOC. I'M GONNA POP UPSTAIRS FOR A FEW.
SORRY, BUT WOULD YOU GUYS MIND WATCHING THE BRIDGE FOR ME?
POINT
HUH?
WE'RE FRIENDS NOW, SO WE GOTTA HELP EACH OTHER OUT, RIGHT? ♪
KLAK
THANKS FOR PITCHING IN. *LAAATER!* ♪
TAP
TAP
PHEW...
SNORE
SNORE
SEE, UZUKI-KUN? IT'S LIKE I SAID, RIGHT?
SHE'S **HORRIFY-ING.** YOU'D CERTAINLY NEVER EXPECT A SCHOOLGIRL TO HAVE SUCH A MURDEROUS AIR.

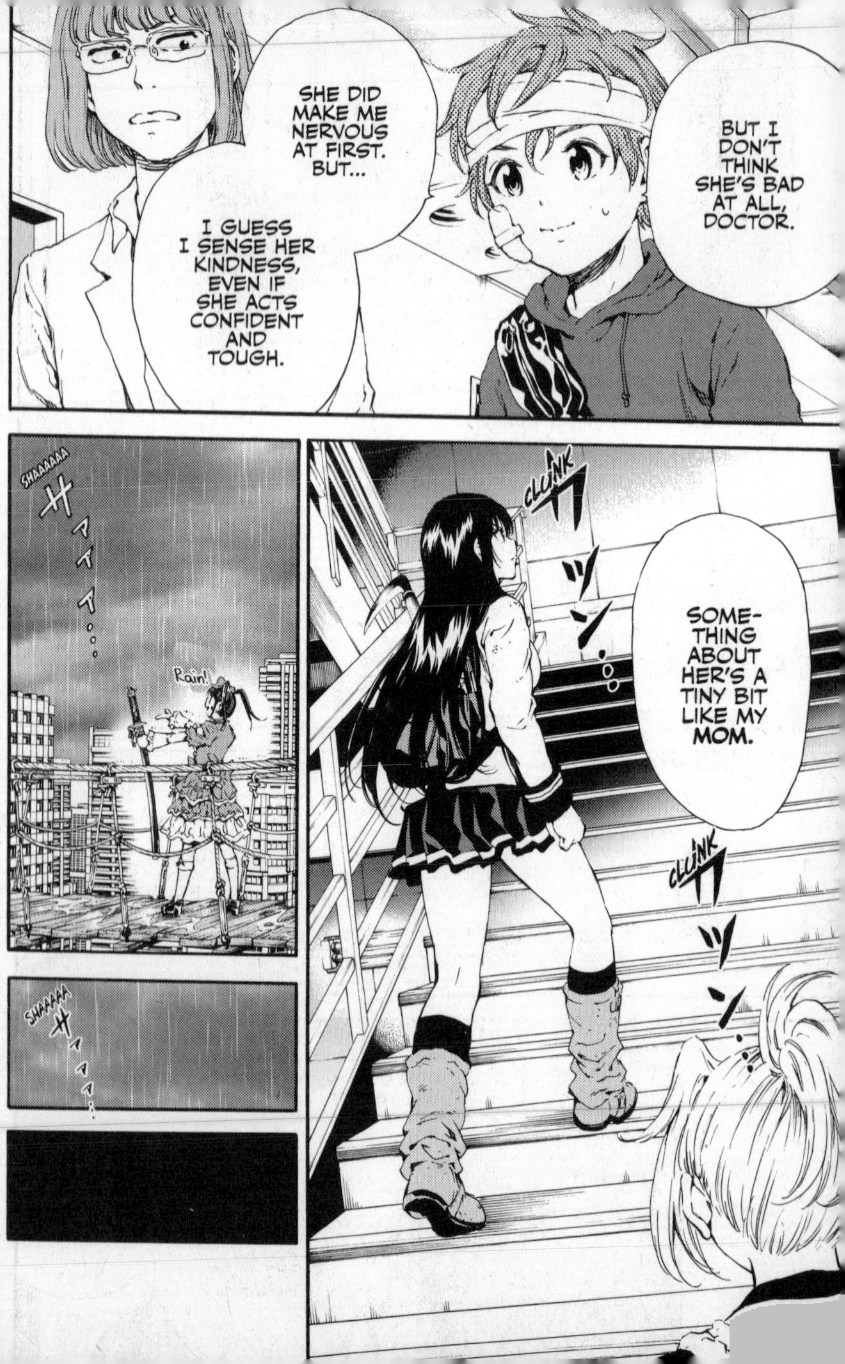
BUT I DON'T THINK SHE'S BAD AT ALL, DOCTOR.
SHE DID MAKE ME NERVOUS AT FIRST. BUT...
I GUESS I SENSE HER KINDNESS, EVEN IF SHE ACTS CONFIDENT AND TOUGH.
CLLINK
SOME-THING ABOUT HER'S A TINY BIT LIKE MY MOM.
CLLINK
SHAAAAAA
Rain!
SHAAAAA

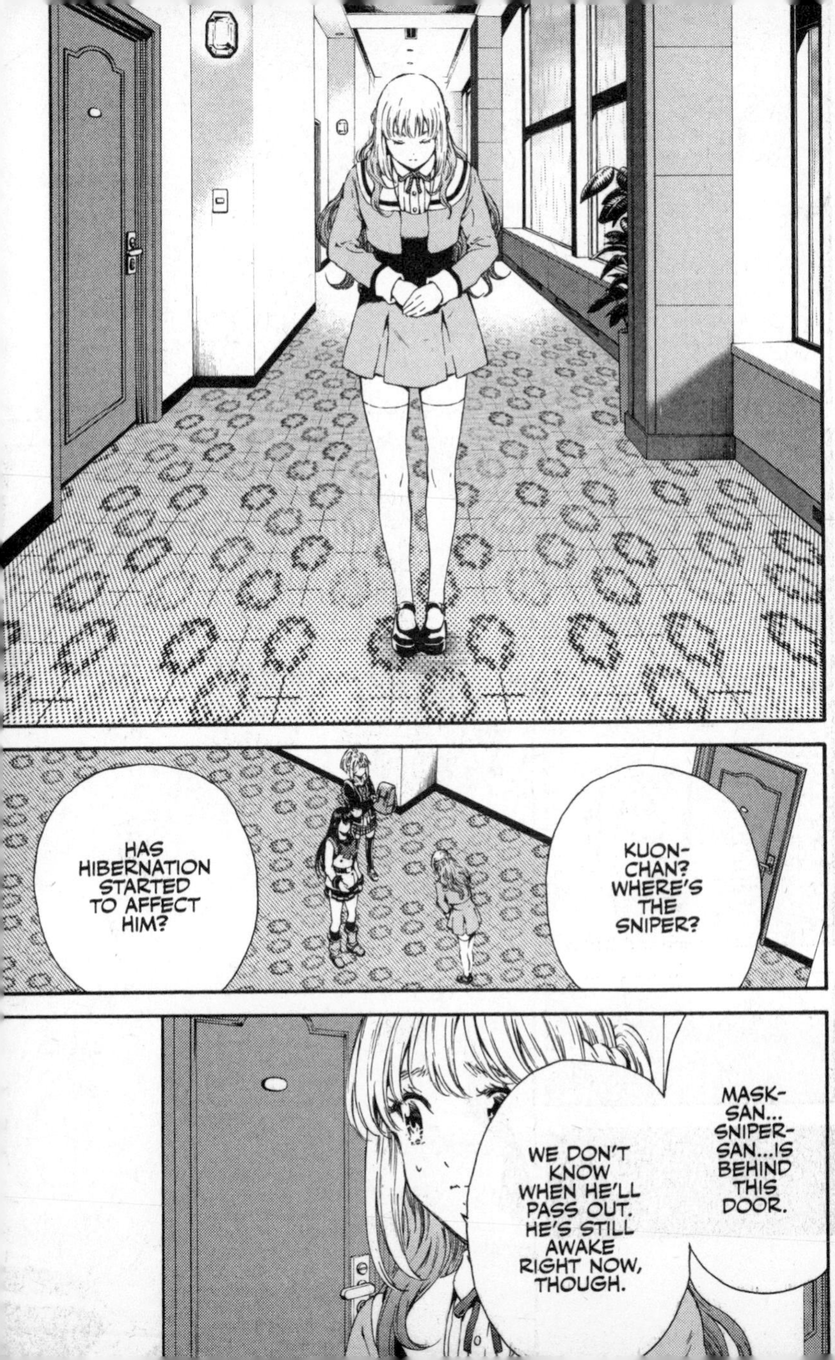
KUON-CHAN? WHERE'S THE SNIPER?
HAS HIBERNATION STARTED TO AFFECT HIM?
MASK-SAN... SNIPER-SAN...IS BEHIND THIS DOOR.
WE DON'T KNOW WHEN HE'LL PASS OUT. HE'S STILL AWAKE RIGHT NOW, THOUGH.

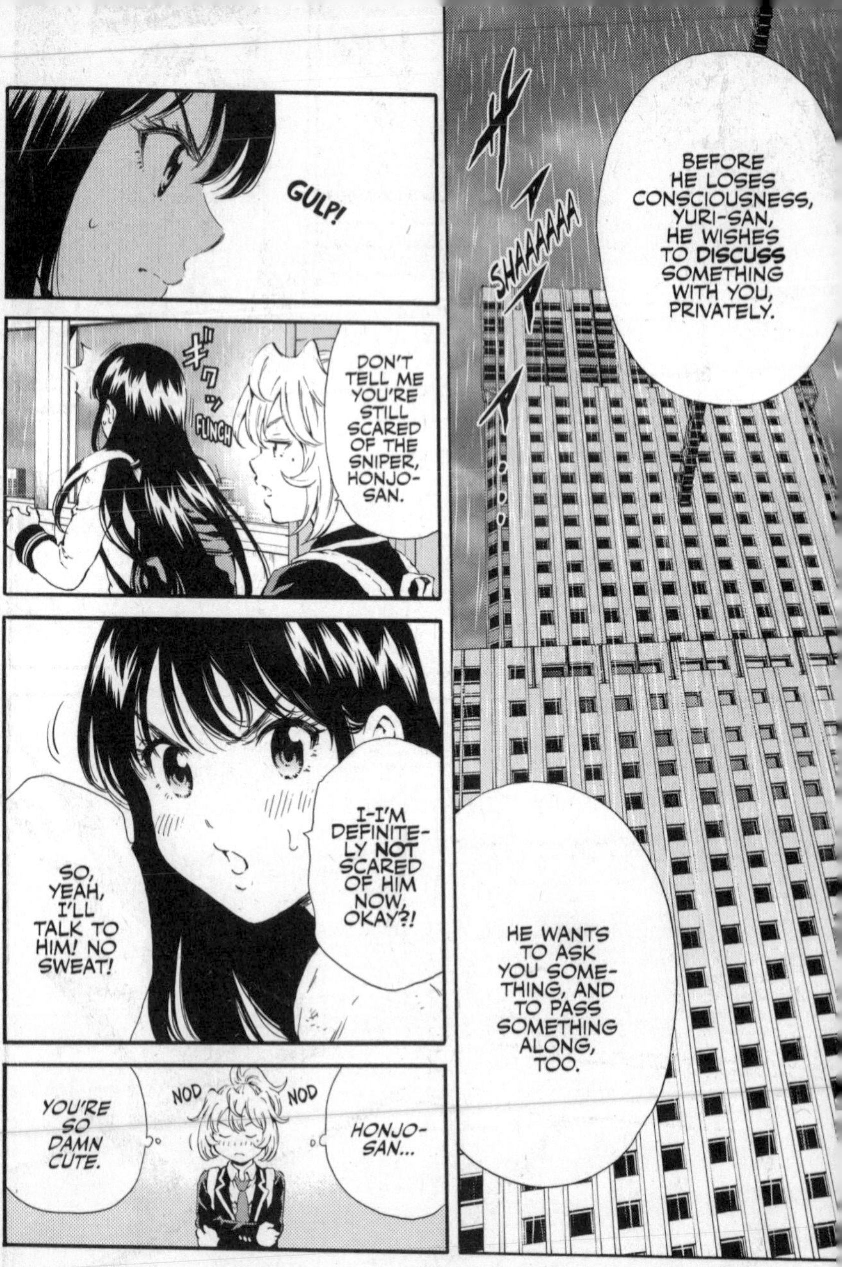
SHAAAAAA
BEFORE HE LOSES CONSCIOUSNESS, YURI-SAN, HE WISHES TO DISCUSS SOMETHING WITH YOU, PRIVATELY.
HE WANTS TO ASK YOU SOMETHING, AND TO PASS SOMETHING ALONG, TOO.
GULP!
DON'T TELL ME YOU'RE STILL SCARED OF THE SNIPER, HONJO-SAN.
FLINCH
I-I'M DEFINITELY NOT SCARED OF HIM NOW, OKAY?!
SO, YEAH, I'LL TALK TO HIM! NO SWEAT!
HONJO-SAN...
NOD
NOD
YOU'RE SO DAMN CUTE.

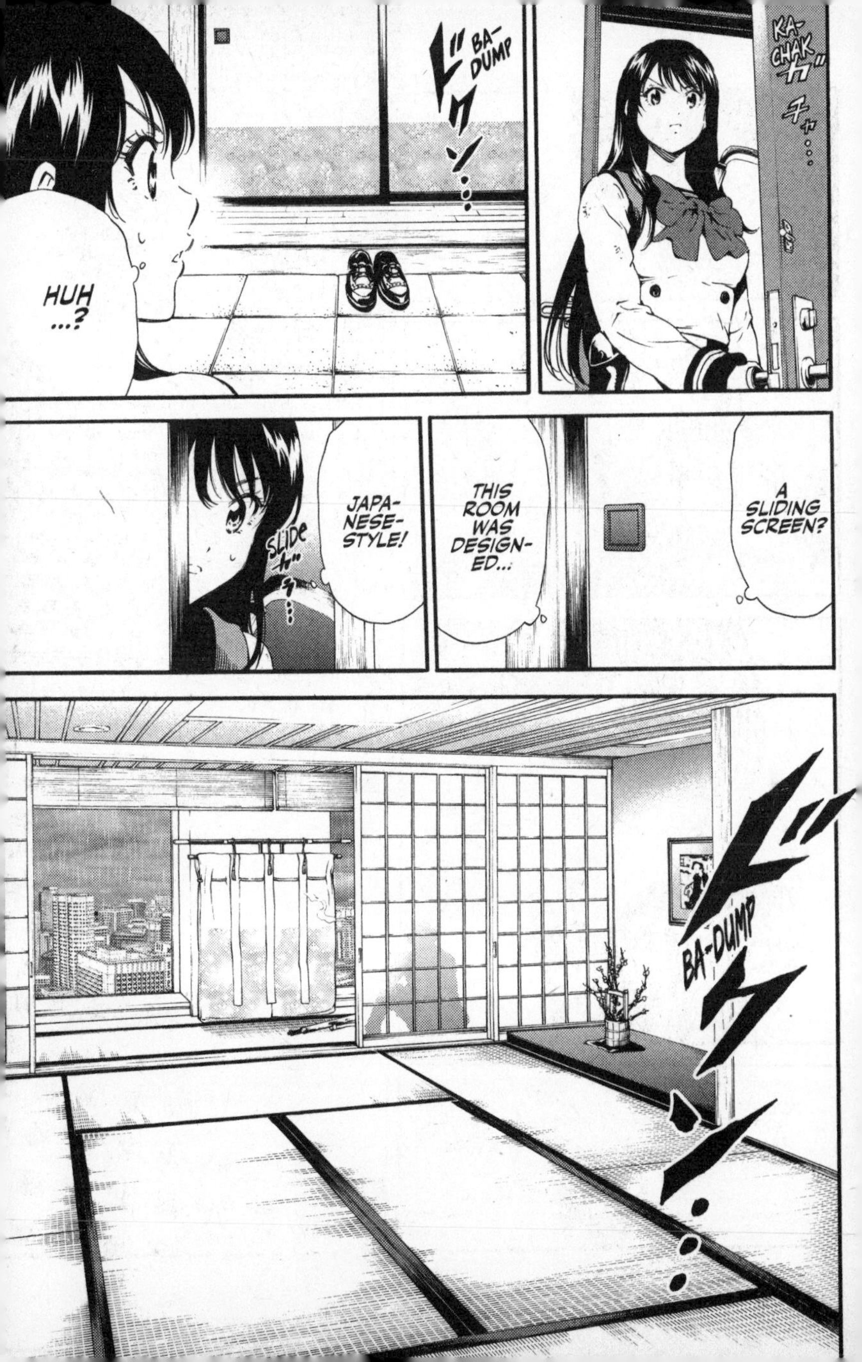
KA-CHAK
BA-DUMP
HUH ...?
A SLIDING SCREEN?
THIS ROOM WAS DESIGNED...
JAPANESE-STYLE!
SLIDE
BA-DUMP

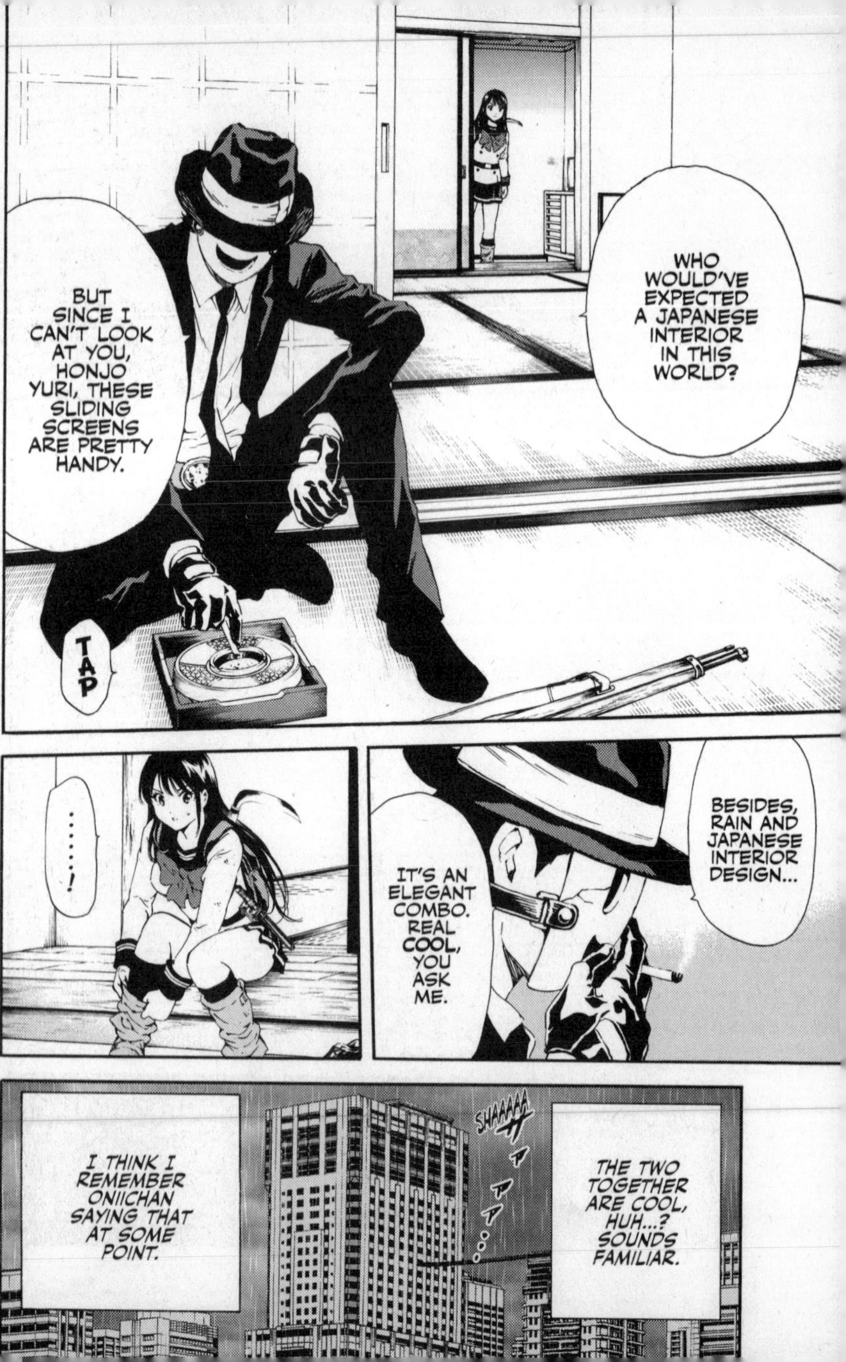
WHO WOULD'VE EXPECTED A JAPANESE INTERIOR IN THIS WORLD?
BUT SINCE I CAN'T LOOK AT YOU, HONJO YURI, THESE SLIDING SCREENS ARE PRETTY HANDY.
TAP
BESIDES, RAIN AND JAPANESE INTERIOR DESIGN...
IT'S AN ELEGANT COMBO. REAL COOL, YOU ASK ME.
......!
THE TWO TOGETHER ARE COOL, HUH...? SOUNDS FAMILIAR.
SHAAAAA
I THINK I REMEMBER ONIICHAN SAYING THAT AT SOME POINT.

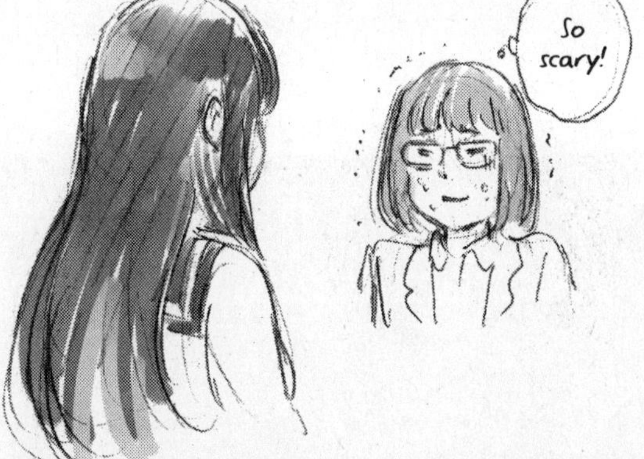
So scary!

HIGH-RISE INVASION

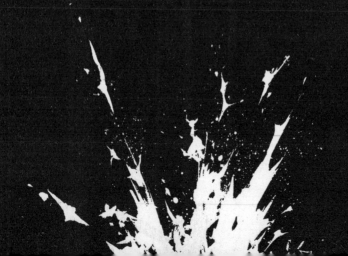

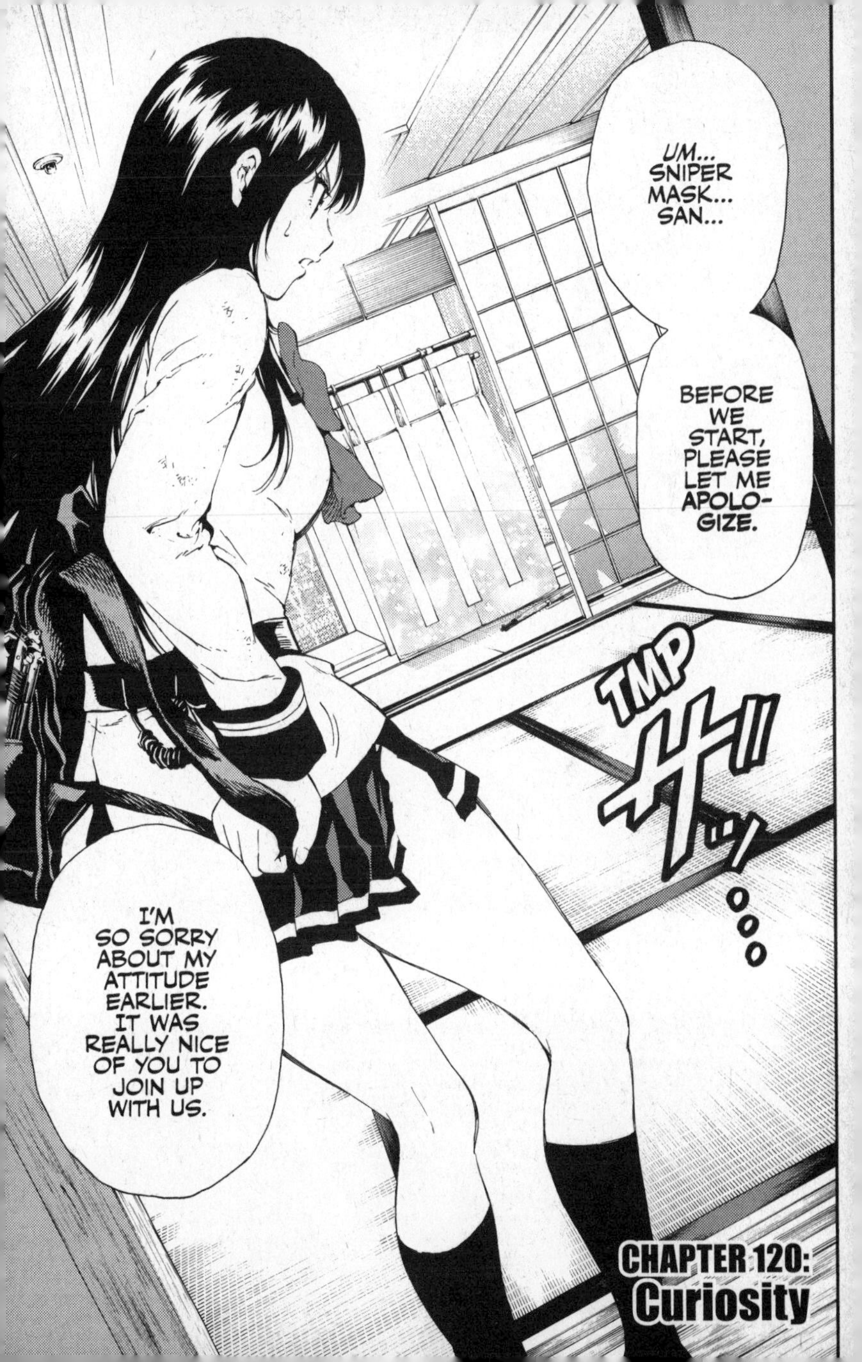
UM... SNIPER MASK... SAN...
BEFORE WE START, PLEASE LET ME APOLOGIZE.
TMP
I'M SO SORRY ABOUT MY ATTITUDE EARLIER. IT WAS REALLY NICE OF YOU TO JOIN UP WITH US.
CHAPTER 120: Curiosity

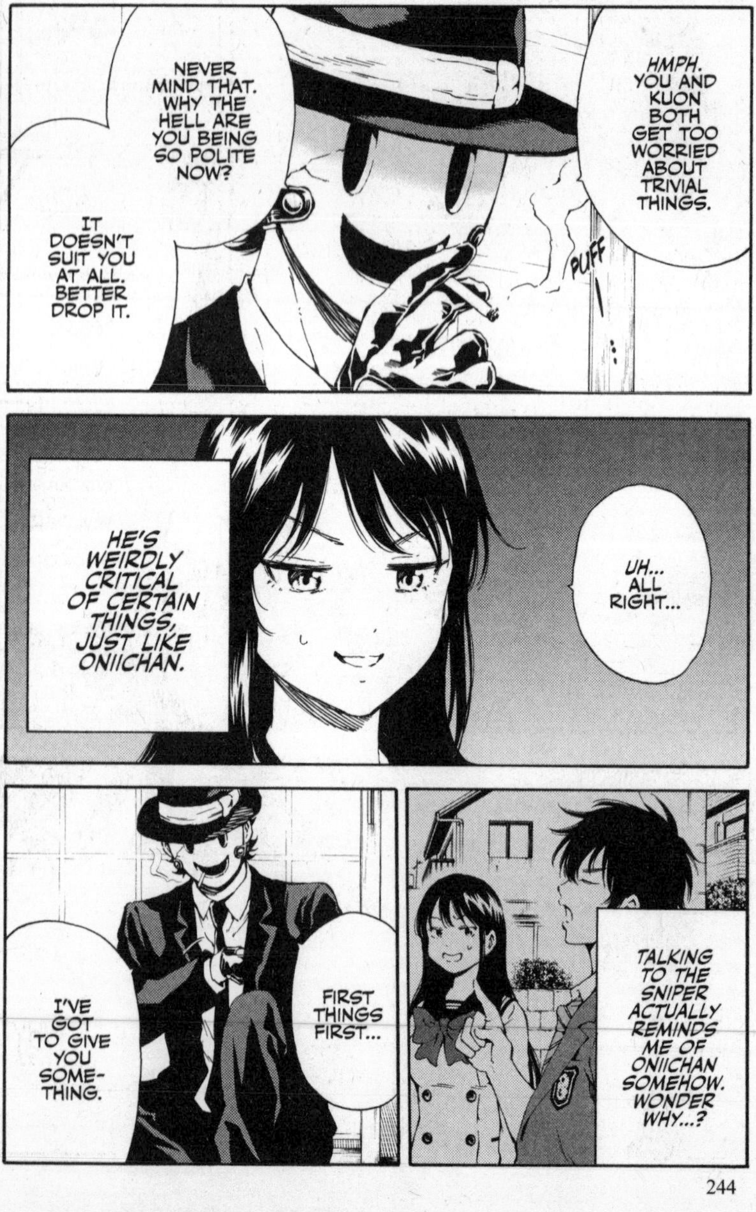
HMPH. YOU AND KUON BOTH GET TOO WORRIED ABOUT TRIVIAL THINGS.
PUFF
NEVER MIND THAT. WHY THE HELL ARE YOU BEING SO POLITE NOW?
IT DOESN'T SUIT YOU AT ALL. BETTER DROP IT.
UH... ALL RIGHT...
HE'S WEIRDLY CRITICAL OF CERTAIN THINGS, JUST LIKE ONIICHAN.
TALKING TO THE SNIPER ACTUALLY REMINDS ME OF ONIICHAN SOMEHOW. WONDER WHY...?
FIRST THINGS FIRST...
I'VE GOT TO GIVE YOU SOMETHING.

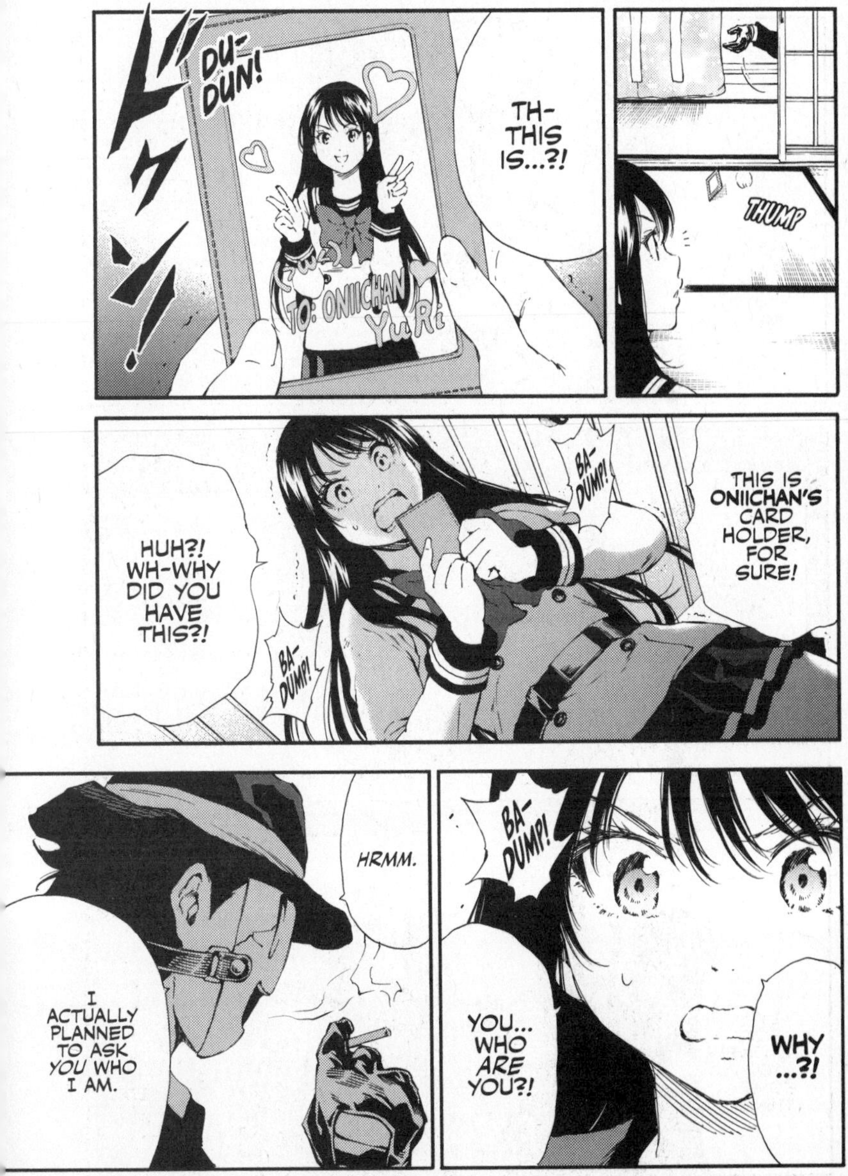
THUMP
TH-THIS IS...?!
DU-DUN!
ドクン!
TO: ONIICHAN
YuRi
THIS IS ONIICHAN'S CARD HOLDER, FOR SURE!
BA-DUMP!
HUH?! WH-WHY DID YOU HAVE THIS?!
BA-DUMP!
WHY...?!
BA-DUMP!
YOU... WHO ARE YOU?!
HRMM.
I ACTUALLY PLANNED TO ASK YOU WHO I AM.

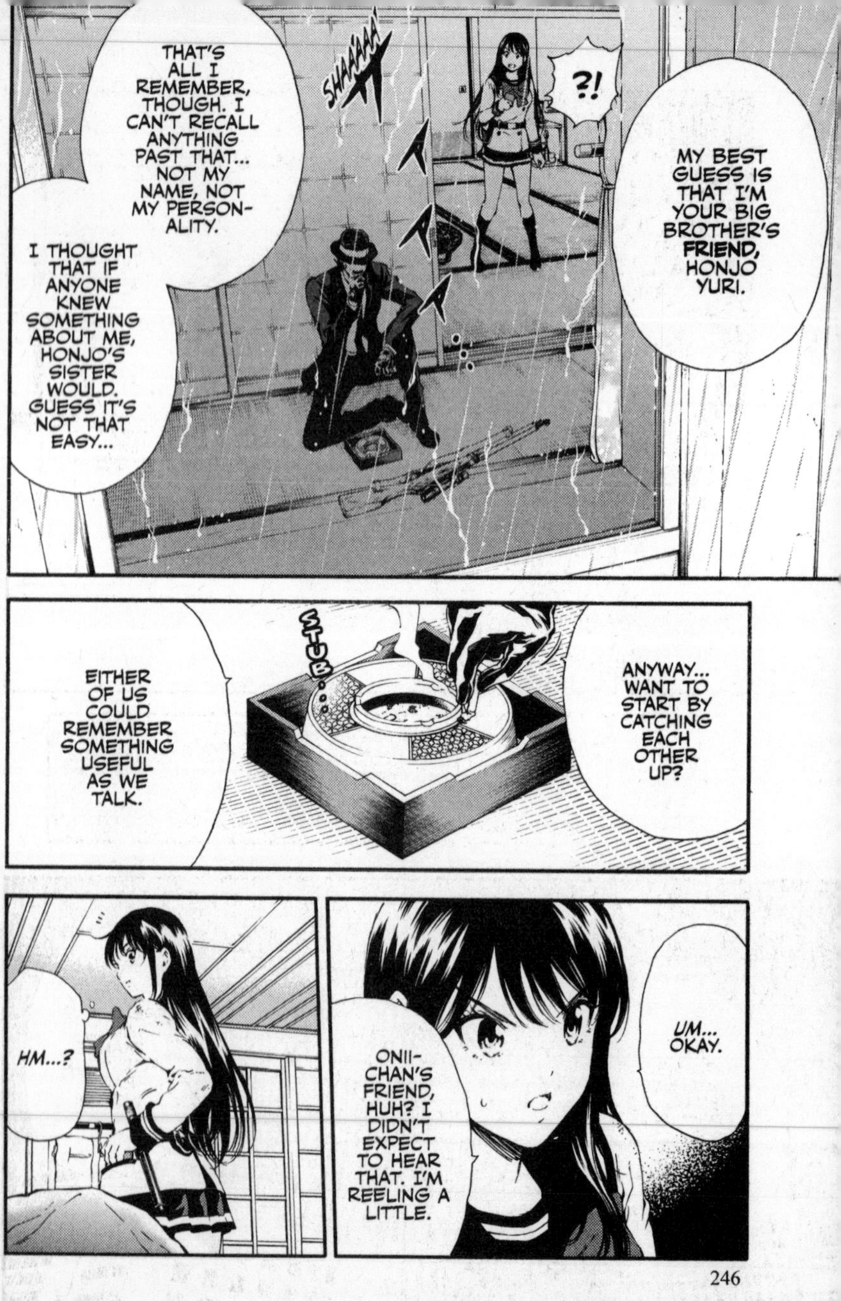
THAT'S ALL I REMEMBER, THOUGH. I CAN'T RECALL ANYTHING PAST THAT... NOT MY NAME, NOT MY PERSON-ALITY.
I THOUGHT THAT IF ANYONE KNEW SOMETHING ABOUT ME, HONJO'S SISTER WOULD. GUESS IT'S NOT THAT EASY...
SHAAAAA
MY BEST GUESS IS THAT I'M YOUR BIG BROTHER'S **FRIEND**, HONJO YURI.
?!
ANYWAY... WANT TO START BY CATCHING EACH OTHER UP?
STUB...
EITHER OF US COULD REMEMBER SOMETHING USEFUL AS WE TALK.
UM... OKAY.
ONII-CHAN'S FRIEND, HUH? I DIDN'T EXPECT TO HEAR THAT. I'M REELING A LITTLE.
HM...?

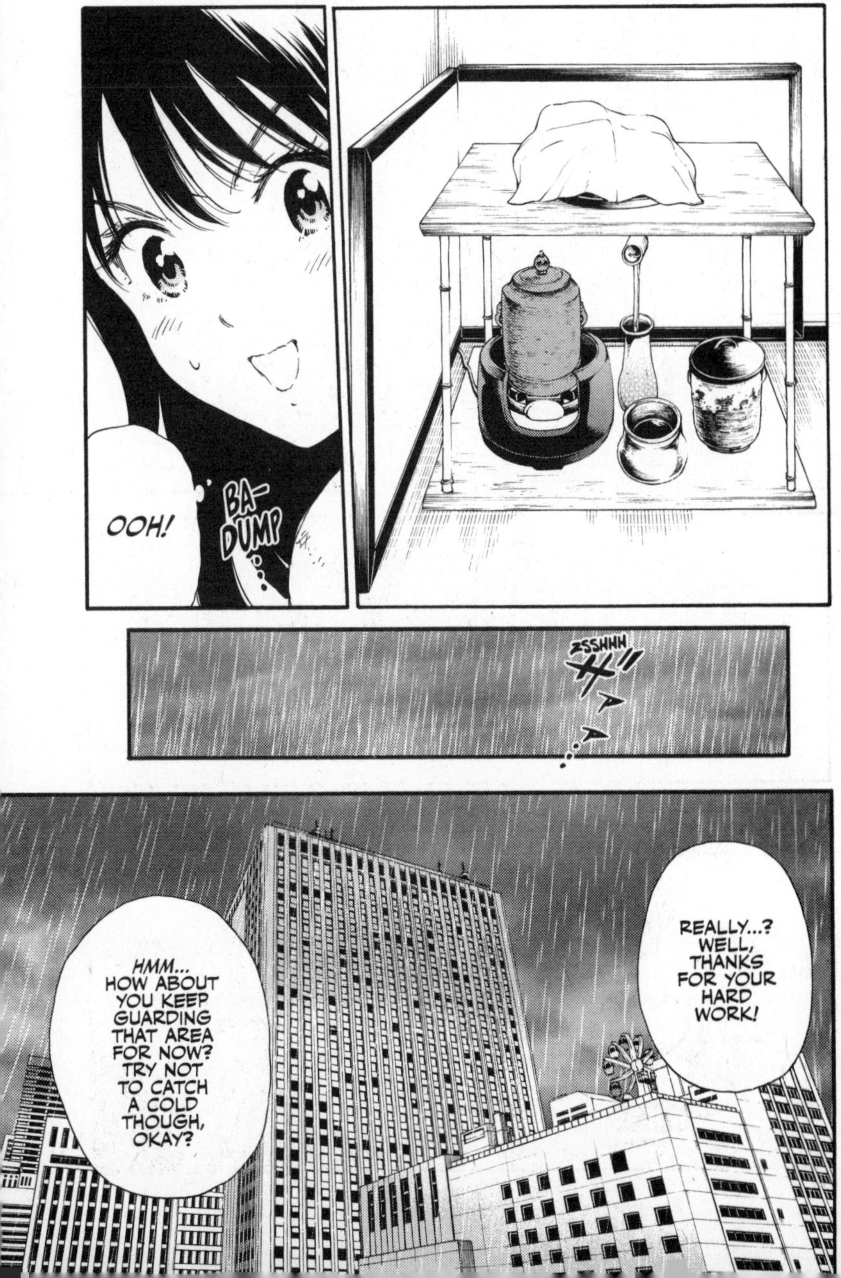
OOH!
BA-DUMP
ZSSHHH
REALLY...? WELL, THANKS FOR YOUR HARD WORK!
HMM... HOW ABOUT YOU KEEP GUARDING THAT AREA FOR NOW? TRY NOT TO CATCH A COLD THOUGH, OKAY?

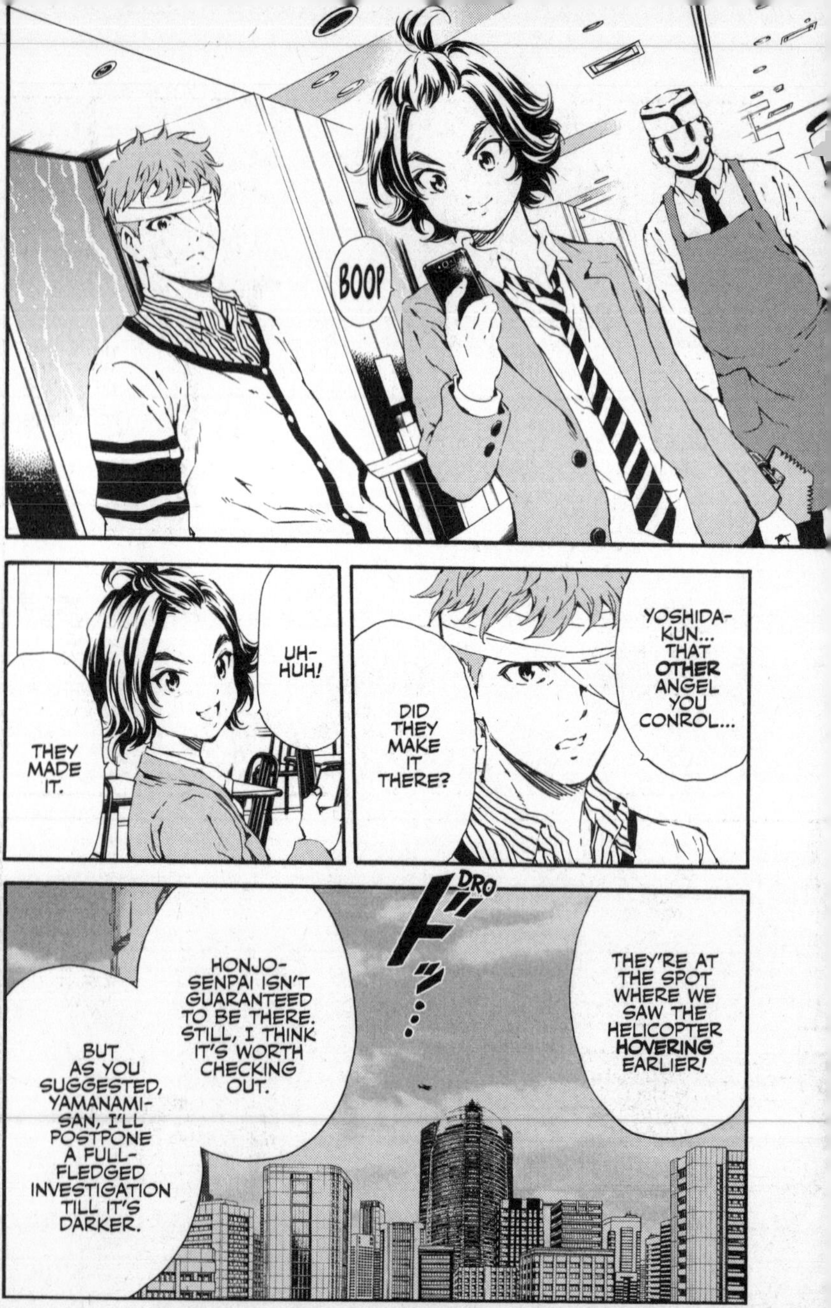
BOOP
YOSHIDA-KUN... THAT OTHER ANGEL YOU CONROL...
DID THEY MAKE IT THERE?
UH-HUH!
THEY MADE IT.
DRO
THEY'RE AT THE SPOT WHERE WE SAW THE HELICOPTER HOVERING EARLIER!
HONJO-SENPAI ISN'T GUARANTEED TO BE THERE. STILL, I THINK IT'S WORTH CHECKING OUT.
BUT AS YOU SUGGESTED, YAMANAMI-SAN, I'LL POSTPONE A FULL-FLEDGED INVESTIGATION TILL IT'S DARKER.

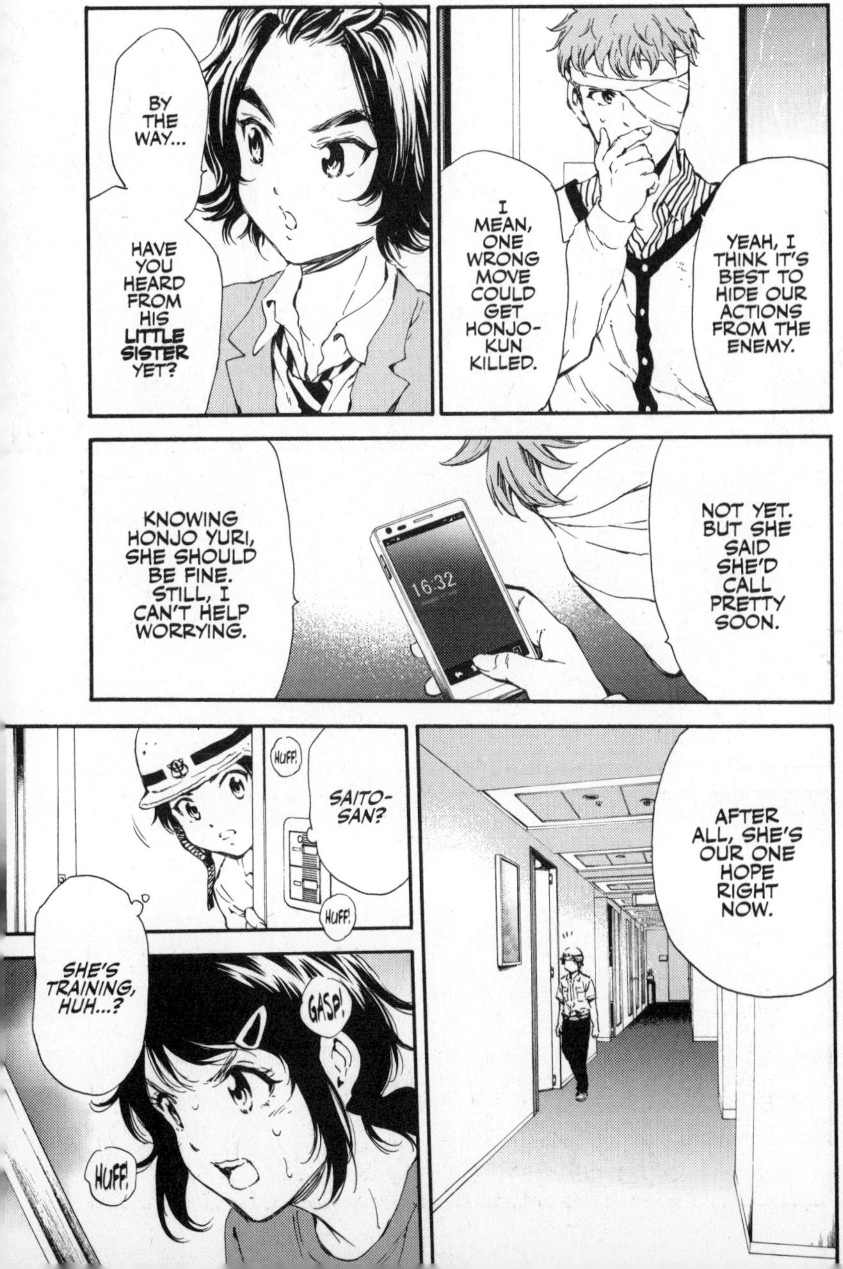
YEAH, I THINK IT'S BEST TO HIDE OUR ACTIONS FROM THE ENEMY.
I MEAN, ONE WRONG MOVE COULD GET HONJO-KUN KILLED.
BY THE WAY...
HAVE YOU HEARD FROM HIS LITTLE SISTER YET?
NOT YET. BUT SHE SAID SHE'D CALL PRETTY SOON.
16:32
KNOWING HONJO YURI, SHE SHOULD BE FINE. STILL, I CAN'T HELP WORRYING.
AFTER ALL, SHE'S OUR ONE HOPE RIGHT NOW.
HUFF!
SAITO-SAN?
HUFF!
GASP!
SHE'S TRAINING, HUH...?
HUFF!

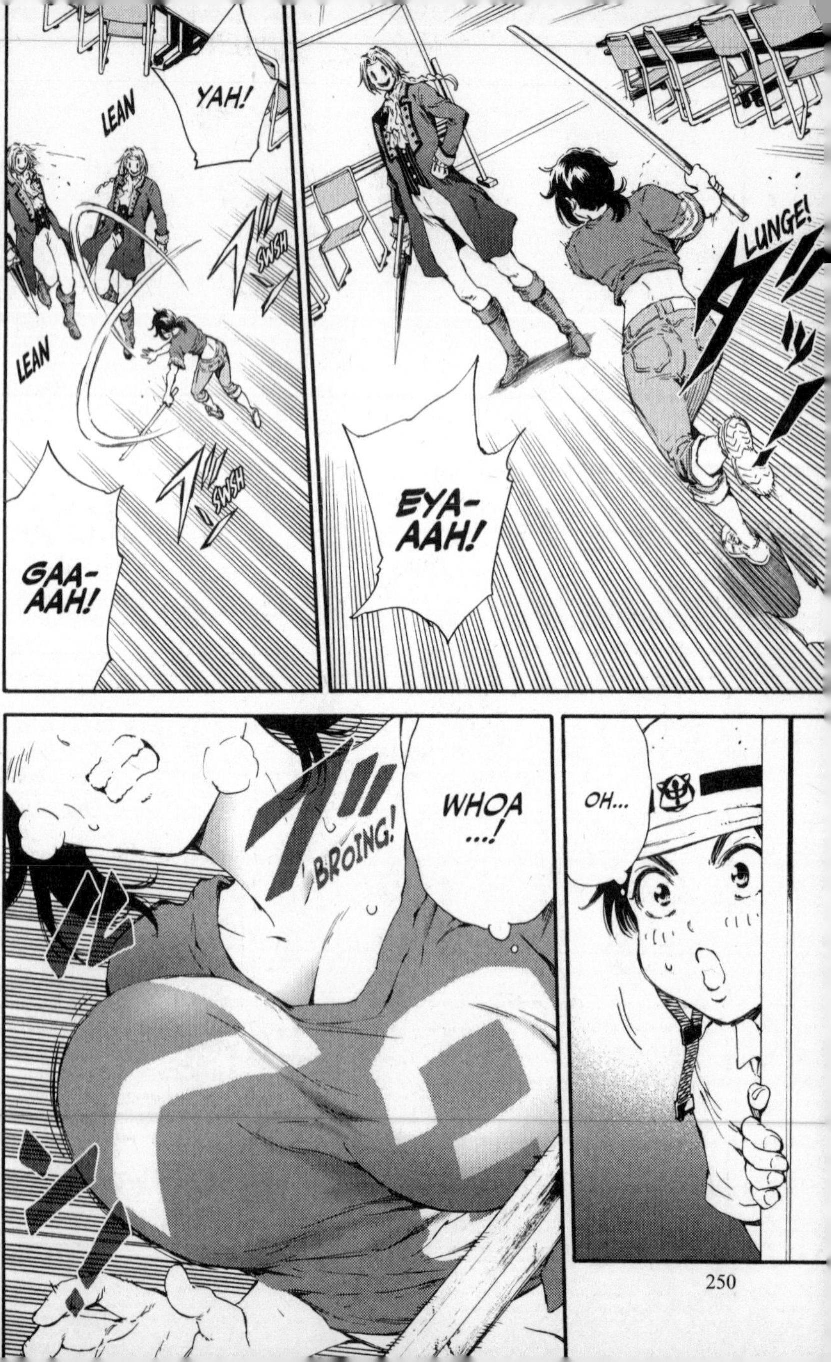
LUNGE!
EYA-AAH!
YAH!
LEAN
SWSH
LEAN
SWSH
GAA-AAH!
OH...
WHOA ...!
BROING!

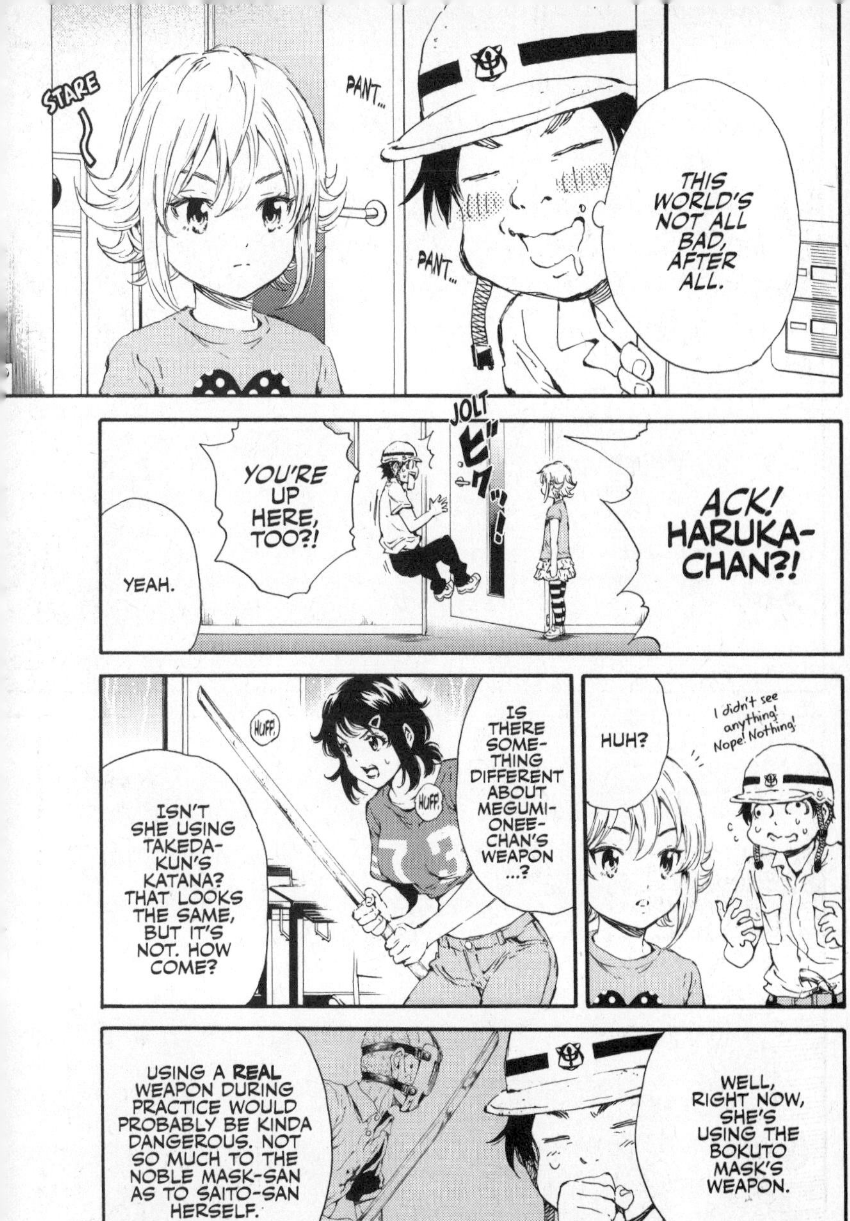
THIS WORLD'S NOT ALL BAD, AFTER ALL.
PANT...
PANT...
STARE
ACK! HARUKA-CHAN?!
JOLT
YOU'RE UP HERE, TOO?!
YEAH.
I didn't see anything! Nope! Nothing!
HUH?
IS THERE SOMETHING DIFFERENT ABOUT MEGUMI-ONEE-CHAN'S WEAPON ...?
HUFF!
HUFF!
ISN'T SHE USING TAKEDA-KUN'S KATANA? THAT LOOKS THE SAME, BUT IT'S NOT. HOW COME?
WELL, RIGHT NOW, SHE'S USING THE BOKUTO MASK'S WEAPON.
USING A **REAL** WEAPON DURING PRACTICE WOULD PROBABLY BE KINDA DANGEROUS. NOT SO MUCH TO THE NOBLE MASK-SAN AS TO SAITO-SAN HERSELF.

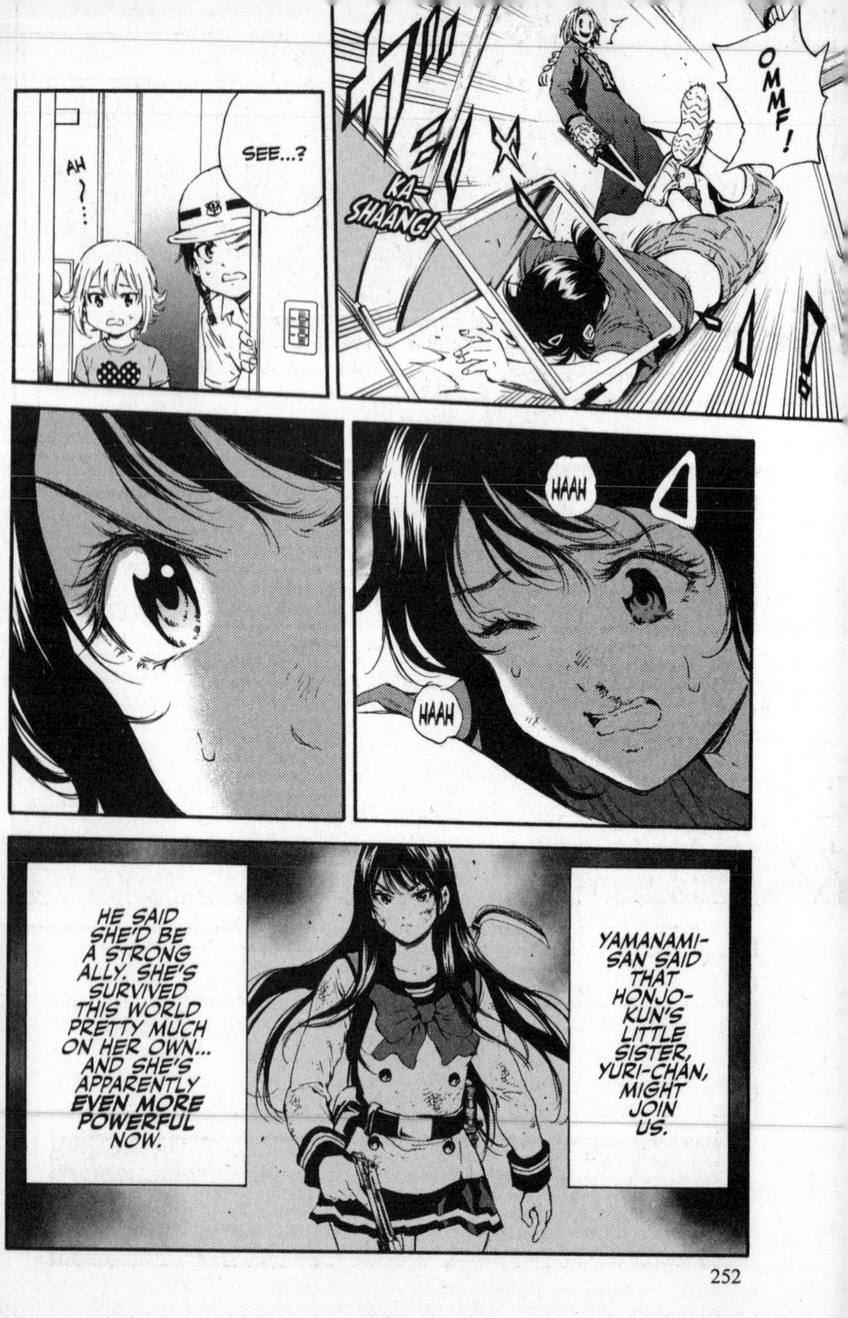
OMMF!
KA-SHAANG!
SEE...?
AH~...
HAAH
HAAH
YAMANAMI-SAN SAID THAT HONJO-KUN'S LITTLE SISTER, YURI-CHAN, MIGHT JOIN US.
HE SAID SHE'D BE A STRONG ALLY. SHE'S SURVIVED THIS WORLD PRETTY MUCH ON HER OWN... AND SHE'S APPARENTLY EVEN MORE POWERFUL NOW.

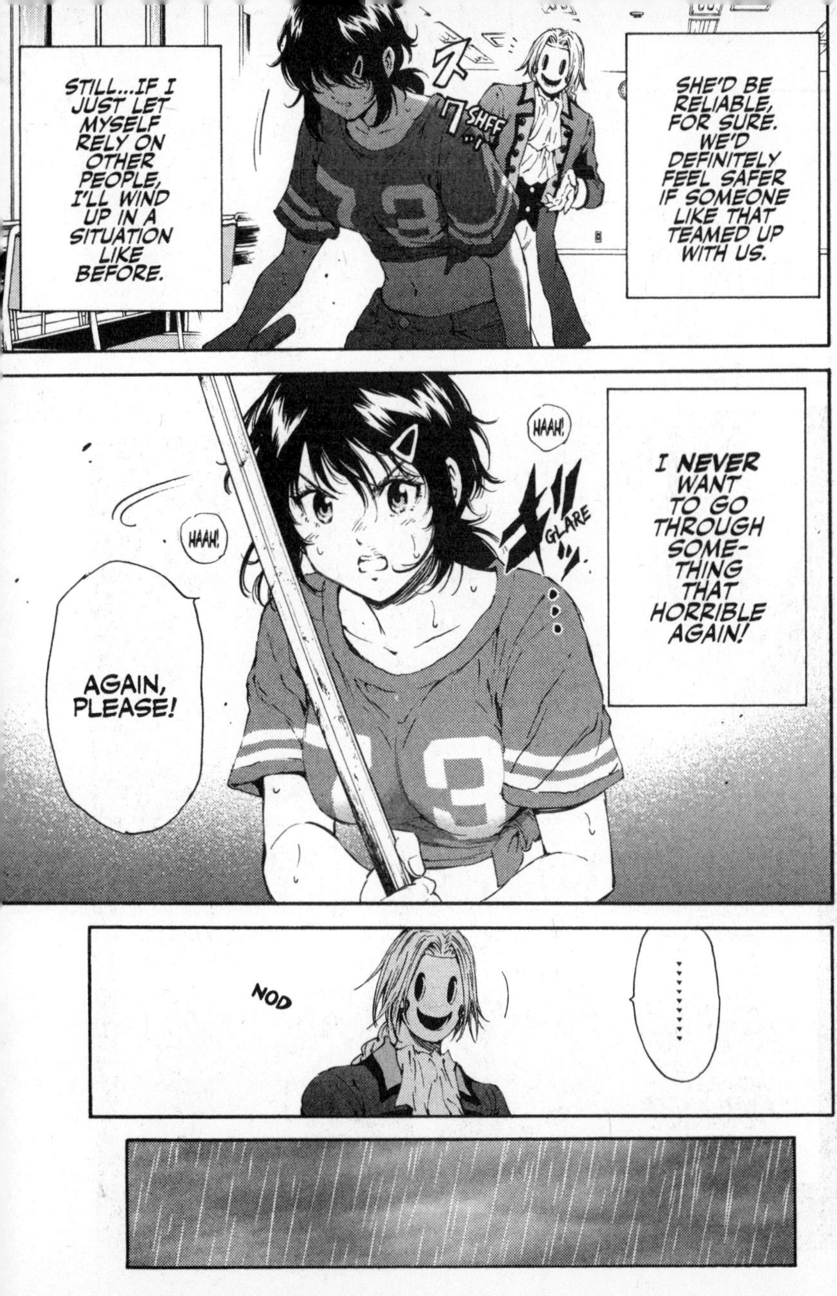
SHE'D BE RELIABLE, FOR SURE. WE'D DEFINITELY FEEL SAFER IF SOMEONE LIKE THAT TEAMED UP WITH US.
SHFF
STILL...IF I JUST LET MYSELF RELY ON OTHER PEOPLE, I'LL WIND UP IN A SITUATION LIKE BEFORE.
I NEVER WANT TO GO THROUGH SOMETHING THAT HORRIBLE AGAIN!
GLARE
HAAH!
HAAH!
AGAIN, PLEASE!
NOD

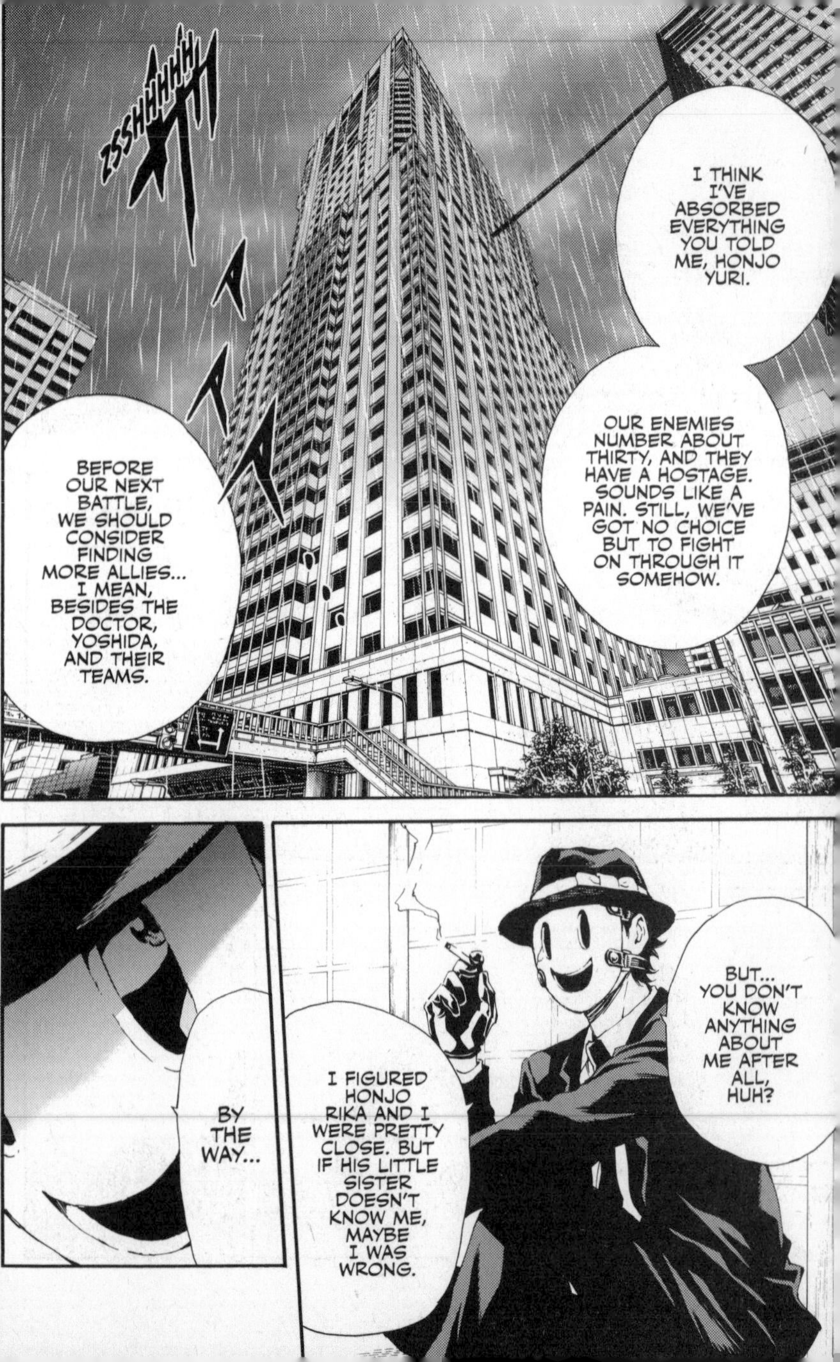
I THINK I'VE ABSORBED EVERYTHING YOU TOLD ME, HONJO YURI.
ZSSHHHHHH
AAA...
OUR ENEMIES NUMBER ABOUT THIRTY, AND THEY HAVE A HOSTAGE. SOUNDS LIKE A PAIN. STILL, WE'VE GOT NO CHOICE BUT TO FIGHT ON THROUGH IT SOMEHOW.
BEFORE OUR NEXT BATTLE, WE SHOULD CONSIDER FINDING MORE ALLIES... I MEAN, BESIDES THE DOCTOR, YOSHIDA, AND THEIR TEAMS.
BUT... YOU DON'T KNOW ANYTHING ABOUT ME AFTER ALL, HUH?
I FIGURED HONJO RIKA AND I WERE PRETTY CLOSE. BUT IF HIS LITTLE SISTER DOESN'T KNOW ME, MAYBE I WAS WRONG.
BY THE WAY...

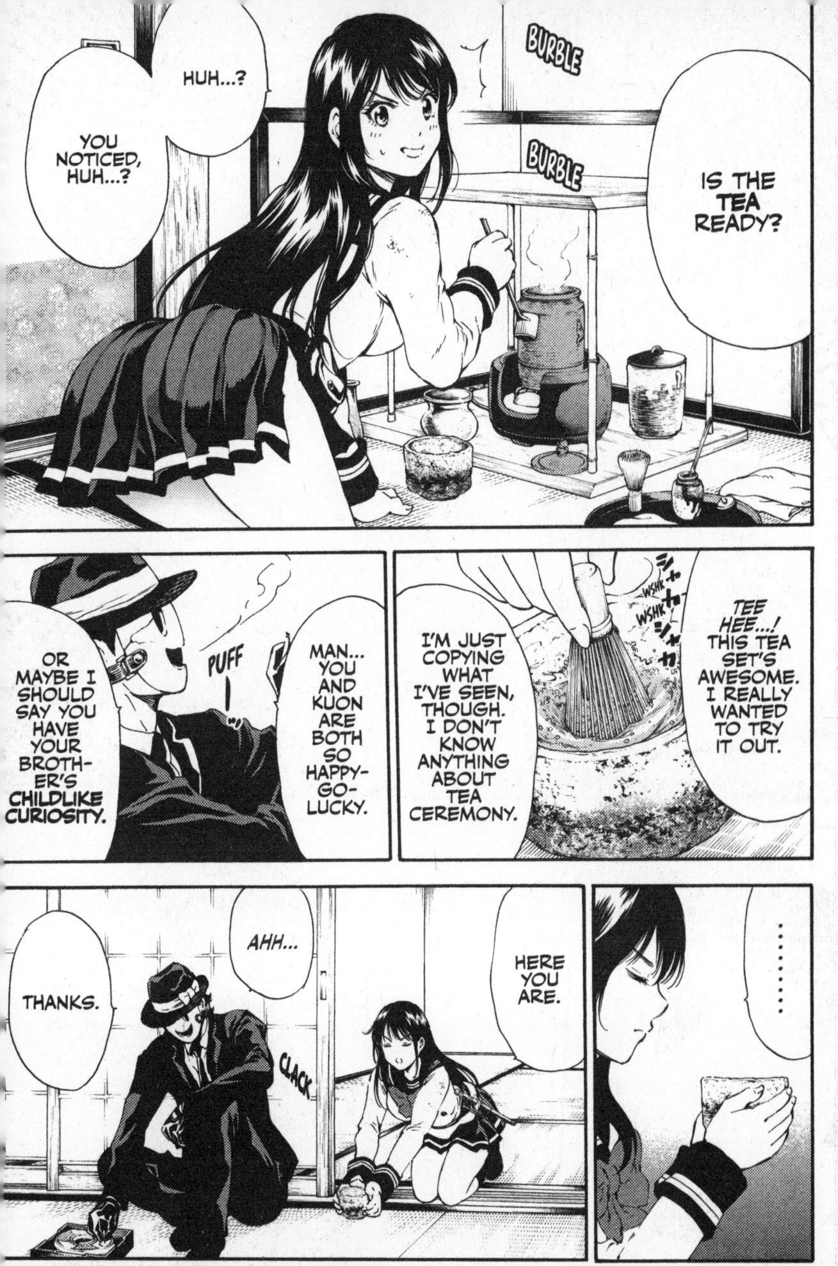
IS THE TEA READY?
BURBLE
BURBLE
HUH...?
YOU NOTICED, HUH...?
TEE HEE...! THIS TEA SET'S AWESOME. I REALLY WANTED TO TRY IT OUT.
WSHK
WSHK
I'M JUST COPYING WHAT I'VE SEEN, THOUGH. I DON'T KNOW ANYTHING ABOUT TEA CEREMONY.
MAN... YOU AND KUON ARE BOTH SO HAPPY-GO-LUCKY.
PUFF
OR MAYBE I SHOULD SAY YOU HAVE YOUR BROTHER'S CHILDLIKE CURIOSITY.
....
HERE YOU ARE.
AHH...
CLACK
THANKS.

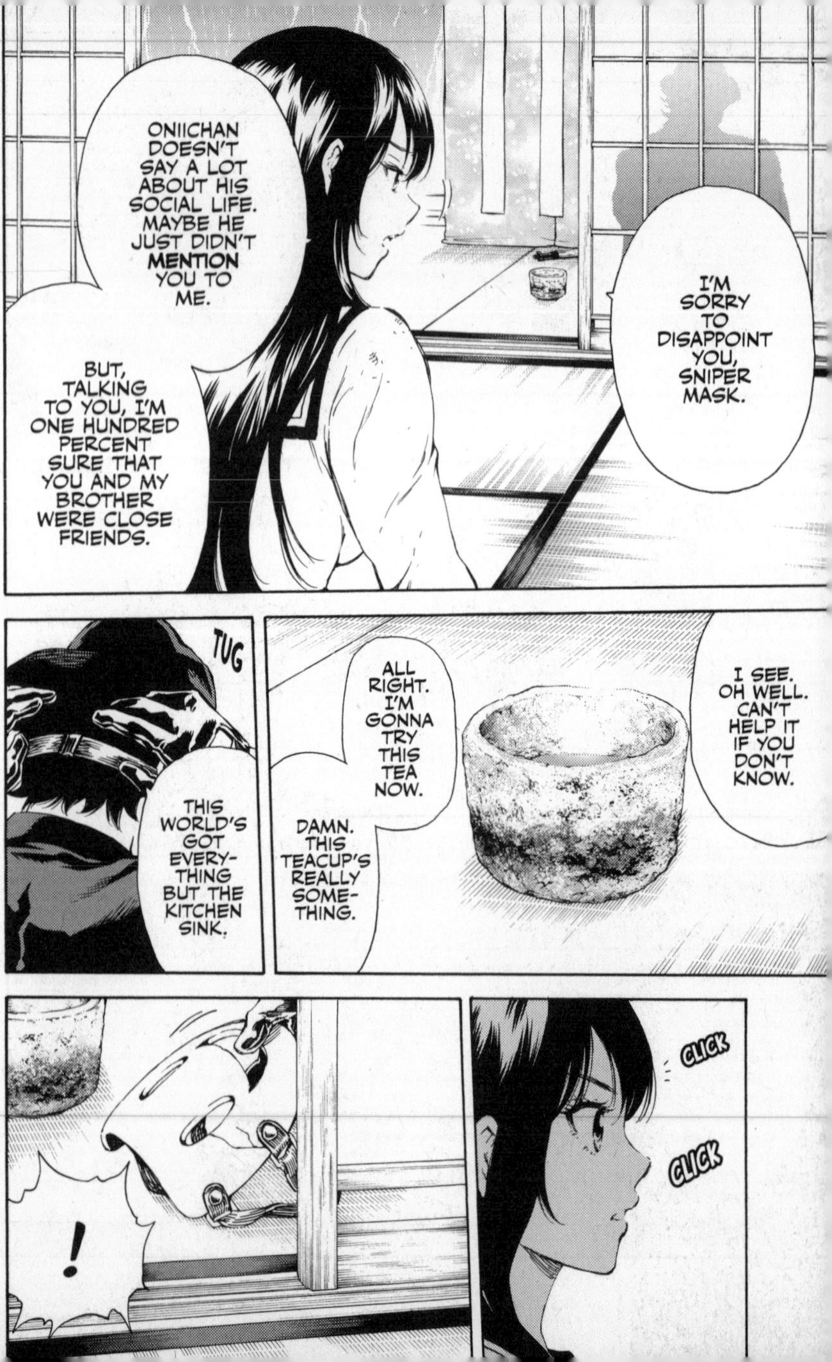
I'M SORRY TO DISAPPOINT YOU, SNIPER MASK.
ONIICHAN DOESN'T SAY A LOT ABOUT HIS SOCIAL LIFE. MAYBE HE JUST DIDN'T **MENTION** YOU TO ME.
BUT, TALKING TO YOU, I'M ONE HUNDRED PERCENT SURE THAT YOU AND MY BROTHER WERE CLOSE FRIENDS.
I SEE. OH WELL. CAN'T HELP IT IF YOU DON'T KNOW.
ALL RIGHT. I'M GONNA TRY THIS TEA NOW.
DAMN. THIS TEACUP'S REALLY SOME-THING.
TUG
THIS WORLD'S GOT EVERY-THING BUT THE KITCHEN SINK.
CLICK
CLICK
!

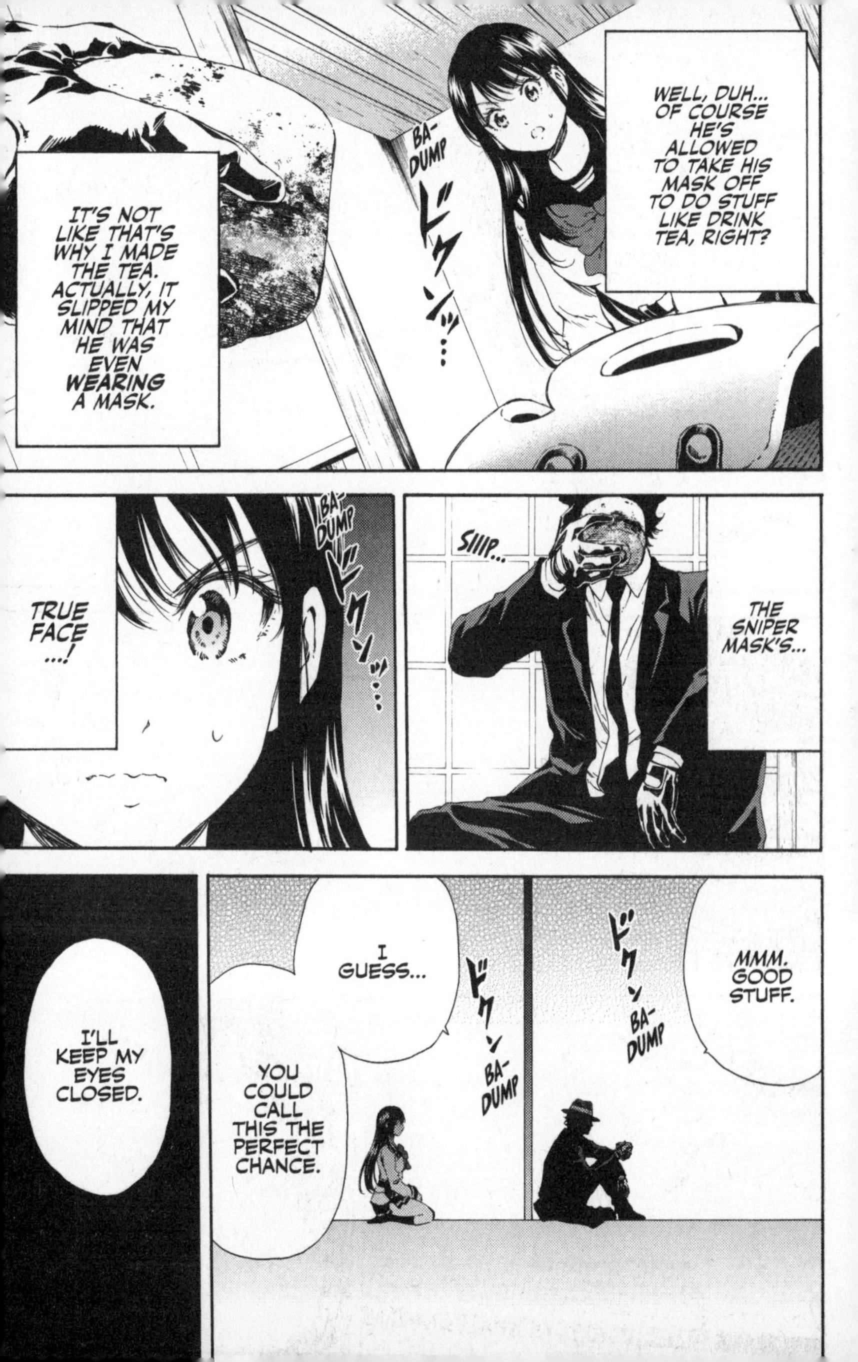
WELL, DUH... OF COURSE HE'S ALLOWED TO TAKE HIS MASK OFF TO DO STUFF LIKE DRINK TEA, RIGHT?
BA-DUMP
ドクンッ...
IT'S NOT LIKE THAT'S WHY I MADE THE TEA. ACTUALLY, IT SLIPPED MY MIND THAT HE WAS EVEN WEARING A MASK.
THE SNIPER MASK'S...
SIIIP...
BA-DUMP
ドクンッ...
TRUE FACE ...!
MMM. GOOD STUFF.
ドクン
BA-DUMP
I GUESS...
ドクン
BA-DUMP
YOU COULD CALL THIS THE PERFECT CHANCE.
I'LL KEEP MY EYES CLOSED.

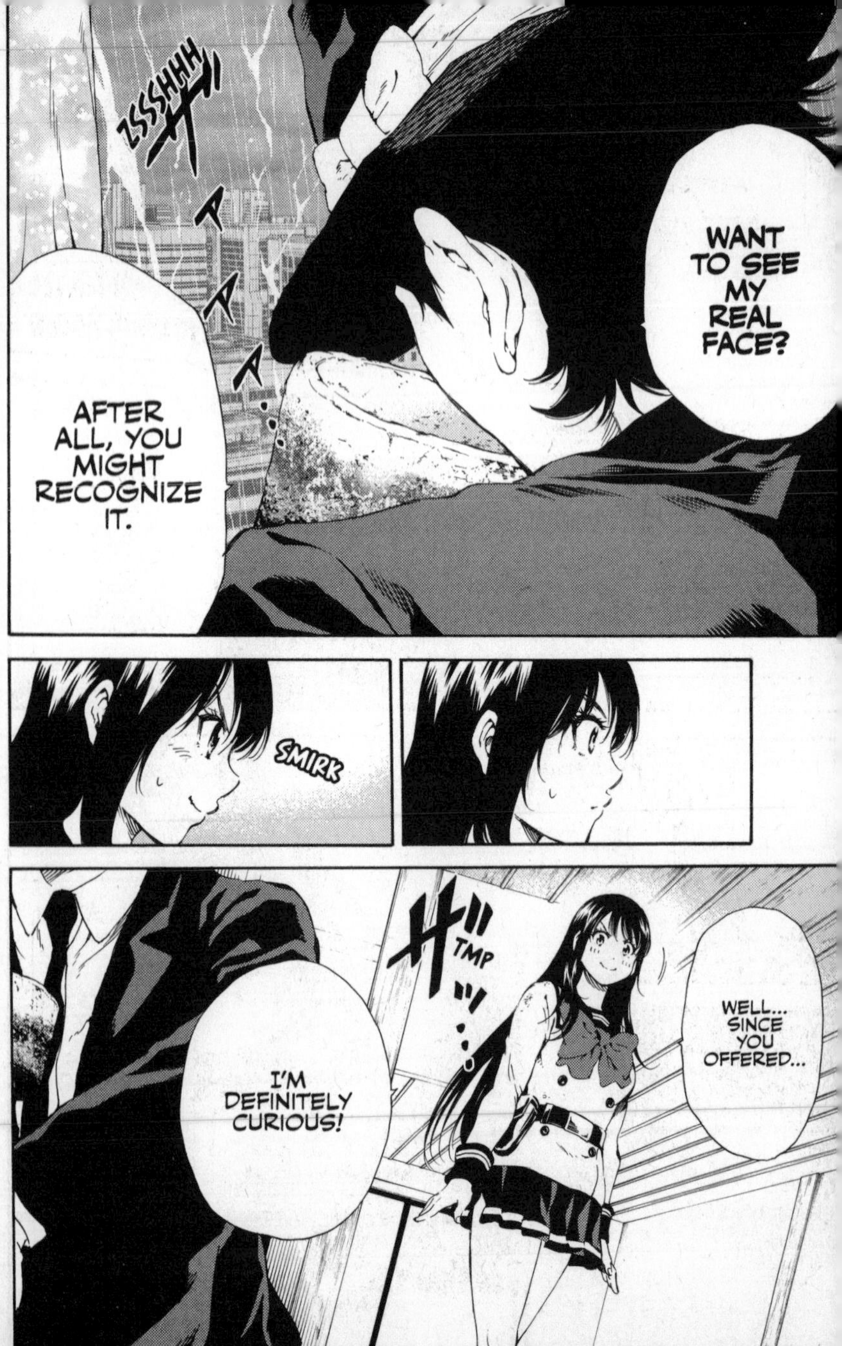
WANT TO SEE MY REAL FACE?
ZSSSHHH
PAPAPA...
AFTER ALL, YOU MIGHT RECOGNIZE IT.
SMIRK
WELL... SINCE YOU OFFERED...
TMP
I'M DEFINITELY CURIOUS!

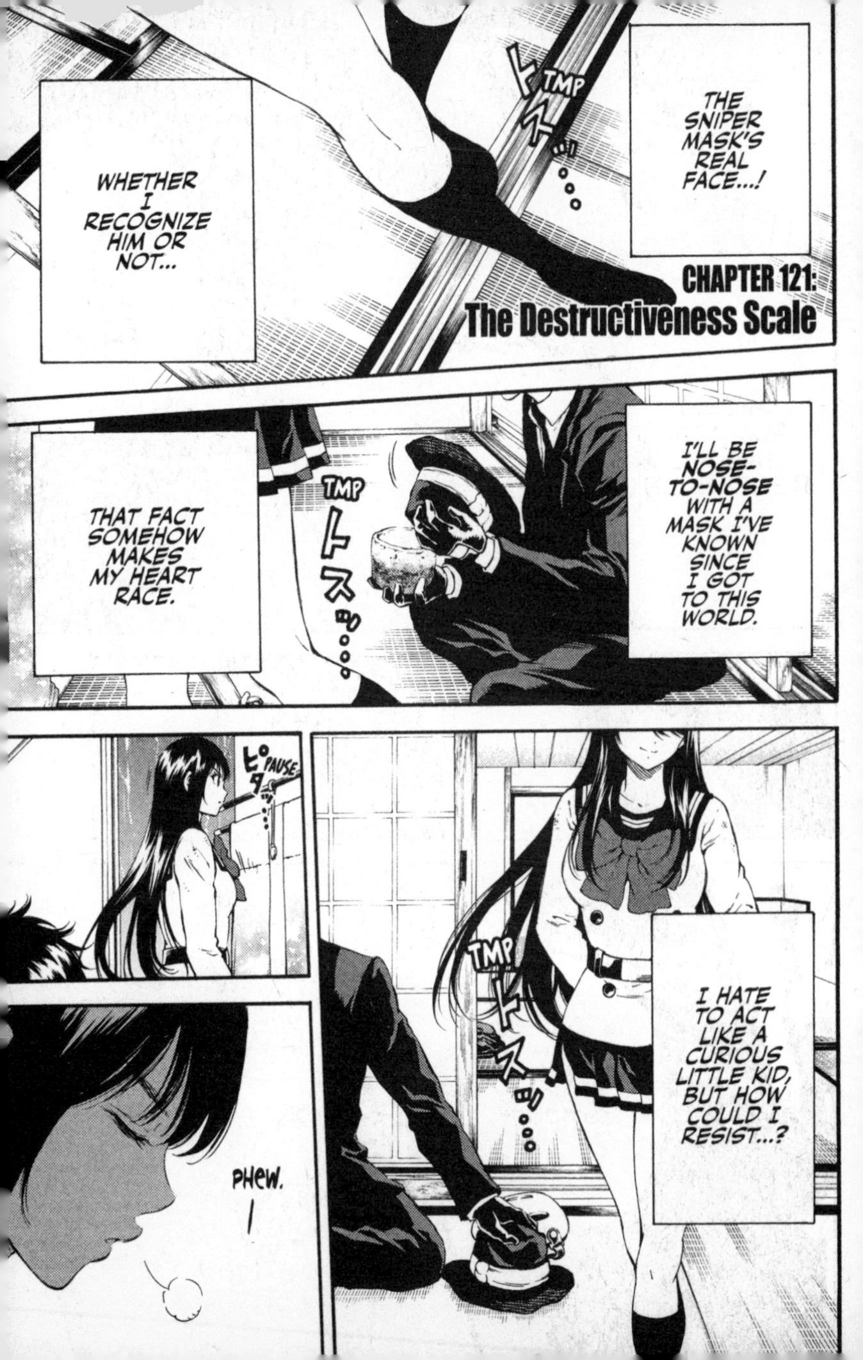
THE SNIPER MASK'S REAL FACE...!
TMP
CHAPTER 121: The Destructiveness Scale
WHETHER I RECOGNIZE HIM OR NOT...
I'LL BE NOSE-TO-NOSE WITH A MASK I'VE KNOWN SINCE I GOT TO THIS WORLD.
TMP
THAT FACT SOMEHOW MAKES MY HEART RACE.
TMP
I HATE TO ACT LIKE A CURIOUS LITTLE KID, BUT HOW COULD I RESIST...?
PAUSE
PHEW.

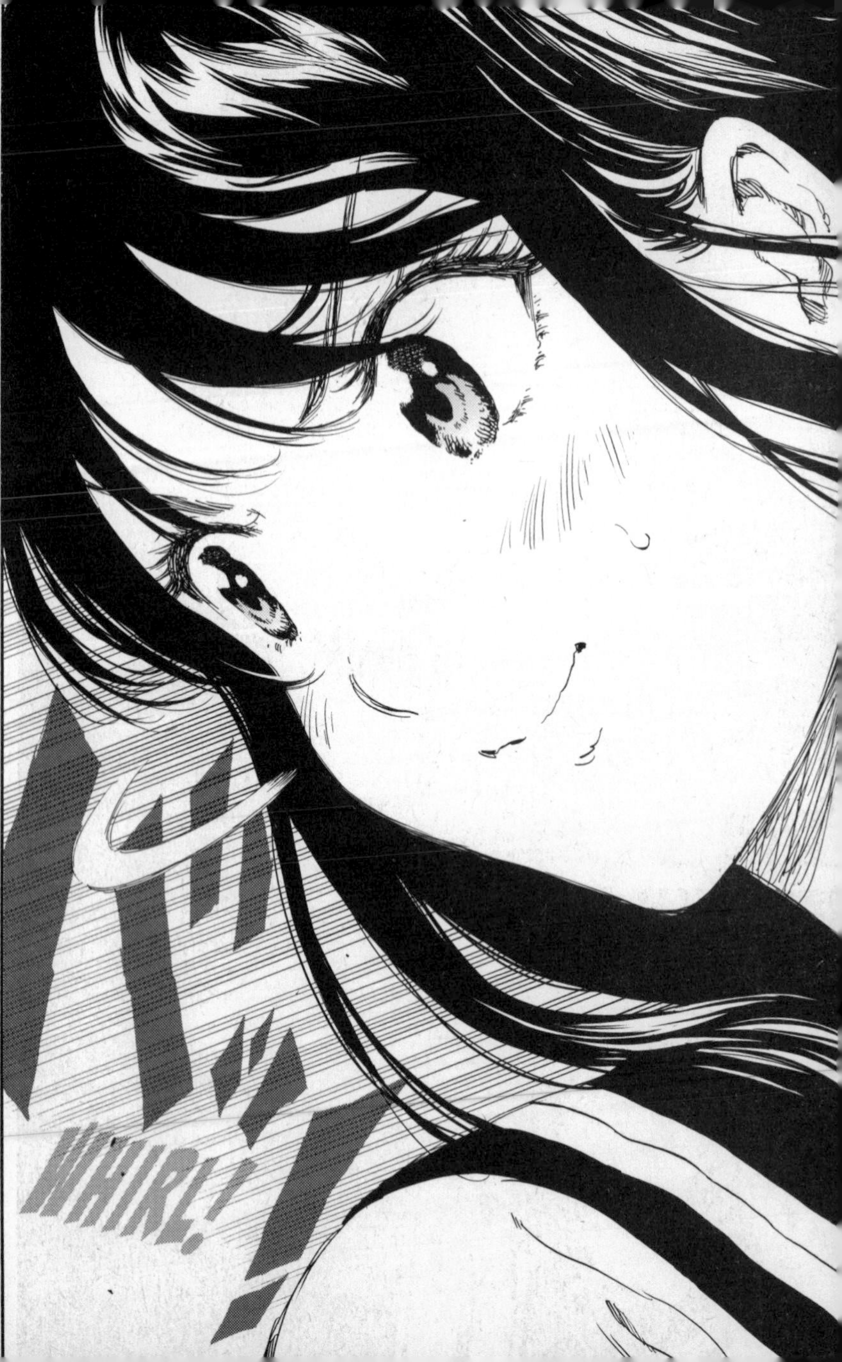
WHIRL!

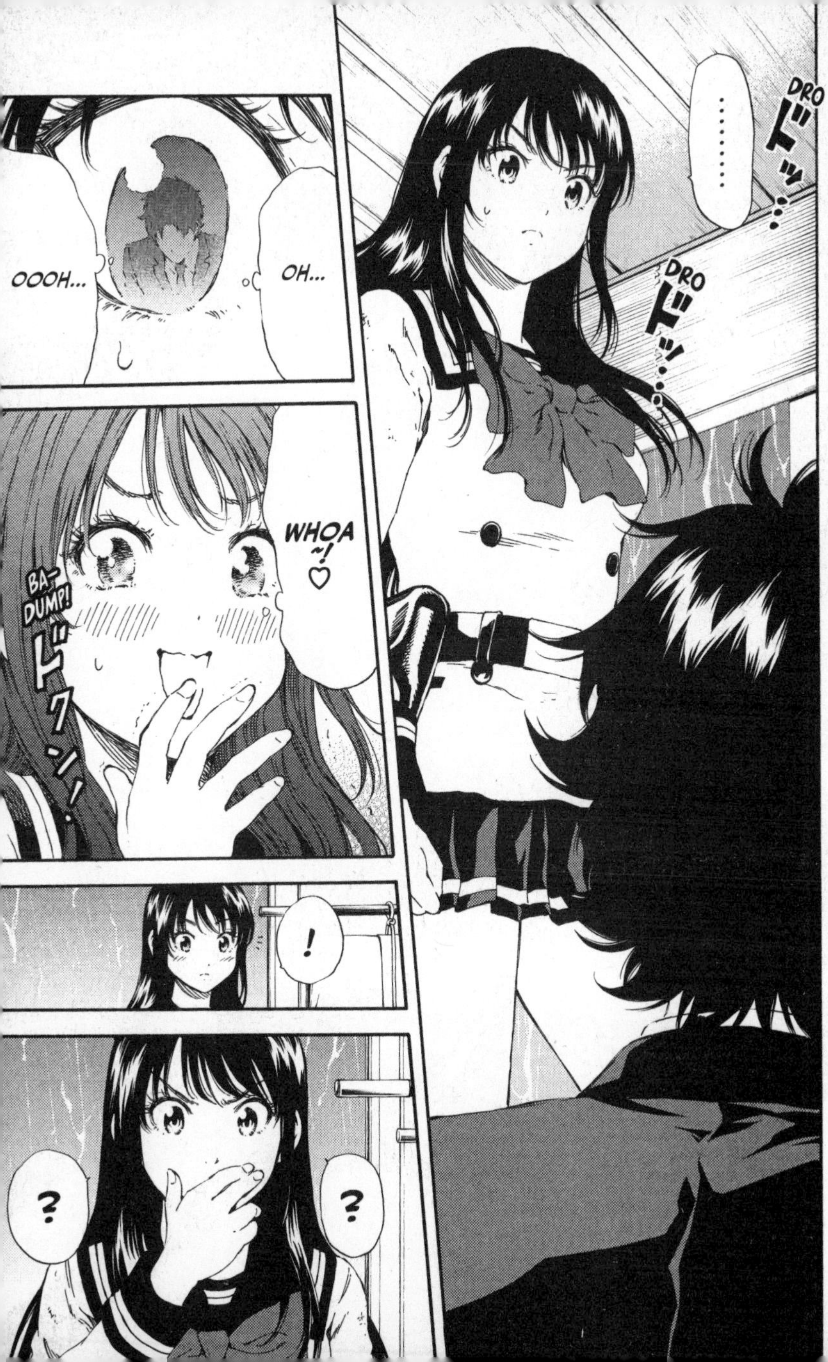

……
DRO ドッ…
DRO ドッ…
OH…
OOOH…
WHOA~! ♡
BA-DUMP! ドクン!
!
?
?

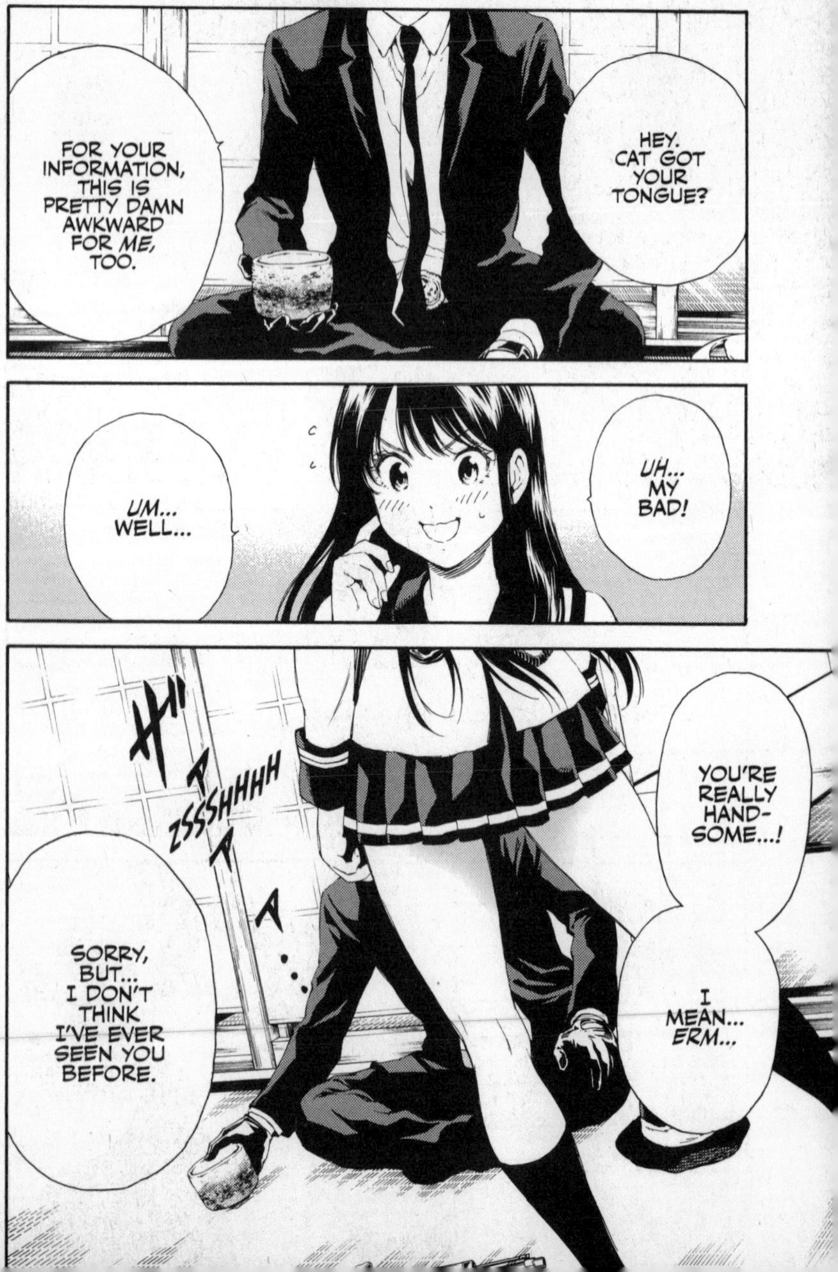
HEY. CAT GOT YOUR TONGUE?
FOR YOUR INFORMATION, THIS IS PRETTY DAMN AWKWARD FOR *ME*, TOO.
UH... MY BAD!
UM... WELL...
YOU'RE REALLY HAND-SOME...!
I MEAN... *ERM...*
ZSSSHHHH
SORRY, BUT... I DON'T THINK I'VE EVER SEEN YOU BEFORE.

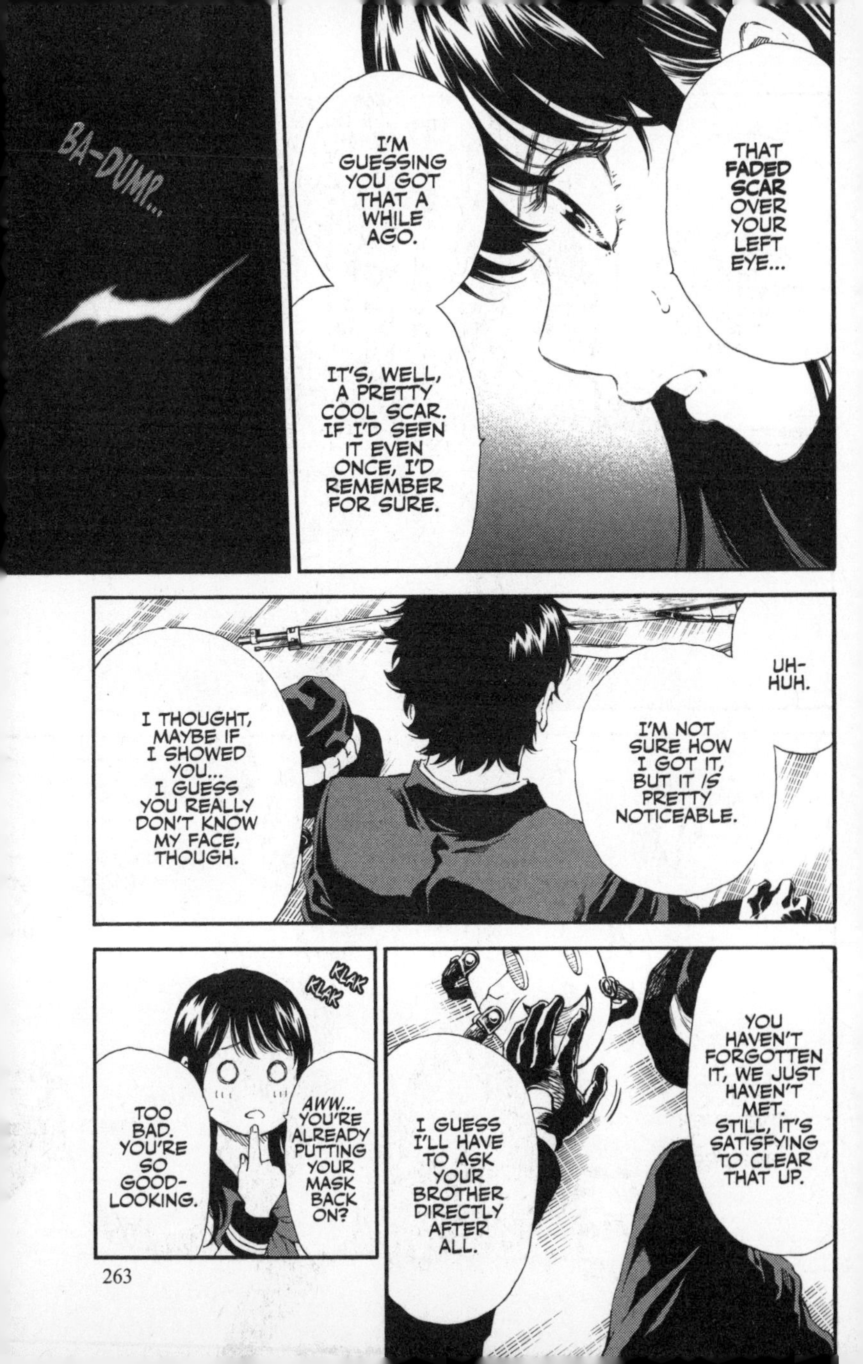
THAT FADED SCAR OVER YOUR LEFT EYE...
I'M GUESSING YOU GOT THAT A WHILE AGO.
IT'S, WELL, A PRETTY COOL SCAR. IF I'D SEEN IT EVEN ONCE, I'D REMEMBER FOR SURE.
BA-DUMP...
UH-HUH.
I'M NOT SURE HOW I GOT IT, BUT IT *IS* PRETTY NOTICEABLE.
I THOUGHT, MAYBE IF I SHOWED YOU... I GUESS YOU REALLY DON'T KNOW MY FACE, THOUGH.
YOU HAVEN'T FORGOTTEN IT, WE JUST HAVEN'T MET. STILL, IT'S SATISFYING TO CLEAR THAT UP.
I GUESS I'LL HAVE TO ASK YOUR BROTHER DIRECTLY AFTER ALL.
KLAK KLAK
AWW... YOU'RE ALREADY PUTTING YOUR MASK BACK ON?
TOO BAD. YOU'RE SO GOOD-LOOKING.

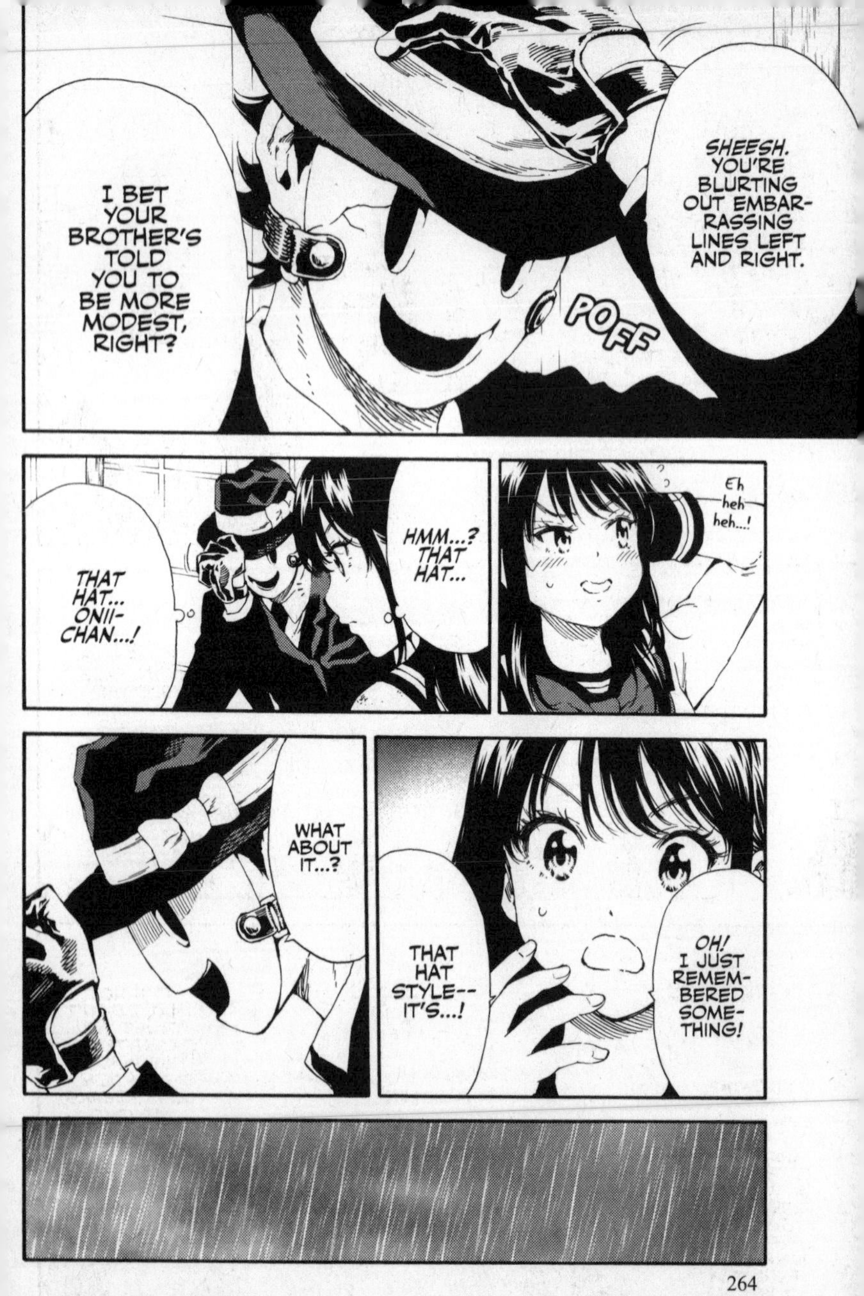
SHEESH. YOU'RE BLURTING OUT EMBARRASSING LINES LEFT AND RIGHT.
POFF
I BET YOUR BROTHER'S TOLD YOU TO BE MORE MODEST, RIGHT?
Eh heh heh...!
HMM...? THAT HAT...
THAT HAT... ONII-CHAN...!
OH! I JUST REMEMBERED SOMETHING!
THAT HAT STYLE-- IT'S...!
WHAT ABOUT IT...?

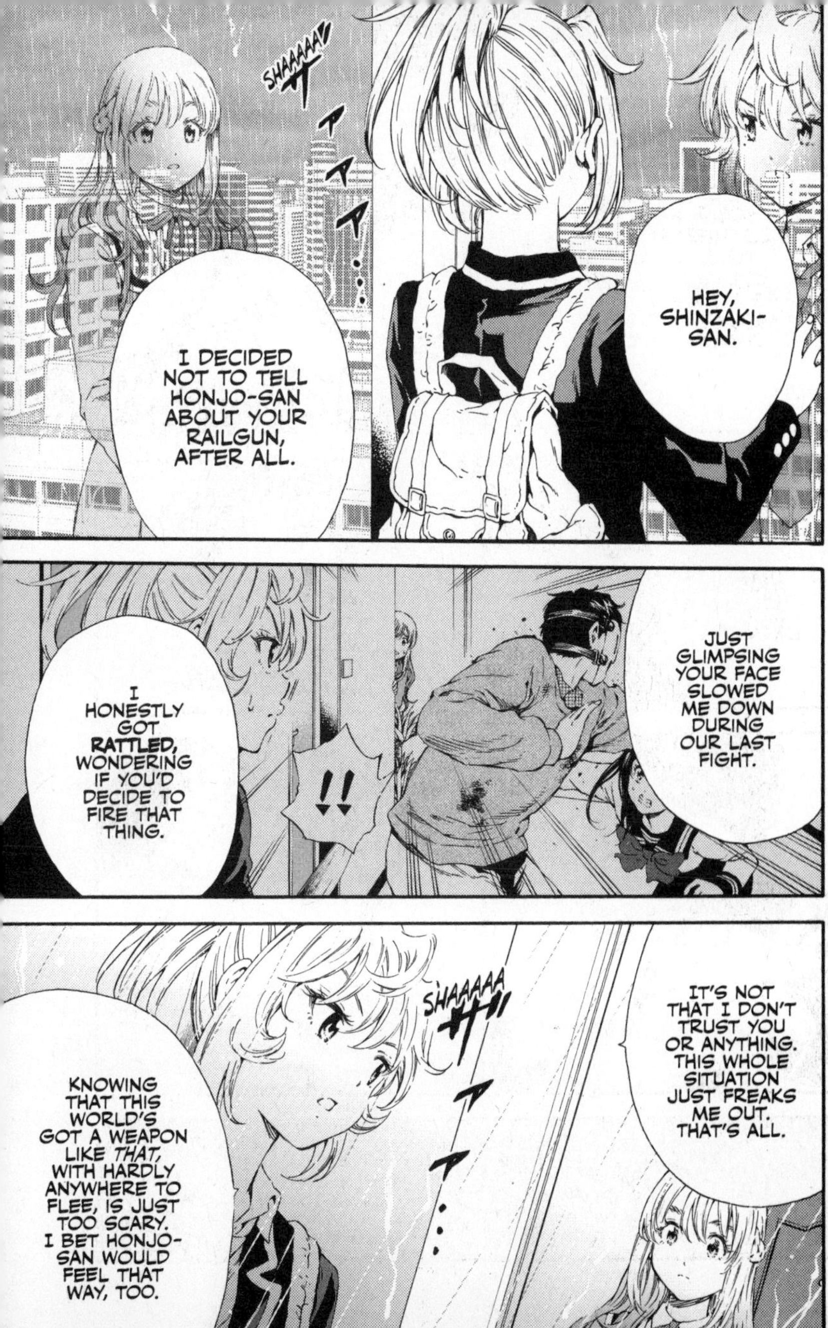
HEY, SHINZAKI-SAN.
SHAAAAA
I DECIDED NOT TO TELL HONJO-SAN ABOUT YOUR RAILGUN, AFTER ALL.
JUST GLIMPSING YOUR FACE SLOWED ME DOWN DURING OUR LAST FIGHT.
!!
I HONESTLY GOT **RATTLED**, WONDERING IF YOU'D DECIDE TO FIRE THAT THING.
IT'S NOT THAT I DON'T TRUST YOU OR ANYTHING. THIS WHOLE SITUATION JUST FREAKS ME OUT. THAT'S ALL.
SHAAAAA
KNOWING THAT THIS WORLD'S GOT A WEAPON LIKE *THAT*, WITH HARDLY ANYWHERE TO FLEE, IS JUST TOO SCARY. I BET HONJO-SAN WOULD FEEL THAT WAY, TOO.

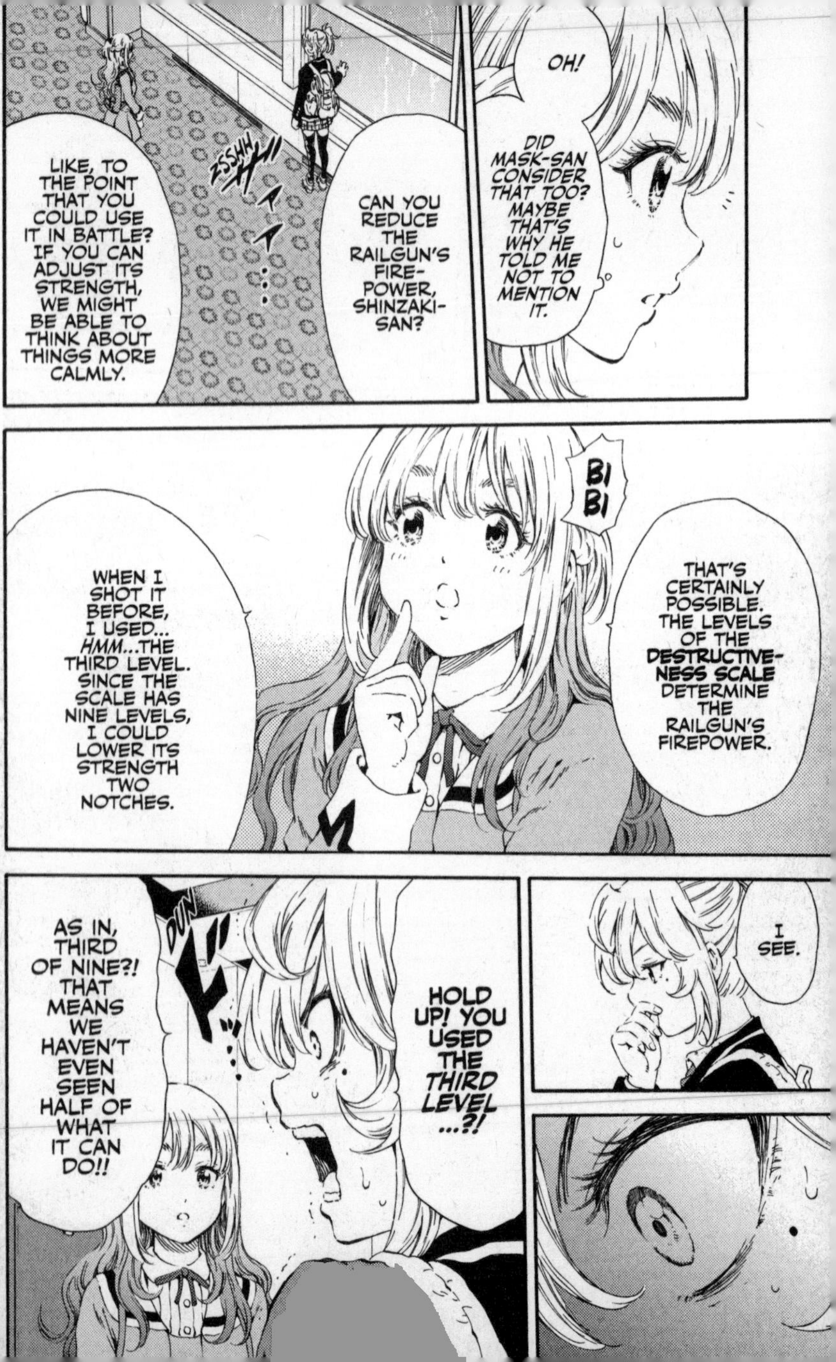
OH!
DID MASK-SAN CONSIDER THAT TOO? MAYBE THAT'S WHY HE TOLD ME NOT TO MENTION IT.
CAN YOU REDUCE THE RAILGUN'S FIRE-POWER, SHINZAKI-SAN?
ZSSHH
LIKE, TO THE POINT THAT YOU COULD USE IT IN BATTLE? IF YOU CAN ADJUST ITS STRENGTH, WE MIGHT BE ABLE TO THINK ABOUT THINGS MORE CALMLY.
BI BI
THAT'S CERTAINLY POSSIBLE. THE LEVELS OF THE DESTRUCTIVE-NESS SCALE DETERMINE THE RAILGUN'S FIREPOWER.
WHEN I SHOT IT BEFORE, I USED... HMM...THE THIRD LEVEL. SINCE THE SCALE HAS NINE LEVELS, I COULD LOWER ITS STRENGTH TWO NOTCHES.
I SEE.
HOLD UP! YOU USED THE THIRD LEVEL...?!
DUN
AS IN, THIRD OF NINE?! THAT MEANS WE HAVEN'T EVEN SEEN HALF OF WHAT IT CAN DO!!

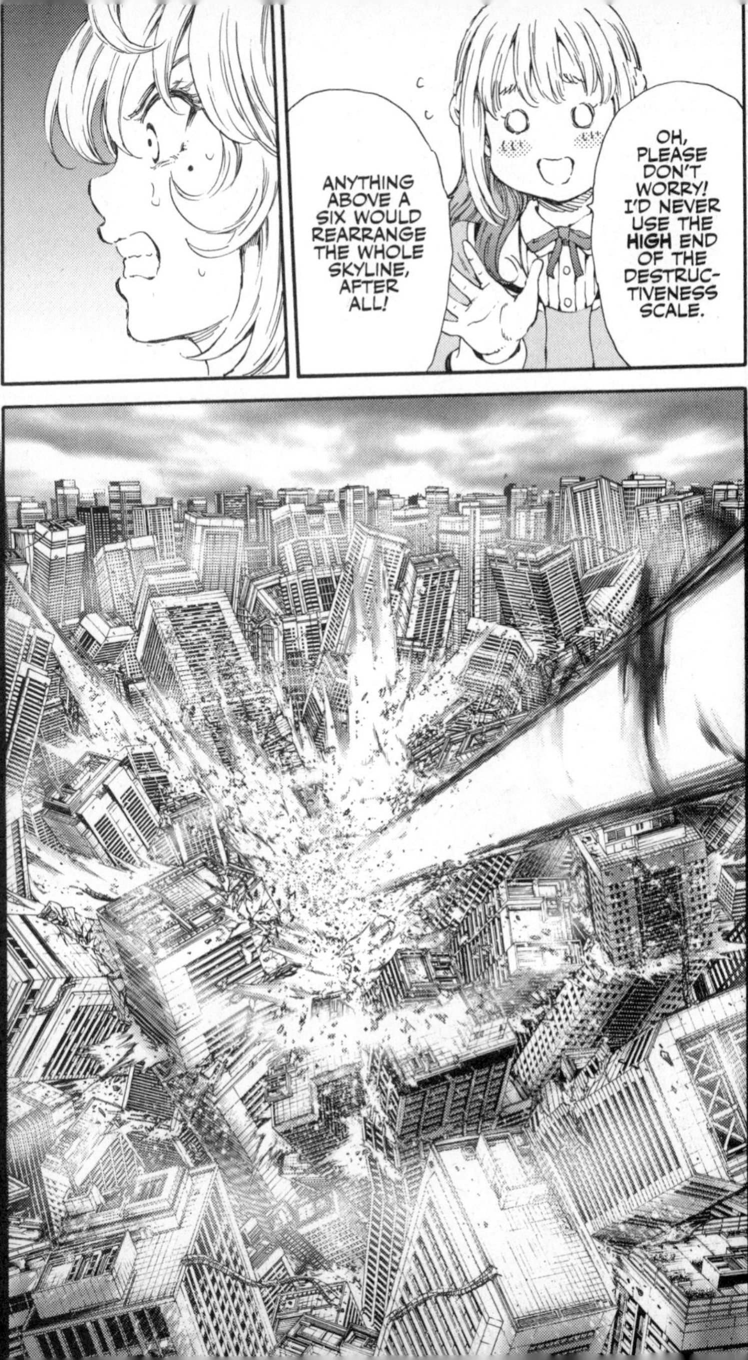
OH, PLEASE DON'T WORRY! I'D NEVER USE THE **HIGH** END OF THE DESTRUCTIVENESS SCALE.
ANYTHING ABOVE A SIX WOULD REARRANGE THE WHOLE SKYLINE, AFTER ALL!

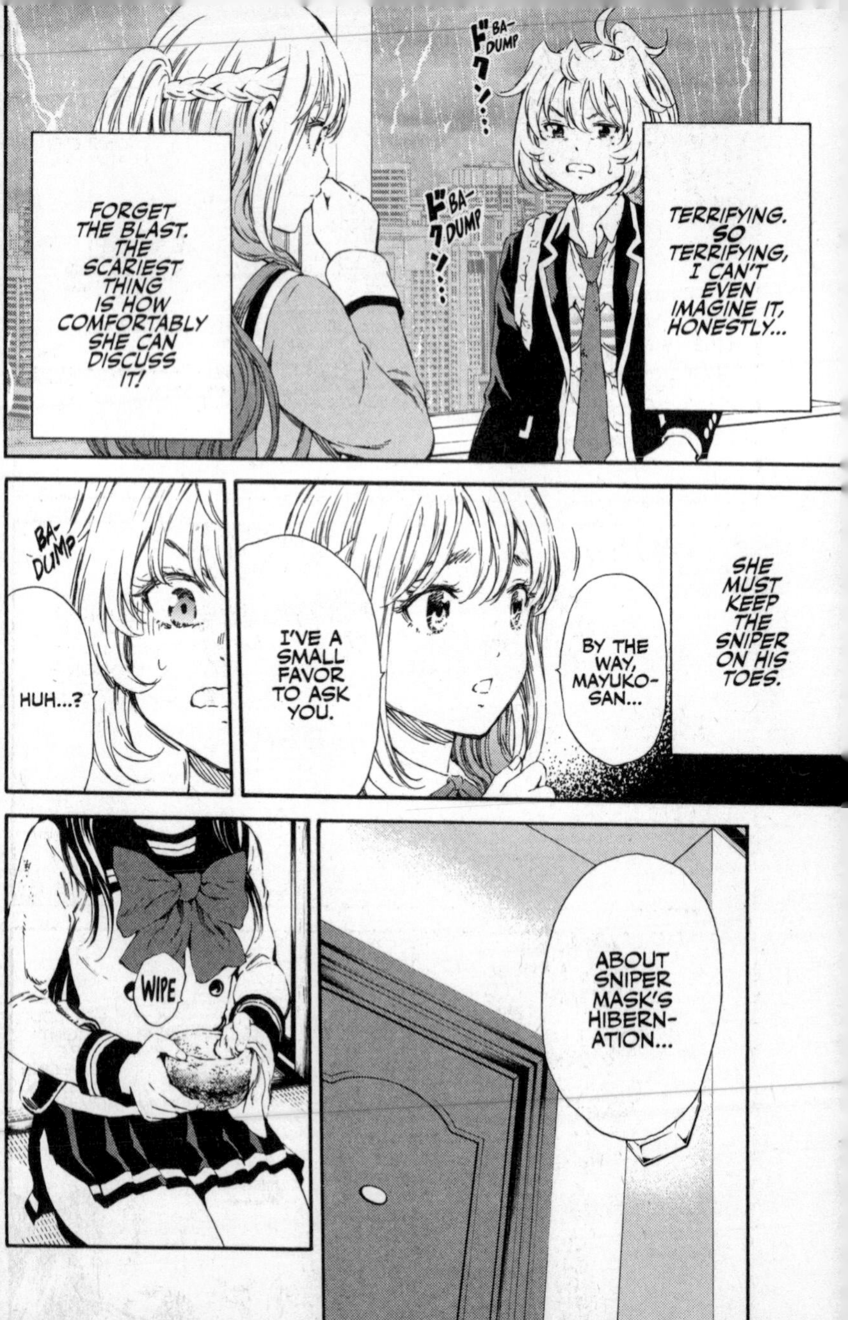
BA-DUMP
TERRIFYING. SO TERRIFYING, I CAN'T EVEN IMAGINE IT, HONESTLY...
BA-DUMP
FORGET THE BLAST. THE SCARIEST THING IS HOW COMFORTABLY SHE CAN DISCUSS IT!
SHE MUST KEEP THE SNIPER ON HIS TOES.
BY THE WAY, MAYUKO-SAN...
I'VE A SMALL FAVOR TO ASK YOU.
BA-DUMP
HUH...?
ABOUT SNIPER MASK'S HIBERN-ATION...
WIPE

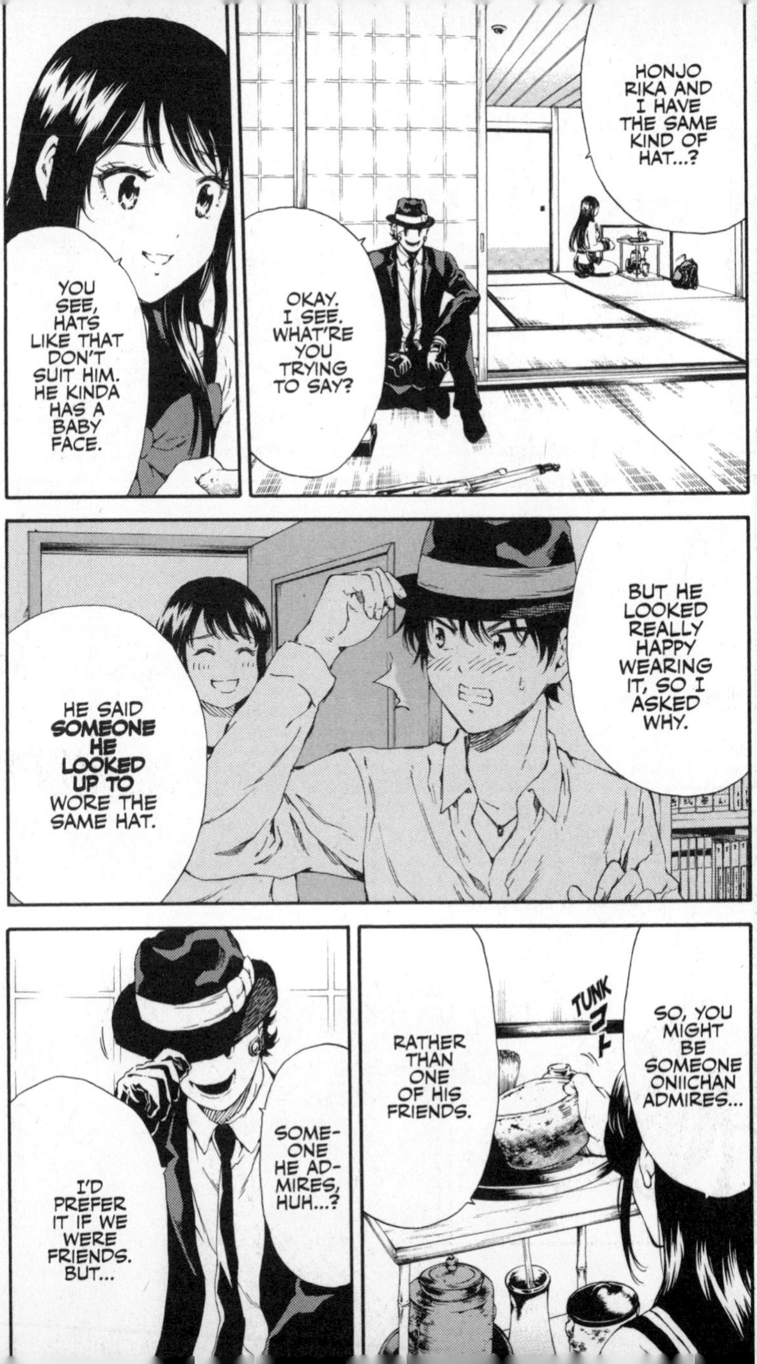
HONJO RIKA AND I HAVE THE SAME KIND OF HAT...?
OKAY. I SEE. WHAT'RE YOU TRYING TO SAY?
YOU SEE, HATS LIKE THAT DON'T SUIT HIM. HE KINDA HAS A BABY FACE.
BUT HE LOOKED REALLY HAPPY WEARING IT, SO I ASKED WHY.
HE SAID **SOMEONE HE LOOKED UP TO** WORE THE SAME HAT.
SO, YOU MIGHT BE SOMEONE ONIICHAN ADMIRES...
TUNK
RATHER THAN ONE OF HIS FRIENDS.
SOME-ONE HE AD-MIRES, HUH...?
I'D PREFER IT IF WE WERE FRIENDS. BUT...

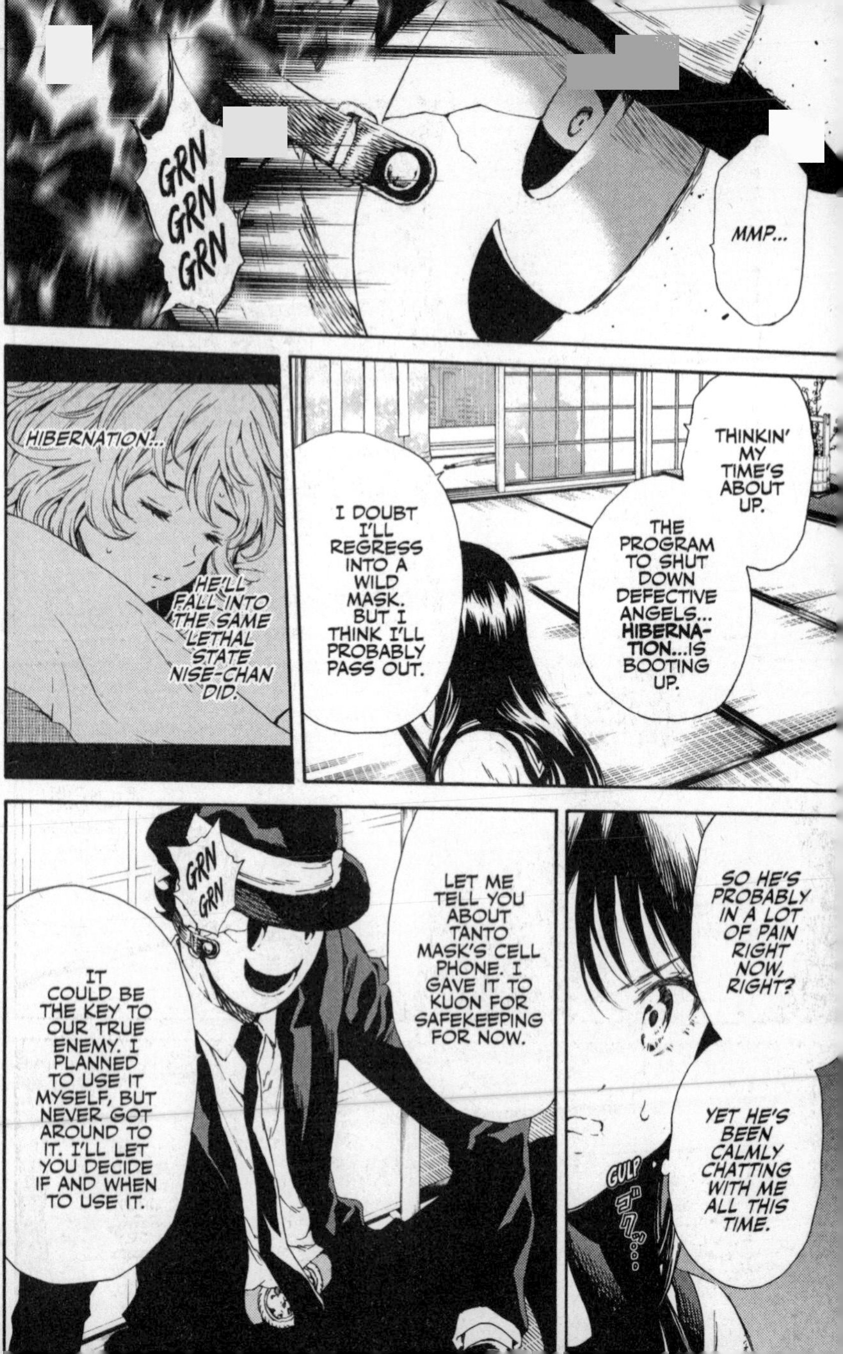
MMP...
GRN GRN GRN
THINKIN' MY TIME'S ABOUT UP.
THE PROGRAM TO SHUT DOWN DEFECTIVE ANGELS... **HIBERNATION**...IS BOOTING UP.
I DOUBT I'LL REGRESS INTO A WILD MASK. BUT I THINK I'LL PROBABLY PASS OUT.
HIBERNATION...
HE'LL FALL INTO THE SAME LETHAL STATE NISE-CHAN DID.
SO HE'S PROBABLY IN A LOT OF PAIN RIGHT NOW, RIGHT?
YET HE'S BEEN CALMLY CHATTING WITH ME ALL THIS TIME.
GULP
LET ME TELL YOU ABOUT TANTO MASK'S CELL PHONE. I GAVE IT TO KUON FOR SAFEKEEPING FOR NOW.
GRN GRN
IT COULD BE THE KEY TO OUR TRUE ENEMY. I PLANNED TO USE IT MYSELF, BUT NEVER GOT AROUND TO IT. I'LL LET YOU DECIDE IF AND WHEN TO USE IT.

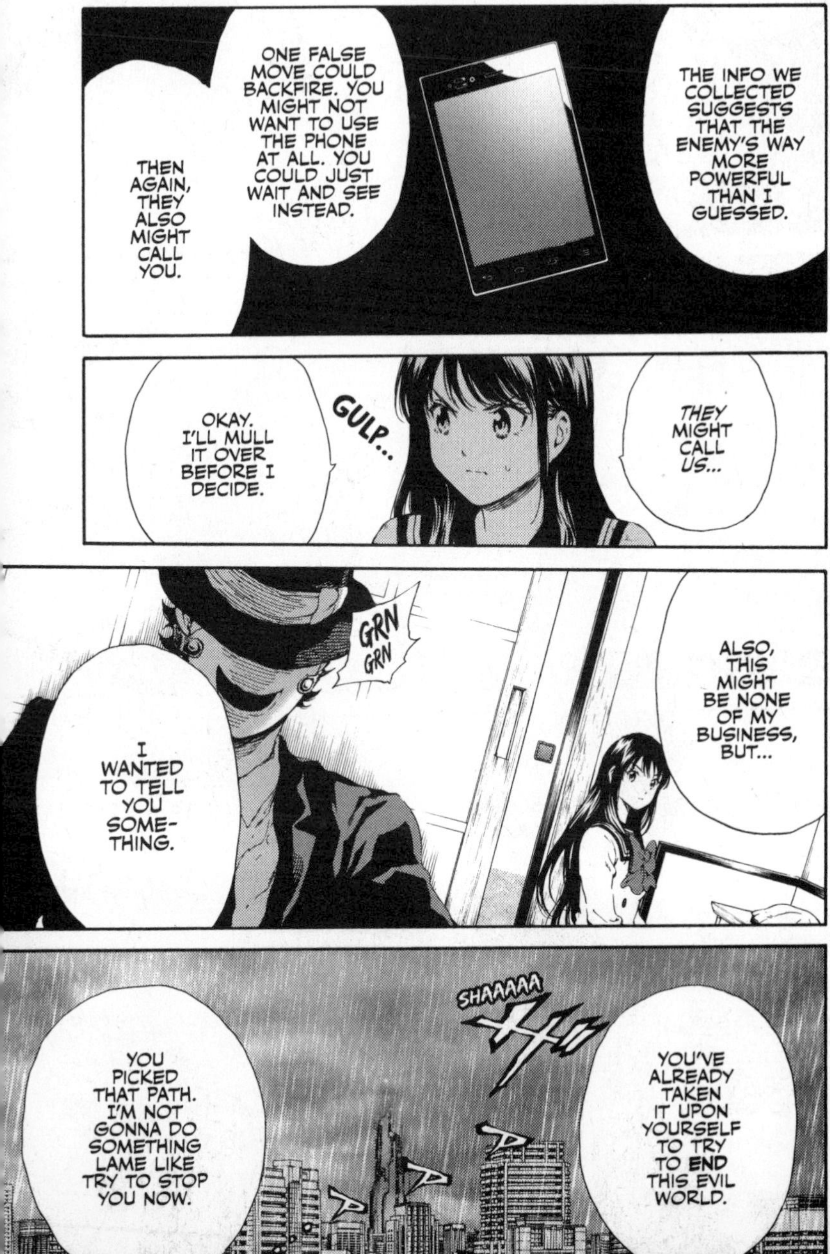
THE INFO WE COLLECTED SUGGESTS THAT THE ENEMY'S WAY MORE POWERFUL THAN I GUESSED.
ONE FALSE MOVE COULD BACKFIRE. YOU MIGHT NOT WANT TO USE THE PHONE AT ALL. YOU COULD JUST WAIT AND SEE INSTEAD.
THEN AGAIN, THEY ALSO MIGHT CALL YOU.
THEY MIGHT CALL US...
GULP...
OKAY. I'LL MULL IT OVER BEFORE I DECIDE.
ALSO, THIS MIGHT BE NONE OF MY BUSINESS, BUT...
GRN GRN
I WANTED TO TELL YOU SOMETHING.
YOU'VE ALREADY TAKEN IT UPON YOURSELF TO TRY TO **END** THIS EVIL WORLD.
SHAAAAA
YOU PICKED THAT PATH. I'M NOT GONNA DO SOMETHING LAME LIKE TRY TO STOP YOU NOW.

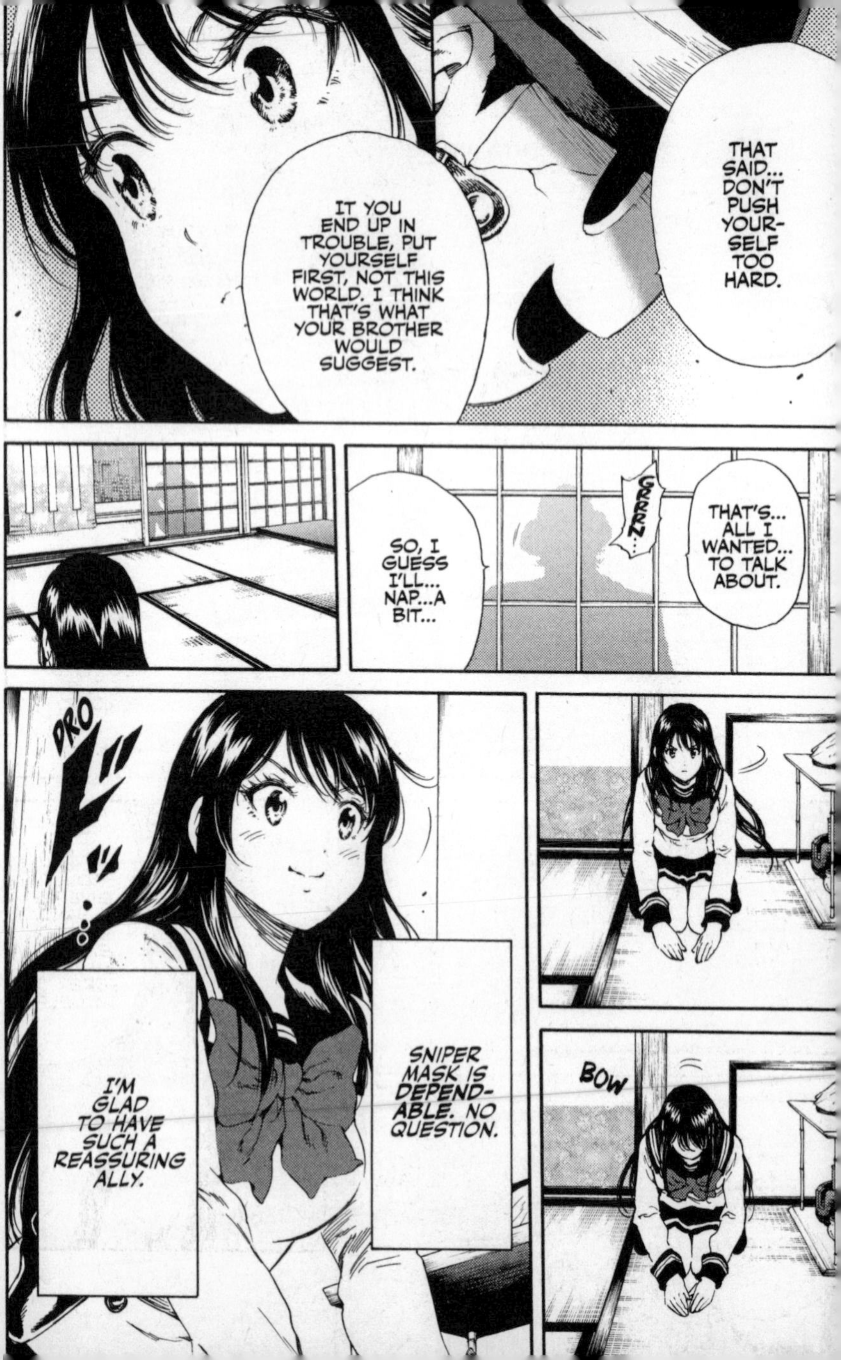
THAT SAID... DON'T PUSH YOUR-SELF TOO HARD.
IT YOU END UP IN TROUBLE, PUT YOURSELF FIRST, NOT THIS WORLD. I THINK THAT'S WHAT YOUR BROTHER WOULD SUGGEST.
GRRRN...
THAT'S... ALL I WANTED... TO TALK ABOUT.
SO, I GUESS I'LL... NAP...A BIT...
BOW
DRO
SNIPER MASK IS DEPEND-ABLE. NO QUESTION.
I'M GLAD TO HAVE SUCH A REASSURING ALLY.

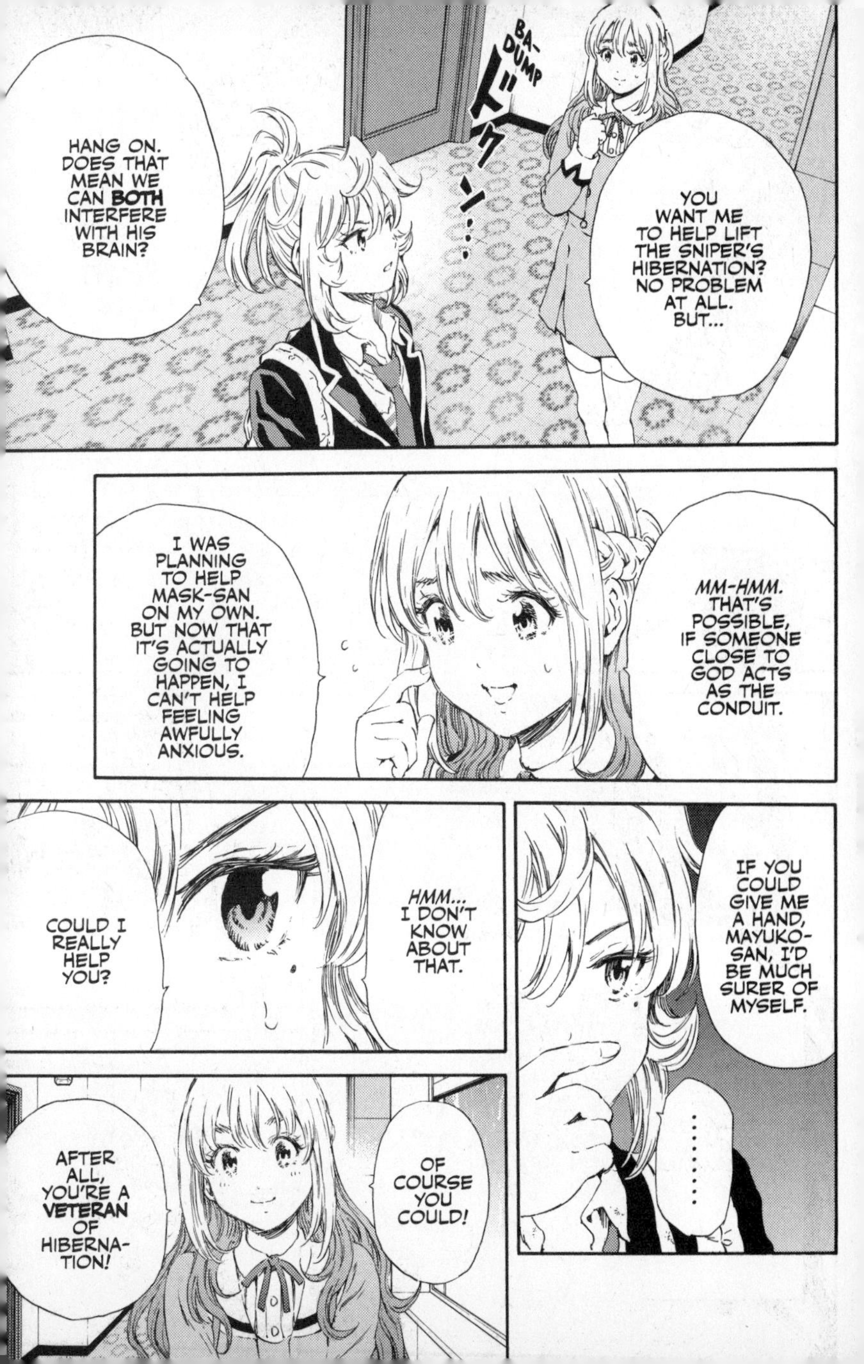
YOU WANT ME TO HELP LIFT THE SNIPER'S HIBERNATION? NO PROBLEM AT ALL. BUT...
BA-DUMP
HANG ON. DOES THAT MEAN WE CAN **BOTH** INTERFERE WITH HIS BRAIN?
MM-HMM. THAT'S POSSIBLE, IF SOMEONE CLOSE TO GOD ACTS AS THE CONDUIT.
I WAS PLANNING TO HELP MASK-SAN ON MY OWN. BUT NOW THAT IT'S ACTUALLY GOING TO HAPPEN, I CAN'T HELP FEELING AWFULLY ANXIOUS.
IF YOU COULD GIVE ME A HAND, MAYUKO-SAN, I'D BE MUCH SURER OF MYSELF.
......
HMM... I DON'T KNOW ABOUT THAT.
COULD I REALLY HELP YOU?
OF COURSE YOU COULD!
AFTER ALL, YOU'RE A **VETERAN** OF HIBERNA-TION!

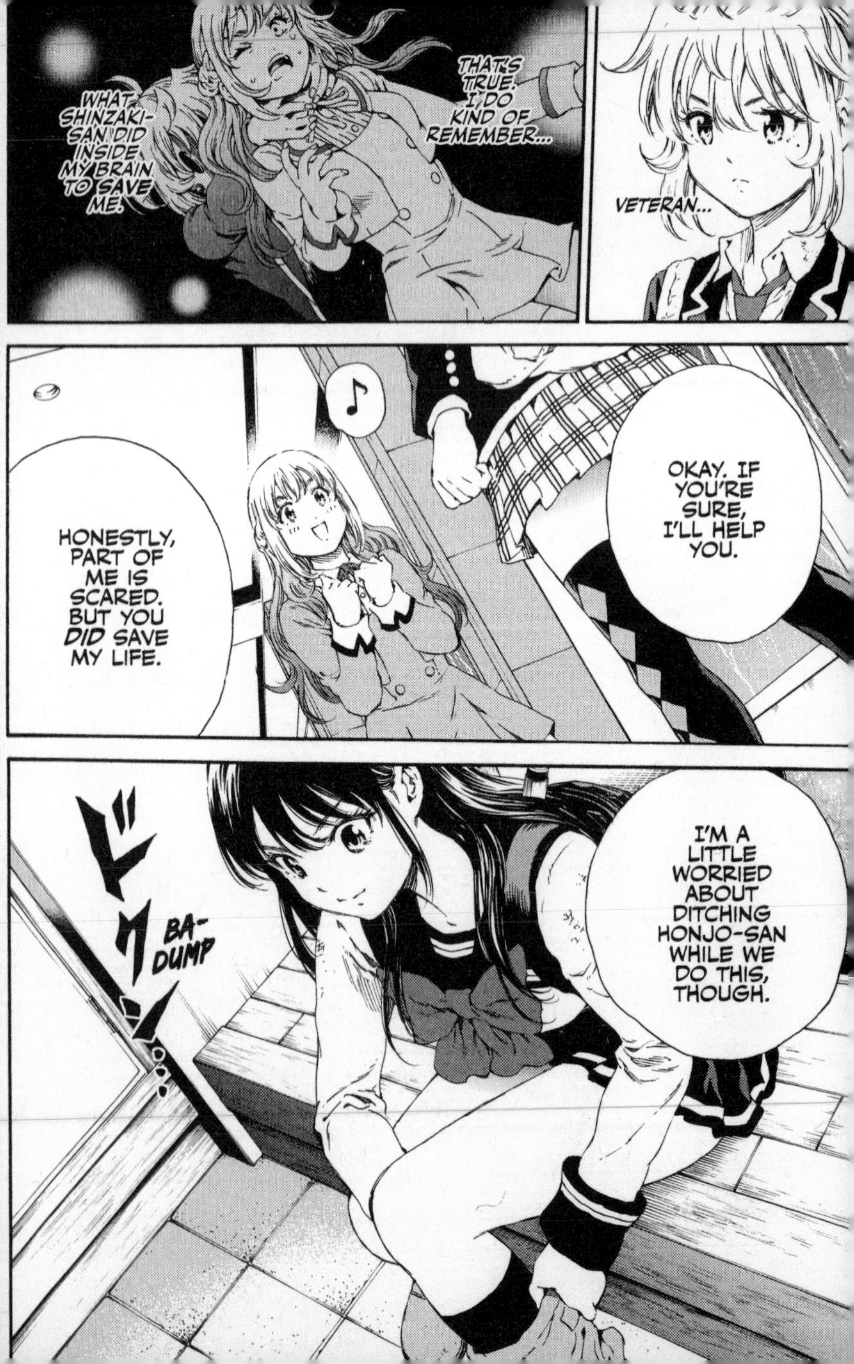
VETERAN...
THAT'S TRUE. I DO KIND OF REMEMBER...
WHAT SHINZAKI-SAN DID INSIDE MY BRAIN TO SAVE ME.
OKAY. IF YOU'RE SURE, I'LL HELP YOU.
♪
HONESTLY, PART OF ME IS SCARED. BUT YOU *DID* SAVE MY LIFE.
I'M A LITTLE WORRIED ABOUT DITCHING HONJO-SAN WHILE WE DO THIS, THOUGH.
BA-DUMP

So scary!

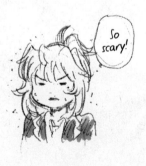

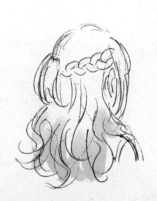

HIGH-RISE
INVASION

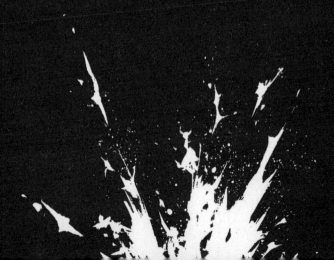

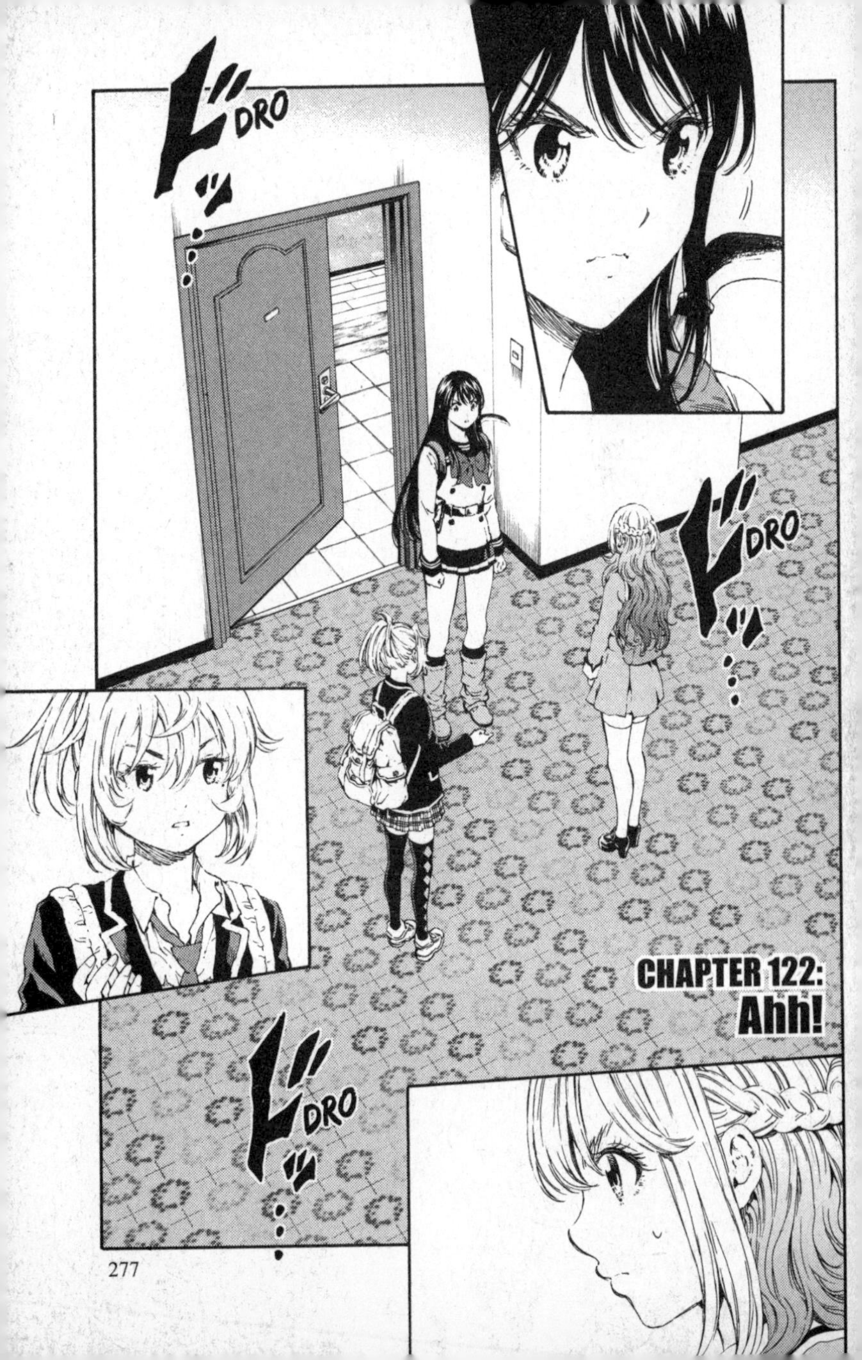
DRO
DRO
CHAPTER 122:
Ahh!
DRO

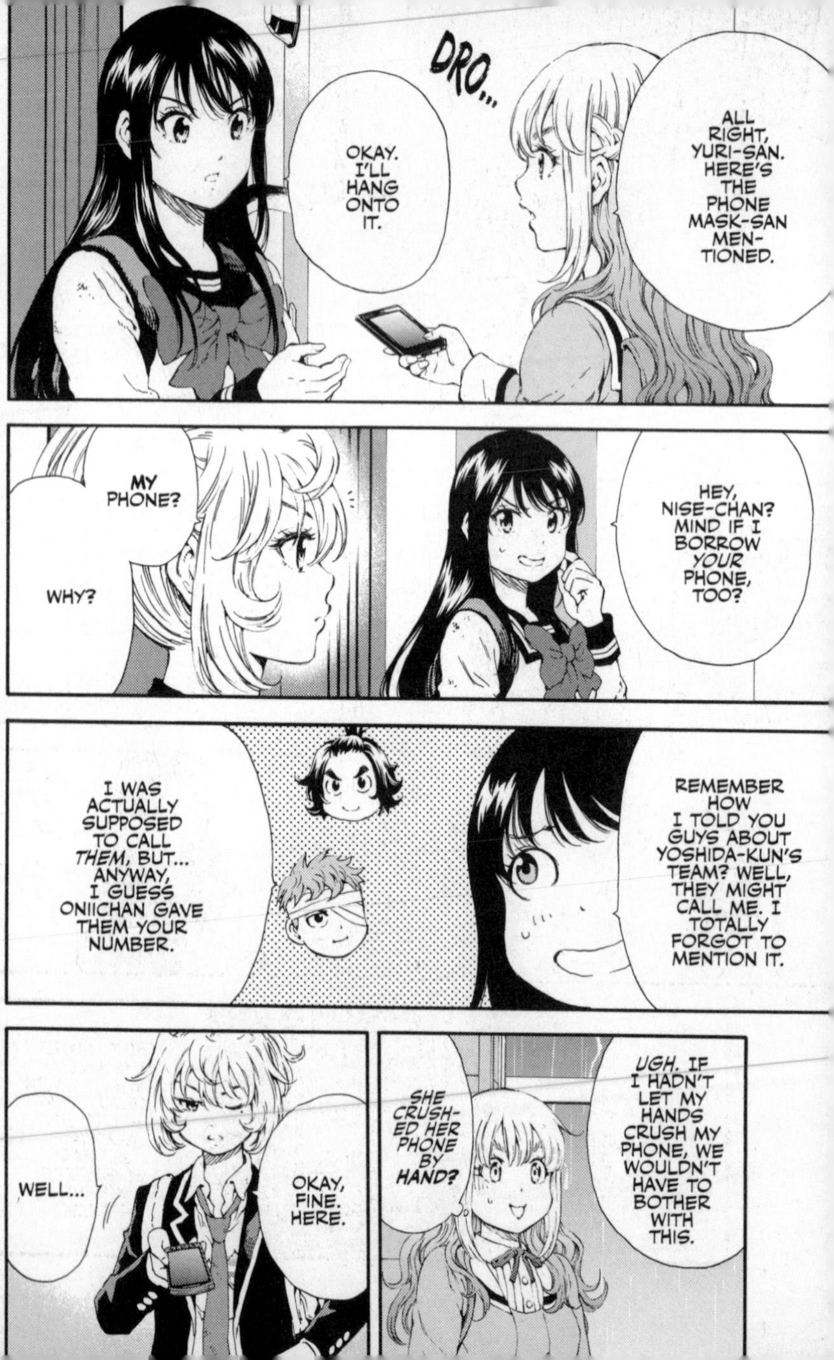
ALL RIGHT, YURI-SAN. HERE'S THE PHONE MASK-SAN MENTIONED.
DRO...
OKAY. I'LL HANG ONTO IT.
HEY, NISE-CHAN? MIND IF I BORROW *YOUR* PHONE, TOO?
MY PHONE?
WHY?
REMEMBER HOW I TOLD YOU GUYS ABOUT YOSHIDA-KUN'S TEAM? WELL, THEY MIGHT CALL ME. I TOTALLY FORGOT TO MENTION IT.
I WAS ACTUALLY SUPPOSED TO CALL *THEM*, BUT... ANYWAY, I GUESS ONIICHAN GAVE THEM YOUR NUMBER.
UGH. IF I HADN'T LET MY HANDS CRUSH MY PHONE, WE WOULDN'T HAVE TO BOTHER WITH THIS.
SHE CRUSH-ED HER PHONE BY ***HAND?***
WELL...
OKAY, FINE. HERE.

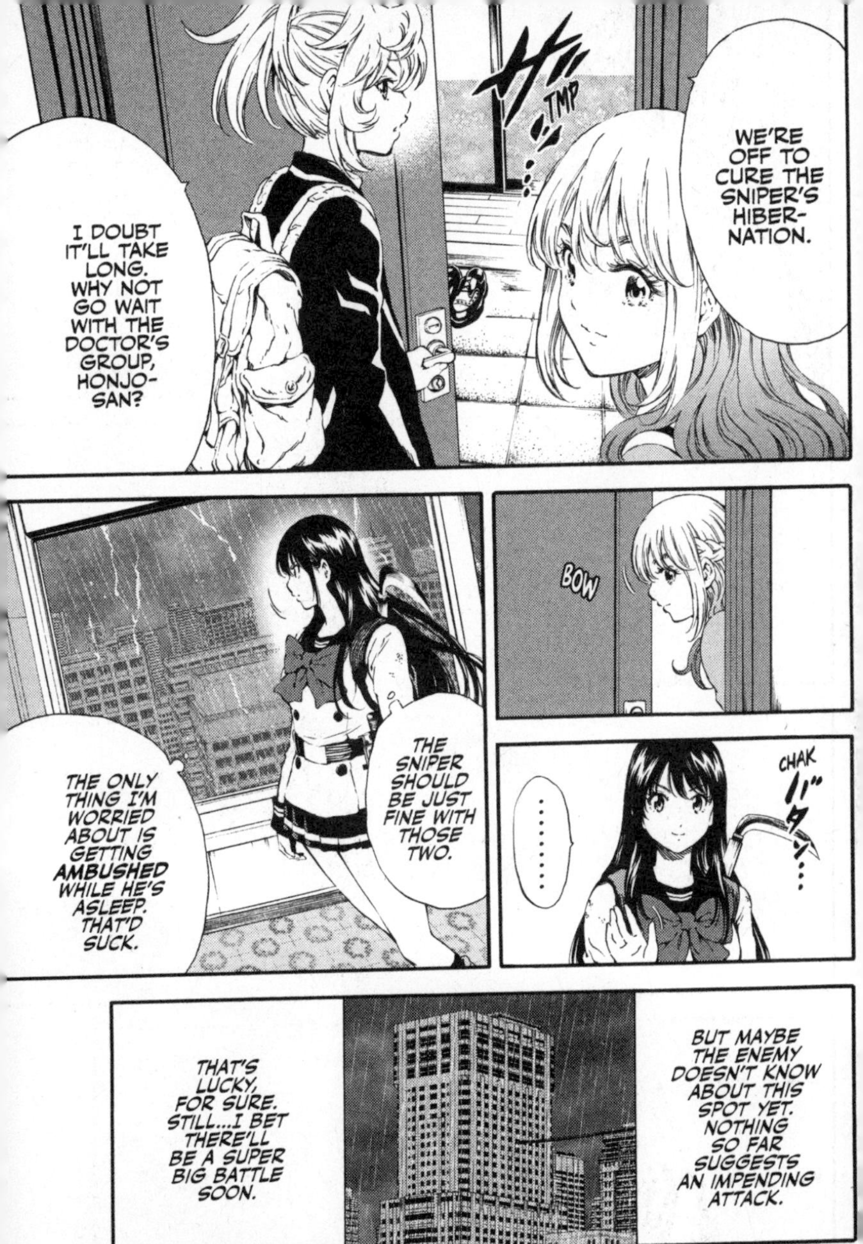
WE'RE OFF TO CURE THE SNIPER'S HIBER-NATION.
TMP
I DOUBT IT'LL TAKE LONG. WHY NOT GO WAIT WITH THE DOCTOR'S GROUP, HONJO-SAN?
BOW
......
CHAK
THE SNIPER SHOULD BE JUST FINE WITH THOSE TWO.
THE ONLY THING I'M WORRIED ABOUT IS GETTING AMBUSHED WHILE HE'S ASLEEP. THAT'D SUCK.
BUT MAYBE THE ENEMY DOESN'T KNOW ABOUT THIS SPOT YET. NOTHING SO FAR SUGGESTS AN IMPENDING ATTACK.
THAT'S LUCKY, FOR SURE. STILL...I BET THERE'LL BE A SUPER BIG BATTLE SOON.

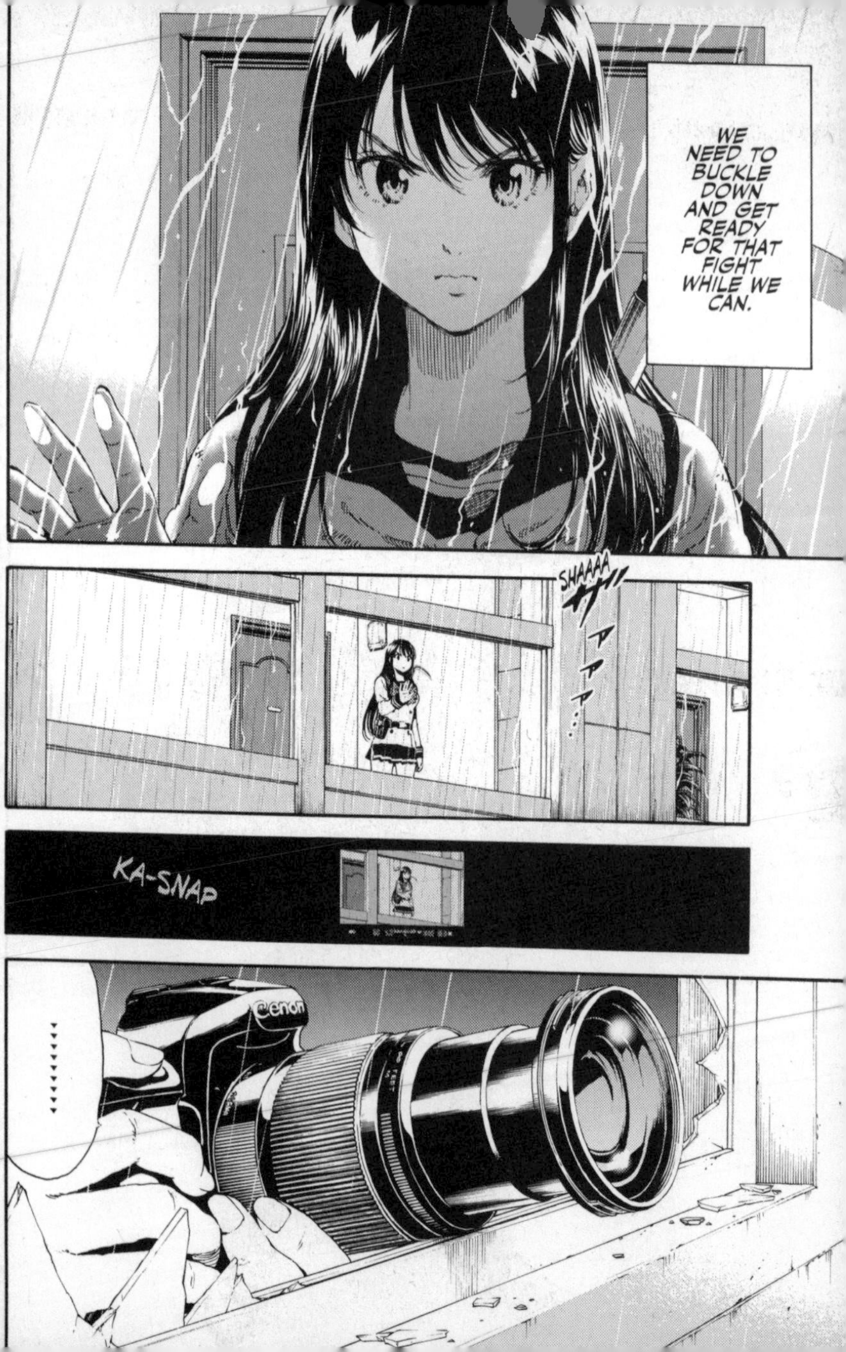
WE NEED TO BUCKLE DOWN AND GET READY FOR THAT FIGHT WHILE WE CAN.
SHAAAA
KA-SNAP
....

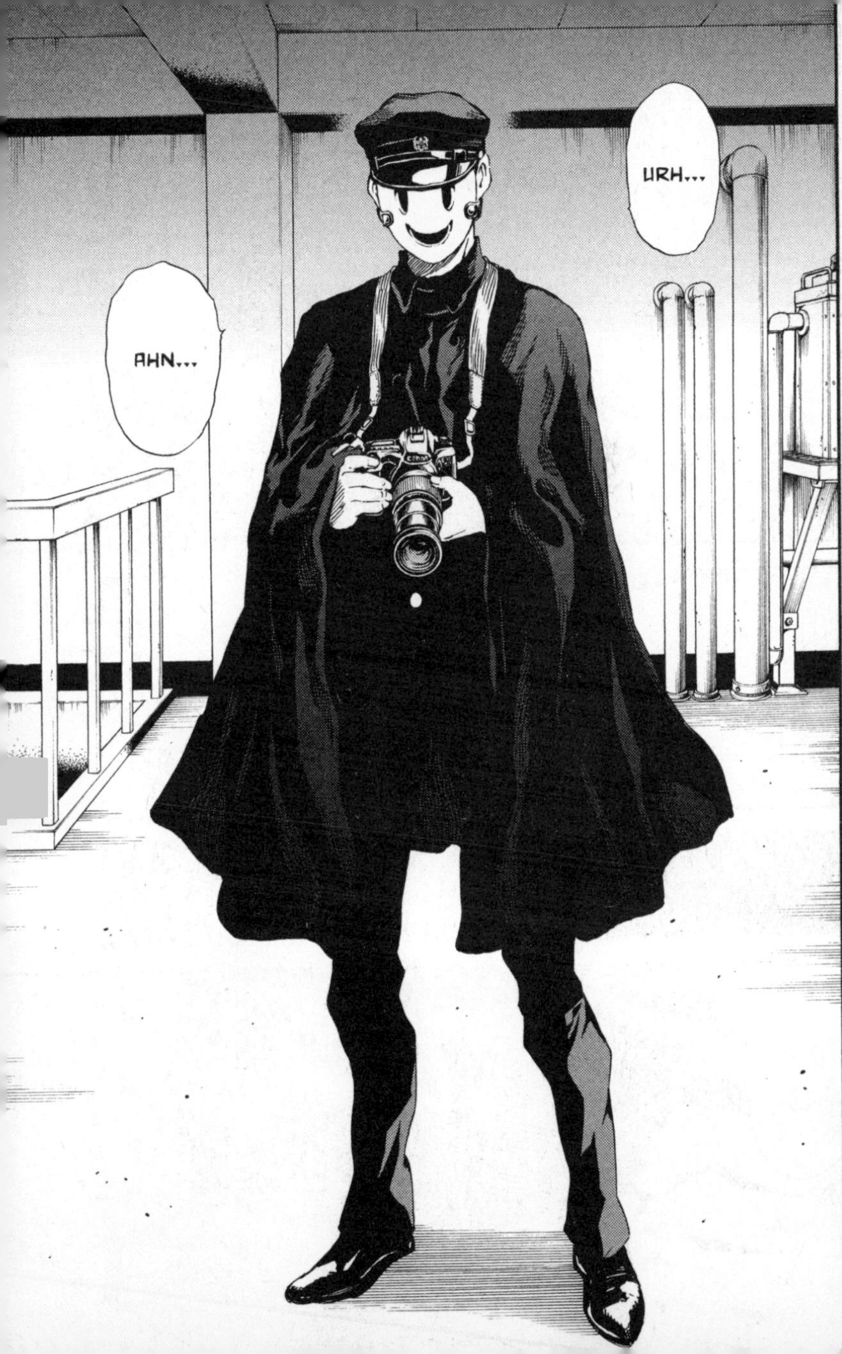
URH...
AHN...

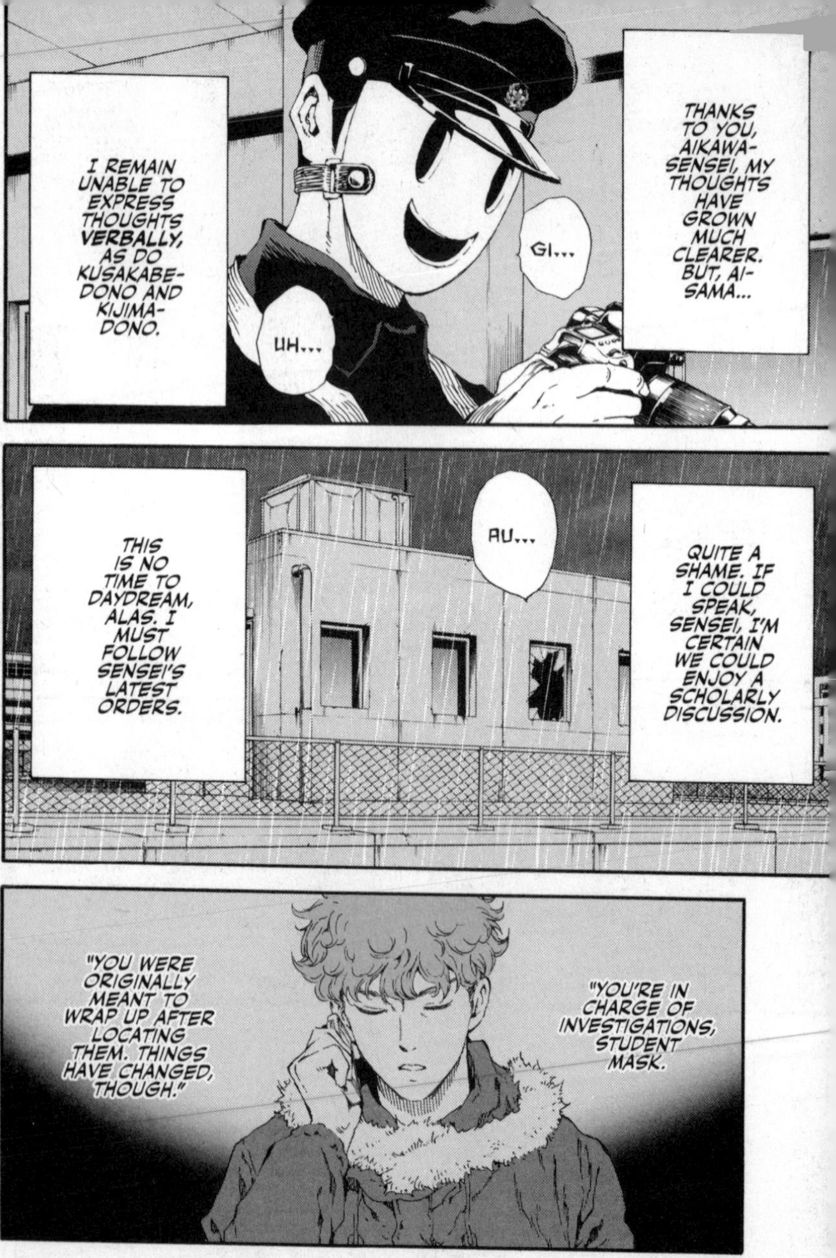
THANKS TO YOU, AIKAWA-SENSEI, MY THOUGHTS HAVE GROWN MUCH CLEARER. BUT, AI-SAMA...
GI...
UH...
I REMAIN UNABLE TO EXPRESS THOUGHTS VERBALLY, AS DO KUSAKABE-DONO AND KIJIMA-DONO.
QUITE A SHAME. IF I COULD SPEAK, SENSEI, I'M CERTAIN WE COULD ENJOY A SCHOLARLY DISCUSSION.
AU...
THIS IS NO TIME TO DAYDREAM, ALAS. I MUST FOLLOW SENSEI'S LATEST ORDERS.
"YOU'RE IN CHARGE OF INVESTIGATIONS, STUDENT MASK.
"YOU WERE ORIGINALLY MEANT TO WRAP UP AFTER LOCATING THEM. THINGS HAVE CHANGED, THOUGH."

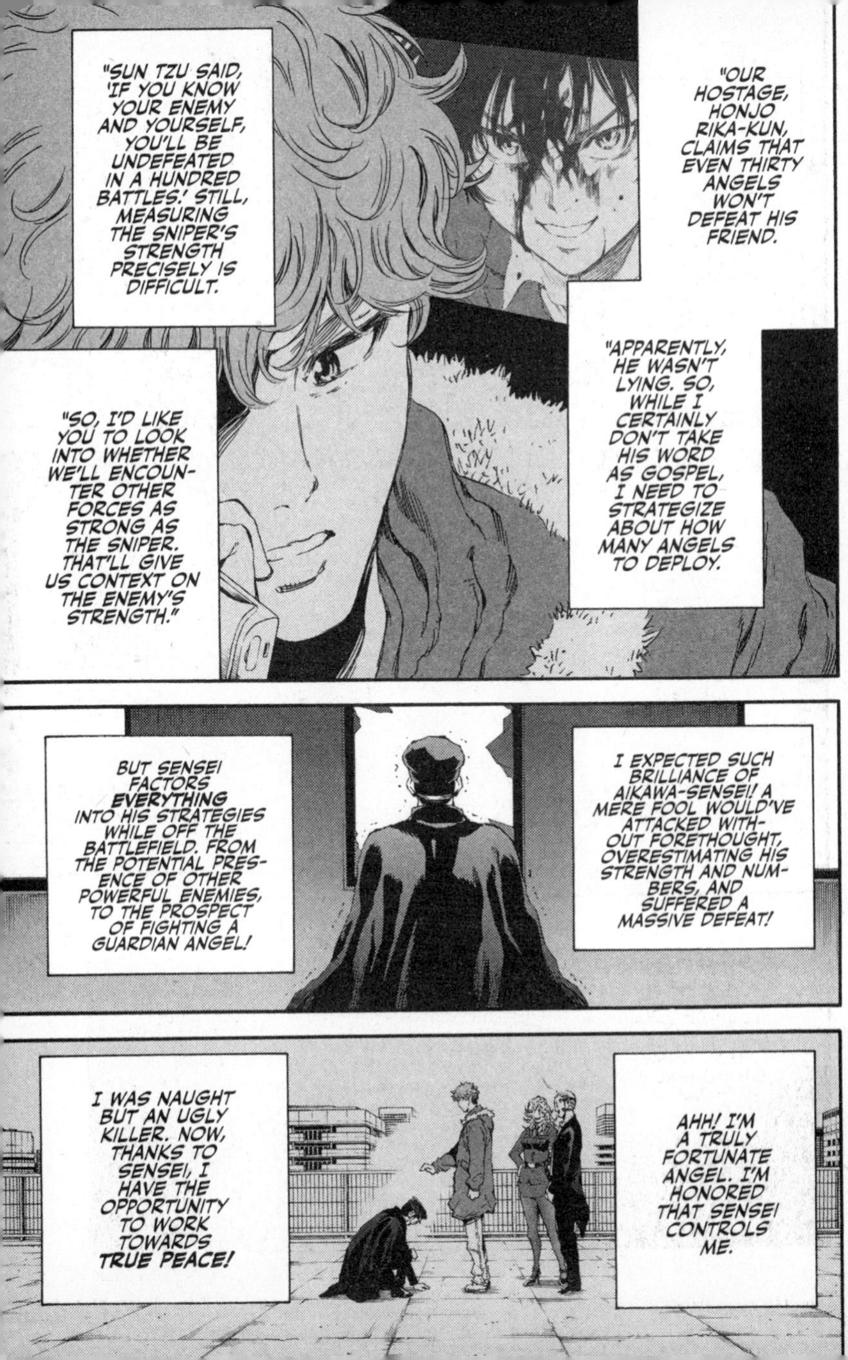
"OUR HOSTAGE, HONJO RIKA-KUN, CLAIMS THAT EVEN THIRTY ANGELS WON'T DEFEAT HIS FRIEND.
"SUN TZU SAID, 'IF YOU KNOW YOUR ENEMY AND YOURSELF, YOU'LL BE UNDEFEATED IN A HUNDRED BATTLES.' STILL, MEASURING THE SNIPER'S STRENGTH PRECISELY IS DIFFICULT.
"APPARENTLY, HE WASN'T LYING. SO, WHILE I CERTAINLY DON'T TAKE HIS WORD AS GOSPEL, I NEED TO STRATEGIZE ABOUT HOW MANY ANGELS TO DEPLOY.
"SO, I'D LIKE YOU TO LOOK INTO WHETHER WE'LL ENCOUNTER OTHER FORCES AS STRONG AS THE SNIPER. THAT'LL GIVE US CONTEXT ON THE ENEMY'S STRENGTH."
I EXPECTED SUCH BRILLIANCE OF AIKAWA-SENSEI! A MERE FOOL WOULD'VE ATTACKED WITHOUT FORETHOUGHT, OVERESTIMATING HIS STRENGTH AND NUMBERS, AND SUFFERED A MASSIVE DEFEAT!
BUT SENSEI FACTORS **EVERYTHING** INTO HIS STRATEGIES WHILE OFF THE BATTLEFIELD. FROM THE POTENTIAL PRESENCE OF OTHER POWERFUL ENEMIES, TO THE PROSPECT OF FIGHTING A GUARDIAN ANGEL!
AHH! I'M A TRULY FORTUNATE ANGEL. I'M HONORED THAT SENSEI CONTROLS ME.
I WAS NAUGHT BUT AN UGLY KILLER. NOW, THANKS TO SENSEI, I HAVE THE OPPORTUNITY TO WORK TOWARDS **TRUE PEACE!**

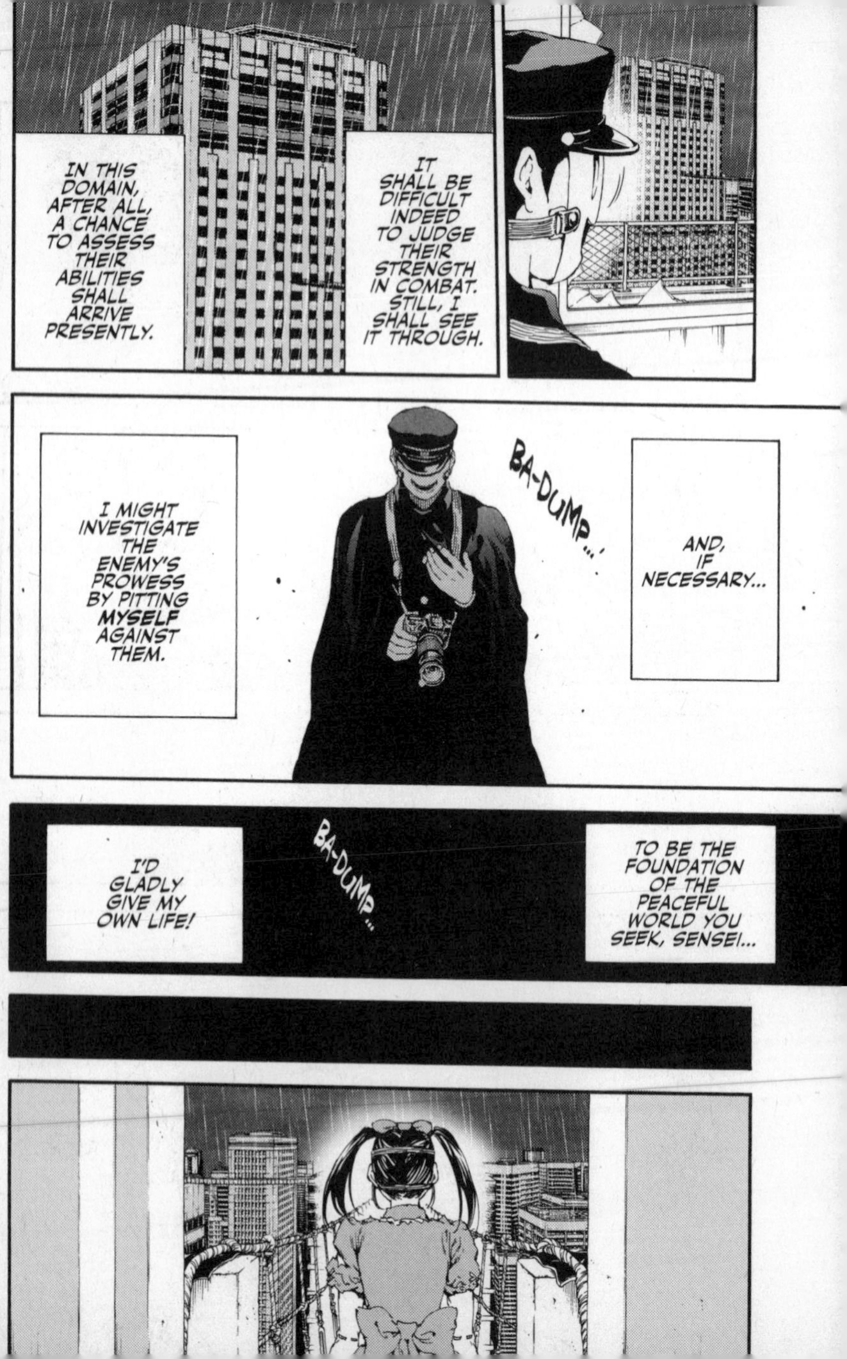
IT SHALL BE DIFFICULT INDEED TO JUDGE THEIR STRENGTH IN COMBAT. STILL, I SHALL SEE IT THROUGH.
IN THIS DOMAIN, AFTER ALL, A CHANCE TO ASSESS THEIR ABILITIES SHALL ARRIVE PRESENTLY.
AND, IF NECESSARY...
BA-DUMP...!
I MIGHT INVESTIGATE THE ENEMY'S PROWESS BY PITTING **MYSELF** AGAINST THEM.
TO BE THE FOUNDATION OF THE PEACEFUL WORLD YOU SEEK, SENSEI...
BA-DUMP...
I'D GLADLY GIVE MY OWN LIFE!

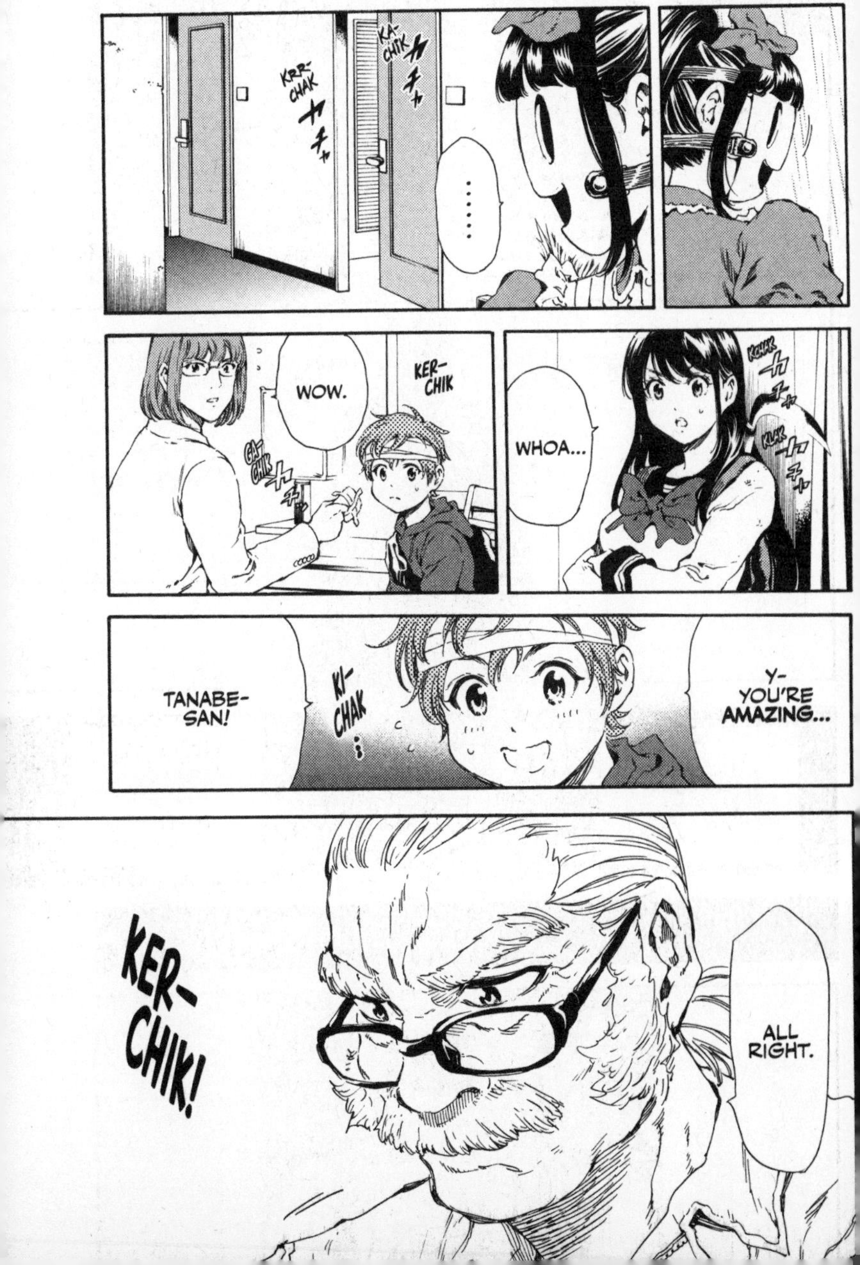
......
KA-CHIK
KRR-CHAK
KCHAK
KLAK
WHOA...
KER-CHIK
WOW.
GA-CHIK
Y- YOU'RE AMAZING...
KI-CHAK
TANABE-SAN!
ALL RIGHT.
KER-CHIK!

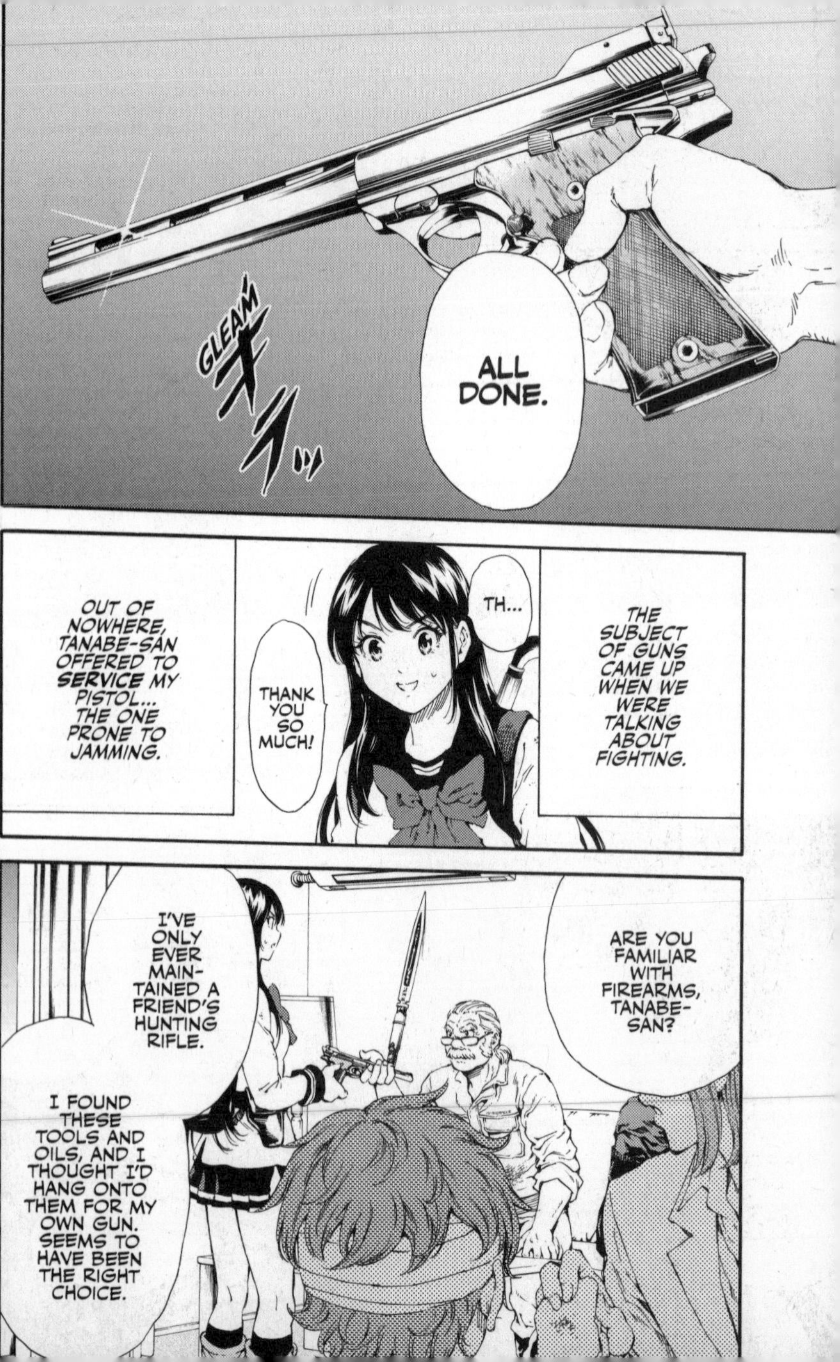
GLEAM
ALL DONE.
THE SUBJECT OF GUNS CAME UP WHEN WE WERE TALKING ABOUT FIGHTING.
TH...
THANK YOU SO MUCH!
OUT OF NOWHERE, TANABE-SAN OFFERED TO SERVICE MY PISTOL... THE ONE PRONE TO JAMMING.
ARE YOU FAMILIAR WITH FIREARMS, TANABE-SAN?
I'VE ONLY EVER MAIN-TAINED A FRIEND'S HUNTING RIFLE.
I FOUND THESE TOOLS AND OILS, AND I THOUGHT I'D HANG ONTO THEM FOR MY OWN GUN. SEEMS TO HAVE BEEN THE RIGHT CHOICE.

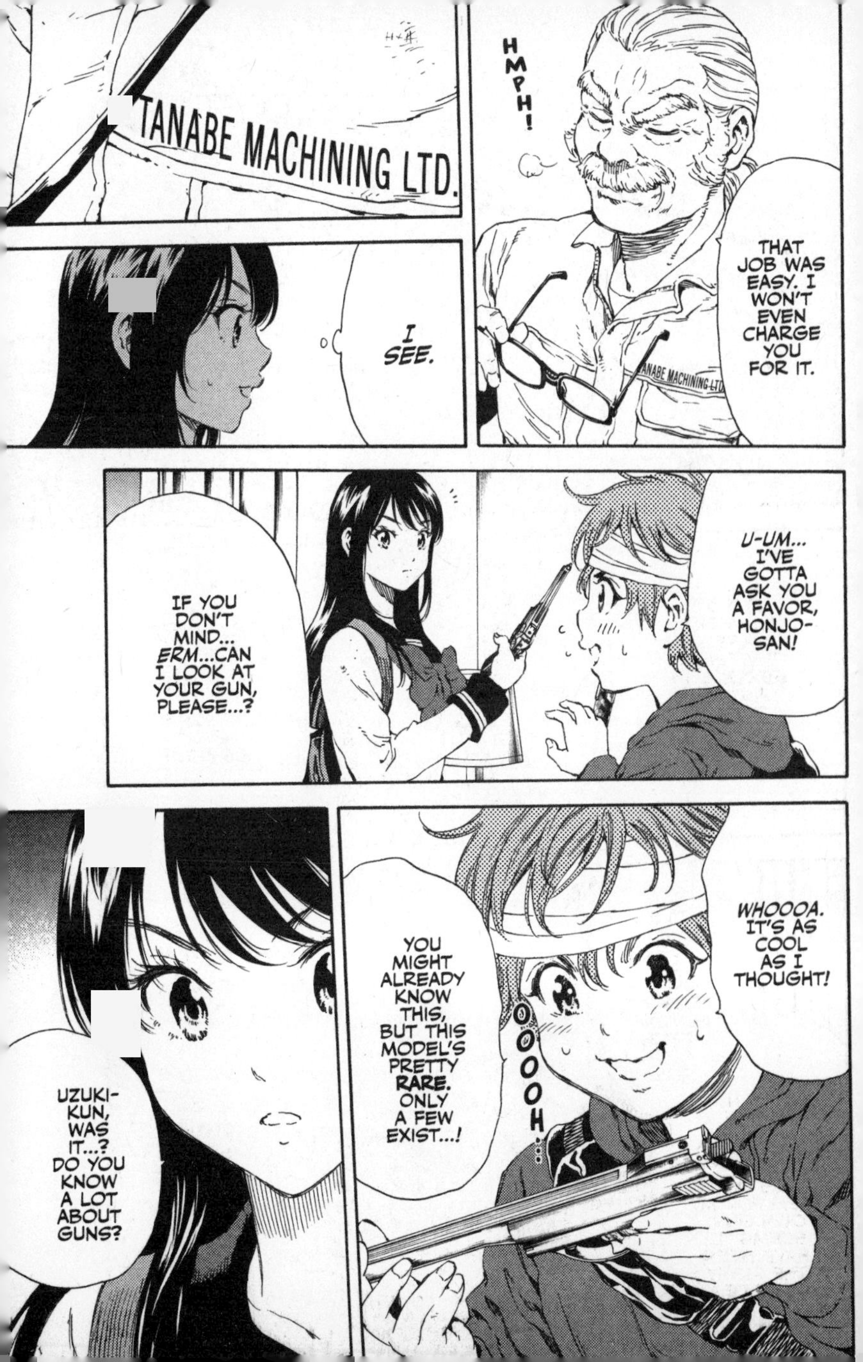
HMPH!
THAT JOB WAS EASY. I WON'T EVEN CHARGE YOU FOR IT.
TANABE MACHINING LTD
TANABE MACHINING LTD.
I SEE.
U-UM... I'VE GOTTA ASK YOU A FAVOR, HONJO-SAN!
IF YOU DON'T MIND... ERM...CAN I LOOK AT YOUR GUN, PLEASE...?
WHOOOA. IT'S AS COOL AS I THOUGHT!
OOOOOH...
YOU MIGHT ALREADY KNOW THIS, BUT THIS MODEL'S PRETTY RARE. ONLY A FEW EXIST...!
UZUKI-KUN, WAS IT...? DO YOU KNOW A LOT ABOUT GUNS?

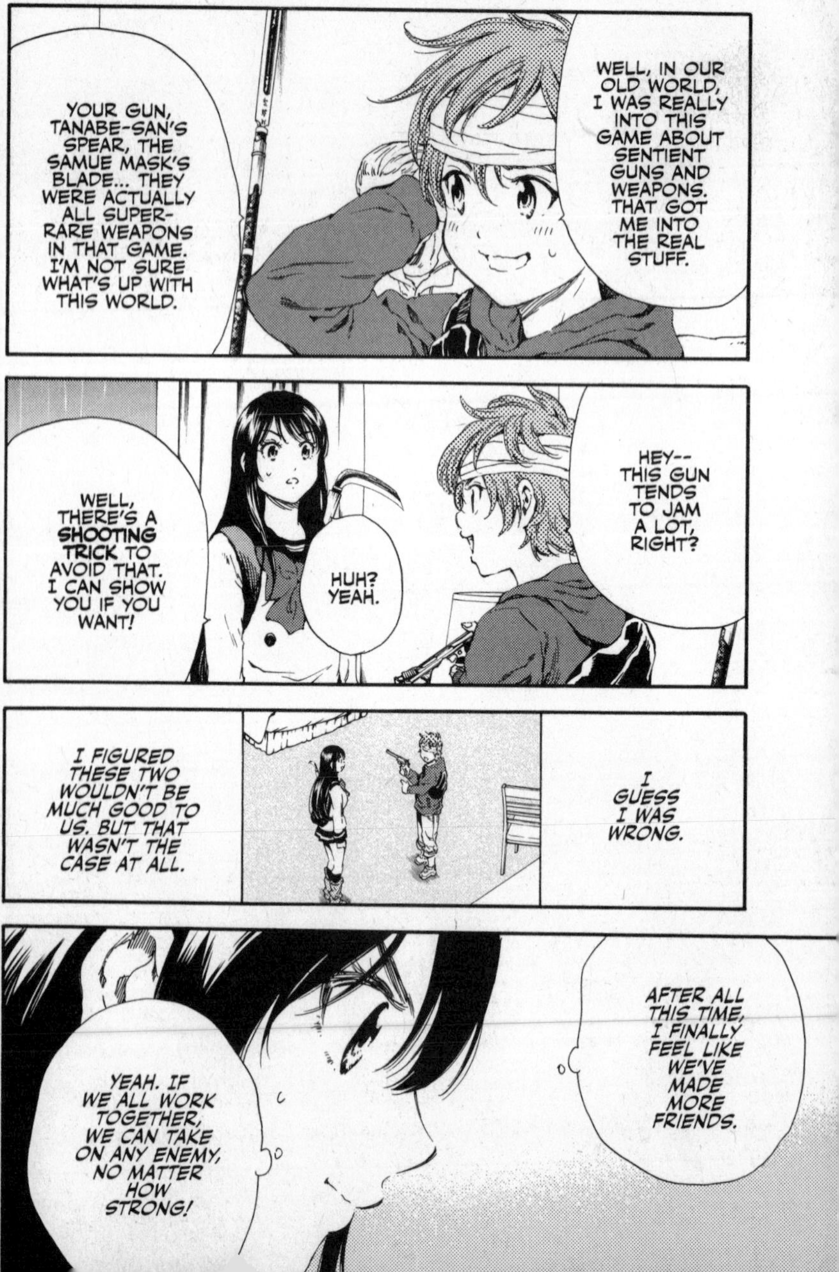
WELL, IN OUR OLD WORLD, I WAS REALLY INTO THIS GAME ABOUT SENTIENT GUNS AND WEAPONS. THAT GOT ME INTO THE REAL STUFF.
YOUR GUN, TANABE-SAN'S SPEAR, THE SAMUE MASK'S BLADE... THEY WERE ACTUALLY ALL SUPER-RARE WEAPONS IN THAT GAME. I'M NOT SURE WHAT'S UP WITH THIS WORLD.
HEY-- THIS GUN TENDS TO JAM A LOT, RIGHT?
HUH? YEAH.
WELL, THERE'S A **SHOOTING TRICK** TO AVOID THAT. I CAN SHOW YOU IF YOU WANT!
I GUESS I WAS WRONG.
I FIGURED THESE TWO WOULDN'T BE MUCH GOOD TO US. BUT THAT WASN'T THE CASE AT ALL.
AFTER ALL THIS TIME, I FINALLY FEEL LIKE WE'VE MADE MORE FRIENDS.
YEAH. IF WE ALL WORK TOGETHER, WE CAN TAKE ON ANY ENEMY, NO MATTER HOW STRONG!

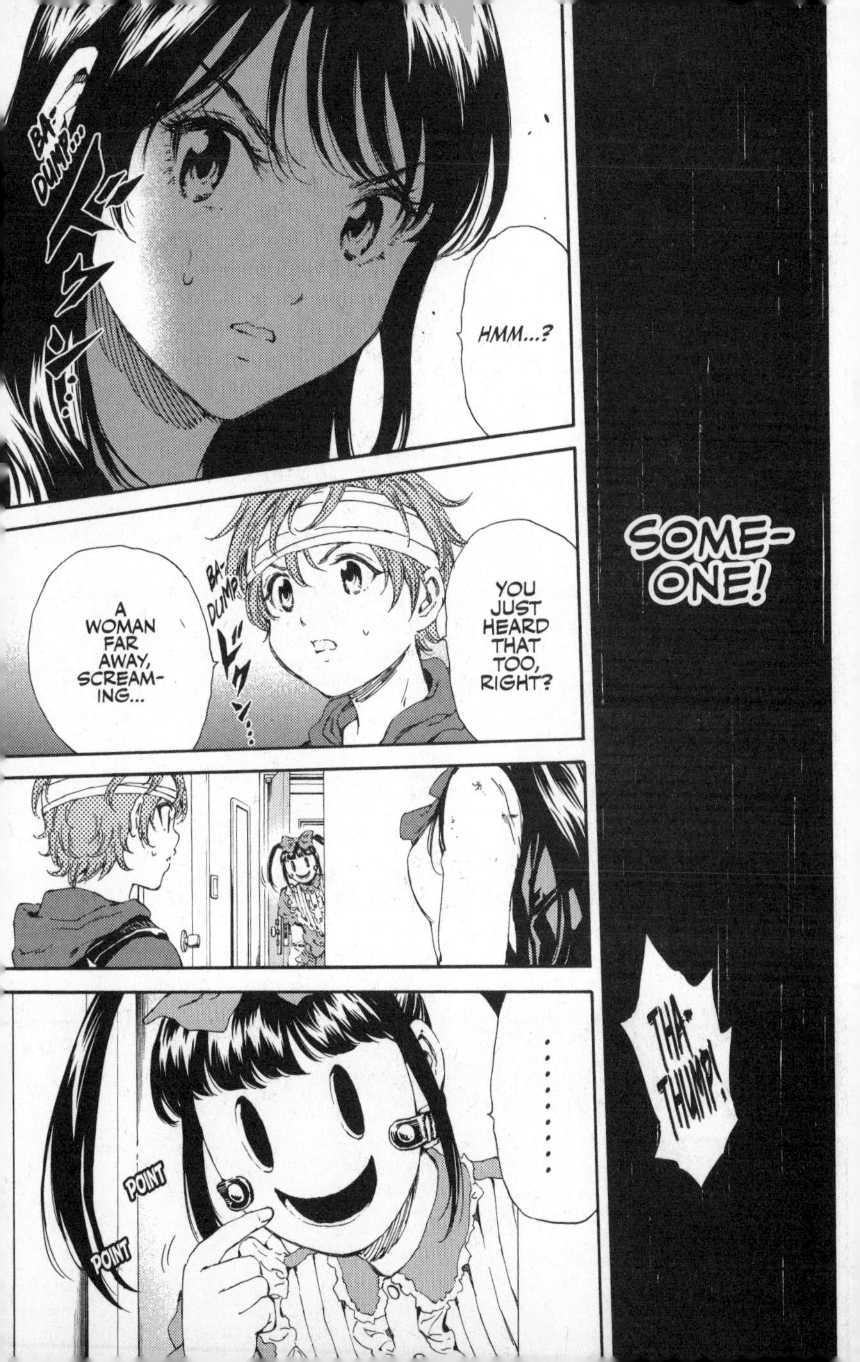
SOME-ONE!
THA-THUMP!
HMM...?
BA-DUMP...
YOU JUST HEARD THAT TOO, RIGHT?
BA-DUMP
A WOMAN FAR AWAY, SCREAMING...
......
POINT
POINT

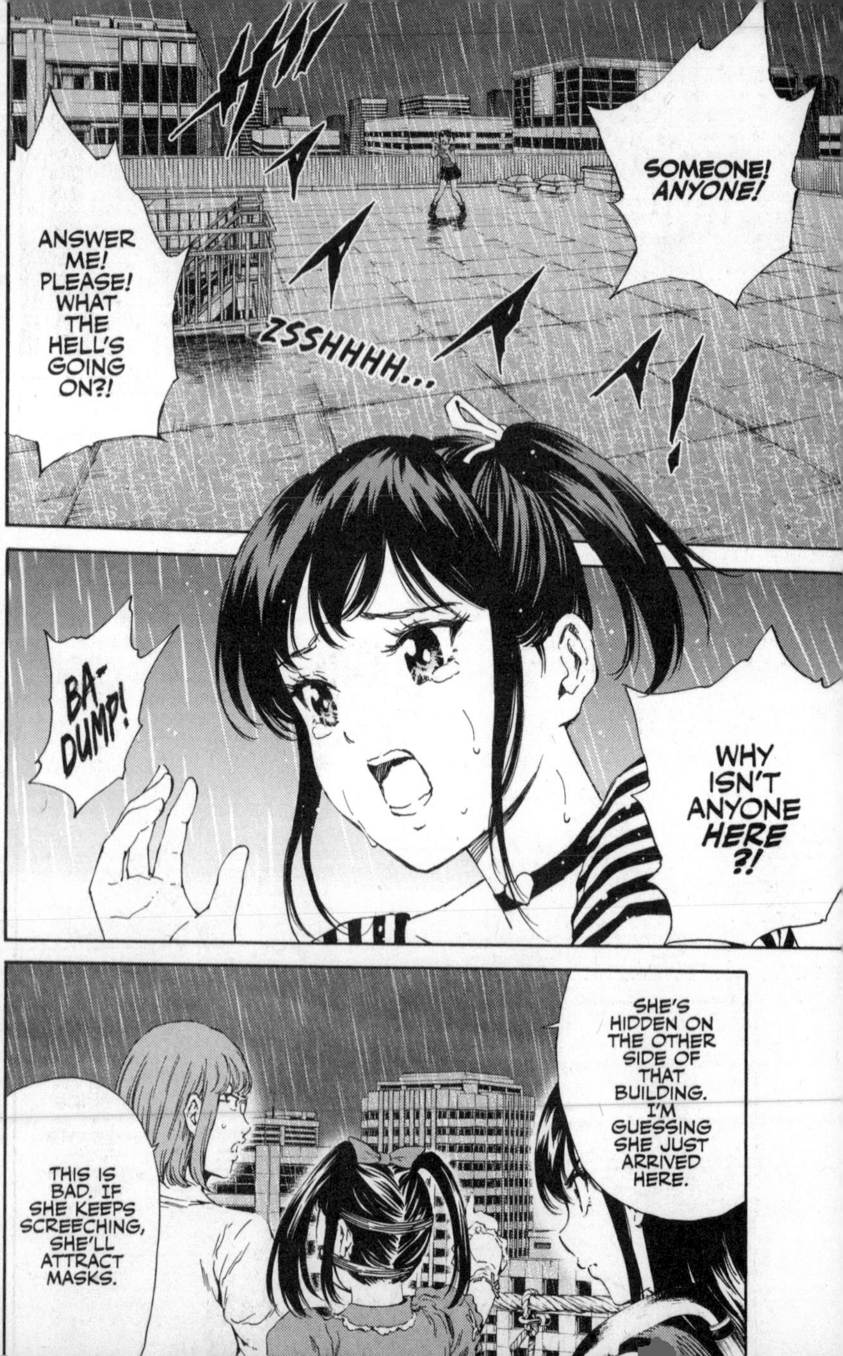
SOMEONE! ANYONE!
ANSWER ME! PLEASE! WHAT THE HELL'S GOING ON?!
ZSSHHHH...
WHY ISN'T ANYONE HERE?!
BA-DUMP!
SHE'S HIDDEN ON THE OTHER SIDE OF THAT BUILDING. I'M GUESSING SHE JUST ARRIVED HERE.
THIS IS BAD. IF SHE KEEPS SCREECHING, SHE'LL ATTRACT MASKS.

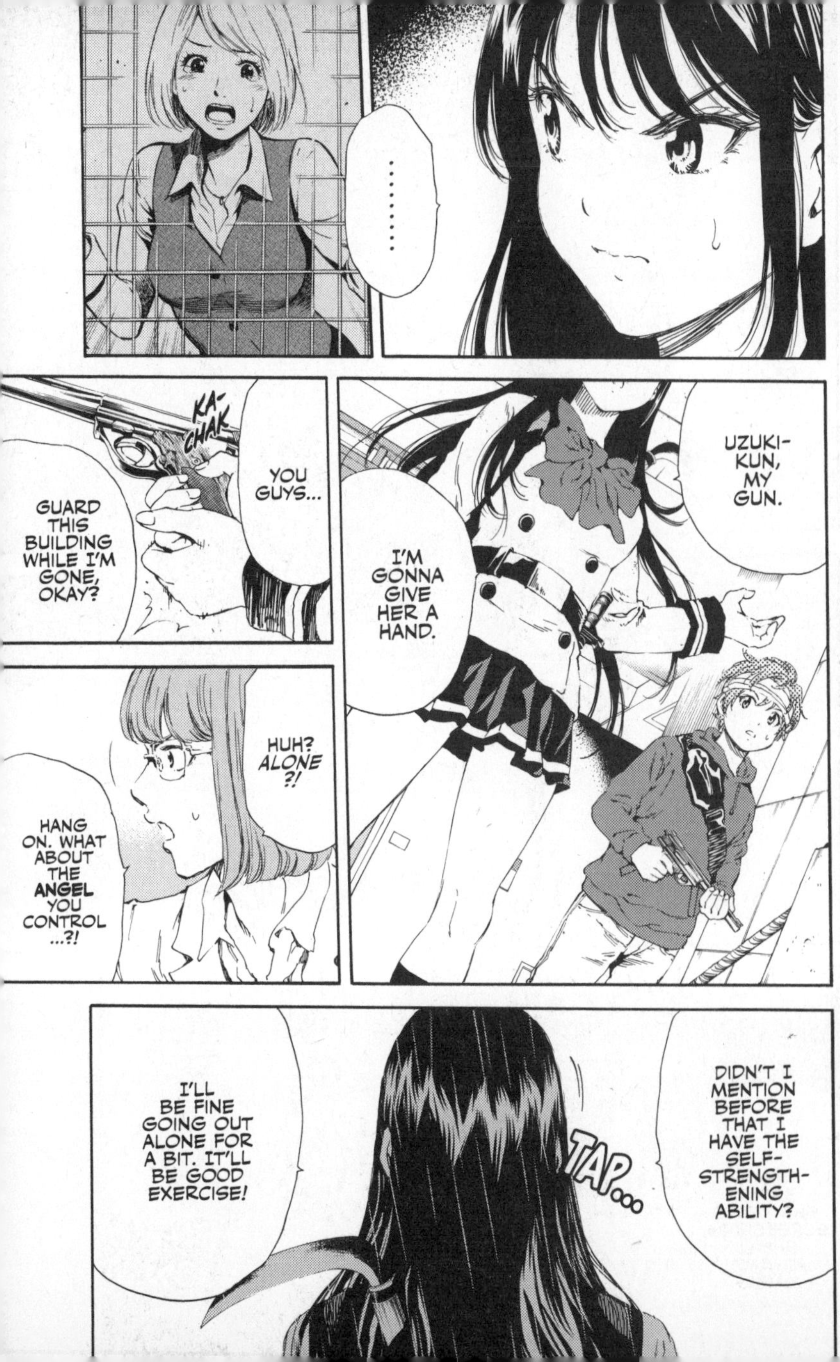
......
UZUKI-KUN, MY GUN.
I'M GONNA GIVE HER A HAND.
YOU GUYS...
KA-CHAK
GUARD THIS BUILDING WHILE I'M GONE, OKAY?
HUH? *ALONE*?!
HANG ON. WHAT ABOUT THE **ANGEL** YOU CONTROL...?!
DIDN'T I MENTION BEFORE THAT I HAVE THE SELF-STRENGTHENING ABILITY?
TAP...
I'LL BE FINE GOING OUT ALONE FOR A BIT. IT'LL BE GOOD EXERCISE!

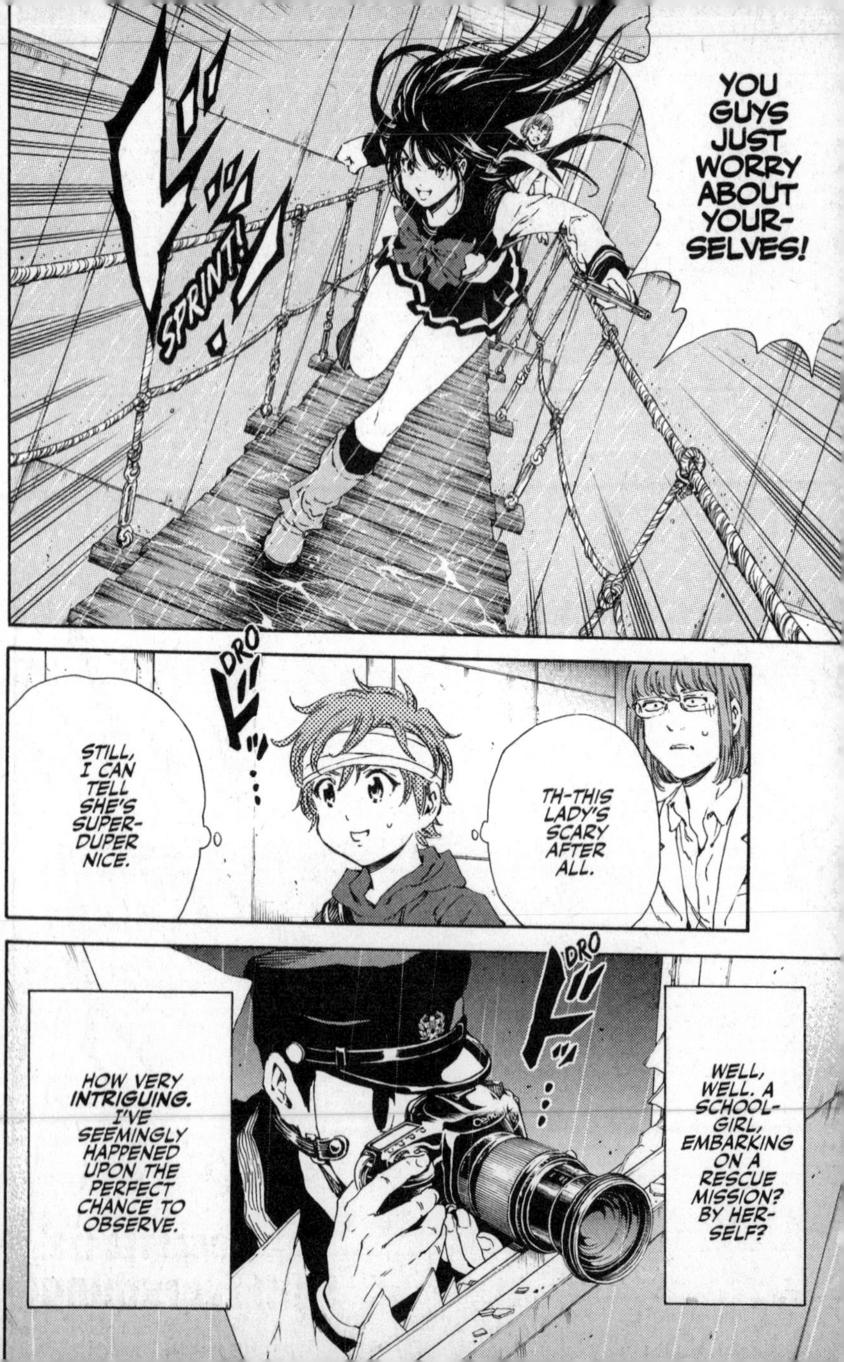
YOU GUYS JUST WORRY ABOUT YOUR-SELVES!
SPRINT!
TH-THIS LADY'S SCARY AFTER ALL.
DRO
STILL, I CAN TELL SHE'S SUPER-DUPER NICE.
WELL, WELL. A SCHOOL-GIRL, EMBARKING ON A RESCUE MISSION? BY HER-SELF?
DRO
HOW VERY INTRIGUING. I'VE SEEMINGLY HAPPENED UPON THE PERFECT CHANCE TO OBSERVE.

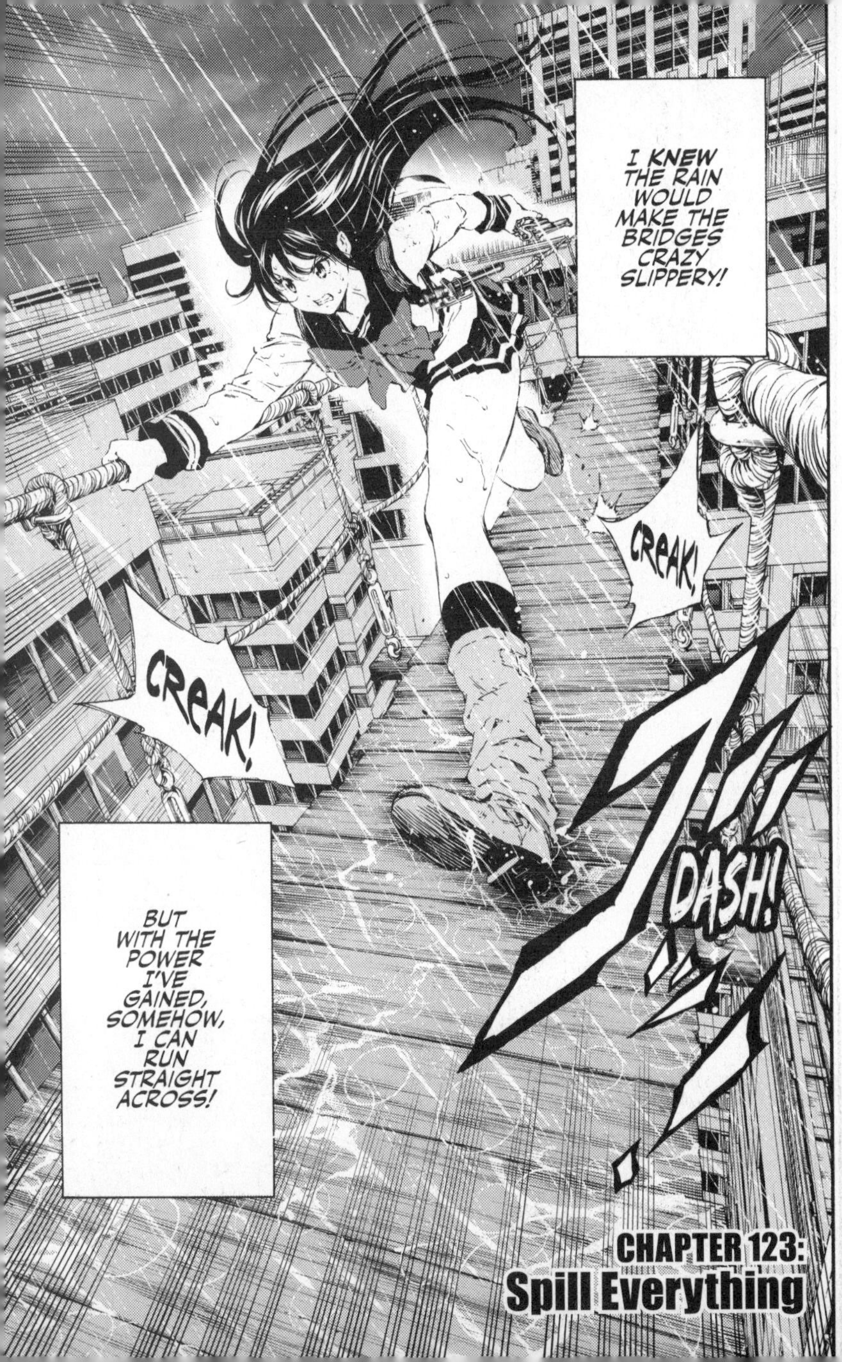
I KNEW THE RAIN WOULD MAKE THE BRIDGES CRAZY SLIPPERY!
CREAK!
CREAK!
DASH!
BUT WITH THE POWER I'VE GAINED, SOMEHOW, I CAN RUN STRAIGHT ACROSS!

CHAPTER 123: Spill Everything

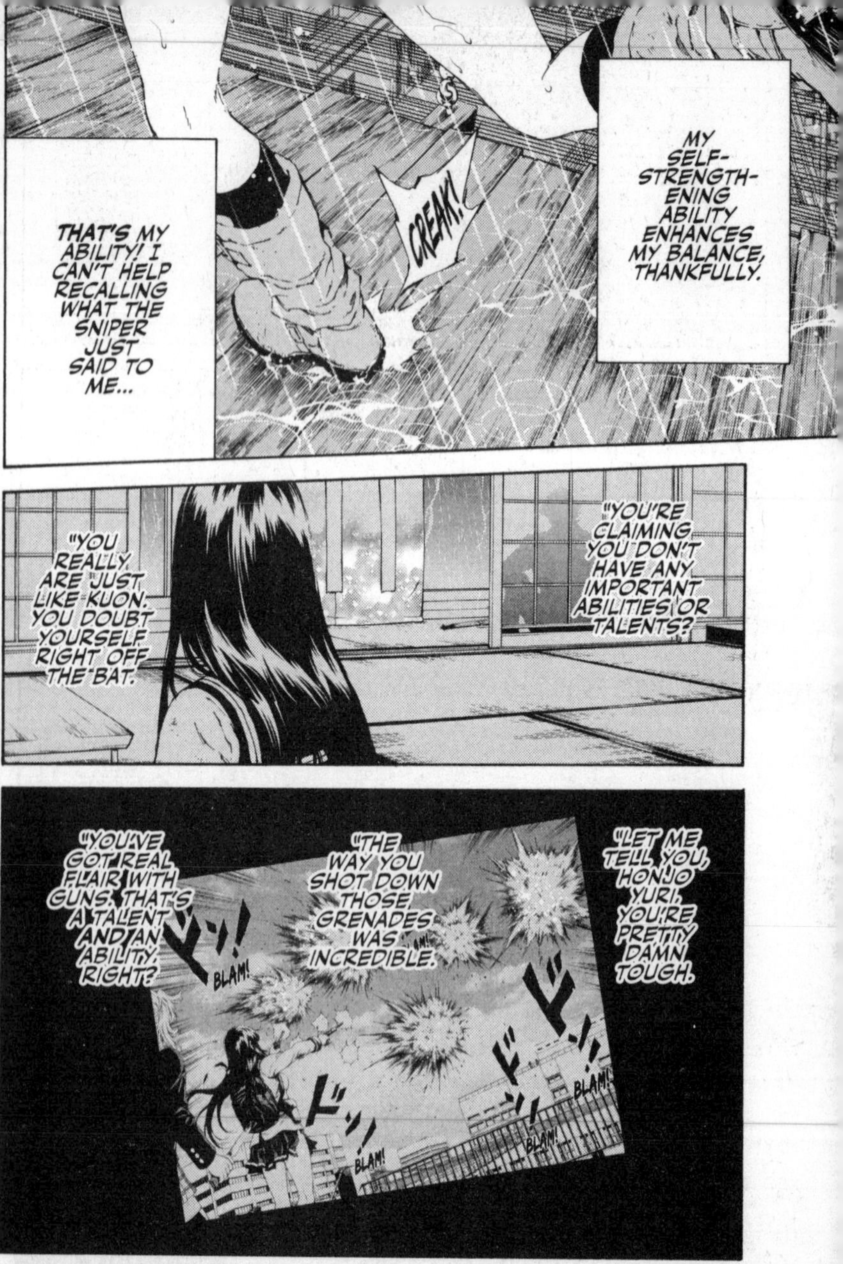
MY SELF-STRENGTH-ENING ABILITY ENHANCES MY BALANCE, THANKFULLY.
CREAK!
THAT'S MY ABILITY! I CAN'T HELP RECALLING WHAT THE SNIPER JUST SAID TO ME...
"YOU'RE CLAIMING YOU DON'T HAVE ANY IMPORTANT ABILITIES OR TALENTS?
"YOU REALLY ARE JUST LIKE KUON. YOU DOUBT YOURSELF RIGHT OFF THE BAT.
"LET ME TELL YOU, HONJO YURI. YOU'RE PRETTY DAMN TOUGH.
"THE WAY YOU SHOT DOWN THOSE GRENADES WAS INCREDIBLE.
"YOU'VE GOT REAL FLAIR WITH GUNS. THAT'S A TALENT AND AN ABILITY, RIGHT?
BLAM!
BLAM!
BLAM!
BLAM!

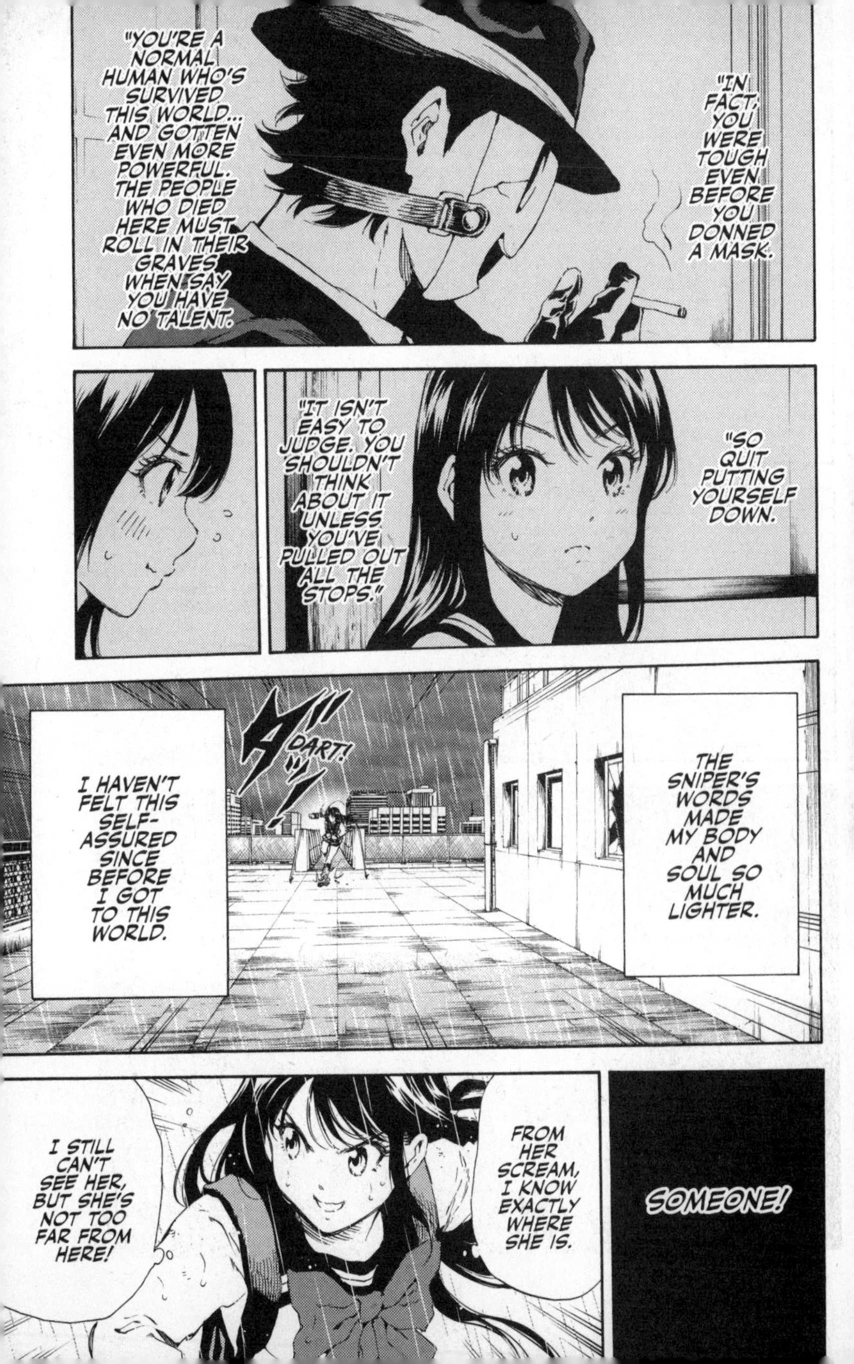
"IN FACT, YOU WERE TOUGH EVEN BEFORE YOU DONNED A MASK.
"YOU'RE A NORMAL HUMAN WHO'S SURVIVED THIS WORLD... AND GOTTEN EVEN MORE POWERFUL. THE PEOPLE WHO DIED HERE MUST ROLL IN THEIR GRAVES WHEN SAY YOU HAVE NO TALENT.
"SO QUIT PUTTING YOURSELF DOWN.
"IT ISN'T EASY TO JUDGE. YOU SHOULDN'T THINK ABOUT IT UNLESS YOU'VE PULLED OUT ALL THE STOPS."
THE SNIPER'S WORDS MADE MY BODY AND SOUL SO MUCH LIGHTER.
DART!
I HAVEN'T FELT THIS SELF-ASSURED SINCE BEFORE I GOT TO THIS WORLD.
SOMEONE!
FROM HER SCREAM, I KNOW EXACTLY WHERE SHE IS.
I STILL CAN'T SEE HER, BUT SHE'S NOT TOO FAR FROM HERE!

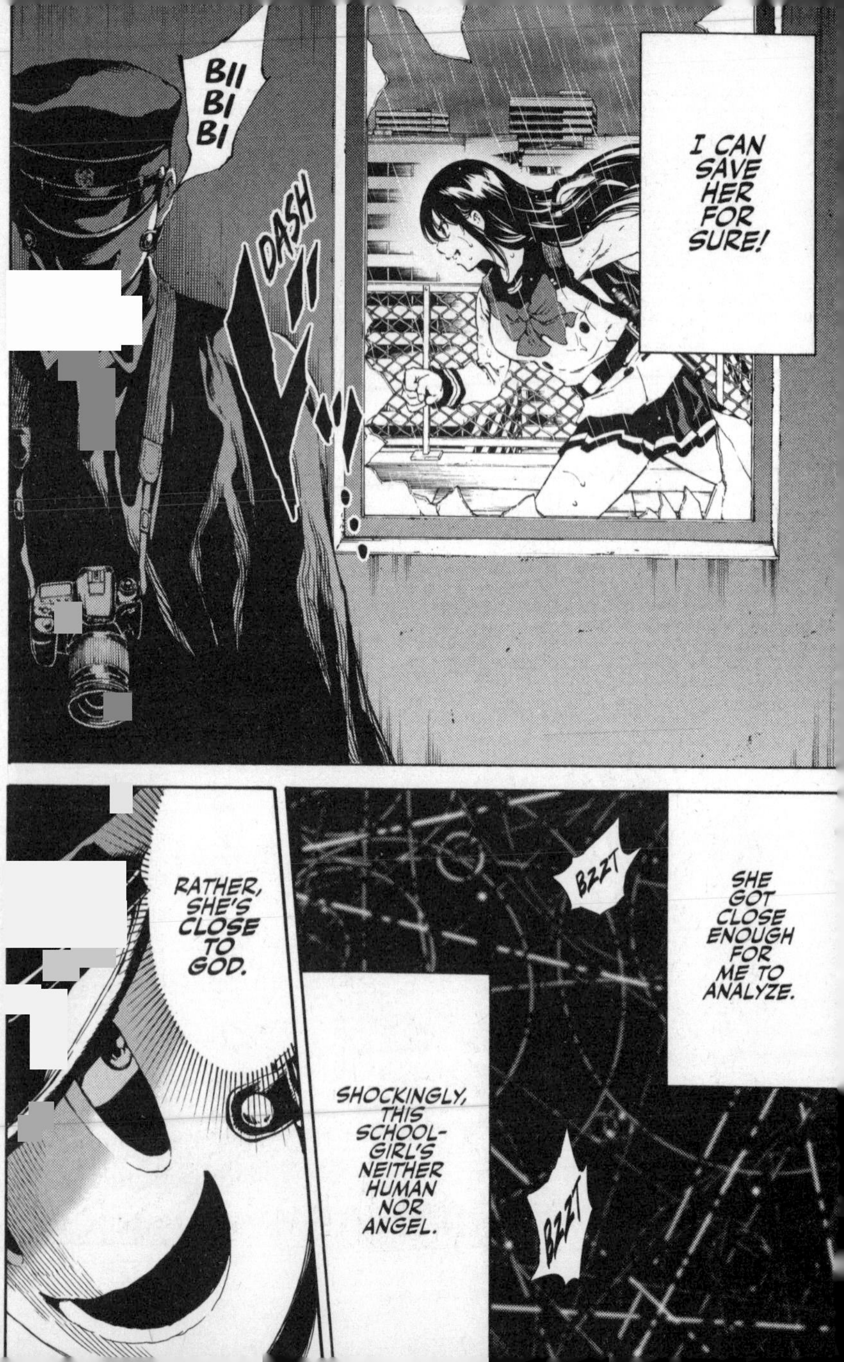
I CAN SAVE HER FOR SURE!
BII BI BI
DASH
SHE GOT CLOSE ENOUGH FOR ME TO ANALYZE.
BZZT
SHOCKINGLY, THIS SCHOOL-GIRL'S NEITHER HUMAN NOR ANGEL.
BZZT
RATHER, SHE'S CLOSE TO GOD.

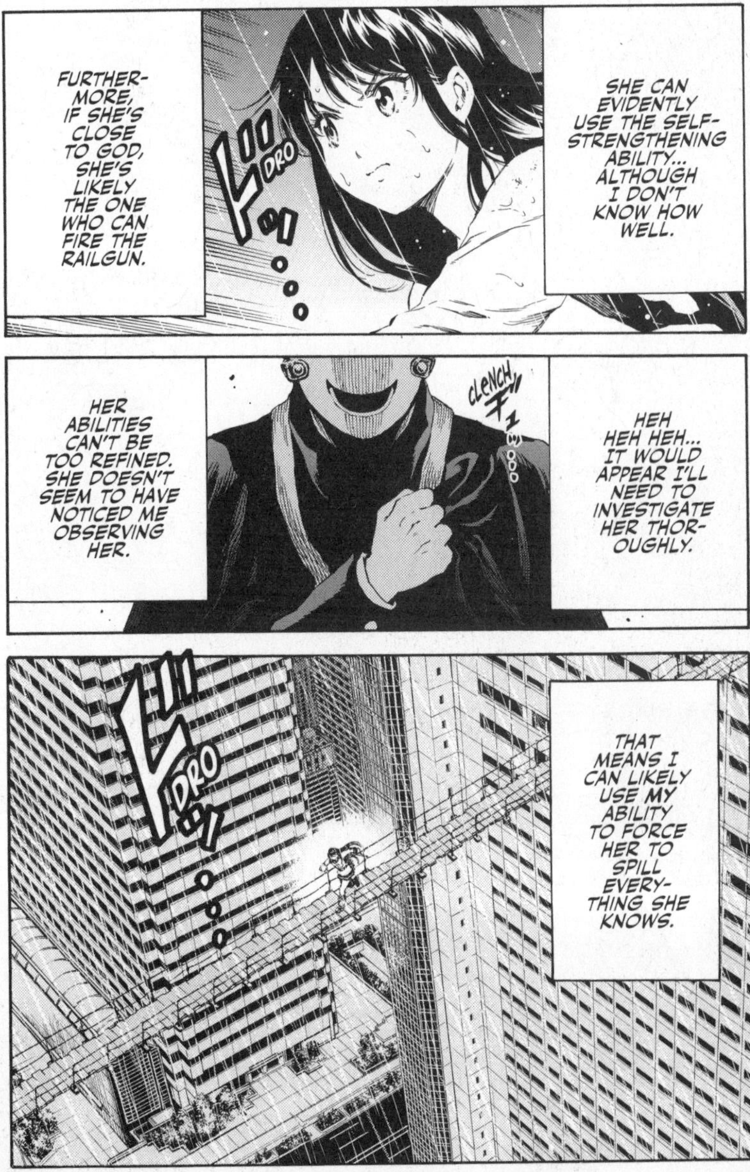
SHE CAN EVIDENTLY USE THE SELF-STRENGTHENING ABILITY... ALTHOUGH I DON'T KNOW HOW WELL.
DRO
FURTHER-MORE, IF SHE'S CLOSE TO GOD, SHE'S LIKELY THE ONE WHO CAN FIRE THE RAILGUN.
HEH HEH HEH... IT WOULD APPEAR I'LL NEED TO INVESTIGATE HER THOR-OUGHLY.
CLENCH
HER ABILITIES CAN'T BE TOO REFINED. SHE DOESN'T SEEM TO HAVE NOTICED ME OBSERVING HER.
THAT MEANS I CAN LIKELY USE MY ABILITY TO FORCE HER TO SPILL EVERY-THING SHE KNOWS.
DRO

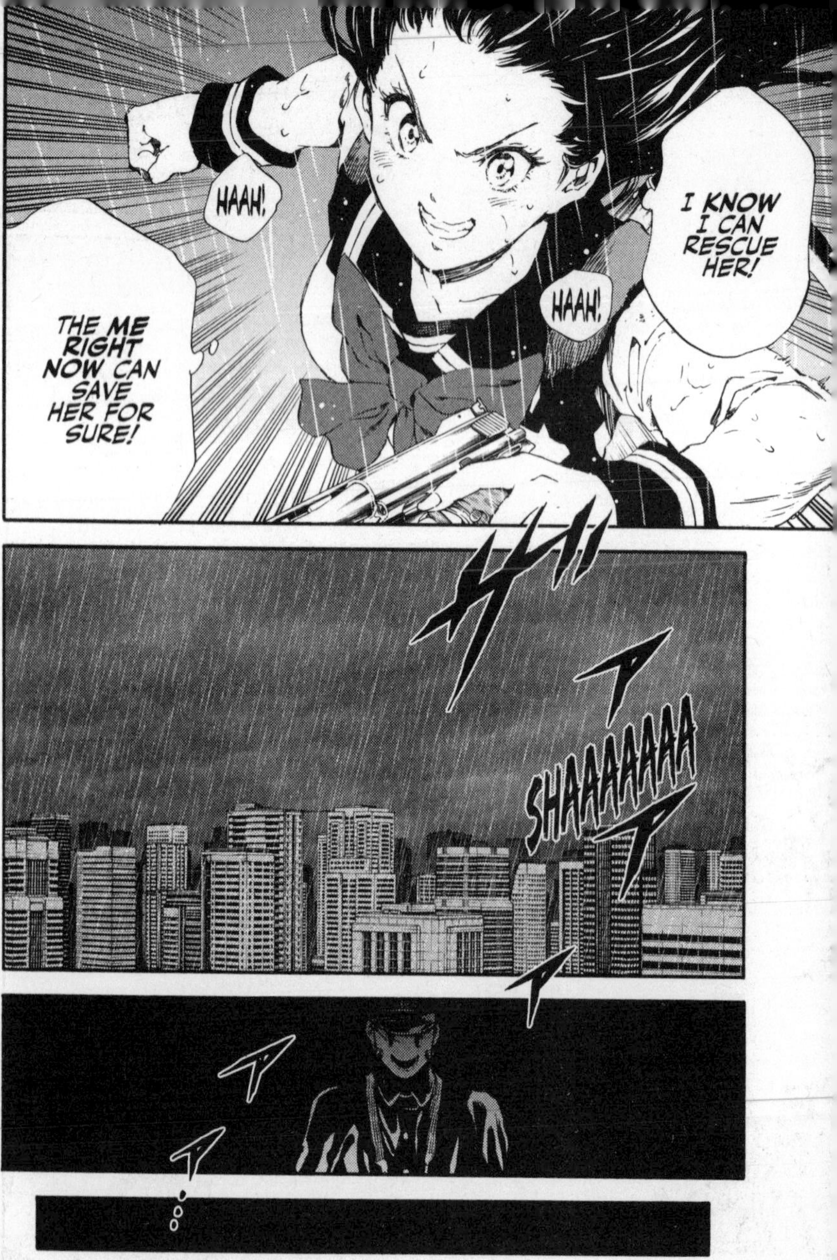
I KNOW I CAN RESCUE HER!
HAAH!
HAAH!
THE ME RIGHT NOW CAN SAVE HER FOR SURE!
SHAAAAAA

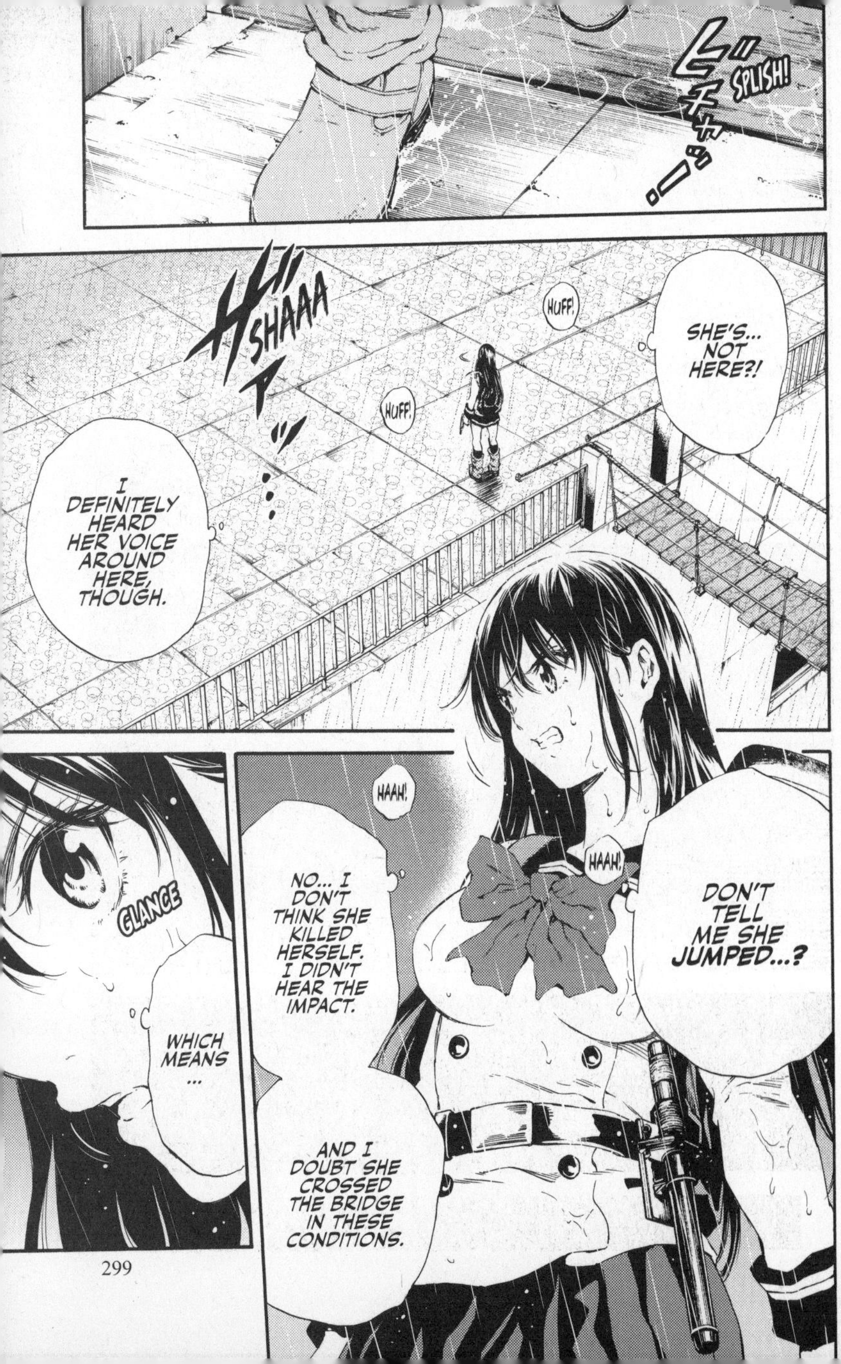
SPLISH!
SHE'S... NOT HERE?!
HUFF!
HUFF!
SHAAA
I DEFINITELY HEARD HER VOICE AROUND HERE, THOUGH.
DON'T TELL ME SHE JUMPED...?
HAAH!
HAAH!
NO... I DON'T THINK SHE KILLED HERSELF. I DIDN'T HEAR THE IMPACT.
AND I DOUBT SHE CROSSED THE BRIDGE IN THESE CONDITIONS.
GLANCE
WHICH MEANS ...

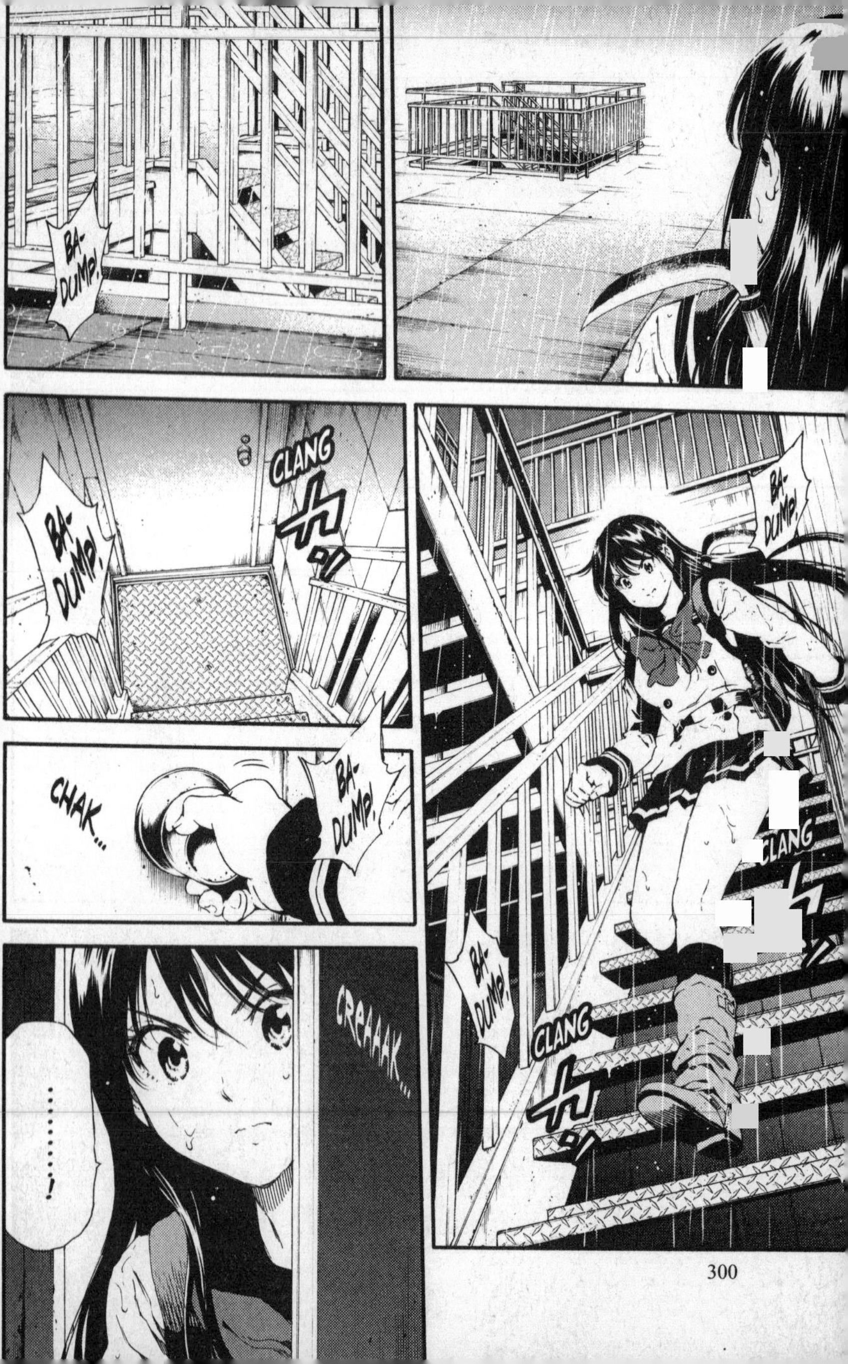
BA-DUMP!
BA-DUMP!
CLANG
BA-DUMP!
CLANG
CLANG
BA-DUMP!
BA-DUMP!
CHAK...
CREAAAK...
.........!

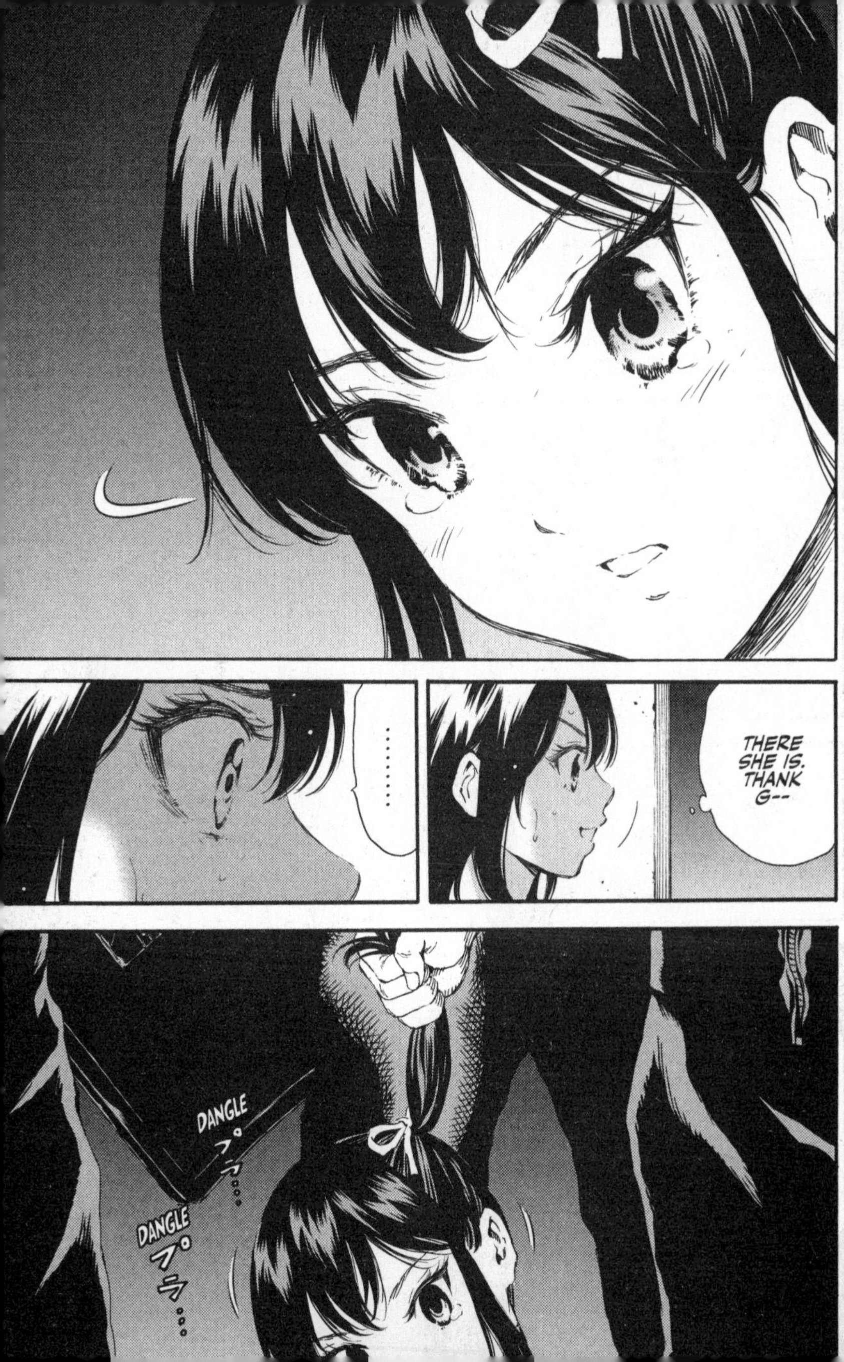
THERE SHE IS. THANK G--
......
DANGLE
プラ…
DANGLE
プラ…

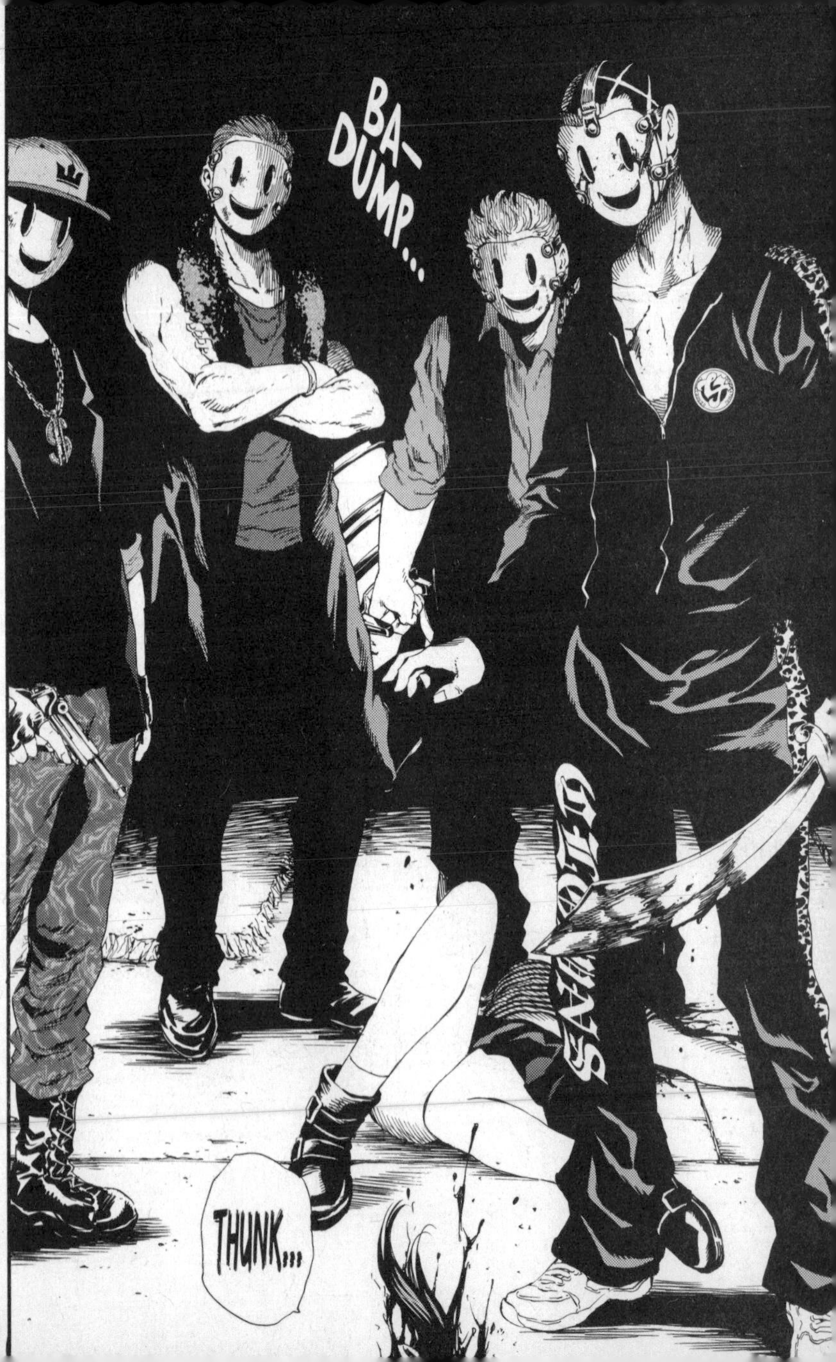
BA-DUMP...
THUNK...

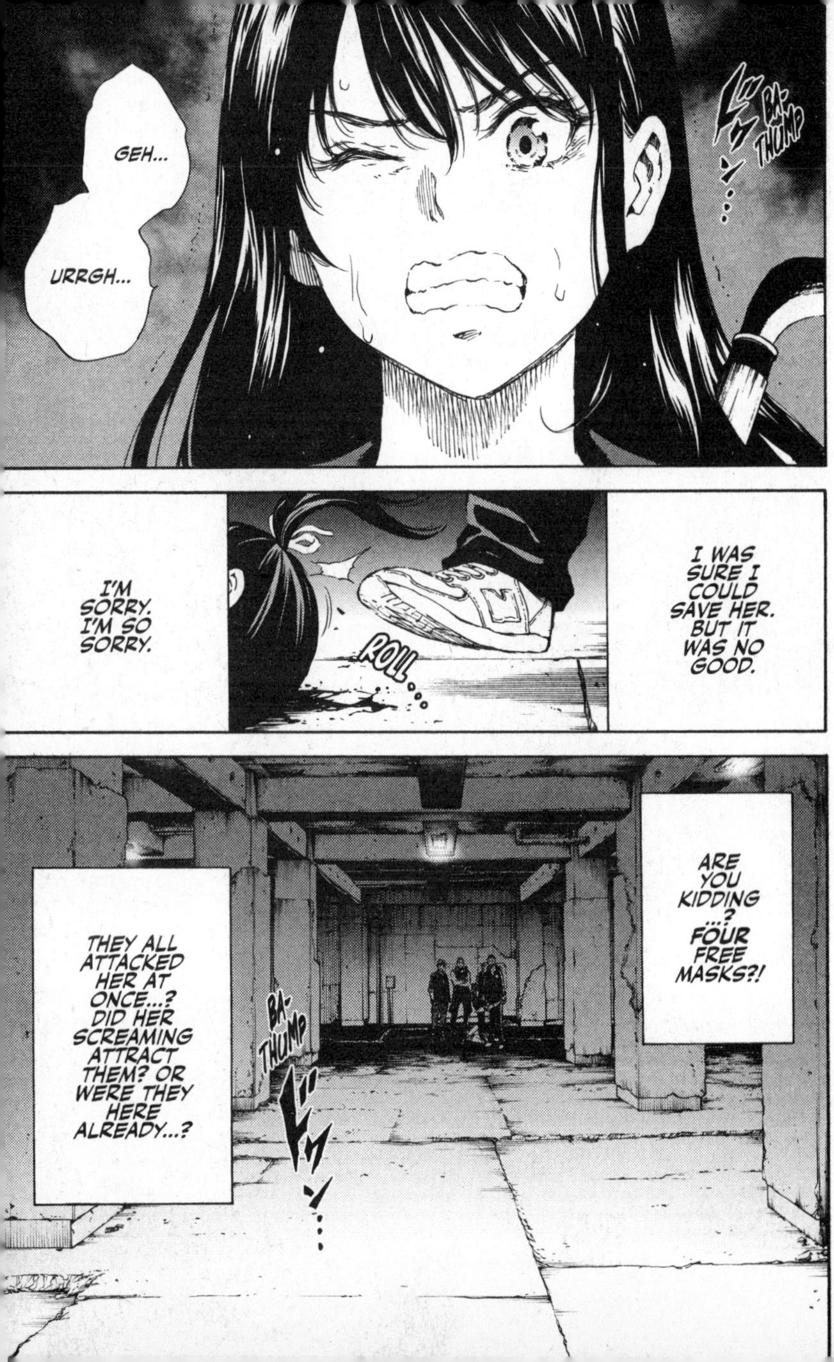
BA-THUMP
GEH...
URRGH...
I WAS SURE I COULD SAVE HER. BUT IT WAS NO GOOD.
ROLL...
I'M SORRY. I'M SO SORRY.
ARE YOU KIDDING ....? FOUR FREE MASKS?!
BA-THUMP
THEY ALL ATTACKED HER AT ONCE...? DID HER SCREAMING ATTRACT THEM? OR WERE THEY HERE ALREADY...?

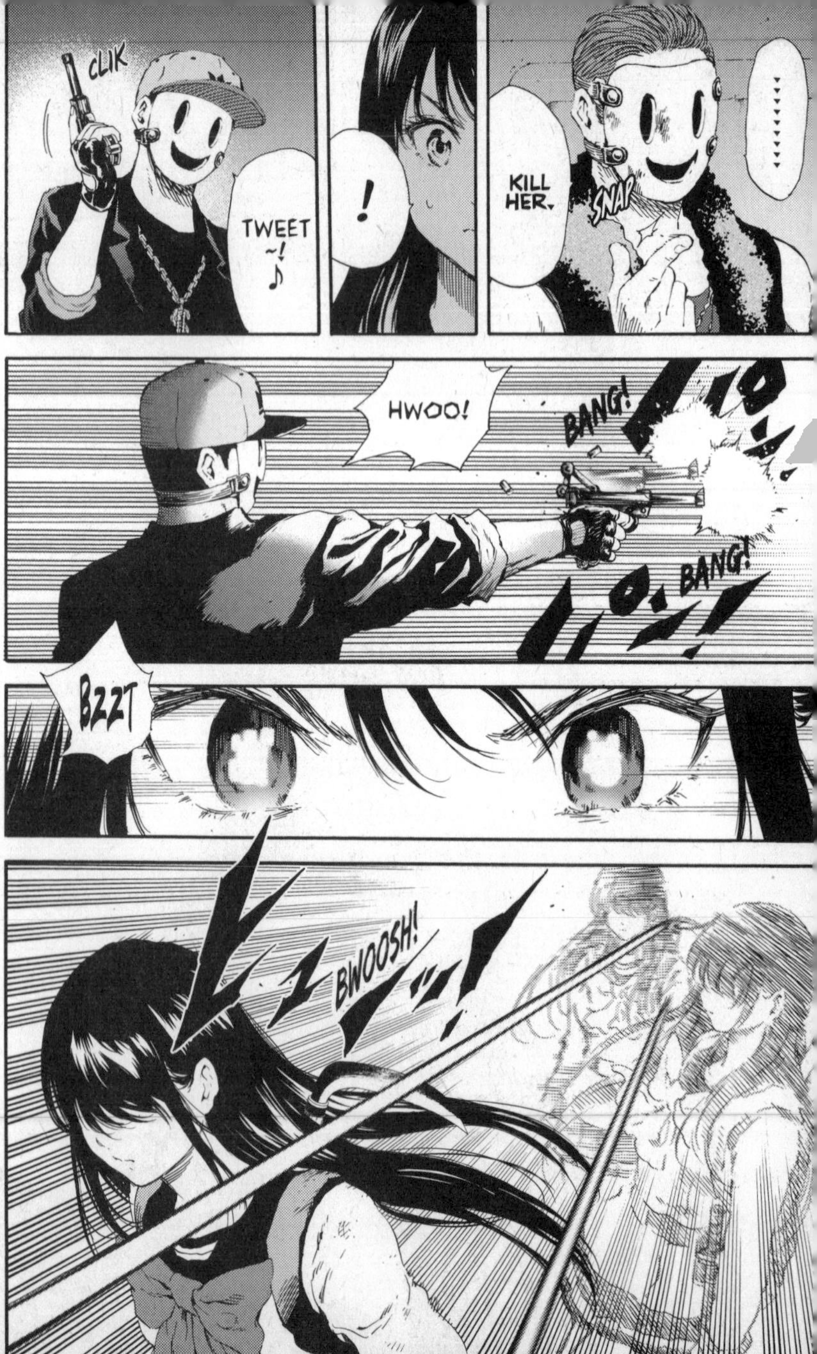
......
KILL HER.
SNAP
!
TWEET ~! ♪
CLIK
BANG!
BANG!
HWOO!
BZZT
BWOOSH!

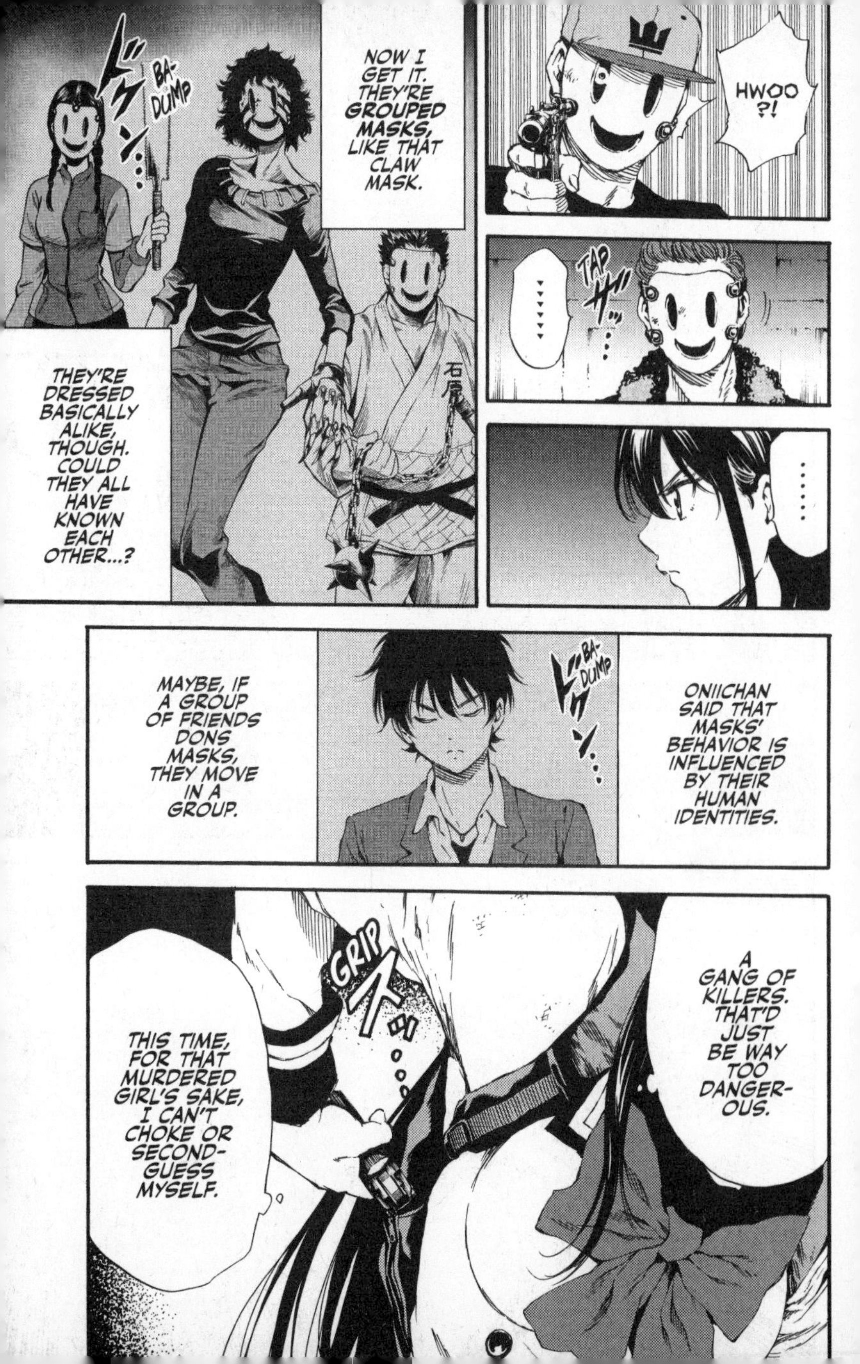
HWOO ?!
TAP
......
......
NOW I GET IT. THEY'RE GROUPED MASKS, LIKE THAT CLAW MASK.
BA-DUMP
THEY'RE DRESSED BASICALLY ALIKE, THOUGH. COULD THEY ALL HAVE KNOWN EACH OTHER...?
ONIICHAN SAID THAT MASKS' BEHAVIOR IS INFLUENCED BY THEIR HUMAN IDENTITIES.
BA-DUMP
MAYBE, IF A GROUP OF FRIENDS DONS MASKS, THEY MOVE IN A GROUP.
A GANG OF KILLERS. THAT'D JUST BE WAY TOO DANGER-OUS.
GRIP
THIS TIME, FOR THAT MURDERED GIRL'S SAKE, I CAN'T CHOKE OR SECOND-GUESS MYSELF.

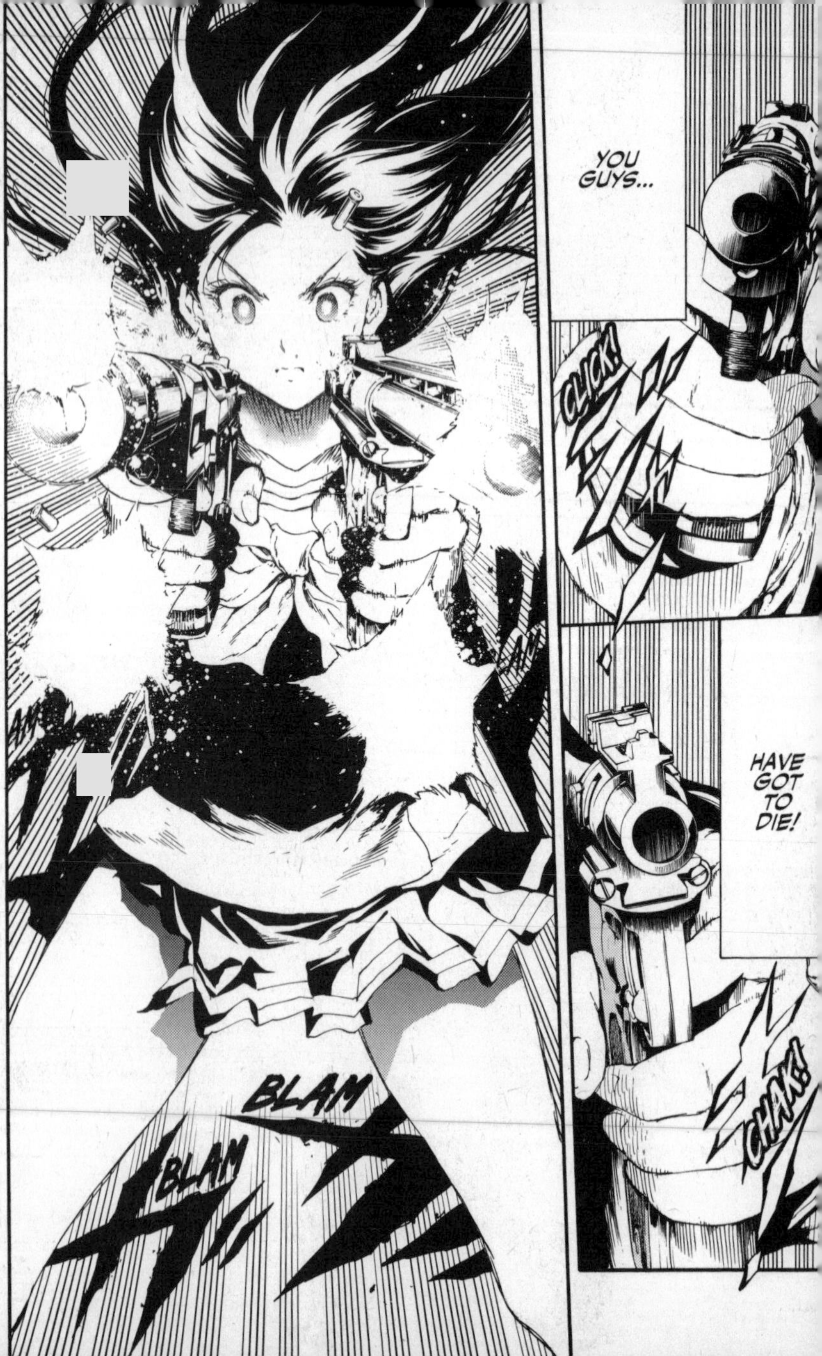
YOU GUYS...
CLICK!
HAVE GOT TO DIE!
CHAK!
BLAM
BLAM

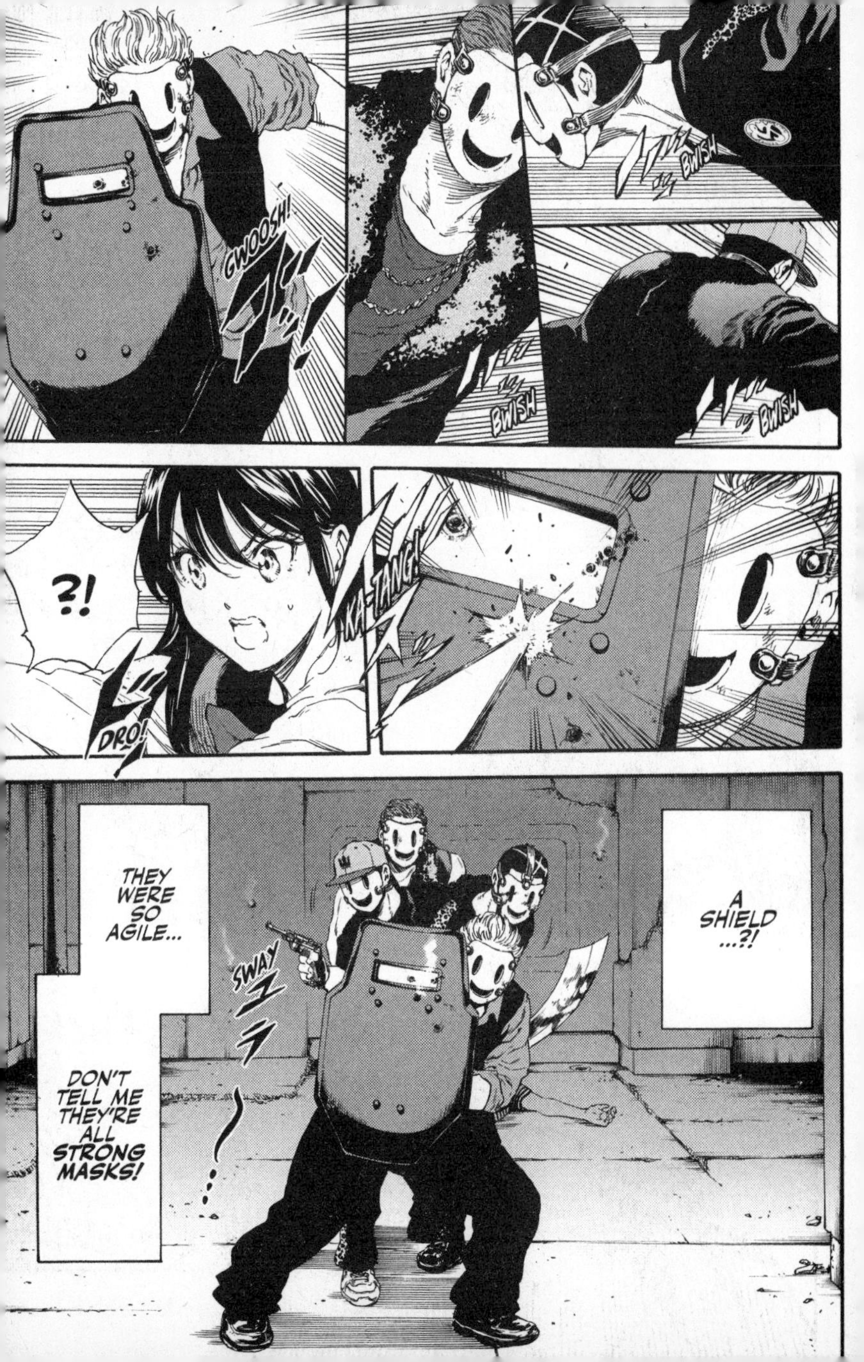
BWISH
BWISH
BWISH
GWOOSH!
KA-TANG!
?!
DRO!
A SHIELD ...?!
THEY WERE SO AGILE...
SWAY
DON'T TELL ME THEY'RE ALL STRONG MASKS!
...

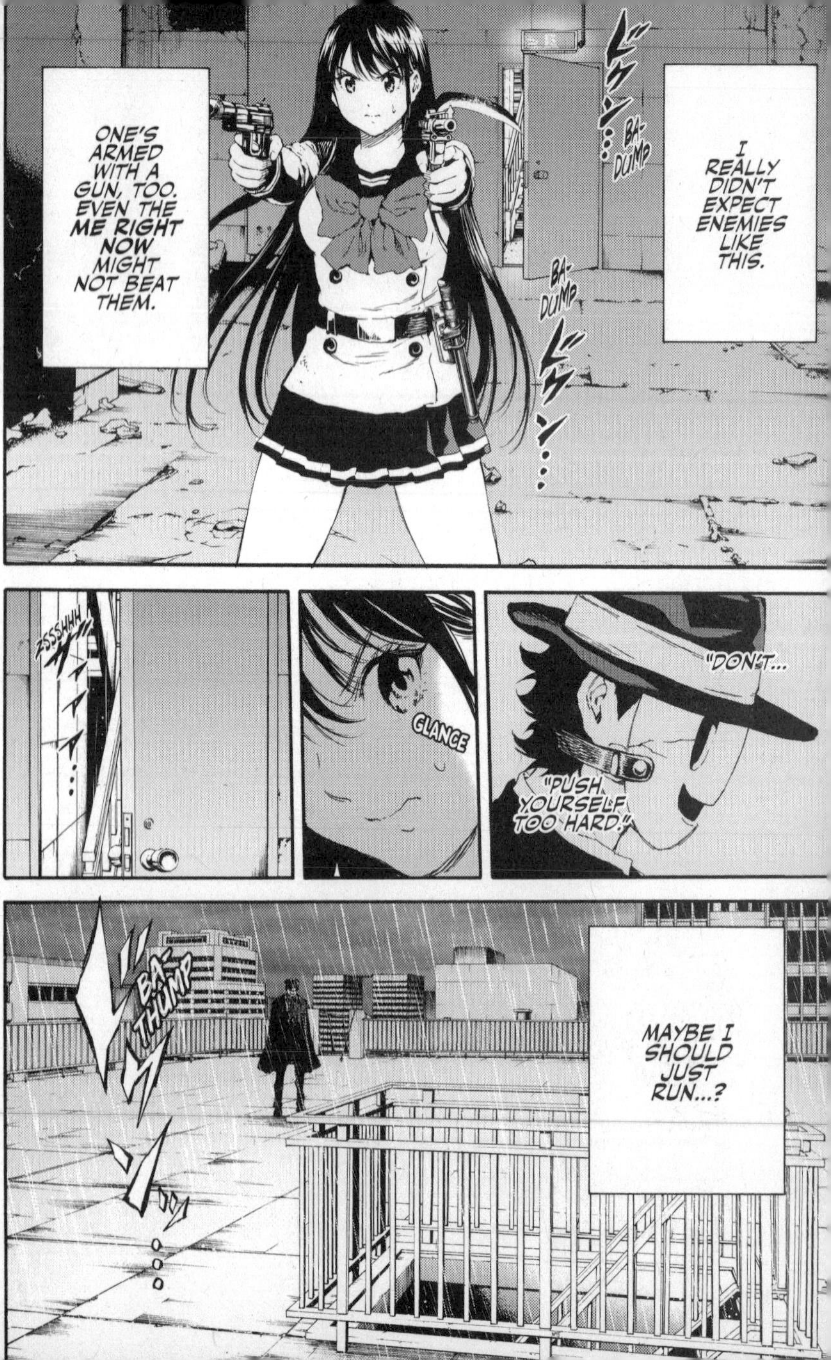
I REALLY DIDN'T EXPECT ENEMIES LIKE THIS.
BA-DUMP
BA-DUMP
ONE'S ARMED WITH A GUN, TOO. EVEN THE ME RIGHT NOW MIGHT NOT BEAT THEM.
"DON'T...
"PUSH YOURSELF TOO HARD."
GLANCE
ZSSSHHH
MAYBE I SHOULD JUST RUN...?
BA-THUMP

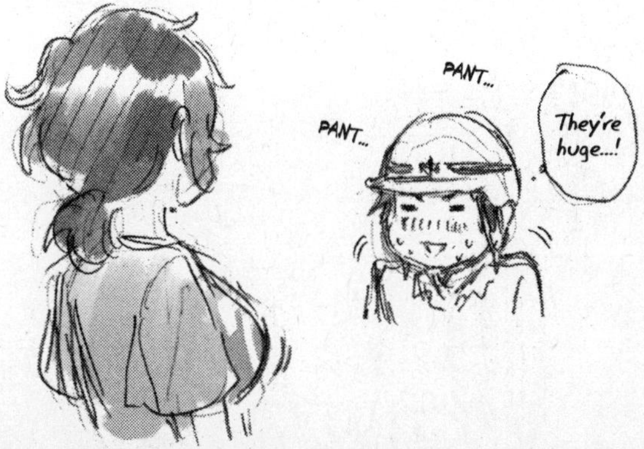
They're huge...!
PANT...
PANT...

HIGH-RISE INVASION

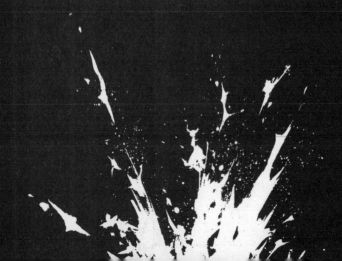

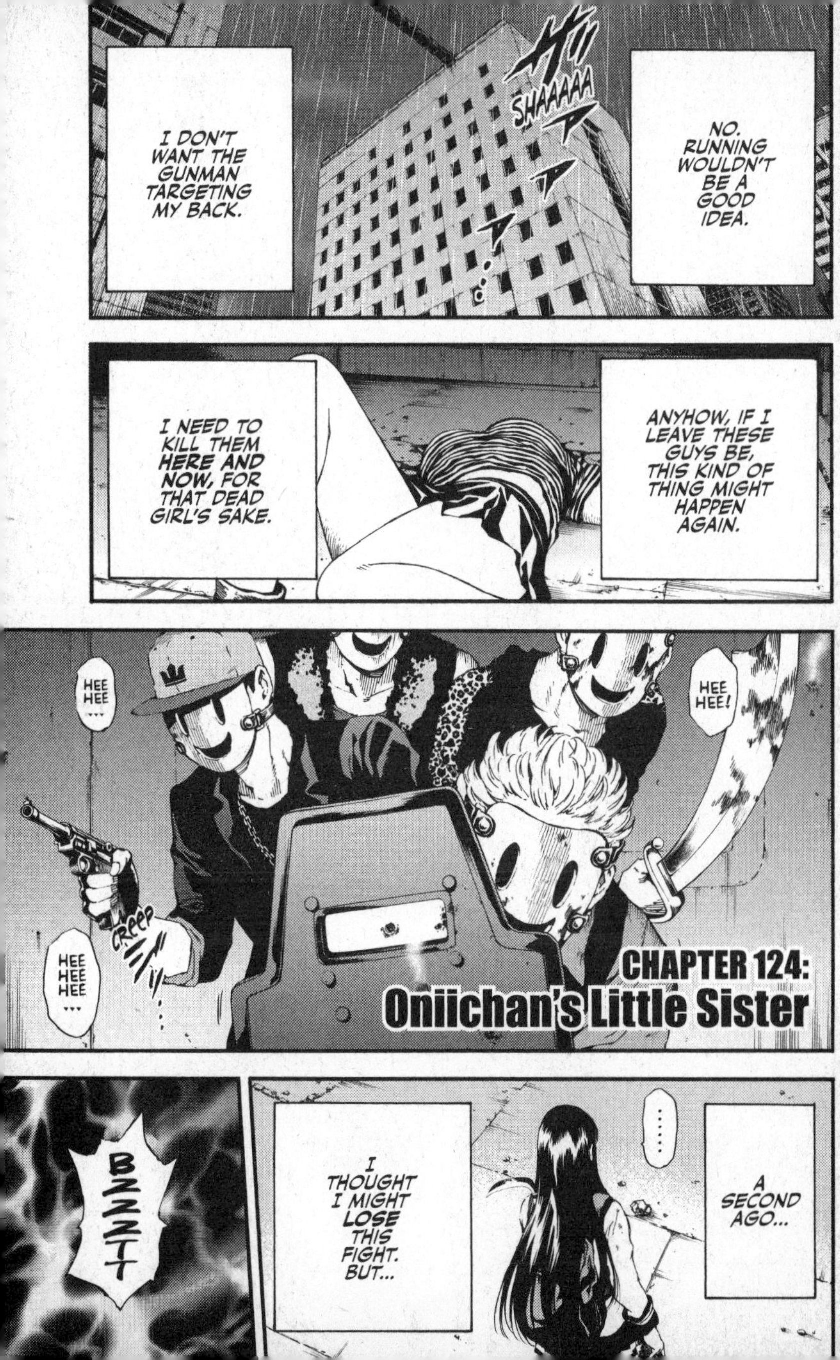
NO. RUNNING WOULDN'T BE A GOOD IDEA.
SHAAAAA
I DON'T WANT THE GUNMAN TARGETING MY BACK.
ANYHOW, IF I LEAVE THESE GUYS BE, THIS KIND OF THING MIGHT HAPPEN AGAIN.
I NEED TO KILL THEM HERE AND NOW, FOR THAT DEAD GIRL'S SAKE.
HEE HEE!
HEE HEE...
CREEP
HEE HEE HEE...
CHAPTER 124: Oniichan's Little Sister
A SECOND AGO...
......
I THOUGHT I MIGHT LOSE THIS FIGHT. BUT...
BZZZTT

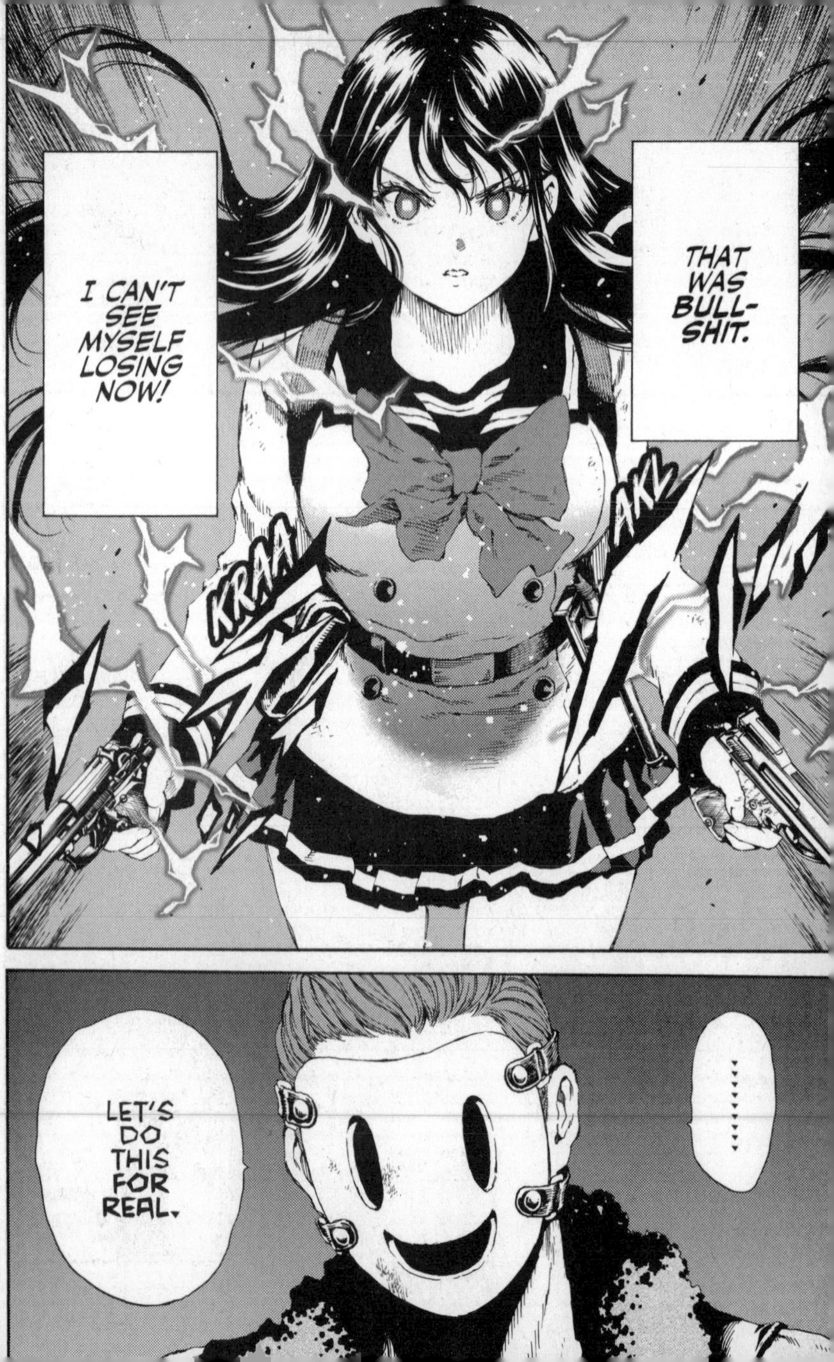
THAT WAS BULL-SHIT.
I CAN'T SEE MYSELF LOSING NOW!
KRAA
AKL
....
LET'S DO THIS FOR REAL.

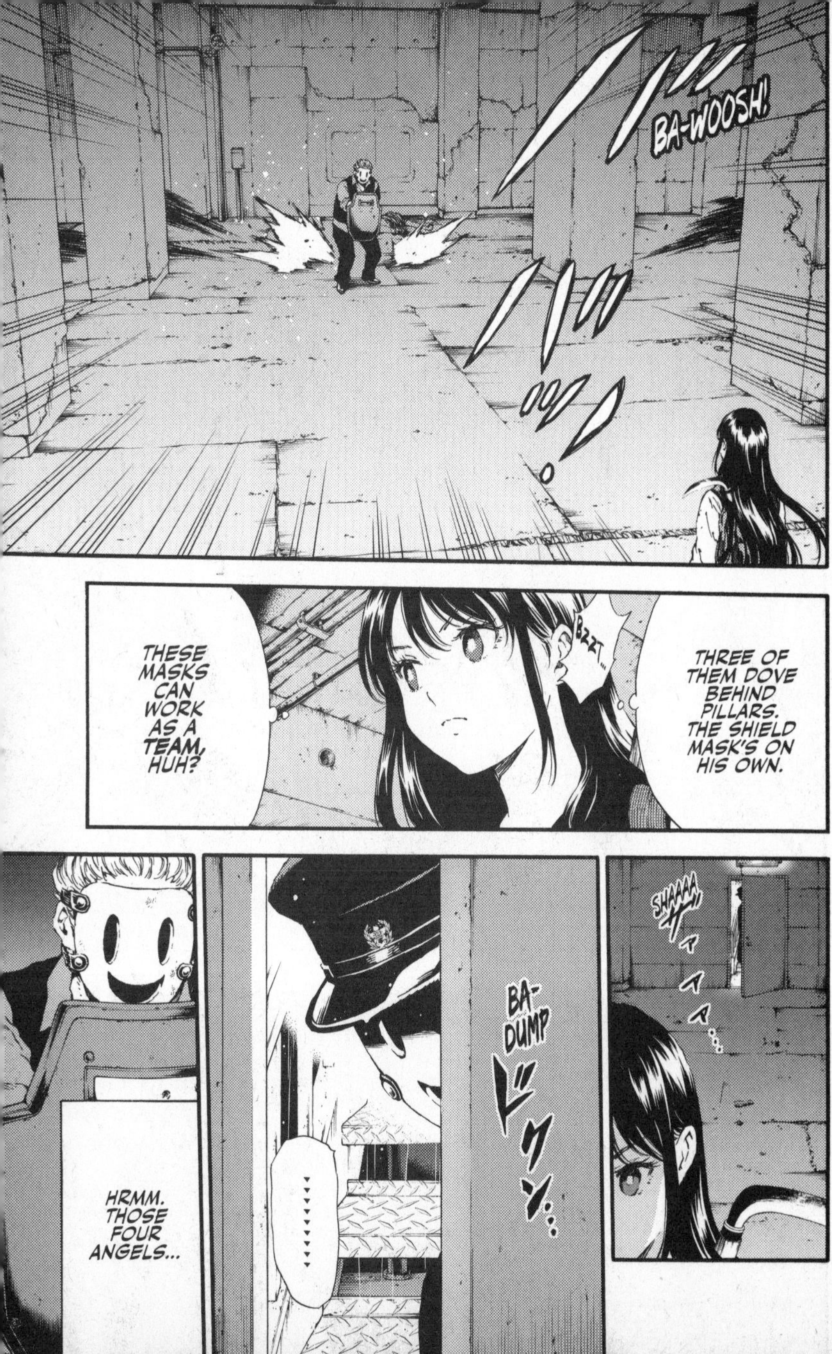

BA-WOOSH!
THREE OF THEM DOVE BEHIND PILLARS. THE SHIELD MASK'S ON HIS OWN.
BZZT...
THESE MASKS CAN WORK AS A TEAM, HUH?
SHAAAA
BA-DUMP
HRMM. THOSE FOUR ANGELS...

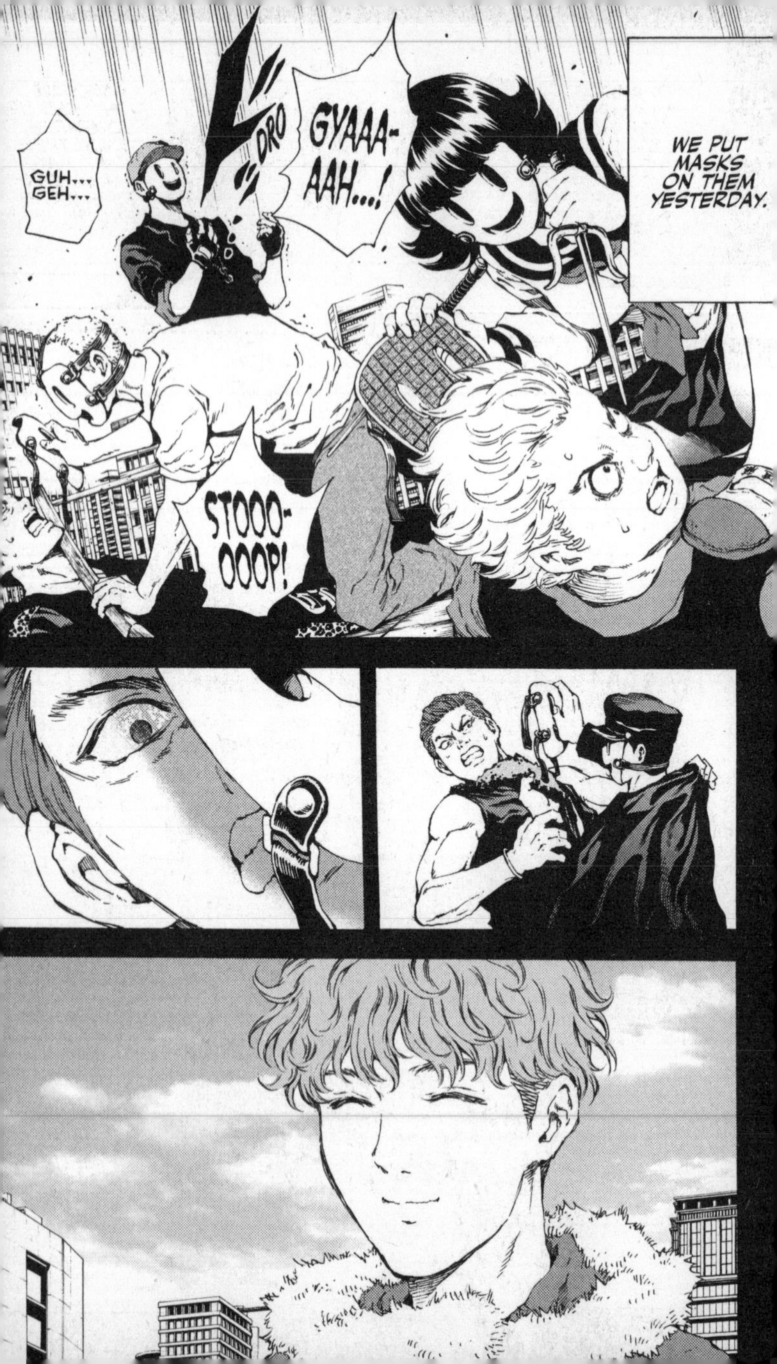
WE PUT MASKS ON THEM YESTERDAY.
GYAAA-AAH...!
DRO
GUH... GEH...
STOOO-OOOP!

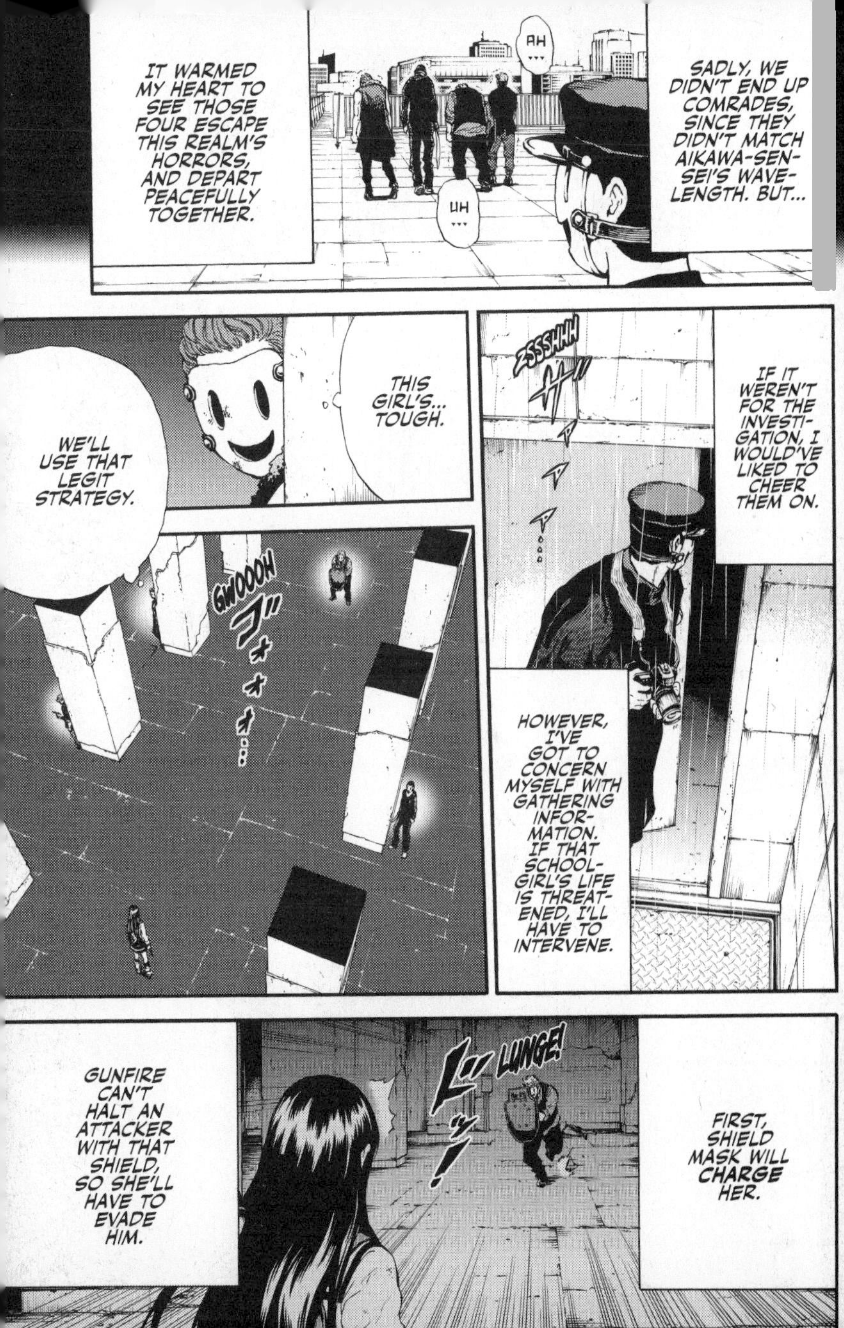
SADLY, WE DIDN'T END UP COMRADES, SINCE THEY DIDN'T MATCH AIKAWA-SEN-SEI'S WAVE-LENGTH. BUT...
AH
IT WARMED MY HEART TO SEE THOSE FOUR ESCAPE THIS REALM'S HORRORS, AND DEPART PEACEFULLY TOGETHER.
UH
IF IT WEREN'T FOR THE INVESTI-GATION, I WOULD'VE LIKED TO CHEER THEM ON.
ZSSSHHH
HOWEVER, I'VE GOT TO CONCERN MYSELF WITH GATHERING INFOR-MATION. IF THAT SCHOOL-GIRL'S LIFE IS THREAT-ENED, I'LL HAVE TO INTERVENE.
THIS GIRL'S... TOUGH.
WE'LL USE THAT LEGIT STRATEGY.
GWOOOH
FIRST, SHIELD MASK WILL CHARGE HER.
LUNGE!
GUNFIRE CAN'T HALT AN ATTACKER WITH THAT SHIELD, SO SHE'LL HAVE TO EVADE HIM.

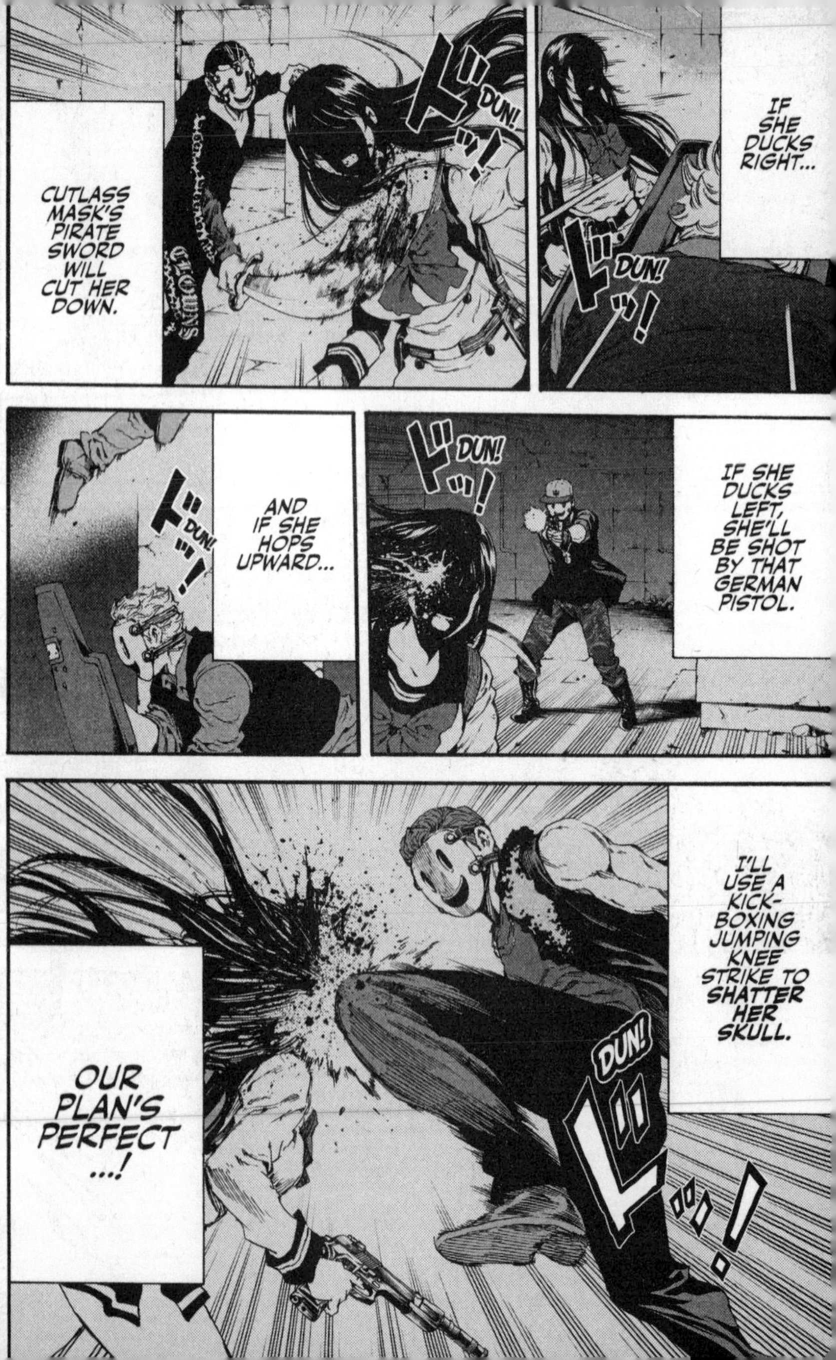
IF SHE DUCKS RIGHT...
DUN!
CUTLASS MASK'S PIRATE SWORD WILL CUT HER DOWN.
DUN!
DUN!
IF SHE DUCKS LEFT, SHE'LL BE SHOT BY THAT GERMAN PISTOL.
AND IF SHE HOPS UPWARD...
DUN!
I'LL USE A KICK-BOXING JUMPING KNEE STRIKE TO SHATTER HER SKULL.
DUN!
OUR PLAN'S PERFECT ...!

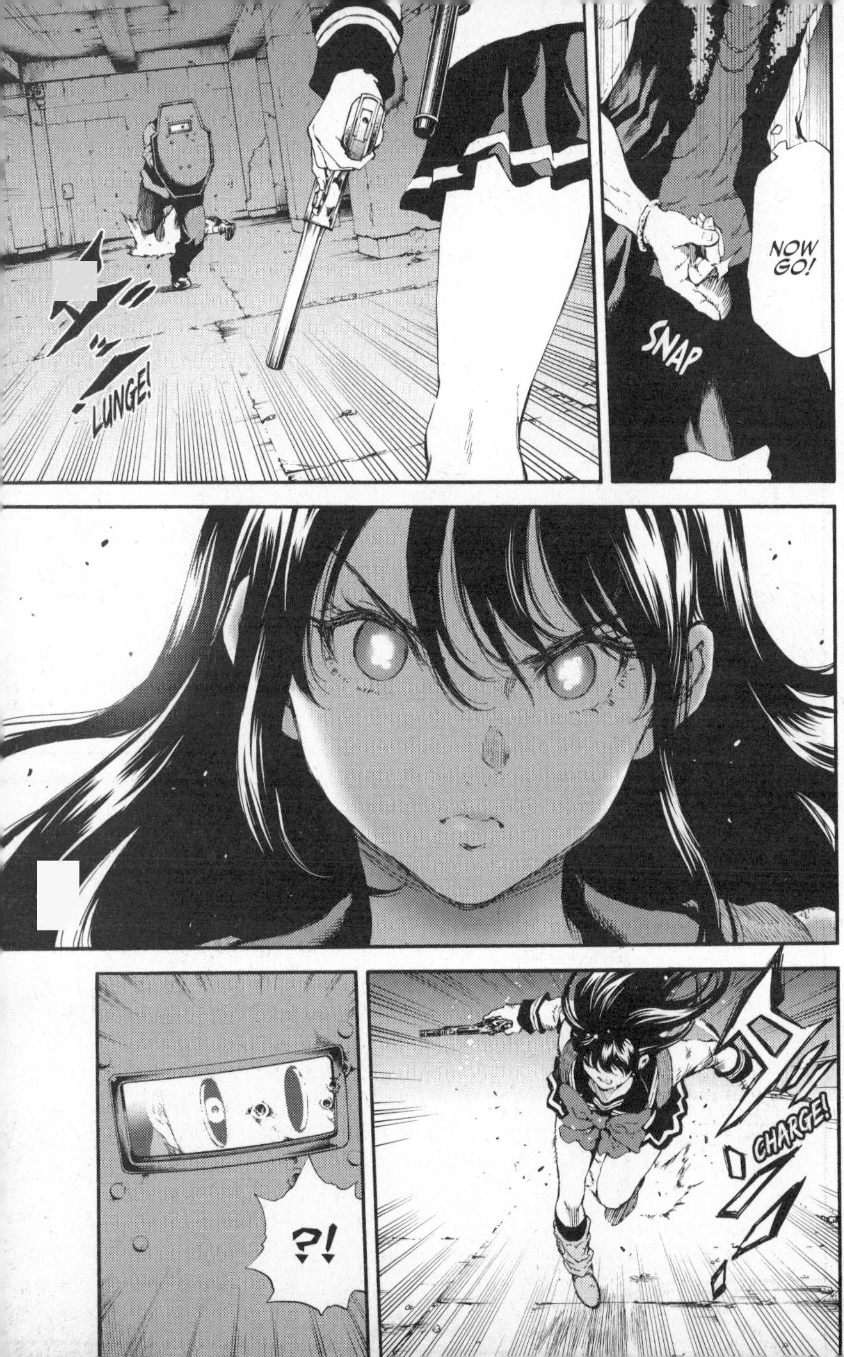
NOW GO!
SNAP
LUNGE!
CHARGE!
?!

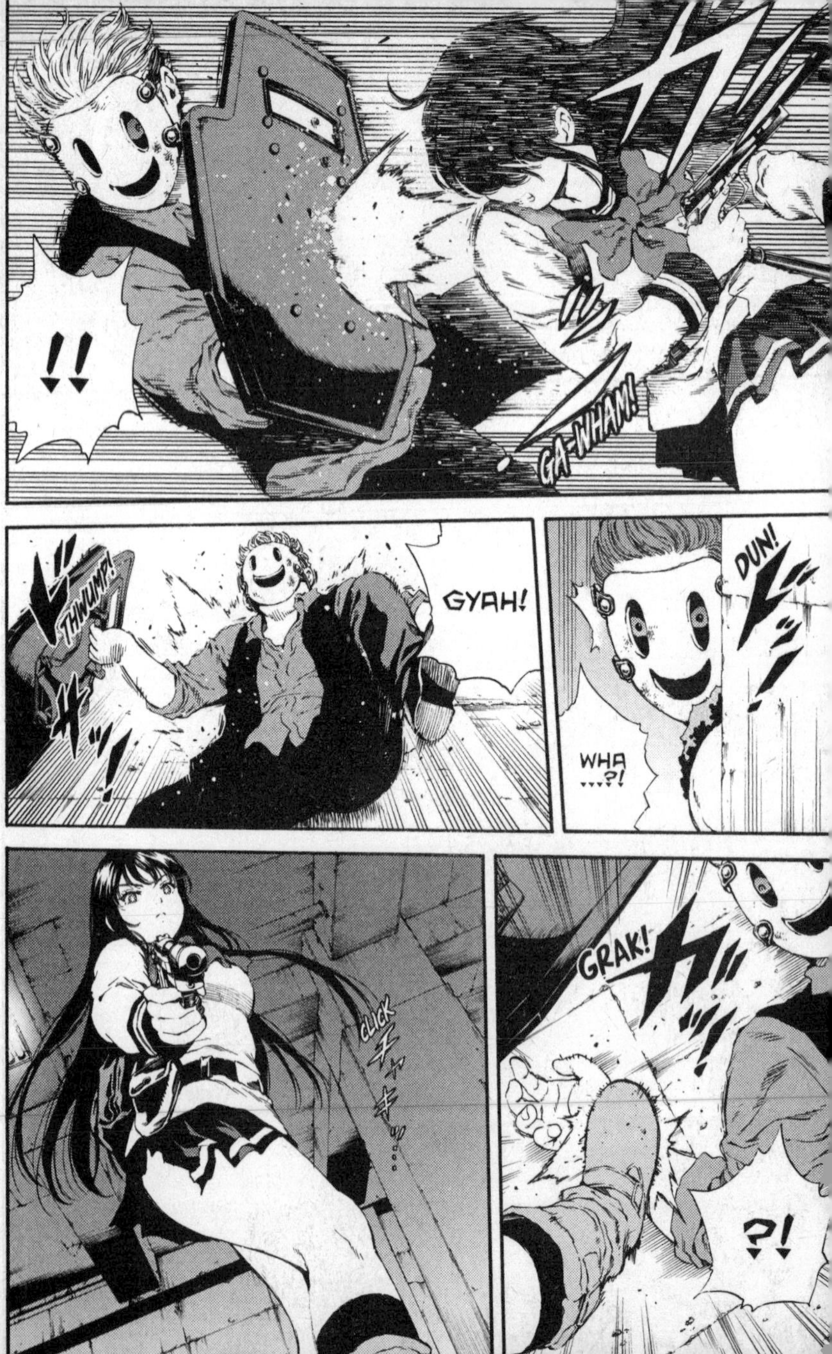

GA-WHAM!
!!
DUN!
WHA ...?!
GYAH!
THWUMP!
GRAK!
?!
CLICK

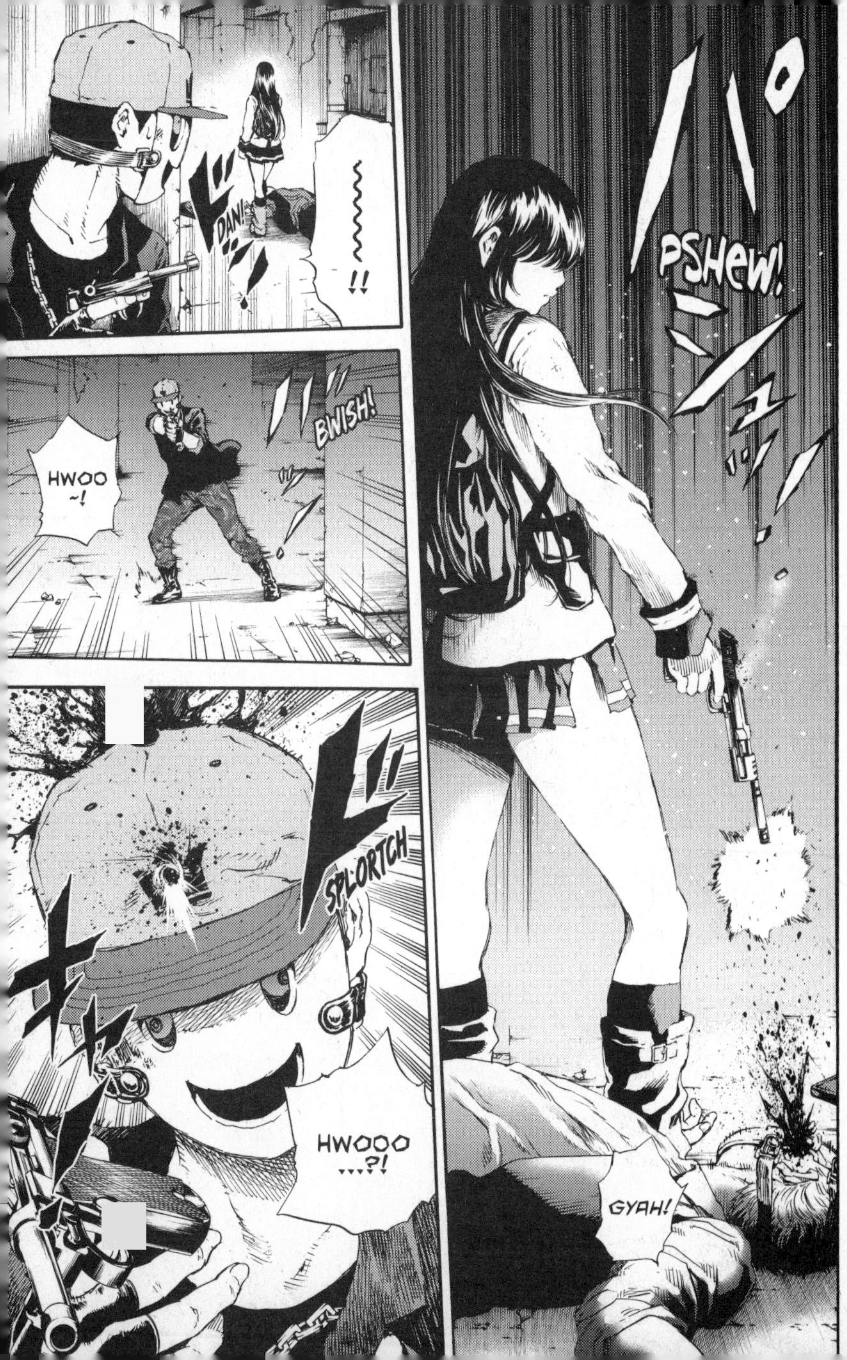
PSHEW!
GYAH!
DAN!
!!
BWISH!
HWOO ~!
SPLORTCH
HWOOO ...?!

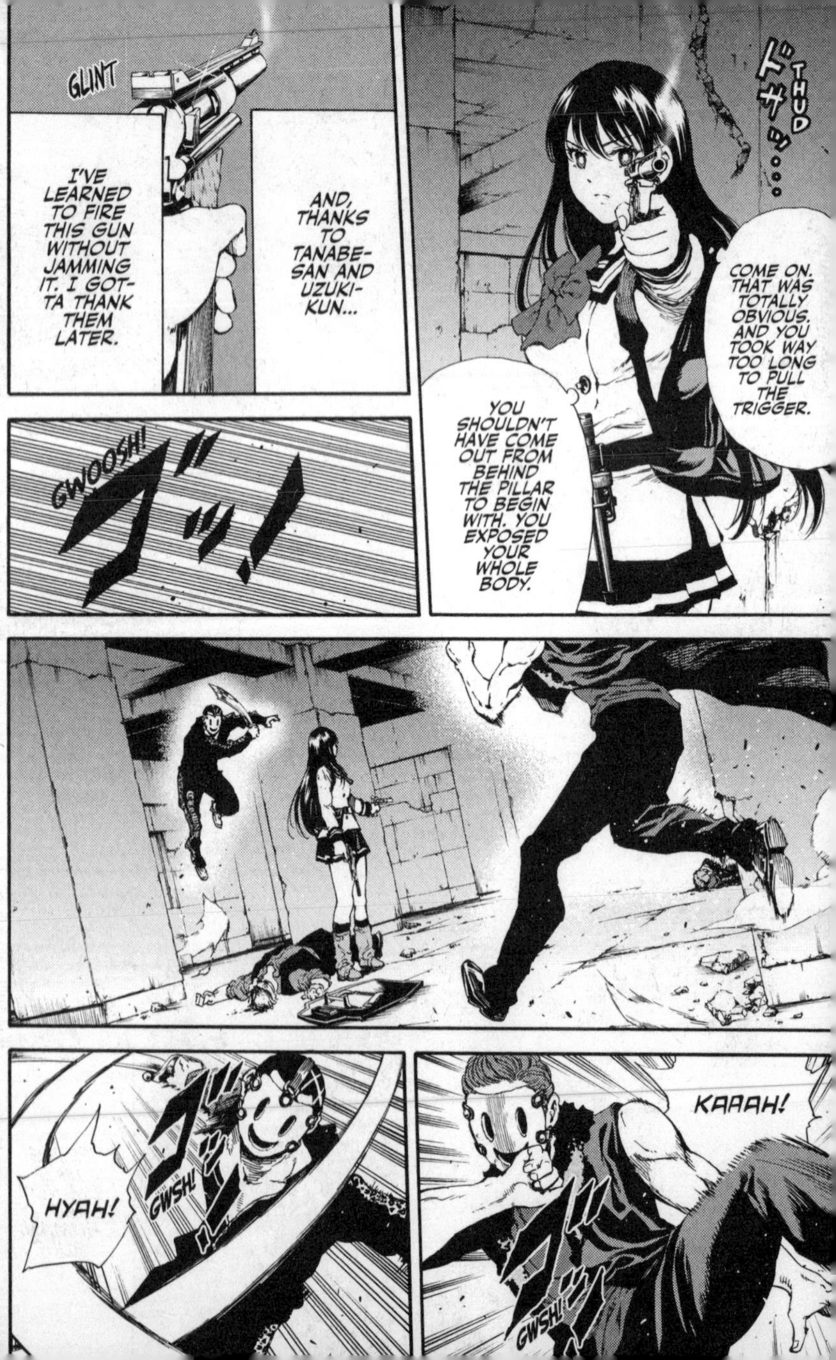
THUD
COME ON. THAT WAS TOTALLY OBVIOUS. AND YOU TOOK WAY TOO LONG TO PULL THE TRIGGER.
YOU SHOULDN'T HAVE COME OUT FROM BEHIND THE PILLAR TO BEGIN WITH. YOU EXPOSED YOUR WHOLE BODY.
AND, THANKS TO TANABE-SAN AND UZUKI-KUN...
GLINT
I'VE LEARNED TO FIRE THIS GUN WITHOUT JAMMING IT. I GOT-TA THANK THEM LATER.
GWOOSH!
KAAAH!
GWSH!
GWSH!
HYAH!

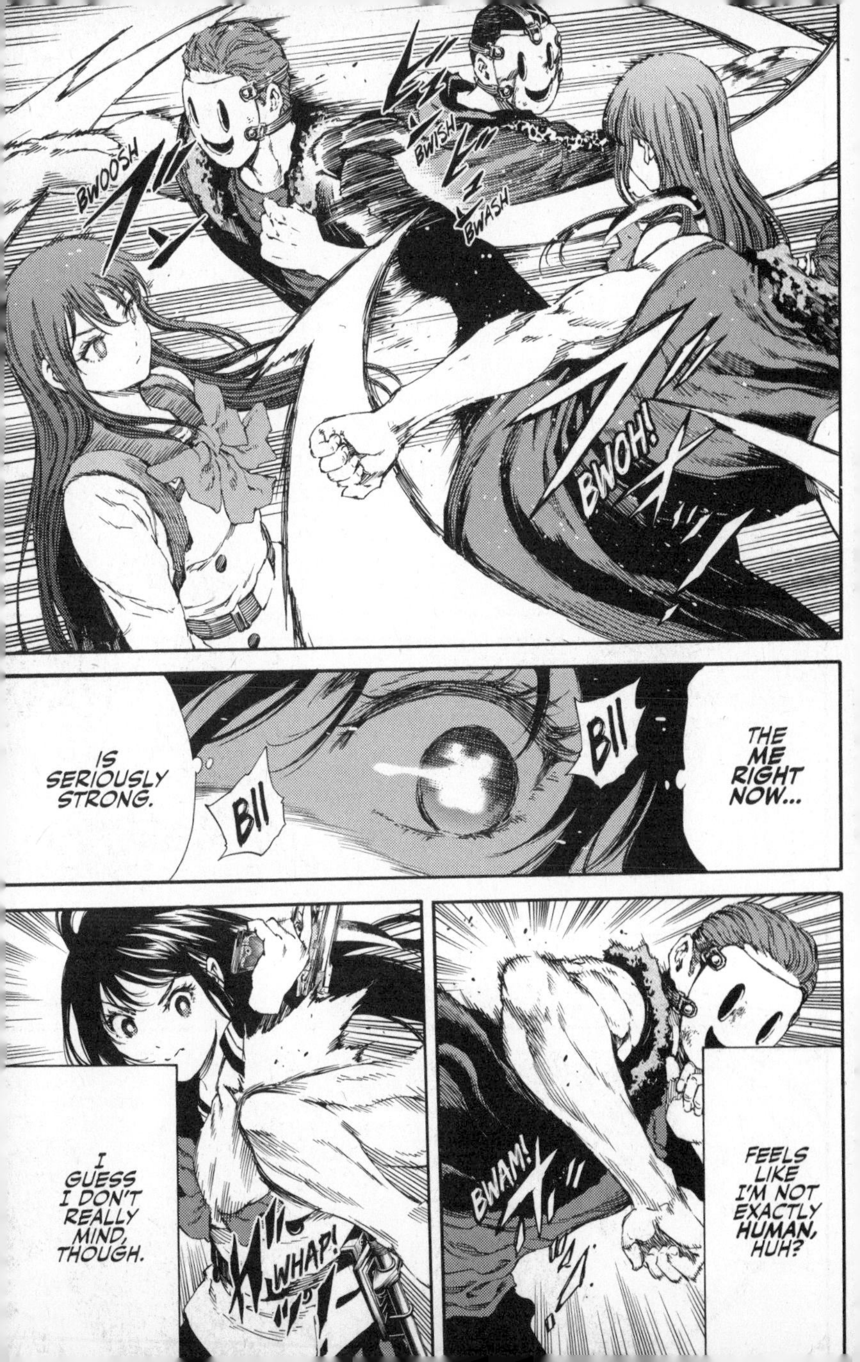
BWISH
BWASH
BWOOSH
BWOH!
THE ME RIGHT NOW...
BII
BII
IS SERIOUSLY STRONG.
FEELS LIKE I'M NOT EXACTLY HUMAN, HUH?
BWAM!
I GUESS I DON'T REALLY MIND, THOUGH.
WHAP!

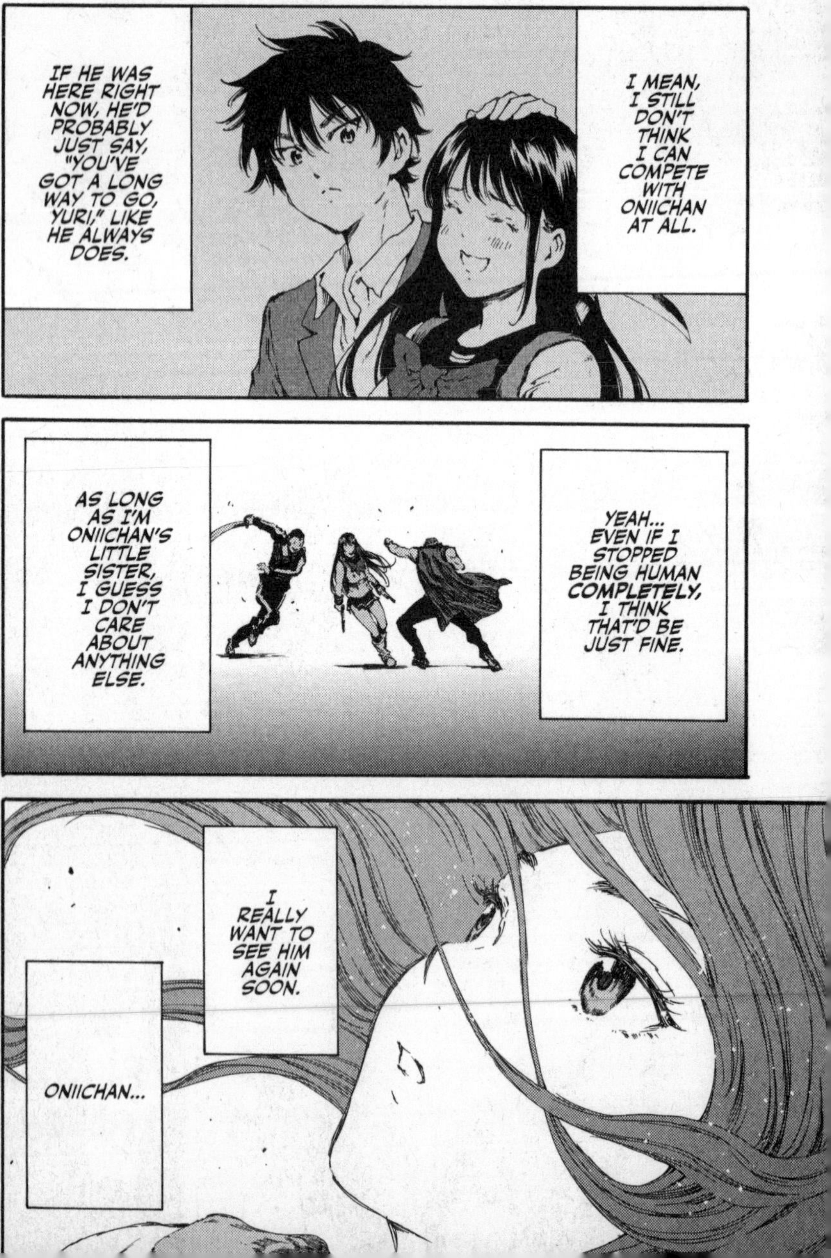
I MEAN, I STILL DON'T THINK I CAN COMPETE WITH ONIICHAN AT ALL.
IF HE WAS HERE RIGHT NOW, HE'D PROBABLY JUST SAY, "YOU'VE GOT A LONG WAY TO GO, YURI," LIKE HE ALWAYS DOES.
YEAH... EVEN IF I STOPPED BEING HUMAN COMPLETELY, I THINK THAT'D BE JUST FINE.
AS LONG AS I'M ONIICHAN'S LITTLE SISTER, I GUESS I DON'T CARE ABOUT ANYTHING ELSE.
I REALLY WANT TO SEE HIM AGAIN SOON.
ONIICHAN...

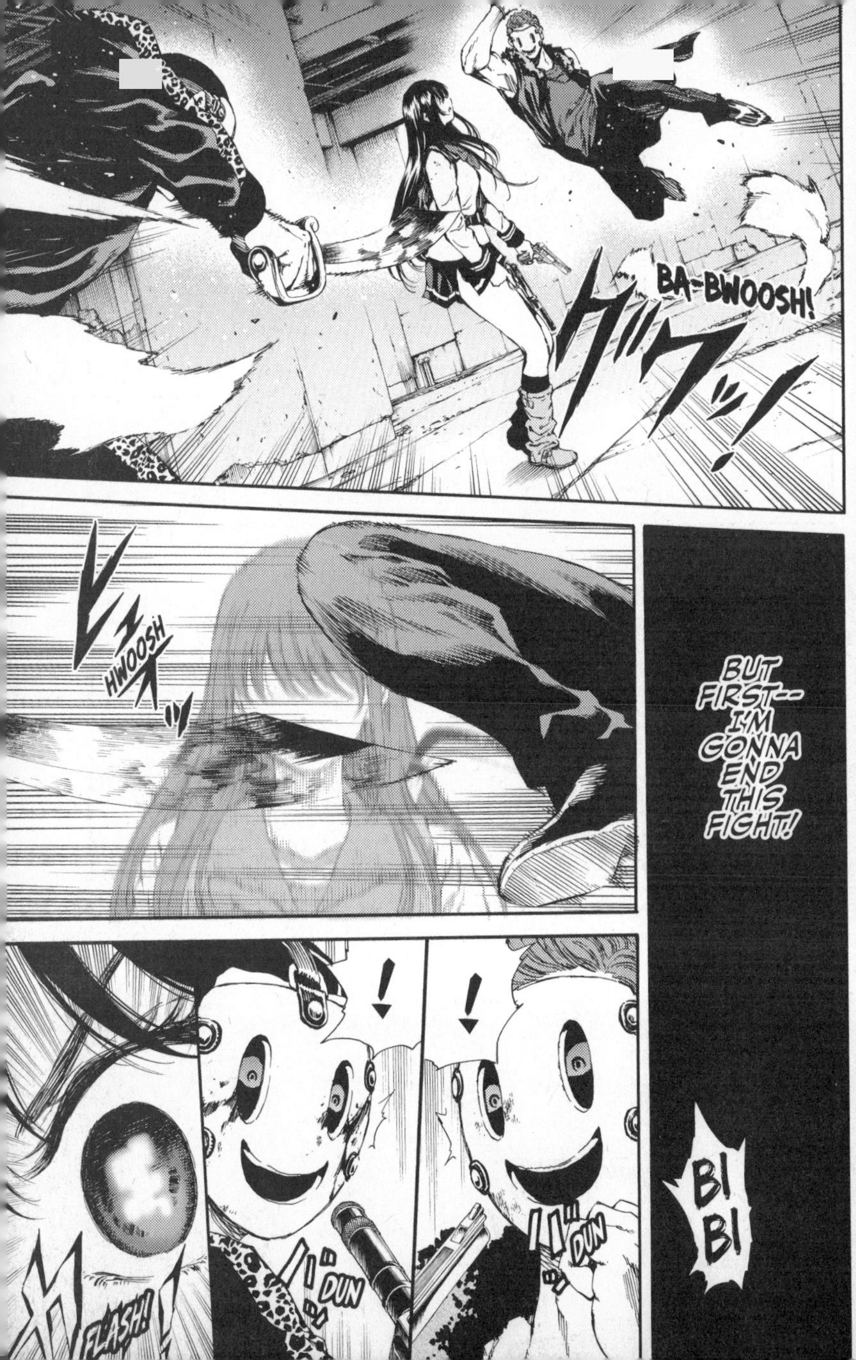
BA-BWOOSH!
BUT FIRST-- I'M GONNA END THIS FIGHT!
BI BI
HWOOSH
DUN
DUN
FLASH!

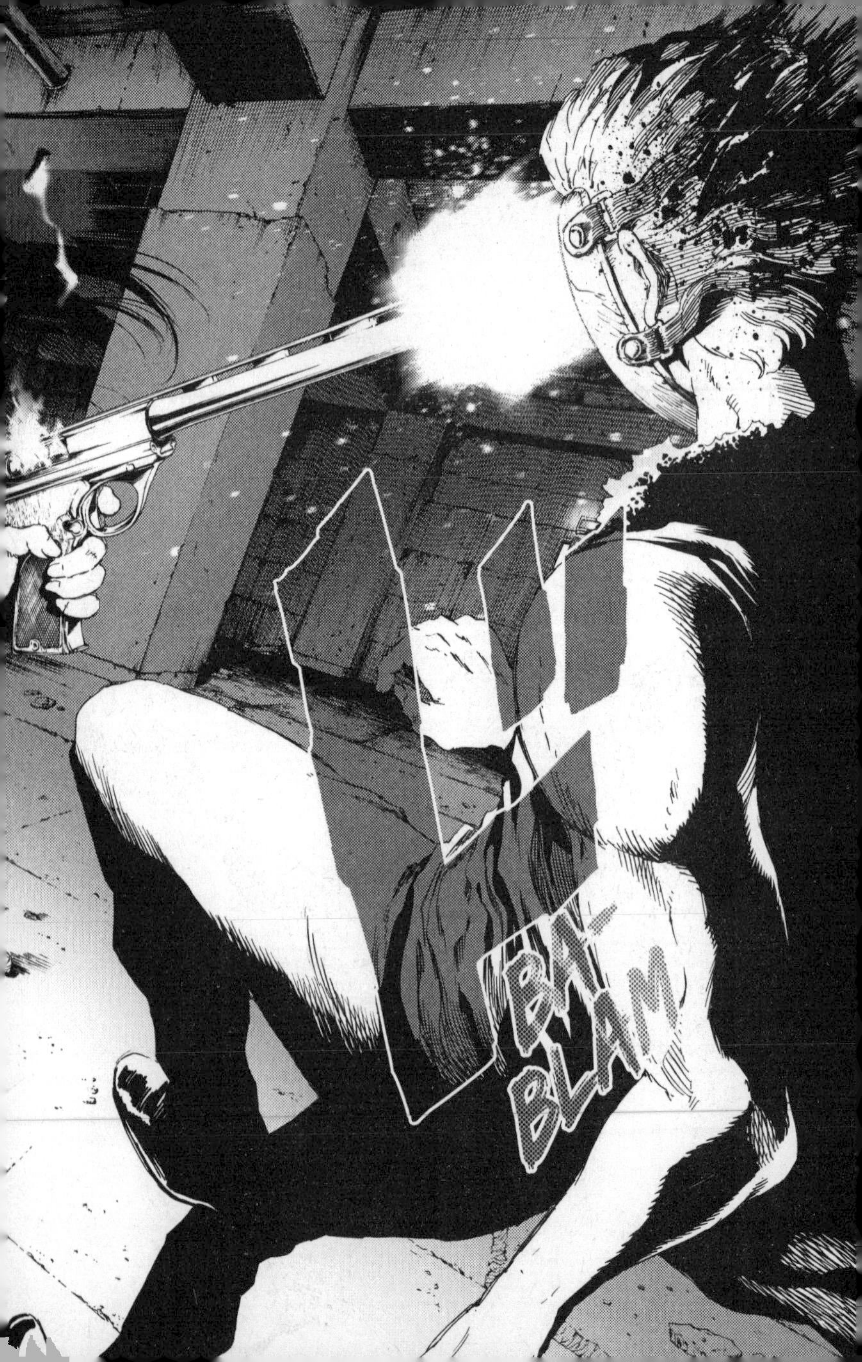
BA-
BLAM

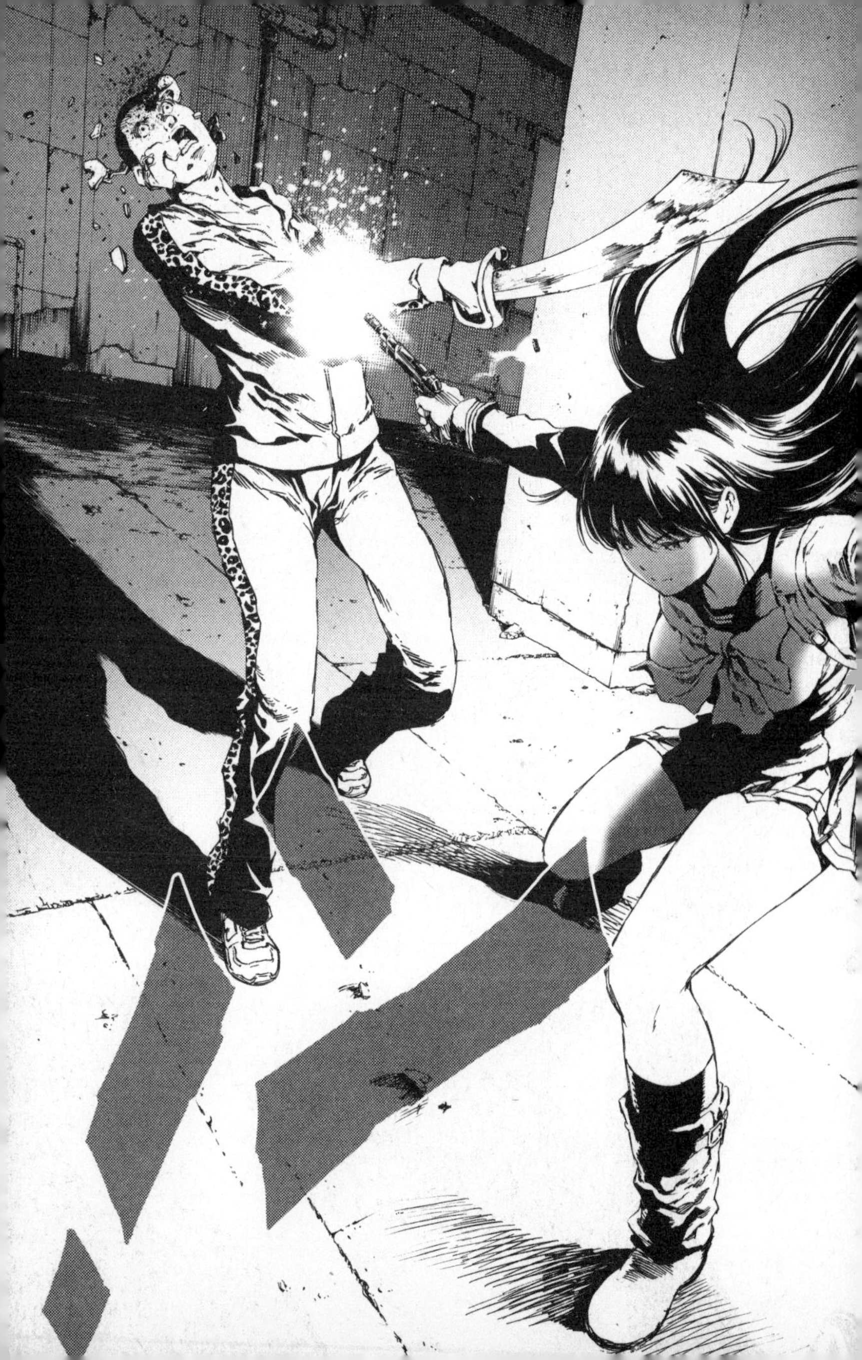

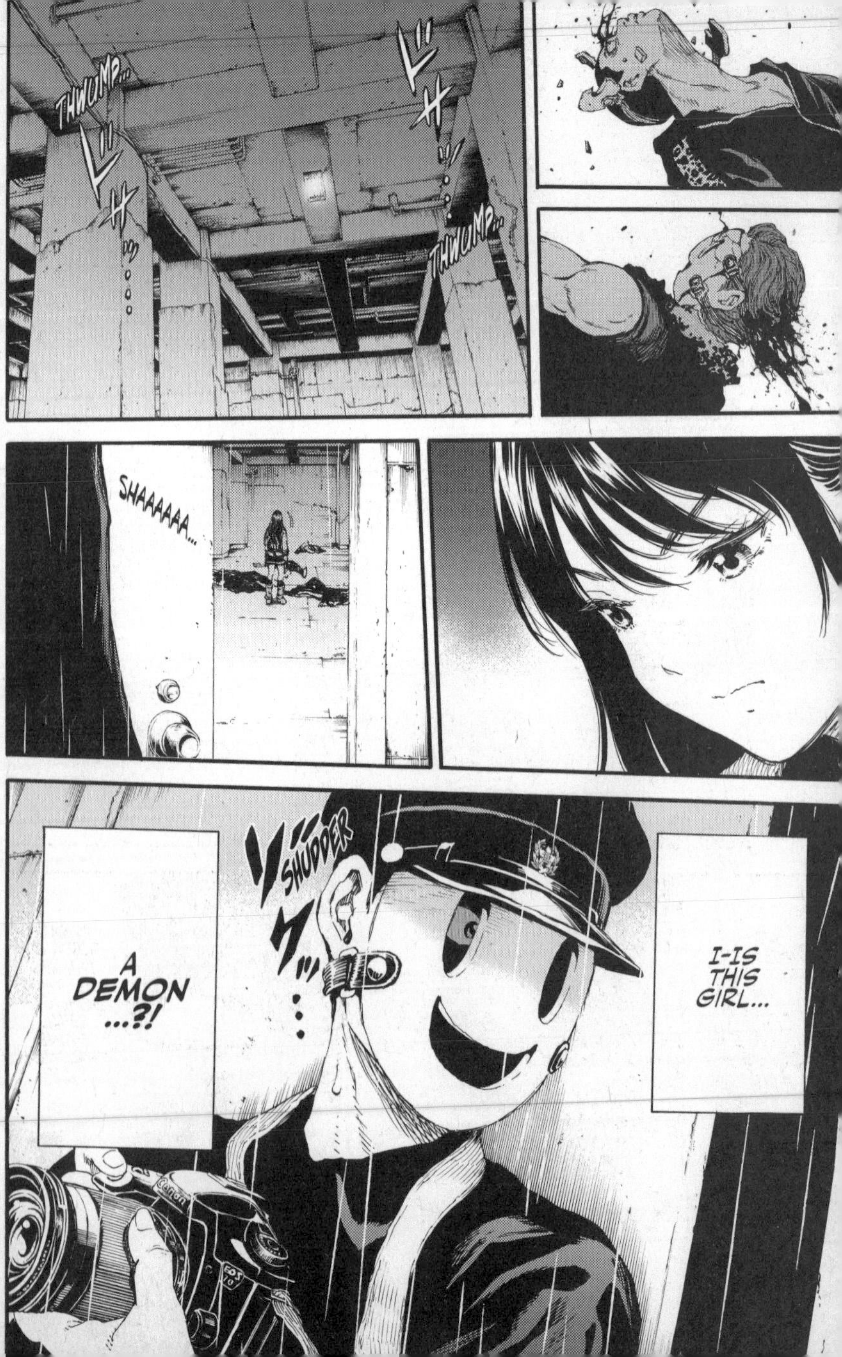
THWUMP...
THWUMP...
SHAAAAAA...
I-IS THIS GIRL...
SHUDDER
A DEMON ...?!

CHAPTER 125: Why Do I Fight?

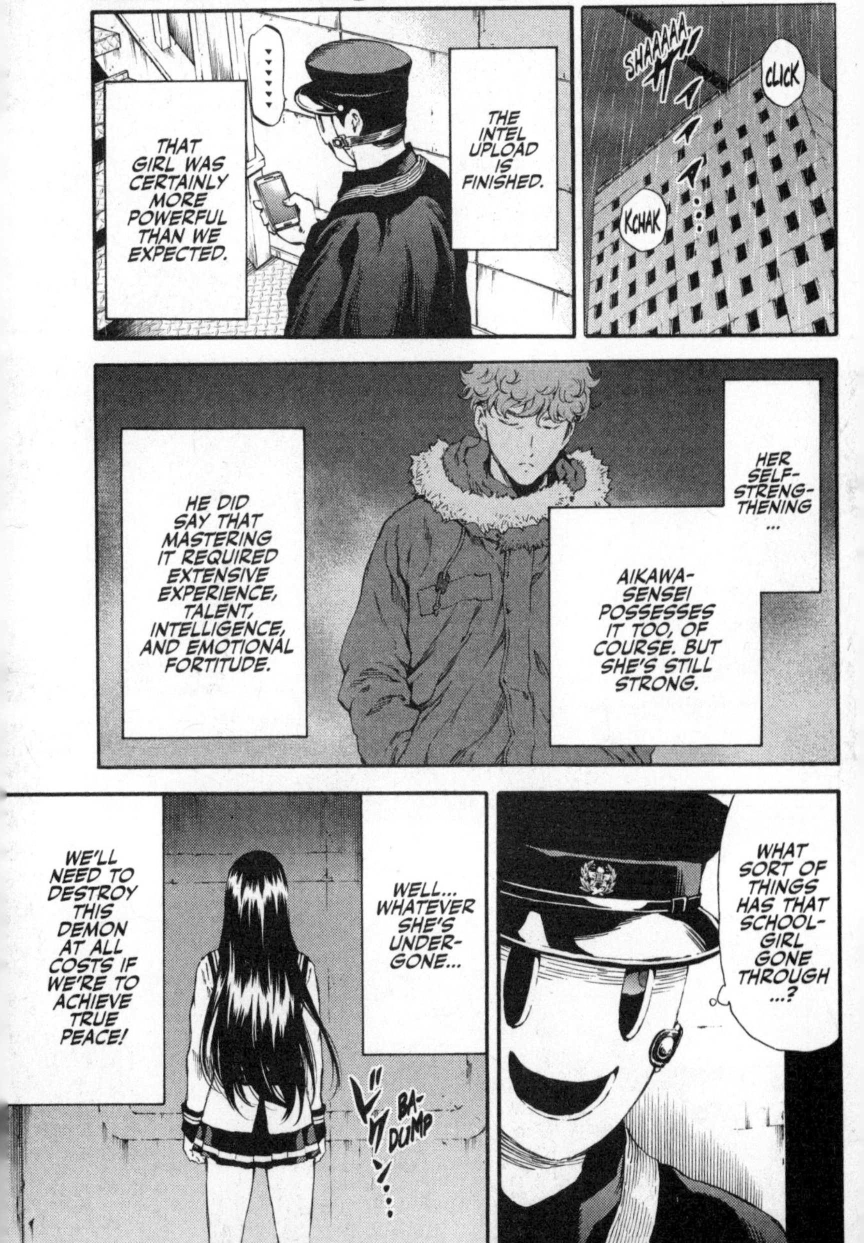
SHAAAAAA
CLICK
KCHAK
THE INTEL UPLOAD IS FINISHED.
......
THAT GIRL WAS CERTAINLY MORE POWERFUL THAN WE EXPECTED.
HER SELF-STRENGTHENING...
AIKAWA-SENSEI POSSESSES IT TOO, OF COURSE. BUT SHE'S STILL STRONG.
HE DID SAY THAT MASTERING IT REQUIRED EXTENSIVE EXPERIENCE, TALENT, INTELLIGENCE, AND EMOTIONAL FORTITUDE.
WHAT SORT OF THINGS HAS THAT SCHOOLGIRL GONE THROUGH...?
WELL... WHATEVER SHE'S UNDERGONE...
WE'LL NEED TO DESTROY THIS DEMON AT ALL COSTS IF WE'RE TO ACHIEVE TRUE PEACE!
BA-DUMP

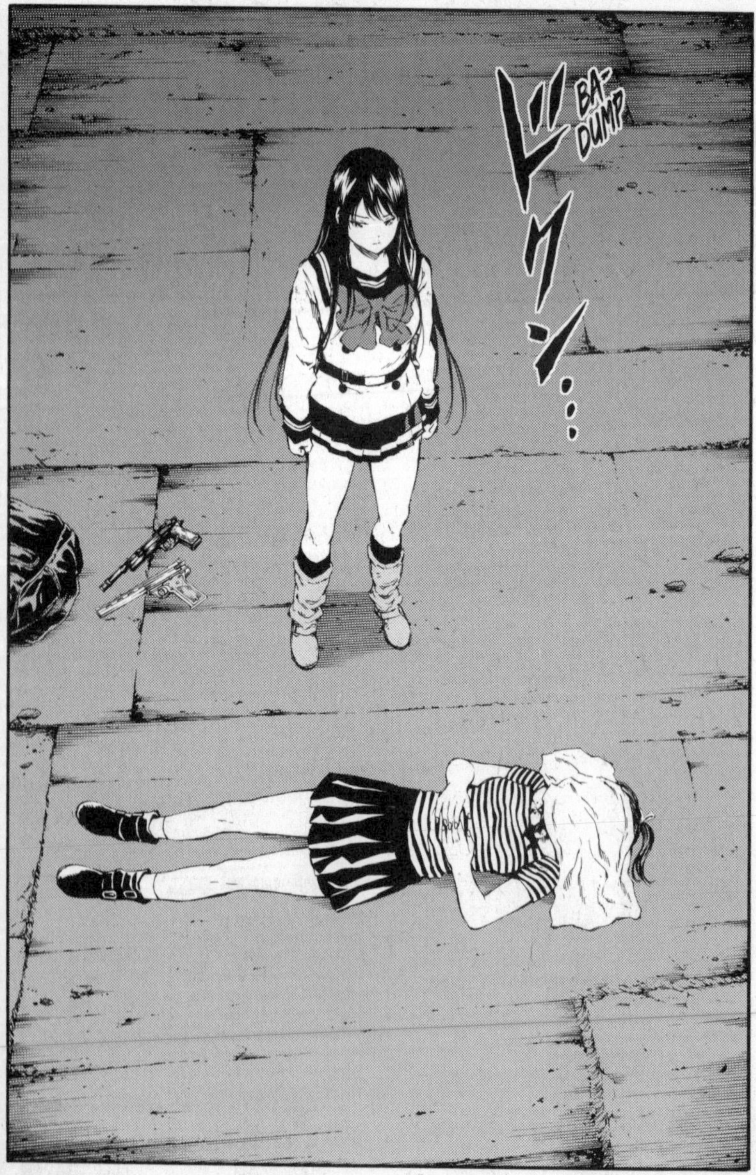
ドクン…
BA-DUMP

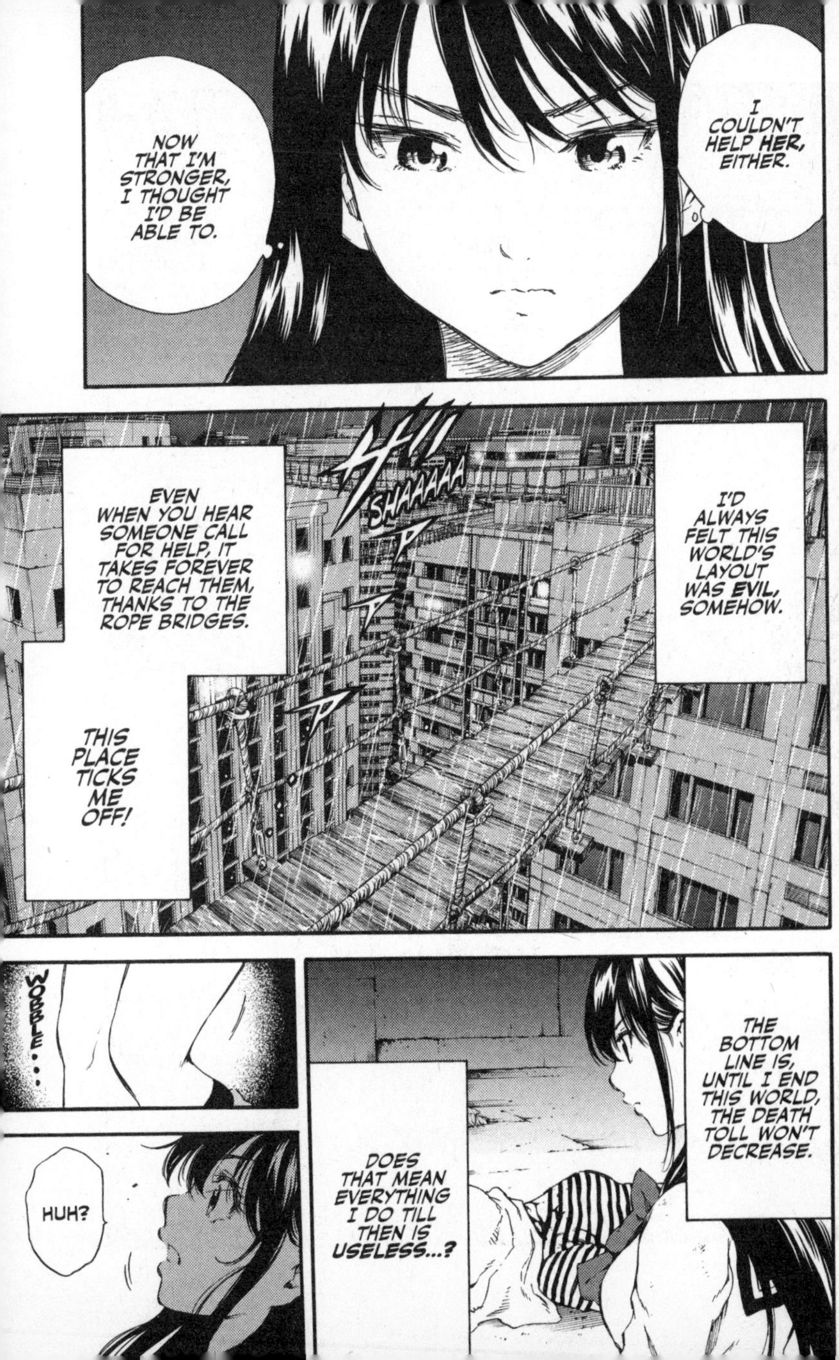
I COULDN'T HELP HER, EITHER.
NOW THAT I'M STRONGER, I THOUGHT I'D BE ABLE TO.
I'D ALWAYS FELT THIS WORLD'S LAYOUT WAS EVIL, SOMEHOW.
SHAAAAA
EVEN WHEN YOU HEAR SOMEONE CALL FOR HELP, IT TAKES FOREVER TO REACH THEM, THANKS TO THE ROPE BRIDGES.
THIS PLACE TICKS ME OFF!
THE BOTTOM LINE IS, UNTIL I END THIS WORLD, THE DEATH TOLL WON'T DECREASE.
DOES THAT MEAN EVERYTHING I DO TILL THEN IS USELESS...?
WOBBLE...
HUH?

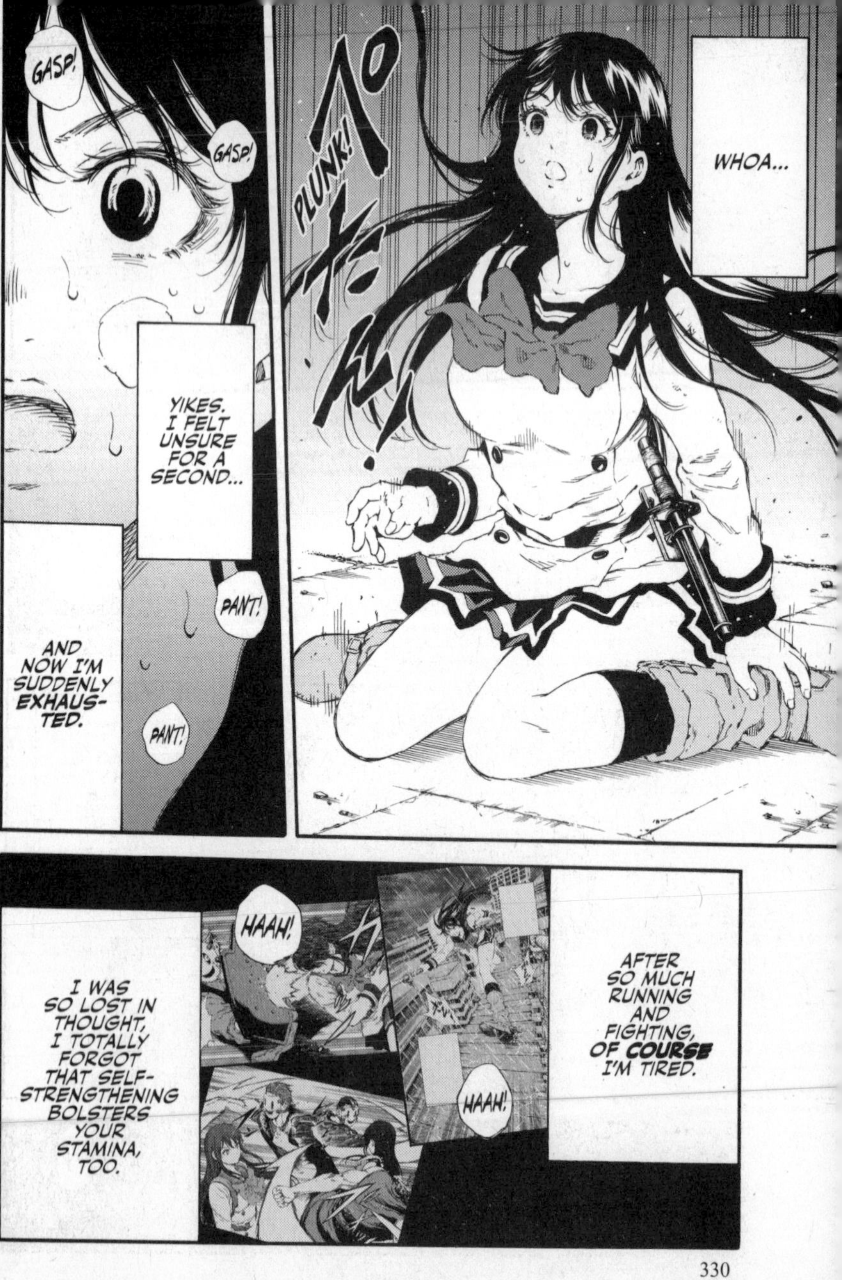
WHOA...
PLUNK!
GASP!
GASP!
YIKES. I FELT UNSURE FOR A SECOND...
PANT!
AND NOW I'M SUDDENLY EXHAUS-TED.
PANT!
AFTER SO MUCH RUNNING AND FIGHTING, OF COURSE I'M TIRED.
HAAH!
HAAH!
I WAS SO LOST IN THOUGHT, I TOTALLY FORGOT THAT SELF-STRENGTHENING BOLSTERS YOUR STAMINA, TOO.

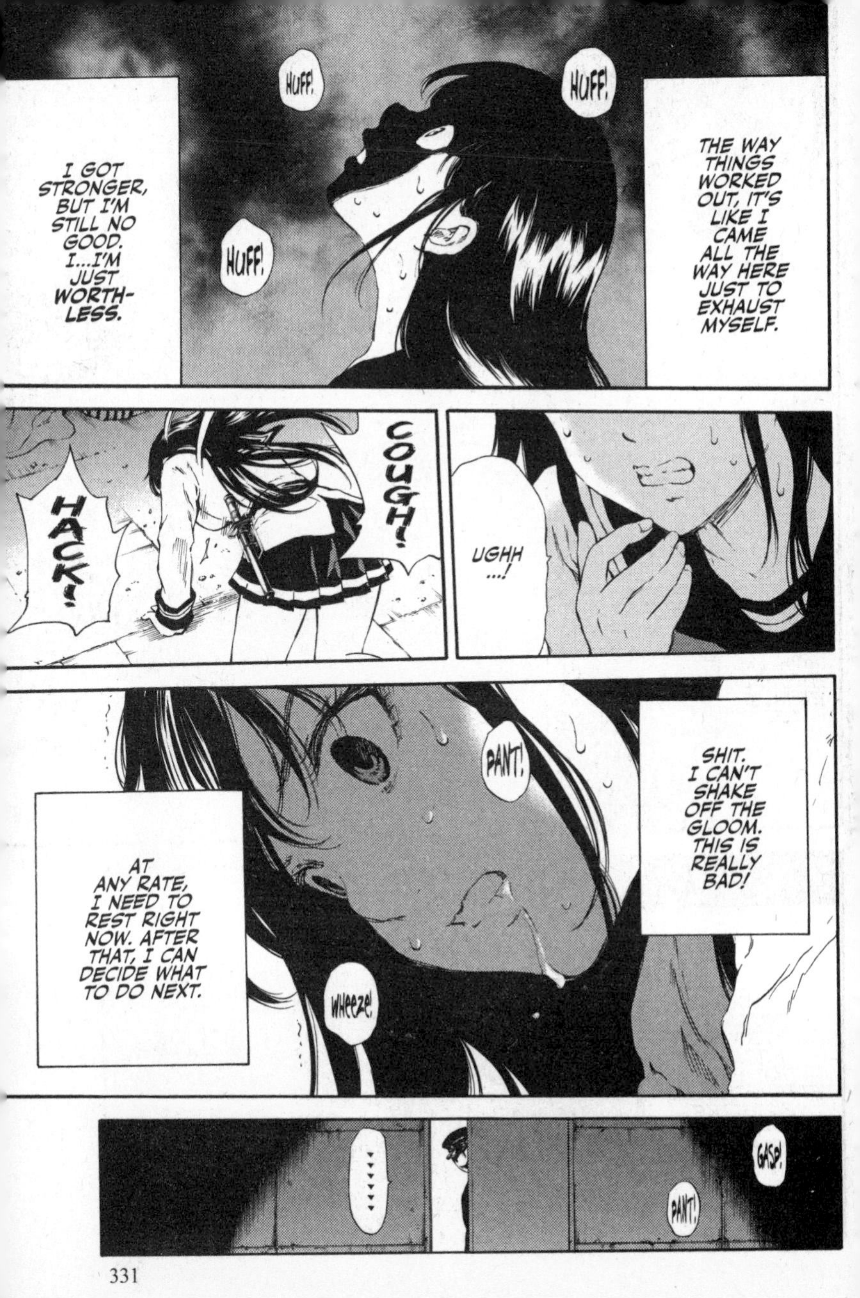

THE WAY THINGS WORKED OUT, IT'S LIKE I CAME ALL THE WAY HERE JUST TO EXHAUST MYSELF.
HUFF!
HUFF!
HUFF!
I GOT STRONGER, BUT I'M STILL NO GOOD. I...I'M JUST WORTHLESS.
UGHH ...!
COUGH!
HACK!
SHIT. I CAN'T SHAKE OFF THE GLOOM. THIS IS REALLY BAD!
PANT!
wheeze!
AT ANY RATE, I NEED TO REST RIGHT NOW. AFTER THAT, I CAN DECIDE WHAT TO DO NEXT.
GASP!
PANT!
......

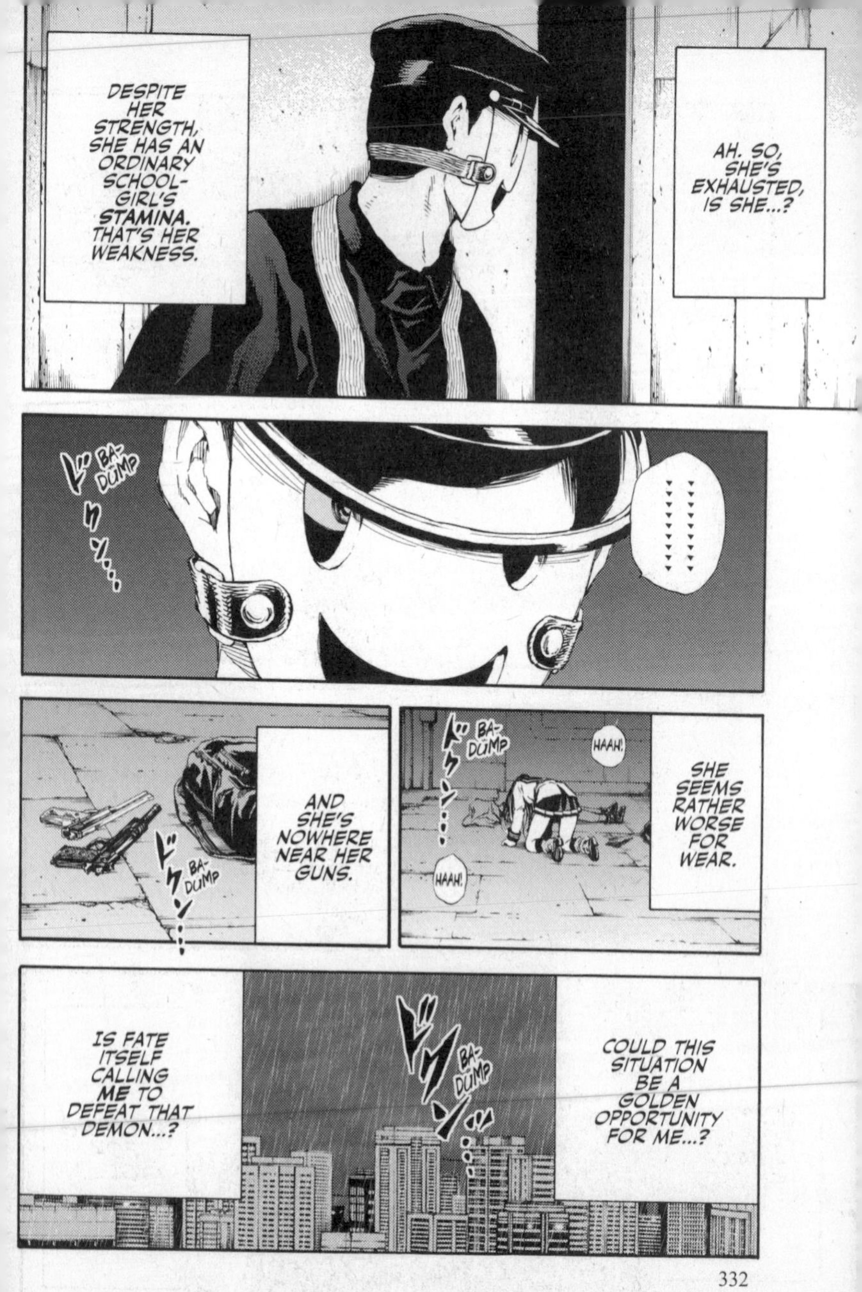
AH. SO, SHE'S EXHAUSTED, IS SHE...?
DESPITE HER STRENGTH, SHE HAS AN ORDINARY SCHOOL-GIRL'S STAMINA. THAT'S HER WEAKNESS.
......
BA-DUMP
SHE SEEMS RATHER WORSE FOR WEAR.
HAAH!
BA-DUMP
HAAH!
AND SHE'S NOWHERE NEAR HER GUNS.
BA-DUMP
COULD THIS SITUATION BE A GOLDEN OPPORTUNITY FOR ME...?
BA-DUMP
IS FATE ITSELF CALLING ME TO DEFEAT THAT DEMON...?

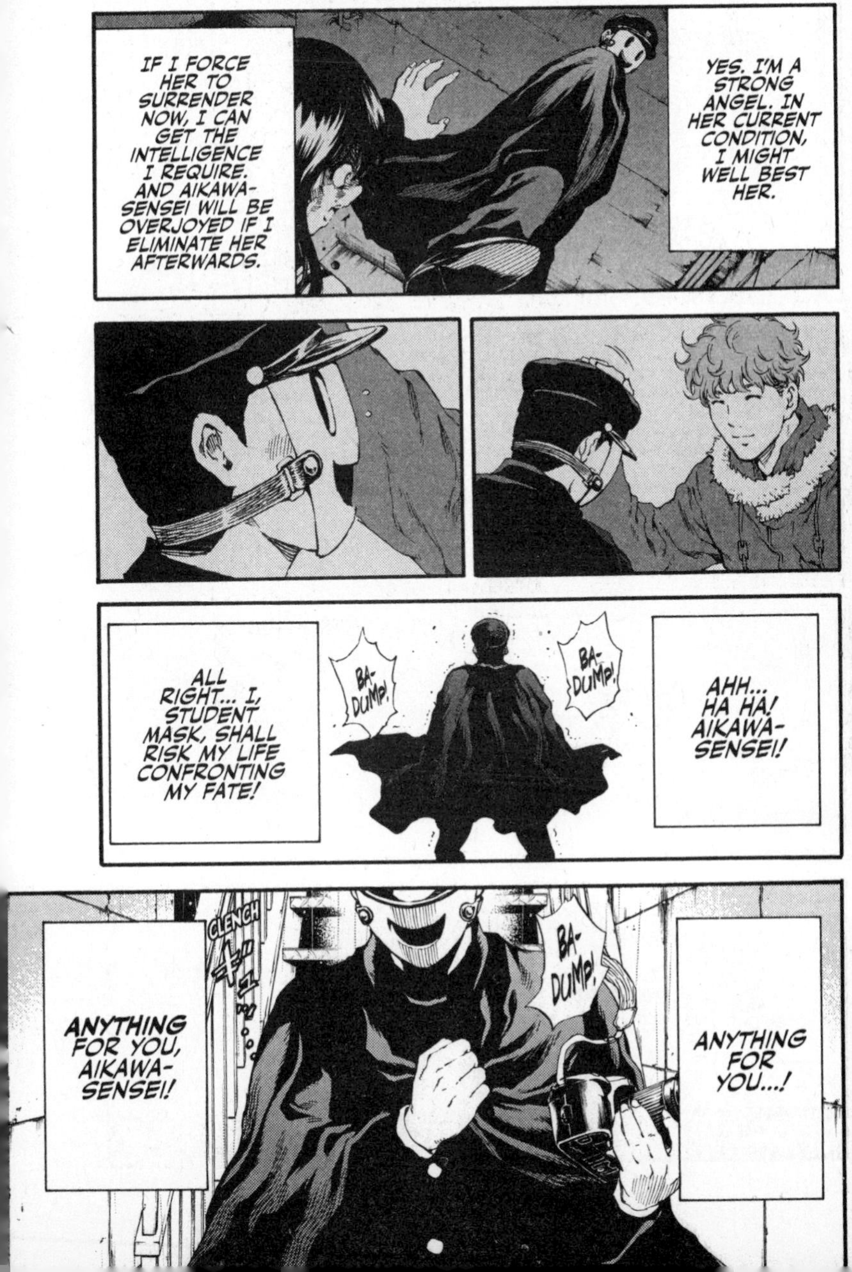
YES. I'M A STRONG ANGEL. IN HER CURRENT CONDITION, I MIGHT WELL BEST HER.
IF I FORCE HER TO SURRENDER NOW, I CAN GET THE INTELLIGENCE I REQUIRE. AND AIKAWA-SENSEI WILL BE OVERJOYED IF I ELIMINATE HER AFTERWARDS.
AHH... HA HA! AIKAWA-SENSEI!
BA-DUMP!
BA-DUMP!
ALL RIGHT... I, STUDENT MASK, SHALL RISK MY LIFE CONFRONTING MY FATE!
ANYTHING FOR YOU...!
BA-DUMP!
CLENCH
ANYTHING FOR YOU, AIKAWA-SENSEI!

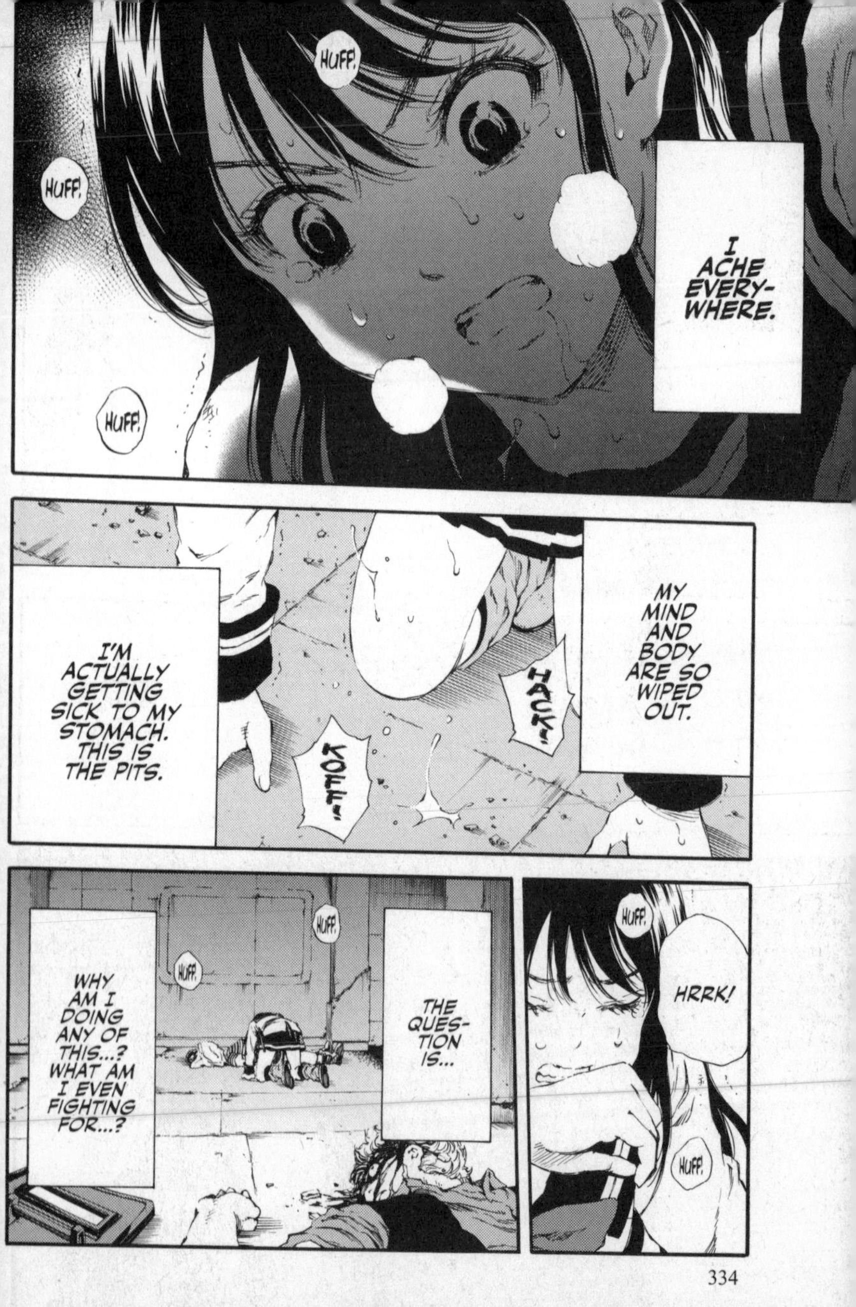
I ACHE EVERY-WHERE.
HUFF!
HUFF!
HUFF!
MY MIND AND BODY ARE SO WIPED OUT.
HACK!
KOFF!
I'M ACTUALLY GETTING SICK TO MY STOMACH. THIS IS THE PITS.
HUFF!
HRRK!
HUFF!
THE QUESTION IS...
HUFF!
HUFF!
WHY AM I DOING ANY OF THIS...? WHAT AM I EVEN FIGHTING FOR...?

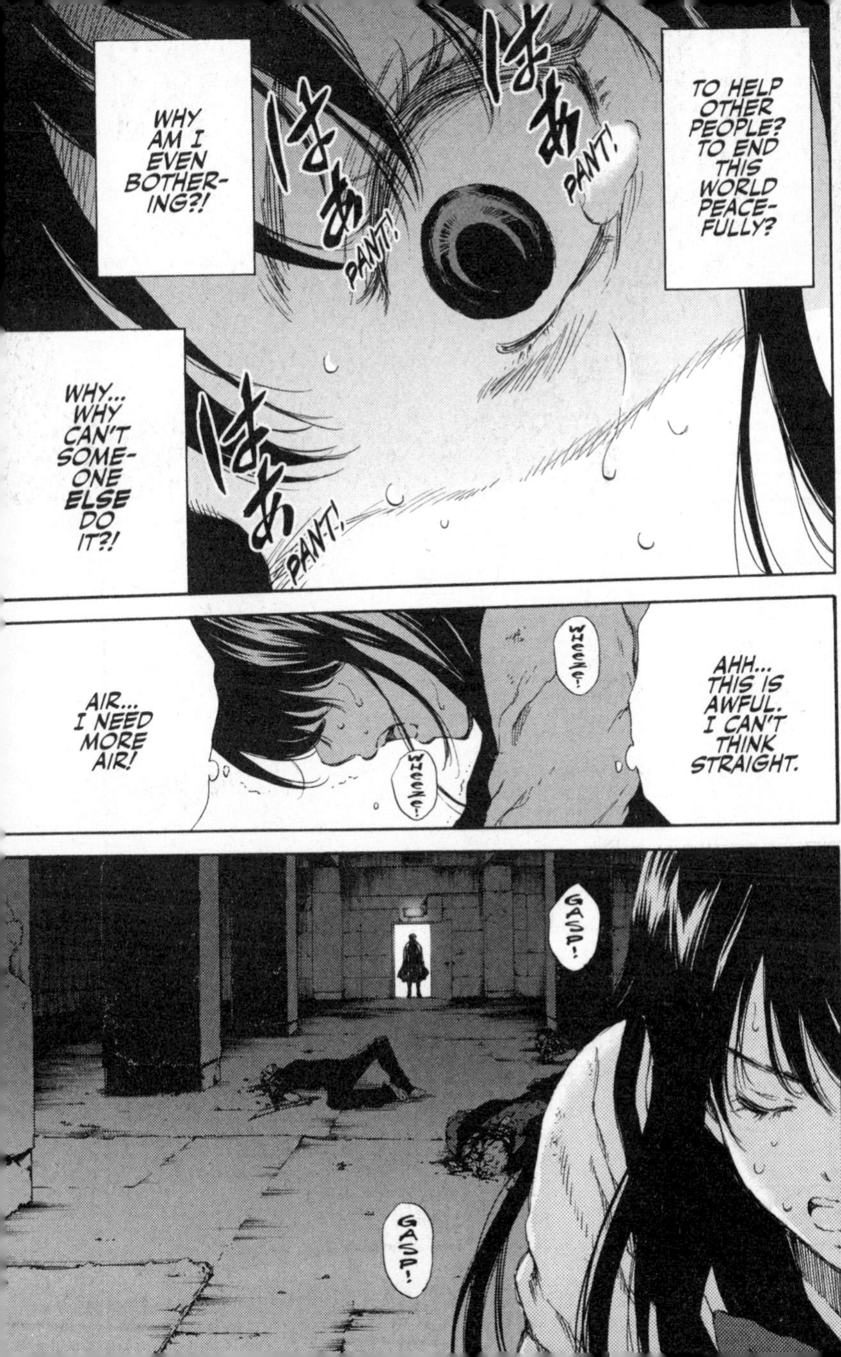
TO HELP OTHER PEOPLE? TO END THIS WORLD PEACE-FULLY?
はあ
PANT!
はあ
PANT!
WHY AM I EVEN BOTHER-ING?!
はあ
PANT!
WHY... WHY CAN'T SOME-ONE ELSE DO IT?!
AHH... THIS IS AWFUL. I CAN'T THINK STRAIGHT.
WHEEZE!
WHEEZE!
AIR... I NEED MORE AIR!
GASP!
GASP!

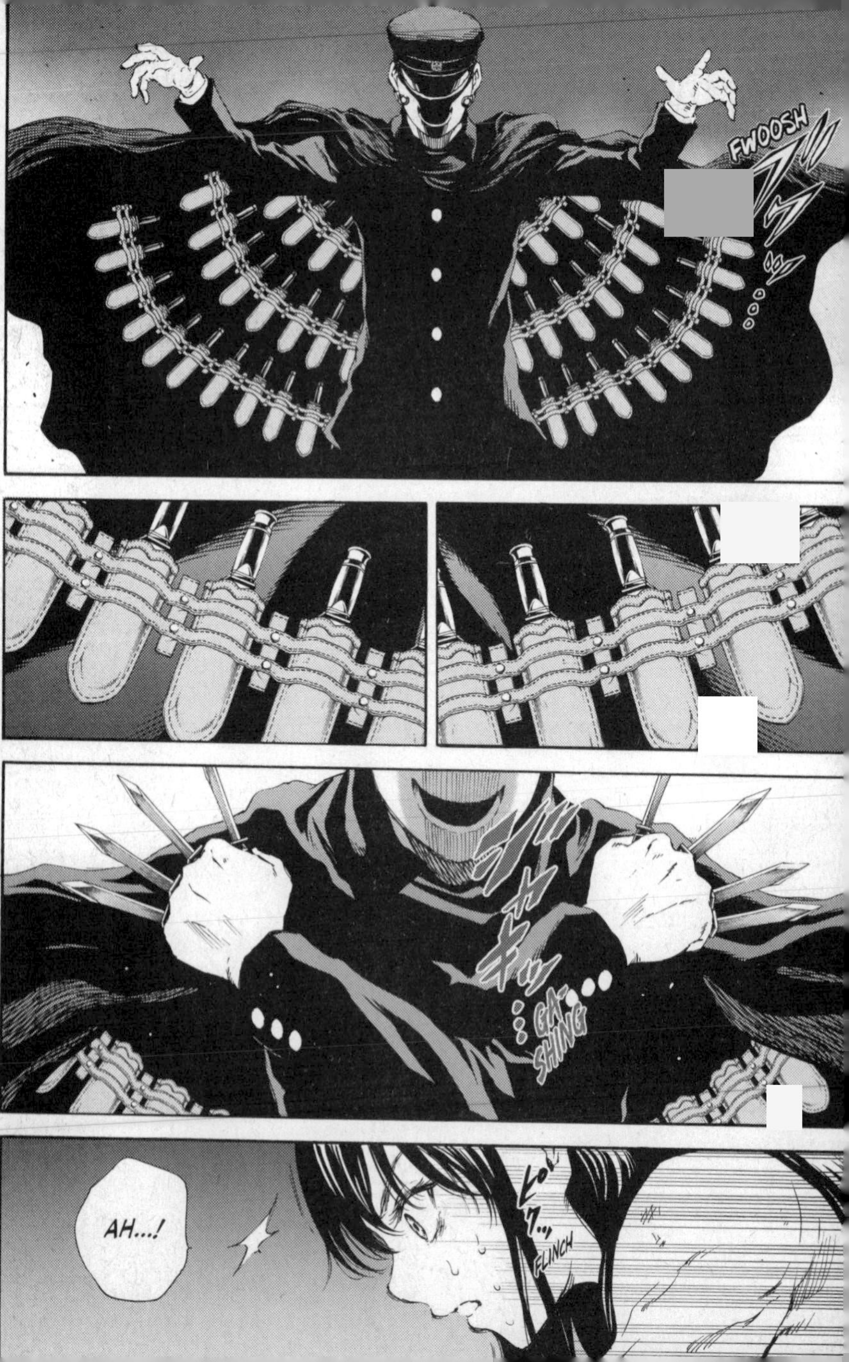
FWOOSH
GA-SHING
FLINCH
AH...!

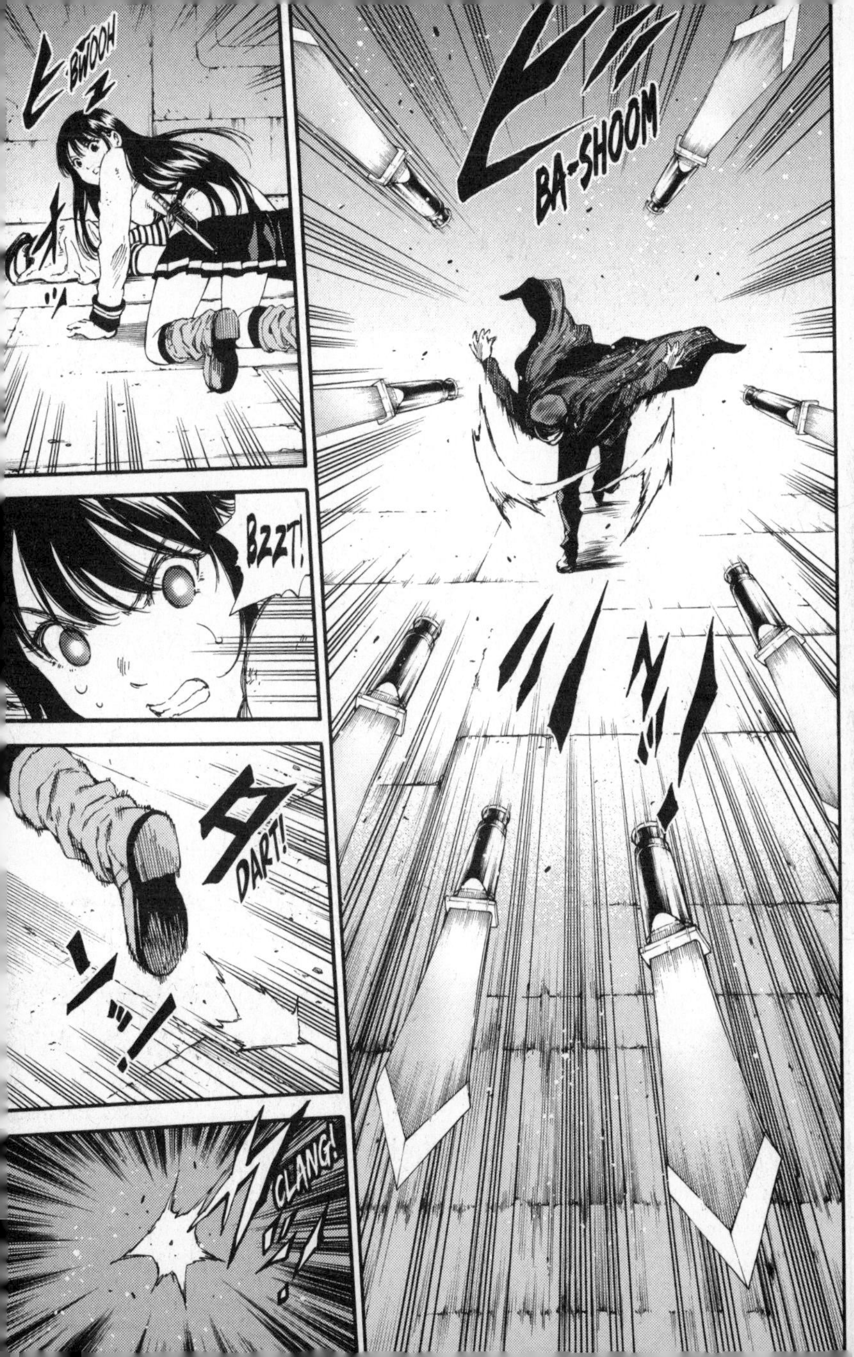
BA-SHOOM
BWOOH
BZZT!
DART!
CLANG!

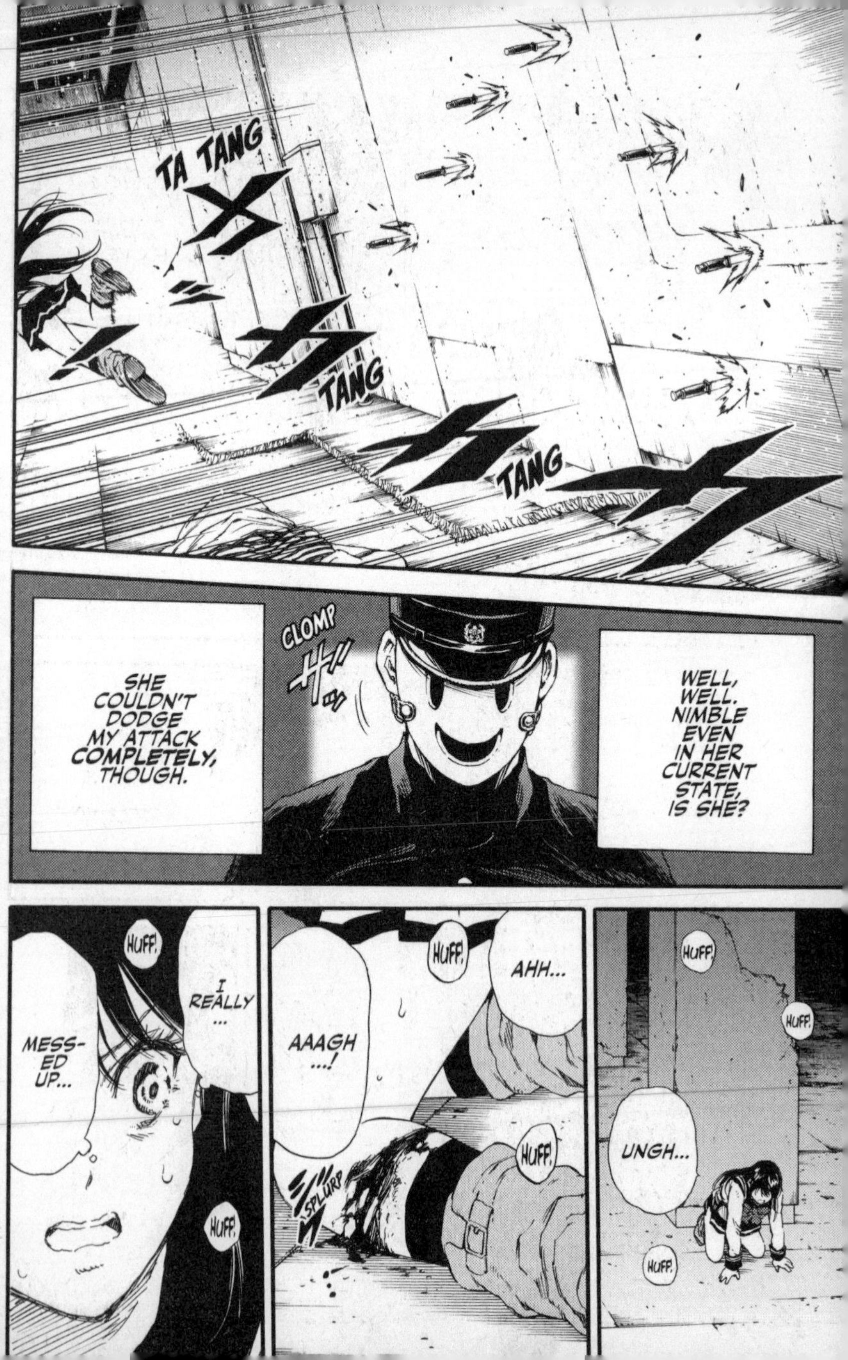
TA TANG
TANG
TANG
WELL, WELL. NIMBLE EVEN IN HER CURRENT STATE, IS SHE?
CLOMP
SHE COULDN'T DODGE MY ATTACK COMPLETELY, THOUGH.
HUFF!
HUFF!
UNGH...
HUFF!
HUFF!
AHH...
AAAGH...!
HUFF!
SPLURP
HUFF!
I REALLY...
MESSED-UP...
HUFF!

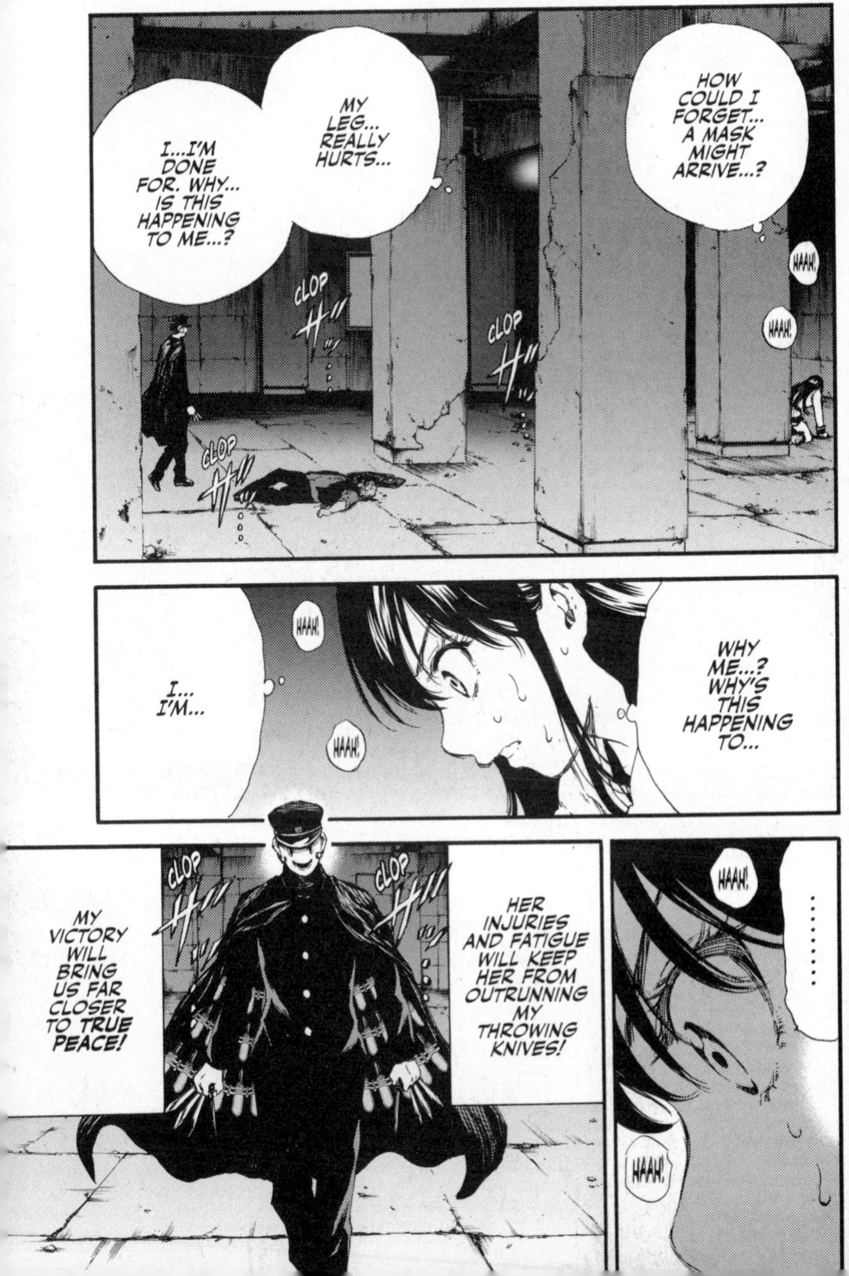
HOW COULD I FORGET... A MASK MIGHT ARRIVE...?
HAAH!
HAAH!
MY LEG... REALLY HURTS...
I...I'M DONE FOR. WHY... IS THIS HAPPENING TO ME...?
CLOP
CLOP
CLOP
WHY ME...? WHY'S THIS HAPPENING TO...
HAAH!
HAAH!
I... I'M...
HAAH!
....
HAAH!
HER INJURIES AND FATIGUE WILL KEEP HER FROM OUTRUNNING MY THROWING KNIVES!
CLOP
CLOP
MY VICTORY WILL BRING US FAR CLOSER TO TRUE PEACE!

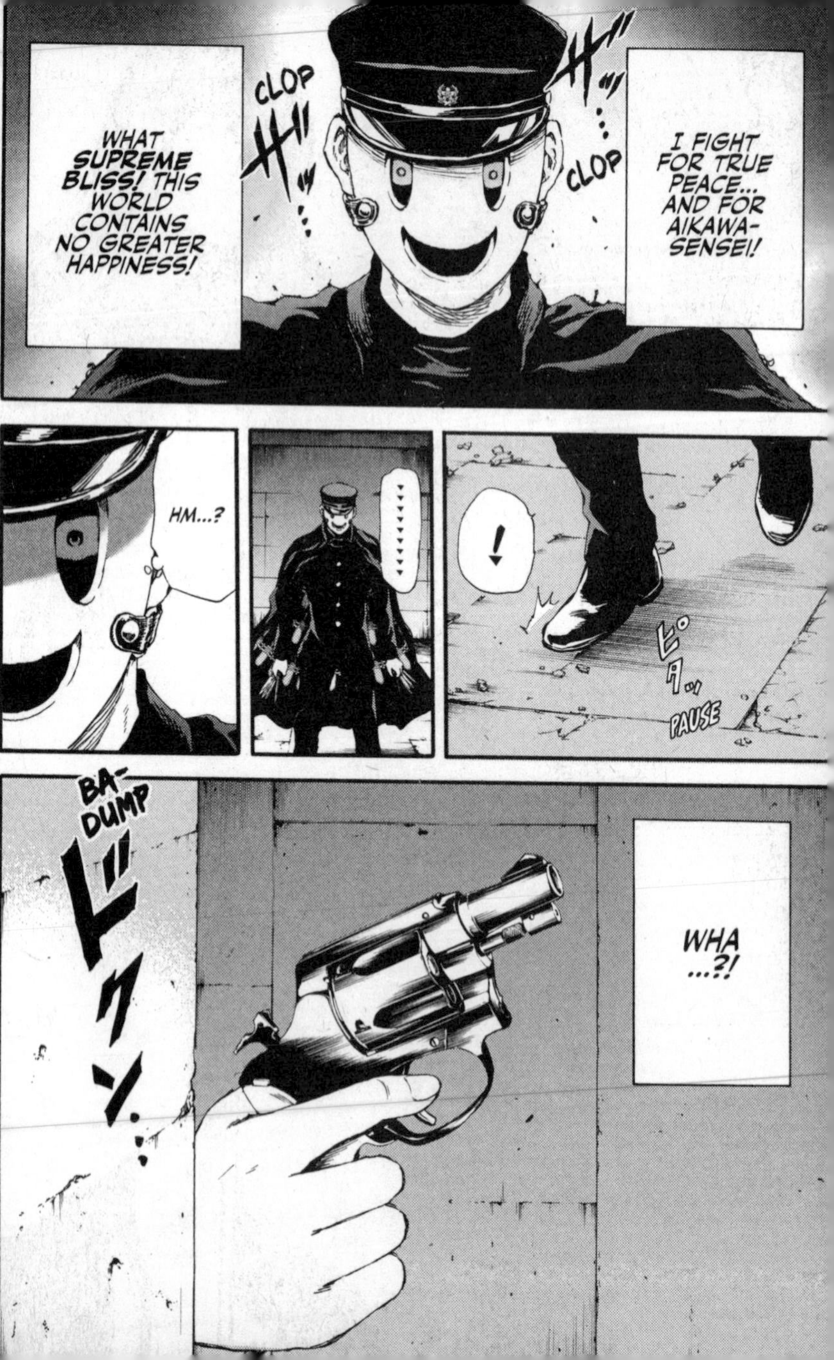
I FIGHT FOR TRUE PEACE... AND FOR AIKAWA-SENSEI!
CLOP
CLOP
WHAT SUPREME BLISS! THIS WORLD CONTAINS NO GREATER HAPPINESS!
!
ピタッ
PAUSE
HM...?
WHA ...?!
BA-DUMP
ドクン…

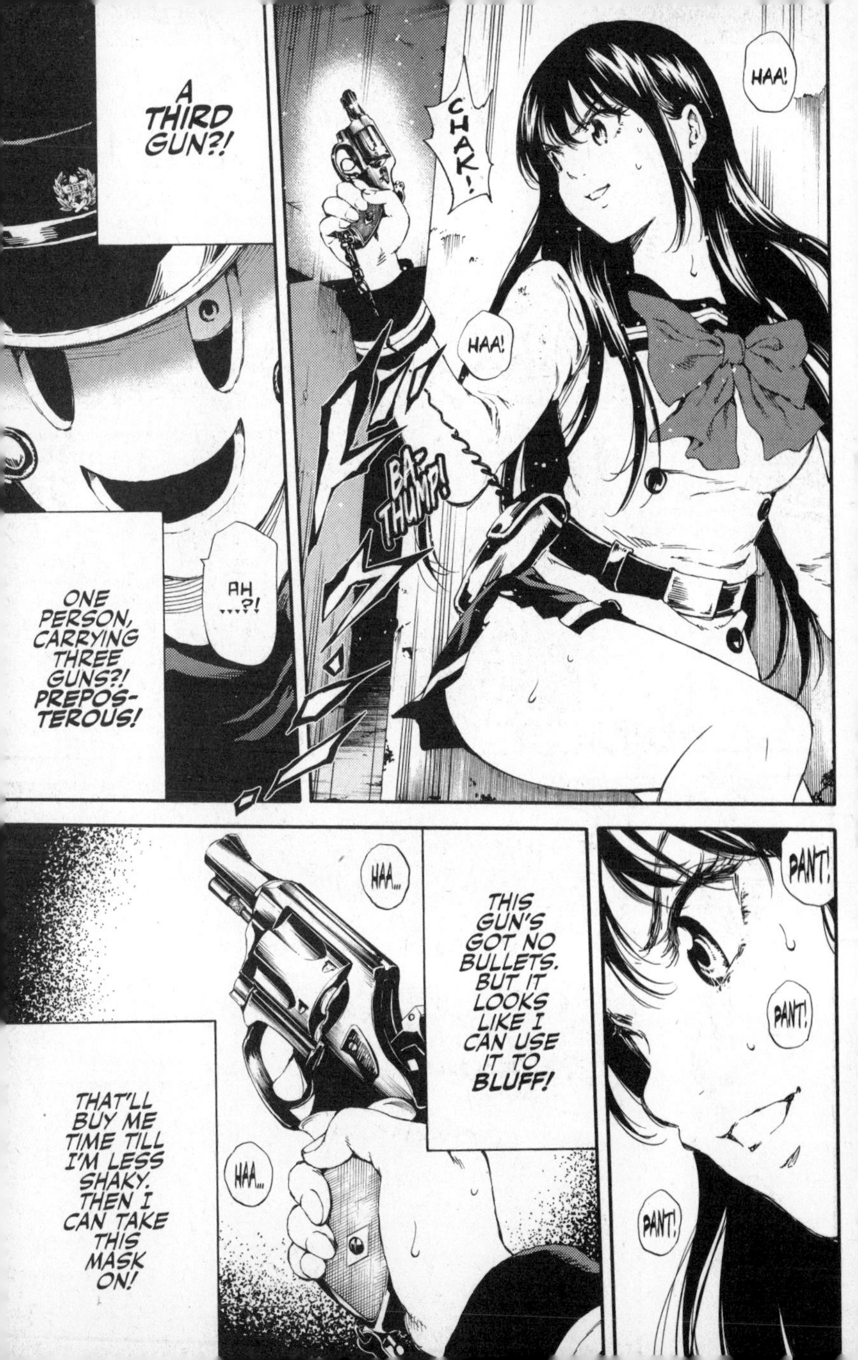

HAA!
CHAK!
HAA!
BA-THUMP!
A THIRD GUN?!
AH ...?!
ONE PERSON, CARRYING THREE GUNS?! PREPOSTEROUS!
PANT!
PANT!
PANT!
HAA...
THIS GUN'S GOT NO BULLETS. BUT IT LOOKS LIKE I CAN USE IT TO BLUFF!
HAA...
THAT'LL BUY ME TIME TILL I'M LESS SHAKY. THEN I CAN TAKE THIS MASK ON!

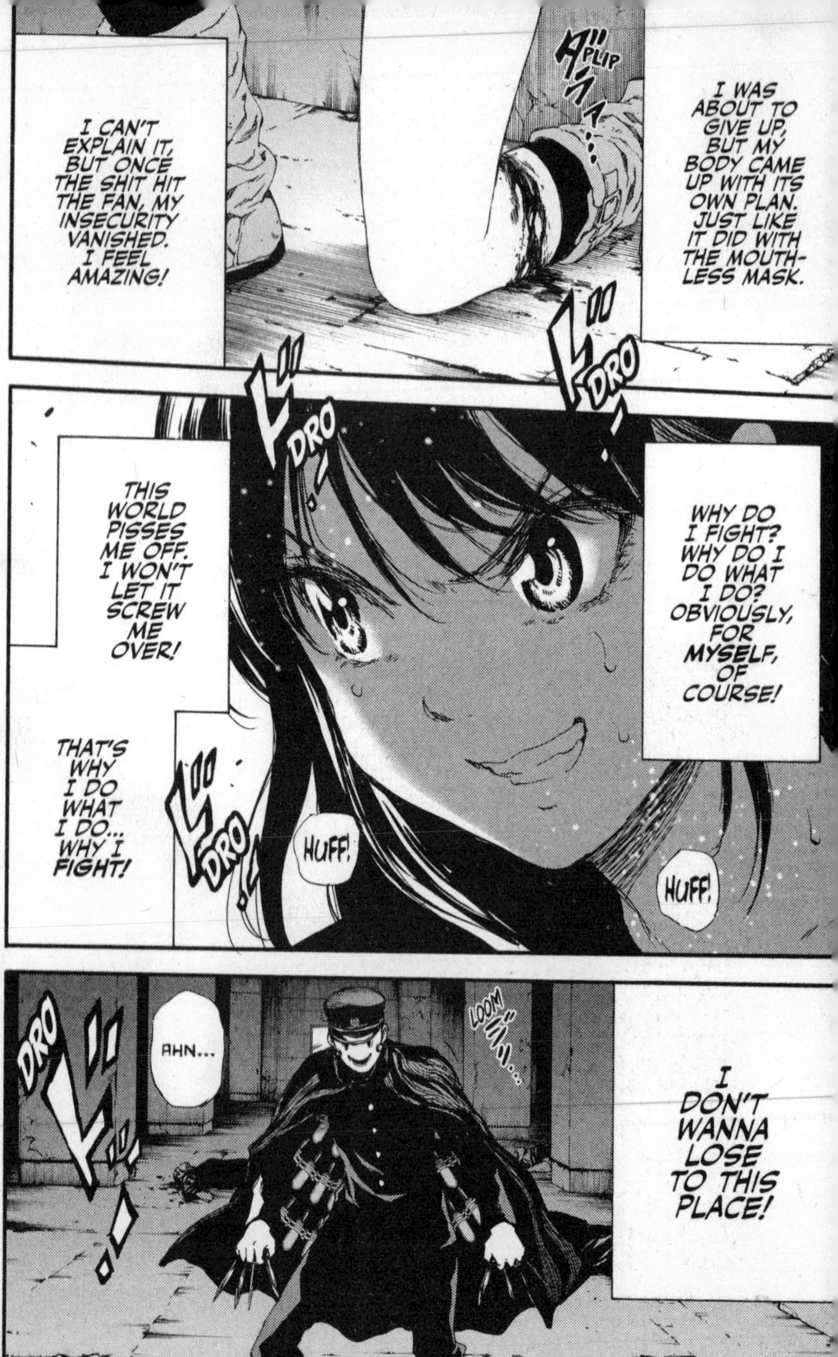
PLIP
I WAS ABOUT TO GIVE UP, BUT MY BODY CAME UP WITH ITS OWN PLAN. JUST LIKE IT DID WITH THE MOUTH-LESS MASK.
DRO
I CAN'T EXPLAIN IT, BUT ONCE THE SHIT HIT THE FAN, MY INSECURITY VANISHED. I FEEL AMAZING!
DRO
WHY DO I FIGHT? WHY DO I DO WHAT I DO? OBVIOUSLY, FOR MYSELF, OF COURSE!
HUFF!
THIS WORLD PISSES ME OFF. I WON'T LET IT SCREW ME OVER!
HUFF!
DRO
THAT'S WHY I DO WHAT I DO... WHY I FIGHT!
I DON'T WANNA LOSE TO THIS PLACE!
LOOM
AHN...
DRO

Volume 10: cover (rough)

HIGH-RISE INVASION

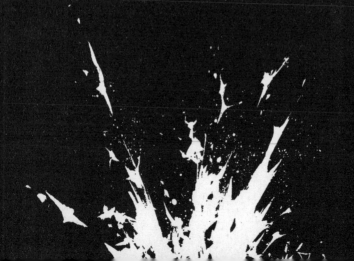

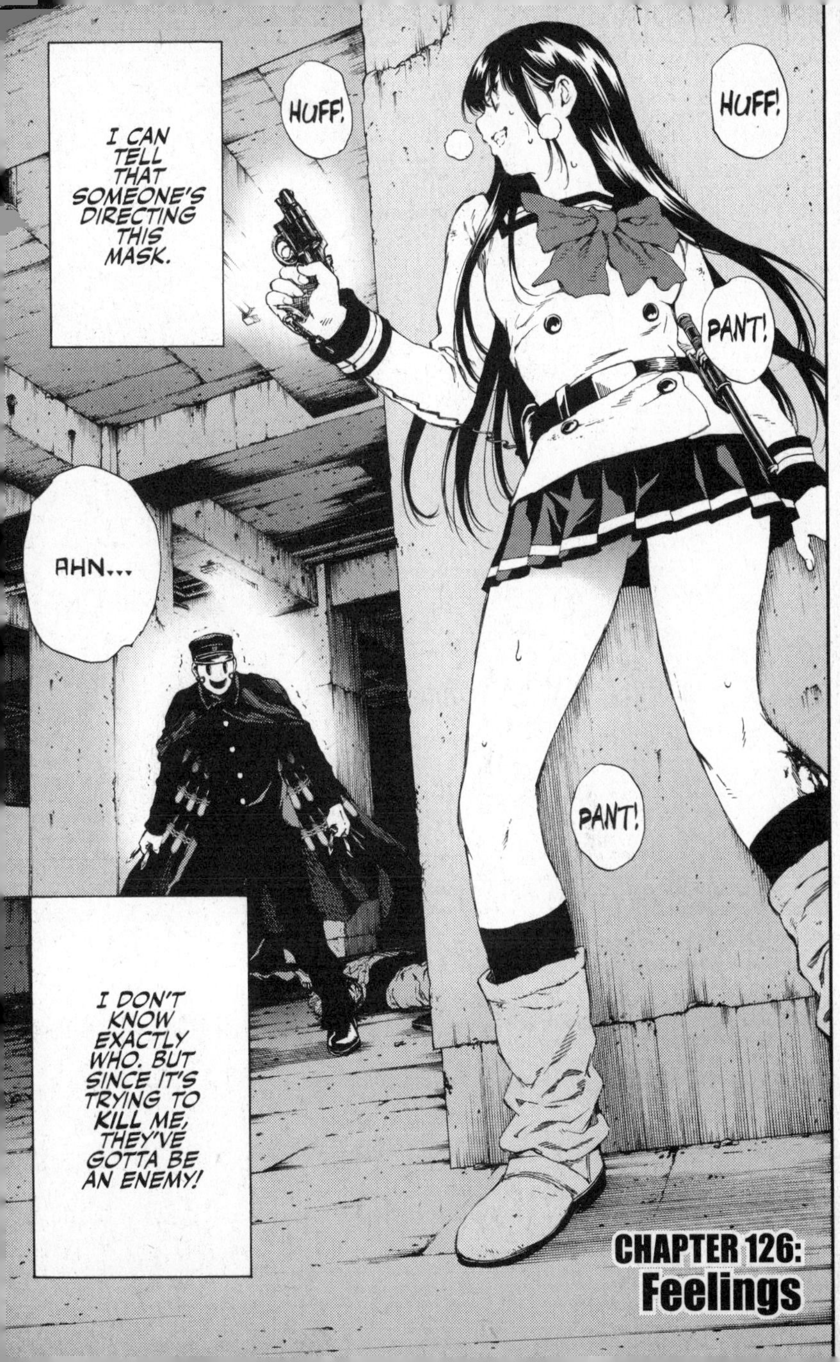
HUFF!
HUFF!
I CAN TELL THAT SOMEONE'S DIRECTING THIS MASK.
PANT!
AHN...
PANT!
I DON'T KNOW EXACTLY WHO. BUT SINCE IT'S TRYING TO KILL ME, THEY'VE GOTTA BE AN ENEMY!

CHAPTER 126: Feelings

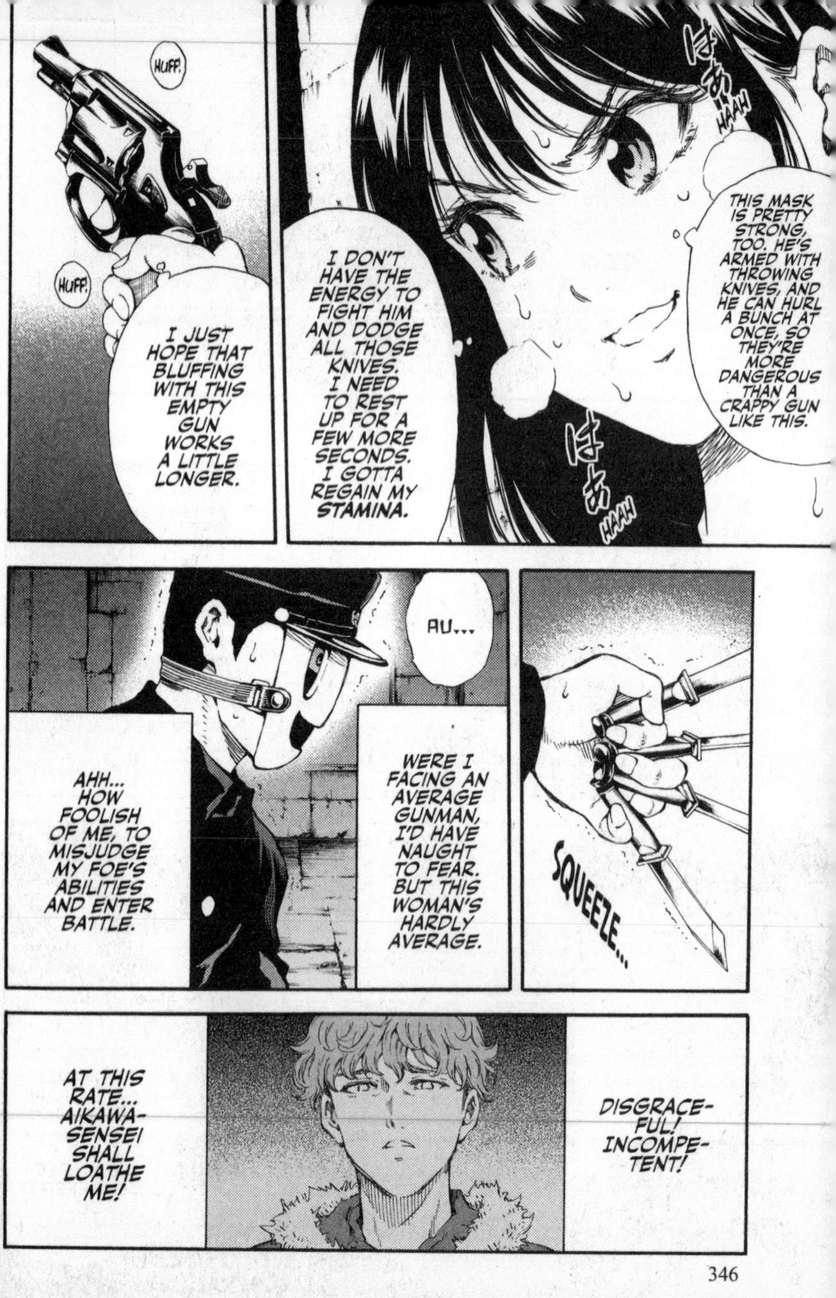

HAAH
THIS MASK IS PRETTY STRONG, TOO. HE'S ARMED WITH THROWING KNIVES, AND HE CAN HURL A BUNCH AT ONCE, SO THEY'RE MORE DANGEROUS THAN A CRAPPY GUN LIKE THIS.
I DON'T HAVE THE ENERGY TO FIGHT HIM AND DODGE ALL THOSE KNIVES. I NEED TO REST UP FOR A FEW MORE SECONDS. I GOTTA REGAIN MY STAMINA.
HAAH
HUFF!
HUFF!
I JUST HOPE THAT BLUFFING WITH THIS EMPTY GUN WORKS A LITTLE LONGER.
SQUEEZE...
AU...
WERE I FACING AN AVERAGE GUNMAN, I'D HAVE NAUGHT TO FEAR. BUT THIS WOMAN'S HARDLY AVERAGE.
AHH... HOW FOOLISH OF ME, TO MISJUDGE MY FOE'S ABILITIES AND ENTER BATTLE.
DISGRACE-FUL! INCOMPE-TENT!
AT THIS RATE... AIKAWA-SENSEI SHALL LOATHE ME!

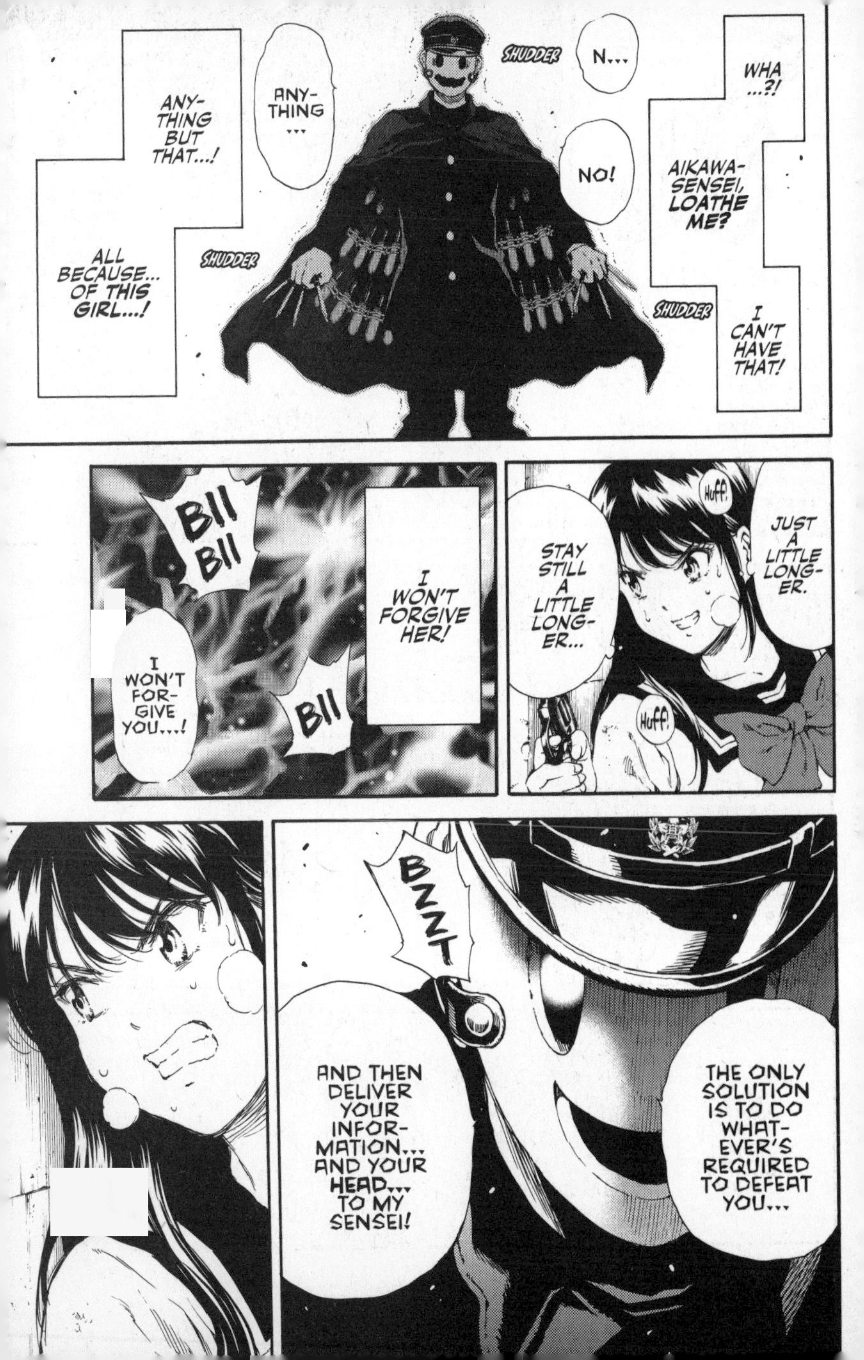
WHA ...?!
AIKAWA-SENSEI, LOATHE ME?
I CAN'T HAVE THAT!
SHUDDER
N...
NO!
SHUDDER
ANYTHING...
ANYTHING BUT THAT...!
ALL BECAUSE... OF THIS GIRL...!
SHUDDER
JUST A LITTLE LONGER.
Huff!
STAY STILL A LITTLE LONGER...
Huff!
I WON'T FORGIVE HER!
BII BII
BII
I WON'T FORGIVE YOU...!
BZZT
THE ONLY SOLUTION IS TO DO WHATEVER'S REQUIRED TO DEFEAT YOU...
AND THEN DELIVER YOUR INFORMATION... AND YOUR HEAD... TO MY SENSEI!

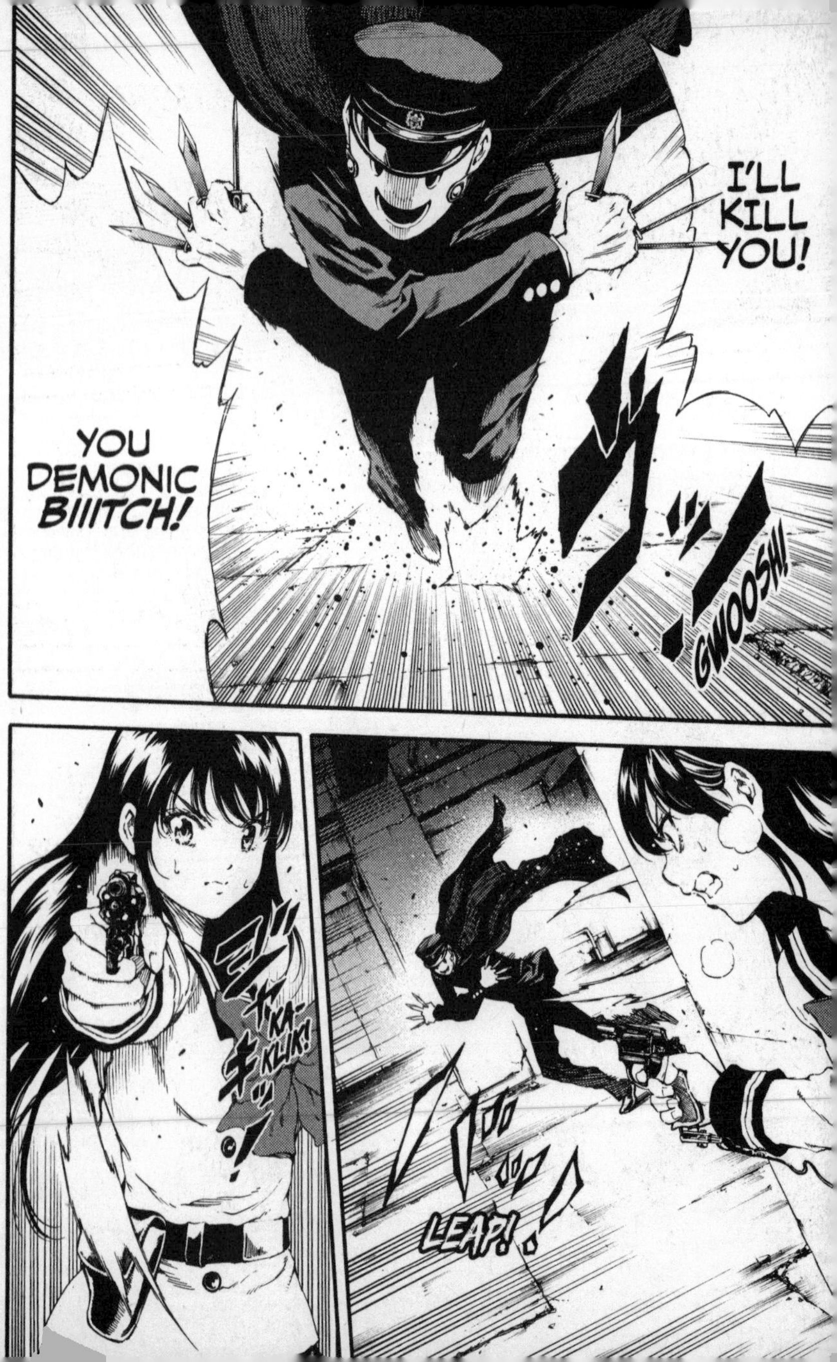
I'LL KILL YOU!
YOU DEMONIC BIIITCH!
GWOOSH!
LEAP!
KA-KLIK!

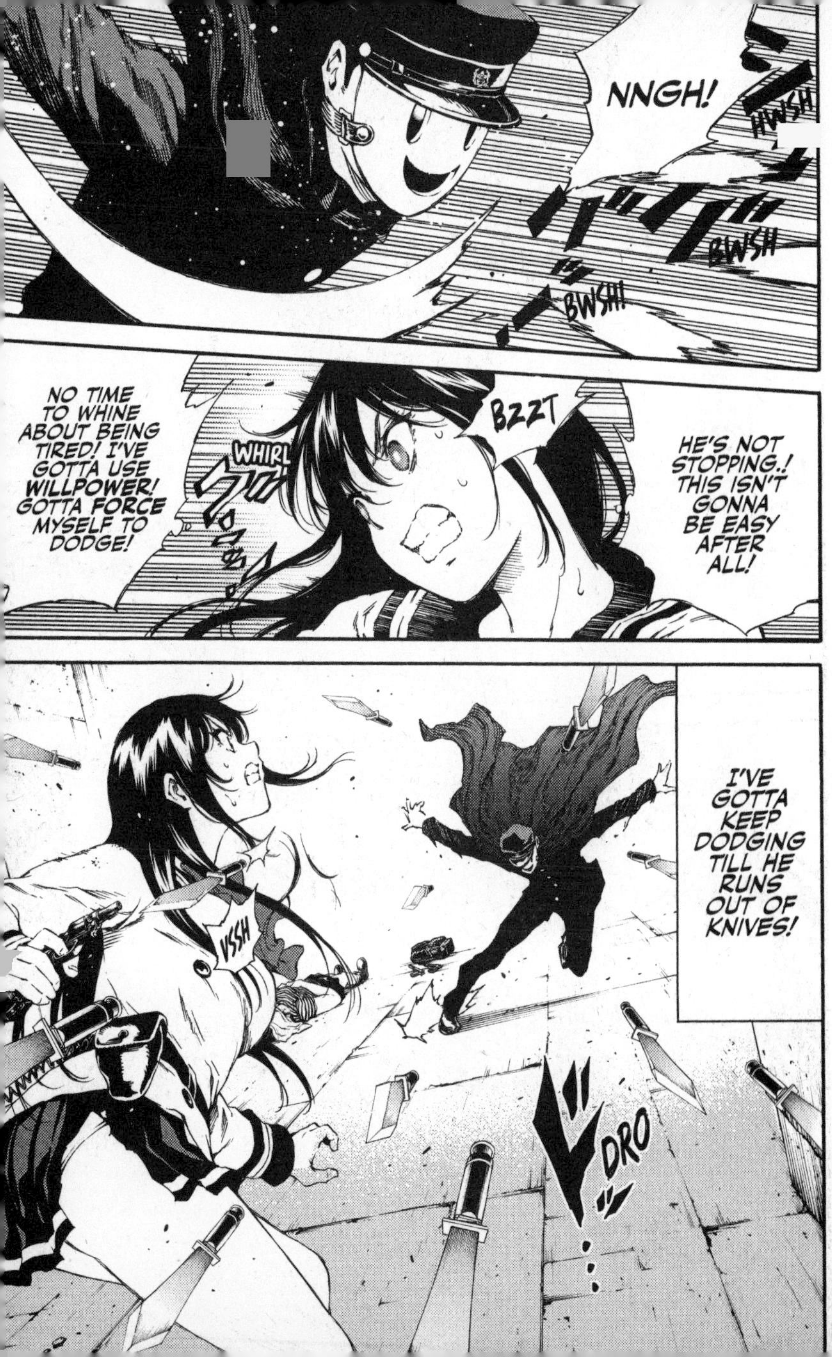
HWSH
NNGH!
BWSH
BWSH!
HE'S NOT STOPPING..! THIS ISN'T GONNA BE EASY AFTER ALL!
BZZT
WHIRL
NO TIME TO WHINE ABOUT BEING TIRED! I'VE GOTTA USE WILLPOWER! GOTTA FORCE MYSELF TO DODGE!
I'VE GOTTA KEEP DODGING TILL HE RUNS OUT OF KNIVES!
VSSH
DRO

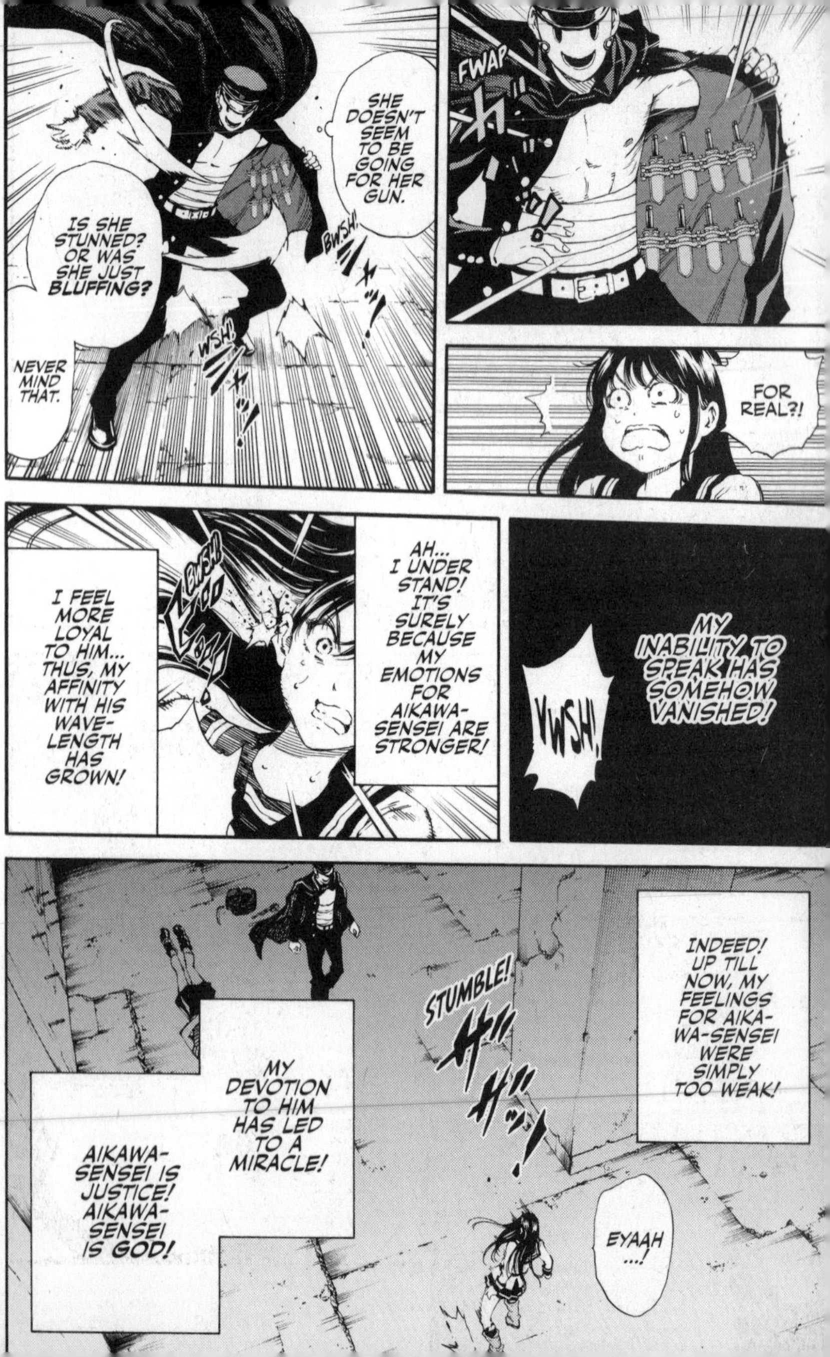
FWAP
FOR REAL?!
SHE DOESN'T SEEM TO BE GOING FOR HER GUN.
IS SHE STUNNED? OR WAS SHE JUST BLUFFING?
BWSH!
WSH!
NEVER MIND THAT.
MY INABILITY TO SPEAK HAS SOMEHOW VANISHED!
VWSH!
AH... I UNDER STAND! IT'S SURELY BECAUSE MY EMOTIONS FOR AIKAWA-SENSEI ARE STRONGER!
BWSH!
I FEEL MORE LOYAL TO HIM... THUS, MY AFFINITY WITH HIS WAVE-LENGTH HAS GROWN!
INDEED! UP TILL NOW, MY FEELINGS FOR AIKAWA-SENSEI WERE SIMPLY TOO WEAK!
STUMBLE!
EYAAH ...!
MY DEVOTION TO HIM HAS LED TO A MIRACLE!
AIKAWA-SENSEI IS JUSTICE! AIKAWA-SENSEI IS GOD!

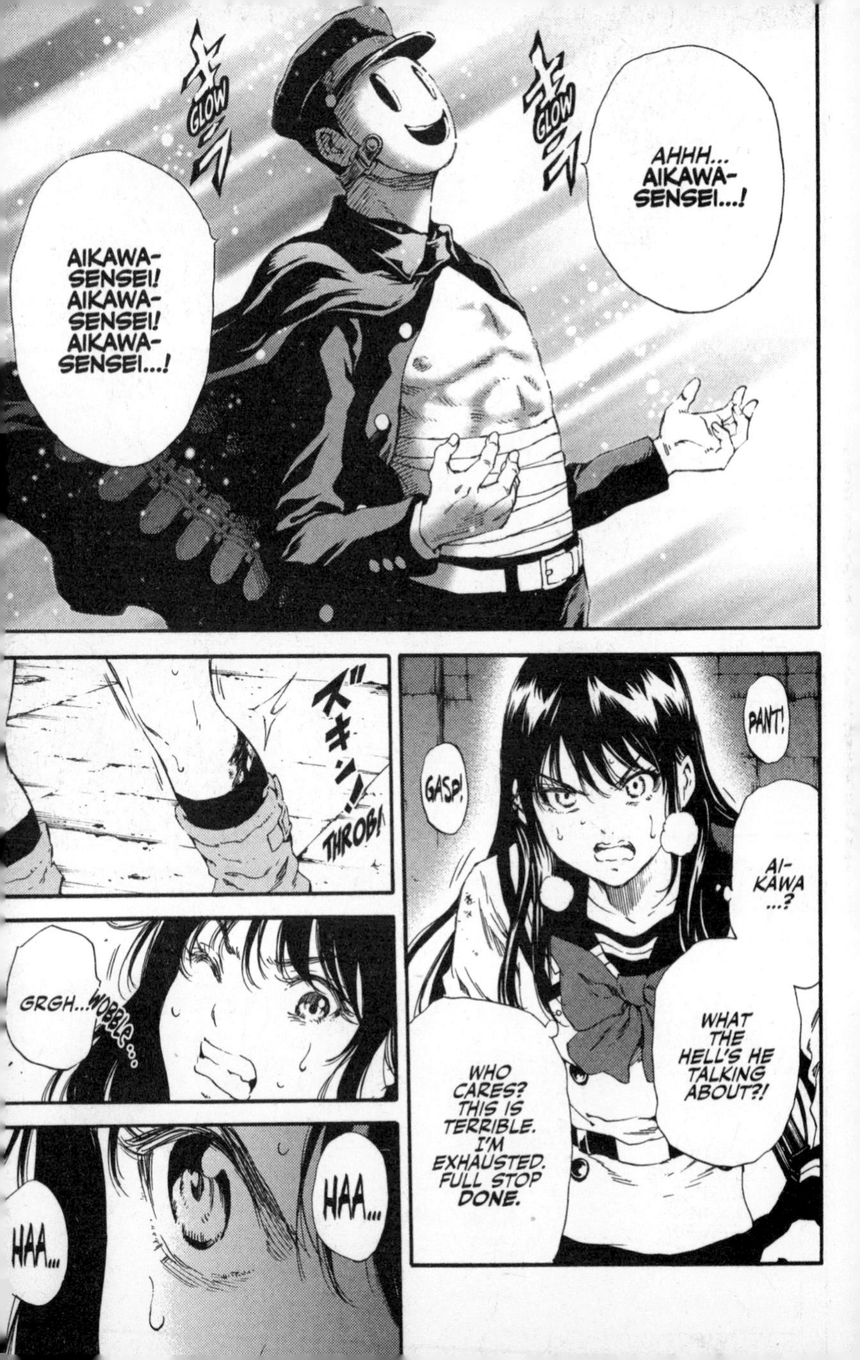
AHHH... AIKAWA-SENSEI...!
GLOW
GLOW
AIKAWA-SENSEI! AIKAWA-SENSEI! AIKAWA-SENSEI...!
PANT!
GASP!
AI-KAWA ...?
WHAT THE HELL'S HE TALKING ABOUT?!
WHO CARES? THIS IS TERRIBLE. I'M EXHAUSTED. FULL STOP DONE.
THROB!
GRGH...
WOBBLE...
HAA...
HAA...

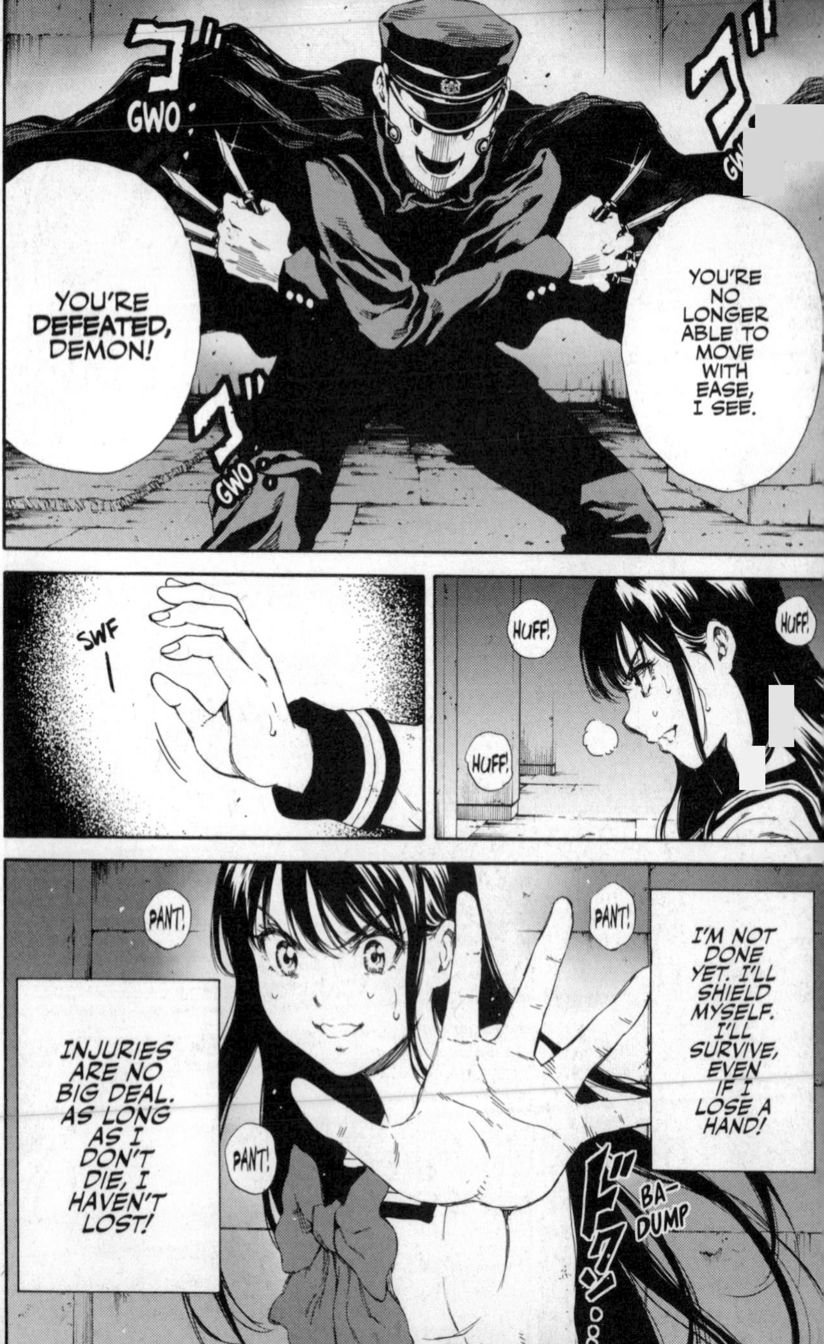
GWO
YOU'RE NO LONGER ABLE TO MOVE WITH EASE, I SEE.
GWO
YOU'RE DEFEATED, DEMON!
GWO
HUFF!
HUFF!
HUFF!
SWF
PANT!
I'M NOT DONE YET. I'LL SHIELD MYSELF. I'LL SURVIVE, EVEN IF I LOSE A HAND!
PANT!
BA-DUMP
INJURIES ARE NO BIG DEAL. AS LONG AS I DON'T DIE, I HAVEN'T LOST!
PANT!

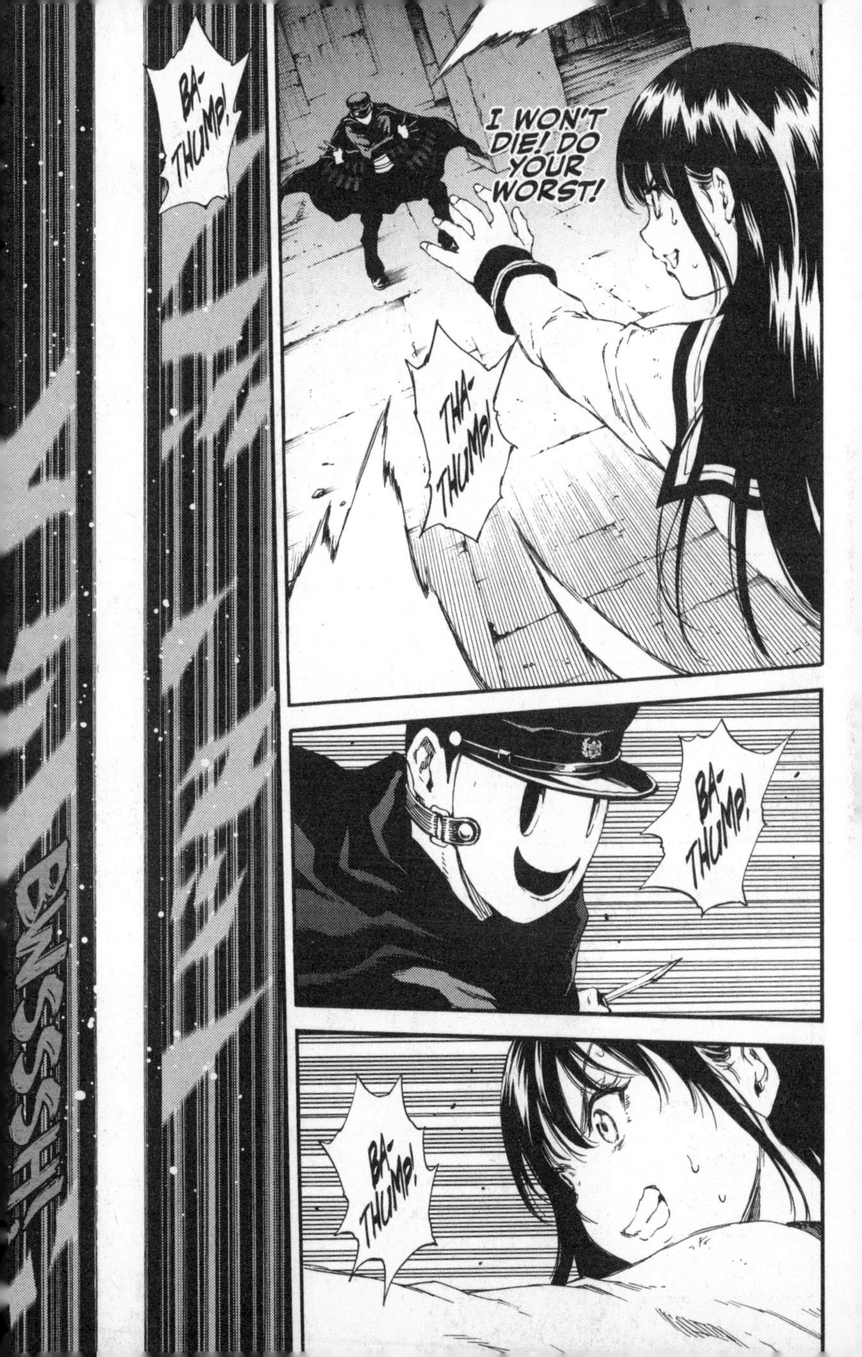
I WON'T DIE! DO YOUR WORST!
THA-THUMP!
BA-THUMP!
BA-THUMP!
BA-THUMP!
BWSSHH!

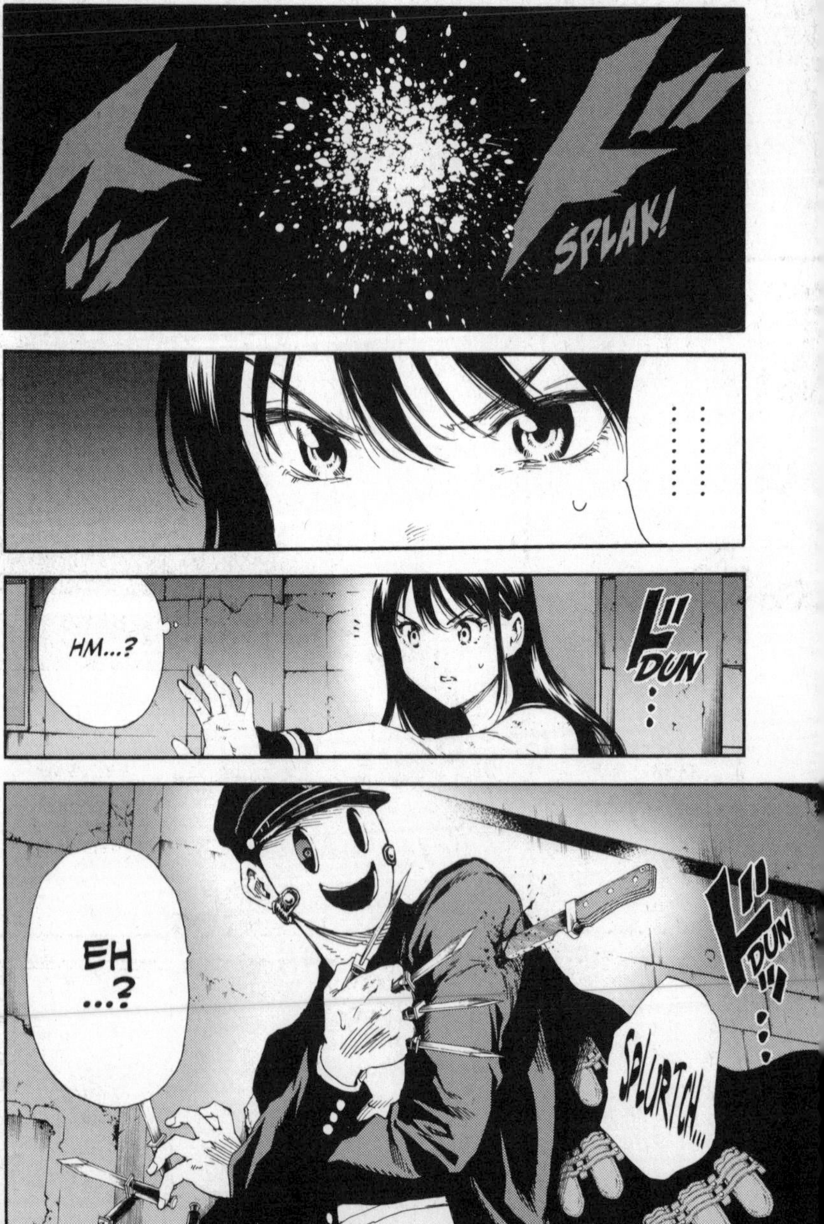
SPLAK!
......
DUN...
HM...?
DUN!!...
SPLURTCH...
EH ...?

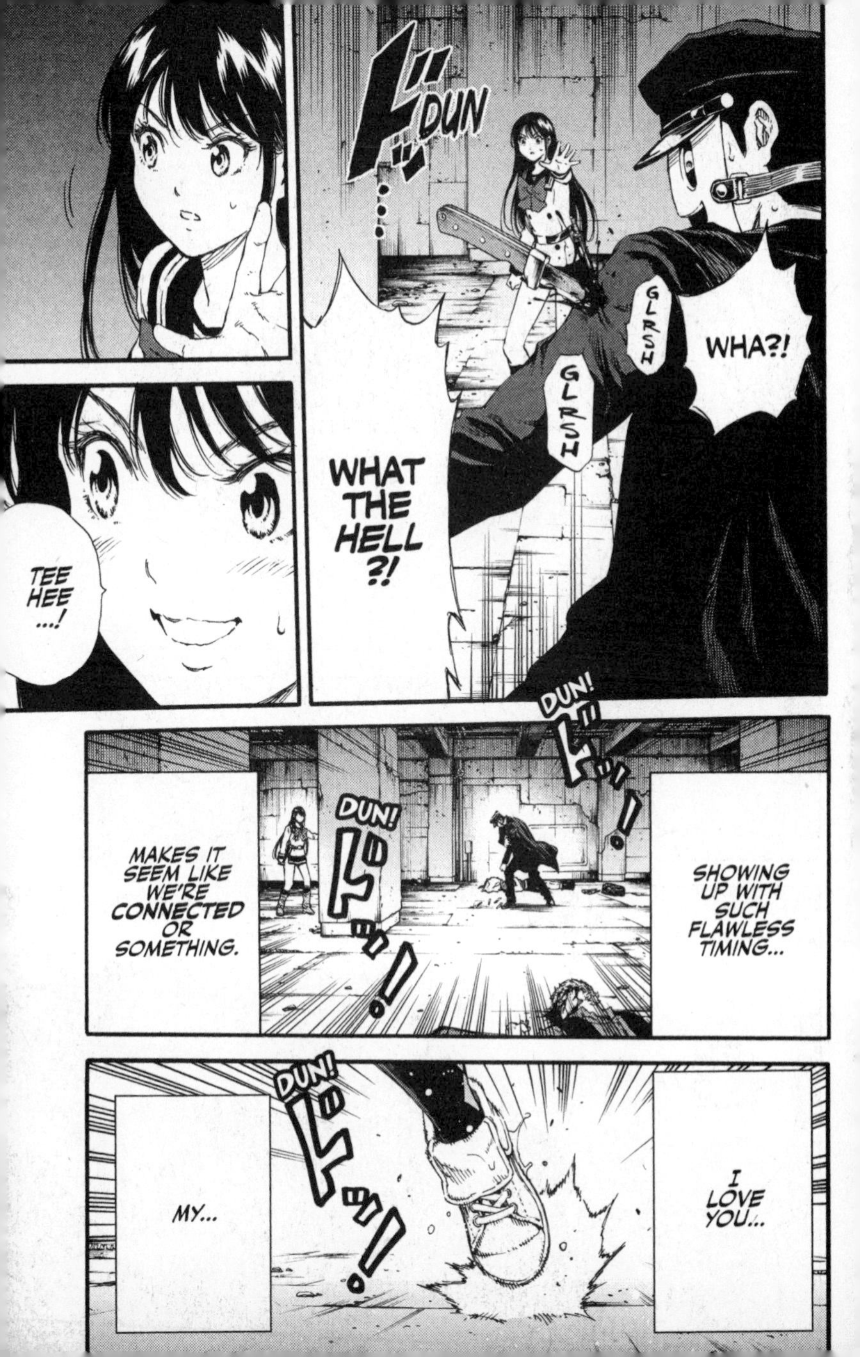
WHA?!
GLRSH
GLRSH
DUN
...
WHAT THE HELL ?!
TEE HEE ...!
DUN!
SHOWING UP WITH SUCH FLAWLESS TIMING...
DUN!
MAKES IT SEEM LIKE WE'RE CONNECTED OR SOMETHING.
I LOVE YOU...
DUN!
MY...

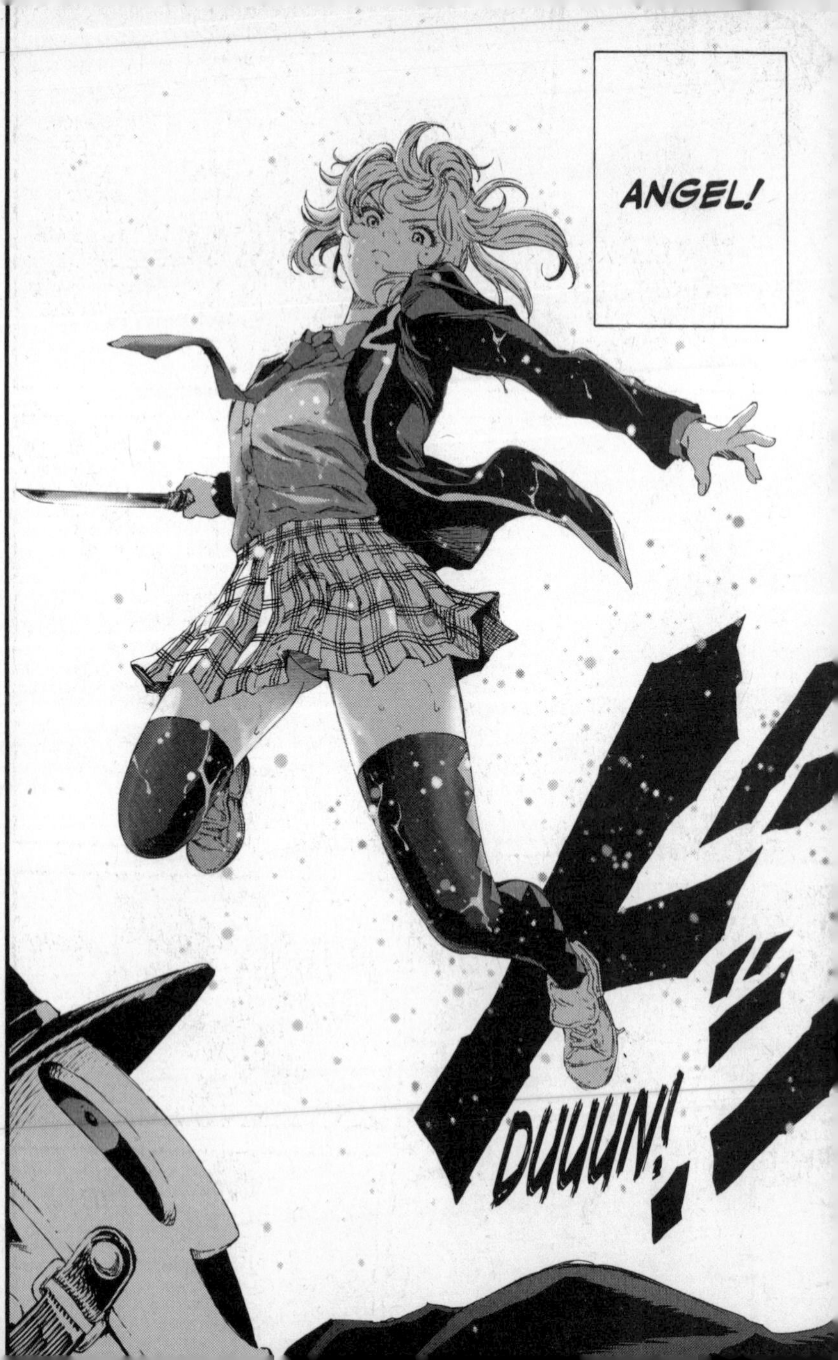
ANGEL!
DUUUN!

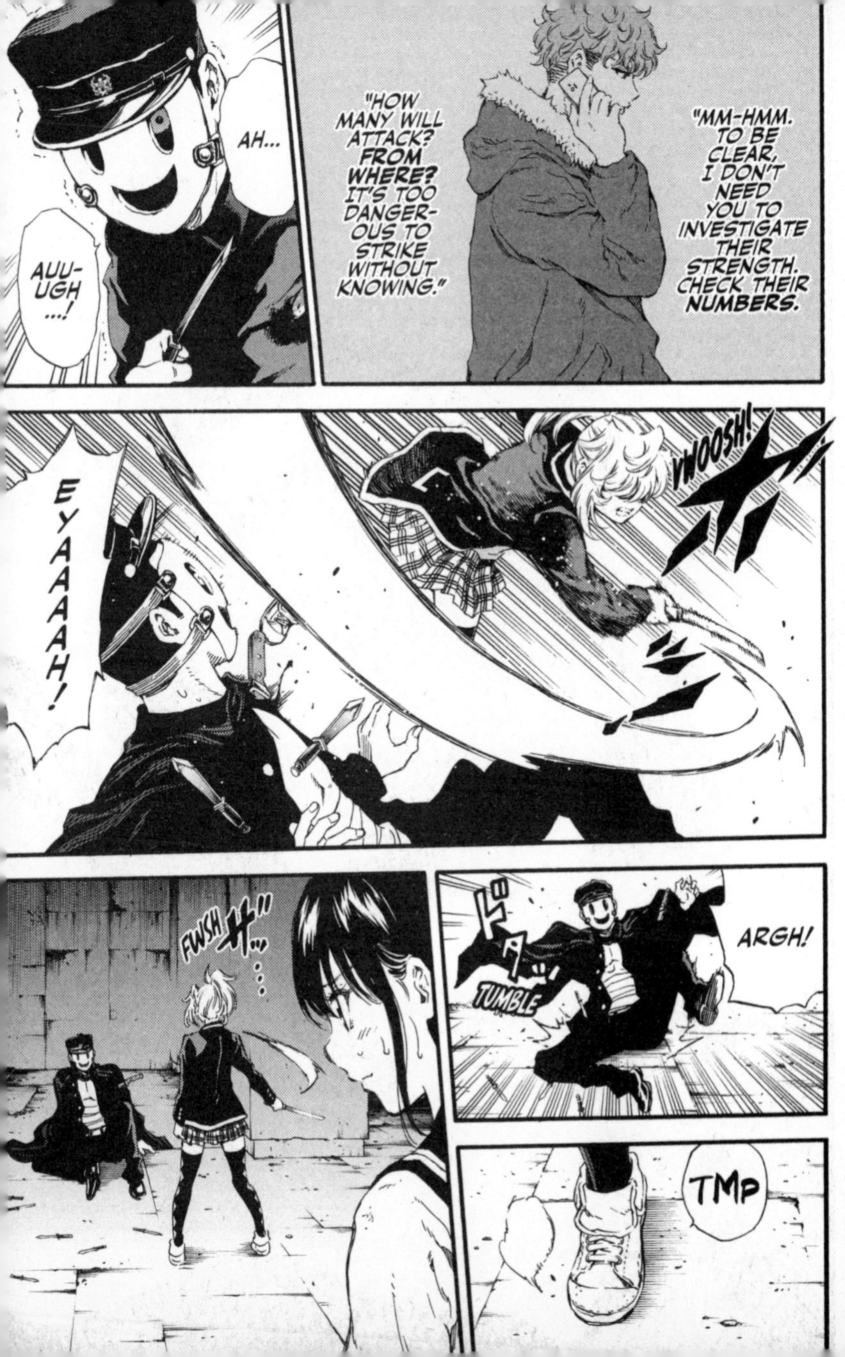
"MM-HMM. TO BE CLEAR, I DON'T NEED YOU TO INVESTIGATE THEIR STRENGTH. CHECK THEIR NUMBERS.
"HOW MANY WILL ATTACK? FROM WHERE? IT'S TOO DANGER-OUS TO STRIKE WITHOUT KNOWING."
AH...
AUU-UGH ...!
VWOOSH!
EYAAAAAH!
ARGH!
TUMBLE
TMP
FWSH
...

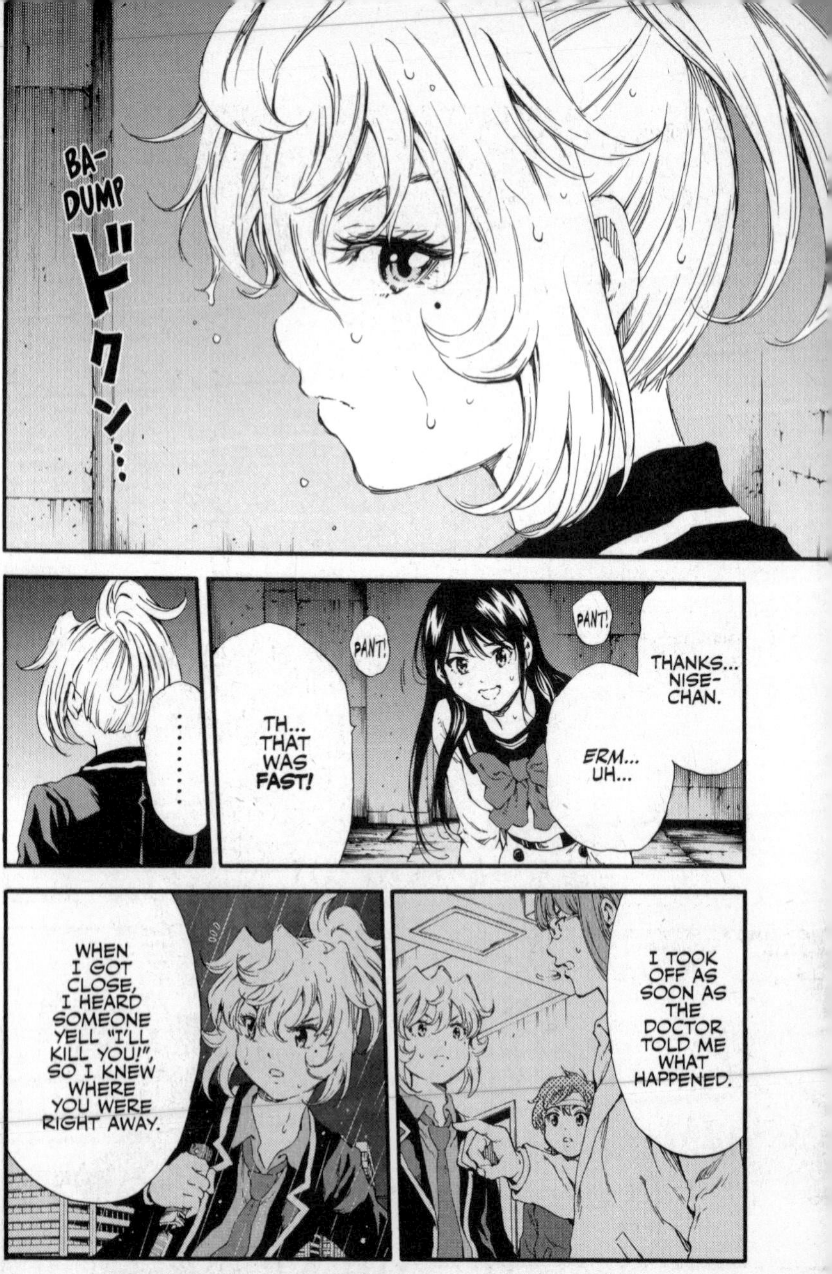
BA-DUMP
ドクン…
PANT!
THANKS... NISE-CHAN.
PANT!
ERM... UH...
TH... THAT WAS FAST!
......
I TOOK OFF AS SOON AS THE DOCTOR TOLD ME WHAT HAPPENED.
WHEN I GOT CLOSE, I HEARD SOMEONE YELL "I'LL KILL YOU!", SO I KNEW WHERE YOU WERE RIGHT AWAY.

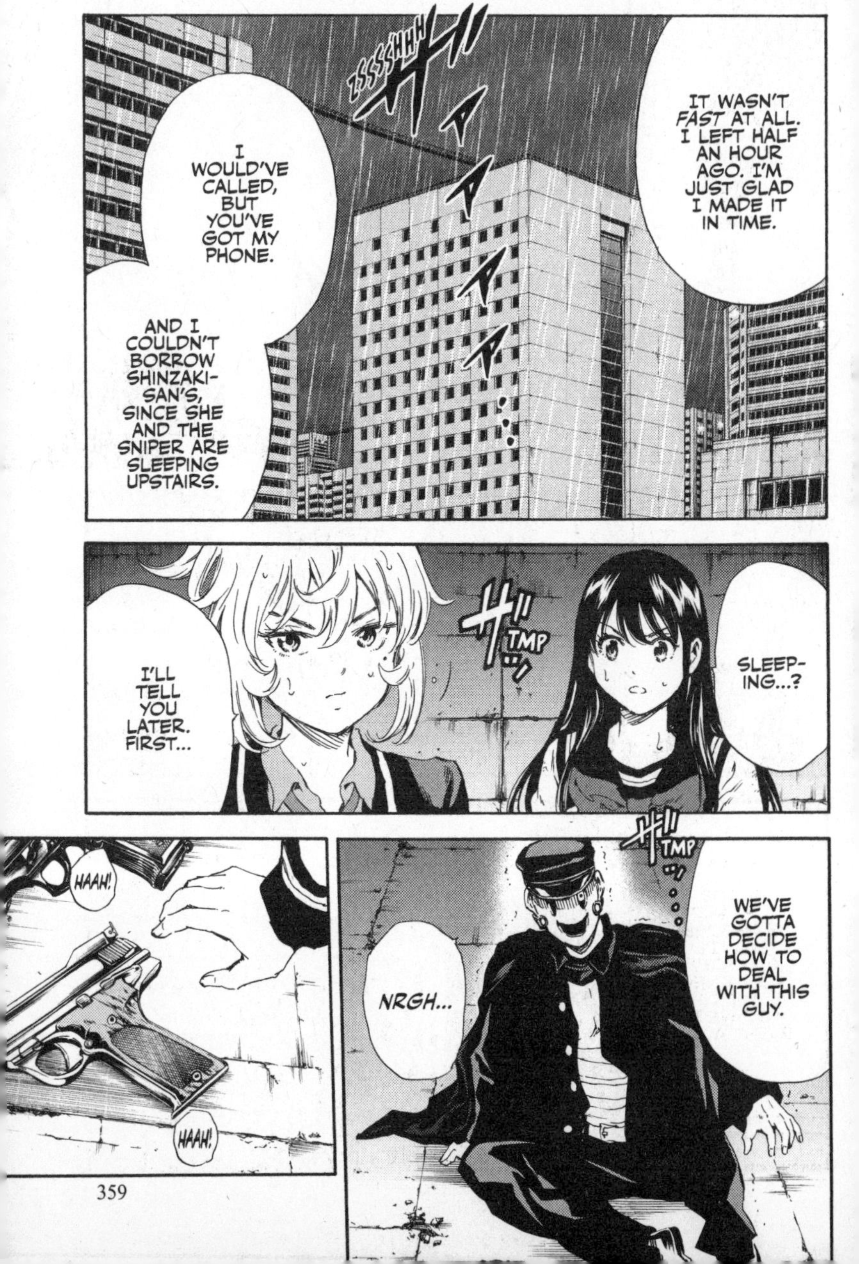

IT WASN'T *FAST* AT ALL. I LEFT HALF AN HOUR AGO. I'M JUST GLAD I MADE IT IN TIME.
ZSSSSHHH
I WOULD'VE CALLED, BUT YOU'VE GOT MY PHONE.
AND I COULDN'T BORROW SHINZAKI-SAN'S, SINCE SHE AND THE SNIPER ARE SLEEPING UPSTAIRS.
SLEEP-ING...?
TMP
I'LL TELL YOU LATER. FIRST...
TMP
WE'VE GOTTA DECIDE HOW TO DEAL WITH THIS GUY.
NRGH...
HAAH!
HAAH!

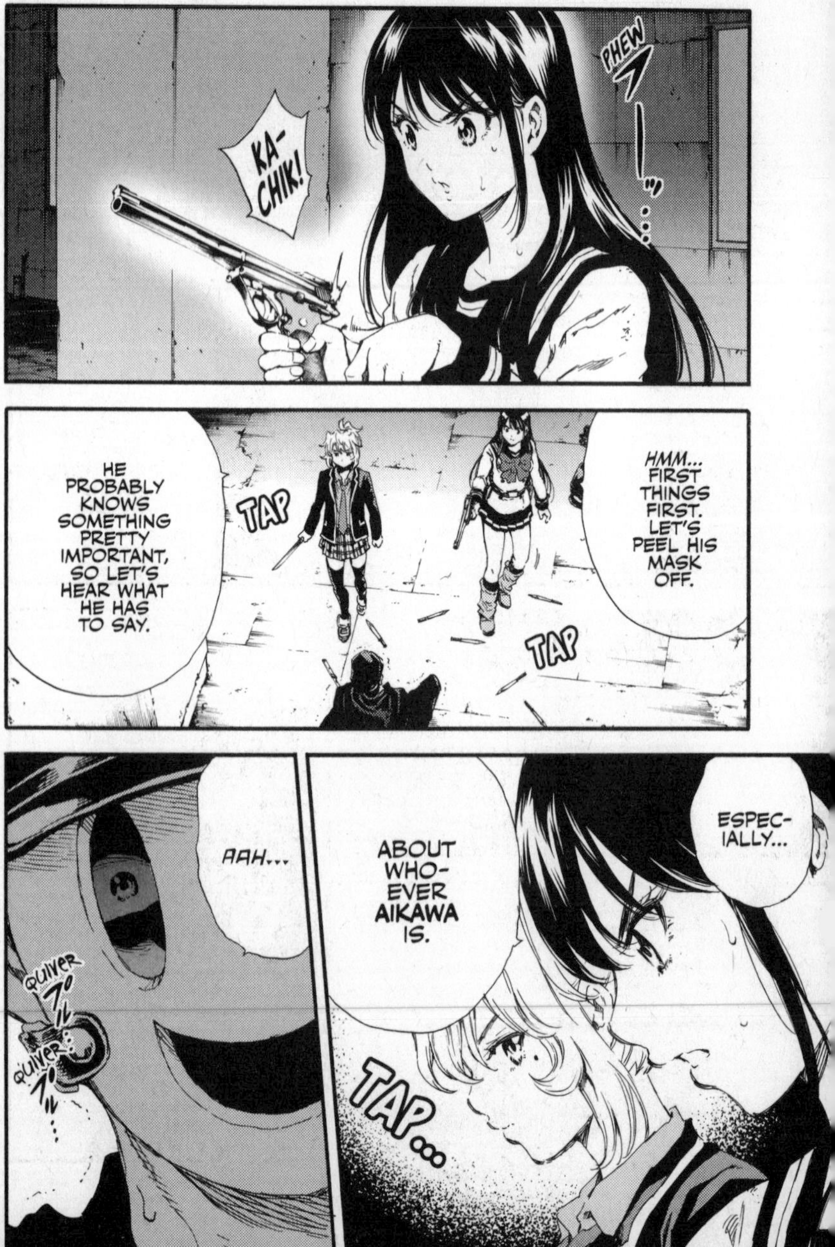
PHEW
KA-CHIK!
HMM... FIRST THINGS FIRST. LET'S PEEL HIS MASK OFF.
TAP
HE PROBABLY KNOWS SOMETHING PRETTY IMPORTANT, SO LET'S HEAR WHAT HE HAS TO SAY.
TAP
ESPEC-IALLY...
ABOUT WHO-EVER AIKAWA IS.
TAP...
AAH...
QUIVER
QUIVER

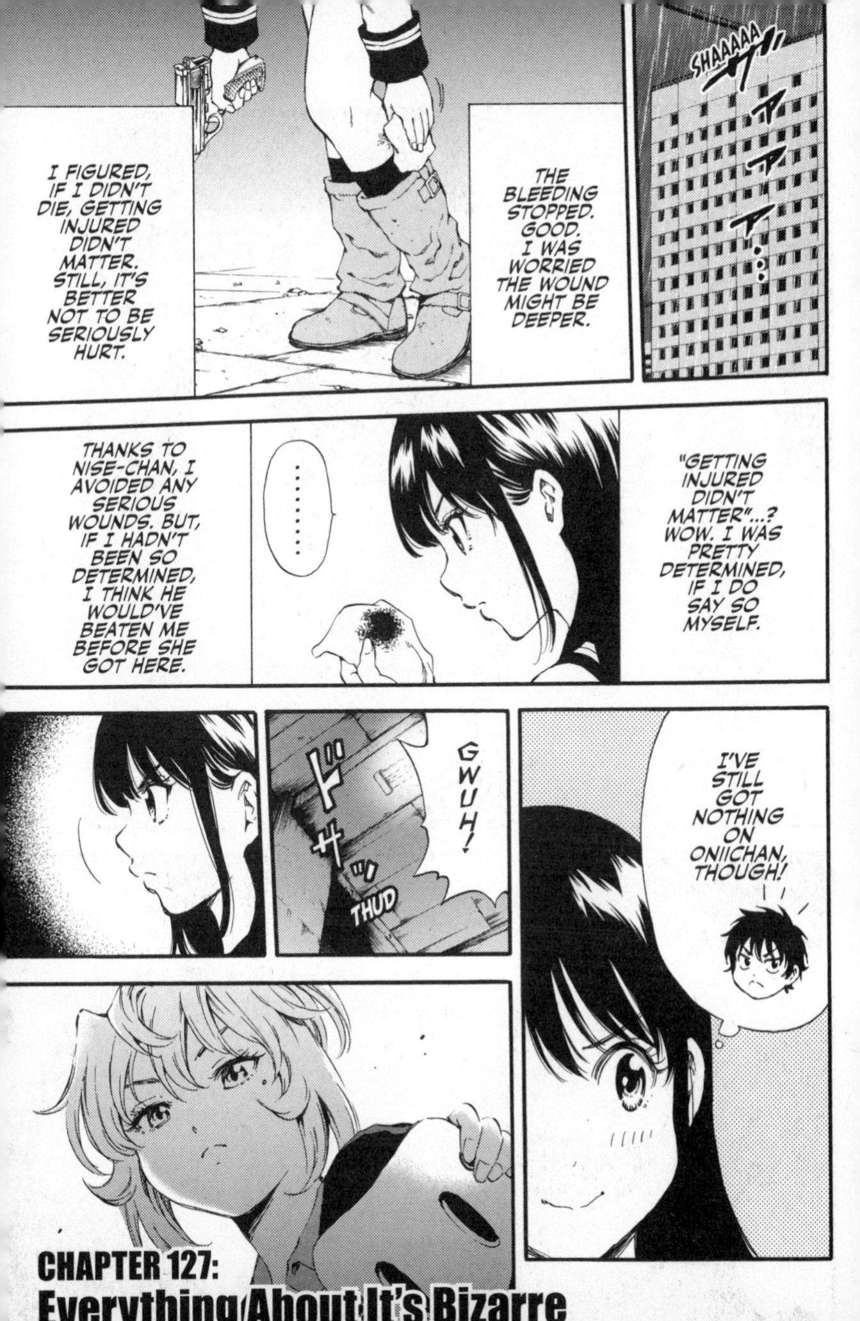
SHAAAAA
THE BLEEDING STOPPED. GOOD. I WAS WORRIED THE WOUND MIGHT BE DEEPER.
I FIGURED, IF I DIDN'T DIE, GETTING INJURED DIDN'T MATTER. STILL, IT'S BETTER NOT TO BE SERIOUSLY HURT.
"GETTING INJURED DIDN'T MATTER"...? WOW. I WAS PRETTY DETERMINED, IF I DO SAY SO MYSELF.
....
THANKS TO NISE-CHAN, I AVOIDED ANY SERIOUS WOUNDS. BUT, IF I HADN'T BEEN SO DETERMINED, I THINK HE WOULD'VE BEATEN ME BEFORE SHE GOT HERE.
I'VE STILL GOT NOTHING ON ONIICHAN, THOUGH!
GWUH!
THUD

CHAPTER 127:
Everything About It's Bizarre

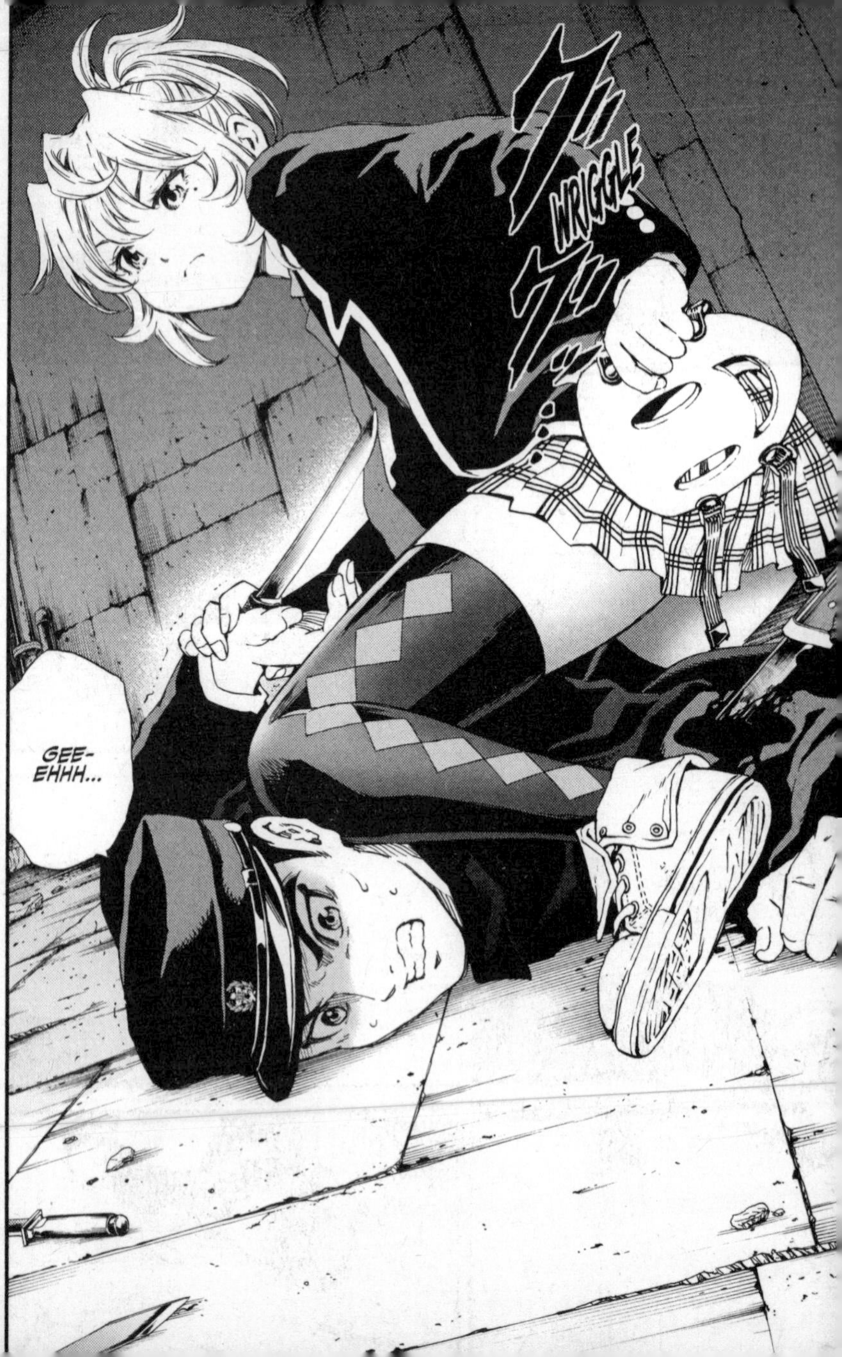
WRIGGLE
GEE-
EHHH...

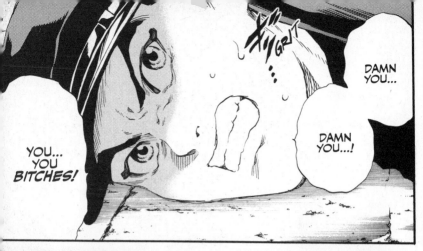

DAMN
YOU...

DAMN
YOU...!

YOU...
YOU
BITCHES!

GAAH!

IF
I HAD
MY WAY,
I'D KILL
YOU
RIGHT
NOW.

BUT
WE'VE
GOT
STUFF
TO ASK
YOU, SO
I'LL LET
YOU LIVE
A WHILE.

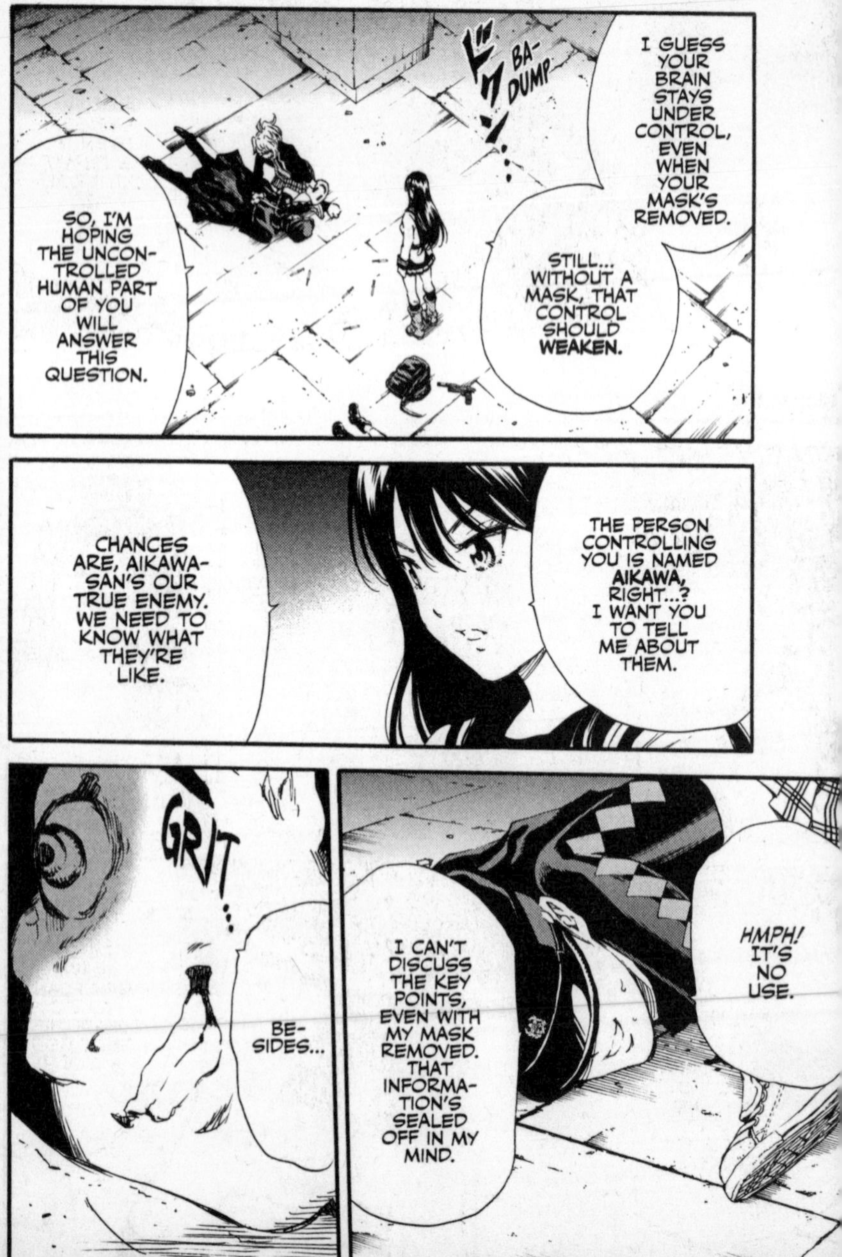
I GUESS YOUR BRAIN STAYS UNDER CONTROL, EVEN WHEN YOUR MASK'S REMOVED.
BA-DUMP
STILL... WITHOUT A MASK, THAT CONTROL SHOULD WEAKEN.
SO, I'M HOPING THE UNCONTROLLED HUMAN PART OF YOU WILL ANSWER THIS QUESTION.
THE PERSON CONTROLLING YOU IS NAMED AIKAWA, RIGHT...? I WANT YOU TO TELL ME ABOUT THEM.
CHANCES ARE, AIKAWA-SAN'S OUR TRUE ENEMY. WE NEED TO KNOW WHAT THEY'RE LIKE.
HMPH! IT'S NO USE.
I CAN'T DISCUSS THE KEY POINTS, EVEN WITH MY MASK REMOVED. THAT INFORMATION'S SEALED OFF IN MY MIND.
GRIT...
BESIDES...

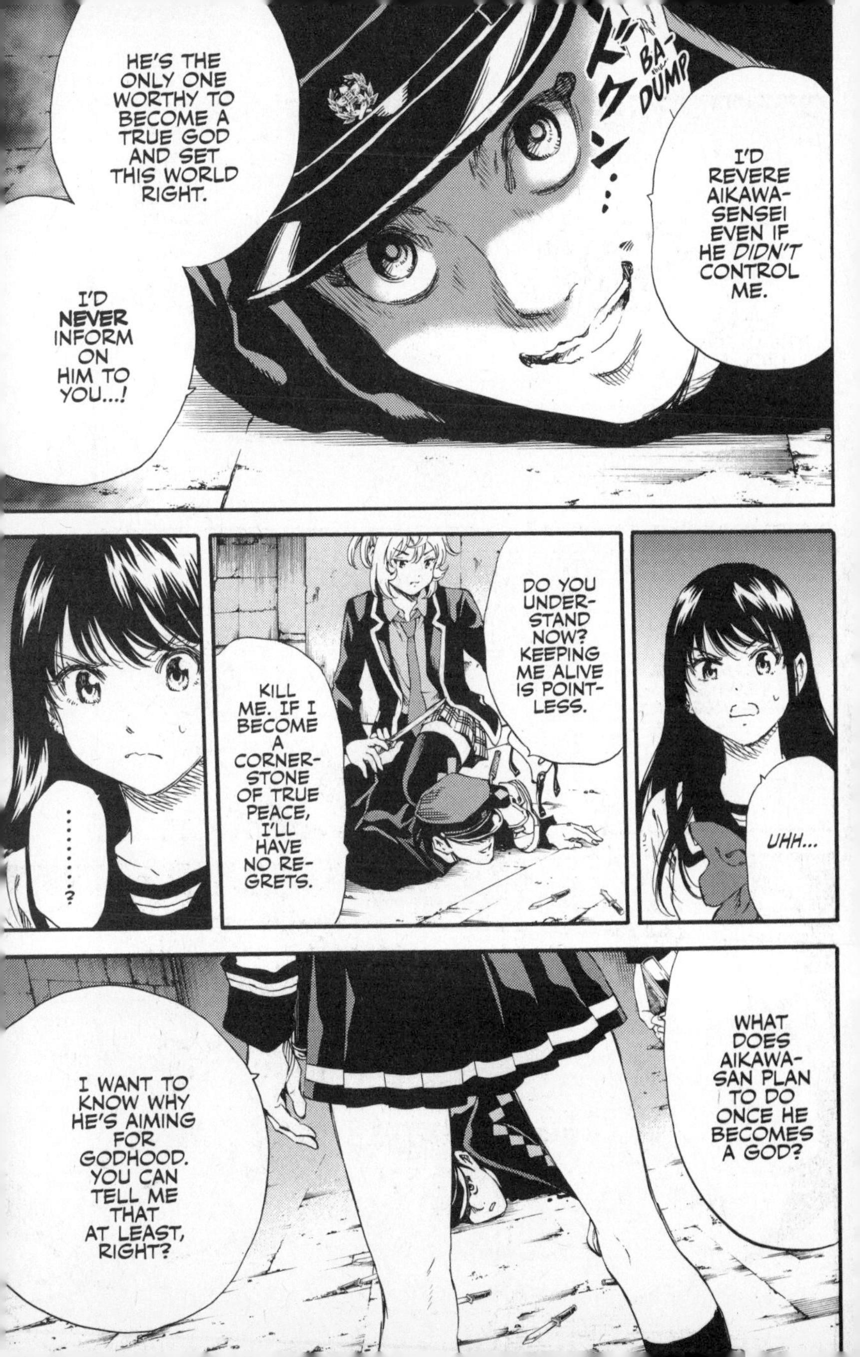
BA-DUMP
I'D REVERE AIKAWA-SENSEI EVEN IF HE *DIDN'T* CONTROL ME.
HE'S THE ONLY ONE WORTHY TO BECOME A TRUE GOD AND SET THIS WORLD RIGHT.
I'D **NEVER** INFORM ON HIM TO YOU...!
UHH...
DO YOU UNDER-STAND NOW? KEEPING ME ALIVE IS POINT-LESS.
KILL ME. IF I BECOME A CORNER-STONE OF TRUE PEACE, I'LL HAVE NO RE-GRETS.
......?
WHAT DOES AIKAWA-SAN PLAN TO DO ONCE HE BECOMES A GOD?
I WANT TO KNOW WHY HE'S AIMING FOR GODHOOD. YOU CAN TELL ME THAT AT LEAST, RIGHT?

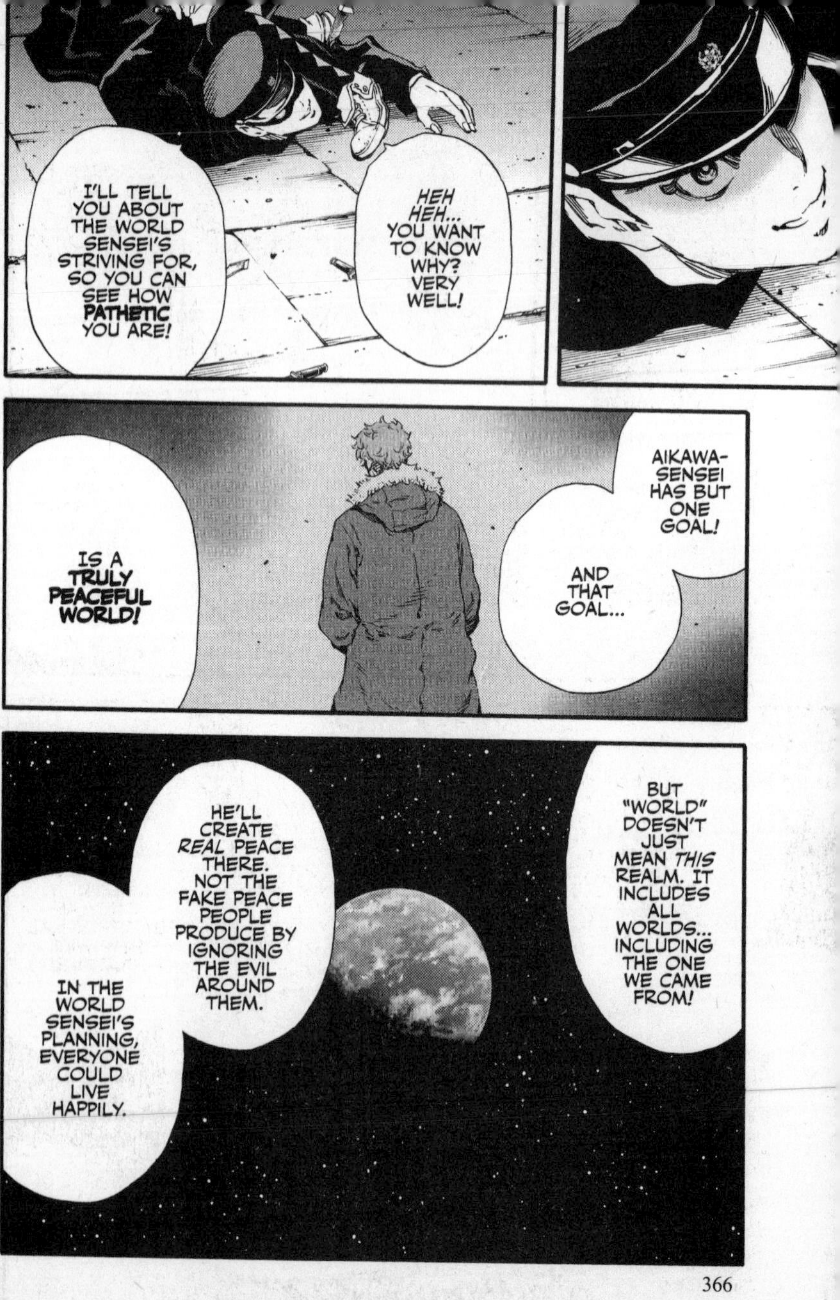
HEH HEH... YOU WANT TO KNOW WHY? VERY WELL!
I'LL TELL YOU ABOUT THE WORLD SENSEI'S STRIVING FOR, SO YOU CAN SEE HOW PATHETIC YOU ARE!
AIKAWA-SENSEI HAS BUT ONE GOAL!
AND THAT GOAL...
IS A TRULY PEACEFUL WORLD!
BUT "WORLD" DOESN'T JUST MEAN THIS REALM. IT INCLUDES ALL WORLDS... INCLUDING THE ONE WE CAME FROM!
HE'LL CREATE REAL PEACE THERE. NOT THE FAKE PEACE PEOPLE PRODUCE BY IGNORING THE EVIL AROUND THEM.
IN THE WORLD SENSEI'S PLANNING, EVERYONE COULD LIVE HAPPILY.

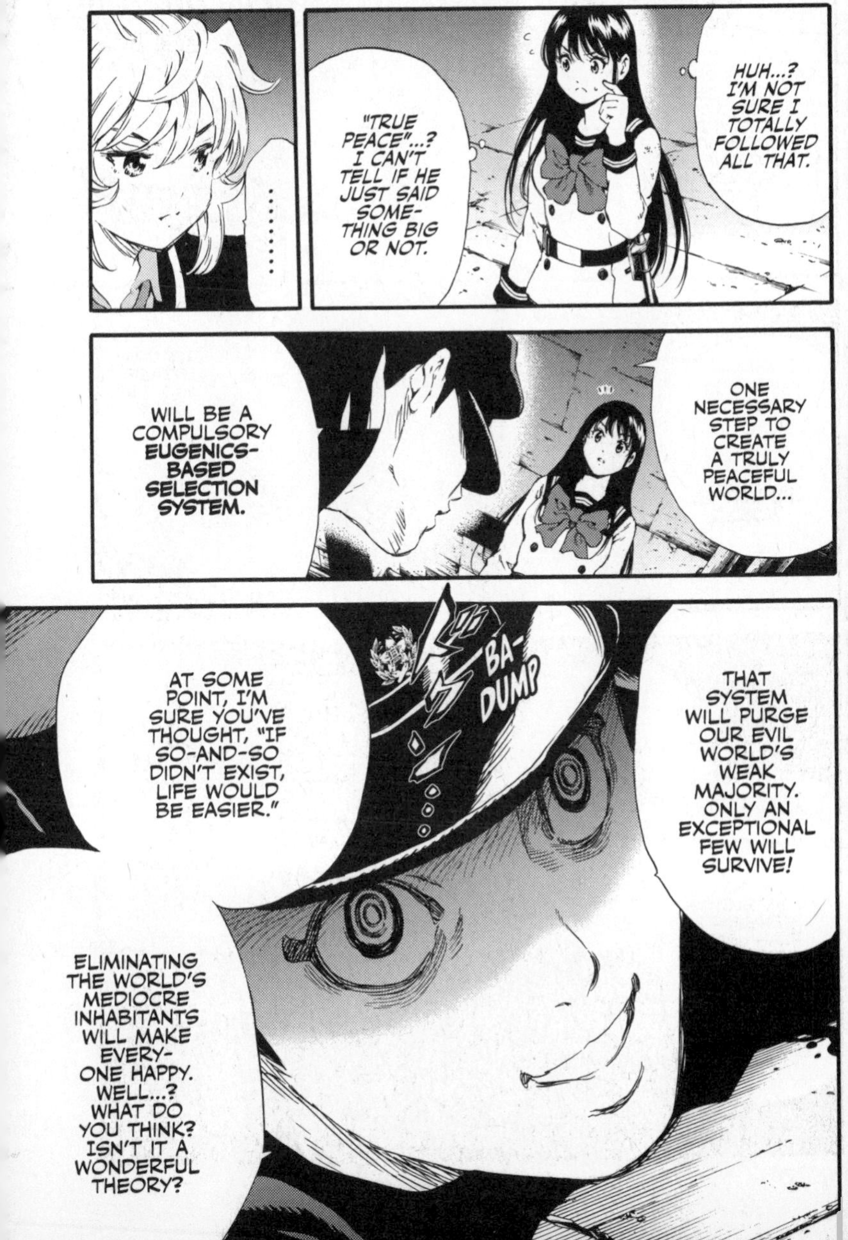
HUH...? I'M NOT SURE I TOTALLY FOLLOWED ALL THAT.
"TRUE PEACE"...? I CAN'T TELL IF HE JUST SAID SOME-THING BIG OR NOT.
....
ONE NECESSARY STEP TO CREATE A TRULY PEACEFUL WORLD...
WILL BE A COMPULSORY EUGENICS-BASED SELECTION SYSTEM.
THAT SYSTEM WILL PURGE OUR EVIL WORLD'S WEAK MAJORITY. ONLY AN EXCEPTIONAL FEW WILL SURVIVE!
BA-DUMP
AT SOME POINT, I'M SURE YOU'VE THOUGHT, "IF SO-AND-SO DIDN'T EXIST, LIFE WOULD BE EASIER."
ELIMINATING THE WORLD'S MEDIOCRE INHABITANTS WILL MAKE EVERY-ONE HAPPY. WELL...? WHAT DO YOU THINK? ISN'T IT A WONDERFUL THEORY?

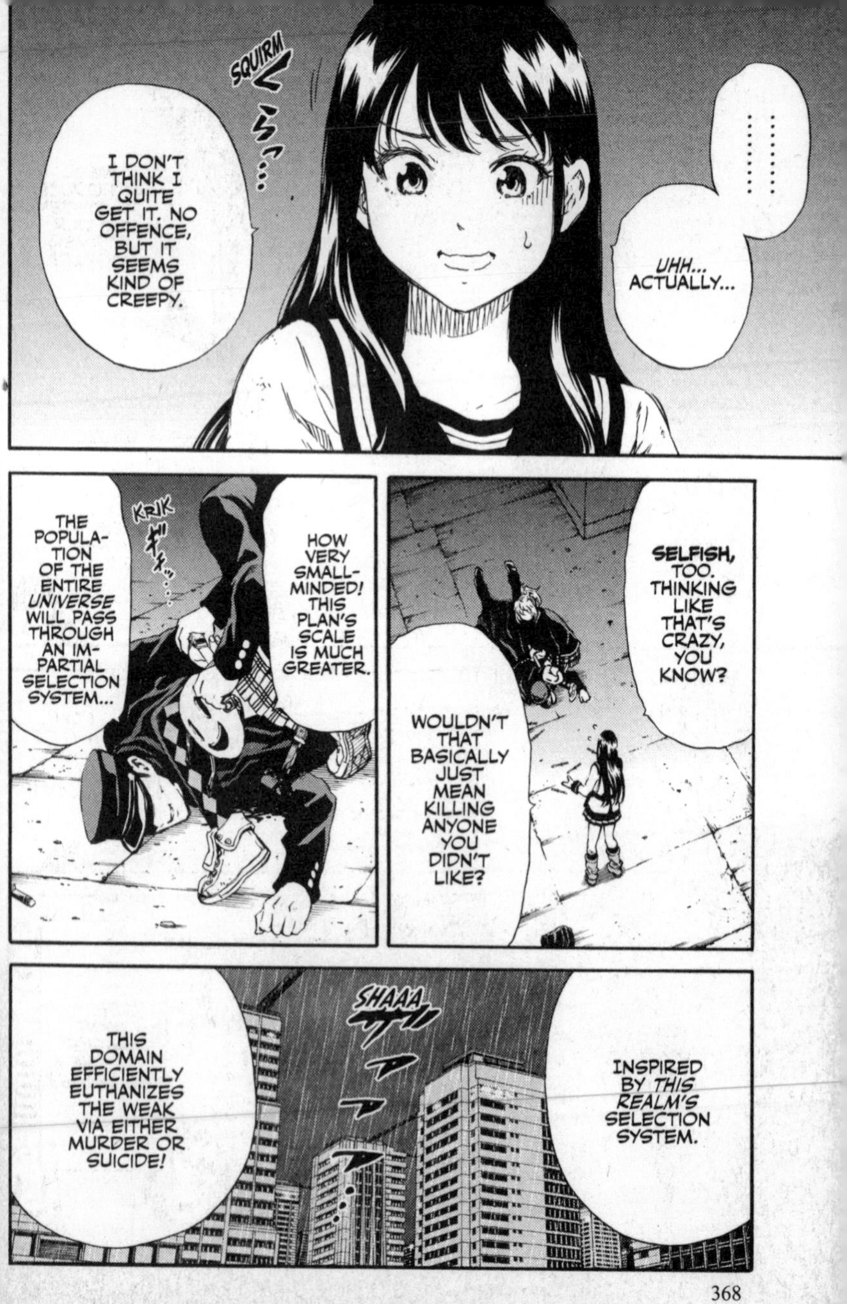

……
UHH... ACTUALLY...
SQUIRM
I DON'T THINK I QUITE GET IT. NO OFFENCE, BUT IT SEEMS KIND OF CREEPY.
SELFISH, TOO. THINKING LIKE THAT'S CRAZY, YOU KNOW?
WOULDN'T THAT BASICALLY JUST MEAN KILLING ANYONE YOU DIDN'T LIKE?
HOW VERY SMALL-MINDED! THIS PLAN'S SCALE IS MUCH GREATER.
KRIK
THE POPULATION OF THE ENTIRE *UNIVERSE* WILL PASS THROUGH AN IMPARTIAL SELECTION SYSTEM...
INSPIRED BY *THIS REALM'S* SELECTION SYSTEM.
SHAAA
THIS DOMAIN EFFICIENTLY EUTHANIZES THE WEAK VIA EITHER MURDER OR SUICIDE!

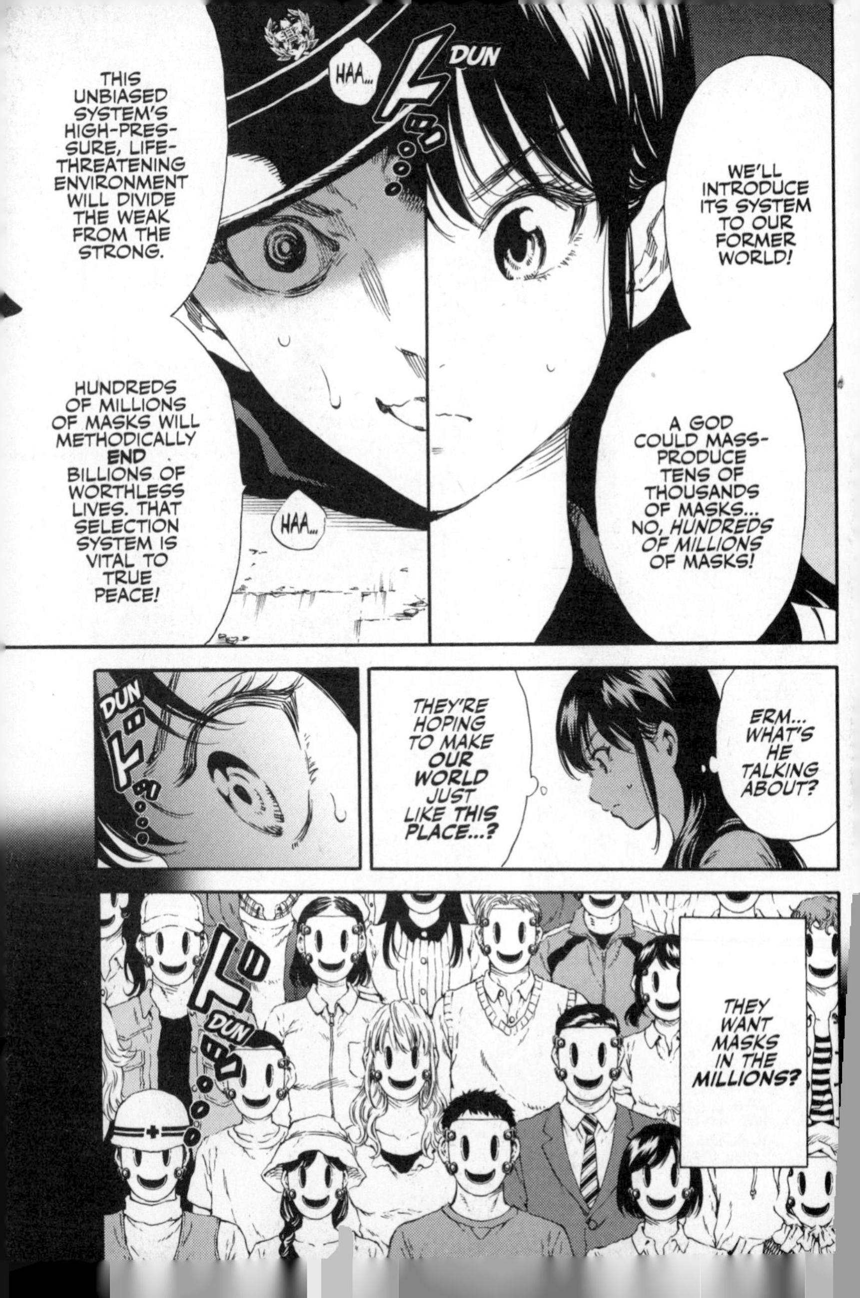
DUN
HAA...
WE'LL INTRODUCE ITS SYSTEM TO OUR FORMER WORLD!
THIS UNBIASED SYSTEM'S HIGH-PRES-SURE, LIFE-THREATENING ENVIRONMENT WILL DIVIDE THE WEAK FROM THE STRONG.
A GOD COULD MASS-PRODUCE TENS OF THOUSANDS OF MASKS... NO, *HUNDREDS OF MILLIONS* OF MASKS!
HAA...
HUNDREDS OF MILLIONS OF MASKS WILL METHODICALLY **END** BILLIONS OF WORTHLESS LIVES. THAT SELECTION SYSTEM IS VITAL TO TRUE PEACE!
ERM... WHAT'S HE TALKING ABOUT?
THEY'RE HOPING TO MAKE **OUR WORLD** JUST LIKE THIS PLACE...?
DUN
THEY WANT MASKS IN THE **MILLIONS?**
DUN

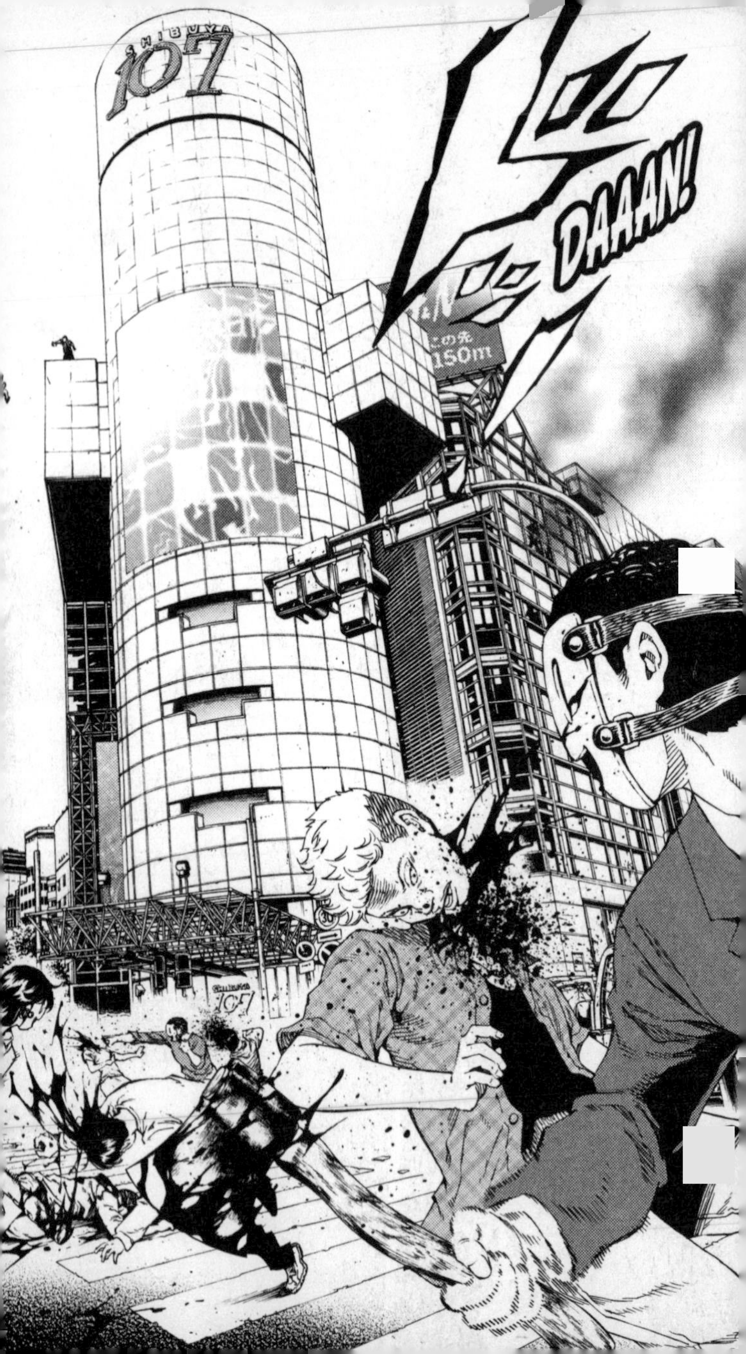
DAAAN!
SHIBUYA
107
この先
150m

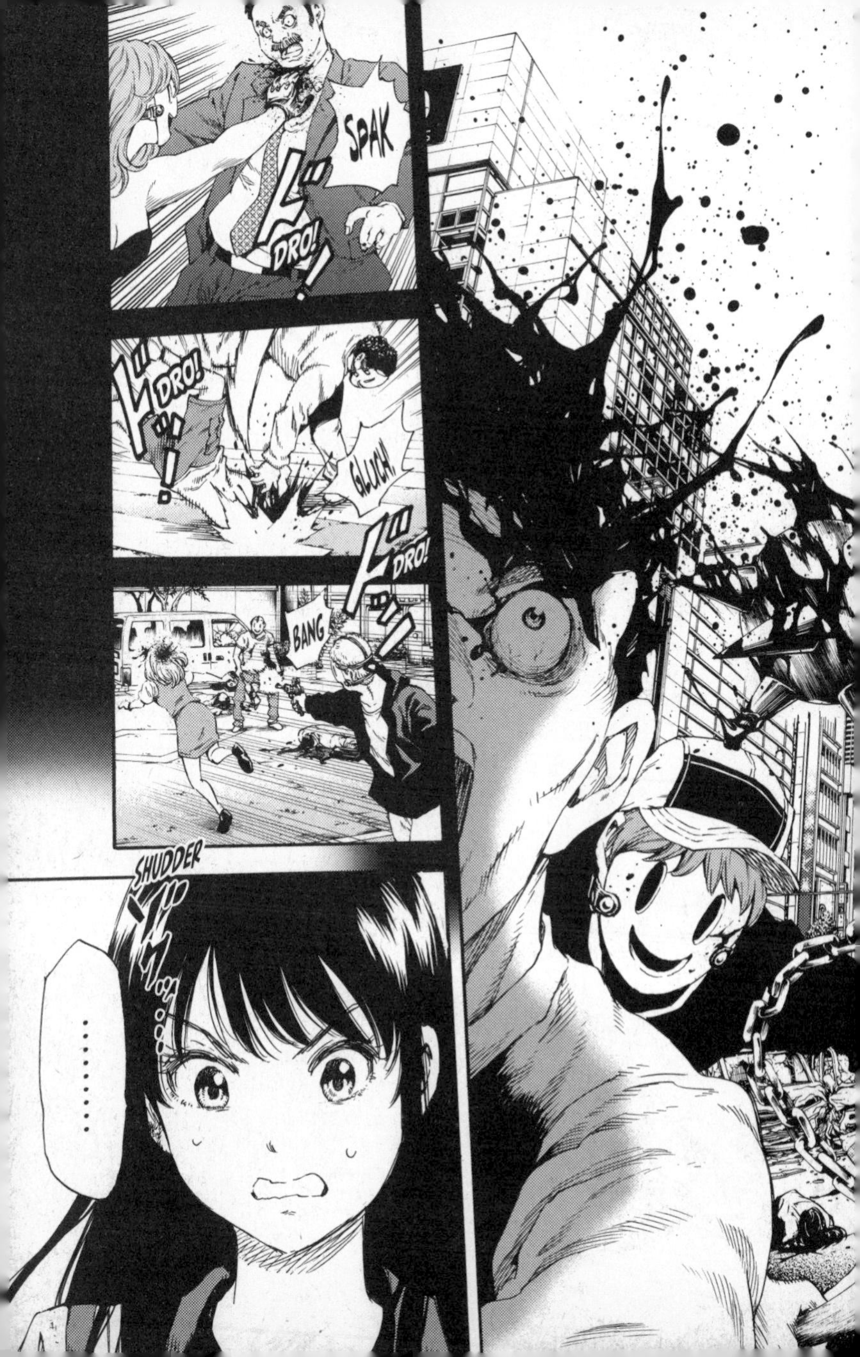
SPAK
DRO!
GLUCH
DRO!
DRO!
BANG
SHUDDER
......

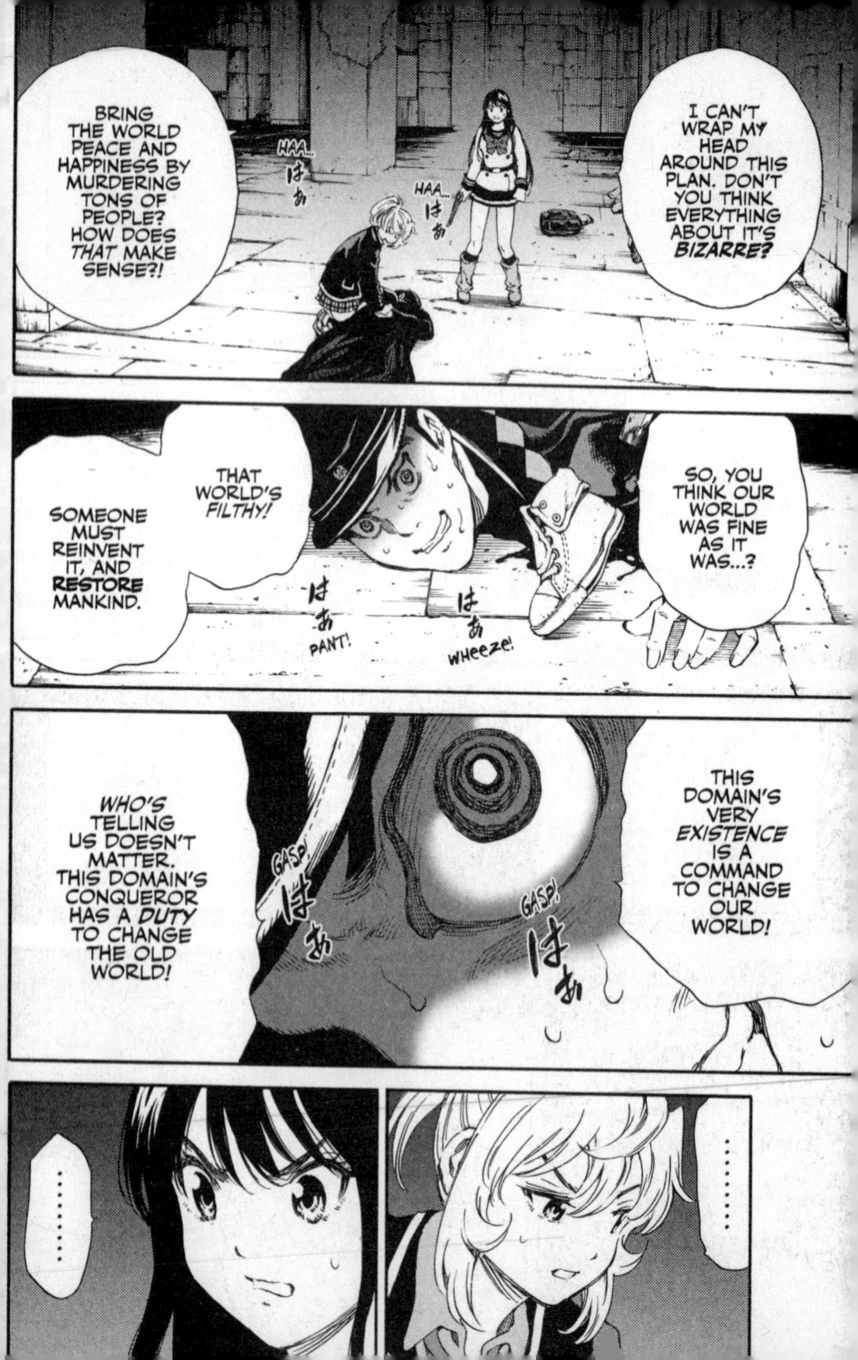
I CAN'T WRAP MY HEAD AROUND THIS PLAN. DON'T YOU THINK EVERYTHING ABOUT IT'S BIZARRE?
HAA... はあ
HAA... はあ
BRING THE WORLD PEACE AND HAPPINESS BY MURDERING TONS OF PEOPLE? HOW DOES THAT MAKE SENSE?!
SO, YOU THINK OUR WORLD WAS FINE AS IT WAS...?
THAT WORLD'S FILTHY!
はあ WHEEZE!
はあ PANT!
SOMEONE MUST REINVENT IT, AND RESTORE MANKIND.
THIS DOMAIN'S VERY EXISTENCE IS A COMMAND TO CHANGE OUR WORLD!
GASP! はあ
GASP! はあ
WHO'S TELLING US DOESN'T MATTER. THIS DOMAIN'S CONQUEROR HAS A DUTY TO CHANGE THE OLD WORLD!
......
......

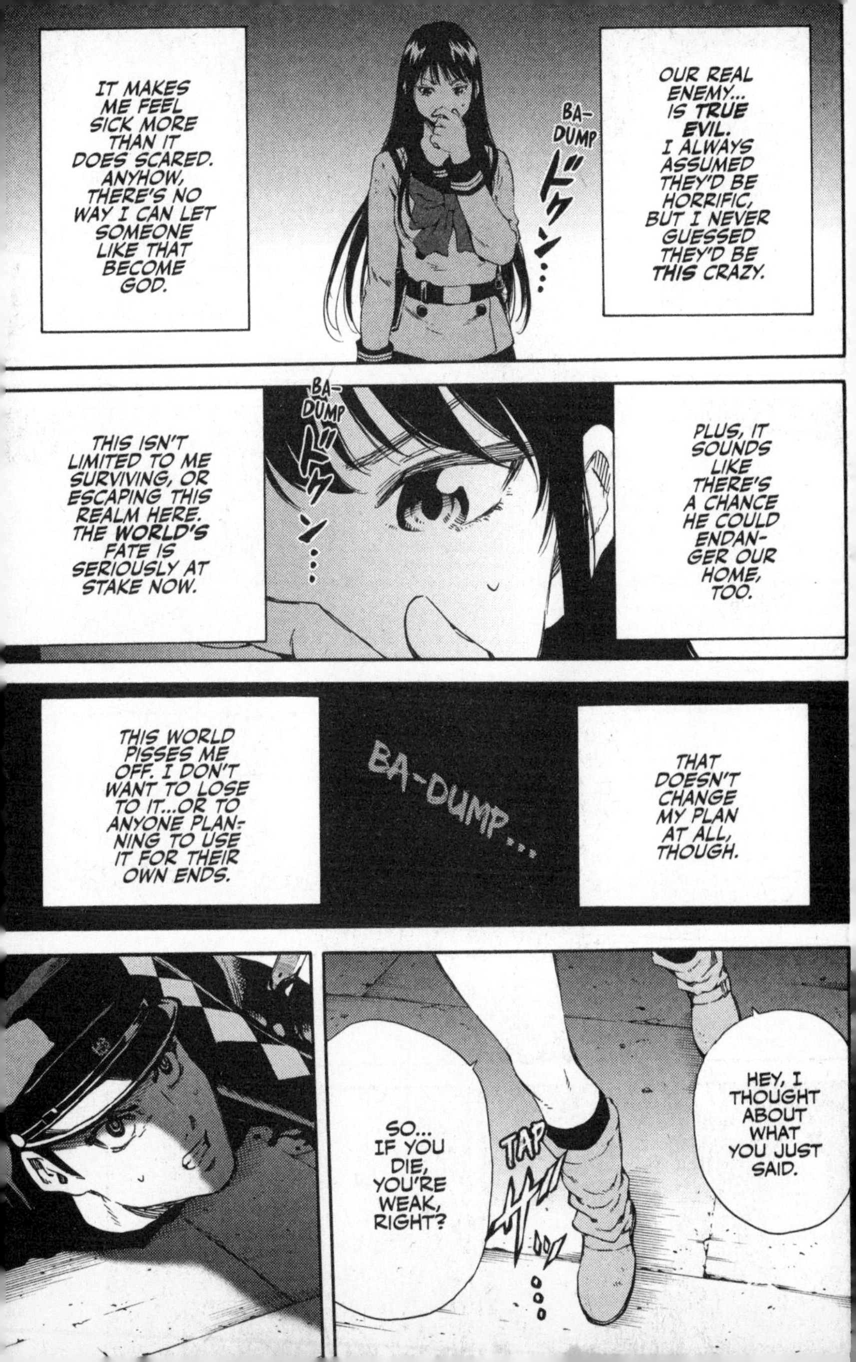
OUR REAL ENEMY... IS TRUE EVIL. I ALWAYS ASSUMED THEY'D BE HORRIFIC, BUT I NEVER GUESSED THEY'D BE THIS CRAZY.
BA-DUMP
IT MAKES ME FEEL SICK MORE THAN IT DOES SCARED. ANYHOW, THERE'S NO WAY I CAN LET SOMEONE LIKE THAT BECOME GOD.
PLUS, IT SOUNDS LIKE THERE'S A CHANCE HE COULD ENDANGER OUR HOME, TOO.
BA-DUMP
THIS ISN'T LIMITED TO ME SURVIVING, OR ESCAPING THIS REALM HERE. THE WORLD'S FATE IS SERIOUSLY AT STAKE NOW.
THAT DOESN'T CHANGE MY PLAN AT ALL, THOUGH.
BA-DUMP...
THIS WORLD PISSES ME OFF. I DON'T WANT TO LOSE TO IT...OR TO ANYONE PLANNING TO USE IT FOR THEIR OWN ENDS.
HEY, I THOUGHT ABOUT WHAT YOU JUST SAID.
TAP
SO... IF YOU DIE, YOU'RE WEAK, RIGHT?

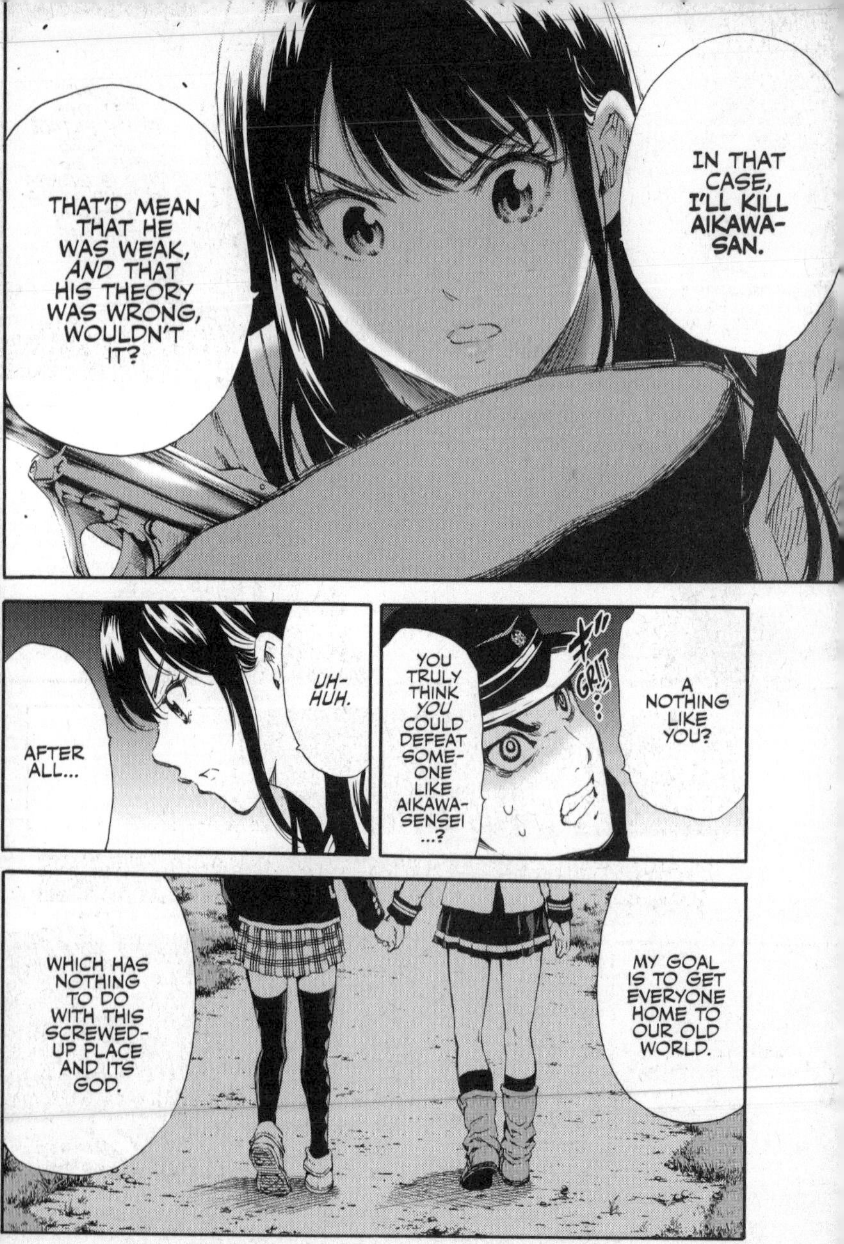
IN THAT CASE, I'LL KILL AIKAWA-SAN.
THAT'D MEAN THAT HE WAS WEAK, *AND* THAT HIS THEORY WAS WRONG, WOULDN'T IT?
A NOTHING LIKE YOU?
GRIT
YOU TRULY THINK *YOU* COULD DEFEAT SOME-ONE LIKE AIKAWA-SENSEI ...?
UH-HUH.
AFTER ALL...
MY GOAL IS TO GET EVERYONE HOME TO OUR OLD WORLD.
WHICH HAS NOTHING TO DO WITH THIS SCREWED-UP PLACE AND ITS GOD.

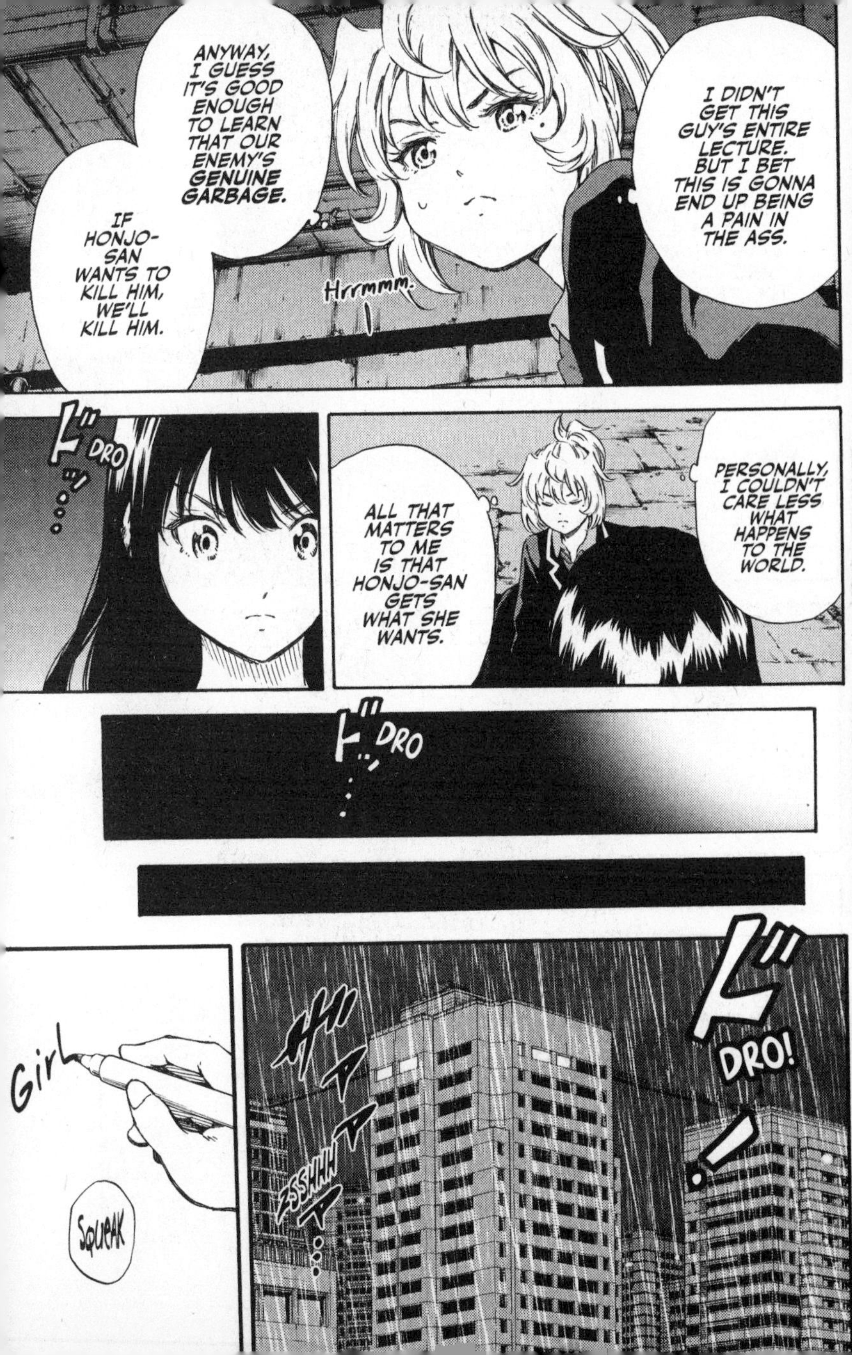
I DIDN'T GET THIS GUY'S ENTIRE LECTURE. BUT I BET THIS IS GONNA END UP BEING A PAIN IN THE ASS.
Hrrmmm.
ANYWAY, I GUESS IT'S GOOD ENOUGH TO LEARN THAT OUR ENEMY'S GENUINE GARBAGE.
IF HONJO-SAN WANTS TO KILL HIM, WE'LL KILL HIM.
PERSONALLY, I COULDN'T CARE LESS WHAT HAPPENS TO THE WORLD.
ALL THAT MATTERS TO ME IS THAT HONJO-SAN GETS WHAT SHE WANTS.
DRO
DRO
DRO!
ZSSHHH
Girl
Squeak

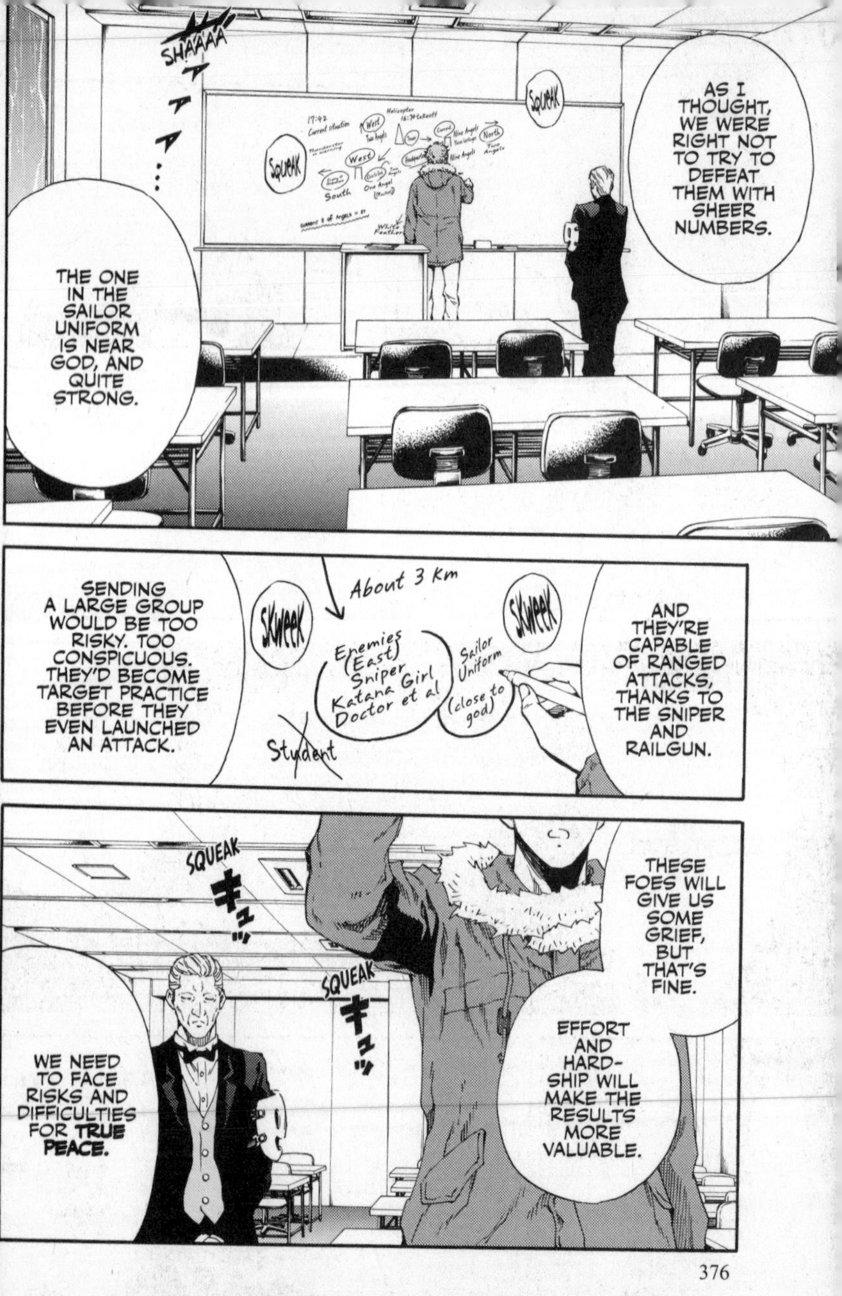
AS I THOUGHT, WE WERE RIGHT NOT TO TRY TO DEFEAT THEM WITH SHEER NUMBERS.
SQUEAK
17:42
Current situation
Helicopter
West
Two Angels
Nine Angels
North
West
South
One Angel
White Feather
SQUEAK
SHAAAA A A A...
THE ONE IN THE SAILOR UNIFORM IS NEAR GOD, AND QUITE STRONG.
AND THEY'RE CAPABLE OF RANGED ATTACKS, THANKS TO THE SNIPER AND RAILGUN.
SKweek
About 3 Km
Sailor Uniform
(close to god)
Enemies (East) Sniper Katana Girl Doctor et al
Student
SKweek
SENDING A LARGE GROUP WOULD BE TOO RISKY. TOO CONSPICUOUS. THEY'D BECOME TARGET PRACTICE BEFORE THEY EVEN LAUNCHED AN ATTACK.
THESE FOES WILL GIVE US SOME GRIEF, BUT THAT'S FINE.
EFFORT AND HARD-SHIP WILL MAKE THE RESULTS MORE VALUABLE.
SQUEAK
キュッ
SQUEAK
キュッ
WE NEED TO FACE RISKS AND DIFFICULTIES FOR TRUE PEACE.

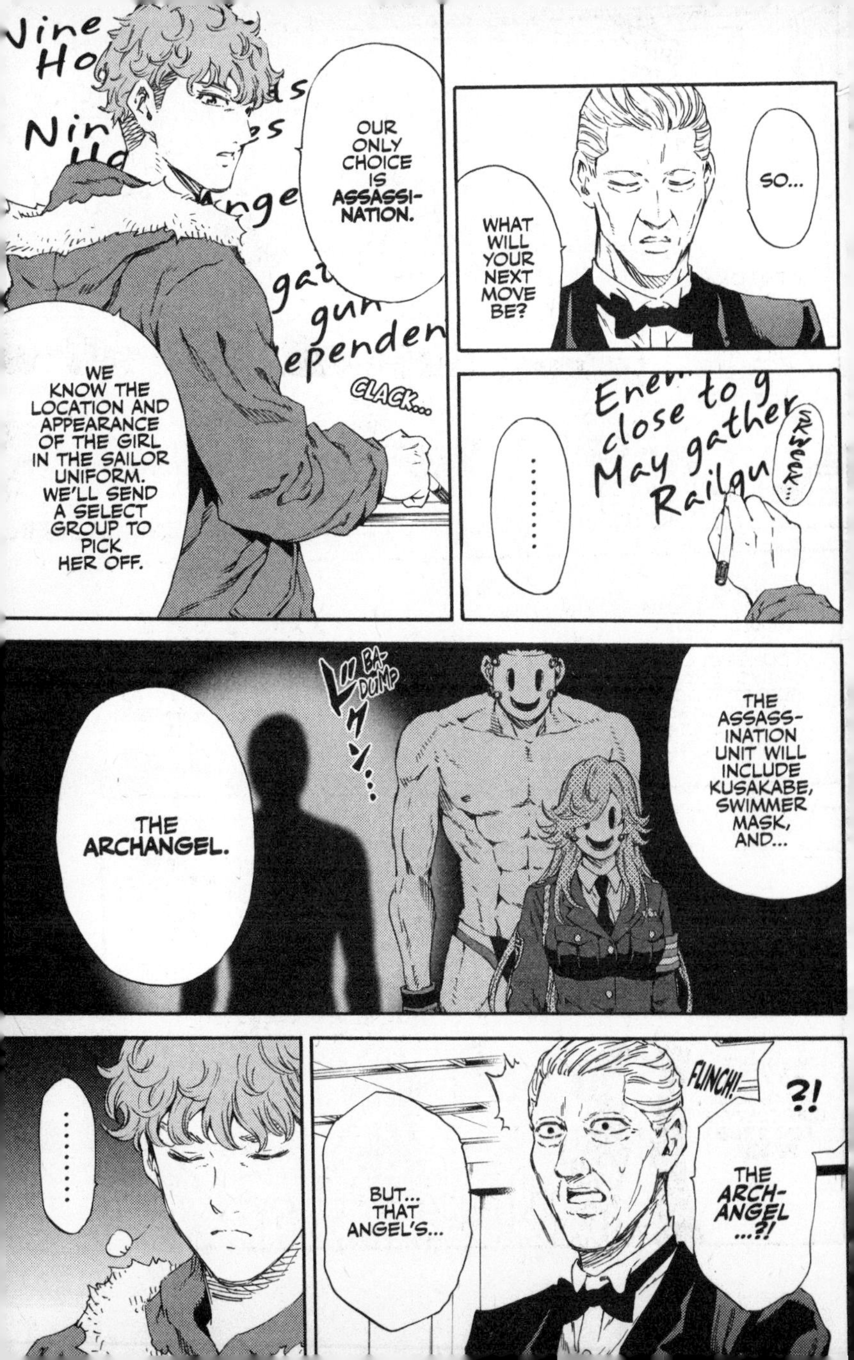
SO...
WHAT WILL YOUR NEXT MOVE BE?
SKWEEK...
Enem
close to g
May gather
Railgu
......
OUR ONLY CHOICE IS ASSASSINATION.
CLACK...
WE KNOW THE LOCATION AND APPEARANCE OF THE GIRL IN THE SAILOR UNIFORM. WE'LL SEND A SELECT GROUP TO PICK HER OFF.
THE ASSASSINATION UNIT WILL INCLUDE KUSAKABE, SWIMMER MASK, AND...
BA-DUMP
THE ARCHANGEL.
?!
FLINCH!
THE ARCHANGEL...?!
BUT... THAT ANGEL'S...
......

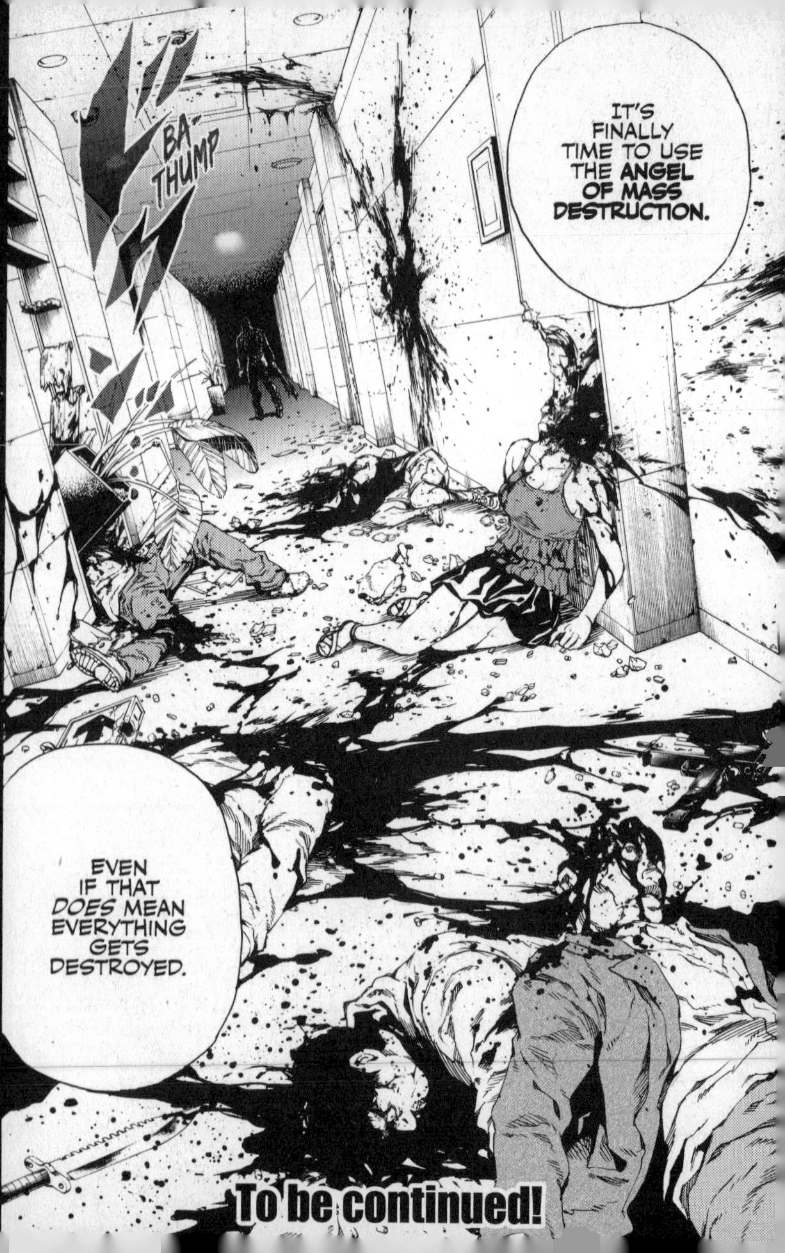
IT'S FINALLY TIME TO USE THE ANGEL OF MASS DESTRUCTION.
BA-THUMP
EVEN IF THAT DOES MEAN EVERYTHING GETS DESTROYED.
To be continued!

HIGH-RISE INVASION

STORY
Tsuina Miura

ART
Takahiro Oba

STAFF
Fukuen Kanako
Saito Yuusaku
Sakurai Hiroshi

EDITORS
Uchida Tomohiro
Kohori Ryuuichi

COMICS EDITOR
Nozawa Shinobu

COVER DESIGN
Inadome Ken

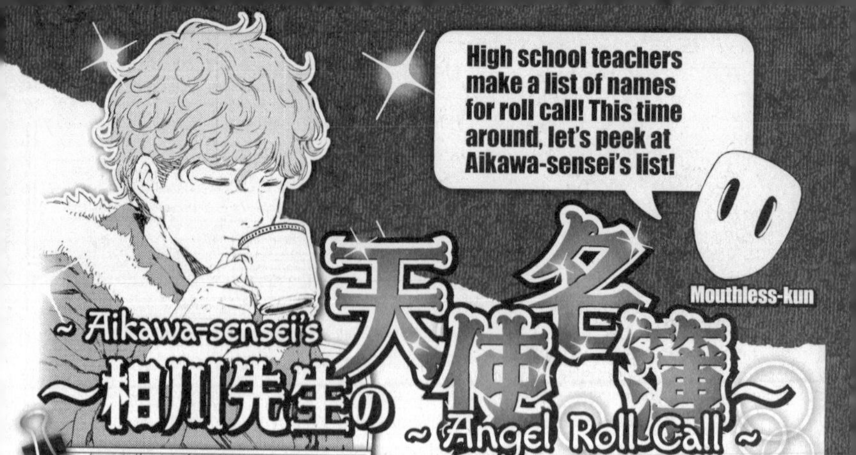
High school teachers make a list of names for roll call! This time around, let's peek at Aikawa-sensei's list!
Mouthless-kun
~ Aikawa-sensei's
～相川先生の天使名簿～
~ Angel Roll Call ~

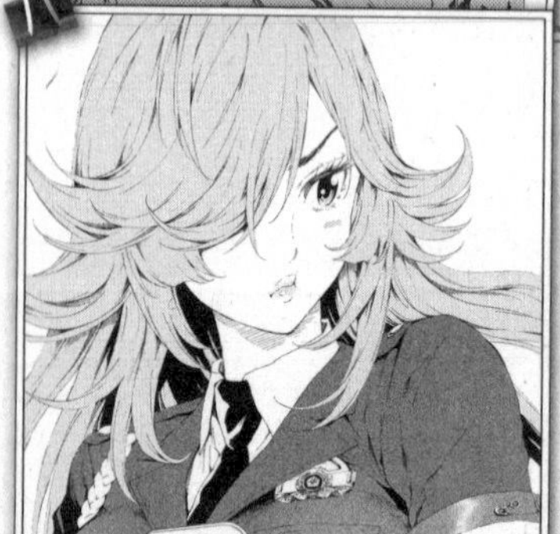

Follower #: 4

Nickname: None (Real Name: Kusakabe Yayoi)

Outfit: Woman's police uniform (Unofficial)

Age: A Self-Reported 18 (Mid to late 20s?)

Speech: Yes

Weapon: Bullwhip

Rating: 6 → 8

Notes: Judging by her badge, she used to be an attorney. Yayoi's wavelength compatibility enhanced her skills, enabling her to speak. Her voice is high-pitched, and it carries well, so she has to be cautious while scouting. Recently, she's taken charge of investigating the area around the tower and supervising the HQ.

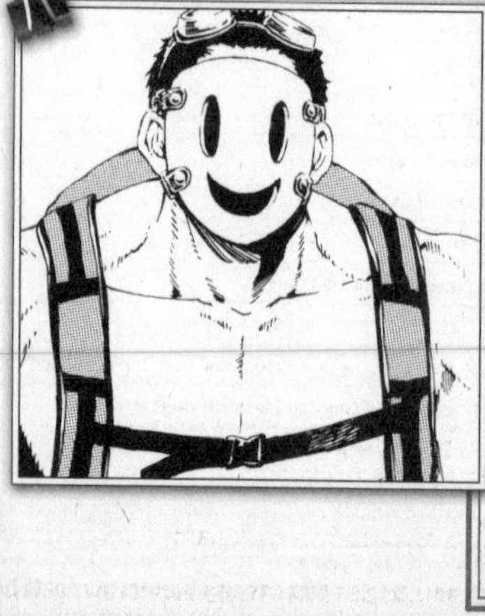

Follower #: 22

Nickname: Swimmer Mask

Outfit: Competition-standard personal swim trunks

Age: Early to mid-20s?

Speech: No

Weapon: MMA

Rating: 8

Notes: Probably a former competitive swimmer. (Very low body fat for a swimmer, though.) His amazing build, alongside his mixed martial arts skills, produced his exceptional combat abilities. Low compatibility with ranged weapons, blades, and poison. He stands out for sometimes not following orders... Maybe due to his human self's influence? I need to be cautious of that.

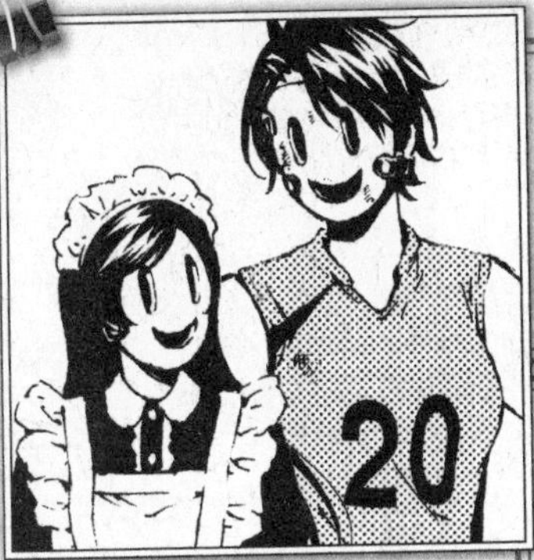
20

Follower #: 16 **Nickname:** Volleyball Mask

Outfit: Personal volleyball uniform

Age: Mid to late teens? **Speech:** No

Weapon: Harpe (Ancient Greek shortsword) **Rating:** 6

Notes: Former volleyball player. Athletes seem to trend towards displaying stronger angelic abilities.

Follower #: 15 **Nickname:** Waitress Mask

Outfit: Maid uniform **Age:** Mid to late teens?

Speech: Limited **Weapon:** Prohibited **Rating:** None

Notes: Probably acquaintances with Volleyball Mask. She can't use a weapon, so I put her in charge of odd jobs around the HQ.

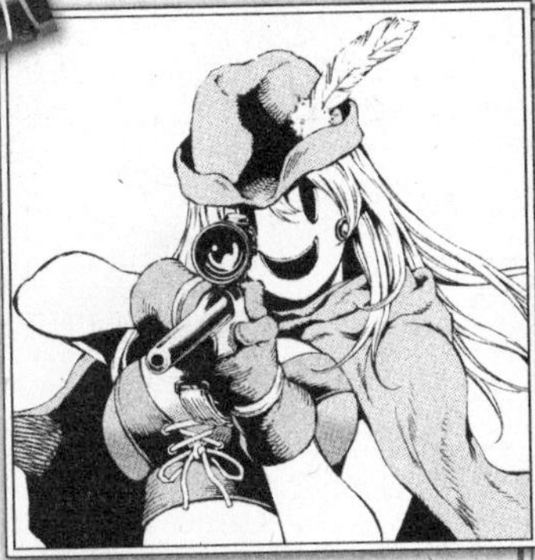

Follower #: 13

Nickname: White Feather

Dress: Western hunting costume (Hat with white feather)

Age: Mid to late teens?

Speech: Limited

Weapon: Rifle (Winchester M70)

Rating: 9

Notes: Caucasian. Speaks English. From her accent, I'd say she's American. Aside from sniping, her other physical abilities are also excellent. Nicknamed for the white feather in her hat, and a famous American Marine sniper. Does that mean my old world's history influences this domain...?

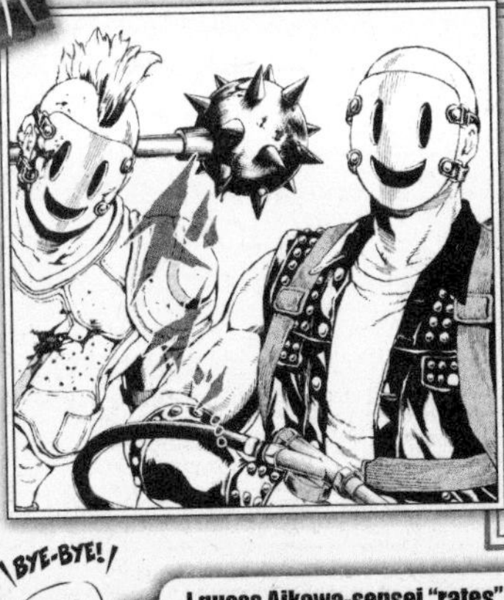

Follower #: 24/25

Nicknames: Ishida/Inoue

Outfits: Movie-influenced

Ages: Early to mid-20s?

Speech: No/No

Weapons: Morning star/flamethrower

Rating: 5/5

Notes: Recruited for their useful weapons and body types. Named after two of my former students, but I honestly don't remember who is Ishida and who is Inoue. Outfits inspired by a certain entertainment franchise. I plan to always use them as a duo.

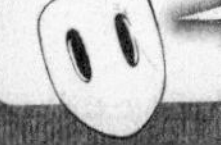
BYE-BYE!

I guess Aikawa-sensei "rates" Angels out of ten...imagine how strong a perfect ten could be!

Text/Tsuina Miura

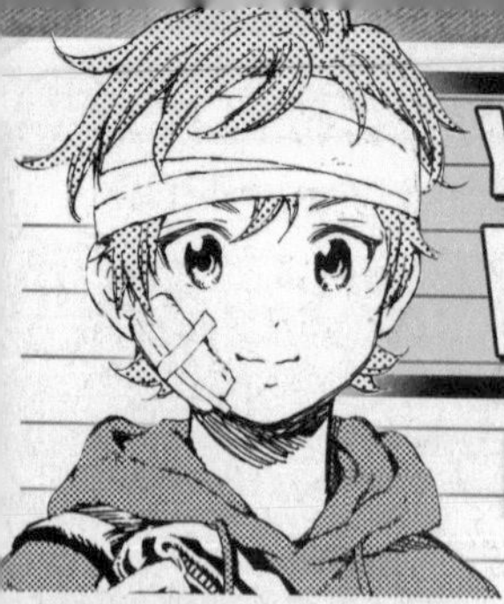

Young Uzaki: The Ultimate WEAPON GEEK

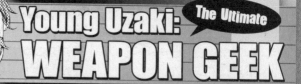

This time around, let's peek at weapon geek Uzuki-kun's notebook!

Mouthless-kun

NAME:

"Sig Sauer Mosquito"

TYPE: Automatic Handgun OWNER: My Mom → Me

Notes: Small handgun. Polymer frame, so it's light, and extremely easy to use. Still, it's weak. And it's pink, so it's really girly. I'd never throw it away, but I'd really like to find a better gun!

RARITY: ★☆☆☆☆

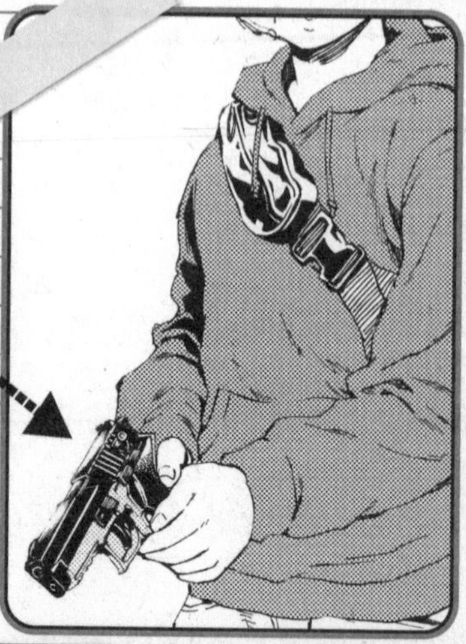

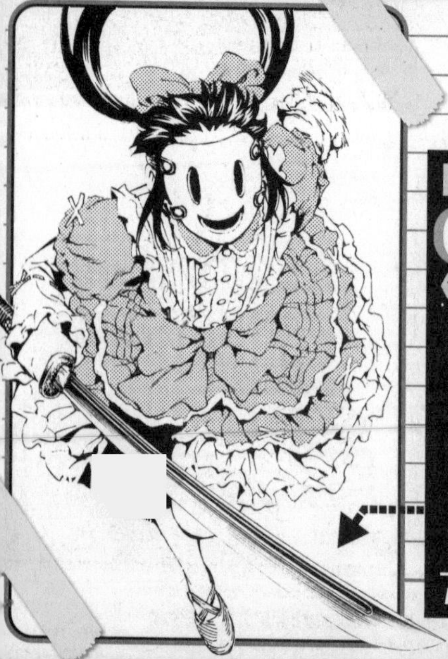

NAME:

Sendai Kunikane

TYPE: Longsword (Japanese) OWNER: Ein-san

Notes: Unfortunately, I can't tell much just from looking at this sword. Ein-san told me about it when I asked her, though. Apparently, Masks are preprogrammed with knowledge about their weapons. Amazing! The Sendai Kunikane is an Edo-period sword, so it might not be too rare. Still, it's pretty cool. And the flower pattern on the guard is super cute.
I think it suits Ein-san perfectly!

RARITY: ★★★☆☆

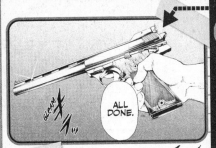

ALL DONE.

GLEAM

KLANK

NAME:

.44 Auto Mag M280

TYPE: Automatic Handgun **OWNER:** Honjo Yuri

Notes: *Super-rare!* Auto Mags are rare to begin with. This special model is even rarer! Shoots magnum bullets, so it's clearly powerful to boot. Its design makes it easy to jam. Still, if you're careful, it should be fine.

RARITY: ★★★★☆

NAME:

Tonbokiri

TYPE: Spear (Japanese) **OWNER:** Tanabe-san

Notes: This spear's super-famous. I recognized it right away! The Sengoku period's strongest military commander used it. It's so sharp, it cut a dragonfly that landed on its blade in two. It's a rarity among rarities! It could be a replica, but knowing this world, it's probably real.

RARITY: ★★★★★

NAME:

Ulfberht

TYPE: Sword (N. European) **OWNER:** Samue Mask

Notes: A legendary Viking sword. Foreign swords are usually weak compared to Japanese ones. But this sword's a special case. Apparently, it's extremely strong. It isn't just rare; a real ulfberht shouldn't exist. This world really is amazing.

RARITY: ★★★★★

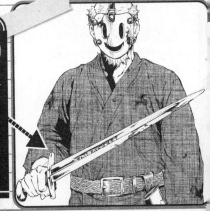

BYE BYE!

Was it too geeky this time? Forgive me... These are just extra pages!

Text/Tsuina Miu

SEVEN SEAS ENTERTAINMENT PRESENTS

HIGH-RISE INVASION Vol. 9-10

story by **TSUINA MIURA** / art by **TAKAHIRO OBA**

TRANSLATION
Nan Rymer

ADAPTATION
Rebecca Schneidereit

LETTERING AND RETOUCH
Meaghan Tucker

COVER DESIGN
KC Fabellon

PROOFREADER
Janet Houck
Cae Hawksmoor

EDITOR
J.P. Sullivan

PRODUCTION MANAGER
Lissa Pattillo

MANAGING EDITOR
Julie Davis

EDITOR-IN-CHIEF
Adam Arnold

PUBLISHER
Jason DeAngelis

TENKUU SHINPAN VOLUME 9-10
© Tsuina Miura 2016, © Takahiro Oba 2016
All rights reserved.
First published in Japan in 2016 by Kodansha Ltd., Tokyo.
Publication rights for this English edition arranged through Kodansha Ltd., Tokyo.

Seven Seas press and purchase enquiries can be sent to Marketing Manager Lianne Sentar at press@gomanga.com. Information regarding the distribution and purchase of digital editions is available from Digital Manager CK Russell at digital@gomanga.com.

Seven Seas and the Seven Seas logo are trademarks of Seven Seas Entertainment. All rights reserved.

ISBN: 978-1-64275-702-6

Printed in Canada

First Printing: September 2019

10 9 8 7 6 5 4 3 2 1

FOLLOW US ONLINE: *www.sevenseasentertainment.com*

READING DIRECTIONS

This book reads from ***right to left***, Japanese style. If this is your first time reading manga, you start reading from the top right panel on each page and take it from there. If you get lost, just follow the numbered diagram here. It may seem backwards at first, but you'll get the hang of it! Have fun!!

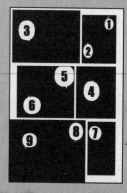